Analysis of Inflation: 1965–1974

NATIONAL BUREAU OF ECONOMIC RESEARCH
Conference on Research in Income and Wealth

JOEL
POPKIN,
Editor

Analysis of Inflation: 1965–1974

Studies in Income and Wealth
Volume 42
by the Conference on Research
in Income and Wealth

Published for the
NATIONAL BUREAU OF
ECONOMIC RESEARCH, INC.
by
BALLINGER PUBLISHING COMPANY
A Subsidiary of J. B. Lippincott Company
Cambridge, Mass.
1977

Library of Congress Cataloging in Publication Data
Conference on Price Behavior, Bethesda, Md., 1974.
Analysis of Inflation: 1965–1974

    (Studies in income and wealth; v. 42)
    The conference was held Nov. 21–23, 1974 in Bethesda, Md.
    Includes index.
    1. Inflation (Finance)—United States—Congresses.
2. Inflation (Finance)—Congresses. 3. Wage-price
policy—United States—Congresses. 4. Price—Mathematical
models—Congresses.
I. Popkin, Joel.   II. National Bureau of Economic Research.
III. Series: Conference on Research in Income and Wealth. Studies
in Income and Wealth; v. 42.

HC106.3.C714   vol. 42 [HG538]   330'.08s [332.4'1]   77-581
ISBN 0-87014-519-3

PREFATORY NOTE

This volume of Studies in Income and Wealth contains the papers presented at the Conference on Price Behavior, held on November 21–23, 1974, in Bethesda, Maryland. We are indebted to the Program Committee, consisting of Joel Popkin, who served as chairman and conference editor, and Ronald G. Bodkin, who assisted with the editing as well as planning; to Franklin Fisher for helpful suggestions at an early planning stage; to the National Science Foundation for its support; and to Ester Moskowitz for preparing the volume for press.

Funds for the economic research conference program of the National Bureau of Economic Research are supplied by the National Science Foundation.

Contents

Analysis of Inflation: 1965–1974

JOEL POPKIN

National Bureau of
Economic Research

Introduction

The subject of this conference volume is the U.S. inflation of 1965–1974 and, to some extent, its interrelationship with inflation in other countries. The period covered is one during which Federal deficits grew and rates of monetary growth were high. There was also an exceptional variety of developments of the kind that are frequently considered in the analysis of inflation. There was the Vietnam buildup, Medicare, a housing boom, devaluation of the dollar and a shift to floating exchange rates, wage and price controls, the rise in crude oil prices and severe bottlenecks in primary product industries. All these developments were associated with both a high rate of inflation and marked changes in relative prices.

It is not my intention in this introduction to summarize each of the papers in the volume. At the conference, discussants were asked to summarize the papers before offering critiques of them. As a result, the reader will find convenient summaries in the discussants' comments, as well as in the concluding sections of many of the papers. Rather, my intention here is to put the conference in perspective in relation to the period of economic history on which it focused, to point out the new ground broken in the papers, to highlight broad areas of agreement and disagreement about the source of the decade's inflation, and to indicate the path of future research suggested both in the papers and by the discussion at the conference.

From the end of 1964 to the end of 1974 the consumer price index rose 66.0 percent, or at an average annual rate of 5.2 percent. In this century only the inflations of 1910–1920 (7.5 percent per year) and 1941–1951 (5.8 percent per year) surpass that of the decade 1965–1974 in terms of intensity. It is interesting that each of these three decades spanned at least one war, which may say more about the disturbing frequency of such outbreaks than about the cause of inflation. To sound a perhaps unwarranted note of optimism, let me also point out that the rate of inflation in the ensuing decade was markedly less: −1.8 percent per year in 1920–1930 and 1.4 percent in 1951–1961.

As one might expect, during 1965–1974 there was considerable fluctuation of the rate of inflation about its average for the period. For changes over twelve-month spans, the rate varied from a low of 1.9 percent to a high of 12.2 percent; it was higher on average in the last half of the decade than in the first half. In terms of the joint variation of the rates of inflation and changes in final output, the ten years can be broken down into several episodes. The year 1965 and the first half of 1966 can be characterized as a period of strong output growth associated with the Vietnam buildup, and of a rekindling of inflation, which had been relatively quiescent since 1958.

Economic activity slowed in 1966–1967 and output was almost flat for one quarter, but this was not tantamount to a recession as usually defined. The expansion of output that began in 1961 was, thus, not interrupted, giving rise to an unusually long expansion and raising the question of whether the business cycle was still alive. It was the 1966–1967 behavior of output that probably gave rise to the interest in growth cycles. But the 1966–1967 experience also had another, perhaps more important, impact—one on policymakers. The overall rate of inflation slowed markedly during the growth slowdown. This suggested anew that policies effecting merely a slowdown in the rate of growth could bring about marked abatement of inflationary pressures. It also brought about renewed interest in Phillips-curve relationships. However, upon closer examination, the bulk of the slowdown in the rate of advance of the CPI during this period turned out to be due to the behavior of farm product prices, which responded, as they usually do in the short run, to the marked changes that often occur in supply. In late 1966, supplies of farm products, particularly livestock, had risen from depressed levels in the preceding twelve months.

The third episode was the resumption of fairly strong rates of output growth from mid-1967 to the third quarter of 1969. This was accompanied by the resurgence of inflation as food prices turned upward and other prices, particularly those of services, increased at an accelerating rate. A key element in the rapid advance of service prices was the continuation of the steep rise in medical care services, a trend that seems to have begun in 1966 and is associated by some with the adoption in 1965 of Medicare and Medicaid.

In 1969 monetary and fiscal policy turned restrictive, and a recession began late in the year. Inflation slowed very little as measured by the fixed weight deflator for gross private output. That measure, unlike the CPI, is not affected by movements in the mortgage interest rate, which dropped sharply between 1969 and 1970. During the recession the fixed weight deflator rose 5.1 percent, compared with an increase of 5.2 percent during 1969.

The recovery began in the first quarter of 1971 with a rise in real GNP that was particularly sharp because auto output had been depressed by a strike in the fourth quarter of 1970. But the growth of real output slowed markedly thereafter, rising at a rate of only 2.9 percent in the second and third quarters. As a result, the unemployment rate hovered at the relatively high 6 percent level that it had reached during the recession. But inflation did not abate; as measured by the fixed weight deflator for gross private product, to exclude the effect of changes in mortgage interest rates, it continued to run at a rate of 5.4 percent during the first two quarters of 1971. In the second quarter, this combination of inflation and unemployment, coupled with a rapid deterioration in the U.S. balance of payments position, created considerable pressure for additional policy measures.

On August 15, 1971, the United States adopted wage and price controls for the first time since the Korean War. The controls began with a ninety-day freeze on wages, prices, and rents. In an equally dramatic step, the United States, for the first time since 1934, suspended the convertibility of the dollar into gold or other reserve assets.

The control program lasted through April 1974 but underwent a number of changes. During the freeze a set of mandatory standards for wage and price behavior was developed. Called Phase II, it was in place from the end of the freeze until January 11, 1973. Phase III followed, distinguished importantly from its predecessor in that emphasis was placed on self-administration of the regulations; the requirements for prenotification of intended wage and price changes were dropped in most sectors of the economy. But as the pace of inflation accelerated in the winter and spring of 1973, the program was made more stringent, chiefly by reintroducing pre-notification requirements. A freeze was put in place once more, on June 13, 1973; it lasted about sixty days. It was followed on August 12 by Phase IV. The rules in this phase were stricter in some respects than those of Phase II after which they had been patterned. But they provided far more flexibility in dealing with shortages and were intended to provide a means of smoothing the transition to an uncontrolled economy. The main vehicle for achieving both objectives was the provision permitting decontrol of specific sectors on a selective basis.

From the third quarter of 1971 to the first quarter of 1973, when the first freeze and Phase II of the control program were in place, real GNP grew at an annual rate of 6.9 percent. This was the fastest pace for any six-quarter period since the one ending in the fourth quarter of 1951, the Korean War period. During the same six quarters, inflation as measured by the deflator slowed to a rate of 4.3 percent. But toward the end of the period there were emerging signs of its acceleration, visible in the price increases for raw commodities, which were particularly sharp for farm products.

Increases in real GNP began to slow in the second quarter of 1973, reflecting some capacity ceilings, and turned negative in the first quarter of 1974 under the impact of the oil embargo and a marked acceleration of inflation. Real GNP continued to decline throughout the year at an increasing rate after the embargo ended. The rate of inflation reached into the double-digit range in the first quarter of 1974, mainly as a result of the rise in crude oil prices. It remained there for the rest of the year, as prices of other primary commodities jumped substantially and wage rate increases accelerated to a rate of more than 10 percent. The larger part of these increases occurred after the sharp runup in crude oil prices and the termination of controls on April 30, 1974.

Analysis of inflation during all or part of 1965–1974 is the subject of the papers in this volume. The diversity of inflationary forces during this period and the policies designed to combat them are reflected in the analytical foci of the papers. As one might expect, considerable attention is given to assessing the impact of controls. The shift to floating exchange rates and apparent increased interdependence of national economies are reflected in the analysis of the effect of U.S. inflation on Canada and of the transmission of inflation and exchange rate change among several industrialized countries. The marked shift in relative prices toward the end of the decade is reflected in the significant extent to which analyses are conducted at a more disaggregated level than has up to now been employed in the analysis of general inflation. But macroanalysis is not eschewed in this volume. It contains aggregative analysis in both Keynesian and monetarist frameworks as well as a focus on the role of expectations in producing inflation.

Administered pricing, another hypothesis about the nature of general inflation, in which prices respond belatedly, if at all, to changes in demand, did not receive much attention from the authors, and the discussants did not criticize them for it. Perhaps this is because administered price hypotheses usually are examined during recessions in an attempt to explain the apparent downward inflexibility of wages and prices during such periods of the cycle. There was only one recession during 1965–1974, the one of 1969–1970. Administered pricing might come to the fore again when economists analyze the behavior of prices in the rather steep recession of 1974–1975.

Much of the diversity in the analyses presented in the volume is a result of the inclusion of the years since 1970. That the developments of those years affect the analysis of price behavior can be seen by a comparison of the topics covered at this conference with those addressed in a comprehensive conference on price behavior held just four years earlier—October 1970. That conference, The Econometrics of Price Determination, was sponsored by the Board of Governors of the Federal Reserve System and the Social Science Research Council.

The main focus of the 1970 conference was on the Phillips curve or the inflation-unemployment trade-off. Wage behavior was accorded the central role in the explanation of inflationary bias in the economy. Recall that this was at a time when the profit share was falling and increases in unit labor costs rather than unit profits were dominating price change. Related issues addressed at that conference included the natural rate hypothesis and the role of expectations. The need was expressed for experimentation with direct measures of price expectations; one paper in this volume reports results of using such measures. Some, but not much, attention was given on that occasion to the role of materials prices and capital costs, particularly in the context of industrial-sector price equations. A similar amount of attention was given to the international transmission of inflation.

While only one paper at the 1970 conference dealt with price behavior at the industry level, the reader of this volume will find that about half the papers are based on disaggregated analysis of price behavior. And the approach to disaggregation varies. Bosworth and Vroman develop their price equations from a stage-of-process approach in which differences are examined in the behavior of consumer price index components and prices of similar products in the wholesale price index. Al-Samarrie, Kraft, and Roberts and also Nadiri and Gupta use breakdowns along SIC lines in manufacturing to help them explain the prices of gross outputs. Nordhaus and Shoven also use gross output prices, analyzing them in an input-output framework. Lawrence Klein reports results of one-digit-sector value-added deflators embedded in the Wharton model, thus establishing a link between sectoral and macroeconomic effects. A similar link between sectoral and macro effects is established in the CANDIDE model of the Canadian economy, as reported by Bodkin, Chabot-Plante, and Sheikh. Hirsch develops an aggregate capacity utilization index that mirrors underlying microlevel bottlenecks in manufacturing industries.

There are two major reasons for the shift to greater disaggregation in the studies of price behavior in this volume. The first is the interest in analyzing the effectiveness of controls in the specific markets in which they were applied. The second reflects interest in explaining the "commodity inflation" of 1972–1974 and in tracing its impact through to the prices associated with final demand.

But admittedly the findings of sectoral analysis cannot be generalized until more is known about the relationship between changes in relative prices and the overall rate of price change. If, for example, price increases were smaller than predicted by structural models for sectors in which prices were controlled, it does not follow obviously that controls were effective for the economy as a whole unless this result is buttressed by findings concerning developments in the uncontrolled sectors. Nor would even this broader analysis support such a final conclusion about controls without an examination of their effect on output, employment, investment, and expectations, as Kosters points out. Similarly, a conclusion that the bulk of the 1972–1974 burst of inflation is attributable to the sharp rise in commodity prices says nothing about the general inflation until the source of the rise in primary commodity prices is understood.

Nonetheless, sectoral price studies must precede attempts to address the broader questions about the nature of inflation regardless of how the inflationary process is viewed at the macro level. For the monetarist, such studies can be of use in explaining the lags found in the workings of monetary policy and the time path of the distribution of a change in money demand between price and quantity in reaching a new equilibrium. For the Keynesian, sectoral studies can be useful in defining the zone of full employment in relation to the aggregate supply curve as well as in determining which, if any, prices are relatively inflexible downward and whether the inflexibility applies only within a certain range of downward shifts in demand.

In addition to their pervasiveness in this volume on price behavior, several other points about the sectoral price studies stand out. In the 1970 Conference on the Econometrics of Price Behavior, sectoral studies were criticized because materials and capital costs were not specified as determinants of prices in the industries under investigation. In the sectoral research presented in this volume, that criticism appears to have been taken seriously. Materials input prices were found to have a significantly large impact on output prices, and the effect of capital costs, though small, was also significant in a number of industries.

Another shortcoming of earlier studies that was remedied in the research presented here relates to the double counting of price change that is implicit in the use of certain aggregate indexes of the wholesale price index system. Research on the behavior of prices for the manufacturing sector (and its major components) usually focused on the WPI for manufactured goods, an aggregate index that includes prices of goods sold within the manufacturing sector as well as outside it. The emphasis in this volume is on input and output price indexes. These, if properly constructed, eliminate double-counting problems.

The analytical findings presented at the conference fall into two categories—those which pertain to the period as a whole and those which pertain to certain subperiods. For the decade as a whole, the results contained here are consistent with those reported elsewhere to the effect that macro models were not accurate in their prediction of wage and price behavior.

Two findings emerge concerning wage determination. The first is that as new observations on wage behavior during 1966–1973 are added in the estimation of Phillips-type wage equations, the coefficient of the price term appears to increase absolutely and relative to the coefficient of the inverse of the unemployment rate. This finding came to light in the 1970 FRB-SSRC conference and was substantiated, using more recent data, by Bosworth and Vroman in their paper. It is also implicit in the finding of Wachtel that the coefficient of the price expectations variable, which he substitutes for lagged price in several wage relationships, becomes significant only after 1965. The same result also appears indirectly in the paper by Bodkin, Chabot-Plante, and Sheikh, in which the sensitivity of

Canadian inflation to U.S. inflation is found to have increased from 1960–1965 to 1966–1970. These empirical results all point to an increasing importance of the feedback from prices to wages in the inflation of 1965–1974.

Another finding about wage determination equations is that there were large prediction errors in 1970–1971. The unusually large increases during those two years in settlements in the unionized sector are examined in the papers by Kosters and by Bosworth and Vroman. The latter quantify the contribution of errors in wage equations for the union-negotiated sector to errors in aggregate wage rate équations. These large residuals declined markedly during controls, making it difficult to assess the impact of the program on wages. If the large residuals were merely aberrations, then controls had no effect. If they marked a significant shift in wage behavior, then the program had the effect of restoring historical relationships between wage rates and their determinants.

With respect to prices, there is no conclusive indication that prediction errors were rising as a percent of actual inflation rates. In the most comprehensive aggregative econometric analysis in the volume, that of Klein, underestimation of price change accelerates in 1968–1971, decelerates in 1972–1973, and accelerates again in 1974. It is only in predicting the level of the price of final output that accelerating errors occur, a finding of both Klein and Anderson and Carlson, the latters' based on the monetarist model of the Federal Reserve Bank of St. Louis.

At the sectoral level, prediction appears to improve when account is taken of the devaluation and the sharp rise in prices of primary commodities, both domestic and imported. Nordhaus and Shoven find that from November 1970 to October 1973, wage rates and import and raw commodity prices explain, both directly and through their impact on other prices, the bulk of the price change observed in the WPI. From October 1973 to July 1974, these prices and wages explain less of the overall rise in the WPI. This suggests that margin widening occurred. Perhaps it was due to an increase vis-à-vis the past in the extent to which firms passed through into prices, the rise in costs associated with the cyclical deterioration of output per man-hour that occurs just before and after the economy reaches a cyclical peak, as it did in 1974.

Nothing in these results suggests the abandonment of any existing theories of wage and price behavior. What they do suggest, however, is that there is, as yet, no single, unique approach to analyzing price behavior, which, when implemented empirically, can explain the inflation of the past decade. The promise of price analysis is that it may lead to the development of a more reliable structure for simulation and prediction. The diversity of inflation-related developments during 1965–1974 has already been remarked. Two that occurred in the latter part of the decade received the bulk of attention at this conference. This first is the wage and price control program that began in 1971; the second is the pervasiveness after 1972 of rapid inflation among industrial countries and its relationship to the devaluation of the dollar and to floating exchange rates.

The effect of controls is explored by Klein, Bosworth and Vroman, Kosters, Nadiri and Gupta, and Al-Samarrie, Kraft, and Roberts. As might be expected, there are differences in the conclusions of each. The differences about the effect of controls would probably be multiplied if the quantitative studies of those effects were broadened to include not only their impact on wages and prices but also on output, foreign trade, and investment. The econometric results reported suggest that the conclusions reached about controls are quite sensitive to the theoretical specification used, the sample period to which the regressions are fitted, and the level of disaggregation at which the analysis is conducted.

The findings of Kwack and of Nordhaus and Shoven, already mentioned, provide some insight into the interrelationships among the rapid inflations of 1973–1974 experienced by most industrialized countries outside the Communist bloc. Kwack finds that a decline in one country's exchange rate worsens its inflation-unemployment trade-off while improving that of its trading partners. Nordhaus and Shoven show that the rise in U.S. import prices after devaluation contributed importantly to the inflation rate of the United States.

While varied in approach and finding, these studies of particular inflation-related developments suggest we are on our way to understanding either the development or its impact, depending on which it is appropriate to focus. It would appear that economists are far from having to "dummy out" periods of economic history such as the Vietnam buildup, wage and price controls, or the 1972–1974 worldwide commodity inflation. What is suggested, however, is that more disaggregation is needed and that national models of various countries should be linked, research strategies that are currently being pursued.

In summarizing the research presented at the 1970 Conference on the Econometrics of Price Determination, James Tobin said, "there is more reason to be optimistic about wage-price econometrics than about resolution of the inflation-unemployment dilemma." Notwithstanding the failure of wage and price equations to predict the intensity of the recent inflation, that conclusion is appropriate for this conference as well. The results reported here suggest that through disaggregation, consideration of international effects, and improvement in specification, tools can be developed to warn of the emergence of significant changes in inflation rates.

1

LEONALL C. ANDERSEN
Federal Reserve Bank of St. Louis

and

DENIS S. KARNOSKY
Federal Reserve Bank of St. Louis

A Monetary Interpretation of Inflation

In this era of shortages, there is a definite glut in at least one market: the supply of explanations for the current inflation greatly exceeds the demand at current prices. It could be that this is just a manifestation of increased specialization in the country. In the old days of 1972, only two products were offered seriously in this market: cost-push and demand-pull inflation. We are now offered a choice among anchovy inflation, interest rate inflation, commodity inflation, imported inflation, wage inflation, gouging inflation, and even divine inflation for those who have lost all hope of finding a worldly explanation.

Our concern in this paper is with the role of the rate of money growth as a factor leading to our nation's accelerating inflation since the mid-1960s. The analysis is based on a modified version of the St. Louis model. The original St. Louis model was based on a monetarist view of the influence of monetary actions (measured by changes in the money stock) and fiscal actions (measured by high-employment government expenditures) on total spending, output, and the price level. The model incorporates a recursive view of the macroeconomic process: monetary and fiscal actions determine changes in total spending (measured by nominal gross national product), which in turn is divided into price and output changes. A research strategy of specifying and estimating reduced form equations was employed in developing the original model.

The recursive nature of the original model is maintained in the modified version used here: one block determines changes in nominal GNP, and a second block determines the division of a given change in nominal GNP into changes in output and in the price level. A major difference is that in each block structural equations are specified and their parameters are estimated in place of direct estimation of reduced form equations. A second difference is that all equations are specified as log-linear instead of linear in the variables. The modified model also includes additional exogenous variables, thereby introducing factors other than the direct influences of monetary and fiscal actions as possible causes of inflation.

The model used in the paper is still in process of development. It is not complete, inasmuch as it does not contain a block explaining the market rate of interest, which is an explanatory variable in the block determining GNP. Also, work is continuing on the structural equations in the other two blocks. The model is used here as an expository device, a means of quantifying a monetary view of the recent inflation.

Our paper is divided into two main sections. In the first, a modified version of the St. Louis model is developed and estimates of the parameters of its structural equations are printed. Then the model, in conjunction with actual events since the mid-1960s, is used to evaluate the role of monetary growth as a cause of the inflation.

THE MODEL

At this point in its development, the model consists of two blocks. The first is for the determination of nominal aggregate spending (nominal GNP). This block is built around the proposition that private nominal spending (consumption plus investment) changes in response to a discrepancy between actual and desired nominal money balances. The second block determines the division of a given change in nominal aggregate spending between changes in the price level and real output. This block has many points in common with the price-level determination process postulated in many large-scale econometric models. It includes structural equations that are intended to explain price, wage, and employment decisions in the private sector of the economy. Unit labor costs are considered explicitly, and various expectations variables play a key role in the model.

Block I: Aggregate Nominal Spending

Aggregate nominal spending (Y_t) in an economy for the acquisition of domestically produced final goods and services is defined as the sum of nominal outlays by domestic households and business firms for consumption and investment (Y_t^d), by all units of government for goods and services (G_t), and by foreigners for domestic product (X_t), less domestic outlays for foreign-produced goods and services (IM_t).

(1) $Y_t = Y_t^d + G_t + X_t - IM_t$

Government spending and exports are assumed to be exogenous variables; and aggregate spending, private spending, and imports are assumed to be endogenous.

It is postulated that the amount of nominal money balances desired (M_t^*) is positively related to the expected level of aggregate nominal spending (Y_t^e) and the nominal short-term rate of interest (r_t), and negatively related to the technical efficiency of the system of making money payments (I_t). The expected rate of inflation is not included as an argument; its influence is presumed to be captured to the extent that the expected rate of inflation is embodied in the nominal interest rate.

Assuming that the function for desired money balances is linear in logarithms, the desired amount of money balances is written in the following form:

(2) $\ln M_t^* = \alpha_1 \ln I_t + \alpha_2 \ln Y_t^e + \alpha_3 \ln r_t$

The coefficients α_1 and α_3 are postulated to be negative; and the coefficient α_2, positive.

Expectations regarding the level of aggregate nominal spending are postulated to be formed on the basis of a weighted average of past levels of aggregate spending:

(3) $\ln Y_t^e = \sum_{i=1}^{n} u_i \ln Y_{t-1}$

It is presumed in this study that the technical efficiency of the payments system, i.e., the amount of nominal money balances required to carry out a given volume of money payments, has increased along with the general rise in the productivity of producing goods and services. It is asserted that, on average, the efficiency of the payments system increases at a constant rate, given by the function $I_t = be^{ct}$. The logarithm of this function is

(4) $\ln I_t = \ln b + ct$

The nominal stock of money (M_t) is assumed to be exogenous, determined by monetary authorities. Therefore, holders of money balances, in the aggregate, cannot adjust their holdings when a discrepancy occurs between actual and desired money balances. Instead, individual holders of money balances attempt to acquire (reduce) money balances by reducing (increasing) their rate of spending on goods and services or selling (buying) financial assets, or both. Changes in quantities or prices, or both, occur in these markets until, in the aggregate, the desired level of money equals the actual level.

When a positive (negative) discrepancy occurs between actual and desired money balances, there is said to exist a positive (negative) "excess supply" of money, which implies positive (negative) "excess demand" in markets for goods and services and for financial assets. It is postulated that private nominal spending (Y_t^d) is the variable that adjusts to eliminate this discrepancy, responding positively to an excess supply of money balances. This adjustment process is assumed to be log-linear. The coefficient π is the response of private domestic spending to an excess supply of money and is postulated to be positive.

(5) $\Delta \ln Y_t^d = \pi(\ln M_t - \ln M_t^*)$

It is assumed that imports are a constant ratio (δ) to $Y_t^d + G_t + X_t$. It is expressed as

(6) $IM_t = \delta(Y_t^d + G_t + X_t)$

At this point, the block for aggregate spending determination consists of seven endogenous variables—four expressed in logarithmic terms ($\Delta \ln Y_t^d$, $\ln Y_t^e$, $\ln I_t$, and $\ln M_t^*$) and three expressed in arithmetic terms (Y_t, Y_t^d, and IM_t).

A new variable, Z_t, is defined as equal to $G_t + X_t$. Using this definition and substituting equation 6 into equation 1 yields:

(7) $Y_t = (1 - \delta)(Y_t^d + Z_t)$

Finally, an identity is developed that transforms equation 7, containing variables expressed arithmetically, into an equation expressed in logarithms. Using the proposition that for small differences the percent change in a variable is approximately equal to the first difference of logarithms of the variable, the following two equations are derived:

(8)　　$\Delta \ln Y_t = w_t \, \Delta \ln Y_t^d + (1 - w_t) \, \Delta \ln Z_t$

(9)　　$w_t = (1 - \delta) \, Y_{t-1}^d / Y_{t-1} = \text{antilog } (\ln (1 - \delta) + \ln Y_{t-1}^d - \ln Y_{t-1})$

Equations 2 through 5 are next solved to yield an equation for changes in private spending in terms of exogenous variables:

(10)　　$\Delta \ln Y_t^d = \pi \ln M_t - \pi \alpha_1 (\ln b + ct) - \pi \alpha_2 \sum_{i=1}^{n} w_i \ln Y_{t-1} - \pi \alpha_3 \ln r_t$

The block for determination of aggregate nominal spending in its final form consists of equations 8, 9, and 10.[1] These equations can be solved for the three endogenous variables ($\Delta \ln Y_t$, $\Delta \ln Y_t^d$, and w_t) in terms of the exogenous variables ($\ln M_t$, $\ln r_t$, $\ln Z_t$, and t) and of the lagged endogenous variables ($\ln Y_{t-1}$) and ($\ln Y_{t-1}^d$).

An examination of the variables in this set of equations indicates that changes in aggregate nominal spending are influenced by changes in five factors: the money stock, government expenditures, exports, the rate of interest, and the average technical efficiency of the payments system. The change in aggregate nominal spending in response to any of these changes is also influenced by initial conditions measured by past levels of spending and the ratio of private spending to total spending. Furthermore, the response of aggregate spending is distributed over time because there is a lagged adjustment to a discrepancy between actual and desired money balances, and expected aggregate spending is postulated to depend on past aggregate spending.

Block I: Estimates of Structural Parameters

A first-difference transformation of equation 10 was estimated as a means of reducing possible statistical problems in regression analysis, stemming from multicollinearity in the level of the variables and from their autocorrelation:

(10′)　　$\Delta \ln Y_t^d - \Delta \ln Y_{t-1}^d = a_0 + a_1 \Delta \ln M_t + a_2 \sum_{i=1}^{n} w_i \Delta \ln Y_{t-1} + a_3 \Delta \ln r_t$

The parameters of equation 10′ are estimated using quarterly observations of the data for 1955I–1973IV. Aggregate nominal spending is measured by nominal GNP. Private nominal spending is measured by GNP minus government spending and exports and plus imports. Money is the sum of demand deposits and currency held by the nonbank public. The nominal interest rate is measured by the 4-to-6–month commercial paper rate. The constant term in 10′ is the response of private domestic spending to the average quarterly increase in the technical efficiency of the payments system $(\pi\alpha_1 c)$ in the sample period. Two zero-one dummy variables are included for the average influence of major strikes on private domestic spending: $D_1 = 1$ for the quarter in which the strike occurs, and $D_2 = 1$ for the quarter following a strike.

An Almon lag is used in estimating the coefficients for lagged changes in aggregate nominal spending. A third-degree polynomial is used, with the coefficient for $t - n - 1$ constrained to zero. The length of the lag (four quarters) is selected to minimize the standard

**TABLE 1 Block I Regression Coefficients
(dependent variable: $\Delta^2 \ln Y_t^d$)**

Variable	With Interest Rate	Without Interest Rate
D_1	−1.871*	−1.979*
D_2	2.144*	2.201*
$\Delta \ln M_t$	0.690*	0.637*
$\Delta \ln r_t$	0.018†	—
$\Delta \ln Y_{t-1}$	−0.841*	−0.697*
$\Delta \ln Y_{t-2}$	−0.076	−0.060
$\Delta \ln Y_{t-3}$	−0.008	−0.020
$\Delta \ln Y_{t-4}$	−0.147	−0.145
$\Sigma\Delta \ln Y_{t-i}$	−1.072*	−0.922*
Constant	1.066*	0.907*
R^2	0.550	0.533
SE	0.898	0.915
DW	2.028	1.999

NOTE: R^2 = coefficient of multiple determination; SE = standard error of estimate; DW = Durbin-Watson statistic. For identification of variables, see description of Block I in the accompanying text. The data are identified in "Block I: Estimates of Structural Parameters."
*Significant at 5 percent level.
†Significant at 10 percent level.

error of estimate. The estimated parameters are presented in Table 1. All the coefficients have the expected signs.

Step-ahead simulations of quarterly percent changes in aggregate nominal spending (at annual rates) over the sample period were conducted for Block I. The import ratio δ (see equation 6) was held at its average value over the sample period. The root-mean-square error for the step-ahead simulation was 2.64 percent at an annual rate.

Block II: Wages, Prices, and Employment

The equations that explain wages, prices, and employment are based on the premise that business firms are on average price searchers in the goods market and price takers in the market for labor services.[2] Consequently, consumers are presumed to determine the current wage rate, subject to their best estimates of the prices that will prevail in the market for goods and services. Thus, prices and wages are presumed to be determined on the supply side in each market, at least in the short run. The actual quantities exchanged at these prices are then determined by demand factors.

Neither firms nor individuals have perfect information about conditions in the goods and labor markets; and, therefore, demand and supply decisions are presumed to be based on expectations in both markets. The interaction of expectations and actual demand provides the dynamics to this section.

Prices are assumed to be determined by wealth-maximizing considerations; and following standard maximizing procedures, prices are derived as a function of unit labor costs. It is not actual output that enters into the calculation of cost, however, but an estimate of the longer-term rate of sales that will maximize net worth at current prices and with the existing capital stock. The price equation is

(11) $\quad \ln P_t = \rho_0 + \rho_1 t + \rho_2(\ln W_t + \ln N_t - \ln \overline{EQ}_t)$

where P_t is the price in the current period t, W_t is the current wage rate, N_t is the amount of labor services employed in the current period, and $\overline{EQ}_t$ is the estimate of the rate of output that will be taken in the market, on average, at the price P_t. Firms are presumed to incur costs in changing prices, and therefore do not change prices in response to short-term changes in demand, even where such changes are expected. Thus, this expected demand $(\overline{EQ}_t)$ is not the amount expected in the current period, which may include some estimate of factors which affect demand in the short run. $(\overline{EQ_t})$ is defined as a distributed lag function of expected demand in the current period (EQ_t):

(12) $$\ln \overline{EQ}_t = \sum_{i=0}^{m} \beta_i \ln EQ_{t-i}$$

The demand for labor services is determined jointly with price in the maximizing decision. With capital stock treated as a completely fixed factor, the amount of labor services demanded is a function of the scale of output only. As in the price equation, the output variable that enters this decision is the longer-term sales expectations of the firm. Labor is treated as a quasi-fixed factor with positive costs of adjustment. The labor demand function is

(13) $$\ln N_t = n_0 + n_1 t + n_2 \ln \overline{EQ}_t$$

The amount of labor services supplied to the market is postulated to be a function of the expected real wage:

(14) $$\ln N_t^s = s_0 + s_1 t + s_2 (\ln W_t - \ln EP_t)$$

where EP_t is the price expected to prevail in the goods market in the current period.

Uncertainty about demand conditions in the labor market is incorporated with the adjustment equation:

(15) $$\Delta \ln W_t = \lambda_1 (\ln W_t^* - \ln W_{t-1})$$

where W^* is the wage rate that would clear the market in the current period. This equation reflects the postulate that labor adjusts its wage demands less than instantaneously to discrepancies between amounts demanded and supplied in the labor market.

This system of equations is in equilibrium only when the price expected by labor, and on which labor supply decisions are based, actually prevails in the goods market, and the amount of goods and services demanded at that price is the rate expected by business firms.

This block of equations is completed by the addition of three functions, two of which define the mechanism by which expectations are formed:

(16) $$\Delta \ln EP_t = \lambda_2 (\ln P_t - \ln EP_{t-1})$$

(17) $$\Delta \ln EQ_t = \lambda_3 (\ln Q_t - \ln EQ_{t-1})$$

(18) $$\ln Y_t = \ln P_t + \ln Q_t$$

The only variable strictly exogenous to this block is the rate of aggregate nominal spending. As in the original St. Louis model, output is determined as a residual.

In this form, this block contains two variables for which no direct measures are available: current labor supply (N_t^s) and the equilibrium wage (W_t^*). In order to get around this problem, equations 13 and 14 are solved for W^* by setting $\ln N_t$ equal to $\ln N_t^s$. The result is then inserted into equation 15. By this procedure both W^* and N^s are eliminated from the system.

(15') $\quad \Delta \ln W_t = \dfrac{\lambda_1}{s_2} [(n_0 - s_0) + (n_1 - s_1)t + n_2 \ln \overline{EQ}_t + s_2 \ln EP_t] - \lambda_1 \ln W_{t-1}$

One further substitution is made. Equations 11, 13, and 15' are solved simultaneously to yield two new equations defining W and P:

(11') $\quad \ln P_t = \gamma_0 + \gamma_1 t + \gamma_2 \ln EP_t + \gamma_3 \ln \overline{EQ}_t + \gamma_4 \ln W_{t-1}$

where

$\gamma_0 = (1/s_2)[s_2(\rho_2 n_0 + \rho_0) + \rho_2 \lambda_1 (n_0 - s_0)]$

$\gamma_1 = (1/s_2)[s_2(\rho_2 n_1 + \rho_1) + \rho_2 \lambda_1 (n_1 - s_1)]$

$\gamma_2 = \rho_2 \lambda_1$

$\gamma_3 = (\rho_2/s_2)[s_2(n_2 - 1) + n_2 \lambda_1]$

$\gamma_4 = \rho_2(1 - \lambda_1)$

(15") $\quad \ln W_t = \omega_0 + \omega_1 t + \omega_2 \ln EP_t + \omega_3 \ln \overline{EQ}_t + \omega_4 \ln W_{t-1}$

where

$\omega_0 = (\lambda_1/s_2)(n_0 - s_0)$

$\omega_1 = (\lambda_1/s_2)(n_1 - s_1)$

$\omega_2 = \lambda_1$

$\omega_3 = \lambda_1 n_2/s_2$

$\omega_4 = 1 - \lambda_1$

This latter transformation allows testing of the specification of the structural equations since several of the parameters in equations 11' and 15" are functionally related. Specifically, $\gamma_4 = 1 - \gamma_2$ and $\omega_4 = 1 - \omega_2$.[3] Empirical tests yielded results which did not contradict these constraints, and thus the following two equations are included in the model:

(19) $\quad \ln W_t - \ln W_{t-1} = \alpha_0 + \alpha_1 t + \alpha_2(\ln EP_t - \ln W_{t-1}) + \alpha_3 \sum_{i=0}^{n} w_i \ln EQ_{t-i}$

(20) $\ln P_t - \ln W_{t-1} = \beta_0 + \beta_1 t + \beta_2(\ln EP_t - \ln W_{t-1}) + \beta_3 \sum\limits_{i=0}^{n} w_i \ln EQ_{t-i}$

One further equation is added, defining unit labor costs (U):

(21) $\ln U_t = \ln W_t + \ln N_t - \ln Q_t$

This block, then, is composed of the seven equations 13 and 16 through 21, where the endogenous variables are $\ln W$, $\ln P$, $\ln Q$, $\ln N$, $\ln U$, $\ln EP$, and $\ln EQ$.

Block II: Estimates of Structural Parameters

The coefficients in this block are estimated using quarterly data for 1955I–1973IV. The wage, price, employment, and output variables are measured by national income accounts data adjusted to remove compensation of government employees. This adjustment is made on the presumption that the behavior postulated in this block is not representative of government employment practices. In addition, this procedure eliminates from the data the artificial effect on price movements of the treatment given government pay increases in the national income accounts. We have not yet incorporated government employment practices into the model, and we treat compensation of government employees (N_g) as an exogenous variable, included in G. Equation 18 is rewritten as $\ln Y_t^p = \ln P_t + \ln Q_t$, where Y^p is aggregate spending on goods and services produced in the private sector. This block is then linked to Block I by the identity $Y_t^p = Y_t - N_{gt}$.

The expectations variables (EP) and (EQ) are derived from the Livingston surveys, using the forecast of the consumer price index and the index of industrial production. The estimates of the coefficients are presented in Table 2.

Step-ahead simulations of Block II as a unit are performed, as in the case of Block I. The root-mean-square errors for percent changes in the endogenous variables (at annual rates) are reported in Table 3.

Blocks I and II: Model Simulations

To ascertain the simulative ability of the model over the sample period, step-ahead simulations combining both blocks are performed. The exogenous variables driving the model are changes in

TABLE 2 Block II Regression Coefficients

Predetermined Variables	Dependent Variables				
	$\ln P - \ln W_{-1}$	$\ln W - \ln W_{-1}$	$\ln N$	$\Delta \ln EP$	$\Delta \ln EQ$
$\ln EQ$	0.004	0.016	0.267*		
$\ln EQ_{-1}$	0.009	0.023*	0.174*		
$\ln EQ_{-2}$	0.011†	0.025*	0.101*		
$\ln EQ_{-3}$	0.010	0.022†	0.047*		
$\ln EQ_{-4}$	0.006	0.013	0.013		
$\ln EP - \ln W_{-1}$	0.874*	0.222*			
$\ln P - \ln EP_{-1}$				0.590*	
$\ln Q - \ln EQ_{-1}$					0.679*
t	−0.001*	0.001	−0.002*		
Constant	−0.107	−0.483*	1.939*		
$\hat{\rho}$	0.290	0.041	0.957	−0.578	−0.583
$\bar{R}^2$	0.999	0.214	0.997	0.571	0.686
SE	0.003	0.006	0.004	0.003	0.008
DW	1.960	1.969	1.731	2.371	2.365

NOTE: For identification of variables, see description of Block II in the accompanying text.
*Significant at 5 percent level.
†Significant at 10 percent level.

money, government spending, exports and government payrolls, and time. The root-mean-square errors for percent changes (at annual rates) are presented in Table 3.

TABLE 3 Step-Ahead Simulation within Sample Period (root-mean-square errors for percent change in quarterly data at annual rates)

Dependent Variable	Block II	Blocks I and II
Price level	1.74%	1.74%
Wage payments	3.11	3.10
Man-hours worked	1.94	2.06
Output	1.74	3.56
Unit labor costs	3.76	4.14
Output per man-hour	2.13	3.19
Aggregate spending	—	2.64

Since this study focuses on inflation, the ability of Block II to simulate the annual rate of change in the price level over four quarters is examined. Overlapping four-quarter dynamic simulations are performed, starting from each quarter between 1955II and 1972III. Root-mean-square errors in the percent quarterly changes (at annual rates) are calculated for all the sets of first-, second-, third-, and fourth-quarter simulations. For the entire sample period, the errors are 1.50, 1.50, 1.27, and 1.31 percent. The model does not take into consideration the imposition and subsequent relaxation of price-wage controls or any special factors; when the simulations are stopped at 1971II, root-mean-square errors of 1.32, 1.26, 0.99, and 0.98 percent are obtained.

MONEY GROWTH AND INFLATION

The model responses of the price level and the other endogenous variables to different growth rates of money are ascertained by hypothetical dynamic simulations for the period 1964–1973. These simulations, to the extent that the model is an accurate portrayal of macroeconomic processes, shed light on the influence of money growth on inflation. They also demonstrate the responses of unit labor costs, wage payments, and productivity—the variables under-lying the traditional cost-push view of inflation—to different growth rates of money.

The simulations start from 1964II. Since the interest rate block is not specified, equation 10' is re-estimated with the interest rate excluded (Table 1). In these simulations it is assumed that no strikes occurred. In the first simulation it is assumed that the exogenous variables increase at their average annual rates from 1955 to 1964; i.e., $\Delta M/M = 3$ percent, $\Delta Z/Z = 6$ percent, and $\Delta Ng/Ng = 7$ percent. In the second simulation it is assumed that $\Delta M/M = 6$ percent, its average annual rate from 1964 to 1973, and that the other two exogenous variables increase as in the previous simulation.

The contribution of the faster money growth to the annual rate of increase in each endogenous variable is measured by the differ-ence between a 3 percent and 6 percent annual rate of money growth. These differences are presented in figures 1 and 2.

FIGURE 1   Differential Response of Endogenous
Variables[a]
(differences in annual rates of
change)

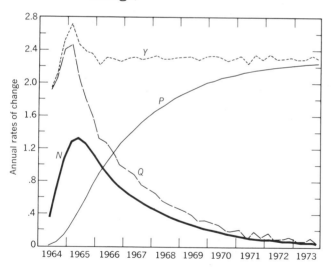

[a] Response to a 6 percent annual rate of money growth minus re-sponse to 3 percent annual rate of money growth. Y = nominal aggregate spending, P = price level, N = employment, and Q = output.

FIGURE 2 Differential Response of Endogenous Variables[a]
(differences in annual rates of change)

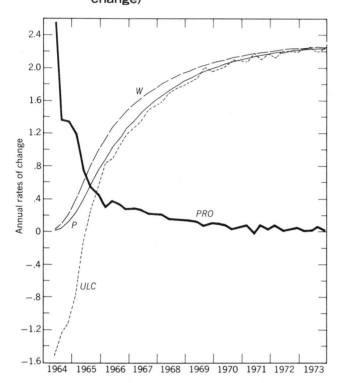

[a] Response to a 6 percent annual rate of money growth minus response to a 3 percent rate. W = wage payments, PRO = output per man-hour worked, ULC = unit labor costs, and P = price level.

Response of Price Level

The model simulations indicate that aggregate nominal spending (Y) would have increased at an annual rate 2.3 percentage points more with a 6 percent rate of money growth than with a 3 percent rate (Figure 1). In addition, the price level (P) would have risen at an annual rate of 2.3 percentage points more by the end of 1973 with 6 percent money growth than with 3 percent growth. Finally, while growth of output (Q) would have been initially greatly affected by the difference between the two rates of money, by the end of 1973, real output would have been rising at the same rate in both cases.[4]

Simulations were also performed holding money growth at 3 percent and assuming that Z grows at a rate of 10 percent, its average annual rate from 1964 to 1973. The results indicate that after a few quarters both the level of Y and its rate of change are virtually the same as in the simulation with 3 percent money growth and 6 percent growth of Z. As a result, the higher rate of growth of Z has little influence on the price level and the other endogenous variables in Block II.[5]

Implications for the Cost-Push View of Inflation

According to the model, changes in the growth of money cause changes in unit labor costs, wage payments, and productivity—the variables underlying a cost-push view of inflation. The hypothetical dynamic simulations produce movements in these three variables and in the price level that are consistent with the cost-push analysis, but these simulated movements are the result of one common factor—changes in the growth of money.

The difference in the rate of increase in wage payments (W) for 6 percent money growth over that for 3 percent growth rises sharply for about two years, then decelerates slowly. By the end of 1973, the difference has stabilized at about 2.2 percentage points higher (Figure 2). On the other hand, the difference in growth of output per man-hour worked (PRO) is substantial in the first quarter of the comparison, dropping sharply for about the next two years. Thereafter, the difference slowly narrows to approximately zero. The difference in the rates of increase of unit labor costs (ULC) are at first substantially below the difference for wage payment, but after the second year, the differences are nearly the same for both. The difference in the rates of increase in the price level (P) closely parallels that for unit labor costs after the second year.

These movements are consistent with the cost-push view of inflation that unit labor costs determine the price level and that an increase in wage payments exceeding growth of output per man-hour worked increases unit labor costs. According to the model, however, the simulated movements in these four variables are the result of the economy's adjustment over time to a higher growth of money. Also, when the results of a 6 percent money rate of growth for 1973 are compared with those for 3 percent money growth, higher rates of increase are indicated in the price level, unit labor costs, and wage payments. The cost-push view would attribute the higher rate of inflation to the higher rate of increase in unit labor costs resulting from the faster rate of increase in wage payments. The monetary view of inflation incorporated in the model would attribute the higher rates of increase in these variables to the faster growth of money.[6]

CONCLUSIONS

A structural model was specified, based on a monetary view of inflation, and its structural parameters were estimated. To the extent that the model captures macroeconomic processes, it demonstrates that the growth rate of money is a basic cause of inflation. An increase in money growth increases aggregate nominal spending. Market behavior of firms and suppliers of labor services, in turn, results in a faster rate of price increase. Model simulations also indicate that the faster growth of aggregate spending produces movements in the price level, unit labor costs, wage payments, and output per man-hour, that typically have been incorporated in a cost-push explanation of inflation. Thus, according to the model, the so-called cost-push phenomenon is to a considerable extent a reflection of the economy's adjustment to changes in the rate of money growth.

NOTES

1. For an earlier version of Block I see Leonall C. Andersen, "Comment on 'A Note on the Effects of Government Finance on Aggregate Demand for Goods and Services,'" *Public Finance*, November 3–4, 1973.
2. The analysis that underlies this section is drawn from previous work. See Denis S. Karnosky, "The Effect of Market Expectations on Employment, Wages, and Prices," Working Paper 17, Federal Reserve Bank of St. Louis, August 1973.
3. The implication of $\delta_4 = 1 - \delta_2$ is that $\rho_2 = 1.0$. This postulate was confirmed in tests not presented here. See ibid., pp. 74–79.
4. Since the difference in growth of real output never falls below zero, the model implies a permanent increase in the level of output from that implied by 3 percent money growth. This characteristic of the model is under further investigation.
5. For an extended report of similar simulations, see Andersen, "Comment."
6. Maximizing behavior and competitive markets underlie the equations in Block II. Empirical estimates of the structural parameters in this block are consistent with those implied by the theory. Consequently, this theory of price level movements is accepted and offered as an alternative to a cost-push theory of inflation based on market behavior of union and business monopolies. See Karnosky, "Effect of Market Expectations."

COMMENTS

Gary Fromm

National Bureau of Economic Research

Complex problems, it appears, often beget simplistic explanations and solutions. In these difficult times of rampaging inflation in the midst of shortages, we are offered a diverse menu of explanatory choices, many of which are cited by Andersen and Karnosky. There is anchovy inflation, agricultural commodity inflation, world business cycle inflation, OPEC inflation, business- and labor-gouging inflation, local government wage-rate inflation, federal-spending inflation, and other more exotic forms. Of course, some analysts still adhere to traditional generalized cost-push or demand-pull inflation causes.

However, Andersen and Karnosky will have none of this and instead offer us their own special concoction. They say that the basic cause of inflation is simply the growth rate of money. Moreover, cost-push phenomena are said to be a reflection of the economy's adjustment to changes in the rate of money growth. Other than hard-core monetarists, it is doubtful that many economists would find these conclusions palatable. It is one thing to say that "money matters" in understanding movements in aggregate price levels. It is another to aver that the root cause of inflation since the mid-1960s is only money.

Andersen and Karnosky reach this conclusion on the basis of simulations with a modified version of the St. Louis Federal Reserve Bank model. The new model, like the old, is recursive. An initial block of equations relates nominal GNP to the nominal money supply, defined as M_1 (demand deposits plus currency). A subsequent block then splits changes in nominal GNP into price and real components, and provides, too, estimates of wage rates, man-hours, unit labor costs, and expected prices and outputs.

There are two major differences between the modified and original models. First, the equations are said to be specified and parameters estimated on a structural basis rather than as reduced forms. Second, most equations are log-linear rather than linear in variables. There are also some different exogenous variables, and interest rates are, at present, treated exogenously, a deficiency which may be removed in subsequent versions.

At this point in its development, Block I of the model takes the

A Monetary Interpretation of Inflation | 27

following form. Total spending is defined by Andersen-Karnosky in their equation 1 as the sum of private domestic spending, government spending, and exports less imports. Desired nominal money balances are made a function of technical efficiency of the monetary system (represented by an exponential time trend), the expected level of aggregate nominal spending (represented by a moving average of past spending), and nominal interest rates (equations 2, 3, and 4). The expected rate of inflation is not explicitly included as an argument, since it is assumed that expected prices are relevant only in periods of hyperinflation. (However, expected prices, of course, enter implicitly, since expected spending must include quantity and price components.)

Actual money balances are assumed to be determined by the Federal Reserve. Therefore, when there is a discrepancy between actual and desired money stocks, holders of money balances in the aggregate are said to adjust their rate of spending and holdings of other financial assets to eliminate the gap. In the present version of the model (equation 5), it is postulated that only private domestic spending adjusts to eliminate the discrepancy (recall that interest rates are exogenous).

In equation 6, imports (IM) are taken to be a constant proportion (δ) of the sum of private domestic spending (Y_t^d) plus government outlays (G_t) plus exports (X_t), with the last two exogenous. Letting $Z_t = G_t + X_t$, the authors can now describe total spending (equation 1) as:

(7) $Y_t = (1 - \delta)(Y_t^d + Z_t)$

or, for small changes (following equation 8),

$$\Delta \ln Y_t = (1 - \delta)\{(Y_{t-1}^d/Y_{t-1}) \Delta \ln Y_t^d + [1 - (1 - \delta)(Y_{t-1}^d/Y_{t-1})] \Delta \ln Z_t\}$$

By combining equations 2 through 5 and performing a first-difference transformation, a final estimating equation is obtained (following 10'):

$$\Delta \ln Y_t^d - \Delta \ln Y_{t-1}^d = a_0 + a_1 \Delta \ln M_t + a_2 \sum_{i=1}^{n} w_i \Delta \ln Y_{t-1}$$

$$+ a_3 \Delta \ln r_t + a_4 D_1 + a_5 D_2$$

Dummy variables (D) are included to account for the average influence of major strikes, and an Almon lag (third-degree polynominal, far-end zero constraint) is used for the aggregate spending term. The length of lag (four quarters) was selected to minimize the standard error of estimate.

The parameters of the equation were estimated using quarterly data for the period 1955–1973. Private spending is taken as nominal GNP less government spending and exports plus imports; money supply, as demand deposits plus currency; aggregate spending, as nominal GNP; and interest rates, as the 4-to-6–month commercial paper rate. $R^2 = 0.55$, and most coefficients are significant at the 5 percent level. The interest rate coefficient is small, and is significant only at the 10 percent level. An ex post dynamic simulation with equations 8 and $10'$ shows that nominal GNP is tracked reasonably well.

Block II of the model explains wages, prices, and man-hours. Prices and wage rates are presumed to be set on the supply side in the short run, with the quantities of output and labor determined by demand factors. Prices are a log-linear function of productivity (represented by a time trend), wage rates, man-hours, and expected sales (at the long-run profit-maximizing price). Firms are presumed to incur costs in changing prices in response to short-run demand shifts, even where such changes are expected. Price and expected sales (EQ) are given by equations 11 and 12, respectively. The demand for labor man-hours depends on a time trend (a proxy for productivity?) and on expected sales or output (equation 13). The supply of labor man-hours depends on a time trend (a proxy for population and increased participation rates of women?), wage rates, and expected prices (equation 14). Since actual wage rates may differ from those which would clear the labor market (demand = supply), there is a partial adjustment mechanism (equation 15).

The second block of structural equations is completed by partial adjustment functions for expected prices (EP) and output and a nominal income-price-output identity (equations 16, 17, and 18).

Since labor supply (N_t^s) and the equilibrium wage (W_t^*) are unobservable, labor demand and supply (equations 13 and 14) are equated and solved for the equilibrium wage. The result is then inserted into the wage adjustment function, yielding equation $15'$. Substituting for expected sales or output (cf. equation 12) in equation $15'$, leads to equation 19.

Similarly, solving for the equilibrium wage rate, substituting for W and N (from equation 13) in equation 11, and using a distributed lag for expected output yields:

$$
(20) \quad \ln P_t - \ln W_{t-1} = \beta_0 + \beta_1 t + \beta_2(\ln EP_t - \ln W_{t-1})
$$

$$
+ \beta_3 \sum_0^n w_i \ln EQ_{t-1} + (\rho_2 - 1) \ln W_{t-1}
$$

(The last term is dropped erroneously from the Andersen-Karnosky formulation because of the assumption that $\rho_2 = 1$.) Finally, in equation 21, unit labor costs are defined.

Taken as a whole, Block II contains five stochastic equations and two identities for the seven endogenous variables: wage rates, prices, man-hours, unit labor costs, real output, expected prices, and expected output. The last two are measured and estimated from the Livingston surveys. The exogenous variables are time and aggregate nominal spending. Lagged endogenous (predetermined) variables are expected prices, expected output, and wage rates.

Equation parameters in this block are estimated using quarterly observations for 1955–1973 with data from the national income accounts, adjusted to remove compensation of government employees (N_g) from all variables (it is not clear how this is done). In the solutions, equation 18 is rewritten as $\ln Y_t^p = \ln P_t + \ln Q_t$, where $Y_t^p = Y_t + N_{gt}$. The coefficients and explained variances obtained in the empirical estimates of the equations in this block reveal reasonable degrees of significance.

In contrast to Andersen and Karnosky's opinion that simulated paths reflect very well actual movements in each variable, ex post dynamic simulations of Block II show relatively large errors compared to simulations with other models for prices, output, man-hours, and unit labor costs over most of the 1955–1973 simulation period.[1] Prices and unit labor costs have large upward biases; and outputs and man-hours, large downward biases. The results generally are slightly worse when blocks I and II are combined in complete model solutions. Only wage rates are predicted reasonably accurately, but these rise along a fairly smooth path. The largest errors in levels of variables are 4.6 percent for prices and for output in the fourth quarter of 1973, 3.6 percent for wage rates in the first quarter of 1961, 7.3 percent for man-hours in the second quarter of 1956, and 6.6 percent for unit labor costs in the fourth quarter of 1973.

Responses of prices and other endogenous variables in the model are obtained from dynamic simulations for 1964–1973. The simulations were run with a growth rate of the sum of nominal government outlays and exports of 6 percent, compensation of government employees of 7 percent, and alternative rates of growth of M_1 of 3 and 6 percent, respectively. With 3 percent money growth, total spending (nominal GNP) increases at a steady 5.9 percent starting in 1967; with 6 percent money growth, the increase is at 8.2 percent. For both rates of money growth, real output grows at 3.9 percent in 1973 (thus, the respective rates of growth of prices at that time are 2.0

and 4.3 percent). Little change was found in the 3 percent money growth simulation when exogenous expenditures (government plus exports) were allowed to grow at 10 rather than 6 percent.

As noted by Andersen and Karnosky, changes in the growth of money cause changes in wage rates, productivity, and unit labor costs. In the 6 percent money growth case for 1973, wage payments rise steadily to a rate of increase of 7.4 percent, and output per manhour first jumps sharply and then declines steadily to a 2.3 percent rate of increase in 1973. As a consequence, unit labor costs rise at a 5.1 percent rate at the same time. Given the nature of the price function, movements of the price level closely parallel those of unit labor costs.

While such movements may be consistent with a cost-push view of inflation, Andersen and Karnosky attribute the impact on prices as a result of the economy's adjustment in 1964–1973 to a higher growth rate of money (6 percent, which approximates the actual M_1 growth rate, in contrast to a hypothetical 3 percent).[2]

Given the instructions of the chairman that discussants are first to summarize authors' papers, I have up to this point for the most part resisted the temptation to criticize the analysis. On its face, it probably seems plausible and perhaps convincing to many, especially to those who have a monetarist bias to begin with. Yet, difficulties with the analysis and its execution abound.

To begin with, there is the fundamental proposition that domestic spending is the variable that adjusts to eliminate discrepancies between actual and desired money balances. Keynesian and portfolio theory would suggest that much, if not all, of the adjustment would occur in the form of shifts in demand for earning assets. Because there is no interest rate block, the present version of the St. Louis model makes no provision for adjustments on the asset side. This is a major deficiency in what is billed as a monetarist model.

Other than to posit that expected price increases are embodied in the nominal rate of interest, little exception can be taken to the specification of the equation for desired money stocks. In fact, when this function is combined with the other equations in Block I, the resultant function relating changes in income to changes in money stocks and interest rates can, when renormalized, be viewed as a typical nominal money demand function. The difficulty with this interpretation is that the terms for expected prices and for time deposit interest rates are missing.

Andersen and Karnosky undertake a first-difference transformation of this equation as a means of reducing possible multicollinearity and serial correlation of residuals. But this procedure is statistically efficient only in highly selected cases. Moreover, it has the effect of creating an unusual dependent variable: $Y_t^d Y_{t-2}^d/(Y_{t-1}^d)^2$.

Estimates of the coefficients of the equation, while they may be statistically significant (it would have been desirable to show t statistics rather than simply to state this) also are unusual. The coefficient of adjustment, with a value of 0.69, is approximately twice the size found in other studies (cf. Stephen Goldfeld's excellent study in *Brookings Papers on Economic Activity*). It gives almost complete adjustment of spending to changes in money stocks within a one-year period. Even more troublesome is the implied income elasticity of desired money balances, which, with or without the interest rate term, appears to be in the neighborhood of 1.5. The size of this coefficient may account for the substantially stronger short-run response of spending to changes in the money stock in the modified St. Louis model than in other models.

Turning to Block II, I find it surprising that no account is taken of the wage-price control program of recent years, especially because ad hoc strike dummy variables are included in the spending function of Block I. While controls may have had little long-run effect on the rate of inflation, it seems inconceivable that they did not have at least a significant short-run impact.

Aside from elimination of a wage rate term in the derivation of the final price function, the basic specification of the initial price equation can be seriously questioned. The purpose of including a time trend is not evident, nor is the absence of materials costs justified.

On the St. Louis model, serious reservations might also be raised on statistical grounds. The authors do not say how parameters are estimated. If the method of ordinary least squares is used, the estimated coefficients for this simultaneous equation system are biased and inconsistent. There are identification problems in both blocks.

Given these and other difficulties, I find it hard to accept the simulation results and the conclusions of the authors. However, they are to be thanked for an interesting and provocative paper, and we should wish them well in the pursuit of their goal of proving that money is the root of all evil, or at least of inflation. In fact, their own simulations would appear to belie this conclusion. The differential long-run response of prices to a 6 percent annual rate of money growth versus a 3 percent rate is 2.3 percent inflation. Since the long-run response of differential real output is negligible, there must be a drop in velocity and, presumably, a smaller increase in interest rates than in the rate of change of prices, which may have consequences for the composition of output. Another fascinating implication of the simulations is that monetary policy is powerful and effective for short-run stabilization of real output and employment. In the first year of a shift in money growth, there are limited price effects but substantial impacts on real output.

NOTES

1. These comments pertain to the original version of the paper, which included charts of predicted versus actual values. Only root-mean-square errors are shown in the present version. Since the model in the latest version is the same as in the original, presumably the errors are identical.
2. Only differential responses are shown in the present version; the earlier one included paths of variables.

2

LAWRENCE R. KLEIN
University of Pennsylvania

Econometrics of Inflation, 1965–1974: A Review of the Decade

The decade ending December 31, 1974, has been a turbulent one in the history of postwar inflation. It is ending on a strong upbeat that has caused econometricians to take some new hard looks at their models because they, together with most other economists, failed to foresee the magnitude of the present spurt.

We often tend to magnify contemporary problems, claiming that present issues are more complicated than ever, making analysis especially difficult. Today's problems are certainly not simple, but it is questionable whether they are any worse than usual, particularly when the outstanding ones are viewed in relation to the others. In analyzing inflation since World War II, we have had to deal with postwar decontrol, the Marshall Plan, the Korean War, the closing of the Suez Canal, major European currency revaluations, U.S. stockpiling, and a number of other major complications.

In the present paper, we are faced with the job of disentangling the effects of Vietnam, New Economic Policy (NEP) controls, dollar devaluation, reclosing of Suez, tripling or quadrupling of crude oil

NOTE: Vincent Su provided much material and insight for the analysis of price and wage relationships during the NEP period.

35

prices, massive crop failures in the USSR, and many other complicating circumstances. It is unquestionably a difficult period, and gives us reason to think again about fundamental model structure, but it is probably not worse by a different order of magnitude than the two preceding postwar decades.

Ultimately, the inflation record gets registered in price statistics; but in order to understand the econometrics of price formation, it is helpful to look simultaneously at other market-determined variables, namely, wage and interest rates. The prices of factors play strategic roles in determining the prices of goods.

In Table 1, annual values are given for three major price indexes, an overall hourly earnings rate, and the Treasury bill rate. In Table 2, some sensitive and strategic components of the various price indexes are separately listed. Although a great deal of econometric analysis is concerned with short-run analysis by quarters or even months, the broad outlines here are given by years for compactness in presentation. The full flavor of the decade's events is given by an annual presentation.

Prices, by any of the three indexes in Table 1, showed the influence of Vietnam War burdens, growing by more after 1965 than in the early 1960s; but they picked up considerably in 1973, and more so in 1974. Wholesale prices appear to have been a leader in 1973 and have kept right on increasing in 1974. Wage rates, according to the hourly earnings series in Table 1, showed a steady, modestly growing increment until 1974 and are shooting up forcefully now in

TABLE 1 A Decade of Market Rates: Prices, Wages, Interest

	GNP Deflator (1958 = 100)	Consumer Price Index (1967 = 100)	Wholesale Price Index (1967 = 100)	Nonagricultural Earnings (dol. per hr.)	Treasury Bill Rate (percent)
1965	110.9	94.5	96.6	2.45	3.95
1966	113.9	97.2	99.8	2.56	4.88
1967	117.6	100.0	100.0	2.68	4.32
1968	122.3	104.2	102.5	2.85	5.34
1969	128.2	109.8	106.5	3.04	6.68
1970	135.2	116.3	110.4	3.22	6.46
1971	141.6	121.3	113.9	3.43	4.35
1972	146.1	125.3	119.1	3.65	4.07
1973	154.3	133.1	134.7	3.92	7.04
1974	170.2	147.7	160.1	4.22	7.89

SOURCE: *Survey of Current Business*, various issues.

TABLE 2   Components of Major Price Indexes

| | GNP Deflator: Import Deflator | Consumer Price Index | | Wholesale Price Index | |
		Food	Services Excl. Rent	Farm Products	Crude Materials
			(1967 = 100)		
1965	103.4	94.4	91.5	98.7	99.3
1966	105.6	99.1	95.3	105.9	105.7
1967	106.5	100.0	100.0	100.0	100.0
1968	107.7	103.6	105.7	102.5	101.6
1969	110.8	108.9	113.8	109.1	108.4
1970	119.2	114.9	123.7	111.0	112.3
1971	125.0	118.4	130.8	112.9	115.0
1972	133.6	123.5	135.9	125.0	127.6
1973	155.6	141.4	141.8	176.3	174.0
1974[a]	219.7	161.7	152.0	187.7	176.0

SOURCE: *Survey of Current Business*, various issues.
[a] Estimate.

order to recoup some lost ground, as a result of a most unusual American situation in which real wages fell during 1974.

Interest rates behave differently from most of the other market variables; they occasionally come down. The pattern in Table 1 is definitely up, but some declines occurred in 1967 and 1971–1972. Basic commodity prices exhibit this kind of behavior, too. They often fall in the short run. Interest rates were not different from prices, however, in that they rose to record high levels in the most inflationary period, 1973–1974.

When we look at component indexes, in Table 2, it is apparent that import prices show strong effects of dollar devaluation and rising commodity prices. Food and crude materials rise much faster than general averages of consumer or wholesale prices, as do many services. The latter index has significant wage and interest components that account for its rapid rise in recent years.

Price behavior in econometric models must respond to movements in raw material prices, factor prices, exchange rates, major world events, and domestic controls if we are to be able to interpret recent events and to be better prepared for future price projections than we have been in the past. In this period, apart from a brief flurry in 1965, there have not been major changes in indirect taxes, but the future may bring value-added taxes (VAT) or analogous policy changes. It is clearly important to be prepared for them.

ECONOMETRIC SPECIFICATIONS

It may appear superfluous to present a paper on the econometrics of inflation at this time, since a book called *The Econometrics of Price Determination*, based on a Federal Reserve–Social Science Research Council conference held in October 1970, was published just a few years ago.[1] It is odd that we appear to be in need of serious rethinking of the subject so soon after the conclusion of a significant and important conference on it, complete with a published record. The fact of the matter is that the considerations of the 1970 conference offered too little guidance on devaluation, food, fuel, and other basic materials costs in the international transmission of inflation.

The dominant specifications for price determination in U.S. econometric models were ably summarized at that conference in overview papers by James Tobin and Saul Hymans. In a very general way, most of the major macroeconometric models determine price as a markup over unit labor cost, with some allowance for demand pressure. In turn, they determine wage change as a function of unemployment rates and price change.

Distinctions between normal and actual unit labor costs, expected and observed price change, demand pressure through special variables like capacity utilization, order backlogs, inventory position, normal and actual labor force occur in the special structural forms of the different models. These are nontrivial refinements of the basic structure, which may be written as

$$p_t = \alpha_0 + \alpha_1 \left(\frac{wL}{X}\right)_t + \alpha_2 \frac{1}{1 - C_p} + e_{pt}$$

$$\frac{\Delta w_t}{w_t} = \beta_0 + \beta_2 \frac{1}{U_t} + \beta_3 \frac{\Delta p_t}{p_t} + e_{wt}$$

where p = price, w = wage rate, L = employment, X = output, C_p = capacity utilization, U = unemployment, and e_p, e_w = disturbance.

This model implies a partial Phillips-curve relation between $\Delta w/w$ and U for a given value of $\Delta p/p$. If we fix the level or the rate of growth of productivity (X/L) and the rate of capacity utilization (C_p), we can, by substitution, derive a trade-off relationship between the inflation rate $(\Delta p/p)$ and U.[2] It is better to take the analysis further and obtain complete system solutions for $\Delta p/p$ and U as functions of all the exogenous variables and initial conditions. At any given time, these two solution values can be jointly varied through common exogenous input changes, producing the trade-off relationship. These are presented for three models by Hymans and individual authors in *The Econometrics of Price Determination*.[3]

It is easy to see how the degree of overall economic performance as measured by the rate of unemployment or capacity utilization will affect inflation according to these equations, and it is also easy to see how wage costs will influence prices. It is less obvious how exchange rates, indirect taxes, food costs, fuel costs, other materials costs, and capital costs will influence the inflation rate. These are all important in the immediate context. In complete system simulations, many of these factors and government policies, including NEP, may affect price solutions by various indirect routes. These are all important but probably not enough to explain the extreme inflation of 1973–1974.

Most macroeconometric models are designed to explain one basic price, say, the manufacturing, nonagricultural, or GNP price level, and then to relate each separate price level to the main price. This is close to the procedure followed in financial analysis. One basic interest rate, the Treasury bill or commercial paper rate, is explained in a market behavorial equation, and other rates are made functions of the basic rate in term structure equations.

The basic price equation is customarily a markup on wage and other costs, with an allowance for demand pressure, like the equation above. Prices of major final demand components such as consumer goods or services (and their subdivisions), producer goods, exports, imports, and public purchases are related either to the central price level directly or to the same explanatory variables that appear in the equation for the central price. Allowance is also made for special factors, such as individual tax rates and subsidies or restrictions in particular markets. There are, however, some basic identities that must be fulfilled, namely

$$X = \sum_{i=1}^{n} G_i$$

$$pX = \sum_{i=1}^{n} q_i G_i$$

$$X = \sum_{i=1}^{m} X_i$$

$$pX = \sum_{i=1}^{m} p_i X_i$$

where X = real GNP, p = implicit deflator of GNP, G_i = ith component of GNP on the expenditure side, q_i = implicit deflator of G_i, X_i = value added in the ith sector, and p_i = implicit deflator of X_i. If there is a direct equation for p, one element of q_i and one element of p_i will be residually computed from the identities. Alternatively, all elements of p_i can be directly modeled, and p will be determined by identities. Import prices will generally be assumed to be exogenous.

Nordhaus[4] has conveniently outlined specifications for price equations corresponding to different production functions: fixed proportions, Cobb-Douglas, and constant elasticity of substitution (CES). There are two significant characteristics of his formulas that should be mentioned separately. He introduces materials inputs explicitly into his production functions; therefore, his output variable should be interpreted as gross real output and not value added, as implied in the preceding formulation. This is important for showing how changes in materials input prices affect output price.

The second feature of Nordhaus's formulation is that his price equations are derived as semireduced forms, obtained by substituting product demand and marginal productivity conditions into the production functions and rearranging terms to express output price as a function of three input prices: wage rate, capital rental, and materials price. Productivity is introduced as a neutral time function that is solved for explicit representation in the price equation.

The usual procedure, outlined in the previous section, is to use unit labor cost (wL/X) as a combined variable showing both wage and productivity (output per man-hour) effects all at once. In the Cobb-Douglas case, there is nothing wrong in using this variable in a price equation, together with other marginal conditions, production functions, and demand functions as separate simultaneous equations. These should give the same system results as Nordhaus's semireduced price equations, provided that all stochastic properties are carefully watched on substitution and reduction. Similar propositions would hold for other production functions. The point is that legitimate transformations and combinations within simultaneous equation systems can be made without having any essential effects on the outcome, although the apparent structure may look different and convey different degrees of information about the underlying system.

There is much simplicity and elegance in Nordhaus's specifications, however, and they are convenient for showing how each input price makes a marginal contribution to final output price, at the same time allowing for overall productivity effects. His general form is $p = f(w, q, v, Y, t)$, where p = output price, w = wage rates, q = capital rental, v = materials price, Y = consumer income, and t = time trend (productivity effect).

This formulation is highly desirable for partial or satellite model studies in which the production process has a small number of materials inputs. Agriculture with feed, seed, fertilizer would be a case in point. Energy industries with intermediate fuel input would be another. However, for outputs in a general system, it will probably be advisable to make use of an input-output approach, as sketched immediately below.

The basic I/O equation, $(I - A) X = F$, relates the gross output vector X to the final demand vector F through the technology matrix A. The matrix I is the identity matrix. We shall define two other matrices, $X = BY$ and $F = CG$, where Y is a vector of values added by the producing sector and G is a vector of GNP components. The matrix B is diagonal and can be obtained from the original I/O matrix as

$$B = \begin{pmatrix} \dfrac{1}{1 - \sum\limits_i a_{i1}} & 0 & \cdots & 0 \\ 0 & \dfrac{1}{1 - \sum\limits_i a_{i2}} & \cdots & 0 \\ \cdot & \cdot & \cdots & \cdot \\ 0 & 0 & \cdots & \dfrac{1}{1 - \sum\limits_i a_{in}} \end{pmatrix}$$

In the present context it is a diagonal matrix of markup factors, showing how value added must be factored up to equal gross output. If we multiply an element of X by an element of B^{-1}, we show how much must be subtracted from gross output in order to obtain value added. The matrix C is constructed from the composition of final demand deliveries by sector. Let us consider m types of final demand, ranging from consumption through investment and public purchases to exports.

$$F_1 = F_{11} + F_{12} + \cdots + F_{1m}$$
$$F_2 = F_{21} + F_{22} + \cdots + F_{2m}$$
$$\cdot \qquad\qquad\qquad\qquad \cdot$$
$$\cdot \qquad\qquad\qquad\qquad \cdot$$
$$F_n = F_{n1} + F_{n2} + \cdots + F_{nm}$$

Elements of the GNP vector G are column sums

$$\sum_{k=1}^{n} F_{kj} \qquad j = 1, 2 \ldots, m$$

If we divide each F_{ij} by its corresponding column sum, we have the matrix

$$C = \left\| F_{ij} / \sum_{k=1}^{n} F_{kj} \right\|$$

From the matrix equation $(I - A)\, BY = CG$, we can derive $Y = B^{-1}(I - A)^{-1}CG$, which expresses how elements of G are transformed into elements of Y. This is called a row transformation because row elements of $B^{-1}(I - A)^{-1}C$ express Y as a weighted sum of elements of G. The sum of Y elements define GNP and so, also, the sum of G elements. We should modify this for appropriate treatment of imports as separate elements of Y, either combined with competitive goods produced domestically or in a separate component if they are noncompetitive. The elements of G, therefore, sum to GNP plus imports, or total supply of goods and services available.

A current-price accounting identity is $p'Y = q'G$. This says that the total of available supply measured as current value added plus imports equals the total current value of GNP plus imports. The row vector p' is a vector of value-added prices, and q' is a vector of implicit GNP deflators.

By substitution we have the identity

$$p'B^{-1}(I - A)^{-1}CG = q'G$$

This identity must hold for all values of G; therefore, we can write

$$\sum_{i=1}^{n} p_i d_{ij} = q_j \qquad j = 1, 2, \ldots, m$$

These are column transformations of p into q. They express each q_j as a column-weighted sum of the elements of p. The weights come from the columns of

$$D = B^{-1}(I - A)^{-1}C$$

The deflators of GNP components, or final demand prices, are, therefore, weighted averages of all sector prices, many of which are intermediate goods and some of which are imported goods. They are elements of p corresponding either to a (noncompetitive) import row or to goods whose characteristics are like those of imported world goods. In general, we would expect movements in domestic prices to follow world prices for nearly identical goods. Equations to explain sector prices in such a model should include international factors that affect domestic prices. Price equations by sector of origin of production should be markup relations on sector costs, as indicated above, but they should be modified by variables representing supply-demand balance. In the cases of sectors that have large competitive import components, it is important to include world price conditions for the commodity line in question. In all cases, indirect tax rates, tariffs, and other special exogenous variables should be included in the sector price relationships.

The price conversion or column problem has been outlined for value-added prices. These are more available in a neat social accounting sense as deflators of gross product originating by sector, i.e., as deflators of X when its elements are measured in current prices. Although data may be less available on a large scale across all sectors, it is more straightforward to explain price of gross output by sector. Let us denote this price vector by p^*. Then we have by definition[5]

$$p_j^* X_j = p_j Y_j + \sum_{i=1}^{n} p_i^* x_{ij}$$

This can be transformed to

$$p_j^* = p_j \frac{Y_j}{X_j} + \sum_{i=1}^{n} p_i^* \frac{x_{ij}}{X_i}$$

$$p_j^* = p_j \left(1 - \sum_{i=1}^{n} a_{ij} \right) + \sum_{i=1}^{n} p_i^* a_{ij}$$

In matrix notation this becomes $p^* = B^{-1} p + A p^*$. The relation between p^* and p can be written as $p^* = (I - A')^{-1} B^{-1} p$.

We thus have a system of equations to transform prices of value added, p, into prices of gross output, or vice versa. As long as the elements of A are constant, it does not matter whether the analysis is carried out in terms of prices of gross output or of value added. The crux of the matter, however, is to model changes in A (and hence B) and also in C. This is needed in order to construct complete models that combine both I/O and macroeconomic analysis. This is the kind of model building and price explanation started in the Brookings model and implemented on a large scale by Ross Preston.[6]

If there are complete equation sets for wage and other costs by sector, in a combined I/O–macromodel system, price equations for each sector with conversion into price deflators of final demand would seem to provide a full explanation of the pricing process. In addition to cost factors in price determination by sector, there should be equations for inventories or other measures of demand pressure, such as order backlogs or capacity utilization, to complete the explanation.

There is, however, another approach to input-output analysis that appears to be feasible and promising for price determination, namely, through the use of rectangular input-output systems.[7]

Let

X_i = output of the ith commodity, $i = 1, 2, \ldots, m$

Z_j = output of the jth sector, $j = 1, 2, \ldots, n$

F = vector of final demand

The basic input-output relations are

$X = AZ + F$

$Z = RX$

Typical elements of A and R are

$a_{ij} = \dfrac{X_{ij}}{Z_j}$ = input of the ith commodity per unit of output of the jth sector

$r_{ij} = \dfrac{Z_{ij}}{X_j}$ = share of sector i in the output of commodity j.

We can compute total output of each commodity from

$X = ARX + F$

$\quad = (I - AR)^{-1} F$

This should give "target" or "desired" amounts of X. Call them X^*. Dynamic price formation equations can then be formulated as

$\Delta p_{it} = \lambda_i (X^*_{i, t} - X_{i, t-1})$

Other adjustment equations would also be possible.

The elements of A and R might, in the first instance, be assumed to be constant. This would be in the spirit of conventional I/O analysis. A more elaborate theory could be constructed to generate time movements of a_{ij} and r_{ij} as direct analogues of the systems that have been developed to generate movements in conventional I/O matrices, assuming a specific underlying production function, such as Cobb-Douglas, CES, or some other.[8]

ECONOMETRIC EXPERIENCE

In the inflationary decade, how did econometric analysis of prices fare? There are several different ways of looking at this question. The first will be to examine the residuals from estimated price equations to see whether "unexplained" variation is random or whether it shows a systematic tendency to be positive and increasing during the period of acceleration of inflation. This tendency can be examined for the whole decade or for any subperiod of particular interest from the viewpoint of inflation. It will be a matter of separating systematic variation that can be "explained" by variables in the price formation equations, as outlined above, from residual variation.

A second approach will be to examine complete system simulation residuals to see how well price movements are interpreted in an inflationary era within the sample period of equation estimation, in extrapolation (ex post), and in genuine forecast simulations.

Finally, system response to external disturbances can be investigated, particularly price responses to disturbances that would be naturally associated with inflation. These responses will be investigated by means of hypothetical simulations.

The vehicle for econometric study in this paper will be the Wharton model. During the period under consideration, this model has gone through three major changes of updating, elaboration, respecification, and comprehensive re-estimation. This means that one single set of price equations, definitions of price variables, or model simulations cannot be used for the whole period of analysis. Also, within a given model, some changes were made in specification of the price equation alone when inflationary problems became so severe that deficiencies were brought to light. Record keeping for actual forecast performance is relatively recent, especially in terms of detail; consequently, more information is available for the past few years than for the whole decade.

There are two principal price variables in the Wharton model. One is the price of manufacturing output, originally the wholesale price index of nonfarm, nonfood products, and later taken to be the implicit deflator of value added in manufacturing.[9] The other is the implicit GNP deflator. As explained in an earlier section, the price of manufacturing output is obtained directly from a behavioral equation for price formation, while the GNP deflator is obtained from a definitional relation as a ratio of nominal to real GNP. The separate deflators of the components of GNP depend principally on the price of manufacturing output or on things related to it. In that sense, both price variables give similar information as indicators of inflation. When residual analysis is considered, the price index of manufacturing output will be the variable to take into account. For system simulation, however, it will be preferable to use the GNP deflator because it has remained as a conceptually stable statistical series through the successive variants of the model, while the manufacturers' price has changed from time to time and provides a variable rather than a fixed standard of reference.

In the latest version of the Wharton model, Mark IV, there are many sector prices, and manufacturing is disaggregated into durable and nondurable components. The equations for these two prices follow the usual markup over normal unit labor costs, pressure of capacity utilization, and lags. The residuals determined in fitting these equations to a given series of price data show no tendency toward acceleration in 1965–1966 or in the most recent period. They do not even show clearly the effects of the freeze and successive phases. Residuals for these periods are not fundamentally different from those of earlier periods. The largest residuals, in absolute value, occur in 1960II and 1953IV (see Table 3 and Figure 1). The root-mean-square residual is 0.97 over the whole eighty-quarter span. In the ten quarters of NEP (through 1973IV), there are five positive and five negative residuals. One is markedly larger (twice as large) and one is markedly smaller (almost zero) than 0.97. It thus appears that standard price behavior

FIGURE 1 Estimated Residuals, Price Equation for Durable Manufactures, 1953III–1973IV

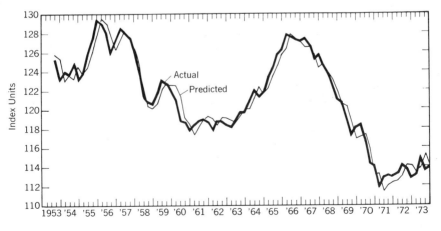

SOURCE: Table 3.

prevailed in the sense that the ratio of prices to normal unit labor cost (adjusted for indirect taxes) changed as capacity pressures and trends changed, without any special effects evident from the control program. It is not to be assumed that controls were ineffective, but only that they did not alter the basic price-wage relationship. The basic movement of durable goods prices was upward in this most recent period, but nondurables showed practically no positive drift (before 1974).

TABLE 3   Estimated Residuals: Price Equation for Durable Manufactures, 1953III–1973IV (1958 = 100.0)

	Actual	Predicted	Residual	Percent Error
1953III	125.4126	125.8060	−0.3934	−0.3137
IV	123.3722	125.4495	−2.0773	−1.6838
1954I	124.0760	123.1132	0.9629	0.7760
II	123.7466	123.6375	0.1091	0.0882
III	124.8748	123.2437	1.6310	1.3061
IV	123.3665	124.5042	−1.1377	−0.9222
1955I	123.9643	123.6431	0.3212	0.2591
II	125.7042	124.5406	1.1636	0.9257
III	127.4427	126.1300	1.3127	1.0300
IV	129.4395	127.7663	1.6731	1.2926
1956I	129.1452	129.4465	−0.3013	−0.2333
II	128.0792	129.1316	−1.0524	−0.8217
III	125.9323	127.8497	−1.9174	−1.5225
IV	127.3130	126.2724	1.0406	0.8173
1957I	128.5383	127.4605	1.0778	0.8385
II	128.0407	128.2416	−0.2008	−0.1569
III	127.4938	127.6005	−0.1068	−0.0837
IV	126.2587	126.4548	−0.1961	−0.1553
1958I	124.2166	124.5767	−0.3601	−0.2899
II	121.4175	122.4966	−1.0791	−0.8887
III	120.7651	120.3612	0.4039	0.3344
IV	120.5551	120.3006	0.2545	0.2111
1959I	121.6083	120.6296	0.9787	0.8048
II	123.0978	122.1443	0.9536	0.7746
III	122.8239	122.7762	0.0477	0.0388
IV	121.8633	122.5775	−0.7142	−0.5861
1960I	120.9747	122.5491	−1.5744	−1.3014
II	118.7809	121.2742	−2.4933	−2.0991
III	118.5744	119.0243	−0.4499	−0.3794
IV	117.7539	118.4637	−0.7098	−0.6028

TABLE 3 (continued)

	Actual	Predicted	Residual	Percent Error
1961I	118.2795	117.3586	0.9209	0.7786
II	118.7195	118.2013	0.5182	0.4365
III	118.9835	118.8409	0.1426	0.1199
IV	118.6437	119.2680	-0.6243	-0.5262
1962I	117.9422	119.0230	-1.0809	-0.9164
II	118.7131	118.4495	0.2636	0.2221
III	118.6416	119.1371	-0.4955	-0.4177
IV	118.4379	119.0582	-0.6203	-0.5237
1963I	118.1565	118.9481	-0.7916	-0.6700
II	118.8988	118.8013	0.0976	0.0821
III	119.5757	119.3902	0.1854	0.1551
IV	119.6642	120.0176	-0.3534	-0.2953
1964I	120.8154	120.0330	0.7824	0.6476
II	121.9981	121.1262	0.8719	0.7147
III	121.3767	122.2236	-0.8469	-0.6978
IV	121.9204	121.5457	0.3748	0.3074
1965I	123.1586	122.3112	0.8474	0.6880
II	124.3382	123.4684	0.8697	0.6995
III	125.6508	124.5686	1.0822	0.8612
IV	126.2353	125.7332	0.5022	0.3978
1966I	127.7717	126.3893	1.3824	1.0820
II	127.5114	127.7793	-0.2679	-0.2101
III	127.3401	127.4034	-0.0634	-0.0498
IV	127.2633	127.0924	0.1710	0.1343
1967I	127.4125	126.5197	0.8928	0.7007
II	126.6686	126.4932	0.1754	0.1385
III	125.2273	125.7032	-0.4759	-0.3800
IV	125.6008	124.3657	1.2351	0.9834
1968I	124.5636	124.7522	-0.1886	-0.1514
II	123.7671	123.8074	-0.0403	-0.0325
III	122.4730	123.0098	-0.5368	-0.4383
IV	121.0939	121.8188	-0.7250	-0.5987
1969I	120.6635	120.6559	0.0076	0.0063
II	118.7186	120.2429	-1.5243	-1.2840
III	117.2443	118.5132	-1.2690	-1.0823
IV	118.0294	116.9108	1.1186	0.9477
1970I	118.3183	117.1710	1.1473	0.9697
II	116.6899	117.4107	-0.7208	-0.6177
III	114.3406	115.8010	-1.4604	-1.2772
IV	113.9969	113.0752	0.9217	0.8085
1971I	111.8324	113.0841	-1.2517	-1.1192
II	112.7720	111.2373	1.5347	1.3609

TABLE 3 (concluded)

	Actual	Predicted	Residual	Percent Error
III	113.0688	112.0307	1.0381	0.9181
IV	112.9439	112.3633	0.5807	0.5141
1972I	113.1587	112.4791	0.6796	0.6006
II	114.0812	113.0315	1.0497	0.9201
III	113.6471	114.1450	−0.4979	−0.4381
IV	112.7246	114.1034	−1.3788	−1.2232
1973I	113.0352	113.4429	−0.4077	−0.3607
II	114.7964	113.8138	0.9826	0.8560
III	113.5130	115.3444	−1.8314	−1.6134
IV	113.8616	113.9509	−0.0893	−0.0785

NOTE: Durbin-Watson statistic = 1.69145.

In the following estimated OLS equation the figures in parentheses are t ratios; the residuals are shown in Table 3:

$$(1 - R)PXMD/NULCD = 10.62 - 0.019t$$
$$(2.82) \quad (3.15)$$

$$+ 8.41 \; (CPMD - NCPMD)/NCPMD + 0.92 \, [(1 - R)PXMD/NULCD]_{-1}$$
$$(5.10) (30.63)$$

$$R^2 = 0.96; \; SEE = 0.97; \; DW = 1.69$$

where

> $PXMD$ = index of the price of output originating in durable manufacturing (1958 = 100)
>
> R = average rate of indirect business taxes (federal)
>
> $NULCD$ = normal unit labor costs (ratio of wage rate to twelve-quarter trailing average of productivity in durable manufacturing)
>
> $CPMD$ = Wharton index of capacity utilization in durable manufacturing
>
> $NCPMD$ = twelve-quarter trailing average of $CPMD$

Another way of looking at residuals is in single-equation extrapolation beyond the sample period, where observed values are substituted for the explanatory variables, and the residual differences between observed and estimated price are tabulated. It is standard practice in forecasting with the Wharton model to evaluate residuals in this manner for the eight quarters just preceding each new set of quarterly forecasts. The purpose of this calculation is to detect drift in behavioral patterns, structural change, or the influence of data revisions. While this procedure is now systematic, older

TABLE 4 Residuals from Equation for Manufacturing Price (Wholesale Price Index of Industrial Commodities)

Date Computed	Span				Quarter				
		1	2	3	4	5	6	7	8
5/21/74	'72II-'74I	-.044	-.054	-.065	-.074	-.079	-.097	-.093	-.069
3/25/74	'72I-'73IV	-.043	-.044	-.054	-.066	-.074	-.079	-.098	-.094
12/13/73	'71IV-'73III	-.042	-.043	-.044	-.055	-.066	-.075	-.082	-.100
9/21/73	'71III-'73II	-.033	-.042	-.043	-.045	-.056	-.068	-.078	-.084
6/14/73	'71II-'73I	-.036	-.031	-.038	-.045	-.055	-.065	-.075	-.061
3/19/73	'71I-'72IV	-.001	.002	.014	.009	.014	.010	.007	.002
12/26/72	'70IV-'72III	.005	.012	.014	.018	.005	.017	.012	.015
8/21/72	'70III-'72II	.006	.005	.012	.014	.018	.006	.017	.013
6/12/72	'70II-'72I	.003	.006	.005	.009	.011	.014	.001	.015
3/20/72	'70I-'71IV	.007	.003	.006	.005	.009	.011	.014	.001
12/16/71	'69IV-'71III	.004	.006	.004	.008	.008	.012	.014	.017
5/26/71	'69II-'71I	.002	.000	.003	.006	.003	.006	.004	.010

.ecords do not exist and, therefore, the values tabulated in Table 4 are given only for the period since May 1971. Each row in the table has two reference times: the date at which the residuals are computed and the period for which the residuals are computed.

There is a break in the tabulated values because a new price equation was introduced in April 1973 in order to take better account of the inflationary impact of import prices under exchange devaluation, to make better estimates of normal unit labor costs, and to sharpen the nonlinear effects of capacity utilization. Prior to April 1973, the price equation used generally underestimated actual prices. After the new equation was introduced, the residuals turned negative, indicating that the new equation overestimated prices.

With the old equation, the residuals show no regular tendency to grow. The residual for the fourth quarter of 1971 is generally quite small. This period has the full effect of the freeze and Phase II. It is the first full quarter after the introduction of NEP (August 15, 1971). The residuals get larger in absolute value after the beginning of 1973, but as they are all negative, they do not show the effects of growing inflation that the price equation might have failed to reflect.

The Mark IV residuals for all separate price equations in the control period provide information both on extrapolation and on aspects of the effectiveness of the controls. Table 5 contains residuals for individual quarters from 1971III through 1974II for each price variable by sector of origin, and the period is blocked off into NEP "phases." The sample period ends in 1971II for these calculations; they postdate those for Mark IV above in that they incorporate some recent data revisions.

This is a mixed pattern. Contract construction shows the restraining influence of wage agreements in that industry through the early part of the extrapolation period. The results are largely negative (price restraint) in agriculture, nondurable manufacturing, finance, and services but are positive or mixed in other sectors. In most cases, these tabulations refer to price movements in relation to wage rates; therefore, it is worthwhile to look into the wage patterns also. In addition, there is a general feeling that NEP was more strongly directed at wage restraint than at overall restraint of prices or nonlabor factor incomes.

Residuals from wage rate equations in the Wharton model, Mark IV, extended beyond the sample, from 1971III through 1974II, are given in Table 6. As in the case of prices, the special wage agreements in the construction sector show through clearly.

TABLE 5 Residuals for Price Variables by Sector of Origin, Wharton Model, Mark IV, 1971III–1974II

NEP Phase	Year and Quarter	Agriculture	Mfg. Durables	Mfg. Non-durables	Transportation	Communication	Electricity and Gas	Contract Construction	Trade	Finance, Insurance, Real Estate	Services
I	1971 III	−4.8	1.2	−0.8	−1.3	1.8	0.4	−5.6	0.2	−1.2	−0.9
	IV	1.6	0.7	−1.4	0.8	−0.6	2.0	−2.6	−0.7	−1.3	−1.2
II	1972 I	−6.7	0.8	−0.9	0.5	1.3	3.8	−1.3	−2.8	−2.4	−3.7
	II	−2.8	1.1	−0.4	0.2	0.2	2.3	−4.2	−1.3	−4.5	−3.6
	III	−0.3	−0.6	−1.7	−0.1	1.6	1.5	−0.6	−0.7	−2.6	−2.8
	IV	−2.6	−1.6	−1.6	−1.0	2.9	2.5	2.7	0.5	−3.2	−2.2
III	1973 I	−6.9	−0.6	−3.0	−0.2	3.5	4.2	3.8	−0.4	−6.3	−7.9
	II	−1.6	0.9	−1.2	1.0	3.9	3.1	5.1	1.1	−3.3	−3.6
	III	−3.4	−2.1	−1.4	−0.2	4.8	2.8	−4.8	0.3	−3.5	−3.7
	IV	−0.2	−0.2	0.0	1.6	6.7	6.2	−7.4	1.9	−2.4	−0.3
IV	1974 I	−29.3	1.8	−0.4	1.9	8.7	11.2	−11.2	1.4	−2.8	−3.6
	II	−30.5	2.9	−6.0	1.6	7.6	10.5	−7.2	1.8	−2.4	−1.9

TABLE 6 Residuals for Wage Variables by Sector of Origin, Wharton Model, Mark IV, 1971III–1974II

NEP Phase	Year and Quarter	Agriculture	Mfg. Durables	Mfg. Non-durables	Regulated Sectors	Mining	Contract Construction	Trade	Finance, Insurance, Real Estate	Services
I	1971III	-.034	.000	.014	.116	.132	-.025	.002	-.008	.031
	IV	.005	-.034	-.012	.018	.260	-.165	-.011	-.010	-.001
II	1972I	.032	.031	.031	.095	.100	-.104	.037	.023	.047
	II	-.015	-.014	.003	-.020	.153	-.022	-.002	-.004	.013
	III	-.105	-.002	.006	-.013	.289	-.105	.007	-.004	-.005
	IV	-.024	.021	.010	-.018	.202	.007	-.002	-.020	-.011
III	1973I	.096	.018	.046	.082	.325	-.062	.022	.025	.044
	II	.025	.009	.002	-.044	.092	-.190	.029	-.073	-.017
	III	-.001	.009	-.003	-.072	.122	-.056	.016	-.026	-.020
	IV	.060	-.012	-.019	-.040	.050	-.181	.010	.009	-.008
IV	1974I	-.016	-.026	-.014	-.014	.192	-.084	.002	-.043	.016
	II	.157	.073	.067	-.070	.147	-.244	.034	-.060	.007

There are predominantly negative residuals in the wage estimates for this sector. The results in mining are for persistent positive residuals. Most other sectors are mixed, although the regulated and finance sectors tend to have negative residuals. There is no clear evidence here that unduly depressed wage rates held down prices or that wage rates were even associated directly with high prices during the NEP period.

If the sample is extended through 1974II so that NEP-phase periods are included, the corresponding tables of residuals are liberally sprinkled with plus and minus entries across all sectors. There is not even a definite tendency for contract construction to have almost all negative residuals. This sector does, however, have strongly negative price residuals through most of Phase II, a period that ended during the last part of 1972.

It is one thing to fit a single equation with small random residuals or even to extrapolate a single equation with correct values for the explanatory variables, and quite another to simulate a whole system with estimated values for all endogenous variables. Three generations of Wharton models have been simulated over historical sample periods, some covering all or part of the period of price acceleration (from 1965 on) within the simulation period and some covering the acceleration period alone.

For reference, let us consider the second generation of Wharton models.[10] For a simulation horizon of one quarter, the root-mean-square error of the GNP deflator in index points for 1949II–1964IV was 0.48; for two quarters, 0.74; for three quarters, 0.89; and for four quarters, 0.99. For the corresponding complete system for Mark III, next generation, for 1960I–1970I, the figure for a one-quarter horizon was 0.25; for two quarters, 0.39; for three quarters, 0.52; and for four quarters, 0.71. This latter is probably a more difficult period to reproduce because it includes the accelerating inflation, but more effort was directed at price determination because of the recognition of forecast difficulties in the applications of the older model. The errors for Mark III are uniformly lower than those of the earlier-generation model. For the earlier acceleration period, 1965I–1970I, alone, the twenty-quarter dynamic simulation of Mark III generated a root-mean-square error of 1.24 index points.

In the extension of the simulation horizon to cover eight quarters, rather than four, the error grows to about one full index point. In extrapolation, however, the error is much larger—about two to three times as large as the within-sample errors. Extrapolation of the Mark III model over the period 1970II–1972IV generates the following root-mean-square errors:

Simulation Horizon (quarters)							
1	2	3	4	5	6	7	8
0.72	0.96	1.04	0.80	1.02	1.41	1.99	2.73

In the first year of extrapolation, it is necessary to reckon with an error of at least one full index point in an inflationary period. In the second year ahead, this error allowance must amount to at least two full index points. It will be seen, below, that these limits are too narrow in application to genuine ex ante prediction during the much stronger inflationary period extending to early 1974.

The latest generation of Wharton models is just being introduced, and preliminary simulations of complete systems show the prevalence of errors amounting to over two full index points in the second year of two-year simulations. The period covered is one of accelerating inflation. When these calculations are extended beyond the range of Table 7, right up to the double-digit periods in 1974, the errors get larger—as much as five index points. A strong effort has been made to improve the mechanism of price determination in the model, but a sizable error persists. Errors greatly in excess of two index points do not occur with any frequency through 1973, but in 1974 the price explosion exceeds model capabilities, and truly large errors appear. The largest discrepancies occur right after the termination of controls, but complications of oil prices, oversized trade deficits, and dollar weakness are not to be neglected in the analysis and in the attempt to draw definite conclusions about the reasons for the underestimate of inflation.

The preceding tabulations have dealt with performance after the fact, either in the sample-fitting period or in a period after that of the sample extrapolation period, but both are hypothetical exercises. It is interesting to examine how well the model as a whole could genuinely predict the rate of inflation in realistic forecast situations. Detailed records are available for Wharton model forecasts from 1967. The forecasts were made regularly from 1963 on, but careful record keeping was not instituted in the earlier years. Some summary statistics are available, but period-by-period forecasts from the "control" solutions are difficult to recover systematically before 1967. The tabulation figures in Table 8 are grouped by quarters into annual forecasts in order to make the presentation more compact. The quarterly record is available but is no more illuminating than the annual results made at each year's end for two years into the future.

TABLE 7 Wharton Model, Mark IV: Actual and Simulated Values of the GNP Deflator

Year and Quarter	Actual	Simulated				
1964 I	108.2	108.3				
II	108.5	108.6				
III	109.1	109.2				
IV	109.6	110.1				
1965 I	110.2	110.3	109.8			
II	110.7	111.1	110.6			
III	111.0	111.8	111.4			
IV	111.5	112.6	112.1			
1966 I	112.4		113.4	112.7		
II	113.5		114.3	113.4		
III	114.5		115.4	114.5		
IV	115.4		116.3	115.2		
1967 I	116.2			115.8	115.6	
II	116.8			116.4	116.2	
III	118.0			117.2	116.9	
IV	119.4			118.5	118.1	
1968 I	120.4				118.2	119.8
II	121.6				118.9	120.6
III	122.9				120.0	121.8
IV	124.3				121.0	122.9

Quarter						
1969 I	125.6	124.2	125.5			
II	127.2	126.3	127.8			
III	129.1	128.6	130.2			
IV	130.9	130.6	132.3			
1970 I	132.9		134.7	132.8		
II	134.4		136.3	134.1		
III	135.8		137.9	135.4		
IV	137.9		139.9	136.7		
1971 I	139.5			137.9	138.8	
II	141.1			139.3	139.8	
III	142.0			140.7	141.1	
IV	142.7			142.0	142.2	
1972 I	144.6				143.6	144.5
II	145.3				144.7	145.7
III	146.5				146.2	147.3
IV	148.0				147.4	148.4
1973 I	149.9					151.8
II	152.6					154.6
III	155.7					159.4
IV	158.9					161.7

The annual story is one of consistent underestimation of inflation, improving at each year's one-year-ahead revision of the prior two-year-ahead forecast but generally yielding a figure below the actual inflation rate. The figures in Table 8 are for the GNP deflator, which gives a good summary picture of inflation running ahead of the model.

In 1970 and 1972 the one-year-ahead prediction was quite close, but in the other years, there was a consistent underestimate. The largest inflationary increment, in 1973–1974, was seriously understated in terms of the level of the variable predicted, but the *increment* between the two years was much closer to the actual amount because both years were systematically biased. This is an example of the general finding that forecasts of change are more accurate than forecasts of level if the latter are systematically biased. This is what has happened in forecasting price movements in recent years.

The main conclusions would not be different if we were to tabulate the results by quarters rather than by years. General results for the whole period, in quarterly forecasting, are shown in Table 9. These show small size and growth of errors in change form but larger error values in level form, especially for the second year of a two-year forecast horizon. A closer examination of the period since the imposition of controls is given in the second and fourth lines of the table. That this is a more difficult period to predict is shown by the enlargment of the error values in most cases. Two years ahead, errors have been as large as four to five index points, while the error of prediction of change has usually been under 1.5

TABLE 8 Wharton Model: Year-End Predictions of Annual Values of GNP Deflator, 1967–1973 (1958 = 100)

Release Date for Prediction	Annual Prediction Period						
	1968	1969	1970	1971	1972	1973	1974
11/12/67	120.7	123.3					
12/23/68		125.2	128.4				
11/26/69			134.2	137.7			
12/10/70				139.3	142.8		
12/21/71					146.4	152.5	
11/29/72						150.6	155.8
12/21/73							164.8
Actual	122.3	128.2	135.2	141.3	146.1	154.3	170.2

TABLE 9 Wharton Model: Root-Mean-Square Error in GNP Deflator
(1958 = 100)

Period	Prediction Horizon (quarters)								First Yearly Average
	1	2	3	4	5	6	7	8	
				Level of GNP Deflator					
1967I–1974I	0.44	0.98	1.76	2.64	3.41	4.11	4.66	5.10	1.35
1971II–1974I	0.46	1.07	1.96	2.96	3.69	4.07	4.04	3.79	1.48
				Change in GNP Deflator					
1967I–1974II	0.44	0.69	0.96	1.06	1.06	1.19	1.19	1.20	0.66
1971II–1974I	0.46	0.82	1.25	1.31	1.37	1.47	1.47	1.50	0.74

index points. The kind of inflation surprises that have disturbed most people—householders, business people, and public authorities—have been unexpected additional rates of five or more index points; therefore these short-run errors are serious. An upper limit of tolerable error should be about 1.5 index points, preferably one index point; therefore, room for improvement exists.

The sensitivity of complete-system solution to external shocks in the form of world price changes is of interest in trying to associate domestic price changes with those in world markets. Accordingly, the Wharton model forecast that was released on July 31, 1974, was chosen as typical. It was used as a baseline case, and four major external prices in the system were changed—the price index of imported goods, the price index of imported services, an average of foreign consumer price indexes, and the price index of world trade. The first is an important explanatory variable in the equation for goods imports and the next two are significant in the imports of services. The fourth index is an important explanatory factor in the export equation. The differences in the exogenous inputs can be seen in Table 10.

In the table the level and growth rate of external prices in the disturbed solution were set so that the input values at the end of the simulation (eight quarters later) would be 98 percent of the baseline cases in all four instances. These lower values reduce the corresponding price indexes of the baseline case by 4.4 to 4.8 index points. The results on a central price variable, the price deflator of output originating in manufacturing, are shown in the last two lines of the table. The price was chosen because it is more sensitive to external import prices. The GNP deflator hardly changes, certainly

TABLE 10 External Price Variables and Manufacturing Deflator in the Wharton Forecast, July 31, 1974 (1958 = 100)

	1974II	1974III	1974IV	1975I	1975II	1975III	1975IV	1976I
Price of imported goods								
Baseline	200.2	207.5	212.0	216.3	220.3	224.4	228.3	232.3
(Disturbed)	(199.7)	(206.4)	(210.4)	(214.1)	(217.4)	(221.0)	(224.2)	(227.5)
Price of imported services								
Baseline	204.7	209.7	213.7	217.7	221.7	225.7	229.7	233.7
(Disturbed)	(204.2)	(208.6)	(212.0)	(215.5)	(218.9)	(222.2)	(225.7)	(229.0)
Foreign consumer prices								
Baseline	200.4	205.2	209.6	213.7	217.5	221.5	225.2	229.0
(Disturbed)	(199.9)	(204.2)	(208.0)	(211.6)	(214.9)	(218.2)	(221.4)	(224.6)
World price								
Baseline	198.0	202.7	207.0	211.1	215.0	219.0	222.8	226.6
(Disturbed)	(197.6)	(201.8)	(205.6)	(209.2)	(212.4)	(215.9)	(219.1)	(222.2)
Mfg. deflator								
Baseline	137.7	141.2	144.3	147.4	150.1	152.7	155.4	158.3
(Disturbed)	(137.6)	(141.1)	(144.2)	(147.1)	(149.8)	(152.3)	(154.8)	(157.6)

not significantly, between the two solutions. This is partly because of the negative treatment of imports in adding up the elements of the GNP. There is a distinct lowering of the price of domestic manufactures if world prices are lowered. The more that external prices are lowered through time, the more domestic prices come down. At the end of the simulation horizon (eight quarters later), when external prices are 98 percent of baseline values, simulation results for the manufacturing deflator come down to 99.6 percent of the baseline case: a fall of approximately 2 percent in external prices results in a fall of approximately 0.4 percent in an important domestic price. Most other deflators of output originating do not change significantly.

DEFICIENCIES AND POTENTIAL IMPROVEMENTS

The recent inflation has been unkind to economists generally. No matter who among them might claim that they saw inflation coming as far back as 1965, they probably did not even consider its present magnitude as a likely possibility. This remark applies to economic analysts generally, whether they be econometricians or non-econometricians, or whether they use monetary tools, fiscal tools, productivity tools, or any other general approach to analysis of the economy. Inflation was underestimated in severity, duration, and general time shape.

In many respects this is a professional failure, and it should provoke a response. To me, the natural response is not to ask for a complete revamping of theoretical and statistical tools of economic analysis, although some popular writers have jumped to this conclusion. As I look at the problem from the viewpoint of econometric model building and attempts to forecast inflation, together with many other performance characteristics of the economy, I see a continuing need to make model formulations more detailed and richer in terms of all the processes that can be accommodated. We have come a long way in the past twenty years in integrating monetary and interindustry materials into econometric models. By themselves, they add to the areas of understanding of the inflation (and other) problems. We have not yet fully integrated national income, input-output and flow-of-funds (F/F) accounts into one complete model although we have made paired combinations of national income accounts (NIA) with I/O and NIA with F/F. As our data and understanding of model building progress, we are gradually achieving this grand synthesis. Our NIA systems provide us with the markups on labor and capital costs and capacity pressures; our I/O systems add markups on materials costs (especially strategic and imported materials); finally, our F/F systems show longer-run influences of money and credit conditions. The present inflation combines all these aspects.

Naturally, any model that encompasses all these factors will have to be large and detailed. This places us in the thousand-equation range. We are just learning how to handle such systems efficiently, and I really believe that this is the route to follow, instead of looking for some breakthrough observation gained by respecification or manipulation of small macro models. Inflation, or price movements generally, are never purely a demand phenomenon, a cost phenomenon, or a monetary phenomenon. The situation always involves a strong mixture of several aspects. It is not generally possible to identify some particular line of the inflationary process in a pure form.

Any narrow approach that concentrates on money supply is going to miss some big influences coming from basic materials markets or industrial capacity pressures. A focus solely on wage movements will be equally liable to failure. We have witnessed so many inflation avenues in the data, modeling, and performance since 1965 that it should be clear that we will have to allow for a wide variety of channels in a large-scale model. This means building more realism and detail into our existing systems and not attempting to build some new macro theory or to add a twist to an existing one.

Given that future econometric research on the price formation sectors of national models should continue along existing lines but be elaborated in detail, as I have argued in this paper, there is still a technical question remaining to be answered: Should we look back historically on the period 1965–1974 in future time series data samples as one that was so disturbed that significant use of dummy variables would be recommended in order to make the equations conform more closely to reality?

This type of question has been finessed, not entirely legitimately, for the Korean War period by starting up most time series investigations in econometric model building after 1954. After that period, there were Kennedy-Johnson guidelines, the Vietnam War, the various phases of NEP, the Soviet wheat deal, and the oil crises. At the time of occurrence of these momentous events, special care and adjustment were made to price-wage equations in order to interpret contemporaneous movements in the economy. Retrospectively, however, we do not find a need for widespread use of dummy variables in order to eliminate outlying observations for the estimation of price equations covering the whole period from 1954 through 1974. It is possible that equations in some specific sectors, like the contract construction sector, would show improvement if these special periods, particularly the eras of Vietnam and NEP, were "dummied out," but the general nature of our findings suggests that these periods will not appear to be so unusual in historical perspective. This is what we are finding in price-wage equations fitted to the whole span.

NOTES

1. Otto Eckstein, ed., *The Econometrics of Price Determination* (Washington, D.C.: Board of Governors of the Federal Reserve System, 1972).
2. *Trade-off* is a better expression for what is meant than *Phillips curve* because the latter usually refers to a structural relation between wage change and unemployment.
3. A. A. Hirsch, "Price Simulations with the OBE Econometric Model"; G. de Menil and J. J. Enzler, "Prices and Wages in the FR-MIT-PENN Econometric Model"; S. H. Hymans, "Prices and Price Behavior in Three U.S. Econometric Models." For the trade-off curve from the Wharton model, see G. I. Treyz, "An Econometric Procedure for Ex Post Policy Evaluation," *International Economic Review*, June 1972, pp. 212–222.
4. W. D. Nordhaus, "Recent Developments in Price Dynamics," in Eckstein, ed., *The Econometrics of Price Determination*.
5. This set of relationships was suggested by E. C. Hwa.
6. J. Duesenberry et al., eds., *The Brookings Quarterly Econometric Model of the United States* (Amsterdam: North-Holland, 1965) and Ross S. Preston, *The Wharton Annual and Industry Forecasting Model*, Studies in Quantitative Economics, no. 7 (Philadelphia: University of Pennsylvania, Economics Research Unit, 1972). Also see Chapter 12, below, on the CANDIDE model of Canada.
7. T. Matuszewski, "Partly Disaggregated Rectangular Input-Output Models and Their Use for the Purposes of a Large Corporation," in A. Bródy and A. P. Carter, eds., *Input-Output Techniques* (Amsterdam: North-Holland, 1972).
8. Systems with Cobb-Douglas production functions have been constructed by M. Saito, "An Interindustry Study of Price Formation," *Review of Economics and Statistics*, February 1971, pp. 11–15. The CES system has been worked out in linear form by B. G. Hickman and L. Lau, "Elasticities of Substitution and Export Demands in a World Trade Model," *European Economic Review* 4 (1973):347–380. This was developed for international trade analysis, but has been adapted for the I/O problem by Ross S. Preston. A translog specification has been proposed by Jorgenson in E. A. Hudson and D. W. Jorgenson, "U.S. Energy Policy and Economic Growth, 1975–2000," *Bell Journal of Economics and Management Science*, Autumn 1974, pp. 461–514.

9. In the 1966 and 1968 versions of the Wharton model, the price of manufacturing output was more central than in the present (Mark III) version introduced in 1970. In the latter, the price of output of the regulated sector and, also, the price of commercial output assumed some importance in overall price determination. In Mark IV, the newest version, there are many more sector prices.

10. L. R. Klein and M. K. Evans, *The Wharton Econometric Forecasting Model*, 2nd enlarged ed. (Philadelphia: University of Pennsylvania, Economics Research Unit, 1968).

COMMENTS

Michael C. Lovell
Wesleyan University

In this paper, Klein reviews ten very difficult years. In part, his paper, like many others at this conference, is an exercise in economic history, for he looks at the evidence concerning the effects of the various game plans, NEPs, and phases of economic policy over the last decade. And his paper is in part a postmortem for econometric models as well as for economic policy, for he reviews the price predictions generated by econometric models over the decade. He also advances certain methodological suggestions as to how we might proceed to do better in the future.

It is fair to say that this was not econometrics' finest hour. The basic structure, summarized by Klein early in his paper, customarily involves one equation relating price changes to labor costs per unit of output and capacity utilization, and another explaining wage changes in terms of unemployment and the speed of inflation. Such a system was not well equipped for analyzing the cost-push effects of currency devaluation and the Organization of Petroleum Exporting Countries (OPEC). Klein reports that the control program did not influence the basic price-wage relationship. However, he does report that the construction industry did indeed exercise restraint. Klein presents evidence showing that the successive refinements of the Wharton model led to improved predictive accuracy, but the annual story is one of consistent underestimation of inflation. Using the most recent Wharton model, Klein presents a two-year simulation showing that a 2 percent moderation in the rate of increase in the price of imports would slow the U.S. inflation by about 0.4 percent.

Perhaps the most intriguing aspect of Klein's paper concerns his buoyant optimism about the future for large-scale econometric models. At the beginning of the paper, he suggests that we should not magnify contemporary problems, and indeed suggests that every decade, not just the one under review, has had its share of disrupting factors to befuddle the analyst. He does not argue that present problems can be patched up with a mendacity parameter reflecting the White House climate, and he warns against any attempt to "dummy out" recent experience. Klein rejects single-cause explanations, pointing out that inflation has involved a mixture of cost-push, demand, and monetary elements. He does argue that we are gradually approaching a Grand Synthesis involving the integration of national income, input-output, and flow-of-funds accounts into one complete model in the thousand-equation range. The Grand Synthesis may involve a structure approaching the complexity of microsimulation models advocated by Guy Orcutt. While the track record for input-output quantity forecasts is such as to suggest that we should not be overly optimistic about the usefulness of these techniques in predicting price movements, Klein will allow for substitution effects by making the input-output coefficients responsive to changes in relative prices. Critics of Klein will doubtless argue that even 999 equations would be too many. My own view is that we should not shave too closely with Bishop Occam's razor. Because of the successive revolutions in computer technology, an econometric model composed of 1,000-plus equations may be no more mind-boggling today than the twelve-equation Model III that Klein published in 1950. But in an era in which research funds are again in short supply, it is interesting to observe that techniques of analysis that competed in earlier decades for foundation support are now appreciated as complementary modes of analysis.

3

BARRY
BOSWORTH
University of California,
Berkeley

and

WAYNE
VROMAN
University of Maryland

An Appraisal of the Wage-Price Control Program

The introduction of the New Economic Plan in August 1971 marked a dramatic change in the United States approach to the problem of inflation. Relative to most countries, the United States had traditionally relied more heavily on policies that depressed resource utilization as the means for curbing inflation. Acceptance of this approach was widespread; and after 1968, fiscal and monetary restraint was viewed as appropriate. Reflecting these convictions, administration officials stuck with their game plan of applying restrictive stabilization policies, giving those policies two and a half years to produce some evidence of success. The inflation rate, however, did not decelerate, and most economic forecasts made during 1969–1971 consistently underpredicted the magnitude of actual wage and price increases.

The initial imposition of a ninety-day wage-price freeze was designed to provide time for developing a control program without introducing the types of inequities that preceded the imposition of the Korean War controls. It was accompanied by a shift toward significantly greater fiscal and monetary stimulus in order to reduce unemployment, and by a major devaluation and a freeing of exchange rates.

Three "phases" of price and wage controls, spanning the years 1972–1973, followed the freeze period. This paper is directed toward an evaluation of the impact of the control program during those two years. A review of price and wage behavior prior to the imposition of controls is presented in the first section. This is followed by a brief outline of the regulations of the control program and an initial summary of price and wage changes during the control period. The major results of the study are given in the third section, which contains a detailed examination of the impact of the controls. Finally, in section four we summarize our major conclusions and discuss some of the lessons learned from this attempt to use an "incomes policy" to moderate the pace of inflation in the U.S. economy.

WAGE AND PRICE BEHAVIOR FROM 1960 TO MID-1971

In this section we review wage and price trends in the decade preceding the imposition of wage and price controls in August 1971. The discussion will be brief, as one of us has described the period in considerable detail elsewhere.[1] Selected wage-price-productivity data for those years appear in Table 1.

The data in panel A illustrate how much wage changes accelerated between 1960 and 1971. From 1960 to 1964, hourly earnings in the private nonfarm economy grew at an average rate of 3.2 percent per year. As output increased rapidly in 1965 and 1966, labor markets tightened; overall unemployment declined and remained below 4 percent of the civilian labor force through 1969. Average wage increases accelerated and reached a rate of 6.5 percent by 1969.

Wage changes by industry exhibit some definite patterns during 1960–1969. Between those dates, manufacturing was not a sector of especially rapid wage advances. Increases in manufacturing were consistently less than the all-industry average; nonmanufacturing had higher than average increases. Within nonmanufacturing, services and construction are also singled out in panel A because they exhibited especially high rates of increase. Rapid output growth (in services) and market power (in construction) probably contributed to those sharp wage increases. Notice also that a rapid acceleration of construction wages took place in 1969.

Through 1969, the wage trends depicted in panel A can be interpreted as largely the result of an increase in the excess demand for labor. To reduce price inflation, which had been accelerating in 1968 and 1969, stabilization policy became restrictive in 1969. Growth in real output and in man-hour productivity dropped sharply during 1969 and 1970. Paralleling the lower real growth in gross national product (GNP) was an increase in the unemployment rate to 5.8 percent by the fourth quarter of 1970. However, the loosening of labor markets in 1970 was not accompanied by a deceleration of wage changes. The all-industry increase in average hourly earnings, in fact, rose from 6.5 percent in 1969 to 6.6 percent in 1970 as manufacturing wage gains accelerated, while nonmanufacturing held steady at its 1969 rate of 6.8 percent. Wage inflation decreased in trade and transportation, but this was offset by continued increases in services and, particularly, in construction.

The data in panel A also show that rapid wage gains continued into 1971. At annual rates, increases for all series except construction equaled or were above their 1970 rates during the first half of 1971. This remained true for manufacturing even after adjusting for the effects of the auto strike in the fourth quarter of 1970.[2] That adjustment, however, did lower the manufacturing increase from 7.5 percent to 6.4 percent for the first half of 1971.

The failure of wage changes to decline in 1970–1971 despite the increasing unemployment led to a widespread public discussion of an adverse shift in the U.S. Phillips curve. Gordon, Friedman, Perry, Phelps, and others have offered different explanations for the observed shift.[3] From this discussion the thesis of the changing nature of labor markets and the accelerationist thesis both gained adherents and have emerged as major competing explanations, though not necessarily mutually exclusive, for the unusually rapid wage advances observed since 1969.

Panel B of Table 1 follows union contract settlements, specifically first-year negotiated increases, in the decade prior to controls. Median percent increases are shown through 1967 (through 1968 in construction), and then means are displayed for 1968 and later periods. From 1960 to 1966, first-year negotiated increases rise at roughly the same rate as average hourly earnings. Negotiated increases consistently exceed gains in average hourly earnings in 1968, and by 1969 a sizable differential between the two is apparent.

TABLE 1 Selected Wages, Prices, and Productivity in the Private Nonfarm Economy, 1960–1971[a] (percent increases at annual rates)

	1960–1964	1965–1966	1967	1968	1969	1970	1971, 1st Half
A. Average Hourly Earnings[b]							
All industries	3.2	3.9	4.9	6.3	6.5	6.6	7.6
Manufacturing	2.8	3.0	4.6	6.1	6.0	6.3	7.5
Nonmanufacturing	3.4	4.4	5.1	6.4	6.8	6.8	7.7
Services	NA	5.1	5.4	6.2	6.9	7.2	7.2
Construction	3.9	4.5	5.6	7.1	8.5	9.4	8.2
B. First-Year Negotiated Wage Increases[c]							
All industries	3.0	4.3	5.6	7.4	9.2	11.9	10.2
Manufacturing	2.5	4.1	6.4	7.0	7.9	8.1	8.9
Nonmanufacturing[d]	3.6	4.4	5.0	7.8	10.8	15.2	11.7
Nonmanufacturing, except construction[e]	NA	NA	NA	NA	9.6	14.3	11.5
Construction[f]	3.7	4.3	7.5	10.1	13.1	17.6	13.9
C. Labor Costs and Prices							
Compensation per man-hour[g]	3.9	4.7	5.6	7.5	6.8	7.1	7.6
Unit labor cost[g]	0.9	2.0	4.3	4.6	7.2	6.4	1.2
Output per man-hour[g]	3.0	2.6	1.2	2.8	−0.4	0.7	6.2
Private nonfarm deflator[h]	1.1	1.8	3.3	3.5	4.5	5.0	3.9
Consumer price index, all items	1.3	2.3	2.9	4.2	5.4	5.9	3.8

NA = not available.

[a] Through 1970 all percent changes are based on annual averages. The 1971 first-half data are based on changes from 1970IV to 1971II in seasonally adjusted quarterly data, except for the consumer price index. The CPI for the first half of 1971 is for the change from December 1970 to August 1971, expressed at an annual rate. Negotiated wage changes are for agreements settled during the period.

[b] Adjusted for interindustry shifts and for overtime in manufacturing. The 1960–1964 observation for construction is not adjusted for interindustry shifts.

[c] Mean first-year adjustments as published by the Bureau of Labor Statistics (BLS) in *Current Wage Developments*. From 1960 to 1967, medians are shown because BLS did not publish means. Data refer to settlements involving 1,000 or more workers.

[d] Before 1966 nonmanufacturing excludes construction, services, and finance.

[e] Derived as a residual by subtracting the effect of construction settlements from all non-manufacturing settlements.

[f] BLS started publishing settlements data for the construction industry in 1969. Observations for 1960 to 1968 are based on Bureau of National Affairs (BNA) data on median

There is a continuing acceleration of negotiated wage changes into 1970; they are widespread and by no means confined to construction. For nonmanufacturing exclusive of construction, the first-year increase rose from 9.6 percent in 1969 to 14.3 percent in 1970. Thus, the gap between negotiated settlements and hourly earnings gains continued to widen in nonmanufacturing in 1970 to the point where the former was twice the latter, i.e., 15.2 versus 6.8 percent.[4]

Average settlements in the first half of 1971 continued to rise in manufacturing, but fell in nonmanufacturing. Yet settlements for all sectors remained above their 1969 levels, and considerably above levels compatible with low rates of inflation for the economy. Finally, the data in panel B dramatically illustrate the acceleration of construction wage settlements in the late 1960s, a trend that continued into 1970.

The implications of accelerating wage changes in the 1960–1971 period for unit labor costs and thus for price inflation are most pessimistic, as illustrated by the data in panel C. Note that increases in compensation per man-hour consistently exceed increases in average hourly earnings throughout the period. This reflects the rapid growth in nonwage compensation, a shift in the employment mix toward white-collar workers and, perhaps, more rapid increases in salaries than in wages during the period. Not only did compensation gains accelerate between 1960 and 1970, but a general slowing of productivity advances is also apparent in panel C. The effects on man-hour productivity of the slowdown in early 1967 and of the 1969–1970 growth stoppage are both dramatic. In 1969 and 1970, this meant that increases in compensation per man-hour were translated almost completely into higher unit labor costs. Consequently, unit labor costs in the private nonfarm economy rose by 7.2 percent in 1969, and by 6.4 percent in 1970. The increase in unit labor costs was reflected in higher prices; but particularly in 1969–1970, the rise in prices was less than that of labor costs.

The data in panel C appear to show some evidence of reduced price inflation during the first half of 1971. Although man-hour com-

---

settlements. These settlements, in cents per hour, were converted to percentages and deflated by 0.84 to be at levels compatible with BLS median settlements. The deflation factor of 0.84 was the average ratio of BNA to BLS median first-year percent increases for 1969–1973.

[g] Based on data for all private nonfarm employees as published by BLS.
[h] Data are for private nonfarm GNP including the household and rest-of-world sectors.

pensation rose at a rate above that of 1970, this was largely offset by very rapid productivity gains.[5] Consequently, the rise in unit labor costs slowed to an annual rate of increase of just 1.2 percent, and increases in both price series fell to annual inflation rates of slightly below 4 percent, a substantial improvement over 1970. The improved price performance of early 1971 merits closer attention, and tables 2 and 3 provide more information about this period.

PRELUDE TO CONTROLS

The question of whether the inflation was coming to an end in early 1971 is crucial to any judgment about the effect of the controls. At first blush, the slower advance of the CPI in early 1971 would seem to offer support for the view that it was decelerating: the annual rate of increase during the first eight months fell to 3.8 percent, compared to an average of 5.9 percent in 1970. As shown in Table 2, however, half of this apparent 2 percent deceleration can be attributed to the reversal of mortgage interest rates as monetary policy shifted toward expansion. Furthermore, while the slower increases of the CPI are mirrored in the finished goods components of the wholesale index, the rate of increase of intermediate materials prices was accelerating.

Turning to a more comprehensive measure of price changes—the private nonfarm deflator—we find an interesting contrast displayed in tables 1 and 2. The use of fixed industry weights sharply reduces the apparent price deceleration of early 1971 from 1.1 percent (5.0 percent to 3.9 percent in Table 1) to 0.4 percent (4.9 percent to 4.5 percent in Table 2). Even this small amount of price deceleration can be traced to a sudden rise in the farm deflator which was not yet fully reflected in finished goods prices. The fixed weight deflators for consumer expenditures, fixed investment, and government purchases show no change from their 1970 rates of increase.

As noted, the aggregate wage indexes continue to increase at their 1970 rates. The fixed weight hourly earnings index rose at an annual rate of 7.6 percent during the first half of 1971 (7.4 percent after adjusting for the auto strike), compared to 6.6 percent in 1970. If the trend productivity gain of about 3 percent is subtracted from this rate of increase, the rise in unit labor costs would be about 4.5 percent. There is a slowing of negotiated wage increases in construction and in the rest of nonmanufacturing in this period. Negotiated increases in manufacturing, however, actually rose above the 1970 rate; and for all sectors, negotiated settlements of early 1971 exceeded the level of 1969 settlements.

Thus, the evidence of a quick end to inflation is limited to consumer finished goods prices, with some indication from intermediate materials prices that even this slowdown was transitory. In sectors outside of contract construction, wage changes showed only minor deviations from 1970 patterns. On the other hand, the costs of aggregate demand restraint were considerable. The unemployment rate stabilized at 6 percent in comparison to the 3.3 percent rate of late 1968, and real GNP growth averaged only 1 percent between the second quarters of 1969 and 1971.

AN OVERVIEW OF THE CONTROL PROGRAM

The thirty-three months of price and wage controls consisted of four distinct phases with significant changes over the period in the basic regulations and enforcement procedures. The first phase, a wage-price freeze, was essentially a transitory period and is not discussed in detail in this paper.[6] We are primarily concerned with the three phases that followed the freeze period.

In this section, the organizational structure of the control program and the basic regulations are outlined. We then summarize the price and wage changes in 1971–1973 as a prelude to the more detailed evaluation given in the subsequent econometric section.

Organizational Structure and Regulations

Only a brief outline of the significant features of the control program will be presented here since more detailed reviews are available elsewhere.[7]

The Cost of Living Council was responsible for administrative control of the Phase II program. It determined which economic units were subject to the controls and classified these units according to the prenotification and reporting requirements to which they were subject. During Phase II, most specific price and wage decisions were made by the Price Commission and the Pay Board. In addition, there were several ancillary committees, including a Committee on Interest and Dividends, and two special advisory committees—the Health Service Industry Committee and the

TABLE 2 Rates of Change in Selected Price Series, Various Periods, 1969–1973 (percent change in seasonally adjusted data at annual rates)

	1969–1970 (annual aver.)	Period of Controls					
		12/70–8/71	8/71–12/71	12/71–6/72	6/72–12/72	12/72–6/73	6/73–12/73
Consumer price index							
All items	5.9	3.8	2.4	2.9	3.9	8.0	9.6
All items[a]	5.5	4.5	2.9	2.8	3.9	8.0	9.4
Food	5.5	4.8	3.0	3.5	6.1	21.5	18.6
Nonfood[a]	5.9	4.7	3.0	3.0	3.2	4.2	6.5
Commodities[b]	4.2	2.8	0.9	2.1	2.5	4.2	6.5
Durables[b]	4.9	2.1	2.5	1.8	2.3	1.4	4.7
Nondurables excl. food	4.0	3.0	1.5	1.9	3.0	5.9	7.8
Services[c]	7.9	7.6	3.4	4.3	3.8	4.3	6.4
Rent[d]	4.1	4.3	2.9	3.6	3.4	5.0	4.7
Medical care services[e]	7.1	6.9	2.0	3.3	4.4	3.7	8.0

Wholesale price index

All commodities	3.7	4.6	2.9	4.1	9.1	20.2	10.9
Farm products, processed foods and feeds	3.4	5.9	6.7	4.5	25.1	45.8	10.4
Industrial commodities	3.8	4.4	0.9	4.0	3.2	10.6	10.9
Consumer goods excl. food	3.0	2.2	1.1	2.3	2.1	6.7	8.1
Producers' finished goods	4.7	3.3	0.5	3.3	1.0	5.4	5.3
Intermediate goods excl. food	3.6	6.1	1.3	4.3	3.7	12.2	11.7
Crude materials excl. food	7.4	2.4	3.2	9.4	12.4	23.0	40.4
Private nonfarm fixed weight deflator[f]	4.9	4.5	2.7	2.8	2.8	5.7	7.5

SOURCE: U.S. Bureau of Labor Statistics and Department of Commerce. The consumer price index excludes the effect of the reduction in the automobile excise tax in 1971.

[a] Excludes used cars and mortgage interest.
[b] Excludes used cars.
[c] Not seasonally adjusted; excludes used cars and mortgage interest.
[d] Not seasonally adjusted; excludes used cars.
[e] Excludes mortgage interest.
[f] Based on quarterly data. Percent changes are for the quarter that includes the first month listed at the top of the column.

TABLE 3 Rates of Change in Selected Wage and Productivity Series, Various Periods, 1969–1973 (percent change in seasonally adjusted data at annual rates)

	1969–1970 (annual aver.)	1971 1st Half	1971 2nd Half	Period of Controls			
				1972 1st Half	1972 2nd Half	1973 1st Half	1973 2nd Half
Private nonfarm[a]							
Employee compensation per man-hour	7.1	7.6	5.6	7.4	6.6	8.7	7.6
Excl. payroll tax increases	–	–	–	–	–	6.5	–
Unit labor cost	6.4	1.2	2.3	3.4	1.8	7.4	8.1
Output per man-hour	0.7	6.2	3.4	3.7	4.7	1.2	–0.5
Average hourly earnings[b]	6.6	7.6	5.6	6.9	6.2	5.8	7.5
Manufacturing	6.3	7.5	5.0	7.2	5.5	5.5	7.6
Nonmanufacturing	6.8	7.7	5.6	7.0	6.3	6.2	7.2
Construction	9.4	8.2	7.8	5.7	4.9	6.4	4.7

Negotiated wages changes[c]						
Over life of contract						
Wages and benefits combined	9.1	8.4	9.0	7.7	6.9	6.1	5.8
Wages only	8.9	8.1	8.2	6.9	5.9	5.4	4.8
First-year adjustments						
All industries	11.9	10.2	12.9	7.7	7.0	5.9	5.6
Manufacturing	8.1	8.9	13.1	7.0	6.4	6.3	5.6
Nonmanufacturing	15.2	11.7	12.8	8.2	7.5	5.7	5.7
Excl. construction	14.3	11.5	13.0	8.0	8.5	5.8	6.7
Construction only	17.6	13.9	12.1	8.7	5.6	5.2	4.7

SOURCE: U.S. Bureau of Labor Statistics, *Current Wage Developments*, various issues; BLS news release, *Major Collective Bargaining Settlements*, various issues; and unpublished BLS data.

[a] Semiannual changes are based on data for the last quarter of each period.

[b] Data are for nonsupervisory employees and are adjusted for interindustry shifts and for overtime in manufacturing.

[c] Average during the period. Data on wages plus benefits refer to units with more than 5,000 employees. Wage adjustments are for units with more than 1,000 employees.

Committee on State and Local Government Cooperation. Beginning with Phase III, the Pay Board and Price Commission were abolished, and their functions were taken over by the Cost of Living Council.

Pay Controls

The Pay Board was initially a tripartite organization with equal representation of labor, business, and the public. After most of the labor members left, it operated as an essentially public board until its dissolution in Phase III. The general wage standard was an overall guide relating wage increases to the trend productivity growth of the economy plus prospective increases in the cost of living. The initial 5.5 percent limit on new wage contracts reflected a target inflation rate of 2.5 percent and a long-run productivity trend of 3 percent. Later action of Congress, exempting fringe benefits, raised the effective standard to 6.2 percent. Congress also excluded the "working poor" and required the board to permit exceptions for agreements which included elements of productivity bargaining to reduce work-rule restrictions.

Although this was a general wage ceiling, the regulations permitted significant departures. Exceptions were allowed in new agreements for historical tandem wage relationships and catch-up allowances for multiyear contracts signed prior to the 1969–1971 acceleration of the price inflation. In addition, deferred increases under existing contracts were not altered in any significant fashion. Thus, the program was focused on new wage contracts rather than existing wage rates. After the initiation of Phase III, the stabilization program moved away from emphasis on a specific wage standard.

Price Controls

The basic approach of the Price Commission was to approve a full percentage pass-through of all allowable cost increases. In general, the definition of allowable costs included all costs—everything except profits. The regulations were later modified to require use of a Price Commission estimate of labor productivity growth rather than that of the individual firms. Exceptions were made for the trade sector, rent, and medical care. In the trade sector, only invoice cost increases, marked up no more than during the freeze, could be passed forward into prices, and for rent and medical care, ceilings were placed on the size of price increases. The commission also limited the allowable wage cost component of a price increase to 5.5 percent. During Phase IV, food manufacturers were placed under a margin control with a pass-through of materials costs on a dollar-for-dollar basis.

Experience with the cost pass-through provisions during Phase II indicated great technical problems because of the need to become involved with the internal accounting practices of individual firms. The allocation of overhead and joint operating costs is a highly arbitrary process. Thus, from a practical point of view, a second fallback regulation on profit margins became of greater importance. That regulation limited profits per dollar of sales to an amount equal to the average of earnings for the highest two out of three fiscal years prior to the establishment of the control program.

Finally, the commission entered into term-limit pricing agreements with some multiproduct firms as a means of reducing administrative burdens. Under those arrangements, firms agreed to hold their average price increases to 1.8 percent but were free to raise individual product prices by larger amounts. The major change during Phase III was a shift to voluntary compliance as opposed to prenotification and prior approval of price increases. Firms were also allowed to include 1972 in the calculation of the profit-margin ceiling. In the middle of 1973 there was a return to the requirement of prior approval for large firms.

Price and Wage Changes during the Control Period

Some progress in reducing the rate of inflation was made in the nonagricultural sector during 1972. As shown in Table 2, the annual rate of increase for nonfood items in the CPI declined from 4.7 percent prior to controls to about 3 percent. The deceleration was particularly large for services—a full three percentage points lower. The nonfarm deflator showed a decline of similar magnitude to that of the nonfood component of the CPI.

Because of a growing problem with food prices, overall price performance during the control period shows less evidence of a slowdown. Thus, the rate of increase of the total CPI was substantially above the target of 2.5 percent and only about one percentage point below the precontrol rate of 4.5 percent. A significant moderation of the inflation is also not evident in the wholesale price index (WPI), which excludes services, as the rate of increase for industrial prices slowed only slightly in 1972.

On the wage side, there was a gradual but steady reduction in the size of negotiated wage settlements—particularly in the construction sector. As shown in Table 3, the slowdown ranged from 2 to 3 percent in the last half of 1972. There were less apparent signs of a slowdown, however, in the hourly earnings data. Employee compensation in the nonfarm sector rose by 6.6. percent in the last half of 1972, compared to 7.6 percent in the first half of 1971, and 7.1 percent in 1970. The fixed weight earnings index shows a slightly larger decline of about 1.5 percentage points from the early-1971 rate of increase.

In 1973, the rate of price inflation accelerated sharply. During the year the CPI rose 8.8 percent, and the WPI rose 15.5 percent. Initially, this inflation was heavily concentrated in the food sector, with a 45.8 percent rate of increase of farm prices in early 1973. At that time, the rate of increase of consumer nonfood items was still only 4.2 percent. However, a very large acceleration was also apparent in wholesale prices for crude and intermediate products other than food. Later in the year, petroleum prices became an additional major source of price inflation. The importance of food and fuel price increases in the last half of 1973 is indicated by data from the national income accounts. While prices of food and fuel were rising at annual rates of 18 and 16 percent, respectively, prices of other consumer items were rising at a 6 percent rate.[8]

Wages were slow to respond to the higher rate of price inflation. Negotiated wage changes continued to decline in size throughout the year. In part because of an increase in social security tax rates, the hourly compensation measure increased more rapidly than in 1972. The hourly earnings index continued to show some deceleration of wage increases in the first half of 1973, but returned to pre-control rates later in the year.

ECONOMETRIC RESULTS

A simple comparison of price and wage increases before and during the period of controls does not provide a very satisfactory basis for evaluating the effects of controls. Only in a few situations is the magnitude of change in the pattern of inflation sufficient for us to conclude that the change was a result of controls. Such a comparison also implies that other economic variables that influence wages and prices remained unchanged. But this was not the case. By late 1973, unemployment had fallen from its August 1971 level of 6.1

percent of the labor force to 4.7 percent; the United States experienced two substantial devaluations with implications for a changed composition of exports and imports and increased pressures on domestic prices; food prices rose sharply in response to crop failures in several major countries; and there was a dramatic shift toward shortages and price increases in world markets for basic commodities.

As an alternative, we made some use of statistical equations to estimate the probable course of prices and wages in the absence of controls. This, too, is not a very satisfactory method of estimating the effects of controls. The wage and price behavior that marked the precontrol period is not well explained by existing statistical equations. Yet similar equations have been used to infer the alternative path of wages and prices over a two-year period. In addition, some of the disturbances during the period of controls, such as devaluation and changes in international commodity markets, are difficult to incorporate into existing price equations, which emphasize domestic factors. Such equations, however, do provide some guidance in summarizing the influence of changes in the underlying economic conditions.

Impact on Wages

Econometric studies of U.S. money wage behavior have proliferated in recent years, and a thorough review of this literature is beyond the scope of our paper.[9] Some of the salient issues in this literature are: (1) the proper measurement of labor-market tightness; (2) the effects of price expectations on money-wage demands; (3) the effects of direct taxes (payroll taxes as well as income taxes) and (4) the effectiveness of income policies (in the 1962–1966 period as well as in the more recent initiatives from 1971–1974) in retarding wage advances. Each of the four issues has generated considerable controversy; and, depending on one's point of view, each has a large effect on how one would specify and estimate an econometric wage equation.

Basic Equations

After experimenting with several more elaborate specifications, we elected to use a relatively simple specification of the wage equation.[10] Except for particular issues discussed later, we found that the alternative specifications considered would not significantly affect our analysis of the control period. The general equation is of the form

$$\%W = a + bUR + c\%\bar{P}_{-1} + dG$$

where

$\%W$ = quarterly percent change in money wage rates
UR = the unemployment rate for civilian men 25 and older
$\%\bar{P}_{-1}$ = a weighted average of recent changes in the CPI, weights being respectively 0.4, 0.3, 0.2, and 0.1 for the four quarters prior to the current quarter
G = a wage-price guidepost dummy variable with a value of unity from 1962II through 1966II and zero in all other quarters

Four wage series were examined: (a) a fixed weight index of straight-time hourly earnings in the private nonfarm economy; (b) a fixed weight index of straight-time hourly earnings in manufacturing; (c) the annual percent increase in wage rates negotiated in manufacturing (first-year increases for multiyear contracts); and (d) the percent increase in wage rates negotiated in the private sector, excluding manufacturing and construction. A description of the sources and derivation of all the variables is contained in Appendix A. Data for these series were used to estimate equations for 1956–1969, and the regressions were then used to predict wage developments for the ensuing four years.

The actual coefficients and summary statistics for the four equations appear in Table 4. The overall fit of these equations is quite good, with all adjusted coefficients of determination ($\bar{R}^2$) exceeding 0.6 and all standard errors 0.22 percent or smaller. On the basis of $\bar{R}^2$ and the standard error, the statistical fit is better in the two negotiated wage-change equations than in the other pair. Positive serial correlation, however, is present in both equations for negotiated wages, particularly equation 3, for manufacturing.' Consequently, there probably is some upward bias in the t statistics shown for those two equations.

The coefficients for the three independent variables are reasonably similar in all four equations, and all are significant by the usual statistical criteria. More weight is attributed to price increases and less to unemployment in equation 4 than in the other three equations, but much of this difference is probably caused by the unavailability of negotiated wage data for 1956 and 1957. All four equations suggest a slowing of wage changes during the period of the Kennedy-Johnson guideposts but the point estimates of -0.22 to -0.35 percent per quarter seem a little large.

TABLE 4 Quarterly Money Wage Increases, 1956I–1969IV
(figures in parentheses are t ratios)

| Dependent Variable | Independent Variables[a] | | | | $\bar{R}^2$ [SE] {DW} |
	a	UR	%$\bar{P}_{-1}$	G	
1. Average hrly earnings, private nonfarm	1.41 (10.49)	−0.14 (5.58)	0.33 (3.37)	−0.22 (3.61)	0.69 [0.19] {1.52}
2. Average hrly earnings, mfg.	1.37 (8.54)	−0.13 (4.53)	0.29 (2.49)	−0.35 (4.88)	0.65 [0.22] {1.81}
3. Negotiated increases, mfg.	1.29 (15.85)	−0.10 (6.68)	0.31 (5.21)	−0.32 (8.66)	0.85 [0.11] {0.60}
4. Negotiated increases, mfg. excl. construction[b]	1.25 (10.54)	−0.06 (2.83)	0.56 (6.49)	−0.23 (4.57)	0.82 [0.14] {1.28}

$\bar{R}^2$ = coefficient of multiple determination adjusted for degrees of freedom.
SE = estimated standard deviation of the disturbance term.
DW = Durbin-Watson statistic.
[a] For definitions, see accompanying text.
[b] Data for the dependent variable are not available prior to 1958.

Although the coefficients agree closely in size and are significant, they are quite sensitive to the period of fit. When earlier data are included, the relative importance of unemployment rises and that of prices declines. Adding later data points further enhances the importance of prices versus unemployment in explaining wage increases.[11] This sensitivity must be kept in mind in estimating the impact of the control program on wage changes during 1972 and 1973.

Results for Wage Controls

Equations 1 through 4 were used to predict quarterly wage changes for 1968–1973, with actual values of the variables appearing on the right-hand side of the equations. Semiannual averages of the residuals expressed at annual rates are shown in Table 5. For comparative purposes, the standard errors of the original regressions appear at the bottom of each column. The construction industry is excluded because of the lack of historical data for union settlements. This industry will be examined separately in the following section.

TABLE 5 Residuals of Wage Equations, 1968-1973 (seasonally adjusted semiannual percent changes at annual rates, actual minus predicted values)

	Estimation Period: 1956–1969				Estimation Period: 1958–First Half 1971			
	Hourly Earnings[a]		Union Negotiated[b]		Hourly Earnings[a]		Union Negotiated[b]	
	Nonfarm	Mfg.	Mfg.	Nonmfg.	Nonfarm	Mfg.	Mfg.	Nonmfg.
1968								
1st half	0.8	1.1	−0.2	−0.3	0.9	1.3	−0.2	−0.5
2nd half	0.5	0.3	0.2	0.8	0.4	0.3	−0.0	0.3
1969								
1st half	−0.2	−0.7	0.4	0.8	−0.4	−0.9	0.0	0.2
2nd half	0.4	0.5	0.4	0.3	−0.2	−0.2	−0.4	−0.6
1970								
1st half	−0.4	0.1	1.0	1.1	−1.2	−0.7	−0.1	−0.2
2nd half[c]	1.8	1.6	1.8	1.9	1.0	0.7	0.7	0.6
1971								
1st half[c]	1.5	1.2	2.4	4.2	0.8	0.5	1.4	3.1

Period of Controls

1971								
2nd half	0.4	0.1	3.0	5.9	0.0	-0.3	2.4	5.2
1972								
1st half	1.8	2.3	1.4	0.2	1.7	2.3	1.2	-0.2
2nd half	1.0	0.6	0.7	-0.2	1.0	0.8	0.7	-0.5
1973								
1st half	0.2	0.2	0.6	-0.3	0.1	0.3	0.3	-0.8
2nd half	0.7	1.1	0.1	-1.7	-0.4	-0.0	-1.4	-3.4
Standard error of regression	0.7	0.9	0.5	0.5	0.7	0.8	0.5	1.0

SOURCE: Equations in Table 4. Residuals are based on projections of observations beyond regression period.
[a] Index of straight-time hourly earnings including interindustry shifts and overtime (in manufacturing).
[b] Bureau of National Affairs data for first-year wage settlements (excluding fringes). Construction industry settlements are excluded.
[c] The data for earnings in late 1970 are adjusted to eliminate the disturbance caused by the automobile strike.

Average residuals based on the equations of Table 4 appear in the first four columns. In all four of these equations, average residuals are uniformly positive in the second half of 1970 and first half of 1971, as actual wage increases exceeded the predicted ones. Further, six of these eight averages are more than twice the standard error of the underlying equation. The residuals in the negotiated wage-change equations become increasingly positive for each period after the second half of 1969 and are especially large for the nonmanufacturing sector. During the period of controls, these positive residuals steadily decline in magnitude.

Residuals in the equations estimated from earnings data decline sharply in late 1971 and then increase in early 1972 in response to the wage freeze and retroactive wage payments. The same type of movement in the residuals is evident in late 1972, and has been related to a bulge of nonunion increases at the beginning of the second year of pay controls.[12] A smoothing of the underlying quarterly data, however, to reduce the impact of these two events, indicates a uniform reduction in the size of the residuals throughout 1972 and early 1973. The gradual movement of actual wage increases back toward the equation predictions is even more evident in the figures for negotiated wage settlements.

The pattern of wage residuals discussed above is illustrated in Figure 1, which shows actual and predicted negotiated wage changes for the manufacturing sector for 1968–1973. Beginning in 1969, actual wage increases begin to exceed those anticipated from historical relationships by increasingly large magnitudes. This pattern is broken with the introduction of the control program, and the two series gradually come back together—primarily because of a reduction in the actual increases.

Because of the sensitivity of the coefficients of prices and unemployment to the period of estimation, a second set of residuals is also shown in Table 5. These are based on an estimation period extending from 1958 through the first half of 1971, with a consequent increase in the weight assigned to the price variable. Qualitatively, these residuals are similar to the first set. The tendency of regressions to average residuals and reduce any extreme error is clearly evident in 1970 and early 1971, but the residuals remain large. The principal change is to raise the level of the predicted increases over the control period, with the result that the smaller positive residuals at the beginning are offset by larger negative residuals in 1973. The predicted increases also accelerate more during the rapid food and fuel inflation of late 1973.

Overall, these results suggest to us the following interpretation.

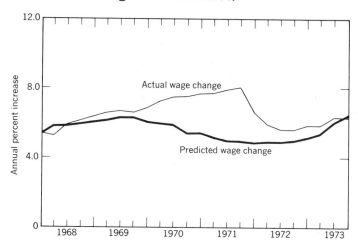

FIGURE 1   Negotiated Wage Increases in
Manufacturing, 1968–1973
(actual and predicted percent rates of
change at annual rates)

NOTE: Predictions are based on equation 3 of Table 4. The equation
was fitted to data for 1956I–1969IV

During 1969–1971, there was a growing tendency for wage changes
—particularly in the union sector—to exceed the rate of increase
that would have been anticipated from historical relationships to
unemployment and price inflation. The magnitude of negotiated
wage changes increased despite an easing of labor market conditions during the recession. By late 1970, this was being reflected in
large increases in average hourly earnings. The particularly large
residuals of late 1970 and early 1971 have been noted by others.
In a 1971 study, George Perry stated that the magnitude of wage
increases from 1970IV to 1971II exceeded predicted levels from his
equations by an average annual rate of about one full percentage
point. The recent paper by Mitchell also shows a similar residual
pattern for these quarters. However, because he did not adjust for
the auto strike of 1970IV, he shows a small residual for 1970IV but
a very large residual for 1971II.[13]
    The wage freeze sharply reduced these increases, but they
showed up again in the postfreeze period. In particular, negotiated
increases in early 1972 were the result of bargaining that had been
started in coal, steel, and the railroads before the freeze and which
was allowed to go through without major change. But during
Phase II, there was clearly a major decline in negotiated settle-

ments: prefreeze residuals were very large and growing, but they were eliminated by mid-1972 and throughout 1973.

Thus, one's view of the effectiveness of wage controls is dependent upon the interpretation of wage behavior prior to the freeze. If these large residuals indicated a permanent shift of wage behavior, the controls succeeded in restoring historical patterns of wage increases. Alternatively, if the wage behavior of early 1971 reflected only a temporary aberration, the controls had very little impact. The change in the magnitude of the residuals after 1971 would suggest a decline during the control period of approximately 0.4 to 0.8 percent in the annual rate of increase for hourly earnings.[14] The estimated reduction in union settlements ranges from 1.5 to 3.0 percent.

Because the control program focused on union settlements and in the short run on newly negotiated contracts, equations based on hourly earnings data may understate the long-run impact of the program. If the unusually large union wage adjustments of 1970–1971 had been permitted to continue into 1972 and 1973, their impact on average hourly earnings would have been larger than in earlier historic periods simply because these adjustments were becoming so large. It is probably safe to say that such large adjustments were tending to widen union-nonunion wage differentials. Had this been permitted to continue into 1972 and 1973, it would have been reflected in more rapid gains in overall average hourly earnings. This acceleration would have been further enhanced if nonunion workers tried to retaliate and to maintain their earlier relative wage position. Thus, the full impact of controls on hourly earnings would extend beyond the initial periods with a cumulative effect.

Construction Industry

Wage changes in construction have exceeded all-industry averages for the past decade. The data in Table 1 showed these wage changes accelerating in the late 1960s and in 1970 with little evidence of abating. Since unemployment rates in construction were already high, rising to 9.7 percent in 1970 from 6.0 percent in 1969, it became widely recognized that traditional market forces were not sufficiently strong to dampen wage increases in that industry. This situation led to the creation of the Construction Industry Stabilization Committee (CISC) in March 1971.

Since regression analysis of construction industry wage changes has not been very successful, we will focus on a tabular presentation of these wage data. In Table 6 we show quarterly percent wage changes at annual rates for 1970–1973. Three wage series are shown: the Bureau of Labor Statistics fixed weight index of hourly earnings; median first-year negotiated wage settlements, as recorded by the BLS for settlements involving 1,000 or more workers; and median negotiated wage settlements effective for the life of the contract for the same series of BLS contracts. Additionally, the number of workers covered in the BLS settlements is shown. These numbers should be considered relative to average industry employment of about 3.5 million during these years.

In this industry, the hourly earnings data show substantial evidence of deceleration. The increases for 1972 and 1973 are more

TABLE 6 Construction Wages, 1970–1973
(percent increases at annual rates)

Year and Quarter	Aver. Hourly Earnings: Fixed Weight Index	BLS Negotiated Settlements		
		First-Year Median Wages	Life-of-Contract Median Wages	Number of Workers (thousands)
1970I	8.9%	15.7%	13.4%	130
II	8.0	14.7	13.9	417
III	11.5	19.0	14.9	112
IV	6.6	19.3	13.7	23
1971I	8.6	18.0	16.7	13
		Period of Controls		
1971II	8.9	13.4	11.0	74
III	8.2	10.9	8.8	171
IV	5.9	10.9	9.3	55
1972I	6.5	15.2	12.7	36
II	4.0	6.1	6.0	161
III	3.4	5.6	5.6	162
IV	9.0	4.6	3.1	97
1973I	6.9	4.2	5.0	154
II	3.2	4.7	5.3	312
III	6.0	4.4	4.6	270
IV	3.5	5.2	5.2	170

SOURCE: Average hourly earnings are from the Bureau of Labor Statistics; negotiated settlements are from BLS, *Current Wage Developments*, June 1974, appendix tables, and earlier issues. Data refer to settlements involving 1,000 or more workers.

than 3 percent below the 9.2 percent rate of increase which prevailed for the 1969–1971I period.

An even more dramatic pattern of deceleration is evident in the settlement data. With the introduction of the CISC in the second quarter of 1971, first-year settlements declined immediately, and then fell to even lower levels in the second quarter of 1972.[15] From the middle of 1972 through the end of 1973 these settlements were closely in line with the original Pay Board guidelines. The life-of-contract data strongly parallel the first-year median settlements. Again there are sharp declines in the second quarters of 1971 and 1972. Similar results are obvious in the data for mean settlements (as opposed to medians) and for compensation (rather than wages). Thus, all the data are consistent with the conclusion of a large and abrupt decline in wage settlements after March of 1971.

Controls and Negotiated Wage Settlements

In the previous sections we stressed the greater impact of wage controls on negotiated settlements relative to average hourly earnings. Because the program focused on union settlements—particularly new contracts—they are explored more fully in this section, using annual data from the Bureau of Labor Statistics on new contracts and effective wage changes.[16] Data for union settlements involving 1,000 or more workers are shown in Table 7 for the period 1966–1973. Consistent industry coverage including construction, services, and finance became available only in 1966.

The percent distribution of first-year wage adjustments and of total wage changes effective during the year are shown in panels A and B, respectively. Between 1966 and 1971, the data in both panels show similar shifts in the distribution of wage changes: a steady decrease in the proportion of workers in the category "under 5 percent" and a rapid rise in the proportion in the "over 9 percent" category. The upward shift was reversed after controls were introduced in 1972 and 1973. This reversal was particularly evident for first-year settlements in panel A. The increased percentage of settlements in the under-5-percent category is not consistent with the view that the general wage standard served as a floor for wage settlements. For first-year settlements, 17 percent were in the under-5-percent category in 1972, and 26 percent were in that category in 1973.[17]

A more systematic display of the shift in effective wage changes is contained in panel C. The second line shows the time pattern of median wage changes; the wage change for the first and third quartiles are shown in the first and third lines. A measure of relative wage dispersion, the interquartile range divided by the median, is shown in the last line. Except for 1969, the median increased steadily throughout the 1966–1971 period. The first-quartile changes, however, rose most sharply in 1968 and 1969, while increases in the third quartile were concentrated in 1970 and 1971. Consequently, the measure of relative dispersion dropped in 1968 and 1969 but was very large in 1970 and 1971.

During the control period, the measure of relative dispersion declined sharply. In contrast to the 1968–1969 episode, however, this decline resulted from a lowering of the third quartile rather than an increase in the first. Thus, the compression of the distribution during the control period is primarily the result of a sharp reduction in the incidence of very large wage increases.

A decomposition of the effective wage changes is shown in panel D. Such increases can be traced to those resulting from newly negotiated contracts, deferred adjustments of contracts negotiated in prior years, and cost-of-living escalator clauses. The primary focus of the wage controls was on newly negotiated contracts. During the first year of controls, the mean effective adjustment fell from 9.2 to 6.6 percent. All of this decline resulted from the smaller role of the first-year adjustments, since deferred and cost-of-living adjustments were unchanged. However, since the number of negotiated contracts varies from year to year, not all of the reduced contribution from first-year adjustments can be attributed to controls or to any other behavioral factors: bargaining in 1972 was light. Of the total decline of 2.6 percent, 1.6 percent was due to the declining proportion of workers negotiating new contracts.[18]

In 1973 the contribution of first-year settlements increased even though their average size declined (5.8 percent in 1973 versus 6.6 percent in 1972). This was the result of a larger volume of contract negotiations in 1973, with a consequent increase in their contribution. The smaller contribution of deferred increases in 1973 reflects both the low level of bargaining activity in the previous year and the reduced size of the settlements.

The acceleration of effective wage adjustments can be traced to the greatly increased contribution of escalator clauses. Escalator clauses are becoming more prevalent, as expectations of large and continuing price increases are now widely held. However, this ascendancy is a consequence of recent inflationary experience and not a response to the control program per se. Mitchell and Weber report that escalator clauses actually declined in frequency during Phase II.[19]

TABLE 7 Aspects of Negotiated Wage Changes Effective in 1966-1973
(private nonfarm agreements covering 1,000 workers or more)

	1966	1967	1968	1969	1970	1971	1972	1973
A. Distribution of Percent Increases for First-Year Adjustments								
Under 5%	53	34	11	6	2	3	17	26
5–7%	35	29	31	30	20	12	41	52
7–9%	8	26	40	20	19	12	21	17
Over 9%	4	11	18	42	59	71	21	4
Not specified	0	2	1	4	0	1	0	0
Mean adjustment	NA	NA	7.4	9.2	11.9	11.6	7.3	5.8
B. Distribution of Percent Increases for Wage Changes Effective in the Year								
Under 5%	68	60	38	38	28	17	25	20
5–7%	25	19	29	35	20	25	37	24
7–9%	4	17	20	10	12	10	18	31
Over 9%	2	5	13	17	39	46	21	24
Not specified	0	1	1	2	1	1	0	0
Mean adjustment	3.7[a]	4.5[a]	6.0	6.5	8.8	9.2	6.6	7.0

C. Quartile Distribution Points[b] and Relative Dispersion of Percent Changes Effective in the Year

First quartile (Q1)	2.3	2.4	4.2	4.3	4.8	5.9	5.0	5.4
Median (Md.)	3.6	4.4	5.5	5.1	7.3	8.0	6.0	7.3
Third quartile (Q3)	5.5	6.5	7.5	7.3	12.4	13.7	8.0	8.9
[(Q3 − Q1)/Md.]	0.89	0.93	0.60	0.59	1.04	0.98	0.50	0.48

D. Mean Percent Adjustment, and Components, Effective in the Year

First-year adjustments[c]	NA	NA	3.2	2.4	5.1	4.3	1.7	3.0
Deferred adjustments[d]	NA	NA	2.4	3.8	3.1	4.2	4.2	2.7
Cost-of-living escalator adjustments[e]	NA	NA	0.3	0.3	0.6	0.7	0.7	1.3
Mean adjustment	3.7[a]	4.5[a]	6.0	6.5	8.8	9.2	6.6	7.0

NA = not available.

SOURCE: U.S. Bureau of Labor Statistics, *Current Wage Developments*, June 1974, and earlier issues.

[a] Estimated by BLS.

[b] Estimates of the first and third quartiles are based on linear interpolation of detailed interval data. The actual intervals published in *Current Wage Developments* are more numerous than those shown in panel B and vary according to the range of settlements effective in the particular year.

[c] Changes negotiated during the year and going into effect within twelve months from the effective date of the agreement. Includes guaranteed minimum adjustments under cost-of-living escalator clauses.

[d] Changes decided upon in earlier years.

[e] Excludes guaranteed minimum adjustments which are treated as deferred adjustments.

Average contract duration has tended to decrease in the 1972–1974 period. For example, the median duration of contracts negotiated during 1973 was 28 months. In the immediately prior round of settlements, these same contracts had a median duration of 32 months.[20] This shortening of contracts, however, should be attributed in part to inflation rather than to effects of the control program. Duration of contracts will probably show a continued decrease this year (1974), especially in settlements where escalator provisions are not part of the package.

Strike activity during 1972 and 1973 was rather low compared to other years. Only 0.15 and 0.14 percent of man-days was lost through strikes in 1972 and 1973, respectively. These percentages were lower than in any year since 1966.[21] Given the unusually heavy bargaining schedule of 1973, it would seem that the control program did not increase the difficulties for labor and management in arriving at mutually agreeable settlements. Perhaps the existence of pay controls even helped by reducing the upper range of feasible wage settlements.

In summary, both the average size of contract settlements and their relative dispersion were sharply reduced during the period of wage controls. The abruptness of this change creates a strong presumption that the controls were a significant causal factor. Finally, although cost-of-living escalators became more common and contract duration became somewhat shorter, these aspects of change seem to be related more to the inflation than to the existence of controls. Both trends have continued since the termination of Phase IV.

Impact on Prices

The price control regulations varied among major sectors of the economy, and for that reason, we have undertaken some disaggregation of the available data. Major distinctions can be made among the controls applied to retail and wholesale trade, services, manufacturing firms, and the food industry. A separate examination of each of these sectors offers an opportunity to evaluate the impact of different types of control regulations.

Retail and Wholesale Trade

Firms in the trade sector were required to maintain a percentage gross markup over invoice costs that was no higher than that of the freeze period. Thus, only increases in the costs of goods to the firm could serve as a basis for an increase in selling price. By not allowing a pass-through of high operating costs, the regulation resulted in some additional restraint beyond a full-cost justification of price increases: productivity growth in the trade sector is less than that of the rest of the economy, while its wage increases match those of other industries. However, this exclusion of operating costs becomes quite unimportant for substantial increases in invoice costs.

Normally, the trade sector would not be viewed as a target for price controls, since it is considered to be quite competitive. The reduction of rates of return below long-run equilibrium levels can only result in a bulge of price increases after controls are removed. On the other hand, the regulation was clear and easy for firms to comply with, since it was designed to follow the pattern of their normal pricing procedures. By exempting firms with fewer than sixty employees, the Price Commission was able to reduce an otherwise overwhelming monitoring burden to manageable size. However, the loose definition of normal margin, shifts in product mix, and conflicts between categorical and item-by-item pricing all made enforcement of the regulations more difficult.

Our efforts to measure the impact on retail trade margins are based upon a comparison of the CPI and WPI indexes for consumer finished goods. Differences in the types of products included in the two indexes and variations in the weights attached to individual items complicate any such comparison. The elimination of food and fuel products from the nondurables component and the removal of used cars and home purchases from the CPI index for durables do improve comparability, but the lists of products included still are not identical. An attempt was made to restructure the WPI index at the four-digit level, using CPI weights, but the results were not significantly different from those obtained using regularly published indexes. The primary effect of the lack of full comparability should be to increase the standard error of any regression equation. There would be no reason to expect a bias in any particular direction during the period of controls. Aggregation should average out some of the individual product differences.

The equations used to relate retail prices to wholesale costs closely parallel those of a pricing model by stage of processing developed by Joel Popkin.[22] The specific equations were estimated for the 1956–1970 period and are presented in Appendix B. These equations were projected through the control period, using other variables such as wholesale prices, wage rates, and capacity utilization at their actual levels. The residuals from these predictions are summarized in Table 8.

TABLE 8 Residuals of Price Equations for Period of Price Controls (seasonally adjusted semiannual percent changes at annual rates; actual minus predicted values)

| | Retail Prices | | | Wholesale Prices | | |
| | CPI Durables[a] | CPI Nondurables[b] | CPI Services[c] | Consumer Goods | | Producer Equipment |
				Durables	Nondurables[b]	
1971						
2nd half	−2.5	+0.1	−0.5	−0.8	−0.1	+0.3
1972						
1st half	−1.2	+0.5	−0.3	+2.1	−0.2	+2.2
2nd half	+1.0	−0.4	−1.2	−3.6	−0.7	−2.0
1973						
1st half	−0.7	−0.2	−1.3	+2.0	−1.9	+0.8
2nd half	+0.7	−0.7	0.0	−3.5	−2.8	−2.2
Average	−0.5	−0.1	−0.7	−0.8	−1.1	−0.2
Standard error of regression	1.0	0.7	0.9	1.3	1.0	1.1

SOURCE: Projections from the price equations of Appendix B.
[a] Excludes used cars and home purchases.
[b] Excludes food and fuel.
[c] Excludes rent.

There is some weak evidence that the margin controls did depress retail prices relative to wholesale costs. For both durables and nondurables, the average of the residuals is slightly negative over the control period. However, the large residual for durables during the last half of 1971 is almost wholly due to the automobile exise tax cut. Elimination of this observation results in a pattern of residuals within the range anticipated from the standard error of the regression, and showing only a slight negative tendency. Thus, the restrictive influence would seem to be of minimal importance. The regulations appear to have allowed firms to do about what they would have done in the absence of controls. From a strictly economic point of view, it is not clear that controls on this sector were worth the effort.

Service Sector

The services component of the consumer price index includes a highly heterogeneous group of industries that were subjected to several distinct types of controls. Medical care services are the most frequently cited example of a substantial impact of the price controls. During Phase II, a 2.5 percent cap on increases in physicians' and dentists' fees was applied. Price increases by medical care institutions had to be cost justified, and they could not be raised above 6 percent without special Price Commission approval.[23]

In the area of regulated utilities, the Price Commission delegated authority to the existing regulatory agencies but retained the right to review their decisions. Finally, a large number of small personal-service firms were exempt from the formal regulations.

As shown in Table 8, the category of services except rent is one that shows a substantial deceleration of inflation throughout the period of price controls. The underlying equation includes variables representing labor costs, mortgage interest rates, and cyclical output. Thus, the indicated slowdown of 0.7 percent is in addition to these cost factors. The residuals are consistently negative throughout the control period, although there is some evidence of a lessening of the restraint near the end of 1973. Among the major components (not shown), medical care and other services had substantial negative residuals. However, household services, which included most of the regulated industries, showed no apparent decline beyond that which could be anticipated from lower mortgage interest rates in 1972. Also, much of the slowdown in the category of transportation services resulted from the adoption of no-fault insurance in several large states rather than representing the effect of controls.

The controls on rent included a 2.5 percent cap on the pass-through of general costs, the full pass-through of taxes, and a recovery of the costs of capital improvements. About half the market was exempt—including all new construction—and the controls were terminated with the introduction of Phase III. The regulations appear to have resulted in a temporary slowing of about 0.5 percent in the rent index. There was an immediate drop in the rate of increase coincident with the introduction of controls and a return to former rates of increase when controls were removed in 1973.

Manufacturing Prices

Our measure of the influence of price controls on prices of manufactured goods is based on equations which are more aggregated than those of Popkin. Three categories of finished goods prices—nondurables except food and fuel, consumer durables, and producer durable equipment—are related to raw materials prices, labor costs, capacity utilization, and cyclical fluctuations in labor productivity. Thus, we have aggregated over the intermediate stages of production.

In all three cases, the residuals of Table 8 show an average negative effect during the period of controls. For both categories of durables, however, the residuals are very erratic, with several large positive residuals. These sharp fluctuations were caused by changes in the timing of automobile price increases. In both years, fall price increases were delayed by the Price Commission into the early part of the following year. Thus, the inclusion of the price increases of early 1974 would substantially reduce the estimated effect of controls. Alternatively, exclusion of the last half of 1973 results in average values of the residuals very close to zero. The pattern of residuals for nondurables except food and fuel is more consistent in indicating a restraining influence of the controls.

Food Prices

Food prices must play a key role in the success of any price-wage controls program. Food costs represent a major portion of consumer spending. But, more important, food prices are likely to become the standard by which the general public will judge the performance of any anti-inflation effort. Price changes for products purchased on a daily or weekly basis are far more visible than those for infrequent purchases, such as automobiles and household durables. Most economists, however, would support the view that food production is a highly competitive sector of the U.S. economy, where the effect of controls would most likely be to replace price increases with rationing. Given the difficulties of operating controls and the limited potential gains, the original decision to exempt raw agricultural products seemed reasonable.

The explosive rise of food prices, which began in late 1972, led to numerous demands that the controls be broadened to cover food products. On the other hand, opponents of price controls argued that the disruption of this market was itself caused by controls. Meanwhile, the Agriculture Department confused the issue further by alleging that the problem resulted from rising consumer demand for food. Claims that the farmer was not receiving the higher prices resulted in numerous investigations of profiteering by middlemen.

Today, it is clear that the rise in food prices had its primary origins in a huge expansion of U.S. agricultural exports. The magnitude of this export expansion and its impact on reserve stocks in the United States are shown in Table 9. World grain production fell sharply relative to expanding demand as adverse weather conditions were experienced in the USSR, South Asia, and Saharan Africa. Since the United States was a supplier of last resort in agricultural products, the dollar value of exports rose by 88 percent in 1973. In the 1972–1973 crop year the volume of feed grain exports rose 58 percent and wheat exports increased 87 percent. However, the United States had become increasingly ill-equipped to fulfill this stabilization function. Grain reserves had been sharply reduced as acreage set-aside programs with direct cash payments to farmers were substituted for the previous system of stockpiling large amounts of grain. This resulted in less flexibility to meet short-run increases in demand. In addition, the United States did not shift toward a policy of stimulating production until reserves had declined to extremely low levels. The grain situation was made worse by the termination of fish-meal exports from Peru, which led to a chaotic market for soybean products, a high-protein feed substitute.[24]

The initial rise of meat prices was related more to cyclical lows in cattle and hog marketings than to world market conditions. The production of meat actually declined in both 1972 and 1973. However, high feed costs did limit substitution of poultry for meat, and with the passage of time high feed costs became a more significant element of the meat supply situation. Price controls in the middle of 1973 made the short-term situation worse in meat because price ceilings were not raised as feed costs increased. Also, the prior announcement of a termination date for the price ceilings caused much of the problem.

Despite the publicized claims, there is little evidence that the rise of retail food prices represented anything more than a simple pass-through of higher farm prices. The recent revision of the na-

TABLE 9 Selected Statistics on Production of Meat and Poultry, Wheat, and Feed Grains, Various Periods, 1960–1973

Status of Product	1960–1970	1970–1971	1971–1972[a]	1972–1973[a]	1973–1974[b]
Meat and Poultry (inspected slaughterings; average annual percent rate of change)[c]					
Meats, total	3.4	4.7	−1.6	−5.9	
Poultry	5.2	1.1	6.2	−2.2	
Wheat (millions of bushels; marketing year[d])					
Beginning carry-over		885	731	863	439
Production		1,351	1,618	1,545	1,711
Total supply[e]		2,237	2,350	2,409	2,154
Domestic disappearance		768	855	786	757
Exports		738	632	1,185	1,148
Ending stocks		731	863	439	249
Feed grains[f] (millions of tons; marketing year[d])					
Beginning carry-over		48.6	33.2	48.4	32.4
Production		160.1	207.7	199.9	205.0
Total supply[e]		209.1	241.4	248.7	237.7
Domestic disappearance		155.2	165.7	173.2	173.4
Exports		20.7	27.3	43.1	43.7
Ending stocks		33.2	48.4	32.4	20.6

SOURCE: *Survey of Current Business*, July 1974, pp. S27–S29, and earlier issues; U.S. Department of Agriculture, *Demand and Price Situation*, August 1974, Table 2.

[a] Figures for wheat and feed grains are preliminary.
[b] Figures for wheat and feed grains are estimates.
[c] Calculated from calendar-year production data, by weight.
[d] Twelve-month marketing year, spanning the pairs of years indicated in the column headings.
[e] Includes imports.
[f] Includes corn, oats, barley, and grain sorghum.

tional income accounts makes clear the rise of farm income, which doubled between the fourth quarters of 1971 and 1973. The Department of Agriculture maintains a price index of farm values using weights identical to those of the CPI series for domestically produced farm products. A comparison of the two indexes indicates that the farm-retail spread rose by 2.0 percent in 1972 and 6.5 percent in 1973. Compared to an average increase of 5.1 percent in the previous two years, and from what can be inferred about increases in labor, transportation, rent, and packaging costs, these increases do not seem large.

We conclude that price controls did not significantly alter food costs. Because of the competitive structure of the industry, controls that allowed for cost pass-throughs were of minor importance. Price controls cannot deal effectively with supply shortages. In the short run, restrictions on grain exports would have been the only effective means of limiting domestic price increases. However, this decision would have involved serious problems for American foreign trade policy.

Summary

In general, the results of this section imply a smaller direct impact of controls on prices than would be inferred from a simple examination of the price indexes of Table 2. Factors other than controls were changing during much of the control period, and, on balance, causing a decline in the predicted price increases. In addition, the disaggregation indicated the importance of special factors such as removal of the automobile excise tax, the adoption of no-fault insurance, and the delay of automobile price increases.

The pass-through of the impact on wholesale prices into the consumer price index implies that the annual rate of price increase was reduced by approximately 0.5 percent during the control period. However, this does not represent the full impact of the controls, because we have used actual wage changes in the price equations. As discussed in the section on wage controls, we find evidence of additional restraint in this area. Finally, the lower rate of price increases would have some indirect feedback effect: slower price inflation resulting in some moderation of wage increases and, thus, of the cost increases to be passed forward in future periods.

The largest direct effect of controls seems to have been in the service sector, where the regulations were tailored to specific industry characteristics. As might be anticipated, controls had little impact on the trade sector, where competitive factors are believed to be quite strong. Within manufacturing, nondurables provided the most consistent evidence of restraining influences. The pattern of residuals for durable prices was more erratic, with some evidence that the greatest effect came from simple delays of automobile price increases.

One interesting result of these equation residuals is that they do not indicate any acceleration of inflation after the shift to Phase III. Although the actual rate of price increase does accelerate, this is more than accounted for by a sharp rise of raw materials costs, the impact on labor costs of the increase in social insurance taxes, and the delayed implementation of the automobile price increases.

On the other hand, this may be too simple a basis on which to conclude that the shift was not important. Certainly, the way in which Phase III was introduced did much to reduce public confidence in and support for the program. In addition, some more detailed components of the wholesale price index indicate a sharper rate of increase after January 1973. Most of these fall within the WPI category of intermediate goods except food, which rose at an annual rate of 16.1 percent between January and April 1973 compared to 3.4 percent in the previous three months. Finding a justification for an acceleration of this magnitude in the underlying cost data is difficult. However, given the size of later increases in food prices, raw materials shortages, and the second devaluation, the shift to Phase III was not a major factor in the 1973 price inflation.

The estimated direct impact of controls on prices is somewhat smaller than that implied by previous studies. A recent study by Robert Gordon provides the best example of the results obtained from an aggregate application of the econometric approach.[25] In addition to estimating the effect of controls on wages and simulating the feedback effect, Gordon obtains an average direct effect on prices of 1.1 percent. In part, the lower estimated impact relative to Gordon reflects differences in the underlying equations and, thus, in the estimates of what the path of the inflation would have been in the absence of controls. In the case of the Gordon study, however, there are significant differences in the data used. His analysis focuses on a fixed weight deflator for the nonfarm sector, taken from the national income accounts, and which is similar to the index presented at the bottom of Table 2. Both indexes show a larger deceleration of the inflation during 1972 than either the CPI or WPI. Some of this difference is attributable to the inclusion of construction prices in the nonfarm-sector index. Except for single-family residential construction, these measures are heavily based on wage rates; and, as shown in the section on wage controls, construction wages decelerated sharply after the introduction of controls. Second, these are value-added deflators, whereas the CPI and WPI measure prices of goods. The deflators include negative effects from import prices and farm products. Since both of these price indexes rose very sharply during the control period, they reduce the value-added deflators relative to finished goods prices.

The private nonfarm deflator is a broader measure of price change, and on a conceptual basis it is preferable to either the CPI or WPI. However, the quality of the price data is very low for both construction and imports. Gordon's index, also, indicates a slower rate of price increase over the controls period than the index of Table 2, which is derived from the Commerce Department fixed weight index for the private sector minus the impact of changes in the farm deflator. The Commerce index involves a more detailed set of weights than those available to Gordon. Some overstatement is also implied by his apparent inclusion of the automobile excise tax as part of the effect of controls.

Most studies do agree, however, that there was some suppression of prices beyond a simple pass-through of the wage restraint. We not only believe that this added price restraint was smaller than implied by other studies, but we are very doubtful that the results can be used to infer that a significant squeezing of profit margins occurred. Since most price equations are based on some measure of "normal" or trend productivity, knowledge of the path of the aggregate price-wage ratio does not provide information about the distribution of income between profits and wages until actual labor productivity has been specified. The extent to which cyclical fluctuations in productivity are incorporated into price changes is a matter of great uncertainty. William Nordhaus indicates that labor productivity change—and thus profits—is critically affected by the distribution of output among industries.[26] In addition, he attributes the decline of corporate profit margins to events that took place before the introduction of price controls. Finally, our own results indicate that much of the restraint on prices was in sectors such as medical care services, where restraint did not have direct implications for the return on capital.

We are reluctant to conclude that a profit squeeze was a major result of the controls. While the statistical results give some evidence for such a view, they are not unambiguous. In addition, the loose administration of the price controls makes it difficult for us to believe that they could have resulted in significant price restraint in the industrial sector.

SOME IMPLICATIONS AND CONCLUSIONS

In general, the interpretation of the control program presented in the previous sections is more favorable than that held by most economists or the general public. Much of the prevalent disillusionment is the result of the 1973 experience, when the rate of price increase exploded despite the existence of controls. However, we feel the events of 1973 illustrate the changing nature of the U.S. inflation problem and not the inevitable collapse of wage and price controls. Widespread crop failures led to a major world food shortage, and a coincident rapid economic expansion in the major industrial countries raised the demand for raw materials at a rate that suppliers could not satisfy in the short run. These two problems were made worse by a second U.S. devaluation and the conversion to flexible exchange rates—events that temporarily increased speculative pressures in the commodity markets. Finally, the oil embargo and the steep price increases that followed sharply intensified inflationary pressures. Not one of these developments was in any way caused by wage and price controls nor were they the types of inflation problems for which controls were a potential cure.[27] Thus, 1973 and 1974 would have been years of accelerating price inflation with or without controls. The rigid application of controls in these circumstances could only have resulted in rationing, black markets, and other distortions. American industrial workers lost substantial real income to farmers and the oil-producing countries, but controls could not be the means for restoring this loss.

The experience of recent years clearly indicates the need to distinguish different types of inflationary processes if we are to select appropriate anti-inflationary policy responses. The classical situation of excessive aggregate demand is but one type of inflation. The 1966–1969 period is one in which demand pressures seem to have been a primary cause of price and wage increases. In such situations, the traditional remedies of demand restraint may be appropriate.

However, the argument for demand restraint is more difficult to make in reference to the situation in 1970 and 1971. Even if this period reflects only a lagged response of prices and wages to prior episodes of excess demand, the long lags imply that restrictive stabilization policies can become very costly in terms of unemployment and lost output. Since most markets had substantial amounts of excess capacity, other factors must have played a role. In the labor market, the Phillips curve was too simple an explanation of wage behavior. In part, the continuation of high rates of wage increases seems to have been related to attempts to catch up for past changes in relative wages or to expectations of continued price inflation.[28] Such a situation may provide justification for controls if they are directed toward stabilizing the relative wage and price structure with less overall inflation. But it is still only a temporary need.

Finally, the situation of 1973 is characteristic of an inflation that is related to supply disruptions in a few basic industries—particularly in food and fuel. Controls cannot effectively deal with real supply shortages; moreover, the application of general restraint can be very expensive unless the demand for such commodities has a very high income elasticity. In the long run, the aggregate impact of these disruptions can be reduced by the holding of adequate reserve stocks. If these stocks do not exist the options for policy are severely limited.

Any conclusion regarding the impact of controls on wages is dependent upon one's interpretation of wage behavior prior to the imposition of controls. If the unexpectedly high level of wage settlements in 1970–1971 represented a permanent shift of behavior, the controls had a substantial restrictive effect. On the other hand, if that was only a temporary development, the controls were not very important.[29] In the case of contract construction, however, the size of the deceleration makes it difficult to disregard the role of the Construction Industry Stabilization Committee.

Second, the focus of the pay controls on new negotiated wage settlements is important in any attempt to measure their impact. The implications for actual wage payments were not immediate and extended beyond the period of controls. Deferred increases, which were a large part of actual wage changes in 1972, were allowed to go through with only minor modifications. Substantial emphasis was placed on eliminating distortions in the relative wage structure even if it meant that some settlements exceeded the general guideline.

The general pay standard was frequently criticized on the basis that it failed to reflect the complexities of relative wages and other factors that are involved in actual wage settlements. In addition, it was alleged that such a standard would serve as a floor rather than a ceiling for wage increases.

Such criticisms of a rigid adherence to a single number may be valid, but this was not the nature of the general standard applied during Phase II. There was recognition of other factors in several exceptions to the 5.5 percent guideline. Examples of this were the catch-up provisions, exemptions for productivity bargaining, and the exclusion of low-wage workers. Furthermore, there is little evidence in the data of the previous sections that the standard did become a floor for wage settlements. Since the United States does not have a labor market dominated by large national unions, some general guide to reasonable wage increases was useful for the smaller union settlements and those in the nonunion area. A pay board cannot be expected to play an active role in every wage negotiation.

On the price side there is some evidence that controls retarded increases by more than would have been expected from a simple pass-through of costs. The most significant slowdown of the inflation was in services—particularly medical care. In the food sector and in retail trade, the behavior of prices appears to have corresponded closely to what would have been anticipated in the absence of controls.

The experience with controls did make evident the major technical problems of administering price regulations. The allocation of resources is more sensitive to changes in relative prices than in relative wages, and problems of shortages can quickly develop. The total cost pass-through provisions were very difficult to enforce because their implementation involved the regulators in the internal cost accounting practices of individual firms. The regulations could also be criticized for using total costs instead of direct or marginal costs. The allocation of overhead costs among individual products involved the greatest technical problems, and fluctuations in sales volume had perverse effects on allowable price changes. It is of interest to note that the greatest impact of the controls appears to have been in the service sector, where direct limitations on market prices were used instead of allowable costs. In contrast, one study concluded that there was no correlation between industrial price increases as reported in the WPI during Phase II and approvals of the Price Commission.[30]

In conclusion, it should be kept in mind that the control program was not one of severe wage and price restraint intended to achieve an immediate end to the inflation. Instead, it was a modest effort with modest results. The focus was on a gradual reduction of the inflation rate. Some initial progress was made. In addition, a major benefit was the justification provided for the redirection of fiscal and monetary policy toward the goal of increasing the level of resource utilization. Subsequent developments—which, however, seem to have been largely independent of the existence of controls—eliminated most of the progress toward lower inflation and unemployment.

APPENDIX A. WAGE EQUATION VARIABLES

The econometric wage equations used four different dependent variables, each measured in quarterly percent changes. They were (a) a fixed weight index of straight-time hourly earnings for the private nonfarm economy; (b) a fixed weight index of straight-time hourly earnings in manufacturing; (c) median negotiated increases in manufacturing; and (d) median negotiated increases in nonmanufacturing exclusive of the construction industry. The two series on average hourly earnings are published by the Bureau of Labor Statistics and are adjusted for interindustry employment shifts and for overtime in manufacturing.

The two series on negotiated settlements are based on quarterly data published by the Bureau of National Affairs (BNA). Lester[31] has described these data in some detail. They are the only quarterly settlement data available for a reasonably long time period. Quarterly median increases, in cents per hour, go back to 1956I for manufacturing and to 1958I for nonmanufacturing exclusive of construction. For multiyear contracts BNA includes just the first-year increase in that quarter's median. These BNA series are closely akin to BLS data on "first-year changes in contracts negotiated during year," which appear in *Current Wage Developments*. BNA median increases were divided by average straight-time hourly earnings of the previous quarter to convert the former to percent changes. The average hourly earnings series for manufacturing is regularly published. An index for nonmanufacturing (1967 = 100) was derived by subtracting the manufacturing index times its weight (0.3384) in the overall index, from the overall private nonfarm index of straight-time earnings. The resulting series was divided by 0.6616 (to index it at 100 for 1967) and then multiplied by 0.0268 (average hourly earnings in the private nonfarm economy in 1967) to convert to a cents-per-hour basis. The median percent change in nonmanufacturing negotiated settlements was then estimated as the ratio of the median negotiated increase for nonmanufacturing to this average hourly earnings series lagged one quarter. Both series of negotiated wage increases are available upon request.

Except for the wage-price guidepost dummy (G), the independent variables used in the Table 4 regressions are based directly on data regularly published by BLS; the dummy equals 1 from 1962II to 1966II and zero in all other quarters. George Perry and Robert J. Gordon kindly supplied us with unemployment and tax-rate data, which were used in initial equation specifications.

APPENDIX B. PRICE EQUATIONS

The price equations used to investigate the impact of the controls are a modification of those published in Popkin, "Consumer and Wholesale Price Increases" (see note 22, below). All the data are seasonally adjusted quarterly percent changes for the period 1956–1970. All price indexes are from the Bureau of Labor Statistics, and all wage rates are fixed weight indexes adjusted to include fringe benefits. Several capacity utilization measures were tried, with the McGraw-Hill index showing the greatest significance. A time trend was used to approximate normal productivity growth, except where some cyclical correction was significant. Highly insignificant co-efficients were deleted from the regressions, and the lag structures are the result of experimentation. In contrast to other published equations in which the Almon polynomial lag estimation technique was used, longer lags were not found to be significant.

Retail Prices (Consumer Price Index)

Durables Excluding Used Cars and Home Purchase

$$DCPID = 0.59\,DWPICD + 0.16\,DWPICD_{-1} + 0.20\,DWRT_{-1}$$
$$\qquad\ (6.3) \qquad\qquad (1.5) \qquad\qquad (2.7)$$

$$+ 0.22\,DWRT_{-2} - 1.17\,DMY6503 - 0.43$$
$$(2.9) \qquad\qquad (4.6) \qquad\qquad (3.8)$$

$$R^2 = 0.78;\ SE = 0.25;\ DW = 1.9$$

The percent change in consumer durable goods prices ($DCPID$) is related to current and lagged changes in wholesale prices of consumer durables ($DWPICD$); wage-rate changes in wholesale and retail trade ($DWRT$), lagged one and two periods; and dummy variables for the 1965 excise-tax reduction ($DMY6503$).

Nondurables Excluding Food and Fuel

Food prices are treated separately elsewhere, and fuel prices are excluded because of the difficulty of getting accurate historical price quotations.

$$DCPINDEFF = 0.48\,DWPINDEFF + 0.22\,DWPINDEFF_{-1}$$
$$\qquad\qquad (4.6) \qquad\qquad\qquad (2.1)$$

$$+ 0.18\,DWRT_{-2} - 10.77\,RU_{-1} + 0.61$$
$$(2.7) \qquad\qquad (3.1) \qquad\qquad (2.6)$$

$$R^2 = 0.83;\ SE = 0.18;\ DW = 1.8$$

The percent change in consumer nondurable prices ($DCPINDEFF$) is related to current and lagged changes in wholesale prices of consumer nondurables ($DWPINDEFF$), wage rate changes in the trade sector ($DWRT$), and the lagged unemployment rate (RU).

Services Excluding Rent

$$DCPISER = 0.41\,DWRPNF + 0.33\,DWRPNF_{-1} + 0.11\,DCPIMIR$$
$$\quad\;\;(2.9) \qquad\qquad (2.3) \qquad\qquad\;\; (4.5)$$

$$-\,9.18\,RU_{-1} - 0.34\,DCS58 - 0.23\,DCS58_{-1} + 1.20$$
$$(2.1) \qquad\quad (4.2) \qquad\qquad (2.7) \qquad\qquad (3.1)$$

$$R^2 = 0.85;\; SE = 0.23;\; DW = 1.6$$

Changes in prices of consumer services ($DCPISER$) are related to current and lagged wage changes in the private sector wage index ($DWRPNF$), changes in mortgage interest rates ($DCPIMIR$), the lagged unemployment rate (RU), and current and lagged changes in the real output of the services sector ($DCS58$).

Wholesale Prices

Consumer Nondurables Excluding Food and Fuel

$$DWPINDEFF = 0.05\,DWPICMEFF + 0.05\,DWPICMEFF_{-1}$$
$$\qquad\qquad\;\;\; (2.0) \qquad\qquad\qquad (2.0)$$

$$+\,0.16\,DWRM + 0.19\,DWRM_{-1} + 0.12\,DWRM_{-2} + 0.03\,KUM_{-2} - 2.41$$
$$(3.5) \qquad\quad (4.3) \qquad\qquad (2.5) \qquad\qquad (3.2) \qquad\qquad (3.5)$$

$$R^2 = 0.53;\; SE = 0.25;\; DW = 1.3$$

Changes in finished goods prices ($DWPINDEFF$) are related to current and lagged changes in prices of raw materials ($DWPICMEFF$), changes in wage rates ($DWRM$) over three quarters, and capacity utilization (KUM).

Consumer Durable Goods

$$DWPICD = 0.04\,DWPICMEFF + 0.10\,DWRM + 0.27\,DWRM_{-1}$$
$$\qquad\quad\; (1.8) \qquad\qquad\quad (1.8) \qquad\;\; (4.9)$$

$$+\,0.25\,DWRM_{-2} - 0.17\,D4PROD_{-2} - 0.38$$
$$(4.2) \qquad\qquad (2.5) \qquad\qquad\;\; (2.5)$$

$$R^2 = 0.53;\; SE = 0.31;\; DW = 1.6$$

Changes in prices of consumer finished goods ($DWPICD$) are related to changes in prices of raw materials, changes in wages rates over three quarters, and a four-quarter change in labor productivity ($D4PROD$).

Producer Finished Goods

$$DWPIPFG = 0.05\,DWPICMEFF + 0.14\,DWRM + 0.29\,DWRM_{-1}$$
$$\ (2.0)\ (2.7)\ (5.7)$$

$$+\ 0.20\,DWRM_{-2} + 0.04\,KUM - 0.18\,D4PROD_{-2} - 3.67$$
$$(4.0)\phantom{DWRM_{-2}}\ (4.6)\ (2.9)\phantom{D4PROD_{-2}}\ (4.8)$$

$$R^2 = 0.66;\ SE = 0.29;\ DW = 1.4$$

Changes in prices of capital goods ($DWPIPFG$) are related to changes in costs of raw materials, changes in wage rates over three quarters, capacity utilization, and a four-quarter percent change in labor productivity.

NOTES

1. See Barry Bosworth, "Phase II: The U.S. Experiment with an Incomes Policy," *Brookings Papers on Economic Activity* 2(1972): 343–383.
2. The observation for 1970IV was replaced by the simple average of 1970III and 1971I, all seasonally adjusted.
3. Four of the major articles are Milton Friedman, "The Role of Monetary Policy," *American Economic Review*, March 1968, pp. 1–17; Robert J. Gordon, "Wage-Price Controls and the Shifting Phillips Curve," *Brookings Papers on Economic Activity* 2(1972): 385–430; George L. Perry, "Changing Labor Markets and Inflation," *Brookings Papers on Economic Activity* 3(1970): 411–441; Edmond Phelps et al., *The Microeconomic Foundations of Employment and Inflation Theory* (New York: Norton, 1970).
4. During 1968–1970, first-year negotiated changes were consistently higher than either life-of-contract changes or effective wage adjustments.
5. A part of the explanation for the rapid compensation and productivity increases of this period is the auto strike of 1970IV. Using the averaging procedure described earlier, the compensation gain was reduced to 7.4 percent and the productivity gain to 4.6 percent. With these alternative measurements, unit labor costs increased by 2.7 percent in the first half of 1971. This rate of increase is still less than half the rate for 1969 and 1970.
6. A detailed review of the freeze period and the problems that were encountered is presented in Arnold Weber, *In Pursuit of Price Stability, Wage-Price Freeze of 1971* (Washington, D.C.: Brookings, 1973).
7. See, for example, the Quarterly Reports of the Economic Stabilization Program, published by the Cost of Living Council.

8. *Survey of Current Business,* July 1974, p. 6.
9. Robert J. Gordon summarized much of this literature in a series of recent papers. He has also made a detailed comparison of his specification with those of others: Robert J. Gordon, "Inflation in Recession and Recovery," *Brookings Papers on Economic Activity* 1(1971): 105–158; and "Wage-Price Controls," cited earlier.
10. Among the set of independent variables tested and rejected for making too marginal a contribution to explained variance were Perry's weighted unemployment rate, his measure of unemployment dispersion, the federal personal income tax rate as used by Gordon, and the tax rate for employer contributions for social insurance.
11. For example, three data periods examined were 1956I–1969IV, 1956I–1971II, and 1958I–1971II. The three pairs of unemployment and price coefficients in the nonfarm hourly earnings equation for these time periods were, respectively, −0.14 and 0.33, −0.11 and 0.48, and −0.08 and 0.64. Thus, an alteration of fourteen quarters from the original data period causes the unemployment coefficient to decline by about half, while the price coefficient roughly doubles.
12. Dan Mitchell, "Phase II Wage Controls," *Industrial and Labor Relations Review,* April 1974, pp. 351–375.
13. See George Perry, "The Success of Anti-Inflation Policies in the United States," in *Conference on Secular Inflation,* Universities–National Bureau Conference 25 (*Journal of Money, Banking, and Credit,* Supplement, February 1973), Table 5. Mitchell's residuals are in his "Phase II Wage Controls," Table 9.
4. These estimates are based on averages of the residuals for the second half of 1970 and first half of 1971 compared to 1972–1973 in Table 5. They are not sensitive to the inclusion of the guidepost dummy and would be increased by eliminating the postfreeze bulge of early 1972.
5. The timing of major reductions with the second quarter is consistent with the industry pattern of initiating annual contract discussions in the spring months.
6. Data from 1973, for example, are published in the June 1974 issue of *Current Wage Developments.*
7. A similar result is obtained if changes in total compensation are examined, rather than just wages, as in Table 7. For first-year settlements of firms employing 5,000 or more workers, the proportions of workers whose total compensation increased by less than 5 percent in the first year were 2 percent in 1970, zero in 1971, 7 percent in 1972, and 6 percent in 1973. These levels are all lower than those shown in Table 7, but the trends are the same, i.e., there were more settlements in this range in 1972 and 1973 than in 1970 and 1971.
8. Because comparatively little bargaining took place in 1972, some reduction in the overall mean between 1971 and 1972 was to be expected. In 1972, the mean of the first-year adjustments was 7.3 percent (panel A). If the mean had remained at its 1971 level of 11.6 percent, the 1972 first-year adjustment in panel D would have contributed 2.7 percent rather than 1.7 percent, and the 1972 mean adjustment would have been 7.6 percent rather than 6.6 percent.
9. Dan Mitchell and Arnold Weber, "Wages and the Pay Board," *American Economic Review,* May 1974, p. 89.
10. *Current Wage Developments,* June 1974, p. 43. Mitchell cites evidence of shorter contracts in his recent paper ("Phase II Wage Controls," p. 373). Dramatic increases in one-year contracts as a percent of all new contracts were

observed in construction in 1971. Outside of construction, however, the increased incidence of one-year contracts was much less pronounced, rising from 6 percent to 15 percent of all new contracts between 1971 and 1972.

21. *Current Wage Developments*, August 1974, p. 35.

22. Joel Popkin, "Consumer and Wholesale Prices in a Model of Price Behavior by Stage of Processing," Research Discussion Paper 13, mimeographed (Bureau of Labor Statistics, 1973).

23. These regulations were altered with the introduction of Phase IV to allow a higher ceiling on price increases, to distinguish inpatient from outpatient services, and to shift the emphasis toward cost per hospital stay rather than individual-service prices.

24. A detailed examination of the 1973 developments in world grain prices can be found in Dale Hathaway, "Food Prices and Inflation," *Brookings Papers on Economic Activity* 1(1974): 63–116.

25. Robert J. Gordon, "The Response of Wages and Prices to the First Two Years of Controls," *Brookings Papers on Economic Activity* 3(1973): 765–781.

26. William Nordhaus, "The Falling Share of Profits," *Brookings Papers on Economic Activity* 1(1974): 169–218.

27. The events of 1973 as they relate to an acceleration of inflation have been previously discussed by one of the authors and will not be extensively reviewed here. See B. Bosworth, "The Inflation Problem During Phase III," *American Economic Review*, May 1973, pp. 93–99. In addition, see William Nordhaus and John Shoven, "Inflation 1973: The Year of Infamy," *Challenge*, May-June 1974, pp. 14–22.

28. An attempt to relate inflation to distortions in the wage structure is illustrated in Arnold Parker and Seong Park, "Distortions in Relative Wages and Shifts in the Phillips Curve," *Review of Economics and Statistics*, February 1973, pp. 16–22.

29. These alternative interpretations are evident in Table 5. During controls the residuals are not generally negative. Instead, they decline toward zero from the large positive residual of the period prior to the controls.

30. H. Boissenian et al., "The Effectiveness of Phase II Price Controls," mimeographed (Santa Monica: Rand Corporation, 1973).

31. Richard Lester, "Negotiated Wage Increases, 1951–1967," *Review of Economics and Statistics*, May 1968, pp. 173–181.

COMMENTS

Edgar L. Feige
University of Wisconsin

The Bosworth-Vroman appraisal of the wage-price control program is disturbingly reminiscent of the play *Six Characters in Search of an Author*. The authors present a myriad of scintillating facts, figures, and questions, all in search of a coherent intellectual framework. As the curtain falls on Pirandello's play, the audience is left struggling to distinguish illusion from reality. Similarly, at the conclusion of the Bosworth-Vroman paper, the issues addressed remain as provocative and essentially unresolved as they were at the beginning. After reading the paper, I was left with a sense of frustration and uncertainty, reflecting not simply the complexity of the issues involved but also the flabbiness of the state of the art and the particular weaknesses inherent in the approach followed by the authors.

The paper begins with a factual description of wage and price behavior from 1960 through the middle of 1971. In the section entitled "Prelude to Controls," the authors raise the question of whether the precontrol inflation was coming to an end as a result of the restrictive stabilization policies embodied in the original "game plan." This issue is seen as "crucial to any judgment about the effect of the controls." The authors conclude that "the inflation rate . . . did not decelerate, and most economic forecasts made during the 1969–1971 period consistently underpredicted the magnitude of actual wage and price increases."

What evidence is brought to bear to sustain the claim that inflation was not decelerating during this period? The gross evidence is as follows:

The rate of increase in the CPI during the first eight months of 1971 fell to 3.8 percent, compared to an average of 5.9 percent in 1970.

The private nonfarm deflator showed a decline from 5 percent to 3.9 percent.

The WPI showed an increase from 3.7 percent to 4.6 percent.

Aggregate wage indexes showed a continuation of wage increases at approximately 1970 rates, while negotiated settlements exhibited modest deceleration.

The authors discount the deceleration in the CPI by claiming that half of the decline is accounted for by the reversal in mortgage interest rates; they minimize the decline in the private nonfarm deflator by citing the smaller decline registered by the fixed weight deflator; and they place an unwholesome weight on the problematic WPI by concluding that "evidence of a quick end to inflation is limited to consumer finished good prices, with some indication from intermediate materials prices that even this slowdown was transitory." Unfortunately, we are not told what specific type of evidence would have persuaded them that inflation was indeed decelerating during this period. This section would have been considerably stronger had it included an analysis of the peculiarities of the construction and weighting patterns of the different inflation indexes along with some conceptual guidance for selecting an "appropriate" measure of inflation. The conceptual issue is particularly acute given the vexing divergences among various measures of inflation.

The next section contains a cursory overview of the controls program, outlining its organization and administration and ending with a recounting of actual price and wage changes during the period of controls. The authors describe the observed dampening in inflation rates during phases I and II and the abrupt acceleration in inflation during 1973 when the CPI rose at a rate of 8.8 percent and the WPI at 15.5 percent.

The main section of the paper, "Econometric Results," is begun with the observation that "a simple comparison of prices and wage increases before and during the period of controls does not provide a very satisfactory basis for evaluating the effects of controls." Nevertheless, in the very next sentence the authors assert that "only in a few situations is the magnitude of change in the pattern of inflation sufficient for us to conclude that the change was a result of controls." Nowhere do we find the basis for such an inference. How large would the observed deceleration in a price index have to be in order to warrant the inference that the controls caused the deceleration?

As an alternative to simply looking at the behavior of observed prices, the authors consider the use of econometric models to generate counterfactual forecasts of the predicted behavior of prices and wages in the absence of controls. This approach, too, is viewed as unsatisfactory because "the precontrol period is not well explained by existing statistical equations." Moreover, "some of the disturbances during the period of controls, such as devaluation and changes in international commodity markets, are difficult to incorporate into existing price equations, which emphasize domestic factors."

Despite their own realistic reservations, Bosworth and Vroman go on boldly to elect a very simple specification of a wage equation to use for generating counterfactual forecasts. They specifically reject a number of the refinements in the wage equation introduced by R. J. Gordon and assert that alternative specifications would not have affected their analysis of the controls. They do not detail the nature of any of the tests performed on alternative specifications and thus the paper offers no real insight into the sensitivity of wage predictions from alternatively specified equations.

The authors depict the percent change in money wages as depending on the unemployment rate, an arbitrarily weighted average of past-quarter changes in the CPI and a wage-price guidepost dummy to give uniform weighting to the 1962–1966 guidepost period. These regressions are estimated by ordinary least squares, and the results are highly suspect. Several of the equations indicate very substantial problems of serial correlation, thus calling into question the adequacy of the specification and the usefulness of conventional tests of significance. The authors mention this problem, but I suspect that they underestimate its importance. Recent simulation results by Granger and Newbold suggest that standard errors might be underestimated by a factor of five, thus raising considerable doubts about the adequacy of the equations presented. The authors also note that their estimated parameters are highly sensitive to the time period selected for fitting the model. The deletion of two earlier years of observations from the data set and the addition of one and a half later years causes a 50 percent reduction in the unemployment coefficient and a doubling of the price coefficient. On the basis of this evidence, I would strongly suspect that if the data set had been more appropriately divided into two subperiods reflecting the years before and after the more rapid inflation of the sixties, the equations would exhibit even greater instability. Furthermore, the confidence ellipsoids on the parameters would be so large that acceptability of the model would be doubtful as a useful counterfactual generator for an assessment of the control period.

The observed parametric instability indicates that the coefficient on past prices seems to rise as actual inflationary experience increases. This finding is probably an echo of the observation made by R. J. Gordon which prompted him to experiment with a variable response coefficient that itself depended upon the severity of the expected rate of inflation. Oi's Tests of the stability of the Gordon wage equation also indicated radical changes in the coefficients between the subperiods 1954–1961 and 1962–1970. It is certainly likely that as expected inflation accelerates, more and more wage contracts will include escalator clauses. Bosworth and Vroman do not, however, pursue this line of inquiry and retain, instead, a simple fixed coefficient model.

The model specifications presented are disconcerting in other regards as well. Nowhere in their paper can I find even a passing suggestion that monetary and fiscal policies might also have some effects on the course of the inflationary process. Neither monetary nor fiscal variables appear in any of the econometric specifications. Given these various problems, it is perhaps not so surprising that the equations grossly underpredict the actual rates of wage inflation in the period immediately preceding the controls.

The authors seem to take some comfort in the finding of a similar pattern of underestimation in models estimated by Perry and Mitchell. Such underestimation raises the question of whether these large residuals reflect a fundamental change in an otherwise stable structure of wage formation or simply an inadequate representation of the historical process generating wages. Since the reported wage equations show little stability over time, I am hard pressed to accept an ad hoc rationalization of this apparent empirical anomaly. While it is true that underprediction of this kind has been reported for the same period in several studies, the latter should not be regarded as each contributing independent evidence of the phenomenon, since they are all based on models that are essentially similar and are estimated from essentially the same body of data.

The predictions used to assess the impact of controls are based on simulations of the simple wage equations, using actual values of the right-hand-side variables, which include lagged prices. To the extent that controls had any effect on holding down prices—for example, during the Phase I freeze—such an effect will be included erroneously in the predicted rate of change in wages for subsequent periods and thereby contaminate the counterfactual forecast with the effects of controls. In general, Bosworth and Vroman find that actual wage increases are substantially above predicted wage increases both before and after the control period. To illustrate, the equations for union-negotiated increases in manufacturing underpredict the actual increase by 3 percent for the second half of 1971 (annual rate) and underpredict the nonmanufacturing increase by a whopping 5.9 percent. The manufacturing equation cited has a reported Durbin–Watson statistic of 0.60 and should probably have been discarded on that basis alone. The large positive residuals only turn negative and greater than 1 percent in the second half of 1973, and this reversal appears due to the burst in prices in the first part of 1973.

Bosworth and Vroman note that the control program focused on settlements and thus "equations based on hourly earnings data may understate the long-run impact of the [control] program." This effect suggests to them that "the full impact of controls on hourly earnings would extend beyond the initial periods with a cumulative effect." This suggestion provides an interesting justification for using data including the 1973 price explosions for assessing the control program. However, upon examining the settlement data, the authors find that the deceleration there is not reflected in average hourly earnings, which in fact rise sharply during the third and fourth quarters of 1973.

In examining the construction industry, the authors simply focus on a tabular presentation of the wage data because "regression analysis of construction industry wages changes has not been very successful." However, if an equation capable of forecasting the behavior of construction wages in the absence of controls cannot be found, it is hard to see what basis of inference can be used to assess the control period.

The next section, "Controls and Negotiated Wage Settlements," again stresses the greater impact of wage controls on negotiated settlements rather than hourly earnings and relies on tabular rather than econometric evidence. Data are presented on the average size of contract settlements and their relative dispersion with the conclusion that "both . . . were sharply reduced during the period of wage controls." The authors assert that "the abruptness of this change creates a strong presumption that the controls were a significant causal factor."

The section dealing with the "Impact of Prices" is motivated by a fascinating issue. The authors note that since control regulations varied among major sectors of the economy, it is possible to evaluate the impacts of different types of control by a study of the separate sectors.

In order to estimate the effects of controls in the separate sectors, the authors utilize a variant of Popkin's stage-of-process framework. Prices in particular sectors are specified to depend upon current and lagged values of wholesale prices, current and lagged wages, an assortment of dummy variables, capacity utilization rates, unemployment rates, and labor productivity measures. No attempt is made to give a theoretical justification for any of the specific equations estimated, and we are simply informed that "highly insignificant coefficients were deleted from the regressions, and the lag structures are the result of experimentation." While such candor about empirical experimentation is refreshing and commendable, the experimentation itself does not inspire much confidence in the inferences derived from equations so selected. The equations are estimated from data covering the period 1956–1970, yet no attempt is made to test the structural stability assumption in spite of the aforementioned instability reported for the aggregate price equations. Once again, counterfactual predictions are generated by using actual values of variables the authorities were trying to regulate, leading to a potential underestimation of the control effect. The authors acknowledge this problem of understatement, but make no attempt to use predicted rather than actual values of those variables, nor do they make any effort to assess the magnitude of the effect.

A recurring feature of these sections is the resort to ad hoc interpretation. While one cannot help but admire the wealth of institutional materials which the authors interweave with their econometric residuals, the collage of assorted findings is unnervingly capricious. A −2.5 percent residual for durables is dismissed as being "almost wholly due to the automobile excise tax cut." Erratic residuals in the manufacturing price series, ranging from −2.1 percent to +3.6 percent, are explained as being "caused by changes in the timing of automobile price increases. . . . Thus, the inclusion of the price increases of early 1974 would substantially reduce the estimated effect of controls. Alternatively, exclusion of the last half of 1973 results in average values of the residuals very close to zero." On the other hand, residuals of −1.9 percent and −2.8 percent for nondurables are regarded as "more consistent in indicating a restraining influence of the controls."

This type of "now you see it, now you don't" empiricism ultimately leads the authors to conclude that "in general, the results . . . imply a smaller direct impact of controls on prices than would be inferred from a simple examination of the price indexes," and that "disaggregation indicated the importance of special factors such as removal of the automobile excise tax, the adoption of no-fault insurance, and the delay of automobile price increases." I find little basis for such inferences in the detailed empirical work presented in the paper. Too many of the authors' rich institutional insights are squandered in attempting to explain residuals from econometric equations in which the authors justifiably have little confidence. Moreover, it is disappointing to discover how little can be inferred about the efficacy of different types of control regulations from their analysis.

On the question of whether the shift to Phase III was responsible for an acceleration of inflation, the authors first argue that the acceleration was "more than accounted for by a sharp rise of raw materials costs, the impact on labor costs of the increase in social insurance taxes, and the delayed implementation of the automobile price increases." We then learn that "this may be too simple a basis on which to conclude that the shift was not important." Finally, we are assured that "given the size of later increases in food prices, raw materials shortages, and the second devaluation, the shift to Phase III was not a major factor in the 1973 price inflation."

In summarizing their findings, the authors claim that their estimated impact of controls on prices is "somewhat smaller than that implied by previous studies." These differences are attributed to differences in both the underlying equations and the data base. A careful study by Kraft and Roberts makes possible an examination of the consequences of different model specifications on the estimates of the effect of controls for a given body of data. However, to date, no one has carefully examined the implications of using different definitions of inflation.

Bosworth and Vroman conclude that their estimate of price restraint "was smaller than implied by other studies," and they are doubtful that a "significant squeezing of profit margins occurred." Given their broad results indicating that controls had virtually no effect, it seems odd that they should begin their final section with the summary statement, "the interpretation of the control program presented in the previous sections is more favorable than that held by most economists or the general public." They then proceed to enumerate the various "causes" of the 1973 inflation including, of course, the oil embargo, devaluation, food shortages, expansion in the industrialized countries, and speculative pressures in the commodity markets. Their favorable impression of the control program is apparently justified by the remark that "not one of these developments was in any way caused by wage and price controls nor were they the types of inflation problems for which controls were a potential cure." If the most favorable observations that can be made about controls are that (a) they did not work to reduce inflation and (b) that they did not cause the oil embargo, the devaluation, the food shortages, etc., then perhaps the time has come to bury controls once and for all. Instead, Bosworth and Vroman gently conclude that the control program was "a modest effort with modest results" and that "a major benefit was the justification provided for the redirection of fiscal and monetary policy toward the goal of increasing the level of resource utilization." Is it not at least conceivable that some of that redirected monetary and fiscal policy has contributed to the exacerbation of our inflationary problems?

4

MARVIN H.
KOSTERS

American Enterprise Institute
in association with
J. DAWSON AHALT
U.S. Department of Agriculture

Controls and Inflation: An Overview

INTRODUCTION

From August 15, 1971, to April 30, 1974, mandatory controls on wages and prices were a component of the economic stabilization policy of the U.S. government. This experiment with "incomes policy" was the first peacetime wage and price control program in the United States. During the period, marked changes occurred in the economic and political environment, in the structure of the program, in the rigor with which controls were administered or were perceived to be administered, and in the rates of price change that emerged. The pace of economic activity ranged from the early stages of a slow cyclical recovery to an extraordinarily vigorous boom in demand, followed by a period of short supply of basic materials, particularly petroleum products, and sharply curtailed production growth. Consumer price inflation initially declined from an

NOTE: The research for this paper was supported by the National Science Foundation (grant GS-43757), the Ford Foundation (grant 740-0510), and the American Enterprise Institute. The full version of the study was presented at the Conference on Price Behavior and was published as *Controls and Inflation: The Economic Stabilization Program in Retrospect* (Washington, D.C.: American Enterprise Institute for Public Policy Research, 1975). The version published here was shortened at the suggestion of the discussant, R. A. Gordon. In particular, a section containing an extensive discussion of the microeconomic effects of controls in specific markets was deleted, but it may be found in the American Enterprise version.

annual rate of slightly below 4 percent in the eight months preceding controls to approximately 3 percent during the first year of controls. But it rose to "double digit" rates of 11.5 percent in the eight months before controls were ended and to 12.2 percent in the eight months after controls were removed.

To assess the influence of controls as an economic policy tool only in terms of what happened to the inflation rate while they were in force would obviously be much too superficial. Price and wage trends occurring under controls are conditioned by the need to allow flexibility for adjustments in response to changes in the market environment, or to adapt the controls so as to contain pressures for significant departures from equilibrium and to keep resources in the channels from which price suppression threatens to divert them. During the period of controls, changes in overall demand levels were of central importance in the market environment, but changes in supply conditions for particular sectors originating from both domestic and foreign sources were also important.

The extent to which controls were intended to affect economic goals other than prices—goals such as output, employment, investment, and efficiency—is relevant in an evaluation of the effects of the controls. Other factors that form part of the context in which controls were administered, and that should be taken into account in evaluating them, are such broader goals as limited bureaucratic intervention in price decisions and collective bargaining, balance-of-payment goals, international trade and foreign policy interests, maintenance of a competitive industrial structure, and preservation of private incentives to promote innovation and efficiency. Finally, a comprehensive assessment of controls should also include a look at economic conditions and prospects prior to the imposition of controls and developments after controls were terminated.

The analysis and discussion in this paper are oriented toward an assessment of controls as a temporary and supplementary "incomes policy" tool. The analysis will look at their possible marginal influence on inflation when they are administered with an emphasis on avoiding serious short-term market disruption and minimizing adverse long-term effects on the economy. Section II is a review of the economic and political developments that preceded the imposition of controls. In section III we look at the design of the control system and changes in the structure of the program. In section IV, the consistency of wage and price behavior with the stabilization regulations is examined by analyzing aggregate data on wage, price, and profit developments. In the fifth section we explore the question of inefficiency and distortions attributable to controls, and in section VI we address some broad issues concerning the role and limitations of direct controls as a stabilization tool.

BACKGROUND

Initially, a policy of gradualism that became known as the "game plan" was put into effect to reverse the rise in the rate of inflation that occurred in the last half of the 1960s.[1] Rapid expansion of aggregate demand from 1964 through 1966, after a period of relatively stable prices, had brought the unemployment rate down to well below 4 percent, a lower rate than had been experienced in the preceding decade. After a pause in 1967, aggregate demand surged again in 1968. By 1969 the unemployment rate was 3.5 percent, with real output growth tapering off and prices rising more rapidly than before.

A gradual slowdown in aggregate demand growth began during 1969. Adjustments in the economy in response to stringent fiscal policy and slower monetary expansion were expected to run in the following sequence:[2] slower growth in total spending in the economy, slower production growth, pressure on profit margins and slower employment growth, smaller wage increases, and finally lower price inflation. The calibration of federal policy instruments necessary to introduce an appropriate degree of disequilibrium and the lags in the process were interrelated and uncertain. It was essential to restrain total spending growth enough to set in motion an adjustment process that would lead to deceleration in price increases, but a longer-than-anticipated lag before prices began to decelerate would result in lower real output levels and higher unemployment than were intended.

By the end of 1970 inflation had proved to be more persistent than had been expected. As a result real output was lower and prices and unemployment were higher than the earlier official projections.[3] These conditions persisted during the first half of 1971. During the first half of 1971 both wholesale prices and the private GNP deflator increased at rates roughly similar to those at which they increased in the previous two years, although consumer prices were increasing less rapidly. The unemployment rate hovered at 6 percent, up from 3.5 percent in 1969. There were no clear indications that unemployment would be reduced appreciably in the ensuing months through more rapid demand growth, and the evidence that inflation was subsiding was tenuous. Furthermore, the rate of price increase, particularly for wholesale prices of industrial commodities, remained high by the standards suggested by the experience of the early 1960s, and the worsening balance of payments was an ominous cloud on the horizon.

The Political Context

There were several indications that the game plan was being played in economic overtime by the beginning of 1971. Unemployment had reached a level that threatened to be politically damaging to the Nixon administration in the absence of firm prospects that it would recede. Public and congressional sentiment became increasingly unfavorable toward the explicitly noninterventionist policies of the administration and shifted toward a preference for direct action to restrain "excessive" wage and price increases.

These conditions provided a climate in which the Democratic Congress enacted legislation in August 1970 authorizing mandatory controls. Whether or not such authority was used, the legislation could be used to embarrass the President and his party.[4] Business attitudes were conditioned by two years in which profits were ground between the millstones of rapidly increasing labor costs and markets in which these costs could not readily be passed through by increasing prices. In October 1970 the Business Council criticized the lack of direct action on wages and prices, a criticism that was reaffirmed in the spring.[5] The Committee for Economic Development, another business group, issued a policy statement in November 1970 recommending establishment of a stabilization body to establish "broad norms" for wage and price behavior.[6] On the labor side, the AFL-CIO had taken a position in support of "equitable" controls if the President determined they were necessary, and George Meany had stated his view that they were.[7] Also, several high officials within the federal government had proposed some form of incomes policy, the most prominent being Arthur Burns, who had become chairman of the Federal Reserve Board in 1970.[8]

Faced with these developments, the administration was increasingly on the defensive in maintaining its noninterventionist stance. In June 1970, the President established the National Commission on Productivity and the Regulations and Purchasing Review Board, and announced that periodic "inflation alerts" would be prepared by the Council of Economic Advisers. In January 1971, the President directed the Cabinet Committee on Economic Policy to analyze conditions in the steel industry in the wake of announced price increases for some steel products. The Council of Economic Advisers was to report immediately to the committee any "exceptionally inflationary wage or price developments"[9] so that appropriate federal action could be considered. The Construction Industry Collective Bargaining Commission had been established in September 1969, and federal action had been taken to reduce construction spending and encourage training of more skilled construction labor, but there had been no relief during 1970 from increasingly large construction wage increases and the pressures they created for similar wage increases in other sectors. On March 29, 1971, the Construction Industry Stabilization Committee was established to place mandatory controls on construction wages. After a review of the economy by the administration in June, decisions were announced not to apply additional stimulus to demand and not to establish an incomes policy. These statements proved to be the last strong official reaffirmation of the game plan.[10] Larger trade deficits and the increased vulnerability of the dollar to massive conversion into other forms of reserves were added to continuing disappointing news on prices and production, triggering the President's dramatic announcement of the New Economic Policy on August 15, 1971.

conomic Conditions in Mid-1971

By mid-1971 the game plan had been successful in bringing about some elements in the sequence of adjustments envisioned for the process of reducing inflation.[11] Slower monetary expansion combined with fiscal policy restraint had reduced the growth of total spending, slowed production and employment growth, squeezed profits, and stabilized or reduced the rate of price inflation. The game plan had succeeded in achieving the early stages of the disinflation process, but further reduction in inflation depended on a trend toward smaller labor cost increases that had not yet emerged. While wages in some sectors were increasing less rapidly than before, very large increases in other sectors kept average hourly labor costs increasing at a roughly stable rate.

These developments raise two issues concerning stabilization policy performance before and after controls were imposed. One is the extent to which the buildup of significant distortions in the wage structure contributed to a slower unfolding of the disinflation process than had been projected. The other is the extent to which improved balance in the wage structure and prospects for more rapid productivity growth pointed to the possibility of improved economic performance after 1971 with or without wage and price controls.

Wages and Collective Bargaining[12]

The unemployment rate rose from 3.5 percent in 1969 to about 6.0 percent in late 1970. However, reduced growth of demand in labor and product markets was not accompanied by smaller wage increases. Adjusted average hourly earnings for the private nonfarm sector rose by 6.7 percent in 1970 and 7.0 percent in 1971, indicating that wage rates were increasing more rapidly than they had when unemployment rates were lower. New first-year wage increases under collective bargaining agreements in manufacturing rose from an average of about 8.0 percent in 1969 to nearly 11.0 percent in 1971 even though the unemployment rate in manufacturing increased from 3.3 percent in 1969 to 6.8 percent in 1971.

Continuing large wage increases under new collective bargaining agreements negotiated in 1970 and 1971 had their roots in earlier trends in prices and other wages. Wages for workers covered by long-term wage contracts negotiated in the late 1960s were depressed relative to those of other workers who received wage increases that more quickly reflected the strong labor market demand and accelerating inflation that prevailed in the later period. When long-term contracts expired, there were strong pressures to restore the relative wage positions of the workers they covered through heavily front-loaded new contracts because the deterioration of their position in the wage structure had resulted primarily from an unanticipated increase in inflation.

The influence of long-term contracts on the wage structure during the period of rising inflation is evident in average hourly earnings changes for industry sectors in which most workers were covered by long-term wage contracts. Data on average wage increases in six major industry sectors in which most workers were covered by long-term collective bargaining agreements with common expiration dates show deterioration in the relative wage position of these workers during the term of their contracts (Table 1). These workers received smaller wage increases than were received by the average private nonfarm worker in the two contract periods shown for each industry between 1966 and 1971. When new agreements were negotiated, average wages in the sectors covered increased by more than average wage increases for private nonfarm workers. In other words, there was a tendency to compensate at the time of negotiation for smaller wage increases during the term of the previous contract.

The data in Table 1 suggest that inflation-induced distortion in the wage structure created conditions leading to unusually large first-year wage increases in major union settlements, particularly in 1970 and 1971.[13] These large negotiated wage increases contributed directly to rapid increases in hourly labor costs and influenced wage changes for related workers, impeding any significant reduction in inflation in spite of considerable slack in labor and product markets.

A major share of the unexpectedly slow decline in wage and price increases in 1970 and early 1971 could have resulted from this

TABLE 1   Increases in Average Hourly Earnings in Selected Industries Mainly Covered by Long-Term Collective Bargaining Agreements and Wage Increases under Collective Bargaining Agreements in Manufacturing, 1966–1971
(annual percent change)

	1966	1967	1968	1969	1970	1971
Private nonfarm	4.5	4.7	6.3	6.7	5.9	6.5
Rubber	3.4	5.6		4.7	5.4	
Autos	2.9	8.6		5.5	13.1	
Trucking	2.9	6.0		6.0	13.8	
Steel		1.1	6.0		3.5	11.9
Metal cans		3.4	10.0		4.2	11.5
Communications		3.2	9.4		3.4	14.7
Collective bargaining agreements (manufacturing only)						
First-year increases			7.0	7.9	8.1	10.9
Deferred wage increases			3.9	4.0	4.6	4.8

NOTE: Changes in average hourly earnings were computed as percent changes in the average from the preceding year, except for the year in which new contracts were negotiated. New contracts were negotiated in the rubber, auto, and trucking industries in 1967 and 1970 and in the steel, metal cans, and communications industries in 1968 and 1971. The percent increase in average hourly earnings in those industries for years in which new contracts were negotiated was computed by comparing average wages for a six-month period after the new contract was negotiated with the average for the same six-month period a year earlier. The particular months chosen are shown in Marvin Kosters et al., "Collective Bargaining and the Wage Structure," *Labor Law Journal*, August 1973, p. 522, Table 3.

much more serious and pervasive pattern of distortion in the wage structure than had been previously experienced during a cyclical slowdown in the economy. Imbalances in the wage structure and the large "catch-up" wage increases in 1970 and 1971 that reduced these imbalances created a transitional lag in wage developments. The pervasiveness of these imbalances also suggests that it would have been extremely difficult to embark on an incomes policy that relied heavily on a simple numerical wage standard, because its credibility could not easily be maintained when pressures for large catch-up wage increases by major unions were so strong.

Productivity and Prices

Extraordinarily slow productivity growth in 1969 and 1970, though a normal cyclical development, was protracted by the depressive effect on real output growth of the sluggish response of wages and prices to demand restraint. Combined with continued large increases in average hourly labor costs, this slow productivity growth produced extremely large increases in labor costs per unit of output. Slack demand in product markets kept businesses from fully recouping the labor cost increases, with the result that profits declined markedly in both 1969 and 1970. Because unit labor cost increases were so large and accounted for such a large share of total costs, the decline in profits could not absorb them, and as a result large price increases continued.

There are several points worth noting here. Pressures for the restoration of balance in the wage structure delayed the arrival of smaller hourly labor cost increases. This delay, and its influence on prices, generated a short-term real output growth path that was lower than had been projected, reinforcing cyclically slow productivity growth and intensifying the pressure of costs on prices. The prevalence of these cost pressures led to a "cost-push" diagnosis of the malady and influenced the design of criteria for price adjustments under the ensuing controls. Slow productivity growth precluded normal increases in real wage and income levels, thereby intensifying pressures for large wage increases, while profits were squeezed to the point where they might be expected to increase significantly in a balanced recovery.

The Outlook in Mid-1971

By mid-1971 conditions had been created for a period of better economic performance. Better performance would require enough strength in aggregate demand to increase the pace of economic activity and enough stability (or some continued decline) in inflation so that stronger demand would raise production and employment levels and would not be dissipated in larger price increases. Prospects were favorable for improved wage and price performance during the cyclical recovery.

On the labor cost side, the period had passed in which pressures for large wage increases under new collective bargaining agreements were most severe. Moreover, deferred wage increases built into existing contracts had stabilized. Deferred increases scheduled to go into effect for 1972 were estimated to be slightly lower than for 1971. While there were some contracts for which large wage increases could be expected—coal miners, railroad workers, and longshoremen—the collective bargaining calendar for 1972 showed fewer workers scheduled to negotiate new agreements and fewer large pattern-setting wage situations than there had been in 1970 and 1971. Moreover, large wage increases were not generally necessary to attract or retain labor in view of the slack in labor markets.

Productivity growth prospects were also favorable during the cyclical recovery in production that was under way. Roughly stable (or even somewhat smaller) hourly labor cost increases combined with more rapid productivity growth could reduce unit labor cost increases, thereby making possible smaller price increases, rising real wages and incomes, and some recovery in profits. Depressed capacity utilization rates suggested ample room for expansion of production without resulting in supply conditions that would create pressure for price increases or generate shortages.[14]

Thus, there was a reasonable prospect for a cyclical rise in productivity growth that would permit real incomes and profits to rise and relieve pressures for large wage and price increases. Realization of this outcome was not assured, however. The trend in newly negotiated wage increases might have been slow to respond to improved balance in the wage structure. Expectations of continued inflation and of possible direct action to restrain inflation might have contributed to persistence in price increases. Expansionary aggregate demand policies might consequently have been disproportionately translated into inflation rather than into real output growth.

THE NEW ECONOMIC POLICY

The three elements of the New Economic Policy announced on August 15, 1971, were (1) suspension of dollar convertibility into gold and imposition of an import surcharge to deal with the balance-of-payments problem, (2) requests to Congress for an investment tax credit and other tax changes to stimulate output and employment, and (3) imposition of a ninety-day freeze on prices, wages, and rents. The New Economic Policy was motivated in large part by high unemployment and was triggered by the international situation—specifically an impending request for conversion of about $2 billion into gold. The element of the New Economic Policy with the most dramatic public impact was the freeze, even though the freeze and the system of controls that followed were intended as a short-term complement to the other policy changes and as a program to speed up the disinflation process already under way.

Structure of the Controls

There were major changes in the organizational structure and administration of controls after the initial freeze, and these changes were widely regarded as marked changes in control policy. The conceptual basis for the regulations applicable to price and wage adjustments remained essentially unchanged, however, for most of the economy during the two and a half years from November 1971 through April 1974, except for the second brief freeze in mid-1973. Both regulations and procedures were modified over time, but the initial wage standard was not formally changed, and the standards for price adjustments generally permitted costs to be passed through with profit margin limitations if prices were increased.

The broad outlines of the standards, procedures, and coverage of the program are summarized in Table 2. The material set forth in the table is amplified in the text by a discussion of some of the salient features of the program's organization and administration.[15] Some of the more detailed technical aspects of the rules and their practical effects are considered in later sections.

Phase II

The Cost of Living Council established the price goals for the stabilization program, exercised authority over procedural issues and issues of coverage, coordinated policies and activities of the other stabilization bodies, and retained planning and policy development responsibility. The goal of reducing inflation to 2 to 3 percent by the end of 1972 was established to permit a gradual reduction in inflation (after an upsurge in the wake of the freeze) and to establish a context within which the Pay Board and Price Commission could develop and administer their standards. Raw agricultural products were the major sector exempt from controls, and coverage remained basically unchanged during the program, except for the small-firm exemption in May 1972 and the decontrol process in late 1973 and early 1974. A stabilization unit within the Internal Revenue Service was established to provide the field organization for the program and to conduct auditing and enforcement activities.[16]

Phase II began on November 14, 1971. One of its distinguishing features was its heavy reliance on self-administration. The formal coverage of the standards was broader than the reach of administrative intervention through formal review of individual wage and price adjustments. A system of differentiated administrative procedures based primarily on the size of firms and employee units was devised to reconcile broad coverage with limited administrative involvement. Administration of the controls was influenced in several ways by the administration's desire to minimize intrusion by a federal bureaucracy into price and wage decisions.

First, heavy reliance was placed on self-administration of the standards for smaller units; these units were subject only to periodic review or a small probability of possible audit. In this respect, the regulations were administered in a way similar to the way the personal income tax is administered. Second, the standards were designed to be generally applicable in order to permit self-administration, even though they were often difficult to apply to particular cases and inevitably much too simple to cover the full range of complex situations in the economy. Third, the regulations were applied to individual firms or employee units with relatively little consideration for industry price and cost patterns or for wage patterns among industries, crafts, and occupations. These characterizations apply with particular force for Phase II. A more varied and complex approach was evolved beginning in 1973, reflecting changes in market conditions and an increased recognition of the inappropriateness of such a simplified approach over time.

Wages

A general numerical standard for wage increases was established, permitting compensation adjustments of up to 5.5 percent without prior notification or review for all except the largest employee units. Although criteria for exceptions were also provided, the wide applicability of the standard left little scope for adjustments in the

TABLE 2 Regulations of the Control Program, Phases II, III, and IV

Program	Phase II: November 14, 1971, to January 11, 1973	Phase III: January 11, 1973, to June 13, 1973	Phase IV: August 12, 1973, to April 30, 1974
General standards *Price increase limitations*	Percent pass-through of allowable cost increases since last price increase, or Jan. 1, 1971, adjusted for productivity and volume offsets. Term limit pricing option available.	Self-administered standards of Phase II.	In most manufacturing and service industries dollar-for-dollar pass-through of allowable cost increase since last fiscal quarter ending prior to Jan. 11, 1973.
Profit margin limitations	Not to exceed margins of the best 2 of 3 fiscal years before Aug. 15, 1971. Not applicable if prices were not increased above base level, or if firms "purified" themselves.	Not to exceed margins of the best 2 fiscal years completed after Aug. 15, 1968. No limitation if average price increase did not exceed 1.5 percent.	Same years as Phase III, except that a firm that had not charged a price for any item above its base price, or adjusted freeze price, whichever was higher, was not subject to the limitation.
Wage increase limitations	General standard of 5.5 percent. Exceptions made to correct gross inequities, and for workers whose pay had increased less than 7 percent a year for the last 3 years. Workers earning less than $2.75 per hour were exempt. Increases in qualified fringe benefits permitted raising standard to 6.2 percent.	General Phase II standard, self-administered. Some special limitations. More flexibility with respect to specific cases. Workers earning less than $3.50 per hour were exempt after May 1.	Self-administered standards of Phase III. Executive compensation limited.

	Phase II	Phase III	Phase IV
Prenotification			
Prices	Prenotification required for all firms with annual sales above $100 million, 30 days before implementation, approval required.	After May 2, 1973, prenotification required for all firms with sales above $250 million whose price increase had exceeded a weighted average of 1.5 percent.	Same as Phase II except that prenotified price increases could be implemented in 30 days unless CLC required otherwise.
Wages	For all increases of wages for units of 5,000 or more; for all increases above the standard regardless of the number of workers involved.	None.	None.
Reporting			
Prices	Quarterly for firms with sales over $50 million.	Quarterly for firms with sales over $250 million.	Quarterly for firms with sales over $50 million.
Wages	Pay adjustments below standard for units greater than 1,000 persons.	Pay adjustments for units greater than 5,000 persons.	Same as Phase III.
Special areas	Health, insurance, rent, construction, public utilities.	Health, food, public utilities, construction, petroleum.	Health, food, petroleum, construction, insurance, executive and variable compensation.
Exemptions	Raw agricultural commodities, import prices, export prices, firms with 60 or fewer employees.	Same as Phase II plus rents.	Same as Phase III plus public utilities, lumber, copper scrap, and long-term coal contracts, initially with sector-by-sector decontrol of prices and wages until April 30, 1974.

SOURCE: Cost of Living Council (CLC).

wage structure. The intellectual roots of this approach can be traced to the rationale for the guideposts of the early 1960s. Its public acceptability as a credible approach owed much to widespread public discussion of the potential contribution of a general numerical norm for wage increases.[17] Moreover, it was compatible with an emphasis on self-administration. Under the wage standard, wages and fringe benefits were treated as perfect substitutes. This treatment was consistent with an emphasis on the cost implications of pay adjustments, but it complicated the treatment of situations in which large increases in fringe benefits were at issue.[18]

While procedural differences in the treatment of wage adjustments were formally based on employee-unit size, in practice the review and formal approval of pay adjustments was restricted largely to increases that exceeded the general standard, with self-administration generally applicable to increases within the limits of the standard. Although the pay standard was widely viewed by the public as setting a limit of 5.5 percent (later recognized to be 6.2 percent under provisions dealing with fringe benefits), the actual standard and the way it was administered were more complex. Pay increases of up to 7.0 percent were permitted for deferred wage increases and as exceptions for tandem relationships, for catch-ups to offset relatively small previous wage increases, and for retaining essential employees. Increases exceeding those explicitly permitted by the regulations could be and were often permitted after review of a particular case.[19]

The regulations covering wage increases were initially developed and administered by a tripartite Pay Board.[20] After four of the five original labor representatives withdrew their participation on March 22, 1972, the Pay Board was reconstituted as a public body with seven members. While a measure of underlying labor cooperation and acquiescence was retained throughout Phase II, organized labor's formal participation in the program was not renewed until the advent of Phase III. Labor participation at a policy level instead of an operating level was obtained through establishment of the Labor-Management Advisory Committee, and a significant impetus for restructuring the program in Phase III came from a recognition that a participatory and cooperative role for labor was essential for any program of wage and price restraint.

Prices

The pricing standards for Phase II were developed and administered by the Price Commission.[21] Price adjustments were permitted if there had been cost increases, subject to the provision that these price increases did not lead to profit margins that exceeded limits established by a base period. Both the cost pass-through and profit margin rules were applied on a firm-by-firm basis, an approach that made self-administration feasible. All firms except the largest could apply the regulations themselves in making price adjustments. The largest firms had to submit requests for price increases and secure approval before those increases could be put into effect. For retail and wholesale operations the cost pass-through regulations permitted maintenance of percentage markups on the cost of merchandise only, while in the manufacturing and services sectors increases in all allowable costs incurred could be passed through on a percentage basis. Price increases to reflect increased merchandise costs for retailers and wholesalers were self-administered even in the largest firms, as were price adjustments for producers of products for which major input costs were exceptionally volatile, for example, in meat-packing operations. More specialized rules, also based on cost pass-through concepts, were developed for health services, insurance, and rents.

The Shift to Phase III

The restructuring of the stabilization program for Phase III was designed to provide a way station out of controls and to secure renewed cooperation in a program of wage and price restraint. From the time they were initially imposed, wage and price controls had been viewed by the administration as a short-term approach. It was repeatedly announced that the goal was to terminate controls as soon as this was feasible.[22] Phase III was intended to be a transitional stage in the process of removing mandatory wage and price controls. At the same time it was intended to contribute toward continued restraint. One element in this restraint involved enlisting the cooperation of organized labor during a year in which the bargaining calendar was heavy and a resurgence of large wage increases was regarded as likely by many observers.[23] The other major element involved special attention to sectors in which continuing inflation problems were regarded as most severe, not only through the application of specialized controls mechanisms but also by an emphasis on federal policies influencing supply, particularly in the agricultural sector. How much Phase III contributed to restraint is a complex problem, but it clearly failed as an attempt to remove controls. Its demise came with the imposition of a new price freeze after five months of retreat from flexibility and self-administration.

The major organizational changes in Phase III were the termination of the Pay Board and Price Commission and the assumption of operational responsibility by the Cost of Living Council.[24] New committee structures were formed for the food and health sectors (an advisory committee with private sector representatives and a government committee to review federal policies influencing inflation for each sector) while the Construction Industry Stabilization Committee continued to operate. Standards and procedures in these three sectors continued basically unchanged from what they were in Phase II.

For other sectors of the economy, the major substantive changes in the program were a modification of the price standard and a change in the administration of price and wage standards. The price standard was modified so as to reduce the constraining influence of profit margin limitations; the profit margin limitation was removed for firms with cost-justified price increases averaging less than 1.5 percent, and the base period that could be used in computing the profit margin limits was extended forward to the most recently completed fiscal year. Prenotification requirements for wages and prices were terminated, although quarterly reports were required for the largest units. Moreover, broad conformance with the standards was required instead of detailed technical compliance with regulations, since detailed technical compliance would need to be accompanied by increasing complexity and detail in the regulations and carefully spelled-out rulings for particular situations. These changes toward "voluntary" and "self-administered" standards were perhaps of most substantive importance and generated most public interest.

On the wage side, John Dunlop, the new director, gave as one of his guiding principles the February 26, 1973, statement by the Labor-Management Advisory Committee that "no single standard or wage settlement can be equally applicable at one time to all parties in an economy so large, decentralized, and dynamic."[25] Although the change in emphasis was widely viewed as a repudiation of the wage norm for Phase II, the main practical effect of the change was to give more explicit attention to wage-structure relationships and patterns but not to raise the average level of wage settlements.[26] On the price side, one of the most revealing indications of the direction in which the program was oriented was the clause in the general price standard permitting adjustments that would otherwise exceed the standards "as necessary for efficient

allocation of resources or to maintain adequate levels of supply."
Apart from the unwinding of delays that had previously been introduced by prenotification requirements, there was little formal change in the substance of the regulations, however, because the regulations, computation procedures, and rulings developed in Phase II were to be used in self-administering adjustments in both prices and wages.

The development and introduction of Phase III had been premised on a view of the price outlook that was far more optimistic than the inflation trend that actually emerged—a failure in prediction that was shared by most professional forecasters.[27] It was also based on the view that the combination of substantive economic conditions in the labor market (particularly the restoration of improved balance in the wage structure) and the cooperative involvement of organized labor in a program to maintain stability made wage restraint during the year a realistic and achievable objective. Wage increases during 1973 were reasonably consistent with prospects as they were viewed in late 1972, in spite of price increases much larger than had been projected.[28]

The surge in food prices, led by large increases in meat prices, began in December 1972. By the end of March, ceilings were imposed on meat prices, based on the expectation at that time that food prices would rise less rapidly later in the year and the view that temporary meat price ceilings could therefore help to maintain restraint in wage settlements. At the beginning of May, the acceleration of price increases had become much broader, and limited prenotification was reinstituted to introduce some delay in the pass-through of increased costs of a wide range of basic materials. By June the earlier optimism regarding food prices later in the year was no longer tenable, and accelerating price increases had become more pervasive throughout the economy. The widespread perception that Phase III was a failure and that a return to a controls structure similar to Phase II could contribute to renewed stability undoubtedly influenced public and congressional attitudes. The decision to terminate Phase III was the policy response.

The sharp acceleration of price increases in 1973 coincided closely in timing with the shift to Phase III but owed little to modifications in the standards of Phase II and their administration. Perhaps the strongest evidence that the shift to Phase III was not responsible for the acceleration is that the acceleration began in food prices, and food prices remained the major contributor to higher living costs throughout most of the year, even though mandatory controls on food prices, including prenotification requirements, were retained throughout Phase III. Moreover, price increases in most other sectors were supported by increased costs (according to the quarterly reports covering the period), most of the largest price increases were within the limits permissible during Phase II, and profits and cost data from other sources show no sharp break with earlier trends. Taken together, this evidence indicates that the problem was not a failure of compliance with the cost pass-through regulations that had been in force since the program began. Consequently, the principal action tool of Phase III, the "stick in the closet" to induce compliance, turned out to be highly inappropriate as an instrument for tempering the kind of inflation that emerged.

Freeze II and Phase IV

The public dialogue on inflation during the first half of 1973 was dominated by discussion of controls and their apparent lack of stringency. In this climate public and congressional pressures rose for strong direct action. A price freeze announced June 13, 1973, was a response to these pressures, despite economic judgments that its disruptive consequences would outweigh its contribution to price stability. The duration of the freeze was not to exceed sixty days; it covered only prices, with wages to be adjusted under existing standards and procedures; and it was to be followed by a stringent program of controls. It was lifted on a sectoral basis as sectors were placed under regulations similar to but somewhat more stringent than those of Phase II, beginning July 18 with the food sector, where market disruptions were most severe.[29] The introduction of Phase IV was also accompanied by announced intentions to decontrol on a sector-by-sector basis.

The standards of Phase IV generally permitted pass-through of increased costs, although there was more differentiation among sectors in the application of this principle. Costs could only be passed through on a dollar-for-dollar basis, however, which had not been the case in Phase II, and prices in a number of sectors were significantly limited because further increases in prices were restricted to increases in costs occurring since the last quarter of 1972 that had not been reflected by price increases during that period. Situations in which price ceilings held prices below market levels were far more numerous in Phase IV than in earlier phases. However, this was mostly attributable to changes in both domestic and world market conditions, to more use of delays in sectors such as steel, and to specialized sectoral regulations, particularly in the petroleum, health, and food sectors.

The difference in market conditions between 1972 and 1973 and the extent to which the actual trend of consumer prices during the year would depend on decisions and developments wholly unrelated to controls is illustrated by two areas singled out by the President in his announcement of the freeze—gasoline and food prices. In the announcement, he referred to strong export demand for farm products, and requested more flexible authority from Congress for export controls. Comprehensive export controls for farm products were not imposed because it was recognized that their imposition would seriously compromise other goals. However, stabilization of food prices at retail was inconsistent with a dramatically rising cost structure that reflected the rise of raw farm product prices on world markets. While the full implications of rising crude oil prices were not evident at this time, prices on world markets were rising above domestic levels well before the embargo, and the U.S. economy was dependent on supplies from foreign sources. Controls could and did play a role in keeping petroleum product prices below levels they would otherwise have reached, but there was no escape from the significant price consequences of the tripling of imported crude oil prices late in the year.

Although the Phase IV regulations were substantively similar for most sectors to those that had been in force in Phase II, the general policy approach of the former differed in two fundamental ways. There was less reluctance to tolerate temporary dislocations resulting from the controls, such as dispersion in domestic prices and instances of domestic prices below prices on international markets. These conditions had been mainly confined to the lumber industry during Phase II. Though they were more prevalent and more severe during Phase IV, remedial adjustments were usually not made unless it could be demonstrated that these conditions would have seriously harmful and costly effects. At the same time, initiatives for the selective decontrol of individual sectors were carried forward, gradually at first and at a faster pace in early 1974. Criteria for decontrol and its timing were never publicly set forth in detail, but they frequently involved commitments from industry representatives with respect to prices, investment, or improvement of industrial relations practices.[30] This approach helped to avoid a disorderly retreat from controls through administrative breakdown or overwhelming pressures from litigation or from congressional initiatives. At the same time the continuing pinch of controls kept counterpressures against decontrol from building.

The elements of the decontrol process are not easily summarized, but it was oriented toward an orderly and cumulative extrication from controls. One of its guiding principles was a general policy of decontrolling both wages and prices in each case. The somewhat paradoxical role played by price prospects is illustrated on the one hand by decontrol of lumber when Phase IV began because prices were declining, and on the other by early decontrol of fertilizer in spite of large price increases because decontrol would contribute to increased domestic supply. The administration's position on extension of the stabilization authority was also designed to facilitate continued decontrol while retaining enough flexibility to promote effective dialogue among private-sector interests, Congress, and the executive branch. By April 30, 1974, more than half of the portion of the economy covered when Phase IV began had been decontrolled, with only 12 percent of the consumer price index remaining under control as against 44 percent before decontrol began. Congressional attitudes had changed so markedly from the previous year that no action was taken to provide for the limited mandatory authority requested by the administration, or even to establish a basis for monitoring the private sector and for analysis and policy review within the executive branch explicitly directed toward longer-term inflation concerns.[31]

IV. CONTROLS AND THE ECONOMY

The effects of controls on the economy, and the effects of developments in the economy on controls, can be approached from various points of view. Each approach can give insight into some aspect of the relation between stabilization actions and economic goals, but regardless of the approach the insights cannot be easily summed up to provide an overall assessment. Careful analyses using different approaches have supported different conclusions on the influence of controls on wages, prices, and profits during the program.[32] In this section, the stabilization program is examined primarily from the point of view of overall consistency of performance with the stabilization rules.

General Performance of the Economy

During the period from 1971 through 1974, wage and price controls were only one component of economic policy, and improved price stability was only one of several goals of that policy. Controls and their administration were regarded as closely linked with the high-priority goal of a vigorous cyclical recovery in 1972. Their influence on this goal was initially uncertain and given close attention.[33]

That controls did not interfere with a resumption of strong cyclical growth and may have contributed to it is an assertion that needs little qualification. Real output rose by about 6 percent in both 1972 and 1973 compared to 3.3 percent in 1971, the first year of the recovery. Although the unemployment rate declined only gradually throughout 1972 and 1973, increases in employment and in the labor force were unusually large. Employment rose by more than 2.5 million workers in 1972 and 1973 compared to an annual average rise of 1.3 million between 1959 and 1969. The period of rapid increase in output that extended through the first quarter of 1973 was accompanied by strong cyclical productivity growth, a short-term development that contributed heavily to the favorable price, income, and profits trends of 1972.

Pressures of labor costs on prices were relieved by the surge in productivity growth, permitting unusually large increases in real earnings with a somewhat less rapid rise in wage rates than earlier. The large increases in output were accompanied by rising profits and some rise in the profits share, although the employee compensation share remained unusually high during the cyclical expansion. These conditions during 1972 help to account for the degree of public acceptance of controls at that time and for the underlying cooperation of organized labor evidenced by the low incidence of work stoppages.

In 1973 price increases accelerated sharply, at the outset mostly for food, and the acceleration in inflation at the consumer level was heavily concentrated in food throughout most of the year. A continuation of relatively moderate wage increases led to a decline in real earnings, even though labor costs per unit of output rose more rapidly when productivity increases tapered off during 1973. Most of the acceleration in price increases, however, can be traced to factors other than larger increases in unit labor costs.

The price surge of 1973 was dominated by developments that were largely outside of the aggregative domestic cost and price relationships that have received most attention in formulating projections of price performance. The main exogenous elements were the decline in world food supply, the further devaluation and subsequent slide in the value of the dollar, the strength and coincidence of the boom in most large industrial countries, and by fall, the oil embargo and action taken by the international cartel to raise prices.

In addition, a number of basic materials industries were operating at capacity production levels, though this was belatedly recognized. While the inflation was supported by a period of rapid monetary expansion, these developments through their influence on domestic supply and prices had a major impact on short-term inflation. It is possible, however, that delays in price increases induced by the controls contributed to the persistence of overly expansionary policies by delaying the recognition of inflationary pressures in 1972 and early 1973.

Wages

Wage increases, as measured by adjusted average hourly earnings, were somewhat smaller in percent terms in 1972 and 1973 than in the preceding four years. The decline in new first-year wage increases under major collective bargaining agreements was much more pronounced. In manufacturing, for example, the average increase declined from 10.9 percent in 1971 to 6.6 percent in 1972. The decline in construction wage increases began in 1971, coincident with the introduction of controls, and new first-year increases declined from an average of 17.6 percent in 1970 to 5.0 percent in 1973. While this shows that wages increased less rapidly under controls than before, the extent to which the slowdown was attributable to the controls is not clear.

Wage-structure developments in the period immediately before institution of controls had created conditions favorable for achieving smaller wage increases by 1972. Deferred wage increases scheduled for 1972 were somewhat lower on average than those for 1971, and most workers with contracts expiring in 1972 had received relatively large increases during the term of their contracts. Their position in the wage structure compared to relative positions of other unionized workers had not deteriorated significantly. Moreover, workers in nonunion manufacturing establishments received smaller wage increases in 1970 and 1971 than those in union establishments. Thus, the wages of most workers with wage agreements scheduled to expire in 1972 were in better balance with wages of other workers in the economy than had been the wages of those covered by contracts expiring in 1970 or 1971. Moreover, the shift from acceleration to a slight deceleration in consumer price increases meant that an improved balance between wage and price increases had emerged after the catch-up process that occurred in the late 1960s.

Wage-structure conditions in 1972 also pointed to the prospect of moderate settlements in 1973. The collective bargaining calendar was dominated by a few large contract situations, and the available evidence indicated that wages under most of the largest contracts expiring in 1973 had increased during the term of these contracts at least as rapidly as had the wages of the average worker. This pattern is illustrated in the tabulation below, which shows the percent increase in average hourly earnings in three industries in which a high proportion of workers were covered by long-term contracts expiring in 1973 (the figures are from the Bureau of Labor Statistics):

Industry Sector	1971	1972
Private nonfarm	6.5	6.4
Rubber	6.5	7.6
Autos	12.3	8.1
Trucking	13.3	10.8

The lack of evidence of deterioration in the relative wage positions of workers under contracts expiring in 1973 is in striking contrast to the pattern in the late 1960s (see Table 1). Moreover, the slower price increases of 1972 permitted unusually large real wage gains for most workers, including those with contracts expiring in 1973.

The wage situation in construction and some other sectors was more complex. First-year wage increases in construction, after accelerating throughout the late 1960s, reached an average rate of increase of over 17 percent in 1970, and normal wage patterns within the industry were severely disrupted. The extremely large wage increases in construction were considered by many observers to be creating wage-structure pressures in other sectors, as workers with comparable skills sought comparable wage increases. The disorderly wage-structure conditions that emerged, both within the construction sector and for wages of workers in other sectors with skills similar to those of construction workers, do not lend themselves to a simple interpretation. They represented developments more complex than simple restoration of a balance in relative wages that had been disrupted primarily through inflation. Consequently, there is no strong basis for confidence that the pattern of leapfrogging and catch-up would have been broken in the absence of controls. The timing and magnitude of the decline in new wage increases in construction in 1971 and 1972 provide strong circumstantial evidence that a significant influence should be attributed to the controls in that sector.[34] Moreover, smaller wage increases in construction under wage controls may have contributed indirectly to wage stabilization in other sectors. Since construction wage levels were already relatively high, it would have been extremely difficult to achieve smaller wage increases in other sectors and a restoration of more normal wage-structure patterns in the absence of a sharp reduction in construction wage increases.

For most sectors, the fact that new wage increases under collective bargaining agreements in 1972 and 1973 were smaller than those in 1970 and 1971 fits the pattern expected on the basis of wage structural developments. Much of the decline in wage increases could have been the result of factors other than the controls, although controls may have facilitated a more rapid realization of smaller wage increases. Wage-structure developments undoubtedly contributed to the acquiescence of organized labor in settlements with smaller wage increases in 1972 and 1973 than had been obtained earlier. The fact that the Pay Board approved higher wage increases in the union than in the nonunion sector, the concentration of wage cutbacks in the union sector, a declining differential between wage increases for union and nonunion workers in manufacturing in 1972, and the reduced dispersion in the size of new wage settlements in 1972 and 1973 are all consistent with the view that an important role should be attributed to changing wage-structure conditions.

Assessment of the contribution of controls to the reduction in the size of new wage increases under collective bargaining agreements in 1972 and 1973 is complicated by the influence of wage structural changes. In Table 3, data on the distribution of wage increases under major agreements show a pronounced reduction in the proportion of increases that exceeded 8 and 10 percent in 1972 and 1973. Although changes in wage-structure conditions provided grounds for expecting fewer very large wage increases after 1971, wage controls may have helped to ensure that restoration of wage-structure balance was accompanied by a reduction in average wage increases.

It has often been suggested that setting a standard or guideline as a ceiling for wage increases also tends to set a floor.[35] The evidence from the data in Table 3 is mixed. A larger proportion of settlements with wage increases below 5 and 6 percent occurred during the two years of controls than during the preceding two years. However, by 1973, wage increases were also far more heavily concentrated in the 5 to 6 percent range than they had been previously. Since the wage standard was implemented for a period too short to assure that its full consequences had become evident, and

TABLE 3 First-Year Wage Rate Changes in Collective Bargaining Agreements Covering 1,000 Workers or More

Percent of Workers Affected

Type of Wage Rate Action	All Industries				Manufacturing			
	1970	1971	1972	1973	1970	1971	1972	1973
No wage increase	–	1	3	1	–	1	2	–
Increase in wages	100	99	98	99	100	99	98	100
Less than 4 percent	1	1	8	8	1	2	4	4
4 to 5 percent	1	1	6	17	1	2	7	5
5 to 6 percent	3	3	20	30	6	4	23	47
6 to 7 percent	17	9	21	22	33	16	26	24
7 to 8 percent	11	5	14	9	18	7	20	7
8 to 10 percent	13	17	15	10	16	15	14	12
More than 10 percent	54	61	13	3	24	53	5	–
Not specified	1	1	–	–	–	–	–	–
Total wage actions	100	100	100	100	100	100	100	100
No. of workers (thous.)	4,675	3,978	2,424	5,320	2,184	1,913	913	2,318
Mean adjustment (percent)	11.9	11.6	7.3	5.8	8.1	10.9	6.6	5.9
Median adjustment (percent)	10.0	12.5	6.6	5.5	7.5	10.1	6.2	5.5

SOURCE: U.S. Bureau of Labor Statistics.

since little confidence can be placed in projections of the proportion of small wage increases that was most likely in the absence of controls, these data provide at best only weak evidence on this issue.

Another issue that has undergone considerable debate is the effectiveness of a simple numerical guideline or standard for wage stabilization. The standards and computational procedures established during Phase II were neither strongly reaffirmed nor explicitly disavowed in 1973; they were, however, used along with other criteria under an approach in which the idea of a single standard applicable to all wage situations was explicitly rejected. These data indicate, however, that the dispersion in actual wage settlements was smaller in 1973 and average increases were smaller, both for all industries and within manufacturing, than in 1972. The standards were apparently administered more flexibly in 1972 than was generally recognized, and they resulted in lower average increases in 1973 than in 1972, in spite of the announced intentions to administer them with more flexibility.

Prices

The goal of a 2 to 3 percent rate of inflation by the end of 1972 was established when controls were introduced. The desired reduction was considerably below the 6 percent increase in consumer prices that took place during 1969. However, the upper range of the goal was a modest target compared to the 3.6 percent rate of increase during the first eight months of 1971. The belief that the goal was within reach was bolstered by the fact that consumer prices were increasing at about a 3 percent rate in mid-1972. More rapid increases in food prices in late 1972, reflected most strongly in the wholesale price index, pointed toward a temporary acceleration in consumer price inflation. But since the acceleration was mainly limited to the farm and food sector, the acceleration in inflation from this source could potentially be reversed relatively quickly by appropriately expansionary farm policies if crop conditions were favorable.

This prospect was shattered by the size and persistence of the increases in farm and food prices, along with the unexpected emergence of tight markets and sharp price increases in several other critical sectors. Thus, the initial promise of progress toward renewed price stability, nurtured in part by the initial apparent success of Phase II, was followed by a surge in inflation to almost unprecedented rates in spite of efforts to restructure the controls to contain it.

Evaluation of the influence of controls on prices is facilitated by examining the sectoral incidence of inflation and of its acceleration during the period. The pass-through of increased costs formed the basis for price adjustments, and in several sectors prices of inputs that accounted for a major share of total costs were exempt from controls. As a result, in those sectors control was exerted only on processing and distribution markups, and prices could rise dramatically under the stabilization rules in contrast to other sectors in which most of the major inputs were domestically produced and subject to controls. Moreover, increases in prices of major inputs and pass-through of those increased input costs to higher product prices were generally permitted when demand conditions in the marketplace supported them. This approach was necessary in view of the limited supplementary role intended for controls and the reluctance to take complementary measures such as subsidization, rationing, or export controls that would have been necessary if a more ambitious role had been assigned to controls.

During 1972, disproportionate contributions to inflation came from the food component of the consumer price index and the farm products and processed food and feeds component of the wholesale price index (Table 4). Increases in wholesale industrial prices were disproportionately concentrated in lumber and hides. In all of these sectors, major inputs were exempt from controls. Demand pressures were transmitted throughout the processing and distribution chain, a process that kept cost increases, except for costs of producing exempt products, roughly consistent with product price increases. In the first three quarters of 1973, food prices rose rapidly, and rapid increases in exempt farm product prices accounted for much of their acceleration. In the last part of the year, the contribution of petroleum and energy prices to inflation was extraordinarily large, even though petroleum and other energy products represented only small components of the indexes.[36] In both sectors, increased costs were quickly reflected in higher consumer prices because the time spent in the production and distribution chain is relatively short. While the prices of both farm products and petroleum products were strongly influenced by developments in international markets, pressure on domestic prices came from export demand in the case of farm products and from rising import prices in the case of petroleum products.

The strength of demand in both domestic and foreign markets and the devaluation of the dollar combined to support higher prices

TABLE 4 Consumer and Wholesale Prices by Phases of the Stabilization Program (percent changes for selected components; seasonally adjusted compound annual rates)

Price Indexes and Components	1969: 12 Months (12/68–12/69)[a]	1970: 12 Months (12/69–12/70)[a]	1971: 8 Months Prior to Freeze (12/70–8/71)	Phase I: 3 Months (8/71–11/71)	Phase II: 14 Months (11/71–1/73)	Phase III: 5 Months (1/73–6/73)	Freeze II: 2 Months (6/73–8/73)	Phase IV: 8 Months (8/73–4/74)	Post-controls: 8 Months (4/74–12/74)
Consumer Price Index									
All items	6.1	5.5	3.6	2.0	3.7	8.3	3.8[b]	11.5[b]	12.2
Food	7.2	2.2	4.7	1.3	6.7	20.8	0.9[b]	17.9[b]	11.7
Meat, poultry, and fish	11.2	-0.6	2.2	6.6	13.0	39.6	-13.5[b]	5.9[b]	3.6
Nonfood commodities	4.5	4.8	2.6	1.0	2.5	4.6	3.0	11.1	12.6
Energy products[c]	3.1	3.6	0.7	-0.7	2.4	18.3	2.5	62.1	3.9
Services[a]	7.4	8.2	4.5	3.1	3.5	4.3	5.3	9.5	12.5
All items except food	5.7	6.5	3.4	2.3	2.8	5.0	3.7	10.4	12.2

Wholesale Price Index

All commodities	4.8	2.2	4.5	2.0	6.8	21.7	-13.7[b]	19.7[b]	19.8
Farm products and processed foods and feeds									
Farm products	7.5	-1.4	5.5	6.5	14.9	50.2	-34.0[b]	13.6[b]	13.8
Processed foods and feeds	8.4	-4.7	7.0	6.9	20.7	75.5	-35.0[b]	12.4[b]	-1.4
Industrial commodities	6.8	0.8	4.6	5.0	11.4	38.2	-34.9[b]	14.8[b]	25.9
Hides	3.9	3.6	3.9	1.1	3.6	10.8	4.8	24.0	22.5
Fuels	3.7	0.5	4.6	3.2	21.0	-6.0	11.6	1.2	0.2
Lumber	4.0	11.1	-0.1	2.5	5.9	19.1	10.4	76.3	51.9
Metals	-8.3	-4.4	29.6	2.4	12.0	46.4	-9.6	14.0	-17.7
	9.8	2.7	6.1	1.0	3.3	10.8	9.5	31.4	25.2
Selected stage-of-processing indexes									
Crude materials except food	10.6	4.7	2.1	2.6		23.9	18.2	69.1	1.1
Intermediate materials except food	3.8	3.2	5.8	1.0		12.9	4.8	25.8	25.4
Consumer goods except food	2.9	3.9	1.9	1.1		7.0	3.6	18.6	17.8

SOURCE: U.S. Bureau of Labor Statistics.

[a] Not seasonally adjusted.

[b] Price changes measured using July 1973 instead of August 1973 to reflect the early release from the sixty-day freeze of food prices on July 18, 1973.

[c] Calculated as a weighted average of the indexes for gasoline, motor oil, fuel oil, and coal, using December 1972 weights.

for a widening range of basic materials. These higher prices were initially reflected primarily in the wholesale price index. In 1973, prices of basic and partially processed materials, which constituted 30 percent of the industrial component of wholesale prices, accounted for about 75 percent of the overall increase in industrial prices. These increased costs for processors and distributors were reflected in the latter part of 1973 and in 1974 by price increases for other commodities in the wholesale price index and higher consumer prices.

There was considerable scope for price increases within the limits of the stabilization rules at the beginning of 1973. The extent to which the prices of commodities in the industrial component of the wholesale price index could rise during 1972 and early 1973 before reaching levels authorized from the outset of the freeze in August 1971 is shown in Table 5. Much of the room for price increases was concentrated in the three sectors shown separately, and the amount of room left was rapidly shrinking in the first part of 1973. The tabulation does not take into account, however, the additional authority for price increases granted by the Price Commission during Phase II. Many companies in each of these sectors, and most of the major companies in the chemical industry, were authorized under term-limit pricing agreements to raise prices by an average of 1.8 to 2.0 percent above the stated levels.[37] By November 1972, after submission of prenotification requests, price increases averaging between 3 and 4 percent had been approved covering a large proportion of the sales of large firms in each of these sectors. Much of the acceleration in wholesale price increases in early 1973 represented increases toward previously authorized levels.

To assess the extent to which price increases during the program were consistent with the cost pass-through rules, actual cost and price trends can be compared. Because labor costs constitute a major share of value added, it is instructive to compare increases in unit labor costs and in the implicit price deflator for the private nonfarm and nonfinancial corporate sectors during the period of controls. There was an unusually close correspondence between price and unit labor cost increases during 1972; price increases were smaller than unit labor cost increases in 1973.[38] The close correspondence during 1972 and early 1973 is particularly striking because in the typical cyclical pattern, at least prior to 1968, price increases exceeded unit labor cost increases when demand and output increases were large. To adjust for this cyclical influence, predicted differences for the period beginning with the last quarter of 1971 were developed on the basis of a regression fitted to the pre-

TABLE 5 Wholesale Prices of Industrial Products below Initial Price Ceilings: Number of Items and Impact, Selected Months, December 1971–April 1973

Industrial Commodities below Apparent Price Ceilings	Dec. 1971	June 1972	Dec. 1972	April 1973
Wholesale industrial commodities (73.162)[a]				
Number of commodities below ceilings	553	496	473	366
Impact of rise to ceilings	1.82%	1.54%	1.46%	0.90%
Chemicals and allied products (5.716)[a]				
Number	69	78	78	69
Impact	0.22%	0.21%	0.21%	0.17%
Metals and metal products (13.439)[a]				
Number	127	113	109	68
Impact	0.74%	0.65%	0.62%	0.25%
Machinery and equipment (12.280)[a]				
Number	138	142	141	120
Impact	0.32%	0.34%	0.34%	0.26%
All other components (41.627)[a]				
Number	219	163	145	109
Impact	0.54%	0.34%	0.29%	0.22%

SOURCE: U.S. Bureau of Labor Statistics.
NOTE: Apparent initial price ceilings are defined as the highest prices of four months: May 1970, June 1970, July 1971, and August 1971. Prices in these months were chosen to approximate the alternate price ceilings of May 25, 1970, in the legislation and those of the base period for the freeze in the thirty days prior to August 15, 1971. Measures of the impact of a rise in prices to apparent initial ceiling levels are estimates of the percent impact of the wholesale price index on the industrial commodities component.
Numbers in parentheses reflect relative importance in December 1971.

---

ceding period and including the unemployment rate and changes in real output.[39] The predicted differences are compared with actual differences in figures 1 and 2, and the charts show substantially smaller price increases relative to unit labor cost increases than predicted throughout the period of controls. Those data strongly suggest that price increases conformed more closely to unit labor cost increases under the cost pass-through rules of the controls than would have been expected at that stage of the cycle in the absence of the pass-through rules.

FIGURE 1   Predicted and Actual Changes in Prices and Unit Labor
            Costs of Nonfinancial Corporations, 1959–1973
            (difference between percent change in prices and
            unit labor costs[a])

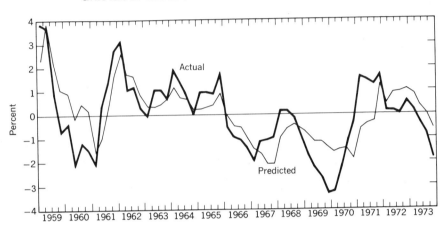

SOURCE: Bureau of Labor Statistics.
[a] Quarterly percent change in prices minus percent change in unit labor costs measured from
four quarters earlier.

FIGURE 2   Predicted and Actual Changes in Prices and Unit Labor
            Costs in the Private Nonfarm Sector, 1950–1973
            (difference between percent change in prices and
            unit labor costs[a])

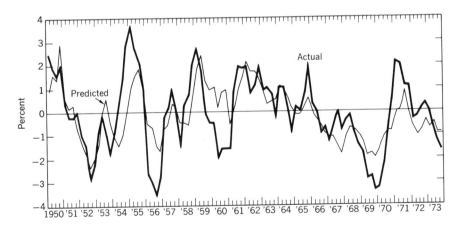

SOURCE: Bureau of Labor Statistics.
[a] Quarterly percent change in prices minus percent change in unit labor costs measured from
four quarters earlier.

Profits

Corporate profits rose by an average of 15 percent per year from 1970 to 1973, after declining by an average of 12 percent per year from 1968 to 1970. The pretax corporate profits share rose from 11.8 percent in 1970 to 13.4 percent in 1972 and 13.6 percent in 1973, but remained well below its average level of 17.4 percent during the 1960s. Profits are highly cyclical, and it is difficult to compare their actual performance in 1971–1973 with performance that would normally be expected in a cyclical recovery. It is instructive, however, to analyze the extent to which profit trends during this period were consistent with the stabilization rules and to examine the relationship between price and profit margin changes.

In the simplest analytic framework, the cost pass-through rules for price adjustments suggest that percent profit margins on sales should remain constant with percent cost pass-through and decline with dollar-for-dollar pass-through of costs. This analytic framework, however, does not take into account possibilities for input substitution, short-term productivity changes that differ from those applied during the program, changes in product mix, and the effect of increased volume on fixed costs per unit of output. Thus, actual profit margins could rise within the framework of the stabilization regulations.

The consistency of profit performance with the stabilization regulations is explored in tables 6, 7, and 8, along with the influence of alternative pricing rules and short-term productivity changes on profits and prices. The analysis is focused mainly on profits, value added, and implicit price deflators for nonfinancial corporations because the coverage and procedural requirements of the controls were concentrated on large firms and the data are readily available. These data permit some judgments to be made about the behavior of costs, prices, and profits in relation to the regulations. The period over which the analysis is made begins with the first quarter of 1971 because price increases under the stabilization regulations could not be linked to cost increases that occurred earlier than the beginning of 1971.

The predominant share of the increase in profits during the entire period from the first quarter of 1971 to the second quarter of 1974 can be attributed to the increase in the current dollar value of output during that period rather than to a rise in percent profit margins. Of the $5.4 billion cumulative increase in profits for nonfinancial corporations during the second quarter of 1974 (column 1, Table 6), $5.2 billion was required to maintain a constant percent profit mar-

TABLE 6 Profits and Profit Margins of Nonfinancial Corporations, Quarterly and Cumulative Changes from 1971I through 1974II

	Actual Change in Profits (1)	Calculated Change in Profits		
		Maintenance of Constant Percent Margin (2)	Departure from Constant Percent Margin (3)	Diff. between Constant Percent and Constant Dollar Margin[a] (4)
Year and Quarter	Quarterly Change in Profits (billions of dollars, annual rates)			
1971II	2.6	1.1	1.5	0.5
III	1.2	0.8	0.4	0.3
IV	0.5	1.2	−0.7	0.1
1972I	5.1	2.3	2.8	0.6
II	2.3	1.8	0.5	0.2
III	2.3	1.2	1.1	0.2
IV	5.7	2.4	3.3	0.5
1973I	2.9	2.8	0.1	0.6
II	0.4	1.8	−1.4	0.9
III	−0.5	1.3	−1.8	0.9
IV	−0.2	1.7	−1.9	1.4
1974I	−4.1	0.5	−4.6	2.1
II	3.2	1.9	1.3	2.2
Cumulative Periods	Cumulative Change in Profits[b] (billions of dollars)			
1971IV	1.1	0.8	0.3	0.2
1972IV	4.9	2.7	2.3	0.6
1973IV	5.6	4.6	1.0	1.5
1974II	5.4	5.2	0.2	2.6

SOURCE: Computed from data from U.S. Department of Commerce, Bureau of Economic Analysis.

NOTE: Profits are measured before taxes and include the inventory valuation adjustment; output is measured in terms of value added as reported in the national income accounts.

[a]This increment to profits is calculated as the difference between the increase in profits that would be sufficient to maintain constant percent profit margins and the increase that would be sufficient only to keep profits per unit of real output constant. It represents the amount by which profits would need to be augmented to compensate for inflation in order to avoid a reduction in the profits share.

[b]Cumulative profit changes are smaller than the sum of quarterly changes by approximately a factor of four, since quarterly changes are expressed at annual rates, and quarterly changes may not sum to totals of four times cumulative changes because of rounding. Cumulative totals for components may also differ because they were calculated on the basis of the percent margin prevailing in the first quarter of 1971.

gin (column 2, Table 6). About half of this component of profits reflected rising prices (column 4, Table 6) with the other half reflecting increased real output. Only a tiny fraction of the increase in profits in this quarter was accounted for by an increase in percent profit margins (column 3, Table 6). Also by the second quarter of 1974, the profits share of gross product originating in nonfinancial corporations was only 10.5 percent, compared to an average of 15.2 percent during the 1960s.

There was a great deal of variation in overall changes in profits during the period, however, and in the extent to which such changes reflected changes in percent profit margins. By the end of 1972, wider percent profit margins accounted for nearly as much of the cumulative increase in profits as the increased value of output at constant percent margins. On the other hand, by the second quarter of 1974 wider margins accounted for only a minute share of the cumulative increase in profits (columns 2 and 3, Table 6). The extent to which profits increase consistent with the objective of maintaining constant percent margins reflected rising real output or rising prices also shifted markedly during the period. The calculated increment to profits resulting from the difference between constant percent and constant dollar profit margins was very small through 1972 ($0.6 billion out of $2.7 billion), but it increased sharply when prices were rising more rapidly during 1973 and early 1974. By the second quarter of 1974, half of the profits increase associated with maintaining constant percent margins was accounted for by higher prices instead of by increased real output.

The difference between constant percent and constant dollar profit margins per unit of real output corresponds closely in concept to the difference between price adjustments to reflect percent pass-through or price adjustments to reflect dollar-for-dollar pass-through of increased costs. Because these calculations (column 4, Table 6) are based on value-added measures of real output, the calculated difference in profits understates the impact on profits of the difference in cost pass-through concepts. The impact of the difference between percentage and dollar-for-dollar cost pass-through may be understated by approximately a factor of two when the costs of materials inputs are rising at about the same rate as costs of the value-added component of prices.

Another limitation in the applicability of these aggregative comparisons of percent and dollar-for-dollar cost pass-throughs is that the cost pass-through regulations were applied in different ways for particular sectors. For example, the retail and wholesale sectors were permitted to apply percent markups to the cost of merchan-

Profit Margins and Changes in Output per Man-Hour of Nonfinancial Corporations, 1971I–1974II

Year and Quarter	Percent Change in Output per Man-Hour (1)	Diff. between Trend Rate and Short-Term Output per Man-Hour Change[a] (2)	Diff. in Rates of Output per Man-Hour Change[b] (3)	Change in Percent Profit Margin[c] (4)
	Quarterly Output per Man-Hour		Quarterly Calculated Increments to Profits (billions of dollars, annual rates)	
1971II	0.9	0.1	0.3	1.5
III	1.6	0.8	2.9	0.4
IV	0.7	−0.1	−0.4	−0.7
1972I	1.8	1.0	3.8	2.8
II	1.0	0.2	0.9	0.5
III	1.1	0.3	1.2	1.1
IV	1.1	0.3	1.2	3.3
1973I	2.0	1.2	5.0	0.1
II	0.2	−0.6	−2.8	−1.4
III	0.2	−0.6	−2.9	−1.8
IV	−0.6	−1.5	−6.7	−1.9
1974I	−1.4	−2.2	−10.3	−4.6
II	0.3	−0.5	−2.3	1.3
Cumulative Periods[d]	Cumulative Output per Man-Hour		Cumulative Calculated Increments to Profits[e] (billions of dollars)	
1971IV	3.2	0.8	0.7	0.3
1972IV	8.3	2.6	2.5	2.3
1973IV	9.9	1.0	0.6	1.0
1974II	8.9	−1.6	−2.5	0.2

SOURCE: Computed from data from U.S. Department of Commerce, Bureau of Economic Analysis, and Department of Labor, Bureau of Labor Statistics.
[a] The trend rate of increase in output per man-hour was calculated as the compound quarterly rate of increase from 1958 through 1969, the period used by the Price Commission for developing rates of productivity growth to be applied in estimating net increases in labor costs. The quarterly trend rate for the nonfinancial corporate sector was 0.8 percent (3.2 percent annually).
[b] Increments to profits attributed to the difference between short-term and trend rates of change in output per man-hour are calculated by applying the differential in output per man-hour changes to the compensation share of value added in the nonfinancial corporate sector.
[c] From column 3, Table 6.
[d] Quarterly changes may not sum to cumulative totals because of rounding.
[e] Cumulative increments to profits are smaller than the sum of quarterly changes by

dise throughout this period as well as in earlier stabilization programs. In certain sectors, such as meat packing, where prices of major inputs were highly volatile, price adjustments were permitted during the entire period only to reflect dollar-for-dollar pass-through of major input costs. It is difficult to be precise about the quantitative influence of constant percent or constant dollar profit margins, but it is worth noting that the impact of the difference between percent and dollar-for-dollar cost pass-through is disproportionately larger for profit margins than for price changes. The increment to profits necessary to maintain constant percent profit margins, by reflecting the rise in prices at a given output level, accounted for about 50 percent of the increase in profits over the entire period but only 1.5 percentage points of the 15 percent rise in prices (columns 1 and 4, Table 8, below).

Short-term changes in output per man-hour resulted in changes in the relationship between revenues and costs that could be reflected in changes in profit margins within the framework of the stabilization regulations. This source of short-term variation in profit margins was most important during the stabilization program, and it is also more readily susceptible to quantification than other possible sources such as changes in product mix or input substitution. In reviewing requests for price increases, changes in short-term production and in sales volume were taken into account to some extent, but their influence was small and difficult to estimate in the absence of information on actual and expected sales volume. Under the stabilization regulations, net increases in labor costs were calculated on the basis of trend rates of increase in output per man-hour. The difference between changes in short-term output per man-hour and these trend rates was used to calculate the potential influence on profits from this source. The results are shown in Table 7 along with actual changes in profit margins. This source more than accounts for the actual widening of profit margins for nonfinancial corporations through 1972, and it accounts for about half of the smaller cumulative rise in profit margins through 1973 (columns 3 and 4, Table 7). After the first quarter of 1973, percent profit margins declined as increases in output per man-hour fell far below trend rates.

---

pproximately a factor of 3 because quarterly changes are expressed in terms of annual ates for compensation and profits. Quarterly changes may not sum to totals of four times umulative changes because cumulative increments to profits were computed on the asis of the percent margin prevailing in the first quarter of 1971.

Changes in profit margins during the entire period seem to be mainly attributable to cyclical developments, including changes in output per man-hour, instead of to changes in the controls. The rise in profit margins from the fourth quarter of 1971 to the first quarter of 1972 may have been influenced by the transition to Phase II, since prices also rose sharply, but it could also be accounted for by the sharp rise in output per man-hour. Similarly, the decline in profit margins in the last half of 1973 might be partly attributable to the second freeze and dollar-for-dollar pass-through of costs in Phase IV, but the decline had begun in the second quarter and could have been expected to continue on the basis of larger increases in costs.

The data on profit margin changes do not support the view that prices increased more rapidly than costs during Phase III. The acceleration of inflation that began in 1973 was in fact accompanied by a sharp reduction in percent profit margin expansion in the first quarter when increases in materials input costs began accelerating. Percent profit margins declined after the first quarter of 1973 as prices, unit labor costs, and other costs rose more rapidly.

Profit data on an annual basis for selected industries indicate that a major part of the 1972 increase in profits was accounted for by manufacturing; and in 1973, by agriculture. In each case, much of the increase in profits could be attributed to wider profit margins. However, the amount of profits attributable to wider profit margins in manufacturing over the entire period, $6.9 billion, was small compared to the amount accounted for by large increases in short-term productivity, $12.4 billion. In addition, because of the large size of the manufacturing sector, the increase in prices that was accompanied by a widening of profit margins was smaller in that sector than in agriculture. With prices of raw agricultural products exempt, almost thirty percentage points of the increase in the price deflator for agriculture was associated with wider margins on value added, mainly during 1973. These data also show a slight narrowing of percent margins for retail and wholesale trade in 1972 and 1973, even though both sectors were formally under regulations permitting constant percent markups over costs.[40]

The profit margin data show a broad pattern of conformity with the regulations during the period of controls. In using profit data to examine the consistency of cost and price increases, it must be recognized that there are limitations resulting from the presence of long-term contracts, the existence of inventories, and the possibilities for hedging in purchasing and pricing policies. The data clearly show the importance of the unusually rapid short-term productivity gains during the early part of the period in providing additional real income that was accrued in the form of a slowing of price increases and a rise in profit margins. They also show that the expansion in profit margins that occurred during 1972 was consistent with the stabilization regulations in force, and that the acceleration in inflation occurring in early 1973 during Phase III was not accompanied by the wider profit margins that would be expected if business firms were raising prices more rapidly than their costs were increasing.

The limited potential of controls as a tool to improve price performance by squeezing profit margins is illustrated by the data on prices in Table 8. A major reason for the insensitivity of prices to profit margin changes is that profits account for only a small fraction of the value of output. Profits accounted for less than 10 percent of output of nonfinancial corporations in 1970. The shift in output per man-hour and profit margin trends in early 1973 reduced the portion of the increase in prices related to changes in percent profit margins, but the shift to more rapid inflation increased the influence on prices of maintenance of percent margins. Expansion of percent margins after the first quarter of 1971, when they were near a cyclical as well as a historical low, accounted for less than one percentage point of the 8.7 percent cumulative rise in prices by the end of 1973, and for only 0.3 of the 15 percent rise by the second quarter of 1974. Maintenance of percent margins, through a rise in profits per unit of real output sufficient to compensate for the rise in output prices, accounted for an additional percentage point by the end of 1973 and 1.5 percentage points by the second quarter of 1974. These data show that the consequences of limiting percent profit margins to their cyclically low level at the beginning of 1971, or reducing percent margins through erosion of the share of profits in real terms, could have significant effects both on the rates of return on investment and on cash flow available for investment in production capacity, even though price inflation in the corporate nonfinancial sector would not have been significantly affected. Moreover, the proportionate effect on consumer prices of a squeeze on profits would have been much smaller than for prices in the corporate nonfinancial sector during 1971–1974 because prices of farm products and imported commodities (which are largely external to the corporate nonfinancial sector) were responsible for much of the acceleration in inflation that occurred in 1973.

TABLE 8 Prices and Their Relation to Changes in Profits and in Output per Man-Hour of Nonfinancial Corporations, 1971I–1974 II

Year and Quarter	Percent Change in Implicit Price Deflator (1)	Change in Percent Profit Margin[a] (2)	Difference in Rates of Change of Output per Man-Hour[b] (3)	Difference between Constant Percent and Constant Dollar Profit Margin[c] (4)
	Quarterly Calculated Increments to Price Change			
1971II	0.8	0.2	0.1	0.1
III	0.6	0.1	0.5	0.1
IV	0.1	−0.1	−0.1	0.0
1972I	0.9	0.5	0.7	0.1
II	0.2	0.1	0.1	0.0
III	0.4	0.2	0.2	0.0
IV	0.6	0.5	0.2	0.1
1973I	0.7	0.0	0.8	0.1
II	1.1	−0.2	−0.4	0.1
III	1.1	−0.3	−0.4	0.1
IV	1.8	−0.3	−1.0	0.2
1974I	2.7	−0.7	−1.5	0.3
II	3.0	0.2	−0.3	0.3

Cumulative Period[d]	Cumulative Calculated Increments to Price Change			
1971IV	1.4	0.2	0.5	0.2
1972IV	3.7	1.5	1.7	0.4
1973IV	8.7	0.8	0.6	0.9
1974II	15.0	0.3	−1.2	1.5

SOURCE: Same as for Table 7.
[a] Calculations based on column 3, Table 6.
[b] Calculations based on column 3, Table 7.
[c] Calculations based on column 4, Table 6.
[d] Quarterly changes may not sum to cumulative totals because of rounding, and cumulative totals for columns 2 and 4 may differ in addition because they are cumulated on the basis of the percent margin prevailing in the first quarter of 1971.

Profit Margin Limitations

Prices could be increased under the stabilization regulations only if an increase in allowable costs could be demonstrated. While cost increases were a necessary condition for price increases, they were not a sufficient condition since limitations on profit margins were imposed in some form throughout the program. Realized profit margins as a percentage of sales were limited to levels achieved during a base period. The limitation was applied to individual firms and computed for the consolidated accounts of the parent firm instead of separately by divisions, profit centers, or other accounting entities. Base-period limits for Phase II were established by computing the average profit margin for the best two of the three fiscal years completed immediately before August 15, 1971, with the inclusion of more recently completed fiscal years permitted after Phase III began in 1973.

Profit margin positions when the stabilization program began and developments during the course of the program can be illustrated in general terms by Federal Trade Commission data for manufacturing corporations (Table 9). These data show that profit margins in the third quarter of 1971, when the stabilization program began, were on average considerably below the apparent base-period limits. For example, profit margins for all manufacturing averaged 8.6 percent in 1968 and 1969 compared to 6.9 percent in the third quarter of 1971 and 7.0 percent for the year. Relative to base-period limits, profit margins were then apparently highest for food and kindred products and tobacco manufacturers, with considerable room for expansion toward base-period limits in most other sectors.

During 1972, manufacturing profit margins rose from 7.1 to 7.7 percent, remaining on average well below base-period limits. Sectors in which margins rose most markedly toward the limits included printing and publishing, rubber and plastics products, and lumber. Profit margins exceeding base-period limits were reported during 1972 mainly by firms specializing in lumber production, although this is not apparent in the aggregate data.

Profit margins on average moved close to base-period levels in 1973, particularly in nondurable goods manufacturing. Early in the year, margins rose markedly in the lumber sector (and later in the year, in several other sectors) to levels apparently above base-period limits. These profit data are not adjusted for inventory profits, in contrast to the data from the national income accounts discussed in the preceding section. In their treatment of inventory profits these profit data are consistent with the computational pro-

TABLE 9 Relation of Profits before Taxes to Sales of All Manufacturing Corporations, by Industry Group, 1968–1974 (percent)

Year or Quarter	All Manufacturing Corporations	Total Nondurable	Nondurable Goods									
			Food and Kindred Products	Tobacco Manufactures	Textile Mill Products	Paper and Allied Products	Printing and Publishing	Chemicals and Allied Products	Industrial Chemicals and Synthetics	Drugs	Petroleum and Coal Products	Rubber and Miscellaneous Plastic Products
1968	8.8	8.4	4.9	11.4	6.1	8.2	7.8	12.5	11.2	18.6	12.0	8.3
1969	8.4	7.9	4.9	10.7	5.7	8.1	9.0	12.1	10.7	18.5	11.7	7.0
1970	6.8	7.3	4.8	11.2	4.1	5.7	8.0	10.7	8.5	17.2	11.0	5.1
1971	7.0	7.2	4.9	11.5	4.6	4.3	7.9	10.8	8.5	17.0	9.5	6.6
1972	7.5	7.2	4.6	11.0	4.8	6.8	8.7	11.2	9.3	17.8	8.5	7.4
1973	8.2	8.2	4.8	11.6	5.3	9.4	8.7	12.3	11.7	18.6	11.1	7.2
1971 III	6.9	7.5	5.2	12.1	4.7	4.5	8.0	11.1	8.5	17.4	10.2	6.5
IV	6.9	6.7	4.6	11.2	5.9	3.2	9.0	10.0	6.5	17.5	8.1	6.8
1972 I	7.1	6.9	4.4	11.0	4.6	5.4	6.3	11.6	9.6	19.0	8.3	7.3
II	7.8	7.1	4.8	11.5	4.6	7.6	8.9	11.1	10.3	18.1	7.1	8.0
III	7.2	7.3	4.7	11.0	4.8	6.5	9.1	11.5	9.0	19.1	8.7	6.9
IV	7.7	7.5	4.6	10.5	5.0	7.5	10.2	10.9	8.5	16.9	9.7	7.3
1973 I	7.9	7.2	4.4	10.3	5.2	8.0	7.5	12.2	11.3	18.6	8.4	6.9
II	8.7	7.9	4.7	10.6	6.0	10.4	8.3	12.3	12.6	17.5	9.6	8.2
III	7.7	7.8	4.8	10.7	5.1	9.8	9.1	12.1	10.9	18.8	10.5	5.8
IV	8.7	9.6	5.2	15.7	4.8	9.2	9.8	12.8	11.9	20.0	16.6	7.7
1974 I	8.9	10.6	4.5	15.2	5.8	10.9	7.3	14.5	14.1	21.0	16.6	7.9
II	9.6	11.1	4.6	18.1	6.5	13.4	9.7	15.6	16.5	20.8	14.5	9.8
Base period limit[a]	8.6	8.2	4.9	11.3	5.9	8.2	8.5	12.3	11.0	18.6	11.8	7.6

TABLE 9 (concluded)

Year or Quarter	Total Durable	Durable Goods												
		Trans-portation Equip-ment	Motor Vehicles and Equip-ment	Aircraft and Parts	Elec-trical Ma-chinery, Equip-ment, and Supplies	Ma-chinery (excl. Elec-trical)	Fabri-cated Metal Products	Primary Metal Indus-tries	Primary Iron and Steel Indus-tries	Primary Non-ferrous Metal Indus-tries	Stone, Clay, and Glass Products	Lumber	Instru-ments and Related Products	Misc. Mfg. (incl. Ord-nance)
1968	9.1	9.1	10.9	6.0	8.1	10.7	7.7	8.4	7.5	9.7	9.3	8.4	15.4	7.7
1969	8.6	7.8	10.1	5.7	7.6	10.8	7.2	8.5	7.0	10.4	8.7	7.9	15.1	7.2
1970	6.3	3.8	4.0	3.5	6.1	9.2	5.8	5.9	3.6	8.9	6.6	4.4	13.7	6.3
1971	6.9	7.1	8.7	3.2	6.4	8.3	5.7	4.3	4.1	4.7	7.7	7.1	13.3	5.9
1972	7.7	7.6	9.1	4.4	7.2	9.3	6.5	5.2	5.0	5.6	8.0	8.0	14.5	6.3
1973	8.3	7.3	8.6	4.9	7.9	10.4	7.4	7.3	6.8	8.0	8.3	10.0	15.4	6.3
1971 III	6.3	4.7	4.8	4.0	6.6	8.0	6.3	0.8	0.2	1.7	9.3	7.9	14.7	7.1
IV	7.0	7.7	9.8	2.6	6.7	8.8	4.5	3.1	3.0	3.4	6.9	6.7	13.6	4.6
1972 I	7.3	8.3	10.4	3.9	6.4	8.8	5.9	4.6	4.0	5.7	5.6	7.0	13.0	5.2
II	8.6	9.4	11.2	5.1	7.1	9.7	7.2	6.2	5.9	6.8	9.6	9.1	14.9	6.7
III	7.1	4.1	4.0	4.3	7.1	9.5	6.9	4.2	4.0	4.6	9.5	9.1	15.5	6.3
IV	7.8	8.0	9.7	4.2	8.0	9.1	6.0	5.7	5.9	5.3	7.0	6.7	14.5	6.9
1973 I	8.5	9.5	11.3	4.9	7.6	10.0	6.9	6.2	5.9	6.8	6.2	9.9	14.4	4.6
II	9.3	9.4	11.2	5.5	7.8	10.6	7.9	7.6	7.3	8.1	9.4	12.8	15.5	6.9
III	7.6	3.8	3.8	4.8	7.8	10.0	7.3	6.8	6.7	7.2	9.3	10.2	16.0	6.6
IV	7.8	5.9	6.8	4.4	8.6	10.9	7.2	8.3	7.4	9.9	7.9	7.2	15.7	6.8
1974 I	7.5	4.6	4.2	5.6	7.5	10.2	7.4	9.1	7.6	11.3	5.7	–	15.9	7.6
II	8.5	5.9	5.7	5.7	7.4	11.1	9.4	12.1	11.4	13.2	9.4	–	15.3	8.1
Base period limit[a]	8.8	8.5	10.5	5.8	7.8	10.8	7.4	8.4	7.2	10.0	9.0	8.2	15.2	7.4

SOURCE: Federal Trade Commission, *Quarterly Financial Reports for Manufacturing Corporations, 1968–1974.*

[a] Estimated for each industry by computing the average percent profit margin for the two years in which profit margins were highest from calendar years 1968 through 1970.

cedures in the stabilization regulations. There are several reasons, however, why these aggregate data on average profit margins for industries provide only a general indication of the degree to which realized profit margins for individual firms were consistent with the requirements for compliance with the stabilization regulations.

Comparisons of base-period profit margin limits for individual firms with their realized profit margins could be significantly different from comparisons of industry averages. Individual firms could choose their most favorable two years, and, in addition, many firms are on a fiscal- rather than a calendar-year basis. Thus, the actual difference between realized profit margins and base-period limits may have been wider than would be suggested by computations based on industry-sector averages for two calendar years. On the other hand, the variability of profit margins for individual firms is much larger than for the averages, and realized profit margins may exceed base-period limits for some firms even though this is not reflected in an industry average.

The data on sales and profits underlying published industry profit margins are also more inclusive than the data specified in the stabilization regulations. For example, subsidiaries based abroad and mainly engaged in foreign operations were excluded from profit margin computations under the stabilization regulations, and the dollar devaluations in 1971 and 1973 significantly increased reported profits for foreign subsidiaries of international corporations. Moreover, farming, life insurance, and public utilities operations were excluded if they were separate accounting entities. In general, the broad definition of firms applied under the stabilization regulations also obscures comparisons with data based on different definitions.

Realized profit margins could, in addition, under certain conditions exceed base-period profit margin limits without violating the stabilization regulations. During Phase II, profit margin limitations were not applied to firms that raised no prices above base-period levels (prices charged in the thirty days before August 15, 1971, or on May 25, 1970). During Phase III, profit margin limits were not applied unless the firm increased prices by at least an average of 1.5 percent above levels authorized on January 10, 1973, and during Phase IV they were not applied to firms that had not increased prices above levels legally prevailing during the mid-1973 freeze. A significant fraction of firms did not raise their prices above base-period levels during 1972, and in late 1973 sales and profits attributable to exempt prices in areas such as exports, lumber, and other sectors exempted later could be excluded from profit margin computations. Firms that had increased prices, but later reduced them sufficiently to compensate for the revenue received from these price increases, were also relieved of profit margin limits. In addition, relief from profit margin limitations or adjustments to base-period limits were often granted through the exceptions process. Relief of this sort reflected well-documented special circumstances experienced by a firm, for example, a major change in its financial structure. The special rules applicable to firms experiencing losses or very low profits could also raise average profit margins without placing the firms at the low-profit end of the distribution in violation of the regulations. It may be concluded that the published aggregate profit margin data cannot be easily translated into evidence on the extent of compliance with the profit margin limits under the stabilization rules.

Beginning in the second quarter of 1972, orders to reduce prices and (when this was possible) to make refunds were issued to firms whose profit margins exceeded base-period levels. Occasionally, there were denials of requests for price increases from firms approaching base-period limits, with the most noteworthy cases being those for two major auto companies in late 1972. By the end of 1972, only a small number of firms showed profit margins in excess of base-period limits, and they were heavily concentrated in the lumber and construction sectors. In construction, the immediate linkage between profit margins and pricing was weak, and special procedures were eventually developed for that sector. In other sectors, remedial actions included refunds where feasible, price reductions where markets would not be unduly disrupted, or payments to the Treasury to reflect profit margin overages. In many instances, the presence of special circumstances that had not been dealt with through the exceptions process led to negotiation of compromise settlements of profit margin overage problems.

The marked acceleration of price increases in early 1973 and the large increases in reported profits for the first quarter of 1973 led many observers to conclude that there was widespread noncompliance with cost-justification and profit margin regulations.[41] Yet reports on prices, costs, and profits for the first part of the year showed few instances of probable violation of the stabilization regulations.[42] In addition, since cumulative profit margins in these reports in most instances did not reflect results for a completed fiscal year, many of the apparent profit margin overages may have been attributable to seasonal factors.

Profit margin limits were applied throughout the remainder of the program, with remedies prescribed when base-period limits were exceeded and denial of requests for price increases when firms were approaching base-period limits. However, the sector-by-sector decontrol process during Phase IV complicated the application of profit margin limits, because exempted activities could be excluded from profit margin computations. Often only crude adjustments could be made by firms with production operations in several sectors, some of which were exempted, and application of profit margin comparisons became increasingly arbitrary and complicated during the decontrol process.

V. CONTROLS AND EFFICIENCY

The concept of efficiency is central to economics, and the general principle that competitively determined prices and wages are consistent with efficient resource usage is well known. Price and wage controls can give rise to inefficient resource use, because suppression of price and wage levels also usually influences interrelationships between them. Controls can introduce inefficient business practices, and lead to patterns of resource use that add to inefficiency arising from existing market imperfections. Moreover, their influence is extended over a major share of the economy. The magnitude of the costs that may be imposed by controls is not easily estimated, but constantly changing conditions in the marketplace make it virtually impossible to manage a system of stringent controls without creating distortions in resource use. Particular instances of market disruptions, misalignment of prices, wasteful business practices, or inequitable wage relationships resulting from controls have usually become evident, but public reaction to these costs builds slowly because most of the costs are hidden and not easily quantified.

Unfortunately, most of the evidence on distortions resulting from controls is fragmentary and anecdotal and does not lend itself to quantification of the resultant costs. Yet the symptoms of inefficiency were sufficiently pervasive and their potential cost sufficiently important to merit a brief general discussion of the problem in addition to that contained in the preceding sections.

Symptoms of Inefficiency

During the first year of controls, there was some evidence that they were interfering with the price adjustments necessary to maintain efficiency and avoid shortages, but the evidence was limited mostly to the lumber sector and to a small number of situations in which pricing to reflect increases in current production costs led either to dispersion in prices for similar products or to prices too low to satisfy current demand.[43] The stabilization regulations were based on the idea that price adjustments should be allowed to reflect cost increases, with shifts in demand in most instances expected to be accommodated through changes in output. It became apparent in the early months of the program, however, that situations would arise in which application of the regulations would forestall some price increases that were necessary to maintain efficiency.[44]

In markets with relatively inelastic supply, short-term demand changes that were large relative to short-term cost increases created one class of problems under cost pass-through regulations. Pricing of radio and television advertising, for example, had traditionally reflected shifts in audience ratings of shows in addition to more stable factors, and these demand-related changes were not accompanied by short-term cost changes. Since export prices were exempt from controls, demand increases for internationally traded products created incentives to export and opportunities to earn windfall profits for traders buying at controlled domestic prices and exporting at higher world prices.

Differences among industries and among the structures of firms within industries sometimes complicated the application of cost pass-through regulations. In the case of sugar, some fruits and vegetables, and, later, lumber, vertically integrated firms often experienced no short-term cost increases that could be used to justify higher prices, while other firms purchasing inputs such as raw agricultural products and standing timber in exempt markets were bidding up raw materials input costs and raising prices proportionately. The presence of large inventories in some cases also weakened the linkage between cost increases and current demand conditions. In some sectors in which prices of major inputs were not exempt, short-term demand increases created an incentive for firms to increase current operating costs (such as wages), both to provide the basis for price increases and to avoid increasing profits above base-period levels. The importance of this indirect influence on wages in the economy is uncertain, but at least one case in which a wage adjustment was apparently motivated mainly by profit margin considerations was brought to the attention of the Cost of Living Council in 1973.[45]

The problem of prices on world markets rising above prices permitted under domestic controls, thus stimulating increased exports, first appeared for cattle hides during the ninety-day freeze. Similar conditions developed when world prices moved above domestic prices for several products (such as lumber, zinc, and molasses) during 1972. While rising prices on world markets posed few difficulties for domestic price controls during 1972, the surge in dollar prices of most commodities traded in international markets during 1973 (including the prices of metals, petrochemicals, and fertilizer) posed problems for any system of domestic controls.

Extension of controls to raw agricultural commodities would have created similar problems in that sector.[46] The stringent limits on domestic prices after the June 1973 freeze, with world prices continuing to rise, threatened diversion of domestically produced supplies to export markets. Exemption from domestic controls was granted for commodities such as copper scrap and a number of other nonferrous metals. Prices of fertilizer and petrochemical products were also exempted so as to reduce incentives for trade diversion, and price adjustments to levels above those generally permitted under the standards were granted for other commodities such as copper and aluminum.[47]

When prices of more and more commodities were held below market clearing levels in late 1973, symptoms of inefficiency became increasingly widespread and diverse. Curtailment of domestic supply was sometimes threatened by increased exports, reduced production to avoid losses, and failure to expand production through use of marginal production capacity. Lack of availability and wide differences in prices of materials inputs complicated production planning and threatened to disrupt production schedules. Distribution and purchasing operations were complicated by multiple prices and instances of bartering in order to reduce costs or obtain scarce materials, and black markets were frequently reported.[48] Such distortions were instrumental in shaping public attitudes toward decontrol.

Cost Pass-Through and Product Mix

Limiting price increases to cost increases, instead of controlling overall processing margins with complete flexibility in relative prices, in some circumstances exacerbated shortages for certain products. For industries operating at capacity levels, incentives to shift the mix of products were created under regulations that linked price increases to cost increases, without permitting increases in some prices to offset reductions in others. These incentives were created even though full pass-through of cost increases was permitted, and price increases to reflect these cost increases could be spread over a broad range of product lines. For cyclical reasons and because of changes in import competition or other factors, profitability of individual product lines may diverge from that of other product lines produced by the same firm. When conditions changed and demand was sufficiently strong to support expanded production of relatively more profitable lines, incentives were created for shifting production toward high-margin product lines and for raising prices for those product lines to the extent justified by overall cost increases.

During 1973, when demand levels pressed strongly on available production capacity, there were several industries in which shortages became severe for product lines that had previously been produced at low profit margins. Some users were forced to switch to higher-quality paper when lower-quality paper became unavailable.[49] Some of the most marked steel shortages were in product lines such as concrete reinforcing bars, mining roof bolts, and baling wire, which had earlier been subject to strong import competition. A wide range of petrochemical inputs and products produced by petroleum refiners were in extremely short supply, after a period in which prices in the chemical industry had been cyclically depressed. The shortages of petrochemical feedstocks were particularly noteworthy, because allocation of a disproportionate share of cost increases to these products was encouraged by the regulations that delayed price increases for gasoline, diesel fuel, and home heating oil.

hortages

Reports of shortages were pervasive in late 1973, and the reports often attributed shortages to the price controls.[50] Shortages are the inevitable counterpart of controls that keep prices below market clearing levels in a simple, static, analytical framework, and the existence of shortages is prima facie evidence that controls are binding. Shortages have sometimes emerged, however, in strong cyclical expansions, and phenomena such as lengthening order backlogs, slower delivery schedules, and temporary unavailability of products or materials have been quite common. Thus, in an environment with rapidly changing supply conditions and strong cyclical demand, shortages and related phenomena may be partially attributable to concern with customer-supplier relationships expressed through maintenance of relative stability in materials availability and prices.

Nevertheless, controls can exacerbate shortages by influencing demand and available supply. If controls are generally thought to be holding prices below market levels, the risk of a decline in prices of materials purchased as inputs and temporarily held in inventory is reduced, and the potential for implicit capital gains if prices are decontrolled or price increases are granted is enhanced. In addition, controls that effectively constrain prices increase the probability that essential materials or products may not be available when they are needed. This encourages users to purchase materials before they are needed and hold them temporarily in inventory as a hedge against possible disruption of production schedules. Legal limits on prices foreclose the possibility of bidding up prices to obtain essential materials when those materials are immediately necessary to maintain production schedules or to avoid delays.

If purchasing policies were significantly influenced by controls in this manner, these policies would have raised demand above normal current production requirements for products and materials in which the difference between price limits and market prices was largest and the potential for shortages greatest. A tendency for inventory buildup would be expected and it might be reflected in somewhat earlier purchases of supplies and materials by final users instead of larger inventories for manufacturers and distributors.

The pattern of inventory accumulation for all manufacturers and distributors indicates that firms were generally attempting to increase inventories in late 1973 and early 1974, even though serious shortages and prices significantly below market levels were concentrated in a limited range of basic materials and products. There were widespread reports of particular instances in which advance material purchases were made and purchasing practices were tailored to shortage conditions. There were reports from construction firms of advance delivery of concrete reinforcing bars to avoid costly delays in projects should these materials not be available on schedule.[51] In the case of petroleum products, there were reports of a buildup of propane inventories and gasoline storage, and gasoline stocks rose toward the end of each month in anticipation of the granting of new price increases.[52] There were also reports of purchases of certain scarce materials for use in bartering for other materials in short supply because prices were kept below market levels.

In 1973, when price ceilings were made applicable to individual firms instead of industry-wide, incentives may have increased for acquiring inventories in excess of immediate production needs. Firms having established relations with suppliers constrained by low price ceilings had a strong incentive to take delivery of all supplies that they were allocated because prices from alternative sources of supply were often higher and further price increases were being granted periodically. In the fall of 1973, for example, price ceilings for domestic copper producers were 60 cents per pound. Moreover, fabricated copper products could be priced on the basis of costs ranging from 60 cents per pound for domestically produced copper or 77 cents per pound for copper scrap to over $1.00 per pound for spot market purchases of imported copper. Similar conditions prevailed for other nonferrous metals such as zinc, lead, and aluminum as well as for a variety of steel and petrochemical products.[53]

It is extremely difficult to distinguish between the influence of controls and the influence of cyclical factors on the widespread incidence of shortages in 1973. The changes in market conditions resulting from shifts in supply or demand were the underlying forces creating pressures for either higher prices or shortages. It is possible that the controls themselves made an independent contribution to the problem by raising demand for inventories, reducing domestic supply through diversion to export markets, and weakening price incentives to expand production. Broad indicators such as unfilled orders and the ratio of unfilled orders to shipments were cyclically strong, but they may themselves have been influenced by the existence of controls. While the unusual pervasiveness of shortages in 1973 is strong evidence that controls contributed to their severity, the controls may in additon have made shortages more visible by providing a focal point for public attention.[54]

Business Practices

There are various ways in which the controls may have altered business practices and decisions in addition to their direct influence on prices. It is difficult to judge the importance of these effects either for their short-term costs or for their longer-term influence. Some effects, such as changes in accounting practices to obtain greater flexibility for price increases or changes in production methods or product mix, mainly involve short-term costs. The costs of other changes, such as those involved in the consequences of changes in investment decisions or pricing practices and market structure, may become evident only after a period of several years.

Straightforward methods can be used to estimate costs imposed by changes in cost allocation or accounting procedures designed to avoid the full impact of controls regulations or that resulted from the need to develop specific information for review by stabilization authorities and supporting data for compliance auditing. Business practices that led to inefficient real resource use in production and distribution imposed costs that are more difficult to measure. Purchasing policies designed to hedge against shortages, or disruption of smooth production flows when shortages were realized, imposed costs that are more obvious but not necessarily more important than the costs of inefficient patterns of input use. The emergence of bartering arrangements as a substitute for transactions in the marketplace contributed to excessively large inventories, complicated marketing by increasing information and search costs necessary to assure timely delivery at the lowest available prices, and led to less efficient distribution than could be expected under uniform prices in the marketplace.

An example from ferrous scrap markets illustrates how controls can reduce efficiency. Steel scrap generated as a by-product of production operations for large firms was subject to price controls, but scrap collected from obsolete or worn-out items was not. Covering all of the junk dealers in the country was impractical, and higher prices in that market could stimulate increased scrap collection. Inefficiency in scrap distribution occurred when scrap subject to controls was sold through bartering arrangements in exchange for scarce items that it was used to produce, such as concrete reinforcement bars. In products produced from steel scrap, distribution inefficiencies occurred in response to wide differences in prices. These prices reflected differences in production costs that depended on the source and cost of the scrap input as well as on the fraction of scrap used in furnaces. Another reported business practice, for which costs imposed are more easily ascertainable, was transshipment of scrap from an industrial plant at one location to steelmaking facilities owned by the same company at another location to avoid sale of the scrap at controlled prices at one market location and purchases of a similar quantity at uncontrolled prices at another.[55]

It was frequently alleged that controls were adversely affecting production levels, particularly when profit margin limits were an effective constraint. Evidence based on production levels attained is ambiguous because the absolute limits on levels of production capability are usually impossible to define precisely for any firm or industry. In addition, firms operate in a dynamic and changing environment in which they must make decisions regarding small adjustments in the production process, expansion of some portion of production operations, or cutbacks in output by scaling down less efficient operations or closing down obsolescent plants. Over time, marginal changes in current production through such decisions could have a significant offsetting influence on price movements. Thus, it is possible that delays in price adjustments and price ceilings could attenuate production responses that would otherwise help to smooth adjustments in prices to changes in demand.

This discussion of controls and their costs can be summarized by brief consideration of two points. The first point is that the short-run costs of controls—at least as they were administered during the Economic Stabilization Program—were apparently not enormous. Evidence of adverse effects during the period of controls is generally not readily apparent in broad measures of production or other indicators either for individual industries or for the overall economy. Thus, in spite of widespread reports of shortages, inefficient business practices, and misallocation of resources, normal measures of economic activity for most sectors did not show pronounced adverse effects that could be directly traced to controls. The second point is that the costs of controls are nonetheless real, and they are not adequately captured by reference only to normal measures of production and economic activity. Resources are used to administer controls, with costs borne both by the government and the private sector. Symptoms of inefficiency that can obviously be traced to controls impose additional real costs, even though these costs are difficult to quantify. In addition, costs of a more subtle type are obscured by normal measures of economic activity because the prices that are used in computing the value of economic output can be less closely identified with the value placed by society on measures of economic output as prices diverge more and more from market values.

I. CONCLUDING DISCUSSION

Whatever direct impact the controls regulations had on wages and prices, controls also influenced the context in which economic policy was made. To the extent that the controls temporarily suppressed price and wage increases, the full influence of market forces became evident to policymakers and the private sector only after some delay. To the extent that market pressures in specific sectors led to rapid price increases or dislocations under the controls, high-level attention was focused on possible policy changes that could influence supply or demand to relieve the pressures placed on controls by a market environment that was forcing prices up. Thus, the controls at times facilitated the development of specific policies that could help to reduce market pressures by shifting supply or demand—policies that were usually more complex but more promising than a simple limitation of short-run price or wage increases. Issues raised by this broad economic role of controls may be of more lasting importance than quantification of their direct effects on prices and wages in any period.

Controls and Demand Management

The possibility that the existence of a program of wage and price controls may have influenced the expansiveness of monetary and fiscal policy is of particular importance for evaluating the full influence of controls on inflation.[56] Indeed, one of the thorniest issues in any attempt to assess the quantitative effects of controls is the issue of what components of economic policy should be treated as independent of controls. It is possible, for example, that controls were viewed as providing some short-run insurance against inflation, thereby shifting the balance toward accepting the risks of more expansionary policies than would have been planned in their absence. Controls may also have suppressed inflation sufficiently to mask for a time inflationary pressures building up in the economy, and consequently they may have delayed a recognition by policymakers that less expansionary policies were called for.

The effect that controls may have had on macroeconomic policy can be explored by examining some evidence concerning the period 1971–1974. Even though no definitive conclusions can be drawn from them, official statements suggest that controls were regarded as providing a measure of protection against inflation, thereby permitting a more expansionary pattern of policies than would otherwise have been considered prudent.[57] The imposition of controls was also accompanied by requests for investment tax credits and tax reductions to stimulate the economy. In addition, the most widely used explanation of the manner in which controls were expected to help reduce inflation was that a major portion of the continuing inflation in 1971 could be attributed to the lingering effects of past inflation. The price and wage projections from standard models made it difficult to account for the rate at which inflation was occurring prior to the control period on the basis of demand conditions prevailing before controls were imposed. The controls were viewed as reducing expectations of inflation by providing a period of lower inflation more consistent with the degree of slack in labor and product markets. Yet the risks of placing too much reliance on controls and moving toward overly expansive policies were also explicitly recognized and cautioned against.[58]

The limits that were placed on prices under controls, along with incentives to keep prices down voluntarily (either out of a spirit of cooperation or to avoid confrontation and possible audit for violations), inhibited market testing. Market signals were muted, and information on accumulating market pressures was received only after delays which added new uncertainty to government policy planning. The importance of this influence of controls during 1971–1974 is uncertain, but it may have delayed a turn toward more restrictive demand management policies.

Both monetary and fiscal policies were expansionary during the early phases of controls. These policies were generally viewed as appropriate for stimulating higher output and employment levels, particularly in the early stages of the recovery when fiscal policy was most expansionary. Federal deficits averaged $19 billion in 1971 and 1972, although the full-employment deficit averaged only $5 billion, and small surpluses were achieved on both bases in 1973.[59] The net expansionary effect on the budget of tax and expenditure changes introduced with the New Economic Policy was estimated as $1.1 billion for fiscal year 1972,[60] a small impact compared to actual deficits at that time. Monetary policy remained expansionary during almost the entire period; the money supply increased at an average rate of about 7 percent, but the most rapid expansion took place in the latter part of 1972. Although in retrospect these policies were overly expansionary, particularly in the latter part of the period, the mistake appears to have resulted mainly from the deficiencies of economic forecasts rather than from policies that differed from those on which the forecasts were based. The upsurge in inflation that began in 1973 was not foreseen by professional forecasters.[61]

ontrols and Other Stabilization Policy Initiatives

The introduction of controls in the U.S. economy, and intermittently of incomes policies of various kinds in other countries, is less a tribute to their demonstrated durability and effectiveness than to the lack of constructive alternatives for responding to public pressures to "do something" that would have a visible and direct effect on inflation. It is appropriate that these pressures should converge on the government in democratic societies, and the government should give high priority to actions and policies that can help to contain inflation. Whether the imposition of generalized wage and price controls is the most constructive response in most instances, however, is open to question. It would be desirable to place more emphasis on the development of imaginative policies that would help to identify and attack the real economic problems of our society. Policy approaches that could help to increase supply, reduce costs, facilitate adjustment, or improve productivity would work more slowly and indirectly to reduce inflation, but such policies would also have less potential for simultaneously imposing costs through reduced efficiency and disappointing public expectations.

The establishment of a system of wage and price controls has, however, facilitated the formation of institutional structures for bringing together representatives of labor, business, the public sector, Congress, and the executive branch, in order to identify and discuss problems and explore possible approaches from different viewpoints. Since the cooperation, support, acquiescence, and expertise of each of these groups is necessary in varying degrees to the success of the effort (particularly the cooperation of organized labor), controls provide a framework for mobilizing public interest and attitudes and promoting a serious exchange of views, statements of positions, and negotiation of compromise approaches. Among the major forums for addressing broad policy issues and individual cases where the Pay Board and advisory committees of Phase II, along with earlier exploratory meetings, the Construction Industry Stabilization Committee, and the Labor-Management Advisory Committee and tripartite committees established in the food and health sectors during phases III and IV.

While the existence of a program of wage and price controls provided the immediate impetus for identifying and bringing together spokesmen representing various interests and involving them in the process of working toward solutions, controls may not have been a necessary precondition for establishing effective structures for policy discussions and problem solving. The Construction Industry Stabilization Committee (which could draw upon authority for direct controls before broader controls were imposed) and the Food Wage and Salary Committee (which could not do this after controls for most sectors were terminated) are examples of structures developed to deal with specific problem areas. It might be possible to establish similar structures in other instances, and these might contribute to the working out of industrial relations problems and the rationalization of wage patterns without their having authority to impose mandatory controls. Structures such as labor-management advisory committees set up to play a consultative and supportive role in the formation of national economic policy have often made modest but valuable contributions. The Conference on Inflation in September 1974 represents another approach to public dialogue on problems and issues. While controls have mobilized active participation and sometimes provided support for compromises by those representing relatively narrow interests to facilitate the achievement of broader goals, cooperation and participation in the resolution of many problems might often be elicited without the spur of comprehensive price and wage controls.

During 1971–1974, the stabilization program also provided structures within the federal government for bringing together cabinet members responsive to different constituencies, a staff capability for identifying discussion policies that contributed to inflation, and a cabinet-level spokesman to focus attention on the inflationary implications of policy decisions. The main forum for internal policy review during Phase II was the Cost of Living Council itself, while the food and health policy committees were the most important forums during other phases of the program.

Controls, with their potential for market disruption, provided strong incentives to search for policy actions that could increase supply or restrain demand and thus reduce inflation. But the development of ways for the federal government to focus more attention on the inflationary consequences of government policy actions should not be dependent on controls. Controls on food prices are certainly not a necessary condition for systematic consideration of the potential impact on inflation of federal farm policy, an area in which federal government policy decisions are of major importance for production and prices. The Council on Wage and Price Stability, in some respects a successor to the Cost of Living Council, may contribute to the evolution of an internal government structure for discussion, review, and action on economic policy issues influencing inflation. The procedures for systematic budget review adopted by Congress may also contribute to improved price stability.

The resurgence of inflation in 1973 gave new impetus to a search for ways in which productivity could be improved to relieve the pressure of rising costs on controls. Stabilization committees often provided a labor-management structure for the discussion of promising approaches and served as a catalyst for their implementation.[62] The rise toward capacity production levels, particularly in early 1973 in many of the industries producing and processing basic materials, focused attention on the question of whether sufficient resources were being devoted to capital investment. Adequacy of capital investment and the contribution that additional new investment could make to improved productivity growth were two considerations that formed the background for the sectoral decontrol process during the last part of 1973 and early 1974. Adequacy of rates of return and willingness to make new investment commitments were factors considered in decontrol decisions. Securing capacity expansion commitments as controls were removed was part of an intricate process to facilitate orderly sectoral decontrol. Investment commitments provided a supporting rationale for sequential decontrol decisions, and they represented a significant effort to coordinate policies for achieving capacity expansion needs with policies for removing controls.[63]

Because the controls imposed limits and delays on price increases and profit margins, investment decisions could have been adversely affected by controls. The influence that controls actually had on business investment, however, is not clear. Several factors suggest that their effects in reducing investment were small: the perceived short-term character of the controls, the influence of longer-term price and cost prospects on many investment decisions, the initial favorable attitude of the business community toward controls, and their apparently small impact on prices during 1972, particularly for industries producing basic materials, in which capacity limitations became most apparent in 1973. Other factors, however, suggest a larger effect: the full effect of prices in signaling increased profitability of investment was reduced to the extent that some prices were held below market levels, cash flow to finance increased investment was reduced, lower profitability impeded external financing, and incremental decisions to alter production operations or keep marginal production facilities in operation may have been affected. In the administration of controls, policies regarding investment evolved from the maintenance of as neutral a policy as possible during the early stages of controls to the explicit encouragement of new investment in decontrol decisions. There was no apparent weakness in business investment during the controls period, a fact that may be attributed mainly to the "temporary" nature of the controls and to their initial favorable effect on public confidence.[64]

The flow of investment decisions in the economy plays a significant role in cyclical movements in demand. The investment tax credit introduced with the New Economic Policy was aimed at least as much toward stimulating demand as toward the need for providing increased productive capacity. Moreover, the capacity problem that emerged in 1973 was concentrated in the basic materials sector instead of being spread throughout the economy. These developments were apparently not foreseen by the firms in the industries concerned, and they were only belatedly recognized by the government. Improved forecasts of capacity needs could have helped to reduce inflation from this source as well as to smooth investment flow and its impact on aggregate demand. Better information on actual production capacity could have contributed to more informed assessments of capacity needs. Moreover, in developing projections of potential output to guide management in setting short-run demand policies, measures of industrial production capacity may be as important as measures of employment conditions. While there is little reason to assume that capacity needs for particular industries could be foreseen any more accurately by a government agency than by firms and investors in the private sector, more detailed and carefully assembled information might contribute to an improved assessment of intentions and prospects by both the government and private sectors.

Controls and the Public

When inflation becomes an issue of public concern, price increases for particular products come to be looked at mainly from the point of view of their contribution to inflation instead of their role in allocating resources in response to reduced supply or increased demand. The existence of formal controls provides a channel for responding to public and political pressures to deal with particular price increases. The temptation is strong to apply rigid controls to specific products, to set limits on the size of individual price increases, or to apply tight rules for sectors in which increased stringency can make no contribution to the real problem. For example, the policy response to the fact that lumber prices were rising more rapidly than other prices in 1972 was to apply more stringent controls, when decontrol might have made a greater contribution toward the underlying problem of supply. Restraining prices in sectors where demand pressures could not be accommodated through short-term supply increases was generally inconsistent with the broad approach of Phase II, but it was as awkward politically to exempt lumber prices then as it was easy to exempt them in 1973 when lumber prices were falling.

The retention of mandatory controls on food prices for Phase III provides an example of control policy oriented more toward the presumed adverse political reaction to voluntary, self-administered controls on products whose prices were expected to rise significantly than toward the economic contribution that continued mandatory controls on such prices could be expected to make. The public impact of retention of mandatory controls on food prices was apparently small because the public was not persuaded by statements explaining how the surge in food prices could not be attributed to the shift to Phase III because mandatory controls on food prices were being continued. Until ceiling prices were imposed for meat, the continuing mandatory controls on food prices were structured to permit pass-through of costs, and they had little disruptive effect on markets because they permitted large price increases. The meat ceilings were addressed in part to another goal—preservation of wage-cost stability—and their influence on wage trends should be weighed against whatever costs they imposed on the economy. Continued mandatory controls on food prices may also have assisted the government in managing its internal policy decisions to increase supply. They may also have increased the acceptability of these policy changes to some segments of the food industry.

The shift in public attitudes reflected by congressional debate and action between the first half of 1973 and the last half of 1973 through early 1974 leads one to ask whether the political process will permit implementation of controls in a manner intended to avoid distortions and inefficiency in the economy.[65] A significant shift in public attitudes toward the merit of stringent controls did not occur until after the graphic illustrations of market disruptions and adverse effects on supply that occurred during the freeze beginning in June 1973. These demonstrations of the futility of stringent controls under the conditions prevailing then and the shortages that emerged later in the year apparently led to increased recognition that stringent controls could be counterproductive.

Limitations of Controls

One of the most fundamental but often misunderstood features of controls is the limited potential they have for contributing to lower inflation, that is, lower inflation than would have occurred in their absence and without the adverse side effects that most of their proponents would prefer to avoid. Under emergency conditions (such as a major war effort) the scale of the diversion of resources that must be accomplished is so large that major strains are inevitable, and the inefficiency and inequity of controls and rationing may be more tolerable than other methods of securing the necessary adjustments. The goals of peacetime incomes policies in Western industrial societies, however, have been much more limited than containment of the inflationary effects of wartime resource diversion. Direct controls on prices and wages to effect the goals of incomes policies have usually been viewed as a supplement to reliance on pricing in the marketplace, although admittedly in some economies they have been viewed as an essential supplement. Draconian systems of controls have generally been avoided, except for short periods, both because their effects are not tolerated for long by the major participants in the economy and because the costs they impose on the economy exceed any benefits that might be achieved through lower inflation.

The manner in which controls are expected to affect the process of inflation is usually not carefully articulated in discussions of the possible contribution of incomes policies. In some instances reference is made to market power and to a range of discretion that may exist in establishing administered prices or negotiating wage increases for large economic units.[66] Of course, the existing structure of markets falls short of fully competitive conditions and results in price and wage relationships that depart from those that would prevail under such conditions. If controls are aimed primarily at offsetting these departures from fully competitive price and wage relationships, their limited influence over inflation and the strains they would be confronted with should be viewed in perspective.

Aiming controls toward offsetting noncompetitive wage-price relationships by squeezing profit margins of firms exercising market power would compel explicit attention to the question of whether rates of return were adequate to support investment and maintenance of production capacity in the sectors affected. A one-time reduction in prices and rates of return of this kind would, of course, make no continuing contribution to reduced inflation.

Similarly, a policy aimed at reducing relative wages in some of the more highly organized high-wage sectors of the economy could be maintained only until the influence on relative wages of labor market power was offset, and there would be no further continuing influence on the rate of inflation. Even if a realignment of relative wage positions could be achieved by use of controls, the forces that generated the prevailing patterns are undoubtedly strong and would pose a continuing threat of labor strife to re-establish the previous wage differentials.

Except for very short periods, the impact on prices of restricting the pass-through of increased costs and squeezing corporate profits is much smaller than seems to be generally recognized. Between the beginning of 1971 and the end of 1973, the cumulative rise in prices attributable to inflation within the corporate nonfinancial sector was 8.7 percent. If profit margins had been held to their low cyclical position at the beginning of the period, the rise in prices would have been reduced by less than one percentage point.

Incomes policies could also be developed that are not oriented toward restructuring broad relative price or wage relationships. These policies could be directed toward a roughly parallel reduction in inflation across all sectors. The controls of 1971–1974, for example, were initially designed to limit price adjustments throughout the economy to the magnitude of short-term cost increases and to influence the size of cost increases primarily by establishing a standard to reduce the size of wage increases. This was viewed as an approach that would help achieve an actual reduction in inflation during a period in which generalized excess demand was not an immediate threat. Revision of expectations and the development of contracts and practices reflecting lower rates of inflation were expected to exercise a stabilizing influence, similar in kind but opposite in direction to the influence that was attributed to the buildup of inflation in the late 1960s on price increases in 1970 and 1971.

Price developments in 1973, particularly the surge in food prices and the large increases in the prices of basic materials and petroleum later in the year, created a vastly different economic environment from what had been projected. These price developments should not necessarily be regarded as a challenge to the validity of the concepts on which the controls were initially based, nor should they necessarily be regarded as a demonstration of the inappropriateness of the limited purposes of the controls under the conditions that were projected in 1971. Instead, they serve as a reminder of the crucial importance for short-term price performance of market developments in a limited number of critical sectors, such as food and energy. More generally, they serve as a reminder of the flexibility of the price system as a mechanism for promoting rapid adjustments to change in the marketplace. The price surge that began in 1973 also indicated that, whatever contribution controls may have made during 1972, they could have little marginal influence under the conditions that emerged in 1973 unless control policy was shifted toward establishing rigid ceilings and supplementing the ceilings with subsidies and non-price-rationing mechanisms as necessary—which would of course have been a policy with an entirely different conceptual basis.

Controls may in some instances make a limited contribution toward facilitating adjustment to lower inflation when no large shifts in supply or demand are projected. Such a contribution could be made by altering public expectations of inflation, for example, if inflationary expectations are an important source of momentum in price and wage increases. Controls are vulnerable to serious failure, however, by neither containing inflation nor avoiding potentially costly inefficiency when major supply or demand shifts occur. The normal function of the market system, of course, is to generate automatic adjustments of prices and consumption to changes in market conditions—changes that are constantly occurring and usually not accurately foreseen. This raises the question of whether the costs that controls may impose before they can be gracefully terminated, or over time if continued indefinitely, may exceed the benefits of whatever limited contribution they may make.

NOTES

1. Paul W. McCracken, "The Game Plan for Economic Policy," *Proceedings of the American Statistical Association*, Business and Economics Section (New York, August 19–22, 1969), pp. 294–298.
2. See, for example, *Economic Report of the President, 1970*, February 1970, pp. 25–27.
3. The disappointing performance and the questions that it raised about reasons for the slow response are illustrated in *Economic Report of the President, 1971*, February 1971, p. 28 and p. 60ff.
4. See also Lloyd Ulman's discussion of this aspect of the politics of incomes policies in "Phase II in Context: Towards an Incomes Policy for Conservatives," in Walter Galenson, ed., *Incomes Policy: What Can We Learn From Europe?* (Ithaca, N.Y.: New York State School of Industrial and Labor Relations, Cornell University, 1973), p. 92.
5. Arnold R. Weber, *In Pursuit of Price Stability* (Washington, D.C.: Brookings, 1973), p. 6.
6. Committee for Economic Development, *Further Weapons against Inflation* (Washington, D.C., 1970).
7. Weber, *In Pursuit of Price Stability*, p. 5.
8. The most widely noted statement by Burns was the Pepperdine speech, "The

Basis for Lasting Prosperity" (address in the Pepperdine College Great Issues Series, Los Angeles, Calif., December 7, 1970).

9. *Economic Report of the President, 1971*, p. 82.

10. The extent to which the public dialogue on inflation had come to be focused on incomes policy and the defensive position in which this placed the administration is illustrated by a statement by Paul McCracken, chairman of the Council of Economic Advisers, that "we have now in effect many elements of what has come rather loosely to be called an incomes policy. We are now considering ways to make these elements more systematic and comprehensive, and to provide more adequately for their management" (Joint Economic Committee, *1971 Economic Report of the President*, 92d Cong., 1st sess., February 5, 9, 17, 18, and 19, 1971), p. 9.

11. For a detailed review of stabilization developments and policy in the period before the introduction of controls, see Phillip Cagan, Marten Estey, William Fellner, Charles E. McLure, Jr., and Thomas Gale Moore, *Economic Policy and Inflation in the Sixties* (Washington, D.C.: American Enterprise Institute, 1972). For examples of discussions raising questions about changes in the response of real output growth and inflation to aggregate demand changes, see Robert J. Gordon, "Inflation in Recession and Recovery," *Brookings Papers on Economic Activity*, no. 1 (1971): 105–158, and the following papers in *Brookings Papers on Economic Activity*, no. 2 (1971): 452–510; Charles L. Schultze, "Has the Phillips Curve Shifted? Some Additional Evidence"; William Fellner, "Phillips-type Approach or Acceleration?"; Arthur Okun, "The Mirage of Steady Inflation"; and Robert J. Gordon, "Steady Anticipated Inflation: Mirage or Oasis?"

12. For a more detailed discussion of the wage-structure developments discussed in this section, see Marvin Kosters, Kenneth Fedor, and Albert Eckstein, "Collective Bargaining and the Wage Structure," *Labor Law Journal*, August 1973, pp. 517–525.

13. This analysis is an application of wage-structure concepts to the particular inflationary conditions of the late 1960s and early 1970s. Wage-structure concepts have been applied in many studies of wage determination under collective bargaining, with concepts in this closely related body of ideas called "wage contours" (Dunlop), "orbits of coercive comparison" (Ross), "wage constellations" (Harbison), and "neighboring strategic wage rates" (Bronfenbrenner and Holzman). See Martin Bronfenbrenner and Franklyn D. Holzman, "Survey of Inflation Theory," *American Economic Review*, September 1963, p. 618.

14. In discussing labor cost, productivity, and price prospects at a Cornell University conference held in April 1972, Lloyd Ulman recognized that these conditions were favorable for an apparently successful incomes policy: "Thus, the policy of restraint could be effective or appear to be effective (if the stimulus to expansion came from other quarters), even if it did not succeed in its conventional task of restraining wage settlements directly. This could be regarded as the Indian Rope Trick Theory of incomes policy" (Ulman, "Phase II in Context," p. 91).

15. This study includes little discussion of Phase I, the wage-price freeze of 1971, which is the subject of a careful study by Weber, *In Pursuit of Price Stability*, cited earlier. Weber was director of the Cost of Living Council during the freeze and served as a public member of the Pay Board during Phase II.

A very brief and lucid sketch of the stabilization program is contained in John T. Dunlop, "Inflation and Incomes Policies: The Political Economy of

Recent U.S. Experience," *Eighth Monash Economics Lecture* (Monash University, Australia, October 1974).

16. The director of the Cost of Living Council was Donald Rumsfeld, who was also counselor to the President. The council chairman was the secretary of the treasury, initially John B. Connally and beginning in the second quarter of 1972, George P. Shultz. In addition to the Pay Board and Price Commission, the Construction Industry Stabilization Committee was continued as an operating unit and the Committee on Interest and Dividends was established. In addition, three advisory committees were created: the Health Services Industry Committee, the Committee on State and Local Government Cooperation, and the Rent Advisory Board.

17. The guideposts outlined in the 1962 *Economic Report of the President* were put forward as a contribution to public discussion, and the impact on public attitudes of widespread discussion of the concept may be illustrated by the opening sentence of the policy statement adopted by the Pay Board on November 8, 1971, establishing the general standard: "Millions of workers in the Nation are looking to the Pay Board for guidance with respect to permissible changes in wages. . . ." It may also be illustrated by the reaction of the press to the statement of the Labor-Management Advisory Committee of February 26, 1973, stating that "no single standard or wage settlement can be equally applicable at one time to all parties in an economy so large, decentralized and dynamic." See, for example, "The Magic Number Is a Blur," New York *Times*, March 4, 1973; and Edward Cowan, "Hocus-Pocus on Wage Guidelines," *Times*, March 11, 1973.

18. Later in 1972, in response to an amendment to the Economic Stabilization Act, provision was made for larger than previously permitted pay increases to reflect introduction of improvements in "qualified fringe benefits," mainly pensions. The coal settlement, the first case reviewed by the Pay Board, included a large increase in labor costs that was necessary to assure the solvency of the pension fund. It provides an example of how wage issues are complicated by circumstances unique to the situation under review.

19. For a perceptive discussion of problems in the administration of wage controls and the emphasis that was placed on a general standard with few exceptions, see Arnold R. Weber, "Making Wage Controls Work," *The Public Interest*, Winter 1973, pp. 28–40.

20. The chairman of the Pay Board was George H. Boldt, and the board was initially composed of fifteen members—five each representing the general public, business, and labor.

21. The chairman of the Price Commission, composed of seven public members, was C. Jackson Grayson.

22. See, for example, the President's address announcing the freeze, and "Background for the Post-freeze Economic Stabilization Program," Cost of Living Council, October 7, 1971.

23. See Don R. Conlan, "1973 U.S. Economic Outlook," New York *Times*, September 3, 1972, and the editorial, "Phase III Controls: Too Vague, Too Narrow, Too Weak," in *Business Week*, March 10, 1973, in which labor leaders were said to be "openly scornful of the idea that wage increases can be held to the 5.5 percent guideline of Phase II."

24. John T. Dunlop became the director of the Cost of Living Council when Phase III was introduced. He had been chairman of the Construction Industry Stabilization Committee since its inception.

25. Statement of the Labor-Management Advisory Committee, February 26, 1973; reprinted in Senate Subcommittee on Production and Stabilization of the Committee on Banking, Housing, and Urban Affairs, "Statement of Dr. John T. Dunlop," *Hearings: Oversight on Economic Stabilization*, 93d Cong., 2d sess., January 30 and 31 and February 1 and 6, 1974, p. A-67. Dunlop's entire statement was reprinted in Cost of Living Council, *Economic Stabilization Program Quarterly Report* for January 1–May 1, 1974 (1974), pp. 129–381.

26. Tripartite committees were established to review wage adjustments in the food industry and the health services sector where self-administration was not permitted.

27. See Senate Subcommittee on Production and Stabilization, "Statement of Dr. John T. Dunlop," App. A, in which a large number of inflation projections for 1973 are tabulated. The actual rise in the GNP deflator was over 5 percent while most projections were between 3 and 4 percent. The difference between the actual and projected rise in consumer prices was even larger because food prices rose much more rapidly than most other prices, and food accounts for a larger share of the consumer price index than of the GNP deflator.

28. For an expression of the administration's view of the wage outlook, see the statement of George P. Shultz, secretary of the treasury and chairman of the Cost of Living Council, in Senate Committee on Banking, Housing, and Urban Affairs, *Hearings on S. 398: A Bill to Extend and Amend the Economic Stabilization Act of 1970*, 93d Cong., 1st sess., January 29, 1973, pp. 11–12.

29. See Marvin H. Kosters, *Controls and Inflation: The Economic Stabilization Program in Retrospect* (Washington, D.C.: American Enterprise Institute for Public Policy Research, 1975), pp. 73–75, for a discussion of the influence of the June 1973 freeze on the food sector.

30. Commitments of some form were made in connection with decontrol for a total of eighteen industry sectors. See *Economic Stabilization Program Quarterly Report* for January 1, 1974–May 1, 1974, Chap. 2; and "Removing Controls: The Policy of Selective Decontrol," in Office of Economic Stabilization, *Historical Working Papers on the Economic Stabilization Program*, Part 2 (Washington, D.C.: U.S. Government Printing Office, 1974), pp. 859–948.

31. See John T. Dunlop, "Toward a Less Inflationary Society" (remarks to the Society of American Business Writers, San Francisco, May 6, 1974), in *Economic Stabilization Program Quarterly Report* for January 1, 1974–May 1, 1974, pp. 599–607, for a discussion of areas in which federal government initiatives could make a contribution toward reducing inflation.

32. See, for example, Robert J. Gordon, "The Response of Wages and Prices to the First Two Years of Controls," *Brookings Papers on Economic Activity*, no. 3 (1973):765–778; and William D. Nordhaus, "The Falling Share of Profits," *Brookings Papers on Economic Activity*, no. 1 (1974):169–208. See also Daniel J. B. Mitchell, "Phase II Wage Controls," *Industrial and Labor Relations Review*, April 1974, pp. 353–375; Michael Wachter, "Phase II, Cost-Push Inflation and Relative Wages," *American Economic Review*, June 1974, pp. 482–491; Edgar Feige and Douglas Pearce, "The Wage-Price Control Experiment—Did It Work?" *Challenge*, July-August 1973, pp. 40–44.

33. See, for example, Milton Friedman's discussion of this question in his *Newsweek* column of November 8, 1971; reprinted in Milton Friedman, *An Economist's Protest* (Glen Ridge, N.J.: Thomas Horton, 1972), pp. 20–22.

34. An estimate of the impact on construction wage increases of the Construction Industry Stabilization Committee was developed by D. Q. Mills in "Explaining

Pay Increases in Construction: 1953–1972," *Industrial Relations*, May 1974, pp. 196–201. His estimate of a 2.5 percent annual effect in reducing construction wage increases is, as he notes, sensitive to the treatment of the significant influence of a wage-structure variable incorporated into his analysis.

35. This argument is noted, for example, in Robert M. Solow, "The Case against the Case against the Guideposts," in George P. Shultz and Robert Z. Aliber, eds., *Guidelines, Informal Controls, and the Marketplace* (Chicago: University of Chicago Press, 1966), p. 45; and Edward Cowan, "U.S. Aide Outlines Tactics on Wages," New York *Times*, March 1, 1973.

36. See Kosters, *Controls and Inflation*, for a discussion of selected sectors in which large increases in prices were concentrated.

37. For an analysis of term-limit pricing agreements, see Frederic L. Laughlin, "An Evaluation of the Price Commission's Policy of Term Limit Pricing during Phase II of the Economic Stabilization Program" (Ph.D. diss., George Washington University, 1975).

38. Means (M) and standard deviations (σ) for the difference between year-to-year changes in prices and unit labor costs were as follows:

	Private Nonfarm		Nonfinancial Corporations	
M	(1950–1973)	−0.11	(1959–1973)	−0.06
σ	(1950–1973)	2.47	(1959–1973)	2.45
σ	(1971IV–1973IV)	0.69	(1971IV–1973IV)	0.82

39. The basic data for the regressions are:

	Constant	Percent Change in Real Output	Unemployment Rate	Standard Error of Estimate
Private nonfarm sector ($N = 90; R^2 = 0.57$)	−5.4	.28	0.89	1.08
Stand. error		(.03)	(0.10)	
Nonfinancial corps. ($N = 51; R^2 = 0.74$)	−6.5	.30	1.01	0.88
Stand. error		(.03)	(0.12)	

Serial correlation was high: the Durbin-Watson statistic was 0.5 for each regression.

40. It was pointed out by Joel Popkin in "Prices in 1972: An Analysis of Changes during Phase II," *Monthly Labor Review*, February 1973, pp. 16–23, that prices of finished goods seemed to have risen by more at the manufacturing level than at the retail level during 1972.

41. Lack of compliance was usually implied, though not explicitly alleged, in calls for stricter controls or a return to controls similar to those of Phase II. New York *Times* editorials calling for stricter controls appeared on average more than twice a month between February and June 1973, usually immediately after wholesale and consumer price increases were announced. The *Business Week* editorial of March 10, 1973, called for a shift from "voluntary" to mandatory rules, better enforcement, and farm product price ceilings. Gardner Ackley in "And Now Phase Four" (*Dun's*, August 1973, p. 11) said that Phase III had "allowed large numbers of firms in many leading industries to violate the profit margin limitations."

42. A preliminary review of reports covering the first four months of 1973 showed only three firms out of nearly 500 without adequate cost increases to support the increased revenues they had received from price increases. An internal analysis of eight industry sectors also showed price increases averaging significantly less than accumulated cost increases, both during the first four months of the year and by June, when the freeze was imposed. By July 12, over 900 reports on costs and profits had been received from firms with annual sales of over $250 million. According to nearly 500 reports from nonfood firms that had been reviewed, price increases averaged less than 1.5 percent above levels authorized when Phase III began for about 450 firms, and only 6 firms that had increased prices by more than 1.5 percent had profit margins exceeding base-period levels. In the food sector only 7 out of almost 150 firms showed profit margins exceeding base-period levels.

43. For example, sugar and certain other food product prices were differentially affected by technical details of the regulations, and modifications in the regulations or exceptions for particular firms were made to alleviate these situations. The influence of controls on lumber markets during Phase II is discussed in Kosters, *Controls and Inflation*, pp. 79–81.

44. During the first week of Phase II, for example, rising cattle prices, with the largest meat-packing firms subject to prenotification and a delay of up to thirty days for price increases, showed the need for special provisions for inputs with volatile prices in order to avoid market disruption and markedly different treatment of large and small firms.

45. In that case, as in many others, the matter was brought to the attention of the Cost of Living Council informally, and it was dealt with without the need for formal action.

46. An extensive discussion of the relationship between farm product prices and food prices, the influence of controls on processing and distribution margins, and the influence of meat price ceilings on prices and supplies is contained in Kosters, *Controls and Inflation*, pp. 61–78.

47. See, for example, Sidney Fish, "Controls Spur Exports of Scarce Commodities," *Journal of Commerce*, December 14, 1973, p. 1.

48. Such instances were frequently reported on the basis of surveys by the National Association of Purchasing Managers and in trade publications and newspapers. Some instances in sectors such as petrochemicals and plastics and nonferrous metals are discussed in Cost of Living Council, *Economic Stabilization Program Quarterly Report* for October 1, 1973–December 31, 1973, Chap. 2 (pp. 5–34). See also Herbert Koshetz, "Black Market in Textile Yarns Is Seen," New York *Times*, January 15, 1974, p. 49.

49. The case of paper is listed among the "proven" distortions in Senate Subcommittee on Production and Stabilization, "Statement of John T. Dunlop," App. Q, p. A-114.

50. Shortages were widely reported in trade publications and in the news media in late 1973 and early 1974. Widespread concern about the incidence and causes of shortages led to three major surveys in late 1973 by the National Association of Purchasing Managers, the National Association of Manufacturers, and the National Association of Business Economists. Long lists of materials in short supply were reported by each, and shortages and black markets were frequently attributed to the controls. See also "Managing in a Shortage Economy," *Business Week*, November 10, 1973, p. 150; and "More and More Scarcities: Who Is Feeling the Pinch," *U.S. News & World Report*, September 3, 1973, p. 15.

51. These practices were reported by construction contractors, who frequently preferred higher prices to shortages. See, for example, "Builders Warn: No Rebars, No Building," *Business Week*, December 8, 1973, p. 37; and Michael K. Drapkin, "Steel Concrete-Reinforcing Bar Shortage May Severely Hurt Nonresidential Building," *Wall Street Journal*, January 21, 1974, p. 24.

52. The behavior of inventories is emphasized in Richard B. Mancke's analysis of the influence of petroleum price controls in *Performance of the Federal Energy Office* (Washington, D.C.: American Enterprise Institute, 1975).

53. Changes in the spread between prices on domestic and world markets between January 1, 1973, and November 30, 1973, for aluminum, copper, lead, and zinc are shown in *Economic Stabilization Program Quarterly Report*, for October 1–December 31, 1973, p. 31.

54. For discussions of specific instances of shortages and inefficiency that were attributed to controls in a wide range of industry sectors, see the statements and testimony of representatives from the private sector in *Hearings: Oversight on Economic Stabilization* (see note 25, above) and Senate Subcommittee on Production and Stabilization of the Committee on Banking, Housing, and Urban Affairs, *Hearings: Economic Stabilization Act of 1974* 93d Cong., 2d sess., February 19 and 21 and March 6, 1974).

55. A brief discussion of price controls in the steel industry and a summary of actions that were taken to modify the regulations is contained in Appendix V of "Removing Controls: The Policy of Selective Decontrol," *Historical Working Papers on the Economic Stabilization Program*, August 15, 1971, to April 30, 1974, Part 2, pp. 942–947.

56. In his foreword to Kosters, *Controls and Inflation*, George P. Shultz observes that "the frequently heard argument that 'needed' fiscal and monetary stimulation will be possible if there is an 'adequate incomes policy' is proof enough of the most pernicious aspect of controls."

57. *Economic Report of the President, 1972*, p. 69, pp. 101–102.

58. *Economic Report of the President, 1973*, p. 53 and *ibid., 1972*, p. 96.

59. *Ibid., 1974*, p. 31.

60. *Ibid., 1972*, p. 71.

61. "Statement of Dr. John T. Dunlop" (see note 25, above), p. A-1.

62. Such initiatives were facilitated by the fact that the director of the Cost of Living Council at that time also served as chairman of the Productivity Commission.

63. See "Removing Controls: The Policy of Selective Decontrol" in *Historical Working Papers on the Economic Stabilization Program*, Part 2, pp. 859–948, for a detailed discussion of the decontrol process.

64. Some evidence of a possible small favorable influence on investment during the controls period is contained in Roland G. Droitsch, "The Impact of the Economic Stabilization Program on Business Fixed Investment," *Historical Working Papers on the Economic Stabilization Program*, Part 2, pp. 949–988.

65. Most of the significant legislative initiatives in Congress before mid-1973 were intended to tighten controls. After mid-1973 most were intended to relieve the pinch of controls; many bills and resolutions to end controls were introduced, and several resolutions or bills were introduced to provide relief from controls in sectors such as food, fertilizer, petrochemicals and steel. See the listing of legislative activities from May 1, 1973, to April 30, 1974 in "Congress and Controls," *Historical Working Papers on the Economic Stabilization Program*, Part 1, pp. 220–243.

66. *Economic Report of the President, 1962*, p. 185.

COMMENTS

R. A. Gordon
University of California at Berkeley

This paper provides a broad and at the same time rather detailed survey of the American experience with wage and price controls during 1971–1974. Several pages of Introduction and Background are taken up in laying the groundwork, reviewing the behavior of aggregate demand, wages, and prices during 1965–1971, and offering some suggestions as to why the accelerating inflation in wages and prices was slow to respond to the deflationary forces that brought on the recession of 1970. This introductory discussion is concluded with the suggestion that there is some reason to believe that by mid-1971 the rate of increase in unit labor costs was beginning to taper off, with the probability of both a deceleration in the rate of price increases and improved profits. The inference, presumably, is that the freeze and subsequent detailed control of wages and prices were not necessary.

A description of the controls through the successive phases then follows, after which Kosters proceeds to consider the effects of the program on the general performance of the economy and on the behavior of wages and prices. The suggestion is offered that "delays in price increases induced by the controls" contributed to an overly expansionary monetary policy in 1972 and the early months of 1973. No supporting evidence for this proposition is offered.

The discussion of the effect of controls on wages does not dig very deeply. The chief emphasis is on the fact that by 1972 the wage structure had come into reasonable balance. Union wages governed by long-term contracts, which had been lagging behind at the end of the 1960s, had finally caught up, and thus the upward pressure on wages was easing, apart from any effect of the controls. In the construction industry, however, wage controls clearly did have a significant influence.

The discussion of the impact of controls on prices does not probe very deeply. One interesting point made is that at the beginning of 1972 there was considerable leeway for industrial prices to rise under the rules initially established, apart from the additional leeway for price increases later granted by the Price Commission. The author also considers the extent to which the relation between price changes and changes in unit labor costs was affected by price controls. The conclusion reached is that "price increases conformed more closely to unit labor cost increases under the cost pass-through rules of the controls than would have been expected at that stage of the cycle." This conclusion is based on rather slender evidence, although other evidence that could be developed might well support it.

Interestingly, in this section of the paper, the author pays more attention to the effect of the controls on profits than he does to their effect on prices and, particularly, on wages. The general conclusion is that rising profits and widening profit margins added relatively little to the rate at which prices were increasing. Percent profit margins did widen somewhat during Phase II, but most of this resulted from increases in man-hour productivity associated with rising output during a cyclical upswing. And profit margins were relatively low when controls were imposed. A further conclusion of this part of the analysis is that the use of percent rather than constant dollar markups during phases II and III added relatively little—not much more than 10 percent—to the rate of inflation.

I shall devote the rest of my comments to the author's "Concluding Discussion." The title of this last section is accurate. It is a "Concluding Discussion," not a clear-cut set of conclusions derived from the data and analysis of the preceding sections. Four broad topics are discussed: (a) the effect of the controls on the management of monetary and fiscal policy, (b) the possibility of developing alternatives to mandatory controls, (c) the influence of public pressures to "do something" about inflation, and (d) the limitations of controls. The discussion is couched in fairly broad terms, and, for the most part, these concluding observations do not depend directly on the detailed empirical presentation in the main part of the paper. I must confess that I found this concluding section not very satisfactory. The presentation is sometimes imprecise; the documentation provided is almost entirely from official sources; and other relevant research is largely ignored.

The paper has relatively little to say about the extent to which the controls might have led to an overly expansionist monetary and fiscal policy in 1972–1973 and thereby contributed to the accelerating inflation in 1973–1974. Indeed, one can hardly begin such a discussion without separating out the relative importance of generalized demand-pull and cost-push forces and of special supply shortages, something which the author does not attempt. One can agree with him, however, that a major problem at the beginning of 1973 was the failure of government and private forecasters to predict the sharp acceleration in prices that was then starting up. This leaves a critical question to which the author does not address himself. If the forecasts had been more accurate, what government actions should then have followed? Tighter monetary and fiscal policy, possibly bringing on a recession earlier than the one that we are now experiencing? Or a decision to stick with Phase II and not move on to the more relaxed controls of Phase III? And/or to take more vigorous action to deal with the specialized shortages that were developing? Or what? An attempt to answer these questions would have extended the paper considerably.

Kosters then goes on to consider possible alternatives to mandatory controls when the public pressure for government action against inflation requires that something be done. Can we develop, in his words, "imaginative policies that would help to identify and attack the real economic problems of our society" and would permit us to avoid the costs of controls—controls which will in any event be certain to disappoint public expectations. Having asked this challenging question, Koster has little to propose except some set of institutional arrangements "for identifying and bringing together spokesmen representing various interests and involving them in the process of working toward solutions. . . ." Some consideration is also given to what the government might do to stimulate investment, particularly in shortage areas; to the effect of controls on investment in 1972–1973 (apparently not very serious); and to the failure of both business and government to predict the capacity shortages that developed in 1973.

After some general observations on the role of public opinion in pushing the government into controls, Kosters concludes with some final observations on the limitations of controls. Among the points made, the following might be mentioned. Holding down profits in oligopolistic industries would have made a trivial contribution to the fight against inflation. Something more might have been gained by reducing relative wages in the more highly organized sectors of the labor market, but the obstacles here are almost insurmountable. Under the circumstances that prevailed in 1973, the Phase II type of controls could not work. By then, for controls to be effective even for a short period, we should have had to move to rigid ceilings supplemented by rationing and subsidies. And, of course, that was never in the cards.

And Kosters ends by asking once again whether wage and price controls in peacetime do not entail costs significantly greater than the benefits they presumably bring. The question is asked in the final sentence but not explicitly answered. But it is fairly clear what he believes is the correct answer.

So much for a summary of the paper. As the former associate director of the Cost of Living Council, Kosters is obviously extremely well informed, and the paper is replete with useful—if sometimes overly detailed—information. Kosters carries out his promise to provide an "overview" of the background and operation of the controls. But this "overview" also takes in a good deal of familiar scenery. In general, there is too much detail, and to some extent too close exposure to the trees obscures the view of the forest.

The presentation is not as analytical as it might be. The quantitative analysis, so far as it goes, does not penetrate very far; sophisticated regression analysis is largely eschewed; and there are surprisingly few references to the work of others who have sought to evaluate the effectiveness of the controls—including some who are at this conference. It might also have been useful to have had some evaluation of the relative extent to which the controls operated to restrain wage increases, on the one hand, and price increases, on the other. Is it true, as has been argued, for example, that the chief effect on wages came through the effect on prices?

On the whole, Kosters is correct in arguing that the sharp acceleration in price increases in 1973 owed little to the relaxation of controls in Phase III. But I think there is evidence that in some industries the relaxation of controls did make an observable difference. The overall impact, however, was not large compared to the push coming from food and raw materials.

5

M. ISHAQ NADIRI
National Bureau of Economic Research

and

VEENA GUPTA
Data Resources, Incorporated

Price and Wage Behavior in the U.S. Aggregate Economy and in Manufacturing Industries

INTRODUCTION

The American economy is in the midst of both a price and a cost inflation of unprecedented magnitude. The causes of these developments are diverse and of unknown power. Substantial increases in the growth of money supply, federal budget deficits, large wage and price settlements, food and fuel price increases, and the prevailing state of expectations about price and wages, among other forces, have been suggested as reasons for the recent inflation. To ascertain the specific roles played by these factors and by certain policy variables, an examination of the behavior of wages and prices at the aggregate and disaggregate industry level is undertaken. The questions we are particularly interested in are:

1. What is the direct response of prices to changes in aggregate demand and to increases in cost factors?
2. Do individual industry prices respond to changes in aggre-

gate demand or are they influenced by industry-specific demand?

3. In contrast to the role of wages, what is the role of the rental price of capital services and of materials prices in determining prices?
4. What is the effectiveness, if any, of government controls in restraining increases in wages and prices?
5. What is the impact of the long-term factors in the commodity and labor markets in contrast to short-run disequilibrium forces?

The policy implications of these questions are very important in designing effective counterinflationary policies. To answer some of these questions, we have constructed a model of price and wage behavior that combines the long-run factors responsible for shifts in equilibrium supply and demand schedules and the short-run disequilibrium forces in the commodity and labor markets. This model is used to estimate price and wage behavior of five aggregates—total economy, private nonfarm, total manufacturing, total durables, and total nondurables—and twelve two-digit manufacturing industries. The data are seasonally adjusted quarterly time series. The estimation period chosen is 1954I–1971II; and for the five aggregates, the period 1971III–1973II is used to test the predictive power of the model beyond the sample period and to assess the effects of the recent controls on wages and prices.

The model is specified in section I. In section II, the econometric specification of the model and the nature of the data are described. In section III, the estimates of the model for the five aggregates are analyzed and their contrasting features are noted. The results for the disaggregate industries are presented and discussed in section IV. The dynamic simulation results for price and wage rates of the aggregate sectors for both the sample and forecast periods are reported in section V, and the effects of recent controls on wage and price behavior are also examined in this section. The summary and conclusions are contained in section VI.

I. SPECIFICATION OF THE MODEL

Assume a Cobb-Douglas production function (1) and a log-linear demand function (2)

(1) $Q^s = AL^{\alpha_1}M^{\alpha_2}K^{\alpha_3}e^{-\lambda t}$

(2) $Q^d = BP^{-\beta_1}Y^{\beta_2}S^{\beta_3}$

where Q^s and Q^d are the quantity produced and demanded; L, M, and K are labor, raw materials, and capital inputs; α_1, α_2, α_3 are the output elasticities of the inputs; and λ is the rate of technical change. P is the output price, Y is total expenditure, S is the price of other goods; β_1, β_2, β_3 are the price, expenditure, and cross elasticities of demand, Q^d. Assuming that the firm maximizes profit, the long-run equilibrium price $P*$ is determined by (3):

(3) $\qquad P* = \theta_0 W^{\theta_1} V^{\theta_2} C^{\theta_3} Y^{\theta_4} S^{\theta_5} e^{\theta_6 t}$

$\qquad \theta_1, \theta_2, \theta_3, \theta_4 > 0; \theta_5 \lessgtr 0; \theta_6 < 0$

where W, V, C are the wage rate, price of raw materials, and rental price of capital services; $\theta_1, \ldots, \theta_6$ are constants.[1] According to (3), increases in factor costs and demand will contribute positively to a price increase; gains in productivity due to technical change will lower prices; and an increase in the price of other commodities may lead to an increase or decrease in the output price, depending on whether they are complementary or substitute products.

The long-run supply of and demand for labor determine the optimum money wage rate and the level of employment. A vast literature on employment demand and labor supply functions is available.[2] It would be useful to specify and estimate structural equations for demand for and supply of labor and solve the reduced form equations explicitly. However, here we shall consider the following reduced form equation

(4) $\qquad W* = \varphi_0 P_C^{*\varphi_1} \left(\dfrac{Q}{L} \right)^{*\varphi_2}$

where P_C^* is the expected price of goods purchased by the workers; $(Q/L)^*$ is long-run average productivity; and φ_1 and φ_2 are elasticities of money wages with respect to expected price and productivity.[3]

Relations 3 and 4 are subject in the short run to disequilibrium forces prevailing in the goods and labor markets. For example, changes in demand for goods may increase or decrease prices, depending on whether excess capacity is present; in the labor market, changes in the unemployment rate or in workers' expectations may influence the short-run course of wage rates. It is also likely that the disequilibrium in one market spills over and generates adjustment in the other market. Government policies such as guideposts and controls, though aimed at correcting some of the existing disequilibriums, may generate some disturbances of their own.

The primary function of these market disequilibrium factors is to modify the moving equilibrium conditions in the commodity and labor markets. Even accounting for these factors, the goods and factor markets may not clear because of search costs, institutional barriers, and so on, which will delay the adjustment of wages and prices to their equilibrium.[4] Combining the market disequilibriums with a simple geometric adjustment process, we obtain the following short-run price and wage equation:

(5) $P_t/P_{t-1} = (P_t^*/P_{t-1})^{\lambda_1}(U_i)^{\gamma_i}$ $(i = 1, \ldots, n)$

(6) $W_t/W_{t-1} = (W_t^*/W_{t-1})^{\lambda_2}(U_j)^{\gamma_j}$ $(j = 1, \ldots, m)$

where P^* and W^* are the equilibrium price and wage rate defined by (3) and (4), λ_1 and λ_2 are the adjustment coefficients, and U_i and U_j are the short-term forces operating in each of the markets. Note that U_i and U_j do not influence P^* and W^* directly. Instead, they modify the rate of adjustment of prices and wages. Guidepost policies and controls can also be considered as part of U_i or U_j.[5]

II. ECONOMETRIC SPECIFICATIONS AND NATURE OF THE DATA

Specification of the Estimating Equations

Before stating the final estimating equations, several specification problems must be considered:

1. The relevant cost variables influencing prices are the *expected* levels of wages, materials price, and user cost; the appropriate demand variable is also the *expected future* level of expenditures. After examining several alternatives, it became clear to us that current factor prices were fairly good representatives of their future values, while a distributed lag of past expenditures seemed to be a good proxy for expected future spending.

2. The most promising short-run variable in the goods market turned out to be either capacity utilization or deviation of productivity from its trend. There were several short-term forces in the labor market, including the level of the unemployment rate or its rate of change, productivity changes, and changes in the consumer price index as a proxy for short-term expectations.

3. The price of substitute goods (S) as a determinant of commodity price was used initially but excluded in further testing of the model since it did not yield satisfactory results.

4. We have not employed any techniques, such as conversion of variables to moving averages, that inevitably improve the goodness of fit of the equations at the cost of introducing or increasing serial correlation. In fact, the Cochrane-Orcutt technique was used whenever evidence of serial correlation was found.

5. To explore the possibility of simultaneous equation bias in the estimating equations, the current wage rate was replaced by its lagged value in the price equation; and current price, by lagged price in the wage equation. Except for some minor changes the results remained the same.[6] The simultaneity issue, however, needs further consideration, especially since movements of other factor costs such as materials prices and the rental price of capital are likely to be endogenous in a complete price-cost model.

The estimating equations based on the above assumptions are the following; both are log-linear:

(7) $$p_t = a_0 + a_1 w_t + a_2 v_t + a_3 c_t + a_4 T + a_5 u_{ct} + a_6 y_t^e + a_7 p_{t-1} + \epsilon_1$$

(8) $$w_t = b_0 + b_1 p_t + b_2 T + b_3(\rho - \bar{\rho}) + b_4 u_t$$
$$+ b_5(p_{t-1} - p_{t-2}) + b_6 D_1 + b_7 w_{t-1} + \epsilon_2$$

where $a_1, a_2, a_3, a_6, a_7 > 0$; $a_4, a_5 < 0$; and $b_1, b_2, b_3 > 0$; $b_4, b_6 < 0$; $b_5, b_7 > 0$. All the lower-case variables are in logs. $w, v,$ and c are the factor cost variables defined earlier, y_t^e is a proxy for the expected level of spending, u_c is the capacity utilization variable, u_t is a proxy for prevailing unemployment conditions; D_1 is the guidepost dummy; and T is the time trend depicting long-run productivity growth; $(\rho - \bar{\rho})$ is the deviation of productivity from its trend value, $\bar{\rho}$; and ϵ_1 and ϵ_2 are the stochastic error terms.

Several features of these equations must be noted:

1. Though prices and costs are two facets of the same inflationary process, a distinction should be made between price and wage inflations. Fundamental causes of each one need to be identified. Therefore, we consider prices to increase initially in response to changes in expected spending, y_t^e, which, in turn, can be related to changes in the stock of money supply or fiscal measures.[7]

2. A full statement of the cost factors that affect price behavior is provided. Unlike most other work on price equations, our model includes materials prices and the rental price of capital in addition to the labor cost and demand variables.

3. Moreover, factor costs and productivity terms are introduced separately, with the result that the data determine whether or not

the contribution of wages is the same as that of productivity. Short- and long-run productivity variables are explicitly included in both price and wage equations.

4. Equations 7 and 8 are formulated in level forms, in contrast to formulations in studies that are concentrated on the rate of change of wages and or prices. Most of the Phillips-type studies are disequilibrium models of the commodity and labor markets aimed at explaining changes in wages and prices around their assumed stationary equilibrium paths. They imply that in the absence of any excess demand, changes in wages or prices will be zero (see Agrawal et al. 1972, for further discussion of this point). However, wages and prices may change due to a moving equilibrium of the supply and demand schedules in those markets. By including both the short- and long-run factors, equations 7 and 8 provide a framework for analyzing the influence of short-term variables in the presence of long-run factors. Also, there is an inherent relationship between the level and first-difference form. The decision to use one or the other is a hypothesis that can be tested (see Bischoff 1969 and Rowley and Wilton 1973 for further discussion). We can predict rates of change of wages and prices from equations 7 and 8 and compare them with the predictions of standard wage and price models.[8]

5. In the labor market, unemployment conditions serve as a disequilibrating force. The level and often the rate of change of the unemployment rate may serve as proxies for these conditions. Note that the relationship between the unemployment rate (or its rate of change) specified in equation 8 is quite different from that postulated in Phillips-type studies. A dynamic Phillips relation is implied in equation 8, where the percent wage rate is related to the *percent* change in the unemployment rate (see Kuh 1967 for further discussion of this subject).

6. The state of expectations is of critical importance in determining price and wage behavior. Formulating the process that generates expectations and identifying the precise magnitudes of the parameters that govern this process are important areas of research.[9] Lack of suitable data on expectations has been a particular difficulty in assessing how prices and wage rates are modified in different expectational environments.

After considering several expectations hypotheses we assumed that expectations affect prices directly through the expected spending decisions depicted by y_t^e and indirectly through their effects on wages. In the wage equation two alternative hypotheses were considered for the effect of short-run price expectations: an extrapolative hypothesis and the Eckstein-Brinner threshold hypothesis (see Eckstein and Brinner 1972 for detailed information on these concepts). The extrapolative hypothesis is of the simple log-linear form:

(9) $$\hat{p}_c^e = \alpha_0' + \alpha_1 p_{ct} + \alpha_2(p_{ct-1} - p_{ct-2})$$

i.e., expected consumer prices depend on actual prices prevailing in the current period and price changes over the two previous quarters. The threshold hypothesis is formulated as

(10) $$D_3 = \frac{p_{ct-1} - p_{ct-9}}{p_{ct-5}}$$

$$D_3 = 0 \text{ if } [(p_{ct-1} - p_{ct-9})/p_{ct-5}] \leqslant 0.05$$

$$= \frac{p_{ct-1} - p_{ct-9}}{p_{ct-5}} - 0.05 \quad \text{otherwise.}$$

In the long run, $p_{ct-1} - p_{ct-2}$ and D_3 will be zero; therefore, they are of interest only in the short run.[10]

7. Guidepost dummy D_1 is introduced in the wage equation to capture the effects of the Kennedy and Johnson administrations' attempts to restrain wage and price increases in 1962–1964. It is assumed that D_1 affects prices indirectly through the wage variable (when D_1 was included in the price equation, its coefficient was either statistically insignificant or had an incorrect sign).

The Nature of the Data

The data used in this study are all seasonally adjusted quarterly time series obtained mostly from published sources. In some cases, new industry-specific data have been constructed from different sources. A brief description of the data is given below.

1. The price series used for the aggregate economy and for the total private nonfarm sectors are the GNP deflator and the implicit price deflator for gross product for nonfarm business sectors. They are seasonally adjusted, with 1967 = 1.00, and are taken from U.S. Department of Commerce, *National Income and Product Accounts of the United States*, 1929–1965, and from various issues of the *Survey of Current Business* (SCB). The output price series for the manufacturing industries are from U.S. Department of Labor, *Wholesale Prices and Price Indexes* and are converted to the base

$1967 = 1.00$. For dissagregate industries, price series were obtained by weighting BLS price series by 1967 sales data.

2. The employment, hours, and wage data are all from BLS, *Employment and Earnings* (1972) and various issues of the *Survey of Current Business*. Two types of wage variable were used: seasonally adjusted average hourly earnings of production workers (W), and straight-time hourly earnings of production workers (W_1); the latter excludes overtime wages. The overtime factor was derived from overtime hours data (published in *Employment and Earnings*) on the assumption that overtime wages equal 1.5 times straight-time wages.[11] For the aggregate and nonfarm private economy a wage series (W_2) excluding the effects of both overtime and industry mix was also constructed, using the method described by Gordon (1972b).

3. The materials prices used for the two aggregate sectors were the wholesale price index for crude materials for further processing, published by the BLS in various issues of the *Wholesale Prices and Price Indexes*, and the implicit price deflator for the product of the private business farm sector, published in the national income and product accounts and in various issues of *Survey of Current Business*. For total manufacturing, total durables, and total nondurables, the materials price is the wholesale price index for intermediate materials, from *Wholesale Prices and Price Indexes*. For the two-digit industries, the materials prices were those constructed by Eckstein and Wyss, which they made available to us.[12]

4. The rental price of capital (c) is constructed according to the formula stated in Hall and Jorgenson (1967):

$$c = [(1 - k)(1 - \omega z)/(1 - \omega)] p_k (r + \delta)$$

z, the present value of depreciation, depends upon r, τ, and the depreciation method used. For the private nonfarm economy, z is a weighted average of present values based on straight-line depreciation and accelerated depreciation methods. For the manufacturing industries, accelerated depreciation was used starting in 1954I. δ is the constant depreciation rate for each industry, taken from Hall and Jorgenson (1967) for the aggregate economy and from Jorgenson and Stephenson (1967) for manufacturing industries. τ is the lifetime of capital for tax purposes based on U.S. Treasury Department (1962). k is the rate of tax credit, equal to 0.05 for the private nonfarm economy, and to 0.037 for the manufacturing industries. The measure of r, the rate of interest, is 1.5 times the AAA corporate bond yield for the aggregate economy and the AAA corporate bond yield as given for the manufacturing industries. This was obtained from various issues of the *Federal Reserve Bulletin*. The price of capital goods is the implicit deflator for gross domestic fixed investment, from U.S. Department of Commerce, *U.S. National Income and Product Accounts, 1929–65*, and subsequent July issues of the *Survey of Current Business*. For the aggregate economy, the same source was used to obtain the implicit price deflators for structures and equipment, and the resulting rental price series for structures and equipment were combined into a weighted average. Differences in the rental prices for various manufacturing industries are due only to varying assumptions of depreciation rates.

5. The utilization rate for the aggregate economy is the Wharton index of capacity utilization for manufacturing, mining, and utilities, from the *Wharton Quarterly*. The utilization indexes for the manufacturing industries are all Wharton's specific-industry utilization rates, which were made available to us. All the utilization rates are seasonally adjusted and are on the base 1967 = 1.00. The methodology of constructing this series is described in Klein and Preston (1967).

6. The productivity variables are constructed as follows: the index of current productivity (X/MH) is defined as the index of output per man-hour and was derived as the ratio of the Federal Reserve index of industry production (X) (from the *Federal Reserve Bulletin*) to an index of man-hours (MH). The latter was constructed for the aggregate sectors and the manufacturing industries as the product of the number of persons employed and the average number of hours worked by production workers. The employment and hours data were obtained from *Employment and Earnings* (1972).

The trend productivity variable was derived by regressing output per man-hour on a linear trend; $\rho = \ln (X/MH)$ and $\bar{\rho} = \ln (\overline{X/MH})$, where X/MH and $\overline{X/MH}$ are the actual and fitted values of productivity per man-hour.

7. Four different unemployment rates were obtained from *Employment and Earnings* (1972). All the data—the unemployment rate for all civilian workers (u_t), for total manufacturing (u_m), for total durables (u_d), and for total nondurables (u_n)—are seasonally adjusted unemployment rates of wage and salaried workers. For the two-digit industries, industry-specific unemployment rates are not available; therefore, we used u_d in the wage equations for the durable industries and u_n in the wage equations for nondurables.

8. Total spending (Y_{t-1}) is lagged GNP in current dollars, from *National Income and Product Accounts* and various issues of the *Survey of Current Business*. y_t^e is the distributed lag of the logarithm of Y_{t-1}.

9. P_c is the seasonally adjusted deflator for personal consumption expenditures (1967 = 1.00), from *National Income and Product Accounts* and various issues of the *Survey of Current Business*.

10. Dummy variable D_1, for the wage-price guidelines of 1962–1967, is constructed following Gordon (1967a). It rises by stepwise increments of 0.25 from zero in 1962I to 1.0 in 1962IV. It remains at 1.0 until 1966IV, and then declines in steps of 0.25 to zero in 1967IV.

11. The variable for inflation severity, D_3 is constructed following the Eckstein-Brinner formulation noted earlier. As indicated, it is equal to the positive excess over 5 percent of the eight-quarter rate of change of the consumer goods deflator. It is equal to zero as long as the eight-quarter rate of inflation is less than 5 percent for two consecutive years.

III. ESTIMATION RESULTS FOR THE TOTAL ECONOMY AND AGGREGATE MANUFACTURING INDUSTRIES

The price and wage equations (7 and 8) were estimated using seasonally adjusted time-series data for the total economy, the total private nonfarm sector, the total manufacturing sectors, total durables, total nondurables, and the twelve manufacturing industries listed by SIC number and name in Table 5, note a. The sample period chosen was 1954I–1971II. The cutoff date was 1971II in order to assess the effects of new economic controls initiated in August 1971. For the period 1971III–1973II, forecasts of price and wage changes were obtained for the five aggregate sectors and industries, using their estimated coefficients. Postsample forecasts could not be made for the disaggregate industries because of data limitations; limitations of data and time also prevented us from extending our forecasts for the aggregates to 1974.

Prices and Wages of the Aggregate Sectors and Industries

Price Equations

The estimates of the aggregate price equations are reported in tables 1 and 2. The difference between the two tables is that the lagged dependent variable (p_{t-1}) is excluded in Table 2. Inclusion

TABLE 1

TABLE 1   Price Equations for Aggregate Sectors[a]
(sample period: 1954 I–1971 II
figures in parentheses are t statistics)

Independent Variables	Aggregate Economy (1)	Private Nonfarm (2)	Total Mfr. (3)	Total Durables (4)	Total Nondurables (5)
c_0	-0.3488	-0.3340	0.0248	0.5073	-0.3691
	(4.485)	(3.605)	(0.1321)	(1.369)	(2.061)
w_t	0.1373	0.1247	0.1418	0.2512	
	(2.386)	(2.411)	(3.780)	(3.666)	
T	-0.0013	-0.0015	-0.0014	-0.0020	
	(4.760)	(4.806)	(5.316)	(2.446)	
$ulcn$					0.1070
					(3.111)
c_t	0.0111	0.0166	-0.0118	0.0138	-0.0369
	(1.734)	(2.148)	(1.336)	(0.9977)	(2.753)
v_t	0.0118	-0.0631	0.2841	0.5612	0.1239
	(1.090)	(0.7903)	(6.296)	(6.256)	(3.873)
u_{ct}	-0.0085	-0.0084	0.0118	-0.0320	-0.2098
	(0.7742)	(0.7067)	(1.588)	(2.595)	(1.053)
p_{t-1}	0.8110	0.8192	0.6361	0.2350	0.7935
	(10.85)	(2.294)	(9.699)	(2.794)	(13.10)
y_t^e	0.0544	0.0585	0.0419	0.0770	0.0327
	(2.745)	(2.555)	(3.199)	(1.970)	(2.785)
ρ_1				0.8424	
R^2	0.9997	0.9995	0.9992	0.9993	0.9932
DW	1.511	1.844	1.550	2.172	1.445
SSR	0.0002	0.0004	0.0003	0.0004	0.0011
SER	0.0021	0.0024	0.0021	0.0025	0.0042

The variables are defined in section II; all are in logs except T. ρ_1 is the autocorrelation coefficient; R^2 is the coefficient of multiple determination; DW, the Durbin-Watson statistic; SSR, the sum of squared residuals; and SER, the standard error of regression.

The standard unit of labor cost, $ulcn = \log [W_t(\overline{X/MH})_t]$, where W is the wage rate and $\overline{X/MH}$ is the trend productivity variable.

The distributed lags of y_t in each equation have the following features:

Total economy	2nd degree polynomial, 6 quarters long, with far end constrained to zero
Private nonfarm	2nd degree polynomial, 6 quarters long, with far end constrained to zero
Total manufacturing	2nd degree polynomial, 10 quarters long, with far end constrained to zero
Total durables	Previous level of aggregate spending
Total nondurables	2nd degree polynomial, 15 quarters long, with far end constrained to zero

of p_{t-1} does not much affect the coefficients of other variables, except that it tends to shorten the length of the distributed lag on the aggregate spending variable (y_t^e). Also, material price (v_t) is collinear with p_{t-1} and, therefore, its coefficient tends to be somewhat unstable. We have used the estimates in Table 1 for simulating price behavior. However, the results were hardly different when the price equations in Table 2 were used.

The results in Table 1 indicate that, with few exceptions, all the variables are statistically significant. This means that the hazards of multicollinearity, which are not unusual in such equations, have been largely avoided. The signs of the coefficients are in accord with theoretical specifications. Factor costs contribute positively to price increase, long- and short-run productivity lowers prices, while expected demand (y_t^e) increases them. The goodness-of-fit statistics of the equations are fairly satisfactory, and R^2, the coefficient of multiple correlation in terms of *changes* of the dependent variable, is 0.50 and over. Existing first-order serial correlation of the residuals is removed by using the Cochrane-Orcutt iterative technique. The autocorrelation coefficient (ρ_1) is near unity in most cases in Table 2, and the Durbin-Watson statistics indicate absence of any serial correlation.

Several observations about the coefficients are in order:

1. The money wage rate is a very significant determinant of the price level. The short-run wage elasticity of prices is about 0.12 in every case except durables, for which it is about 0.25. In nondurables, the coefficients of w and the productivity trend were constrained to equality. The short-term elasticity of price with respect to standardized unit labor cost *ulcn* is about 0.11.

2. The long-run productivity growth variable (T) has a negative and statistically significant coefficient in all cases. The magnitude of this coefficient is much smaller than that of the wage variable in all cases except nondurables. Even if the effect of short-run productivity changes captured by the utilization rate (uc_t) is taken into account, the total contribution of productivity growth in lowering prices is more than offset by wage increases.

3. The rental price of capital contributes positively to price increases in all cases except total nondurables, where its coefficient is negative. The short-term impact of this variable seems to be about 0.01, a rather small effect.[13]

4. Materials costs are very important in the manufacturing industries. Reasons for the statistical insignificance of v_t in

TABLE 2 Price Equations for Aggregate Sectors and Industries[a] (sample period: 1954 I–1971 II; figures in parentheses are t statistics)

Independent Variables	Aggregate Economy (1)	Private Nonfarm (2)	Total Mfr. (3)	Total Durables (4)	Total Nondurables (5)
c_0	−3.127	−3.181	1.289	0.9108	−2.736
	(3.907)	(3.656)	(3.576)	(2.405)	(2.568)
w_t	0.2916	0.2328	0.2002	0.3274	
	(4.102)	(2.803)	(3.273)	(4.834)	
T	−0.0056	−0.0067	−0.0021	−0.0032	
	(2.505)	(2.855)	(2.885)	(2.746)	
$ulcn$					−0.0032
					(0.0022)
v_t	0.0407	0.0281	0.5927	0.6388	0.5641
	(1.742)	(1.024)	(8.780)	(6.975)	(3.669)
c_t	0.0229	0.0394	0.0204	0.0246	0.0076
	(2.166)	(3.186)	(1.660)	(1.665)	(0.3360)
u_{ct}	−0.0363	−0.0412	−0.0401	−0.0468	−0.0983
	(2.609)	(2.556)	(4.957)	(4.129)	(2.392)
y_t^e	0.5298	0.5719	0.1221	0.1425	0.0936
	(3.543)	(3.541)	(2.406)	(2.234)	(3.805)
ρ_1	0.9513	0.9399	0.8017	0.8806	0.8991
R^2	0.9960	0.9992	0.9971	0.9992	0.9934
R_X^2	0.6080	0.4980	0.7966	0.8025	0.4414
DW	1.338	1.354	1.568	1.836	1.515
SSR	0.0004	0.0005	0.0027	0.0004	0.0011
SER	0.0026	0.0030	0.0021	0.0026	0.0042

The variables are defined in section II; all are in logs except T. The goodness-of-fit variables are identified in Table 1; R_X^2 is the coefficient of multiple correlation in terms of change in the dependent variable.

The distributed lag variable y_t^e is specified as follows:

Total economy	2nd degree polynomial, 15 quarters long, with far end constrained to zero
Private nonfarm	2nd degree polynomial, 15 quarters long, with far end constrained to zero
Total manufacturing	2nd degree polynomial, 15 quarters long, with both ends constrained to zero
Total durables	2nd degree polynomial, 10 quarters long, with far end constrained to zero
Total nondurables	2nd degree polynomial, 15 quarters long, with far end constrained to zero

the aggregate economy could be the inadequacy of our measures of cost of materials and possibly the collinearity between v_t and p_{t-1} and y_t^e. In the manufacturing industries, prices are quite sensitive to changes in v_t, especially for durables. The elasticity of prices with respect to v_t exceeds its elasticity with respect to w in those industries.

5. The utilization rate captures the effects of short-term changes in productivity. Similar results were obtained when a variable measuring the productivity deviation from its trend was substituted for uc_t in the price equations. The consistently negative signs of the utilization rate variable in equations shown in tables 1 and 2 are in sharp contrast to the positive effect of the utilization rate on price changes reported in the literature. (See Nordhaus 1972 for a summary of the empirical evidence on the effect of the utilization rate.) It can be interpreted to mean that when demand increases, higher utilization of existing capacity results in lower costs; that is, an increase in utilization depicts movement along the unit cost curve, and that leads to lower prices when there is excess capacity.

6. The expected demand variable (y_t^e) captures long-run changes in demand. It has a positive and statistically significant coefficient in each regression. The sum of the distributed lag coefficients is reported for each equation in tables 1 and 2; the distributed lag on GNP is a second-degree polynomial of varying lengths with the far end often constrained to zero. However, the distributed lag coefficients, though not reported here, were positive and statistically significant, and they usually traced a geometric lag structure.

Thus, in determining price behavior, both costs and demand factors play important roles; their quantitative influence and the timing of their effects is quite different. The evidence that aggregate spending affects manufacturing prices significantly stands in contrast to results reported in the literature. Also, this effect is in addition to the short-run industry-specific demand increase depicted by the utilization rate.

The Aggregate Wage Equations

The dependent variables in Table 3 are average hourly earnings. Series such as compensation per man-hour or average hourly earnings adjusted for overtime and interindustry shifts might be better measures of labor costs. These series were constructed, and the

TABLE 3 Wage Equations for Aggregate Sectors[a]
(sample period: 1954I–1971II;
figures in parentheses are t statistics)

Independent Variables	Aggregate Economy (1)	Total Mfg. (2)	Total Durables (3)	Total Non-durables (4)
c_0	−1.661 (3.393)	−0.1962 (0.7446)	−0.4301 (2.140)	−0.384 (1.272)
u^{-1}				0.006 (2.175)
$u_t - u_{t-1}$	−0.0094 (1.333)	−0.0305 (3.979)	−0.0157 (3.717)	
$\rho - \bar\rho$	0.0603 (2.745)	0.0864 (2.573)	0.1143 (3.358)	0.0747 (1.679)
T	0.0022 (3.556)	0.0005 (1.306)	0.0011 (2.251)	0.0005 (1.174)
p_c	0.4232 (3.492)	0.0869 (1.412)	0.1358 (2.724)	0.0976 (1.459)
D_1	−0.0039 (2.218)	−0.0038 (2.133)	−0.0046 (2.376)	−0.0041 (2.507)
$p_{ct-1} - p_{ct-2}$	0.5617 (3.049)	0.5111 (2.761)	0.4032 (1.705)	0.8111 (1.389)
w_{t-1}	0.6190 (5.977)	0.8932 (12.83)	0.8153 (11.77)	0.8991 (13.25)
ρ_1				0.1893
R^2	0.9998	0.9996	0.9995	0.9998
DW	1.964	2.533	2.418	2.104
SSR	0.0008	0.0009	0.0013	0.0004
SER	0.0026	0.0038	0.0046	0.0026

[a]The unemployment rates are industry-specific. For total aggregate economy, total civilian unemployment rate (u_t) is used. For the manufacturing industries u_m, u_d, and u_n are used in the equations for total, durables, and nondurable manufacturing industries, respectively.

P in all cases is the implicit price deflator for personal consumption expenditures, and $p_{ct-1} - p_{ct-2}$ is the difference in the logs of this deflator.

The variables are defined in section II; all are in logs except T and D_1.

The wage equation for the private nonfarm sector is the same as that reported in column 1.

The results were quite similar when the regressions were run excluding w_{t-1} and taking account of first-order serial correlations; the regression for total non-durables, however, was the exception.

wage equations were re-estimated. The results were not much different from those reported in Table 3. However, we consider that average hourly earnings including overtime is a more comprehensive wage cost; it includes the short-term rise in wage rates due to business expansion. This cost, which is due to higher utilization of the labor force, is in contrast to the capacity utilization rate, which reflects the spreading of overhead costs.[14]

The estimated coefficients in Table 3 are all statistically significant and have the theoretically correct signs, and the fit of the model in every case is fairly good. It is clear that long-term variables such as trend productivity and the price level and the short-term market disequilibrium variables—changes in the unemployment rate and price expectations—and guidepost policies exert significant influence on money wages.

The impact of unemployment conditions on wage behavior differs among the various sectors: the reciprocal of the unemployment rate was statistically insignificant in every case other than total nondurables, but the rate of change of the unemployment rate was significant in other cases, particularly in total manufacturing and durables. As we noted, the relation of the wage rate and unemployment variables, $u^{-1} = \ln(1/U)$ or $u_t - u_{t-1} = \ln(U_t/U_{t-1})$, in the regressions of Table 3 implies a dynamic relation where the percentage change in the wage rate is associated with percent change in the unemployment rate. If we write wage equation 8 in a simplified form, $\ln W_t = a + b \ln(U_t/U_{t-1})$, and differentiate with respect to time, we get

$$(11) \quad \frac{\dot{W}}{W} = b \left(\frac{\dot{U}_t}{U_t} - \frac{\dot{U}_{t-1}}{U_{t-1}} \right)$$

where $\dot{W}$ and $\dot{U}$ are the time derivations of the level wage rate and unemployment and b is the coefficient of $u_t - u_{t-1}$ in Table 3. (11) is in contrast to the Phillips-type analysis which relates *change* in the money wage rate to the unemployment rate $\dot{W}/W = b_0'(1/U)$. Our finding is in the spirit of Kuh's productivity theory of wage levels; (see Kuh 1967 for further discussion of this subject).

Continuing, we see that the productivity trend contributes significantly to growth of the wage rate, particularly for the aggregate economy and durables. Short-term productivity measured as a deviation of actual (ρ) to trend productivity ($\bar{\rho}$), i.e., $\rho - \bar{\rho}$, is fairly significant in all cases, especially in the manufacturing industries. The behavior of this variable, which is often a proxy for profits, indicates that cyclical increases in demand for output exert strong effects on wage movements.

The government guidepost effects seem to have been significant in modifying the growth of the wage rate in all the aggregate sectors and in the manufacturing industries. The magnitudes of the coefficients of D_1 are similar among the various equations, with a slightly larger impact in the durables.

The short-term effects of price on the wage level consist of two terms, the level effect and the rate-of-change effect. The coefficients of p_{ct} and $p_{ct-1} - p_{ct-2}$ are both positive, statistically significant, and less than unity. The coefficient of the acceleration term is substantially smaller than unity,[15] and the short-term elasticity of wage with respect to the price level is also less than unity. Note that a dynamic relationship between changes in the money wage rate and changes in consumer prices is embedded in the model.[16]

The coefficient of w_{t-1} can be interpreted as either an adjustment coefficient or a first-order serial correlation coefficient. A test to identify the role played by w_{t-1} in the model suggested, though not conclusively, that it serves as an adjustment mechanism (see Griliches 1967 for the description of this test). The regression coefficients of w_{t-1} indicate that wage adjustment is much stickier in the manufacturing industries than in the aggregate economy. This may be due to aggregation of individual-industry adjustment processes of varying patterns whose convolution creates a much shorter adjustment for the aggregate wage rate.

Long-Run Estimates

The implied long-run elasticities of prices and wages with respect to their long-run determinants can be deduced from the regression results reported in tables 1 and 3. The short-term market disequilibrium variables, such as the utilization rates in the price equations and the unemployment rate and price expectations variable in the wage equations, will take their stationary values in the long run. That is, in the long run, prices will be determined by factor costs and long-run productivity; wages will be determined by the long-run expected price level and long-run productivity growth.

The long-run elasticities of price with respect to costs and expected demand and the long-run elasticity of wages with respect to changes in consumer prices and productivity growth are shown in Table 4. Some interesting patterns emerge. In the aggregate sectors, the wage rate elasticity of prices is about 0.70. The elasticities of prices with respect to rental price of capital are certainly low, and in nondurables the sign of the rental price is negative. In the manufacturing industries, it is materials costs that play the dominant role.

TABLE 4 Long-Run Elasticities of Prices and Wage Rates with Respect to Long-Term Determinants[a]

	Price Equation						Wage Equation	
	w_t	t	$ulcn$	c	v	y^e	p_c	t
Total economy	0.68	−0.007		0.058	0.063	0.284	1.10	0.0057
Total private nonfarm	0.667	−0.008		0.089	0.3318	0.313	1.10	0.0057
Total manufacturing	0.378	−0.003		−0.033	0.781	0.112	0.814	0.0044
Total durables	0.355	−0.003		0.018	0.732	0.101	0.735	0.0059
Total nondurables			0.504	−0.1789	0.600	0.1583	0.967	0.0049

[a]These statistics were calculated by dividing the approximate coefficients shown in tables 1 and 3 by $1 - \lambda'$, where λ' is the estimated coefficient of the lagged dependent variable.

These patterns closely correspond to factor shares reported by Nordhaus (1972).[17]

The long-run contribution of productivity in lowering prices is more than offset by the increase in factor costs, while the contribution of productivity growth to wages is about 0.005 to 0.006. Expected demand has a powerful effect on the price level in every case, but the elasticity of price with respect to changes in spending is well below unity. This suggests that an increase in demand leads to an increase partly in prices and partly in output in the long run. The long-run response of the wage rate to the consumer price index varies among the aggregates. For the aggregate economy and nondurables, the elasticity is unity, but it is less than that in total manufacturing and durables. It seems that a severe money illusion is present in the durable industries, even in the long run.

V. DISAGGREGATE MANUFACTURING INDUSTRIES

The price and wage equations (7 and 8) were fitted for the same period to the data for the twelve two-digit manufacturing industries described earlier. Price and wage behavior in these industries is quite divergent, and the estimates suggest that the response of industry prices and wages to changes in aggregate and industry-specific variables differs among industries.

The results for individual industries are summarized in tables 5 and 6. Some of the variables were omitted because of multicollinearity. As can be seen from the tables, the fit of the regressions is fairly good. With some exceptions, the explanatory variables have the correct signs and are statistically significant. The industry results can be summarized briefly.

Industry Price Behavior

The long-term productivity trend has a negative and statistically significant effect in all cases except textiles, petroleum, and primary nonferrous metals. It plays a somewhat larger role in the durables than in nondurables, with the largest impact in the primary ferrous, nonferrous, motor vehicles, petroleum, and paper and allied products industries.

TABLE 5 Price Equations for Disaggregated Manufacturing Industries[a] (sample period: 1954I–1971II; figures in parentheses are t statistics)

Variables	Nondurable Manufacturing Industries					
	SIC 20	SIC 22	SIC 26	SIC 28	SIC 29	SIC 30
c_0	−1.128	2.528	−3.415	−4.630	−1.601	−6.213
	(4.288)	(6.399)	(4.203)	(26.35)	(3.222)	(3.909)
T	−0.0022	0.0020	−0.0117	−0.0018	0.0043	−0.0205
	(2.523)	(3.313)	(4.203)	(4.543)	(2.114)	(4.868)
w_t	0.1379	0.5667	0.2780	0.0512	−0.5120	0.5035
	(1.939)	(7.836)	(1.491)	(2.250)	(2.418)	(2.143)
v_t	0.3078	−0.0755			0.2801	
	(9.816)	(1.725)			(2.154)	
c_t	−0.0350	−0.0368	0.0563		0.1077	0.0013
	(1.965)	(4.006)	(1.890)		(2.41)	(0.0208)
p_{t-1}	0.4583	0.6864		0.9119	0.8203	
	(8.450)	(12.59)		(20.76)	(10.45)	
y_t^e	0.1718	−0.4837	0.6442	0.0886	−0.0784	1.158
	(4.039)	(6.510)	(4.347)	(3.805)	(0.9325)	(3.650)
u_{ct}	−0.0144			−0.0156	0.6009	
	(0.8331)			(1.689)	(5.046)	
ρ			0.9126			0.8875
R^2	0.9952	0.9168	0.9888	0.7679	0.8644	0.9962
R_X^2			0.4046			0.4485
DW	1.481	1.035	1.532	1.615	2.045	1.731
SSR	0.0022	0.0018	0.0024	0.0004	0.0239	0.0016
SER	0.0060	0.0053	0.0062	0.0027	0.0189	0.0057

SIC = Standard Industrial Classification.

[a] All the variables except T are in logs. The distributed lag variable y_t^e is specified as follows:

SIC No. and Description	
20	Food and kindred products	2nd degree polynomial, 6 quarters long, both ends constrained to zero
22	Textile mill products	2nd degree polynomial, 10 quarters long, far end constrained to zero
26	Paper and allied products	2nd degree polynomial, 6 quarters long, far end constrained to zero
28	Chemical and allied products	2nd degree polynomial, 10 quarters long, far end constrained to zero
29	Petroleum and allied products	Previous level of total spending
30	Rubber and allied products	2nd degree polynomial, 10 quarters long, far end constrained to zero

	Durable Manufacturing Industries					
Variables	SIC 32	SIC 331	SIC 333	SIC 35	SIC 36	SIC 371
c_0	−0.1892	−5.650	1.105	−0.0791	−0.1185	−1.238
	(0.9450)	(4.330)	(1.234)	(0.3986)	(0.4822)	(2.435)
T	−0.0017	−0.0178	0.0093	0.0011	−0.0014	−0.0056
	(2.583)	(4.445)	(2.752)	(1.399)	(2.047)	(3.053)
w_t	0.2303	0.4707	−1.100	−0.0749	0.0762	0.2313
	(3.143)	(5.511)	(3.898)	0.7784	(0.9113)	(3.539)
v_t	0.2530	0.1395	0.3803	0.2197	0.1169	0.3618
	(2.676)	(2.598)	(5.365)	(3.957)	(2.972)	(2.879)
c_t	−0.0131	0.0336	0.1751	0.0105	0.0473	−0.0101
	(1.013)	(1.051)	(3.392)	(0.5576)	(2.138)	(0.2533)
p_{t-1}	0.7375		0.7542	0.7472	0.7997	
	(10.27)		(14.80)	(13.42)	(15.19)	
y_t^e	0.0036	1.032	−0.0488	0.0065	0.0086	0.2344
	(0.0950)	(4.331)	(0.3816)	(0.1680)	(0.2546)	(2.599)
u_{ct}	0.0068	−0.0335	0.0759	0.0140		−0.0378
	(0.5661)	(3.795)	(3.546)	(1.123)		(3.394)
ρ		0.9390		0.4233		0.9202
R^2	0.9980	0.9973	0.9834	0.9995	0.9848	0.9917
R^2_X		0.6075		0.7375		0.3619
DW	1.902	1.160	1.272	1.905	1.323	1.904
SSR	0.0009	0.0199	0.0200	0.0005	0.0018	0.0023
SER	0.0039	0.0057	0.0179	0.0031	0.0055	0.0061

SIC No. and Description	
32	Stone, clay, and glass — Previous level of total spending
331	Primary ferrous — 2nd degree polynomial, 10 quarters long, far end constrained to zero
333	Primary nonferrous — Previous level of total spending
35	Nonelectrical machinery — 2nd degree polynomial, 10 quarters long, far end constrained to zero
36	Electrical machinery — 2nd degree polynomial, 10 quarters long, far end constrained to zero
371	Motor vehicles and equipment — Previous level of total spending

TABLE 6 Wage Equations for the Disaggregated Manufacturing Industries[a]
(sample period: 1954I–1971II; figures in parentheses are t statistics)

Variables	Nondurable Manufacturing Industries					
	SIC 20	SIC 22	SIC 26	SIC 28	SIC 29	SIC 30
C_0	−0.4988 (0.9480)	−2.032 (2.803)	−0.0682 (0.5615)	−0.0980 (0.4343)	0.5628 (2.703)	−0.1321 (0.6423)
T	0.0019 (3.408)	0.0002 (0.6069)	0.0018 (3.657)	−0.0003 (1.033)	0.0026 (4.292)	0.0019 (4.375)
u^{-1}		0.0223 (2.392)			0.0077 (3.069)	
$u_t - u_{t-1}$			−0.0079 (1.982)		−0.0239 (2.266)	−0.0216 (2.353)
$\rho - \bar{\rho}$	0.1096 (0.9892)	0.1495 (2.467)	0.0400 (1.770)	0.0187 (1.473)	−0.0541 (1.374)	0.0762 (1.833)
D_1	−0.0074 (2.564)	−0.0055 (1.595)	−0.0052 (4.493)	−0.0020 (1.340)	−0.0027 (0.7910)	−0.0052 (1.557)
D_3	0.6691 (1.489)		0.5287 (2.551)	0.3410 (2.434)	1.296 (3.501)	0.7128 (2.578)
p_{ct-1}	0.0808 (1.747)	0.3180 (2.120)	0.0855 (3.080)	0.0059 (0.1300)	0.1271 (3.699)	0.0518 (1.487)
w_{t-1}	0.8376 (16.13)	0.8030 (10.10)	0.7926 (13.62)	1.028 (31.23)	0.6835 (9.390)	0.7410 (12.34)
ρ_i		−0.1278		−0.2697		
R^2	0.9989	0.9986	0.9997	0.9998	0.9981	0.9982
R^2_X		0.3633		0.5596		
DW	2.738	2.021	2.169	2.079	2.033	2.485
SSR	0.0032	0.0033	0.0010	0.0005	0.0042	0.0031
SER	0.0071	0.0073	0.0039	0.0029	0.0082	0.0071

The wage rate is a very important explanatory variable in every case except petroleum, primary nonferrous, and nonelectrical machinery, where the sign of the wage is negative. This is mainly due to the multicollinearity between the wage rate and the lagged dependent variable, p_{t-1}. When p_{t-1} is dropped, the coefficient of w_t becomes positive and statistically significant. The short-run elasticity of price with respect to the wage rate varies among the different industries, ranging from a high of 0.57 for textile mills products

Variables	Durable Manufacturing Industries					
	SIC 32	SIC 331	SIC 333	SIC 35	SIC 36	SIC 371
C_0	−0.2242	−0.0407	0.2853	0.2810	−0.1416	−3.631
	(1.192)	(0.3555)	(2.387)	(2.084)	(1.195)	(4.170)
T	0.0019	0.0018	0.0010	0.0015	0.0020	0.0019
	(3.089)	(4.690)	(2.948)	(2.616)	(5.227)	(2.418)
u^{-1}	0.0056				0.0076	0.0083
	(2.426)				(0.3596)	(1.631)
$u_t - u_{t-1}$		−0.0193	−0.0207	−0.0074	−0.0008	−0.0487
		(2.560)	(3.905)	(2.627)	(2.609)	(4.680)
$\rho - \bar{\rho}$	0.0766	0.0908	−0.0269	−0.0119	0.0546	0.0513
	(2.166)	(6.075)	(1.293)	(0.5337)	(2.136)	(1.435)
D_1	−0.0058	−0.0068	−0.0040	−0.0018	−0.0038	0.0055
	(3.355)	(2.256)	(1.303)	(1.094)	(2.609)	(1.085)
D_3	1.077	0.2136	0.5015	0.7994	0.8674	
	(5.211)	(0.7297)	(2.010)	(3.623)	(4.730)	
p_{ct-1}	0.0992	0.2357	0.0074	0.1174	0.0352	0.8975
	(1.553)	(5.336)	(0.6388)	(2.898)	(4.110)	(4.904)
w_{t-1}	0.7397	0.6570	0.8805	0.7469	0.7421	0.3935
	(7.999)	(10.10)	(23.69)	(8.706)	(14.77)	(3.600)
ρ_1	−0.2192				0.0642	−0.2843
R^2	0.9995	0.9983	0.9992	0.9997	0.9997	0.9965
R_X^2	0.5421				0.5780	0.5831
DW	2.021	1.996	2.081	2.128	1.861	2.009
SSR	0.0011	0.0037	0.0018	0.0008	0.0007	0.0102
SER	0.0044	0.0077	0.0055	0.0036	0.0033	0.0139

All variables except T, D_1, and D_3 are in logs. In nondurables industries the unemployment rate for total nondurables is used for u_t, and in durables, the unemployment rate for total durables is used for u_t. The industries are identified by name in Table 5, note a.

to a low of 0.05 for chemicals. Also, this is invariably greater than the elasticity of price with respect to the productivity variables. This implies that an increase in productivity has to be very large to compensate for wage increases; otherwise, there might be a general tendency for industry prices to drift upward.

Materials price is the most important explanatory variable for price behavior in several industries, especially the durables. The short-run elasticity of prices with respect to v_t is about 0.40 in primary nonferrous (SIC 333) and motor vehicles (SIC 371) and 0.12 in electrical machinery (SIC 36).[18]

The utilization rate in the disaggregate industries plays different roles: it has a negative sign in some industries and a positive sign in others. The positive sign indicates a demand effect, while the negative sign, as mentioned before, stands for movement along the average cost curve before capacity output is achieved. It is interesting to note that whenever the utilization rate is positive and significant the expected demand variable (y_t^e) is negative and insignificant, suggesting that u_{ct} captures the effect of expected demand in those industries. Generally, the utilization rate is not a very important variable in the nondurables, except petroleum (SIC 29), where it has a positive coefficient of 0.6. In durable industries, it is usually significant with a negative sign in primary ferrous (SIC 331) and motor vehicles and positive and significant in primary nonferrous.

The rental price of capital services is statistically significant in several industries and enters with a positive sign in most, with the exception of two nondurables (food and kindred products, SIC 20, and textiles, SIC 22) and two durables (stone, clay, and glass, SIC 32, and motor vehicles, SIC 371). However, the coefficients of c_t in the two durable industries are not statistically insignificant. If we were to interpret this variable as a proxy for a fair rate of return, the negative coefficients would suggest that firms would raise prices in order to maintain a given rate. Changes in rental price play a very important role in the durables, particularly in primary nonferrous, where the short-run elasticity of price with respect to c_t is about 0.2. Among the nondurables, petroleum prices seem to respond strongly to changes in the rental price of capital.

Total spending, y_t^e, exerts an important influence on prices in several industries. Except for the industries where the utilization rate enters positively, y_t^e has a statistically significant positive coefficient. The effect of aggregate spending seems to be large and highly significant in the durable industries.[19]

The coefficient of p_{t-1} varies somewhat among industries, from a high of 0.9 in chemicals to a low of 0.46 in food and kindred products. However, in most cases, it is about 0.7 or 0.8, implying an average of four quarters for prices to adjust to their equilibrium values, which are calculated as $(1 - \lambda)/\lambda$, where $1 - \lambda$ is the coefficient of p_{t-1} in the industry regression.

Long-run elasticities of the price level with respect to factor costs, productivity growth, and expected demand can be calculated using the estimates in Table 5. Tentative calculations indicate that a majority of the industries respond strongly to wage rate and materials price changes in the long run. The effect of the rental price of capital is rather small, and the long-run elasticity of prices with respect to expected demand is large but less than unity, and it varies among industries.

Industry Wage Behavior

The response of wages to the explanatory variables differs considerably among the industries. The main features of the results in Table 6 can be summarized briefly.

The labor market disequilibrium variables, u^{-1} and $u_t - u_{t-1}$, and sometimes both, have statistically significant effects on wages in every industry except food and kindred products.[20] The reciprocal of the unemployment rate has a positive sign and is statistically significant in textiles, chemicals, and stone, clay, and glass. The rate of change of the unemployment rate is significant in all other industries. Both unemployment variables are significant in two industries—nonelectrical machinery and motor vehicles. Note the dynamic characteristic of the wage rate and unemployment rate, which we discussed before. This relationship is sustained at the disaggregate level as well (see the section, Aggregate Wage Equations, above).

The long-run productivity trend, T, and the short-run productivity changes contribute significantly to wage increases in most industries, except in chemicals, where the coefficient of T is negative and statistically insignificant. The coefficients of trend productivity generally cluster around 0.0018 except for petroleum, for which the figure is especially high (0.0026). The contribution of the short-run productivity variable $(\rho - \bar{\rho})$, which is often a proxy for profits, varies among industries. In some nondurable industries, such as rubber products and textiles, short-term productivity contributes significantly, while in nonferrous and in nonelectrical machinery it is not significant.

The guidepost dummy (D_1) is statistically significant in every case except petroleum, nonelectrical machinery, and motor vehicles. The negative sign of this variable in all industries except motor vehicles suggests that guidepost policies effectively dampened the growth of the wage rate in the majority of U.S. manufacturing industries. This finding is complementary to the evidence found by Perry (1970) and to our results for the aggregate sectors and industries of the economy reported in Table 3.[21]

The threshold variable (D_3) plays an important role in the wage behavior of the disaggregate manufacturing industries. Except for textiles, primary ferrous, and motor vehicles, D_3 always has a positive and statistically significant coefficient, but the magnitude of the coefficient varies considerably among industries. Nonetheless, it seems that industry wage rates are quite sensitive to changes in prices after a certain critical level.

The short-run elasticity of wages with respect to the price level varies considerably. In a majority of cases, the coefficient of p_{t-1} is positive and statistically significant, and it is always less than unity. The largest coefficient—0.90—is for motor vehicles.

The lagged wage rate is statistically significant, but its coefficients vary in magnitude among industries. Its largest value occurs in chemicals, and its lowest value, in motor vehicles. The implied adjustment process of wages to their equilibrium value seems to be about one year in most industries other than motor vehicles, where the adjustment is much faster.

Tentative long-run elasticities of wages with respect to price and productivity can be derived from the estimates of Table 6. Generally, the price elasticity of wages varies among industries and is smaller than unity except in textiles and motor vehicles. The long-run elasticity of wages with respect to trend productivity also varies considerably among industries. Food, paper, petroleum, and most durables have elasticities that range between 0.007 and 0.010. All these results on long-run elasticities should be considered tentative, since some specification errors could be present in estimating industry wage equations.

V. GOODNESS OF FIT, FORECASTING ABILITY, AND EFFECT OF CONTROLS

Comparison with Autoregressive Models

A useful test of the overall explanatory power of the estimated equations is to compare them with a set of autoregressive models. This comparison is a stringent test for the analytical models (see Jorgenson-Hunter-Nadiri 1970 for a discussion and tests for such comparisons). We shall compare the price and wage equations both at the aggregate and disaggregate levels with a set of second-order autoregressive models of the form:

$$(12) \qquad p_t = \alpha_0' + \alpha_1' p_{t-1} + \alpha_3' p_{t-2} + \epsilon_p$$

$$w_t = \beta_0' + \beta_1' w_{t-1} + \beta_3' w_{t-2} + \epsilon_w$$

All variables are in logarithms, and ϵ_p and ϵ_w are the residuals.

The F statistics computed from the sums of squared residuals of the analytical and autoregressive models are shown in Table 7. For the calculations shown in the table, the critical value of F with degrees of freedom (1, 60) is 7.08 at the 1 percent level of significance and 4.00 at the 5 percent level. It is clear that in every case, the analytical model performs much better than its autoregressive counterpart. This is quite impressive, since autoregressive models have an edge over analytical models whenever the data are highly serially correlated, as is the case with price and wage series.

Forecasts of Prices and Wages for Rates for Aggregate Sectors and Industries

The estimated equations can be used to dynamically simulate price and wage behavior for the sample period 1954I–1972II and the forecast period 1971III–1973II. Also, it is possible to examine the effectiveness of price and wage controls which were imposed during the latter period. Because of the unavailability of data on materials prices at the disaggregate industry level after 1971III, we cannot generate forecasts of individual-industry prices and wages, but we have been able to do so for aggregate sectors and industries. To save space, we shall present certain summary statistics on the simulation results for the sample period, but for the forecast period, the absolute and percent errors will also be reported and analyzed.

The summary statistics of the simulation of prices and wages over the sample period are reported in Table 8. The predictions are very good. The root-mean-square error ($RMSE$) for prices is often about 0.002, while that for wage rates is about 0.012. The mean absolute error (MAE) and mean errors (ME) are also very small. The largest error as a percent of the actual rates is seldom more than 0.01 for both prices and wage rates; the largest error in absolute terms seldom exceeds two to three cents. We also calculated quarterly and four-quarter percent changes of the actual and predicted values of the variables and obtained their percent forecast errors.[22] In prices, the largest absolute quarterly percent error in the sample period was in the private nonfarm sector (about 0.016); for the wage rate, it was in durables (about 0.015). The summary statistics of the forecast errors for the period 1971III–1973II are also shown in Table 8.

TABLE 7 F Statistics for Comparison of Regression Equations in Tables 1 and 3 with Their Autoregressive Counterparts[a]

Industry	F Statistics		Industry	F Statistics	
	F_p	F_w		F_p	F_w
Aggregate economy	100.00	60.00	Chemical and allied products	20.00	40.00
Private nonfarm	42.85	60.00	Petroleum and allied products	23.00	33.86
Total mfr.	80.00	45.00	Rubber and allied products	52.4	38.00
Total durables	85.11	70.00	Stone, clay, and glass	60.00	55.00
Total nondurables	20.00	28.57	Primary ferrous	13.25	33.33
Food and kindred products	18.00	11.00	Nonelectrical machinery	50.00	50.00
Textile mills and products	13.33	23.33	Electrical machinery	16.66	50.00
Paper and allied products	10.50	23.41	Motor vehicles	15.59	49.00

[a] In calculating these F statistics for various industries, appropriate adjustments were made to take account of variations in the degrees of freedom.

TABLE 8 Analysis of the Residuals of the Aggregate Price and Wage Equations over the Sample and Forecast Periods[a]

(residuals as quarterly differences between actual and simulated level of prices and wages)

	Aggregate Economy		Private Nonfarm		Total Manufacturing		Total Durables		Total Nondurables	
	p_t	w_t	p_t	w_t	p_t	w_t	p_t	w_t	p_t	w_t
	Sample Period: 1954I–1971II									
RMSE	.0010	.012	.002	.012	.0034	.012	.0063	.012	.004	.0029
MAE	.0082	.010	.0016	.010	.0028	.010 ·	.0055	.010	.003	.0023
ME	−.0018	$.4 \times 10^4$	$.18 \times 10^{-5}$	$.4 \times 10^{-4}$	$.2 \times 10^{-4}$	$-.4 \times 10^{-3}$	$-.9 \times 10^{-4}$	$-.13 \times 10^{-3}$	$.6 \times 10^{-5}$	$.22 \times 10^{-2}$
	Forecast Period: 1971III–1973II									
RMSE	.0043	.035	.0075	.035	.019	.023	.0016	.032	.030	.0065
MAE	.0036	.028	.0062	.028	.012	.017	.0010	.029	.018	.0051
ME	.0018	.023	−.0061	.023	−.011	−.015	$-.2 \times 10^{-3}$	.014	.017	.0007

RMSE = root-mean-square error.
MAE = absolute mean error.
ME = mean error.
[a] All price indexes are on base 1967 = 1.00, and the wage rates are in dollars.

TABLE 9 Absolute and Relative Forecast Errors of Prices and Wages for the Aggregate Economy and total Manufacturing[a]

Year and Quarter	Aggregate Economy				Total Manufacturing			
	Prices		Wages		Prices		Wages	
	A	B	A	B	A	B	A	B
1971 III	.0079	−.0016	−.0041	−.0014	.0005	.00003	−.020	−.0053
IV	.0035	−.0037	−.0138	−.0012	−.0015	−.0017	−.029	−.0023
1972 I	.0068	.0022	.0612	.0078	−.0007	.0007	.015	.0085
II	.0034	−.0023	.0290	−.0068	.0026	.0029	.052	.0009
III	.0009	−.0020	.0192	−.0021	.0080	.0046	−.014	−.0051
IV	−.0019	−.0023	.0247	.0011	.0100	.0016	.0011	.0041
1973 I	−.0042	−.0018	.0651	.0079	.025	.0123	−.086	−.0044
II	−.0011	.0025	.0077	−.0114	.0462	.0168	−.051	−.0088

[a] In each case, column A contains the absolute magnitude of the errors recorded. For prices, column A shows $P_t - P_{t-1}$ and for wages, $W_t - W_{t-1}$. Column B contains the percent rates of change of quarterly forecast errors of prices and wages. For prices, the relation-

They are generally small and trace the same pattern as those observed for the sample period. As is to be expected, they are generally larger in magnitude than the corresponding statistics in the sample period.

In Table 9, the absolute and percent forecast errors for the aggregate sectors and industries are presented.[23] In columns A, the absolute magnitudes of the errors are recorded; and in columns B, the percent changes of quarterly forecast errors of price and wages. Several observations are in order: In general, the size of errors is fairly small; the forecast errors are larger in the individual industries than in the aggregate economy; the percent forecast errors for prices and wage rates seem to increase in the manufacturing industries after 1972III; and there seems to be a jump in the errors in 1972I and 1973II, dates which correspond to the lifting of controls.

It is difficult to evaluate the relative predictive performance of our model against alternative models for individual industries because industry forecasts of wages and prices are not readily available. However, we can compare our price forecasts for the aggregate economy with the recently published projections of the Federal Reserve Bank of St. Louis; the figures shown in the following tabulation are absolute errors in forecasts of percent changes in the GNP price deflator at annual rates:[24]

Year and Quarter	Total Durables				Total Nondurables			
	Prices		Wages		Prices		Wages	
	A	B	A	B	A	B	A	B
1971III	.0120	.0049	−.030	−.0074	−.0028	−.0030	.0135	−.0003
IV	.0079	−.0035	−.032	−.0005	−.0016	.0015	.0077	.0080
1972I	.0062	−.0016	.014	.0122	−.0003	.0007	.0180	.0089
II	.0071	.0007	.0279	.0033	−.0006	−.0003	.0175	−.0021
III	.0087	.0013	.0189	−.0023	.0048	.0047	.0147	−.0023
IV	−.0076	−.0129	.0461	.0066	.0211	.0442	.0152	.0036
1973I	−.016	−.0076	.0482	.0003	.0470	.0115	.0147	.0073
II	−.019	−.0023	.0182	−.0074	.0683	.0159	.0088	−.0121

ship shown is $[(P_t - P_{t-1})/P_{t-1}] - [(\hat{P}_t - \hat{P}_{t-1})/\hat{P}_{t-1}]$. The relationship for wages is the same, with W substituted for P and $\hat{W}$ for $\hat{P}$ in each case.

	Forecast Errors	
Period	St. Louis Model	Equation 3
1971I	2.4%	−0.64%
II	2.8	−1.48
1972I	1.7	0.88
II	1.9	−0.92
III	1.8	−0.80
IV	1.6	−0.92
1973I	1.2	−0.72
II	0.6	1.00
Average absolute error	1.75	0.736

It is clear that except in 1973II, the prediction errors of our model are much smaller than those generated by the St. Louis model. In fact, the average error of our model over this period seems to be less than half that predicted by the St. Louis one.

The Effectiveness of Controls

Price and wage controls were imposed in August 1971, and they were continued in some modified form until August 13, 1973. Prices and wages were frozen in Phase I (August 15 to November 12, 1971), in Phase II (November 12, 1971, to January 11, 1973) a set of mandatory but flexible controls was imposed; in Phase III (January 11 to June 13, 1973), a policy of voluntary restraints was pursued, that was followed by Phase III and a half (June 13 to August 13, 1973), in which the second freeze on wages and prices was decreed. Finally, in Phase IV, a policy of mandatory but flexible controls was followed.

The question is whether the incomes policies pursued were effective. Our model can be used to throw some light on this question. We can introduce dummy variables in our regression equations to capture the effects of price controls, or we can look at the dynamic forecasts generated by the model for the control period and compare them with the actual values of prices and wages; the difference between those predicted and actual values constitutes a measure of the effectiveness of the income policies. That is, if the model overpredicts prices and wages in this period, the magnitudes of the overpredictions will be considered as a measure of the effectiveness of the wage-price controls.

We did not re-estimate the original equations by introducing dummy variables for controls; rather, we followed the second alternative of comparing the actual and predicted values of the series for 1972III–1973II in order to obtain some feeling for the degree of effectiveness of the controls.

In Table 9 the differences between actual and predicted percent changes in prices and wage rates for the aggregate economy and the three aggregate manufacturing industries are reported in columns B. The negative sign means that percent rates of price and wage change projected by the model exceed their actual values, and the magnitudes indicate the extent of overprediction. For the aggregate economy, the percent change in the GNP deflator is overpredicted for each quarter during the period 1971III–1973II, except for 1972I and 1973II, which are associated with termination or modification of the control policies. In those two quarters, the jump in actual prices was quite substantial, and the model underpredicts the amounts. Similarly, controls in phases I and II were fairly important in restraining wage increases. After each of these two periods, the wage rate seems to shoot up, indicating a catching-up phenomenon. The magnitude of this effect is particularly significant after the termination of Phase I. In Phase III, the percent change in the wage rate is underpredicted in 1973I and overpredicted in 1973II, while the opposite is true of prices. Thus, the actual rise in the wage rate continues its momentum in 1972I and 1973I in spite of controls, while for prices, the influence of Phase II controls continues up to the beginning of Phase III. For the entire period of the controls, aggregate-economy prices and wages are overpredicted by the model to such an extent that in spite of overreaction of the economy to the termination of phases I and II, controls seem to have had a net dampening effect.

In the case of the manufacturing industries, the effectiveness of the controls is not very clear. In Phase I, the model generally overpredicts both prices and wages. Actual prices and wages respond to the lifting of Phase I controls, and there is a consistent pattern of price and wage bulges in 1972I. This catching-up phenomenon is very strong in total manufacturing and total durables. There is a difference in the effect of controls on wages and prices in phases II and III. In total manufacturing and nondurables, prices seem to continue to rise irrespective of the controls: prices are underpredicted throughout the period 1972II–1973II. In durables, the controls seem to exert some influence in 1972IV–1973II. The effect of controls on wages in that industry grouping does not exhibit a systematic pattern, except that at the end of Phase II, wage rates bulge, i.e., actual wage rate increases are substantial, and the model underpredicts them. In Phase III there is evidence that wage rates in the manufacturing industries have been affected by the controls. For the whole period 1971III–1973II, it seems that wage and price controls have been fairly ineffective in controlling price increases in total manufacturing and nondurables but have had partial success in the durables. This success of the controls was more visible on the wage side, though the pattern, timing, and magnitude of their influence have varied considerably.

Thus, it seems that both the Kennedy-Johnson and Nixon control policies had some effect on wage rates and prices. The guideposts influenced wages directly and strongly and prices only indirectly through wages.[25] Although the recent controls did exert a direct effect on the growth of general price level and had some effect on manufacturing prices, there is reason to believe that the controls were more successful in restraining wages. When the controls were lifted or modified, prices and wages reacted sharply in response to efforts to recoup the losses incurred during the controls. The magnitude and timing of the influence of guideposts and of recent control policies in restraining price and wages increases differed substantially among various sectors of the economy.

VI. SUMMARY AND CONCLUSIONS

We have constructed a model that integrates the long-run determinants of equilibrium price and wage rates with short-run disequilibrium factors operating in the commodity and labor markets. We have tried to take account of all the relevant factor costs, productivity changes, and demand considerations that enter into the determination of the price level. In formulating the wage equation, long-run factors such as the growth of productivity and prices were integrated with short-term phenomena such as controls and changes in unemployment conditions, price expectations, and productivity. The wage and price equations were fitted using data for the total economy and for fifteen manufacturing industries for 1954I–1972II. Price and wage forecasts were generated for the aggregate sectors and for manufacturing industries for 1971III–1973II, covering the period when economic controls were in effect.

Several important conclusions are derived from the analysis:

1. Factor costs such as wage rates, rental price of capital services, and materials prices are important determinants of prices in both aggregate and disaggregate industries. Their individual contributions vary among sectors and industries, but the usual practice of omitting materials prices and, particularly, the rental price of capital in price equations was found to be unwarranted.

2. Capacity utilization has a significant negative effect on prices in the aggregate economy and in a large number of individual industries. This finding is in contrast to the positive relationship found by other investigators. Our results suggest that higher utilization of existing capacity, everything else remaining the same, will reduce costs and lead to lower prices. Thus, up to a point, policies designed to increase resource utilization will not be inflationary.

3. An important finding of our analysis is that aggregate spending influences prices at both the aggregate and industry levels. This is in contrast to the findings of several studies which imply no influence of the economy-wide variables on individual-industry price behavior. The pervasive effect of aggregate spending on the level and structure of prices has important policy implications.

4. A combination of long- and short-term factors determines the course of money wages. Long-run productivity growth and consumer prices play important roles in determining long-run wage rates. There is considerable variation in the response of wage rates to these two variables in different sectors and industries. In a majority of cases, the long-run elasticity of wages with respect to prices was found to be less than unity.

5. There is a dynamic relationship between the wage rate and the unemployment rate at the aggregate and industry levels; the unemployment rate or its rate of change, depicting short-term disequilibria in labor markets, influences wages in almost all industries. The precise relationships between wage changes and unemployment variables and the magnitudes of their effects vary considerably among industries. On the whole, the results suggest that wage increases could be slowed down to some extent if the unemployment rate is rising at an increasing rate.

6. Prices and price expectations play an important role in determining wage behavior. The elasticity of the wage rate with respect to prices is below unity in the short run. In many cases, even in the long run, money illusion seems to prevail in several industries. Short-run price expectations affect wage behavior both at the aggregate and disaggregate levels. The expectation phenomenon is best captured by an extrapolation hypothesis at the aggregate level and by a nonlinearity relation in the form of a threshold effect at the disaggregate levels.

7. The results indicate that guideposts have significant effects on aggregate and disaggregate industries. Their effects on wage rates have been quite pervasive and of varying magnitudes.

8. Productivity changes play an important role in wage determination in the sectors and industries considered. The trend productivity has a significant effect on wages of the aggregate and individual manufacturing industries, while deviation from productivity contributes importantly to all the aggregate wage regressions and some of the durables and nondurables.

9. For dynamic simulations of the model within the sample period, at both the economy and industry levels, the errors were smaller and wages and prices tracked far better than for a set of autoregressive models. The forecasts generated by the model are close to actual prices and wages for the aggregate sectors and manufacturing industries during the period 1971III–1973II. Moreover, the percent rates of change of prices and wages generated by the model satisfactorily track the actual values during the period when controls were in effect.

10. The effects of controls on price and wage rates of the aggregate sectors and manufacturing industries seem to have been mainly on the wage side; aggregate price increases were slowed down by the controls in phases I through III; in the manufacturing industries the controls were effective mainly in Phase I but ineffective in phases II and III. However, this assessment is only tentative.

11. The overall policy implication of our findings is that simple counterinflationary policies will be inadequate in stabilizing prices and wages. A combination of policies should be considered that will combat not only short-run inflationary conditions but also the effects of the underlying forces of secular inflation in the economy. A complex set of strategies is needed, which would involve management of total spending, promotion of long-run productivity growth, dampening excessive expectations, better utilization of the existing capacity, and effective wage and price controls.

NOTES

1. See Nordhaus (1972) for the details of the deviation of similar price rules under different technological constraints.
2. See Fair (1969) for a survey of the literature on labor-demand functions and Mincer (1970) for a general survey of the research on labor supply behavior.
3. We can specify log-linear demand and supply functions (4a) and (4b):

   (4a) $L^d = a_0 P^{*a_1} X^{*a_2} W^{-a_3}$

   (4b) $L^s = b_0 P_C^{*-b_1} W^{b_2}$

   P^* is the expected output price, X^* is the expected output, P_C^* is the expected price of consumer goods: Solving for equilibrium wage, we get

   $$W^* = \gamma_0 P^{\gamma_1} X^{\gamma_2} P_C^{\gamma_3}$$

   where $\gamma_0 = (a_0/b_0)[1/(a_3 + b_2)]$; $\gamma_1 = a_1/(a_3 + b_2)$; $\gamma_2 = a_2/(a_3 + b_2)$; $\gamma_3 = b_1/(a_3 + b_2)$.
   In principle, therefore, both output price and price of goods purchased by the workers should determine equilibrium wage rate. The problem is that P_C and P are highly collinear and one of them must be excluded from the regressions. Of course, it is possible that either the specific industry output price or the consumer price index may best represent the price effect. At the individual industry level, it is labor's negotiation strategy that determines whether the specific commodity or the general price level should be used as a determinant of wage rate settlements.
4. There is the question of whether the adjustment factors and the short-term factors are interdependent. We have assumed that some part of the adjustment to the equilibrium condition can be identified explicitly by the short-term factors and that the rest may be associated with the adjustment coefficient specified in the model.
5. However, certain fiscal measures such as investment tax credits, reductions in income tax rates on corporations, and taxes on depreciation allowances are part of the cost structure. They are transmitted to prices through the market forces; in the model, their effects are incorporated through the rental price of capital. Guideposts and controls, on the other hand, are superimposed on the market adjustment process.
6. The experiments were performed using aggregate price and wage equations. Therefore, the conclusion may hold only tentatively for other sector and industry results.

7. We did not have enough time to attempt to specify the determinants of y_t^e. However, using Christ (1973) and Anderson and Carlson (1972), it is possible to estimate a reasonable function explaining total spending y_t^e in terms of monetary and fiscal variables.

8. The problems of multicollinearity that will be present in estimating level equations can be treated by using the Ridge regression estimation technique (see Hoerl and Kennard 1970 for a discussion of this method). Some preliminary efforts showed that in the regressions for the aggregate economy, the coefficients were fairly stable. Also, most of the coefficients as shown in tables 1 to 3 are statistically significant, which suggests that multicollinearity is not very severe in the aggregate sectors and industries.

   The rate-of-change formulation has severe shortcomings. First, by construction, the influence of short-run factors is emphasized, sometimes at the expense of long-run factors; the latter may be the most important determinants of wage and price movements. Second, various arbitrary moving average arrangements are often used to obtain better fits and sensible results, but such attempts introduce serial correlation in the estimating equations, and that leads to biased parametric estimates. (See Black and Kelejian 1972, Oi n.d., and Rowley and Wilton 1973 for further discussion.)

9. See Turnovsky (1972), Mincer (1969), and Juster and Wachtel (1972) for further discussion of the issues concerning formulation and effects of expectation on various economic decisions.

10. The expectational variables p^e and D_3 were used as alternatives in the wage equations for the aggregate and industry regressions. The results generally favored using p^e in the aggregate equations and D_3 in the industry ones.

11. For the disaggregate industries overtime hours are not available for 1953–1957. The regression technique was used to extrapolate backward the straight-time earnings series.

12. The methodology used to construct this data set, which is based on the input-output tables for the United States, is fully described in Eckstein and Wyss (1972).

13. The existence of collinearity between this variable and p_{t-1} may explain some of the instability of its coefficient.

14. Using adjusted wage series would have made it difficult to distinguish the effects of labor utilization and capacity utilization; also, it would be difficult to distinguish the effects of trend increase in wages (because of removal of overtime component) and a trend increase in productivity.

15. The coefficient of $p_{ct-1} - p_{ct-2}$ for the nondurables is rather high but statistically not significant.

16. Differentiating a truncated version of the wage equation

$$\ln W_t = a_1 + a_2 \ln P_{ct} + a_3 \ln \left(\frac{P_{ct-1}}{P_{ct-2}} \right)$$

with respect to time and rearranging terms, we get the expression

$$\frac{\dot{w}}{w} = a_2 \left(\frac{\dot{P}_{ct-1}}{P_{ct-1}} \right) + a_3 \left(\frac{\dot{P}_{ct-1}}{P_{ct-1}} - \frac{\dot{P}_{ct-2}}{P_{ct-2}} \right)$$

This implies a short-term price elasticity of less than 1.0 when a_2 and a_3 are less than 1.0; therefore, our results are consistent with those reported by Solow (1968), Gordon (1972), Perry (1970), and others.

17. Nordhaus (1972) reports factor shares as follows:

Sector	Factor Shares (percent)		
	Labor	Capital	Materials
Manufacturing			
Nondurables	.24	.08	.68
Durables	.40	.13	.47
Total	.45	.13	.42
Private nonfarm	.61	.19	.20
GNP	.73	.22	.05

The GNP figures are from the national income accounts; those for manufacturing for 1958 are from the input-output table in *Survey of Current Business*, 1965.

18. In some of nondurables, such as chemicals (SIC 28) and paper products (SIC 26) materials do not enter significantly and are excluded. However, this may be caused by the high collinearity of m_t and p_{t-1} in those industries.

19. Several experiments with industry output variables suggested that aggregate expenditure is a better measure of demand in industry price equations. In most cases, the short-run elasticity of prices with respect to y_t^e ranges from about 0.08 to 0.60. In primary nonferrous, the coefficient of y_t^e depicts the long-run elasticity, since the lagged dependent variable p_{t-1} has been excluded from the regression.

20. Time-series data on unemployment rates for individual industries are not available. Therefore, the unemployment rate for total durables is used in each durable industry and that of total nondurables for each nondurable industry.

21. In the literature the evidence on guideposts has been challenged; see, for example, Gordon (1972b) and Wachter (1970).

22. These were calculated as

$$x_1 = \frac{z_t - z_{t-1}}{z_{t-1}} - \frac{\hat{z}_t - \hat{z}_{t-1}}{\hat{z}_{t-1}}$$

and

$$x_2 = \frac{z_t - z_{t-4}}{z_{t-4}} - \frac{\hat{z}_t - \hat{z}_{t-4}}{\hat{z}_{t-4}}$$

where z_t is the actual and $\hat{z}_t$ is forecast value of levels of prices and wage rates.

23. The results for the private nonfarm sector are not reported because the wage equation is identical to that for the total economy, and the price forecasts are quite similar to the ones presented in the first two columns of Table 9.

24. See Federal Reserve Bank of St. Louis *Review*, September 1974, p. 20, Table 1. These figures are calculated by taking the difference between actual and ex ante projections of the St. Louis Model. The signs of the forecasts errors generated by equation 3 are ignored for comparison purposes.

25. These results are in accord with the recent evidence reported by de Menil (1974).

REFERENCES

Agrawal, R., et al. 1972. "The Neoclassical Approach to Determination of Prices and Wages." *Econometrica*, August: 250–263.

Anderson, L. G., and K. M. Carlson. 1972. "An Econometric Analysis of the Relation of Monetary Variables to the Behavior of Prices and Unemployment." In Eckstein, ed., 1972.

Bischoff, C. W. 1969. "Hypothesis Testing and the Demand for Capital Goods." *Review of Economics and Statistics*, August: 354–368.

Black, S. W., and H. H. Kelejian. 1972. "The Formulation of the Dependent Variable in the Wage Equation." *Review of Economic Studies*, January: 55–59.

Christ, C. 1973. "Monetary and Fiscal Influences on U.S. Money Income 1891–1970." *Journal of Money, Credit and Banking*, February: 279–300.

de Menil, G. 1974. "Aggregate Price Dynamics." *Review of Economics and Statistics*, May: 129–140.

Dowling, J. M. 1973. "Wage Determination in the Two-Digit Manufacturing Industries, Theory Test and Forecasts." *Quarterly Review of Economics and Business*, Spring: 27–35.

Eckstein, O., ed. 1972. *The Econometrics of Price Determination*. Washington, D.C.: Board of Governors of the Federal Reserve System.

Eckstein, O., and R. Brinner. 1972. *The Inflation Process in the United States*. Study prepared for Joint Economic Committee, 92d Cong., 2d sess.

Eckstein, O., and G. Fromm. 1968. "The Price Equation." *American Economic Review*, December: 1159–1183.

Eckstein, O., and D. Wyss. 1972. "Industry Price Equations." In Eckstein, ed., 1972.

Fair, R. 1969. *The Short-Run Demand Function for Workers and Hours*. Amsterdam: North-Holland.

Federal Reserve Bank of St. Louis. 1969. *Review*, September.

Gordon, R. J. 1972a. "Inflation in Recession and Recovery." *Brookings Papers on Economic Activity*, no. 1: 105–106.

———. 1972b. "Wage-Price Controls and the Shifting Phillips Curve." *Brookings Papers on Economic Activity*, no. 2: 385–430.

Griliches, Z. 1967. "Distributed Lags: A Survey." *Econometrica*, 35: 16–49.

Hall, R., and D. Jorgenson. 1967. "Tax Policy and Investment Behavior." *American Economic Review*, June: 391–414.

Hoerl, A. E., and R. W. Kennard. 1970. "Ridge Regression: Applications to Nonorthogonal Problems." *Technometrics*, February: 69–82.

Jorgenson, D., J. Hunter, and M. I. Nadiri. 1970. "The Predictive Performance of Econometric Models of Quarterly Investment Behavior." *Econometrica*, 213–224.

Jorgenson, D., and J. A. Stephenson. 1967. "Investment Behavior in U.S. Manufacturing, 1947–60." *Econometrica*, April: 169–200.

Juster, F. T., and P. Wachtel. 1972. "Inflation and the Consumer." *Brookings Papers on Economic Activity*, no. 1: 71–122.

Klein, L. R., and R. S. Preston. 1967. "The Measurement of Capacity Utilization." *American Economic Review*, March: 34–58.

Kuh, E. 1967. "A Productivity Theory of Wage Levels—An Alternative to the Phillips Curve." *Review of Economic Studies*, October: 333–360.

Mincer, J. 1970. "The Distribution of Labor Incomes: A Survey with Special Reference to the Human Capital Approach." *Journal of Economic Literature*, March: 1–26.

Mincer, J., ed. 1969. *Economic Forecasts and Expectations: Analysis of Forecasting Behavior and Performance.* New York: National Bureau of Economic Research.

Morley, S. n.d. "Interest and Prices in U.S. Manufacturing." Mimeographed. University of Wisconsin.

Nordhaus, W. D. 1972. "Recent Developments in Price Dynamics." In Eckstein, ed. 1972.

Oi, W. n.d. "On Measuring the Impact of Wage-Price Controls: A Critical Appraisal." Mimeographed. University of Rochester.

Perry, G. L. 1970. "Changing Labor Markets and Inflation." *Brookings Papers on Economic Activity*, no. 3: 411–441.

———. 1967. "Wages and the Guideposts." *American Economic Review*, September: 897–904.

Phillips, A. W. 1958. "The Relationship between Unemployment and the Rate of Change of Money Wage Rates in the United Kingdom, 1861–1957." *Economica.* New Series. November: 283–299.

Rowley, J. C. R., and D. A. Wilton. 1973. "Quarterly Models of Wage Determination: Some New Efficient Estimates." *American Economic Review*, June: 380–384.

Solow, R. "Recent Controversy on the Theory of Inflation: An Eclectic View." In S. W. Rousseas, ed., *Inflation, Its Causes, Consequences and Control.* New York: Calvin K. Kazanjian Economics Foundation, 1968.

Turnovsky, S. J. 1972. "The Expectations Hypothesis and the Aggregate Wage Equation: Some Empirical Evidence for Canada." *Economica*, February: 1–17.

U.S. Department of Commerce. *National Income and Product Accounts of the United States, 1929–1965.*

———. *Survey of Current Business*, various issues.

U.S. Department of Labor. *Employment and Earnings Statistics for the United States, 1909–1965* (1965), and more recent editions for later years.

———. Bureau of Labor Statistics. *Monthly Labor Bulletin*, various issues.

———. Bureau of Labor Statistics. *Wholesale Prices and Price Indexes.*

U.S. Treasury Department. Internal Revenue Service. 1962. *Depreciation Guidelines and Rules.* Pub. 456, July.

Wachter, M. L. 1970. "Relative Wage Equations for U.S. Manufacturing Industries." *Review of Economics and Statistics*, November: 405–410.

COMMENTS

Samuel A. Morley
Vanderbilt University

The Nadiri-Gupta paper is an ambitious attempt to separate and identify the forces driving wages and prices in the United States. The novelty of their approach lies in their including capital costs, and in their attempt to integrate both the long- and short-run disequilibrium factors operating in factor and commodity markets into a single model or set of reduced form estimating equations. While this approach is a standard one in labor markets, this is the first time, to my knowledge, that the same disequilibrium approach has been followed in goods markets. The authors have firms and workers adjusting actual wages and prices toward their long-run equilibrium levels by a simple geometric adjustment process, where the amount of the adjustment is assumed to be influenced by the indicators of short-run disequilibrium, unemployment, and idle capacity.

Solving the profit and utility maximum conditions and combining them with ad hoc short-run adjustment functions, the authors arrive at short-run reduced form estimating equations for prices and wages which show P to be a function of the variables influencing equilibrium price (demand, wages, raw materials, and capital cost) and the short-run adjustment factors (capacity utilization and lagged price level). Similarly, wages are a function of the factors influencing the demand and supply curves of labor (productivity and the cost-of-living index) and the disequilibrium factors (unemployment rates and lagged wages).

The resulting equations are fitted to quarterly observations for 1954I–1971II, using single-equation ordinary least squares or, where autocorrelation is a problem, generalized least squares. The equations are estimated for several aggregates: the aggregate economy, private nonfarm, manufacturing; and several disaggregated subsectors of manufacturing. Separate equations for wages and prices are estimated for each of these sectors. The fitted equations are then used to project prices and wages over the price control period to determine the effect of the control program.

In general, the fits of the model are very good, although this is hardly surprising, since we are fitting time series with a strong time trend. Most of the variables, with the significant exception of capacity utilization, enter the regressions with the expected sign. Wages are the most significant determinant of prices, although the short-run elasticity of prices with respect to wages is only 0.12 in the aggregate. The rental price of capital, a variable generally left out of investigations of inflation, enters positively in most equations, although quantitatively its effect is small.

Demand also enters positively, although there appears to be an unavoidable bias in the aggregate regression since it in effect regresses prices on themselves multiplied by quantity. Note that the coefficients on the demand variable are much smaller in the disaggregated regressions. Also, these coefficients do not capture the entire influence of demand on prices, for demand also has an influence through capacity utilization, a variable that enters negatively and significantly in all the aggregate regressions, in marked contrast with previous studies. Hence the net relationship between prices and aggregate demand remains somewhat unclear.

In the wage equation, the effect of unemployment is as expected, although the additional explanation afforded by the unemployment variable is rather small. In the authors' words: "On the whole, the results suggest that wage increases could be slowed down to some extent if the unemployment rate is rising at an increasing rate."

The model generates long-run elasticities if the regression coefficients are divided through by the adjustment coefficient, which is the coefficient on the lagged endogenous variable. In the long run, the elasticity of prices with respect to demand appears to be quite low (0.28 for the total economy), especially considering the possible bias in the short-run coefficient alluded to above. Productivity enters as a positive influence on wages and a negative influence on prices. According to the model, the first effect outweighs the second, which implies that wages fully capture rising productivity over time. In the long run, the reaction of wages to changes in expected prices is close to if not greater than unity, as can be seen in the right-hand columns of Table 4. Curiously enough, the long-run price coefficient on wages is smaller in manufacturing than in the aggregate economy, which is the opposite of what one might expect, given the extent of union power in the two labor markets.

The model was also run for twelve subsectors of manufacturing. In general, the results are parallel to those at the aggregate levels. Wages and capital costs contribute positively to prices in most cases. The utilization rate is somewhat peculiar. It is positive in four cases, negative in four, and not entered in four. The short-run adjustment coefficients seem to show a tendency to faster adjustment in the more competitive industries.

The model is tested by comparing its goodness of fit during the sample period to a second-order autocorrelation scheme, a test which it passes with flying colors. Having jumped that hurdle, it is then put to work to determine whether price and wage controls had any dampening effect. This is done by running a dynamic simulation of the model over the period 1971III–1972II. If the model overpredicts price or wage levels or both over this period, the authors will conclude that the control program had some effect. However, this procedure will not work if some of the effect of the program finds its way into the supposedly exogenous variables in the model. One such variable is the Consumer Price Index (CPI), an important determinant of wage levels in the short run. If the control program reduces the CPI, then it will have had an effect on wages that will not be captured in the test used by the authors. It could also be the case that the existence of the controls encouraged the authorities to set aggregate demand higher than it would otherwise have been. Since aggregate demand is a positive determinant of prices, the test used will overstate the *net* effect of the control program on prices. Given these conditions, the results indicate that controls had some dampening effect on prices, although its size appears to be small, and a larger, though still small, effect on wage rates. For manufacturing, the controls do not appear to have been effective, particularly as regards prices. It would be useful to the reader if the authors were to provide some cumulative index of predicted and actual prices and wages here, so that a somewhat better judgment could be made about the quantitive importance of the controls program. It certainly does not appear to be large.

Turning now to some comments on the paper, on the theoretical level the most significant departure of this paper from previous work is its attempt to provide a model capable of distinguishing between long- and short-run influences on prices and wages. While that represents a worthwhile advance over the ad hoc models used in previous research, I believe that certain problems still remain in the way that excess capacity and unemployment, the indicators of market disequilibrium, appear in the model. In the first place, it turns out that in the goods market equation, capacity utilization generally enters the regressions with a negative sign. That is, the lower is capacity utilization, the higher prices are likely to be. The authors justify these findings by reference to U-shaped average cost curves. While that explanation may well be right, and while it may be consistent with a markup pricing model, it does not fit very well with equations 5 and 6. If the market systems represented by those equations are dynamically stable, the rates of change of prices and wages should be positively, not negatively, related to the indicators of excess demand.

I have another problem with equations 5 and 6. Because actual and equilibrium prices are explicitly allowed to differ, disequilibrium quantities implicitly influence prices, even if they are not put into the regressions directly. To avoid this, there must be a side relationship between U_i and the difference between P_t and P_t^*. Now, U_i has been put into the regressions as a determinant of the speed of adjustment of prices and wages to their long-run equilibrium levels, an adjustment process which is also partially captured by the other indicator of disequilibrium in the model, namely, P_t^*/P_{t-1}. As far as I can make out, there is nothing in the system guaranteeing that the two indicators are consistent, or to put it another way, there is nothing to guarantee that the system will stop at equilibrium. For example, suppose that prices last period were at their long-run equilibrium level, P^*. Unless $U_{i,t} = 1$ (i.e., excess demand is equal to zero), prices according to the model will continue to change, moving away from their equilibrium level. In order for the model to be consistent, there must be a side condition relating $U_{i,t}$ to the difference between P_t^* and P_t. That being the case, $U_{i,t}$ does not give us any independent information and could be eliminated by a respecification of the model.

Another of the main thrusts of this paper is its disaggregation within the manufacturing sector. Given the work and expense involved, one wonders whether the disaggregation is worth the trouble. That depends on what the disaggregation is intended to accomplish. If one is interested in testing for different models of price setting in manufacturing, the results for individual industries are useful in their own right. If, however, one is primarily trying to improve his predictions of aggregate inflation rates, he will only be interested in disaggregation if the prediction errors he gets by summing up the industry indexes are smaller than those obtainable through some aggregate scheme. Since the paper does not have a complete disaggregation, one cannot judge how worthwhile disaggregation is in this case. However, before researchers plunge off into such work, they ought to stop and ask themselves—and make clear to their readers—just what the purpose of the disaggregation is.

My second category of comments has to do with econometric problems in the paper. One can think of at least three different kinds of simultaneous equation biases in these regressions. The most obvious is that between wages and prices. At the aggregate level there is surely a reverse relationship operating between prices and wages that is affecting coefficient estimates, and I cannot see any reason for not re-estimating the wage and price models simultaneously. Another possible source of bias, as I have already mentioned, is between the demand variable and prices. The demand variable is nominal GNP. Hence, in the aggregate regressions one is very close to regressing prices on themselves. Still another source of bias lies in the possible endogenicity of capacity. Following Hay,[1] if one conceives of firms with market power setting both their production levels and prices as functions of the level of expected aggregate demand, then the capacity variable will not be independent of the error term in the price regression equation and its coefficient will be biased. Finally, given the undoubted serial correlation in all of these time series, I am uncomfortable about using the lagged endogenous variables on the right side of the regression equations.

Assuming that these econometric and structural problems do not invalidate the results, the paper has a basic and very important policy implication that I think bears emphasizing. Though the authors have not given us a way of doing so, it appears that if we were to calculate the effect of a stabilization program on price and wage levels, we would reach the conclusion that demand management is a poor way to try to reduce inflation. The reason is that even though demand enters the regression equations positively, it does so with a rather small sign and is likely to be overshadowed at least in the short run by the behavior of the capacity utilization variable, which would tend to drive prices up as demand was pushed down by the government. There is nothing much to hope for from the labor side, where we see that the unemployment rate has a very weak influence on wages. It is unfortunate that the authors have not worked out a dynamic simulation using their results to show explicitly the effect of demand reduction on prices and wages. I believe that such a simulation would show that restraining aggregate demand would only reduce inflation with a long lag if it reduced it at all.

Furthermore, the simulation would dash the sanguine hopes of some that wage reactions in the labor market would make the stabilization policy effective even if prices react perversely to reductions in capacity utilization. Even though the authors do not quite agree, I think that this paper provides additional evidence on the uncertain relationship between demand and prices in our economy. If that evidence finally leads policymakers to question the assumptions on which they continue to advocate recessions to fight inflation, the paper will have made an important contribution.

NOTES

1. George A. Hay, "Production, Price and Inventory Theory," *American Economic Review*, September 1970, pp. 531–545.

6

AHMAD
AL-SAMARRIE
U.S. Office of Management
and Budget

JOHN
KRAFT
Federal Energy
Administration

BLAINE
ROBERTS
University of Florida

The Effects of Phases I, II, and III on Wages, Prices, and Profit Margins in the Manufacturing Sector of the United States

Dissatisfaction with our ability to achieve reasonable compromises between competing national objectives has reached crisis proportion in recent years as, in country after country, a high rate of inflation has continued to exist side by side with below-potential economic growth and an unacceptably high rate of unemployment. In such a climate, the clamor for direct government intervention to influence wage and price decisions tends to be strong. The United States, England, France, Australia have found it necessary or convenient to resort to some kind of incomes policy or wage and price controls to alleviate inflationary pressures.

The U.S. experimentation with wage and price policy in peacetime goes back to the Kennedy-Johnson guideposts of 1962–1966, although formal wage and price restraint was implemented only with the inauguration of the Economic Stabilization Program (ESP) by the Nixon administration in August 1971. The forces that brought about the new program were varied and complex, including primarily the deterioration in the U.S. balance of trade and payments, the repeated runs on the U.S. dollar in foreign money markets, and the failure of prices and wages to respond quickly and adequately to the anti-inflationary demand-management policies of the 1969–1971 period.

A cursory look at the record during the controls period shows moderate price increases in 1972 but sharply rising prices in 1973. Do these diverse price trends reflect the relative success or failure of the various phases of the ESP, or are they largely the result of external market forces that overwhelm any impact emanating from wage and price controls? What are the theoretical considerations in assessing the effectiveness of the regulations on the pricing practices of different types of firms? Given these theoretical considerations, how can we estimate the effects on prices and wages of the various phases of the control program, and what degree of disaggregation is required to provide meaningful results? In cases where wages and prices were found to have been significantly affected by the control program, was this achieved at considerable costs in terms of market distortions?

Our purpose in this paper is to provide answers to some of these questions, using phases I, II, and III of ESP as a frame of reference. The focus is on the manufacturing sector of the economy, on which the program was supposed to have had its heaviest impact. The paper contains two main parts, one theoretical and the other empirical. In the theoretical section we explore the possible effectiveness of the regulations on firms with different pricing practices. In the empirical section we present the results of an integrated wage-price model focused on the manufacturing sector. The model contains wage, price, and profit margin equations for seventeen manufacturing industries. These are aggregated on a fixed weight basis to create aggregate equations for manufacturing. Dummy variables are used to capture specific structural shifts that may have occurred during the various phases of controls. One dummy variable, covering the eight-quarter period, is used for the wage equations, and two dummy variables are used in the price equation to capture the separate impacts of phases II and III. Dynamic simulations are then used to compare the aggregate performance of the manufacturing sector with what would have occurred without price controls.

I. THE THEORETICAL EFFECTIVENESS OF PRICE AND WAGE CONTROLS

Our purpose in this section is to explore the implications of the price, wage, and profit regulations of phases I, II, and III. We examine the price regulations of the three phases for manufacturing firms from the partial equilibrium viewpoint of the theory of the firm. While this is far from a complete picture of the effect of the price regulations, it is a natural first step. In order for there to be any aggregate effects in a dynamic general equilibrium context, there must be some effect at the microeconomic or firm level. Further, the theoretical development offers a number of suggestions that can be combined with econometric analysis of past price changes and with data gathered by the price control agencies to produce tentative conclusions.

Prices

To facilitate the theoretical analysis of the effect of the price regulations on the determination of prices, assume that the firm faces a stable, downward-sloping demand curve[1] and makes a decision at the beginning of each phase of controls that determines the quantity of all inputs hired, the prices of all outputs, and the quantity that will be produced over the period. In other words, at the beginning of each phase the firm chooses inputs, outputs, and prices, and these remain fixed over the period of the regulations. Further, the plan for prices, inputs, and outputs is independent of future periods. The firm bases its decision on certainty expectations about input prices and demand (i.e., the variance of expected input prices and quantities sold at various output prices is zero).

Phase I

On August 15, 1971, President Nixon announced a New Economic Policy commencing with a freeze on most wages and prices for a period of not more than ninety days.[2] Many firms had either announced price increases or planned price increases that were delayed by the freeze.[3] To the extent that these price increases were in response to cost increases already incurred, the profitability of the firm would have been adversely affected during Phase I. The effect on production decisions would, however, depend upon the relation between demand and marginal costs. If some unit costs had risen before the freeze, but had not been recouped by higher prices, then clearly average costs would be higher. However, the effect on marginal costs, in both the short and long run, is ambiguous: marginal costs could either rise or fall for specific levels of output (see Truett and Roberts 1973). It seems likely, however, that marginal costs would be higher. With prices frozen at prefreeze levels, the firm would face a kinked demand schedule, with the kink at the frozen price level. Thus, marginal costs could increase without the firm changing its output. The degree to which marginal costs could change without having an effect on output would depend upon the elasticity of the firm's demand curve and, hence, the extent of discontinuity in the marginal revenue function. Thus, there is some theoretical support for the hypothesis that the freeze caused no change in output or prices relative to prefreeze levels, that price increases should have been near zero, and that profit margins should have been somewhat below what they would have been without the freeze.

Phase II

Phase II price regulations classified firms into three tiers: Tier I—firms with over $100 million in annual sales; Tier II—firms with between $50 million and $100 million in annual sales; and Tier III—firms with less than $50 million in annual sales. Tier I firms were required to "prenotify" the Price Commission of price increases unless they had a term limit pricing agreement (TLP).[4] The prenotification requirement meant, in effect, a delay of thirty days.[5] Tier II firms were required only to postnotify the Price Commission. Tier III firms were required merely to keep appropriate records for auditing and monitoring purposes.

The basic regulations that applied to manufacturing firms stated simply:

> A manufacturing firm may charge a price in excess of the base price only to reflect increases in allowable costs that it incurred since the last price increase in the item concerned, or that it incurred after January 1, 1971, whichever was later, and that it was continuing to incur, reduced to reflect productivity gains, and only to the extent that increased price does not result in an increase in its profit margin over that which prevailed during the base period.[6]

From the beginning of Phase II, one major stumbling block in this regulation was the meaning and measurement of productivity. At first, the forecasted productivity rise used to offset the rise in wage rates was calculated by each firm. The situation was entirely unsatisfactory from the standpoint of the Price Commission because no uniform productivity measurement was used by Tier I firms (some used output per man-hour as a measure of productivity, while others used total factor productivity) and because many firms showed zero or unacceptably low productivity figures, either because of oversight, ignorance, or a deliberate policy of justifying higher price increases. To remedy the situation the Price Commission, beginning in April 1972, required that instead of using their own estimates, firms should apply a set of productivity factors developed by the staff of the commission for most four-digit Standard Industrial Classification (SIC) industries. The commission's productivity factors were based on the Bureau of Labor Statistics (BLS) trends in output per man-hour for 1958–1969. In addition to using these productivity estimates as offsets to allowable labor cost increases, firms were also required to subtract from cost increases an appropriate amount of reduced fixed costs due to increased volume of output. However, the projected volume was solely up to the firm, rarely challenged by the operations staff of the Price Commission, and generally quite low.

Other steps were taken by the Price Commission to limit "allowable" cost increases. Allowable labor cost increases resulting from contracts signed after August 15, 1971, were limited to the Pay Board standard of 5.5 percent plus 0.7 percent for fringe benefits. Other limits were placed on discretionary cost increases (overhead and advertising) incurred to avoid the intent of the regulations. For several reasons, the impact of the limitation on labor cost increases was not very significant for manufacturing firms. First, workers under expiring contracts accounted for no more than one-fourth of the total labor force of major unions (those representing 1,000 workers or more) during 1972; since unionization accounted for about two-thirds of production workers on manufacturing payrolls and about two-fifths of all production workers on private non-agricultural payrolls, the relative importance of expiring contracts was much reduced. Second, during Phase II the Pay Board approvals averaged 5.5 percent for new wage agreements, 5.3 percent for deferred agreements in durable manufacturing, and 5.3 percent for deferred agreements in nondurable manufacturing (Mitchell 1974).

Firms were constrained by two control policies, one on allowable costs and one on the base-period profit margin (generally referred to as the second line of defense). If the firm had only *one* product, granted "allowable" wage increases, and based its decision on an assumed gain in total productivity roughly equivalent to the productivity and volume offsets required under Phase II, the two control policies were reduced to one basic restriction—a constant profit margin limit: either the profit margin in effect just prior to cost increases occurring after January 1, 1971, or the profit margin in the base period,[7] whichever was lower.

The effect of such a regulation under the foregoing assumptions will depend on the pricing practices of the firm. Accordingly, we shall consider three types of firm: the profit-maximizing firm, the sales-maximizing firm, and the target-return-pricing firm. In each case, the firm is assumed to produce only a single product.

The Profit-maximizing Firm A single-product firm that is constrained by a constant profit margin rule has a profit margin curve that is parabolic to the average cost curve, reaching a minimum and being closest, in absolute terms, to the average cost curve at its minimum. The profit-maximizing firm would not necessarily be constrained by the Price Commission rules. Specifically, it would not be affected if the marginal revenue curve cut the marginal cost curve at the point at which the desired price was less than the allowable cost curve.[8]

During Phase II it was often argued that the allowable cost rules provided an incentive for firms to incur higher costs. Generally, the argument ran as follows: since an x percent increase in unit costs (assuming such cost increases were not detectable by the Price Commission as discretionary) entitled the firm to an equivalent x percent increase in price, margins would remain constant, but absolute profits would rise. There is clearly some merit to this argument, especially when such cost increases can be shown on the books to be current but actually are productive expenditures to be recouped later. However, the argument is only valid under a limited set of circumstances.

First, suppose the firm considers cost expenditures that are purely wasteful. The firm will have an incentive to incur such costs if the allowable price under the constraints of a given profit margin is at a point on the firm's demand curve that is inelastic.[9] In such cases, the profit-maximizing firm will allow costs to increase until the allowable price is such that marginal revenue is zero. By letting average unit costs rise by x percent, the firm is entitled to an x percent increase in price. If demand is inelastic, the quantity demanded will fall by less than x percent, providing the percent increase in profit is precisely equal to the percent increase in revenue. However, the regulations always cause the profit-maximizing firm to produce as much or more than it otherwise would have and at a price equal to or less than the uncontrolled price, even when the firm expends monies on nonproductive but allowable costs.

The firm will, however, have no incentive to engage in purely wasteful expenditures when the allowable price is in an elastic portion of the firm's demand schedule. In this case, there will be no distortion of the optimal capital-labor relation, in contrast to typical public utility regulation based upon rate of return on capital. As is well known, rate-of-return regulation causes an excessive investment in capital (see Averch and Johnson 1962, Baumol and Klevorick 1970, and Stein and Borts 1972).

If the unnecessary cost increases are allowable cost increases but do generate some present-valued revenue, it then follows that the constrained profit-maximizing firm will let cost rise more than if such expenditures generated no revenue.[10] Under such conditions, the firm will reach an equilibrium in maximizing profits at some point between unconstrained output and the point where marginal revenue is zero, depending upon how much additional revenue is generated per dollar of unnecessary cost increases.

he Sales-maximizing Firm   The implied effectiveness of the control program is much different for a firm that maximizes sales (revenues) than for one that maximizes profits. A sales-maximizing firm earns no pure economic profits, that is, revenue is maximized subject to the condition that total revenue must be greater than or equal to total costs. Of course, accounting profits would be positive, since they are, in part, returns to factors of production that are not measured in the accounting process. If all unmeasured costs in the accounting sense are fixed, then the allowable price curve may lie everywhere above the average total cost curve, intersect it once, or intersect the average total cost curve twice. For the sales-maximizing firm, the price control strategy must either be ineffective or the firm must be forced to operate at a loss, since by definition the firm just covers average total cost.

te Firm That Pursues Target Rate-of-Return Pricing   Since the work of Kaplan, Dirlam, and Lanzillotti (1958), pricing to achieve a target rate of return on investment has become widely regarded as the most prevalent short-run business pricing practice. Usually target rate-of-return pricing is construed to mean that the price is set so that if the firm produces at "normal" output (generally defined by management as 70–80 percent of capacity), it will earn its target rate of return on investment (net worth plus long-term debt). If net worth and long-term debt are constant, then repricing in response to increased unit costs of production is equivalent to maintaining a constant dollar profit per unit of output when the firm is operating at its "normal" rate. Price adjustments that maintain a constant dollar profit at normal output are referred to as "dollar-for-dollar pass-throughs" of cost increases, a rule in effect under Phase IV of the ESP. Phase II regulations allowed an equal percent increase in unit profits to be tacked onto cost increases.

If capital investment is unchanged, the same dollar profits would achieve the target rate of return. It follows, therefore, that if the firm had no volume offset for fixed costs (either because all accounting costs were variable or because the firm projected no change in volume), then the allowable price increase permitted by the Price Commission would be greater than the price increase desired by the firm using target rate-of-return pricing. If the firm did experience an increase in volume and had a volume deduction for allowable increases in variable costs, then the permitted price increase may be greater than, equal to, or less than the desired price increase, depending upon the magnitude of the volume offset, the increase in allowable costs, and the profit margin of the firm.[11] Since the volume offset was entirely up to the firm, it would seem likely that the requested price increase was "greater than or equal to" rather than "less than" for the firm using target rate-of-return pricing. The firm would have no incentive to incur unnecessary costs unless its projected volume increase was too high. In that case, if it did incur additional costs, the percent increase in profits would be commensurate with both. Thus, if the volume projection was too high (which is unlikely), unnecessary costs could be incurred to raise profits at the normal level of output to achieve the target rate of return. This analysis does not consider current demand conditions but, in general, the target rate-of-return rule is not a profit-maximizing rule of thumb.

To summarize the import of the foregoing analysis, the effect of Phase II controls depended upon the specific conditions of the market. It seems likely that in several industries there was no change in historical relationships among prices, output, and costs. Furthermore, in cases where structural shifts can be identified empirically, the analysis should offer an explanation.

Phase III

Guided by its avowed policy of ridding the economy of the fetters of wage and price controls, the Nixon administration took advantage of the observed improvement on the inflationary front in late 1972. Phase III, which lasted for nearly half a year, abolished both the Price Commission and the Pay Board, dropped the prenotification requirements in most sectors of the economy, maintained the report-filing requirements for only the largest economic units, exempted the rent sector from control, made the profit margin rule much less stringent, and allowed considerable flexibility in the standards.[12] These steps gave Phase III the appearance of "a dash back to the market" despite repeated references by various government spokesmen to the ultimate use of the "stick in the closet" to restrain undue wage and price increases. Assuming the management of the firm interpreted the new steps as the death knell of controls, then the firm would resume historical pricing practices. Thus, if any structural shift was identified for Phase II, it should disappear for Phase III.

Wages

The first freeze, in August 1971, applied to virtually all wages and salaries, including those with increases scheduled by contract to take effect during the freeze. Initially the Cost of Living Council ruled that wage increases scheduled to go into effect during the freeze could not be paid retroactively after the freeze was over. This was later overturned by the courts, and many wage increases were paid retroactively after Phase II began. This fact has two principal effects on the data. First, because of the bunching of these increases, the data should show a bulge for the beginning of Phase II. Second, the increase in the wage indexes will lag behind the actual increase in labor costs in those cases where wage payments were made retroactive to the freeze.

Phase II

Phase II regulations were comprehensive, although some exceptions were later made in the program for small units (those employing fewer than 60 workers) and for low-wage earners. Employee units were classified into three categories: Category I firms, those with 5,000 workers or more, were required to prenotify the Pay Board of all wage increases regardless of whether they were above or below the pay standard; Category II firms, employing 1,000 to 5,000 workers, were only required to submit quarterly reports to the Pay Board about pay increases, the same as for Category I units; and

Category III firms, those with under 1,000 workers, were subjected to little or no control. A pay standard of 5.5 percent per year for contracts negotiated or determined after November 14, 1971, was set by the Pay Board. This standard was, however, allowed to go higher (up to 7 percent) in those special cases where higher wage increases were deemed necessary to promote faster productivity growth, to correct a gross inequity in the relation between the pay of one group of workers and another group with which the first group had a well-established parity, to allow for legitimate fringe benefits, or to honor contracts written prior to Phase II and scheduled to go into effect during the phase.

Phase III

The Phase III regulations generally de-emphasized wage regulations apart from food, health care, and construction. Officially, the regulations published on January 12, 1973, still contained the 5.5 percent standard, but latitude for exceptions was greatly increased. With the primary emphasis on a self-administered control program, the prenotification requirement of wage increases by large units was removed.

Relevant to this paper is the potential effect of the Pay Board regulations on wage determination. This effort is somewhat unclear, for the regulations may tend to decrease or increase the rate of change in wages in specific industries depending upon prevailing economic conditions. One of the consequences of the establishment of an incomes policy is to add bargaining strength to those contracts with pay provisions closest to the control program's pay standard. For example, in an industry where, without a Pay Board, the increase in wage rates may have been held to 4 percent by management, the increase in wage rates, under a 5.5 percent pay standard, would be higher with controls than without them. However, in industries where management would have offered, say, 8 percent without a standard, the rate of increase in wage rates would probably be constrained by the existence of a wage control program with a 5.5 percent standard. Thus, the institution of a standard tends to shift the bargaining on the distribution of income from the industry to the national level. With an incomes policy that is "in the national interest," the role of the labor union is to follow the "national interest" with respect to the overall goals of reducing inflation, although the brunt of the anti-inflationary strategy should fall on tougher price regulations, particularly as they apply to those industries most able to absorb cost increases.

Wage increases granted during Phase II were not significantly different from the 5.5 pay standard (see Mitchell 1974 for a discussion of this point). While this is revealing, it does not answer the pertinent question of whether wage increases would have been different without wage controls. Although no definitive answer can be provided, wage equations with dummy variables can be employed roughly to assess the relative impacts of the wage regulations on different industries.

II. FORMS OF THE VARIOUS AGGREGATIVE EQUATIONS

In the preceding section, microanalysis at the firm level was used to suggest the various effects a control program might have. However, because of aggregation and data gaps, it is difficult to derive aggregative equations for major economic sectors or a specific industry from the theory of the firm. At the more aggregative level, it is necessary to resort to less rigorously derived theoretical models if one is to make any attempt at quantifying determinants of wages and prices and the effect that controls may have had.

Prices, profit margins, and wage rates are not only interrelated but they depend on similar economic forces. For example, an increase in the overall price index for goods and services usually provokes an upward pressure on wages in various industries. In addition, the relative rates of increase in prices and wages, together with changes in demand and nonlabor unit cost, will largely determine whether the profit margins of specific industries will increase or decrease. Moreover, both prices and profit margins are heavily affected by such things as the scale of production, the intensity of demand, and the efficiency with which inputs are used in the production processes. These interrelationships should be kept in mind in setting the analytical framework and in interpreting and estimating equations relevant to the three variables.

The Price Equations

In theory, price changes are a function of changes in demand and supply forces. Demand changes are caused by shifts in consumers' incomes, consumers' tastes, and relative prices. Changes in supply, on the other hand, largely reflect changes in technology and input prices, both of which affect productivity and unit costs. The manner by which these demand and supply forces affect price adjustment depends heavily on the relative sizes of supply and demand elasticities. The latter, in turn, are a function of the degree of competition in commodity and labor markets, the degree of substitution among inputs, the length of the production process, the reliability and speed of information, and the institutional arrangements governing the production and distribution of goods and services.

A priori, one would expect large differences among manufacturing industries in the way in which supply and demand forces affect their prices. Whether or not the responses of industry prices to these forces can be adequately measured by use of regression equations is an open question. For one thing, most of the factors with a bearing on member firms' pricing decisions lack available quantitative measures. And since these factors are continuously interacting, no neat hypothesis exists that can be tested with available data.

While theory and available data are so far apart in the case of price adjustments that no meaningful tests can be performed, it is still possible to use the correlation-regression approach to identify stable relations among the prices of key manufacturing industries (the object of the price restraint program) and other explanatory variables which, at least to a degree, run the gamut of supply-demand factors. The objective of such an approach is not so much to test a theory of market behavior but to predict price changes. The basic form used here is

$$(1) \qquad \frac{dp}{p} = a_0 + a_1 \frac{dy}{y} + a_2 \frac{dy^d}{y^d} + a_3 \frac{dw}{w} + a_4 \frac{dv}{v} + a_5 \frac{dr}{r} + a_6 \frac{di}{i}$$

where p is an index of the price of output, y is an output variable, y^d is an excess demand variable, w is a wage rate variable, v is an index of materials prices, r is a rate of return variable, and i is an interest rate variable.

The Profit Margin Equations

Profit margins are, by definition, a function of output price, level of output, and unit (or average) costs of production. Hence, equations that explain changes in profit margins do not suffer from the same theoretical morass of confluent unmeasurables as optimal price adjustment. They do, however, suffer from inadequate profit data. Therefore, the parametric values we obtain in estimating an equation of the form given in (2) do tell us something about the industry.

Furthermore, where the standard error is sufficiently small, such equations should also be useful in assessing the potential impact of a system of price controls that relies, in part, upon profit margin limitations.

The equation for profit margins is

(2) $$\frac{dm}{m} = a_0 + a_1 \frac{dy}{y} + a_2 \frac{dp}{p} + a_3 \frac{dw}{w} + a_4 \frac{dv}{v} + a_5 \frac{di}{i} + a_6 \frac{dk}{k}$$

where m is the ratio of pretax profits to sales, and k is a depreciation rate variable. Other variables are defined in equation 1.

The Wage Equations

The basic Phillips-curve hypothesis (which serves as an initial point of departure for the specification of our wage equations) states that when the supply of and demand for labor in terms of money wages is not in equilibrium, the rate of change of wages is proportional to the excess demand for labor. The relationship between money wage change and the unemployment rate is convex. This is but one of several possible nonlinearities in the determination of the rate of change in money wages (for a discussion of non-linearities in wage equations, see de Menil 1969). This convex relationship between the unemployment rate and the rate of change in money wages is approximated by the inverse of the unemployment rate. Labor market tightness is characterized by extremely large wage changes at low unemployment rates. The opposite is true for a fluid labor market.[13]

The relationship between prices and wage change can be established in two ways. First, wage bargaining is more in terms of real wages than money wages, and thus money wages are influenced by prices. Second, money wage determination is based on money wage expectations as measured by future price expectations. In the absence of a money illusion, individuals should fully anticipate price changes and translate them into wage gains. This would imply a vertical long-run Phillips curve and a coefficient of unity on the expectations variable. In most empirical tests of the expectations hypothesis the coefficient has been statistically less than unity.[14] The real wage associated with any increase in money wages varies inversely with the rate of change in the prices workers pay as consumers, and thus workers adjust their wage demands according to the size of the price inflation they expect. A coefficient of less than unity would imply that workers are either unwilling or unable to translate the price increases into wage demands.

The effect of the wage regulations on econometric wage equations over the various phases of controls depends to some extent upon how such equations are specified. In recent years, a number of alternative hypotheses of wage determinations have been advanced, all of which apparently have approximately the same explanatory ability.[15] However, the type of specification does affect the significance of dummy variables included in an equation. This is evident by comparing some recent studies of wage determination at the aggregate level. Perry (1970) used a modified Phillips-curve approach for wage determination by emphasizing labor market variables that differ from the conventional aggregate rate of civilian unemployment. Using a weighted unemployment rate and an unemployment dispersion index, Perry was able to track movements in wages during the late 1960s that were above the rates predicted by previous conventional models. Perry's approach yields a significant guidepost dummy variable. Eckstein and Brinner (1972) explain the apparent outward shift in the Phillips curve by using an inflation severity variable with the usual aggregate rate of unemployment. This approach also yields a significant dummy variable for the period of the guideposts. Gordon (1971, 1972) uses three labor market variables along the lines of Perry's and rejects the significance of a guidepost dummy variable. Wachter (1974) takes into account the change in the relative structure of wages over the business cycle, uses the conventional rate of unemployment, and rejects the significance of a dummy variable.

Often profits or the profit rate are included in the wage equation on the presumption that profits influence the bargaining power of unions and management in the determination of wages. Kuh (1967), however, argues that profits are actually a proxy for productivity, and that workers bargain for higher wages on the basis of increased productivity and its associated reduction in unit labor costs.

In summary, we hypothesize that the rate of change in money wage rates is a function of labor market tightness, price expectations, and labor productivity. The general form of the equation estimated for each industry is as follows:

$$\frac{dw}{w} = a_0 + a_1 \frac{dp}{p} + a_2 \frac{dE}{E} + a_3 \frac{dQ}{Q} + a_4 \frac{1}{U} + a_5 Z + a_6 L + a_7 GPD$$

where w is the industry wage rate, p is the consumer price index, E is the industry employment, Q is the productivity index for all manufacturing, U is the aggregate rate of unemployment, Z is the level of industry profits, L is the layoff rate for all manufacturing, and GPD is a guidepost dummy variable; its value for 1962I is 0.25; for 1962II, 0.50; 1962III, 0.75; 1962IV–1966IV, 1.0; 1967I, 0.75; 1967II, 0.50; 1967III, 0.25; and zero for all other quarters.

III. DATA TECHNIQUES AND METHOD OF ESTIMATION

Form of the Variables and the Data

For several reasons, we elected to use the four-quarter percent change in each variable, which we then corrected for autocorrelation. All the rate variables were expressed in decimal as opposed to percent form. All lags were introduced as either fixed weighted averages of past variables (rather than being estimated freely) or as lag adjustments. For the weighted average, weights of 0.4, 0.3, 0.2, and 0.1 were used for periods t through $t - 3$.[16]

The data used to estimate the price equations are at the two-digit Standard Industrial Classification (SIC) level of compilation. The variables are largely self-explanatory except for the indexes of output and input prices. All are defined in the appendix below. The variables were constructed in a manner similar to that employed by Eckstein and Wyss (1972).[17] However, the final series were constructed with slightly different groupings and thus are not comparable with theirs.

Estimation Procedures

The wage, price, and profit margin equations were estimated for the time interval from 1959III to 1971II. The initial date was chosen primarily because of data limitations, and the closing one was selected so as to avoid the influence of the Economic Stabilization Program.

The use of four-quarter rates of change reduces the multicollinearity among variables in a statistical sense, although it does not eliminate the problem. In using four-quarter rates, we do not assume that a constant fraction of the dependent variable changes every quarter with the same parametric response to the same variables (or the equivalent) as postulated, for example, by Perry (1964). For a discussion of the problems generated by the Perry-type assumption, see Black and Kelegian (1972) or Rowley and Wilton (1974).[18]

The estimated wage, price, and profit margin equations were corrected for autocorrelation, using nonlinear least squares estimation and the Hildreth-Lu technique.[19] The latter was used to search a grid of values to insure a global minimum rather than only a local minimum for the residual sum of squares. The wage equations were corrected for first-order autocorrelation; and the price and profit margin equations, for second-order autocorrelation.

IV. EMPIRICAL RESULTS FOR 1959III–1971II

A summary of the results for the estimated price, profit margin, and wage equations for the seventeen industries is presented in tables 1, 2, and 3. Initially, each equation was estimated with all the hypothesized variables included. Variables were then retained in an equation on the basis of two considerations: one, that the variable was significant prior to the correction for serial correlation; two, that the variable also proved to be significant in other periods of estimation and the estimated coefficients appeared to be robust both prior to and after the correction for serial correlation. Variables were retained in the estimated equations on this basis even if their estimated coefficient was not significantly different from zero; variables that did not satisfy conditions one and two were dropped from the estimated equations. Within any general category of variables, such as output or demand, the specific forms of the variables may differ, as indicated in the tables.

The Price Results

As would be expected, price changes are positively and significantly affected by wage and materials cost pass-throughs in most of the sample manufacturing industries. However, the results do not provide clues to the market structures of specific industries. They are capable of supporting either a competitive pricing model or the other widely held hypothesis: target-rate full-cost pricing. At least in part, this is because of the broad level of industry aggregation with which we are working (two-digit SIC) and because of the variables chosen for making the analysis. Most of these variables enter into the pricing decisions of both competitive and noncompetitive firms. Variables such as capital costs that would be useful in discriminating between competing theories are either not available in accurate form or are rendered ineffective by the presence of more powerful cost factors with which there may be strong multicollinearity.

The output variable has an impact on the dependent variable in textiles (SIC 22), lumber (SIC 24), paper (SIC 26), and electrical machinery (SIC 36). For textiles and lumber, the positive output coefficient taken in conjunction with the positive association between the price variable and the profit margin (Table 2), implies that price increases in those two industries tend to exceed average cost increases when output is rising, with the result that consumers do not always share in the fruits of cyclical increases in productivity. Or put another way, prices in those industries are responsive to the market cyclical changes associated with those industries. For paper and electrical machinery, the negative correlation between changes in output and variations in price would suggest that those industries pass on cost declines during periods of increasing productivity. This phenomenon seemed to have characterized the 1959–1966 period when, because of increased capacity utilization, the electrical machinery industry was able to maintain relative price stability.

As an explanatory variable, excess demand seems to be important in only four industries. In three of them (food processing, lumber, and nonferrous metals), the regression coefficient has the correct sign, i.e., there is a negative association between the inventory-to-sales ratio (a proxy for excess demand) and the four-quarter rate of change in output price. In chemicals and fabricated metals, prices tend to fall when demand becomes excessive.

In only one instance is there a negative relation between changes in wages and changes in prices. Adjusted average hourly earnings were not available for nonferrous metals (SIC 33). For this industry, both unadjusted wage rates and wage rates adjusted for overtime and interindustry shifts were tried. The latter gave a superior fit. A 1 percent increase in average hourly earnings, excluding overtime, results in a decline of 0.77 percent in output prices, but in a lagged manner over sixteen quarters. The negative coefficient is difficult to explain.

Materials prices are significant in eight industries. The negative coefficients on input prices in textiles and rubber are extremely small—0.01 and 0.04 percent, respectively.

A decline in cash flow in tobacco is associated with price increases. The four-quarter rate of change in Moody's Aaa bond rate

TABLE 1 Industry Price (PQF) Equations,[a] 1959III–1971II
(figures in parentheses are t statistics)

SIC No.	Industry	Constant	Output (QF)	Demand (DINSF)	Wages (WF)	Materials Prices (PIQF)	Bond Rate (BAAF)	ρ_1 [ρ_2]	$\bar{R}^2$ [DW] {SEE}
20	Food processing	.0160 (2.57)		−.1040 (−1.76)		.4812 (8.25)		0.77	0.91 [1.78] {0.0008}
21	Tobacco	.0028 (0.27)			.3050[b] (2.29)		.1086 (3.21)	0.76	0.79 [1.74] {0.0104}
22	Textiles	−.0679 (−2.09)	.1356 (1.36)		1.5158[c] (2.42)	−.0118 (−0.29)		0.79	0.54 [1.97] {0.0204}
23	Apparel	.0084 (2.11)				.2708 (2.22)		1.37 [−0.70]	0.82 [2.03] {0.0090}
24	Lumber	−.0385 (−1.07)	.2086 (0.95)	−.3001 (−2.48)	1.3611[d] (1.96)			1.18 [−0.51]	0.80 [2.28] {0.0381}
25	Furniture	−.0066 (1.90)			.6998[d] (8.18)	.0782[c] (1.75)		1.09 [−0.45]	0.94 [2.26] {0.0038}
26	Paper	−.0095 (−0.85)	−.0101 (−0.14)		.3532 (1.56)	.1898[b] (2.11)		1.03 [−0.44]	0.75 [2.19] {0.0088}
28	Chemicals	−.0061 (−0.67)		.0533 (3.43)	.1853[b] (1.26)			0.90	0.87 [2.19] {0.0035}
30	Rubber	−.0149 (−0.84)			.7214[c] (1.58)	−.0441[d] (−0.32)		1.11 [−0.40]	0.72 [1.92] {0.0181}

Code	Industry	(A)	(B)	(C)	(D)	(E)	ρ	$\bar{R}^2$ / DW / SEE
32	Stone, clay, and glass	−.0265 (−5.32)			1.1129[c] (9.87)		1.17 [−0.48]	0.95 [2.08] {0.0044}
331	Ferrous metals	−.2709 (−0.49)				.0791 (1.48)	1.25 [−0.25]	0.96 [1.79] {0.0049}
333	Nonferrous metals	.5081 (2.31)		−.0415 (−3.67)	−.7745[b] (−1.313)		1.53 [−0.77]	0.86 [1.98] {0.0224}
34	Fabricated metals	.0060 (1.84)		.0175 (1.29)	.1082 (1.15)	.6730 (2.72)	1.08 [−0.46]	0.96 [1.90] {0.0039}
35	Nonelectrical machinery	−.0004 (−0.04)			.4897[c] (2.93)	.2310 (3.06)	0.88	0.96 [1.74] {0.0030}
36	Electrical machinery	.0022 (0.37)	−.1293 (−2.67)				1.43 [−0.62]	0.90 [2.15] {0.0078}
371	Motor vehicles	−.0053 (−1.15)				.9351 (4.83)	0.94 [−0.31]	0.82 [2.18] {0.0084}
38	Instruments	.0049 (0.93)				.3193 (2.40)	0.82	0.73 [1.72] {0.0059}

ρ_1 = first-order autocorrelation coefficient.
ρ_2 = second-order autocorrelation coefficient.
$\overline{DW}$ = Durbin-Watson statistic.
$\bar{R}^2$ = coefficient of multiple determination, adjusted for degrees of freedom.
SEE = standard error of estimate.

[a] For identification of variables and sources of data, see appendix.
[b] For wages, signifies use of *WF*, lagged one period; for materials prices, signifies *PIQF*, lagged one period.
[c] For wages, signifies use of *WFWA*; for materials prices, *PIQF*, lagged two periods.
[d] For wages, signifies use of *WFWA*, lagged one period; for materials prices, *PIQF*, lagged four periods.

TABLE 2 Industry Profit Margin (PMF) Equations,[a] 1959III–1971II (figures in parentheses are t statistics)

SIC No.	Industry	Constant	Output (QF)	Output Prices (PQF)	Wages (WF)	Input Prices (P/QF)	Interest Costs (BAAF)	ρ_1 [ρ_2]	$\bar{R}^2$ [DW] {SEE}
20	Food processing	.0087 (0.66)		-.4297ᵇ (-0.62)				0.60	0.45 [1.71] {0.0311}
21	Tobacco	-.0359 (-1.84)	.4349 (2.59)	1.572ᵇ (3.13)				0.60	0.42 [2.00] {0.1442}
22	Textiles	-.0558 (-2.32)	2.524 (7.89)	2.265 (3.36)			-.5889 (-2.11)	0.23	0.82 [1.91] {0.0963}
23	Apparel	-.1731 (-2.63)	4.236 (5.04)	1.545ᵇ (1.04)	3.263ᵇ (2.34)				0.34 [1.40] {0.2071}
24	Lumber	-.3166 (-2.23)	6.689 (5.26)	.8463 (0.99)	4.018 (1.49)			0.43	0.66 [1.88] {0.3116}
25	Furniture	-.0782 (-2.19)	3.974 (6.87)			-.7323ᵇ (-1.74)			0.50 [1.73] {0.2197}
26	Paper	.0345 (0.39)	1.974 (5.32)	1.741 (2.20)	-4.669 (-2.59)		.0050ᵇ (0.02)	0.73	0.86 [1.63] {0.0528}
28	Chemicals	-.1862 (-4.01)	1.333 (5.94)	-2.762 (-2.40)	1.265 (1.46)			0.60	0.76 [1.92] {0.0352}

SIC	Industry							
30	Rubber	−.2502 (−4.96)	1.715 (6.77)		2.142[b] (1.74)	−5.623 (−3.83)	0.25	0.66 [1.42] {0.1086}
32	Stone, clay, and glass	−.1025 (−3.18)	2.285 (4.74)				0.30	0.44 [1.99] {0.1442}
331	Ferrous metals	.0740 (0.75)	1.500 (4.67)		−4.460[c] (−1.94)		0.39	0.59 [1.49] {0.2300}
333	Nonferrous metals	−.0670 (−1.60)	1.578 (7.99)	1.369 (4.10)	−1.809[d] (−1.50)		0.30	0.73 [1.95] {0.1059}
34	Fabricated metals	−.0882 (−2.15)	2.522 (6.18)				0.60	0.68 [1.99] {0.1076}
35	Nonelectrical machinery	−.0573 (−1.97)	1.007 (3.13)				0.89 [0.29]	0.72 [2.05] {0.0745}
36	Electrical machinery	−.1076 (−2.37)	1.471 (4.31)				0.70	0.62 [1.83] {0.0872}
371	Motor vehicles	no statistical relationship						
38	Instruments	−.0608 (−1.80)	1.070 (3.77)				0.68	0.71 [1.65] {0.0654}

[a] Summary statistics are identified in notes to Table 1. For identification of variables and sources of data, see appendix.

[b] For output prices, signifies use of PQF, lagged one period; for wages, WF, lagged one period; for input prices, $PIQF$, lagged one period; for interest costs, SPD.

[c] WF, lagged four periods, was used.

[d] $WFWA$ was used.

TABLE 3 Industry Wage (WF) Equations,[a] 1959III–1971II (figures in parentheses are t statistics)

SIC No.	Industry	Constant	Consumer Prices (PRF)	Employment (EMF)	Productivity (QMF)	Unemployment (1/u)	Guideposts (GPD)	ρ_1	$\bar{R}^2$ [DW] {SEE}
20	Food processing	.0271 (6.08)	.7347[b] (6.86)	-.2426 (-3.60)			-.0105 (-2.63)	0.70	0.94 [1.90] {0.0040}
21	Tobacco	.0100 (0.86)	1.0870[b] (3.55)	-.3667 (-0.88)	.2261[b] (1.85)			0.53	0.65 [1.72] {0.0178}
22	Textiles	.0048 (0.35)	.6487[b] (14.51)	.2061[b] (2.05)		.0939[b] (1.31)		0.44	0.82 [1.85] {0.0077}
23	Apparel	.0840 (3.85)	-.3914[c] (-0.92)			-.0071[c] (-0.96)	-.0385 (-3.08)	0.96	0.83 [1.53] {0.0096}
24	Lumber	.0299 (2.75)	1.0057[b] (3.82)	.1988 (2.45)			-.0220 (2.19)	0.64	0.82 [1.74] {0.0114}
25	Furniture	-.0214 (-2.84)	.5545[b] (5.22)	-.1307 (-3.82)		.2216[b] (5.29)		0.55	0.94 [1.82] {0.0047}
26	Paper	.3020 (6.75)	.6794[b] (15.07)	-.0773 (-2.57)			-.0085 (-5.17)	0.31	0.96 [1.65] {0.0032}
28	Chemicals	.0151 (0.36)	.0974[b] (0.76)				-.0040 (-0.88)	1.02	0.96 [1.72] {0.0032}

30	Rubber	.0252 (2.48)	.5513[b] (2.35)	.1512 (5.10)			$-.0250$ (-2.85)	0.74	0.80 [1.82] {0.0083}
32	Stone, clay, and glass	.0251 (6.19)	.4726[b] (2.28) .3686[b] (2.14)	.0607 (2.00)			$-.0055$ (-1.46)	0.41	0.91 [1.92] {0.0054}
331	Ferrous metals	$-.0304$ (-1.66)	.4225[c] (0.21)	$-.0518$[b] (-1.45)	.6408 (5.56)	.1697[b] (1.82)	$-.0179$ (-1.88)	0.49	0.71 [1.45] {0.0135}
333	Nonferrous metals	.0472 (2.89)	.4715[c] (0.21)	.0472 (1.19)	.4275 (5.95)	$-.0102$[c] (-2.77)	$-.0157$ (-2.02)	0.61	0.80 [1.77] {0.0082}
34	Fabricated metals	.0196 (4.50)	.8494[b] (7.91)	.0782 (2.89)			$-.0113$ (-2.66)	0.33	0.93 [1.68] {0.0046}
35	Nonelectrical machinery	.0217 (6.88)	.8386[d] (9.97)	.0248 (0.28)			$-.0085$ (-2.65)	0.48	0.93 [1.99] {0.0046}
36	Electrical machinery	.0250 (3.47)	.6269[d] (3.05)	$-.1050$ (-3.69)				0.80	0.91 [1.64] {0.0043}
371	Motor vehicles	.0121 (0.51)	.8632 (2.93)	.1452 (4.03)	.5614 (2.88)	$-.0091$[c] (-0.81)	$-.0167$ (-2.09)	0.24	0.69 [1.94] {0.0057}
38	Instruments	.0201 (3.58)	.7049 (4.63)	$-.0980$ (-4.14)				0.85	0.96 [1.32] {0.0164}

a Summary statistics are identified in notes to Table 1. For identification of variables and sources of data, see appendix.
b For consumer prices, signifies use of PRF, lagged one period; for employment, EMFWA; for productivity, QMF, lagged one period; for unemployment, 1/u, lagged one period.
c For consumer prices, signifies use of PRFWA; for productivity, QMF.
d PRFWA, lagged one period, was used.

in tobacco is positively related to price movements as well as cash flow. For other variables there is no significant relationship with price changes in all the other industries.

The Profit Margin Results

The demand and cost variables are much weaker in explaining the variations in the profit margins of food processing (SIC 20), apparel (SIC 23), furniture (SIC 25), and stone-clay-glass (SIC 32) than those of ferrous metals (SIC 331), fabricated metals (SIC 34), nonelectrical machinery (SIC 35), and instruments (SIC 38). The explanation may lie in the degree of market power exercised by different industries and in the ability and willingness of those industries to absorb cost increases. By and large, the first group of industries is relatively competitive, operates with narrow margins, and is often forced to absorb some cost increases when demand is weak. The other group of industries, on the other hand, tends to pass on to consumers the bulk of cost increases, irrespective of the state of the business cycle.

Increased output raises profit margins in every industry except food processing, where it is not significant, and transportation (371), where we could not obtain a fit. And except for those industries, the estimated elasticity of profit margins with respect to output is greater than 1.00. For example, at a profit margin of 0.07, a 1 percent increase in output in textiles would increase margins 2.5 percent, to 0.0718.

Price increases in food processing and chemicals are associated with falling margins. This indicates that price increases do not fully compensate for rising average costs. For example, it is well known that when farm food prices are rising, processors do not mark up and pass through all the increases. In the chemical industry, price reductions are associated with increased margins, indicating that while productivity gains do lower prices, the price reductions do not match unit cost declines, with the result that margins increase.

The constant term is relatively large and negative for the majority of industries covered in this report. This is probably because we have not estimated the precise profit margin identity: $\Pi/px = 1 - (WL/px) - (rk/px)$. Instead we have abstracted from the identity the main economic variables that influence profit margins.

The Wage Results

For all industries except apparel, chemicals, and nonferrous metals, a form of the rate of change in the consumer price index (CPI) is significant at the 10 percent level. In tobacco and lumber, a 1 percent increase in price induces an increase of more than 1 percent in wages. The CPI is particularly important during periods of rapid inflation when, in their desire to catch up, union leaders usually have strong support among workers to push for higher wages. The role of the CPI in wage determination has become much more important of late as labor contracts increasingly contain cost-of-living escalator clauses, and as nonunion wages tend to follow union wage patterns, though often with some lags.[20]

Profits do not seem to be significant in explaining wage changes, perhaps because of their high collinearity with consumer price changes and with productivity. The role of productivity in wage settlement seems to be unimportant, except in such industries as tobacco, primary metals, and motor vehicles. In these industries, there is some information on productivity trends that can be considered along with other variables in determining hourly wage rate increases, even though labor and management do not always agree on the size and measurement of productivity growth. Moreover, the fact that there has been a significant application of labor-saving technology in these relatively highly unionized and concentrated industries makes consideration of the productivity variable highly relevant in any meaningful wage negotiations.

Changes in production worker employment is another variable that may have an impact on variations in the hourly wage rate. During periods when the labor market is relatively tight, an industry that must expand its labor force in order to perform efficiently may have to pay higher wages in order to attract workers from other industries or discourage its existent workers from leaving in search of more attractive pay. For several of the industries covered in this paper, the coefficient on the employment variable has the expected positive sign. However, the coefficient is negative for several other industries—food, tobacco, ferrous metals, and electrical machinery. In these industry groups, the trend of production worker employment has been downward, largely because of automation. The negative sign can be explained by the existence of strong union pressure for higher wages as a partial compensation for reduced employment. This is true in electrical machinery, where a 1 percent decrease in employment would increase average hourly earnings by 0.10 percent.

In most cases, the measures of labor market tightness were ineffective in explaining movements in wages. The aggregate unemployment variable had the expected positive sign in textiles, furniture, and ferrous metals, while layoffs had the expected negative sign in apparel, nonferrous metals, and transportation. It would appear that national indicators of labor market tightness have minimal impact in explaining the movement of wages on the disaggregated two-digit manufacturing industries.[21]

The guidepost dummy variable is significant and negative in eleven industries, its impact ranging from 0.4 to 3.85 percentage points.[22]

V. DIRECT IMPACT OF PHASES I, II, AND III ON PRICES, PROFIT MARGINS, AND WAGES IN SEVENTEEN MANUFACTURING INDUSTRIES

In this section of the paper we attempt to measure the *direct* impact of the Economic Stabilization Program on the determination of prices and wages in specific manufacturing industries. The direct impact is to be distinguished from the *total* impact, which includes feedbacks between prices and wages. The mechanism for measuring the total impact will be discussed in section VI.

Obtaining the direct impact of controls is possible by re-estimating industry equations for 1959III–1973II so as to include the eight quarters of the ESP. The dummy variable $ESP1$ was added to all the wage equations and has the value of 1.0 in the eight quarters from 1971III to 1973II, and zero in all other quarters. The price and profit margin equations have two dummy variables: $ESP2$, which equals 1.0 in the period 1971III–1972IV, and zero otherwise; and $ESP3$, which equals 1.0 in 1973I and 1973II. The approach is analogous to the one used for the guidepost dummy GPD.[23]

Using the estimated coefficient for a dummy variable in an equation for prices, wages, and profit margins leaves a great deal unanswered about the program. First, it assumes that the program was totally responsible for any change that occurred. Second, to determine the total impact, a model should be constructed that would compare simulated values without controls to simulated values with controls or with actual data where there exist interactions between wages and prices.[24] This exercise was far too complicated and required too many questionable assumptions to be undertaken here. However, an aggregate model for the manufacturing economy is presented in section VI.

The results of the re-estimated equations are shown in tables 4, 5, and 6. In general, there was very little change in the value of the coefficients for the independent variables or the general statistical properties of the equations. The control dummies, ESP1, ESP2, and ESP3, were retained regardless of their significance.

The listing in Table 7 highlights the cases in which the dummy variables in the price, profit margin, and wage equations were significant at the 5 or 10 percent level. A negative coefficient suggests that controls may have been effective in restraining prices and wages, and a positive coefficient would imply at least the absence of restraint. Several inferences can be drawn from this table and from tables 4 through 6.

The control program seemed to be totally ineffective in constraining price inflation in those industries that experienced demand-pull inflation during phases II and III, namely, lumber (SIC 24), ferrous metals (SIC 331), and nonferrous metals (SIC 333). The explanation lies, perhaps, in the nature of capacity utilization in these industries and in the manner in which wage and price controls work during various phases of the business cycle. It is generally recognized that controls tend to be much more effective in restraining prices when there are significant amounts of unused capacity in various industries than during periods of capacity constraints. The experience of the lumber industry from the second half of 1972 through most of 1973 reflected the influence of the housing boom and the resulting pressure on lumber prices. Similarly, the acceleration in general economic activity in this period put undue pressure on productive capacity and prices within the metals industry and made evasion of price controls by some Tier I firms much easier.

Despite its attractiveness as a resource-saving device for the Price Commission staff, term limit pricing (explained in note 4) was a factor in the lack of any significant impact of the control program on the pricing decisions of such key industries as chemicals (SIC 28) and electrical machinery (SIC 36). Many of the companies that elected the TLP arrangement were in these two industries, and their productivity growth during the 1971–1972 business recovery was above average. This productivity improvement, coupled with the significantly high rate of profits, should have resulted in more moderate price performance by the chemical and electrical machinery industries than what actually occurred. It is conceivable that the TLP arrangement (which gave

TABLE 4 Industry Price (PQF) Equations,[a] 1959III–1973II (figures in parentheses are t statistics)

SIC No.	Industry	Constant	Output (QF)	Demand (DINS)	Wages (WF)	Materials Prices (PIQF)	Rate of Return (BAAF)	Phases I and II (ESP2)	Phase III (ESP3)	[ρ_2]	$\bar{R}^2$ [DW] {SEE}
20	Food processing	.0143 (2.10)		-.1194 (-1.35)		.4393 (8.47)		-.0068 (-0.64)	.0270 (1.68)	0.76	0.93 [1.74] {0.0111}
21	Tobacco	.0040 (4.26)			.2449[b] (3.34)	-.0034 (-1.29)	.1086 (3.40)	-.0205 (-2.22)	-.0030 (-0.24)	0.75	0.78 [1.84] {0.0101}
22	Textiles	-.0703 (-2.03)	.1275 (1.43)		1.7818[c] (2.94)	-.0069 (-0.17)		.0227 (1.04)	.0049 (0.16)	0.81	0.72 [1.96] {0.0231}
23	Apparel	.0086 (2.08)				.3511 (3.95)		-.0113 (-1.37)	-.0230 (-2.03)	1.34 [-0.67]	0.81 [2.17] {0.0096}
24	Lumber	-.0026 (-1.57)	.5367 (3.03)		1.7669[d] (2.24)			.0965 (2.63)	.0884 (1.70)	1.21 [-0.51]	0.83 [2.07] {0.0417}
25	Furniture	-.0086 (-2.81)			.7557[d] (8.00)	.3641[c] (1.39)		-.00001 (-0.00)	-.0066 (-1.29)	1.27 [-0.65]	0.92 [2.14] {0.0043}
26	Paper	-.0111 (-1.10)	-.0044 (-0.06)		.3817 (1.89)	.1843[b] (2.25)		.0084 (1.11)	.0165 (1.57)	1.05 [-0.45]	0.81 [2.10] {0.0085}
28	Chemicals	-.0030 (-0.34)		0628 (4.60)	.1251[b] (0.95)			.0014 (0.35)	.0136 (2.46)	0.70 [-0.21]	0.84 [1.74] {0.0043}

30 Rubber	−.0155 (−0.95)	.7520^d (1.81)	.0196^d (0.17)	−.0098 (−0.59)	−.0080 (−0.36)	1.06 [−0.36]	0.70 [1.91] {0.0174}
32 Stone, clay, and glass	−.0250 (−2.84)	1.0161^c (5.24)		−.00001 (−0.02)	.0081 (0.89)	1.20 [−0.50]	0.89 [1.75] {0.0078}
331 Ferrous metals	.0134 (1.31)		.1298 (1.52)	.0319 (4.25)	.0325 (3.12)	1.41 [−0.52]	0.93 [1.77] {0.0079}
333 Nonferrous metals	.0502 (2.05)	−.0404 (−3.50)	−.5598^b (−0.11)	.0292 (1.43)	.0408 (1.43)	1.52 [−0.76]	0.85 [1.83] {0.0225}
34 Fabricated metals	.0044 (1.43)	.0190 (1.50)	.1854 (2.30)	.5984 (8.79)	.0009 (0.26)	−.0033 (−0.69)	1.01 [−0.42]	0.96 [1.94] {0.0039}
35 Nonelectrical machinery	−.0008 (−0.11)	.4636^c (2.84)	.2474 (3.31)	−.0034 (−0.95)	−.0071 (−1.46)	0.83	0.94 [1.78] {0.0035}
36 Electrical machinery	.0051 (0.83)	−.0543 (−1.71)		.0016 (0.24)	.0201 (2.03)	1.47 [−0.61]	0.89 [1.93] {0.0078}
371 Motor vehicles	−.0056 (−1.10)	.8449 (4.88)		.0025 (0.31)	−.0086 (−0.33)	0.81 [−0.24]	0.79 [2.16] {0.0095}
38 Instruments	.0056 (1.26)	.3689 (2.84)		−.0074 (−1.34)	.0029 (0.40)	0.96 [−0.16]	0.73 [2.07] {0.0057}

[a]Summary statistics are identified in notes to Table 1. For identification of variables and sources of data, see appendix.

[b]For wages, signifies use of WF, lagged one period; for materials prices, $PIQF$, lagged one period.

[c]For wages, signifies use of $WFWA$; for materials prices, $PIQF$, lagged two periods.

[d]For wages, signifies use of $WFWA$, lagged one period; for materials prices, $PIQF$, lagged four periods.

TABLE 5 Industry Profit Margin (PMF) Equations,[a] 1959III–1973II
(figures in parentheses are t statistics)

SIC No.	Industry	Constant	Output (QF)	Output Price (PQF)	Wages (WF)	Input Prices (PIQF)	Interest Costs (BAAF)	Phases I and II (ESP2)	Phase III (ESP3)	ρ_1	$\bar{R}^2$ [DW] {SEE}
20	Food processing	.0070 (0.58)		-.3878[b] (-1.61)				-.0220 (-0.80)	.0363 (0.92)	0.54	0.40 [1.85] {0.030}
21	Tobacco	-.0076 (-0.46)	.0621 (0.47)	.2951[b] (0.71)				-.0301 (-1.01)	.0142 (0.38)	0.59	0.37 [1.84] {0.037}
22	Textiles	-.0684 (-2.02)	2.699 (6.91)	1.157 (1.56)			-.5474 (-1.77)	-.1566 (-1.68)	.0524 (0.43)	0.38	0.71 [1.90] {0.118}
23	Apparel	-.1276 (-1.72)	3.287 (3.62)	-.9202[b] (-0.58)	3.197 (2.01)			-.0491 (-0.43)	-.2550 (-1.12)		0.15 [1.34] {0.237}
24	Lumber	-.3148 (-2.31)	6.729 (5.73)	.8108 (1.04)	3.893 (1.51)			-.1256 (-0.57)	.0183 (0.06)	0.44	0.67 [1.82] {0.295}
25	Furniture	-.5065 (-1.51)	3.666 (6.86)			-1.892[b] (-1.59)		.1136 (0.92)	-.3524 (-1.96)		0.47 [1.68] {0.218}
26	Paper	-.0672 (-0.28)	2.754 (2.82)	4.271 (1.93)	-2.771[b] (-0.59)		.1362[b] (0.91)	.3400 (1.83)	-.3255 (-1.42)	0.76	0.66 [2.05] {0.156}
28	Chemicals	-.1732 (-3.83)	1.265 (5.48)	-2.170 (-1.87)	1.079 (1.30)			.0441 (1.32)	.0524 (4.83)	0.56	0.73 [1.85] {0.038}

30 Rubber	−.1892 (−3.46)	1.299 (4.57)	1.963[b] (1.57)	−2.480 (−3.56)	.1276 (1.59)	−.1154 (−1.03)	0.16	0.55 [1.86] {0.131}
32 Stone, clay, and glass	−.1003 (−2.94)	2.179 (4.42)			.0451 (0.46)	−.1085 (−0.76)	0.33	0.41 [2.02] {0.147}
331 Ferrous metals	.0045 (0.08)	1.638 (7.35)	−2.988[c] (−2.18)		.4022 (3.36)	.6603 (2.68)	0.09	0.60 [1.98] {0.147}
333 Nonferrous metals	−.1479 (−1.21)	2.242 (4.82)	−.4902[d] (−0.15)	1.501 (1.98)	.1518 (0.84)	−.2134 (−0.89)	0.24	0.45 [2.00] {0.253}
34 Fabricated metals	−.0896 (−2.23)	2.499 (4.82)			.0886 (1.10)	−.2591 (−2.41)	0.60	0.69 [1.98] {0.252}
35 Nonelectrical machinery	−.0567 (−1.67)	.9191 (2.98)			−.0015 (−0.02)	.0472 (0.55)	0.64	0.67 [1.58] {0.101}
36 Electrical machinery	−.110 (−2.51)	1.384 (4.24)			.0804 (1.08)	−.0501 (−0.58)	0.70	0.63 [1.89] {0.079}
371 Motor vehicles	no statistical relationship							
38 Instruments	−.0604 (−1.93)	1.053 (3.76)			.0293 (0.51)	−.0812 (−1.11)	0.61	0.64 [1.89] {0.070}

a Summary statistics are identified in notes to Table 1. For identification of variables and sources of data, see appendix.
b For output price, signifies use of *PQF*, lagged one period, *SPD*. For wages, *WF*, lagged one period; for input prices, *PIQF*, lagged one period; for interest costs, *SPD*.
c *WF*, lagged four periods, used.
d *WFWA* used.

TABLE 6 Industry Wage (WF) Equations,[a] 1959III–1973II (figures in parentheses are t statistics)

SIC No.	Industry	Constant	Consumer prices (PRF)	Employment (EMF)	Productivity (QMF)	Unemployment (1/u)	Guideposts (GPD)	Phases I, II, III (ESP1)	ρ_1	$\bar{R}^2$ [DW] {SEE}
20	Food processing	.0307 (6.88)	.6500ᵇ (6.12)	−.2054 (−3.60)			−.0123 (−3.05)	.0060 (0.16)	0.70	0.94 [1.93] {0.0042}
21	Tobacco	.0121 (1.02)	1.0852ᵇ (3.49)	−.2718 (−3.33)	.2997ᵇ (2.04)			.0021 (0.15)	0.51	0.64 [1.88] {0.0189}
22	Textiles	.0056 (0.44)	.6213ᵇ (4.55)	.2408ᵇ (2.65)		.0938 (1.39)		.0026 (0.14)	0.37	0.79 [1.90] {0.0082}
23	Apparel	.0829 (4.39)	−.2529ᶜ (−0.64)			−.0087ᶜ (−1.30)	−.3813 (−3.24)	−.0070 (−0.77)	0.85	0.82 [1.59] {0.0093}
24	Lumber	.0324 (2.74)	.9852ᵇ (3.48)	.1877 (2.37)			−.0246 (−2.27)	−.0198 (−1.81)	0.68	0.80 [1.72] {0.0114}
25	Furniture	−.0161 (−1.68)	.6211ᵇ (4.90)	−.0891 (−2.32)		.1897 (3.72)		.0110 (2.20)	0.61	0.91 [1.88] {0.0055}
26	Paper	.0307 (14.35)	.6639ᵇ (12.50)	−.0476 (−1.47)			−.0093 (−4.79)	.0089 (4.08)	0.32	0.94 [1.76] {0.0038}
28	Chemicals	.0586 (1.96)	.0598ᵇ (0.41)				−.0052 (−0.87)	−.0033 (−0.79)	0.97	0.94 [2.24] {0.0040}

		.0235 (2.87)	.4638 (2.33)	.1360 (4.76)			-.0234 (-2.99)	-.0049 (-0.64)	0.69	0.81 [1.93] {0.0083}
32	Stone, clay, and glass	.0247 (6.57)	.5420[b] (2.81) / .2893[b] (1.87)	.0617 (2.10)			-.0065 (-2.01)	.0099 (2.72)	0.31	0.90 [1.90] {0.0065}
331	Ferrous metals	-.0148 (-0.68)	.5158[c] (1.51)	-.0740[b] (-1.81)	.4550 (3.98)	.1130 (1.05)	-.0154 (-1.39)	.0473 (4.04)	0.75	0.78 [1.41] {0.0171}
333	Nonferrous metals	.0664 (4.30)	.3712[c] (1.79)	.0641 (1.73)	.3119 (5.43)	-.0242[c] (-3.86)	-.0202 (-2.85)	.0083 (1.24)	0.57	0.87 [1.69] {0.0086}
34	Fabricated metals	.0211 (5.06)	.8087[b] (7.86)	.0752 (2.95)			-.0120 (-2.91)	.0013 (0.30)	0.61	0.93 [1.74] {0.0048}
35	Nonelectrical machinery	.0219 (7.75)	.8294[d] (10.95)	.0196 (1.21)			-.0083 (-3.00)	.0014 (0.49)	0.40	0.93 [1.99] {0.0045}
36	Electrical machinery	.0271 (3.57)	.6072[d] (2.85)	-.0940 (-3.57)				-.0032 (-0.59)	0.81	0.90 [1.62] {0.0058}
371	Motor vehicles	.0305 (1.30)	.8276 (3.12)	.1474 (5.76)	.4440 (3.23)	-.0194[b] (-0.20)		.0067 (0.67)	0.25	0.74 [1.90] {0.0165}
38	Instruments	.0231 (4.01)	.6260 (3.74)	-.0973 (-3.31)				-.0033 (-0.70)	0.78	0.91 [1.71] {0.0049}

a Summary statistics are identified in notes to Table 1. For identification of variables and sources of data, see appendix.
b For consumer prices, signifies use of PRF, lagged one period. employment, 1/u, lagged one period.
c For consumer prices, signifies use of PRFWA; for unemployment, L.
d PRFWA, lagged one period, used.

EMFWA, for employment; QMF, for productivity, lagged one period; QMF, lagged one period; for unemployment, L.

TABLE 7 Two-Digit SIC Manufacturing Industries in Which Dummy Variables Were Significant

ESP1$_t$		ESP2$_t$		ESP3$_t$	
Positive	Negative	Positive	Negative	Positive	Negative
		Price Equation			
		SIC 24†	SIC 21*	SIC 24†	SIC 23*
		SIC 331*	SIC 23†	SIC 26†	SIC 35†
		SIC 333†		SIC 28*	SIC 38†
				SIC 331*	
				SIC 333†	
				SIC 36*	
		Profit Margin Equation			
		SIC 26*	SIC 22*	SIC 28*	SIC 25*
		SIC 30†		SIC 331*	SIC 26†
		SIC 331*			SIC 34*
		Wage Equation			
SIC 25*	SIC 24*				
SIC 32*					
SIC 331*					

*Significant at 5 percent level.
†Significant at 10 percent level.

companies much flexibility in raising individual prices so long as their weighted average price increases were within the prescribed limit of 1.8 percent) could have resulted in the circumvention of a significant downward impact on prices that otherwise would have been obtained because of the control program. Moreover, with the relaxation of the control program under Phase III, and with the significant reduction in the level of unused capacity experienced during the first half of 1973, demand pressures asserted themselves, thereby rendering unlikely any effective price restraint in these and several other industries. Small wonder then that the coefficients on the dummy variables turned out to be positive in the price equations for several industries. Output prices in the tobacco industry (SIC 21) and in apparel (SIC 23) were somewhat lower under Phase II than would have been the case without controls.

The dummy variables for the wage equations, if significant, are generally capturing shifts arising from other causes. Most of the major contracts in manufacturing were not negotiated during phases I and II, having been signed prior to mid-1971. The only industries in which the Pay Board played a major role during the control period were lumber and glass. The Pay Board's action is reflected in the negative coefficient on the wage dummy variable for SIC 24 (Table 7). The Pay Board's action is not reflected in a similar wage constraint for SIC 32, which incorporates the glass industry subgroup. This is because the wage behavior of the other subgroups of SIC 32 (namely, stone and clay) was subject to little or no control due to the preponderance of small firms in these two.

The positive coefficient for ferrous metals in the wage equation is perhaps more indicative of the distortion hypothesis than the effects of the control program. The wage settlement in this industry was negotiated prior to the August 1971 freeze. It is interesting that average hourly earnings in ferrous metals were "out of line" by about 4.7 percent. However, an examination of the profit margin equation seems to suggest that the advances in the wage variable may have been more than compensated by price increases, since the profit margin dummy variable is positive and significant for the ferrous metals industry.

Finally, according to the equations, wages were held down in lumber, while prices were pushed above their normal relation with the independent variables, though without any impact upon the profit margins. This can perhaps be explained by the proposition that large lumber firms used wage increases as a trigger to raise prices, and that such wage increases are correlated positively with margins. In other words, if wages are held down, this will tend to reduce profit margins.

I. AGGREGATE WAGE-PRICE EQUATIONS AND THE TOTAL IMPACT OF CONTROLS

Microanalytic data and disaggregated industry equations are indispensable to any meaningful understanding of the wage-price control experiment. However, in most of the literature, the impact of controls is assessed through the use of aggregate wage-price relations for the manufacturing or private nonfarm sector of the economy. Following this practice, the seventeen industry variables were aggregated into macroeconomic wage and price variables for total manufacturing. The purpose of this exercise was twofold: to determine if the aggregate results were consistent with the industry results and to ascertain the results of the program in terms of the movement of macroeconomic variables.

The manufacturing wage and price equations were estimated for the period 1959III–1971II to determine the aggregate historical relation, and simulated from 1971III through 1973II to provide a basis for assessing the movement of wages and prices in the absence of controls. The equations were then re-estimated with dummy variables from 1959III through 1973III to determine the direct impact of controls on manufacturing input prices in phases II and III. The model was then simulated over the control period to allow for feedbacks between wages and prices, so that we could measure the total impact of controls. The method of aggregation entails weighting average hourly earnings, output prices, and input prices for each of the seventeen manufacturing industries by the appropriate relative value of shipments in 1958. The other variables in the estimated wage and price equations were taken from data relevant to the manufacturing sector.

Variables shown as four-quarter rates of change are marked by an F suffix. Variables with the suffix FWA are defined as four-quarter rates of change with an imposed weighted average of that variable for periods t through $t - 3$ (see appendix). The wage and price equations are estimated with the identical autocorrelation correction procedure that was used to estimate the industry wage and price equations of section V.

Estimated Equations

The results for the estimated wage and price equations appear in Table 8. The estimated coefficients all have the correct signs and the correct magnitudes. In the wage equation, the coefficient on the price expectations variable ($PFWA$) is significantly different from zero but not significantly different from unity, indicating that workers attempt to recover loss of real income in the form of higher money wages. The other two variables in the wage equation that are significant at the 5 percent level are the wage guidepost dummy variable (GP) and changes in output per man-hour in manufacturing ($QFWA$). The aggregate unemployment[25] rate (u) has the correct sign but is insignificant at the 5 percent level. Changes in prices are explained by changes in labor and nonlabor input costs. In particular, standard unit labor costs ($WFWA_{t-1} - 0.03$) and input prices ($IPFWA_t$) explain 94 percent of the movement of prices. A 1 percent change in standard unit labor costs induces a change of 0.36 percent in prices.

For manufacturing wage and price equations to capture the feedbacks of inflation, it is necessary to treat wages and prices as endogenous variables. While wages (WF_t) and output prices (PQF_t) are endogenous to the model, consumer prices are exogenous. To close the model, consumer prices (PF_t) are made a function of output prices (PQF_t). The equation linking output prices and consumer prices (PF_t) is estimated for the period 1959III–1971II by using an Almon lag. The estimated equation implies that the partial adjustment mechanism will translate 95 percent of output prices into input prices in eight quarters. The estimated linking equation is[26]

$$PF_t = \underset{(14.62)}{0.01161} + \underset{(21.21)}{0.95212} \sum_{i=D}^{7} PQF(-i)_t$$

$$\bar{R}^2 = 0.91; DW = 0.412; SEE = 0.00410$$

The simulations are based on the four-quarter price and wage equations, fitted to the period 1959III–1971II (equations 1 and 3 of Table 8). Over the entire period, the full model has a tendency to underpredict wages by 0.061 percentage points. The error measures provide the first warning that the model will not perform with complete accuracy. While the estimated wage and price equations have significant coefficients and strong explanatory power, the structural equations when combined into a model fail to perform with any real consistency. First, the model tends to slightly underpredict wages. This problem is compounded by the failure of the model to track the wage increases of the late 1960s.[27] Second, the root-mean-square errors for the wage and price simulations are larger than the standard errors for the estimated wage and price equations. This implies that the variances of the residuals of the simulations are larger than the variances of the residuals of the estimated equations. The interpretation of the mean absolute errors is that at each discrete simulation the average error, irrespective of sign, is 0.5352 percentage points for wages and 0.3978 for prices.

ᴛhe Wage–Price Control Program

The actual movement of wages and prices during the control period can be compared with the performance of the model in simulations from 1971III to 1973II under the influence of identical exogenous factors. Comparisons are made on the basis of average performance of controls for 1971III–1973II, which corresponds

TABLE 8 Estimated Wage and Price Equations for Total Manufacturing, 1959III–1971II and 1959III–1973II (figures in parentheses are t statistics)

Wage Equations (WF_t)	Constant	$PFWA_t$	$1/u_t$	GPD_t	$QFWA_t$	$ESP2$	$ESP3$	ρ_1	$\bar{R}^2$ [DW] {SEE}	ME^a [RMSE] {MAE}
1. 1959III–1971II	0.0046 (0.755)	0.987 (8.54)	0.0349 (1.23)	−0.0109 (−3.69)	0.3220 (5.16)			0.4271 (2.77)	0.921 [2.14] {0.0045}	.000613 [.007256] {.005352}
2. 1959III–1973II	0.0061 (0.958)	0.8874 (7.17)	0.0436 (1.46)	−0.0133 (−4.11)	0.3313 (5.13)	0.0056 (1.41)	−0.01169 (−2.47)	0.450 (2.78)	0.926 [2.00] {0.0049}	

Price Equations (PQF_t)	Constant	$WFWA_{t-1}$ −0.03	WF_t −$WFWA_t$	$IPFWA_t$	$ESP2$	$ESP3$	ρ_1	ρ_2	$\bar{R}^2$ [DW] {SEE}	ME^a [RMSE] {MAE}
3. 1959III–1971II	0.0059 (2.22)	0.3636 (2.65)	0.09175 (1.31)	0.5858 (7.28)			0.9481 (6.21)	−.1604 (−1.02)	0.963 [1.93] {0.0030}	−.000097 [.005377] {.003978}
4. 1959III–1973II	0.0054 (1.67)	0.2185 (1.10)	0.0252 (0.279)	0.5966 (7.08)	0.0011 (0.301)	−0.0007 (−1.80)	1.1612 (8.07)	−.3595 (−2.21)	0.958 [2.04] {0.0037}	

$\bar{R}^2$ = coefficient of multiple determination adjusted for degrees of freedom.

DW = Durbin-Watson statistic.

SEE = standard error of estimate.

NOTE: Variables used in the equations are identified in the accompanying text, and the data sources are given in the appendix.

[a] ME = mean error; $RMSE$ = root-mean-square error; MAE = mean absolute error. The mean of WF_t is 0.03978, and the mean of PQF_t is 0.01331. The error measures are calculated as follows, where A_t defines the actual value, S_t the simulated value, and N the number of observations in the interval of the simulation:

$$ME = \frac{1}{N} \sum_{t=1}^{N} (A_t - S_t)$$

$$RMSE = \sqrt{\frac{1}{N} \sum_{t=1}^{N} (A_t - S_t)^2}$$

$$MAE = \frac{1}{N} \sum_{t=1}^{N} \left| A_t - S_t \right|$$

roughly to the period of the initial wage-price freeze, the controls of Phase II, and the more flexible controls of Phase III. The exogenous variables retain their actual values (historical values) for this period, while the endogenous wage and price variables assume the values of 1971II as their initial values and the simulated values thereafter. By beginning the dynamic simulation in 1971III, we avoid the cumulative underpredictions exhibited by the 1959III–1971II simulation.

If wages and prices were determined in the same manner after controls as in the period prior to 1971III, then our model would accurately predict the movement of wages and prices during the control period. If the mechanisms that generated wages and prices prior to controls were operating in an unrestrained fashion during the control period, then the errors generated in the latter period should be of approximately the same magnitude as those before.

Table 9 contains the simulated wage and price changes predicted for 1971III–1973II. These results are characteristic of an economy without controls, while the actual wages and prices are for an economy with controls. The average difference between the simulated and actual values could serve as a crude approximation for the total impact of controls.[28]

Since this approach is unable to distinguish between simulation error and error due to controls, the alternative—to estimate the direct impact of controls by including dummy variables in the wage and price equations—has also been used. The dummy variables measure the influences on the residuals of an estimated equation. We have associated these structural influences with the efforts of the Economic Stabilization Program by defining ESP to coincide with the establishment of wage and price controls.

Equations 2 and 4 of Table 8 were estimated for 1959III–1973II. They include the ESP dummy variables, which reflect the partial derivative of the change in wages and prices with respect to the actions of the Economic Stabilization Program. The coefficients are only a measure of the direct impact of controls, since the equations are not allowed to interact. Controls resulted in a significant 1.17 percentage point annual reduction in wages in the manufacturing sector of Phase III. The impact on manufacturing prices also was negative (an annual percentage point decrease of 0.074), but not significantly different from zero. Phase II and Freeze I exerted a positive pressure on wages and prices, which is consistent with the industry results. On the other hand, the significant downward impact on wages in Phase III contradicts our previous results for the disaggregated industries. However, the disaggregated equation did not include a Phase III wage dummy, and this could account for the inconsistency.

Because they do not include the interaction of wages and prices, the dummy variable coefficients fail to measure the total impact of controls. The total impact can be measured by simulating the re-estimated wage and price equations (2 and 4). It has been indicated that the model used to simulate an economy without controls produced a bias in the predicted value of wages and prices because of the errors generated in each of the discrete simulations. To measure the total impact of controls by comparing the simulated values for an economy without controls against the actual values for an economy with controls would result in an error because of the presence of bias in the simulated series. A more consistent measure of the total impact of controls is to compare two simulated series of wages and prices. It may then be assumed that simulation bias is present in both models and, hence, that the total impact would be net of any simulation bias. Therefore, the total impact is measured by comparing the simulated values for an economy without controls against the simulated values for an economy with controls. These simulated values appear in Table 9.

If the mechanism generating wages and prices had operated as it did prior to the establishment of the control program, then the equations for an economy without controls would provide predictions of wages and prices. However, if the control program had any influence on the determination of wages and prices, then the equa-

TABLE 9   Comparison of Simulated Values of Wage (WF$_t$) and Price (PQF$_t$) Equations for an Economy with Controls and for an Economy without Controls[a]

	Simulated without Controls		Simulated with Controls	
	WF$_t$	PQF$_t$	WF$_t$	PQF$_t$
1971III	7.48	3.85	8.02	3.87
IV	7.55	4.61	8.06	4.54
1972I	7.35	5.48	7.81	5.32
II	7.39	5.91	7.91	5.67
III	7.84	6.22	8.16	5.87
IV	8.51	6.36	8.74	5.89
1973I	9.04	7.08	7.96	5.74
II	9.48	8.73	8.19	7.21

[a]Simulations begin in 1971III.

tions with the control-program dummy variables would yield the appropriate predictions for an economy with controls. The differences in these two simulations would reflect the total impact of the control program. It appears that the control program raised manufacturing wages by 0.03 percentage points on an annual basis and lowered prices by 0.52 percentage points on an annual average, above what would have occurred in the absence of controls.

On the whole, it can generally be concluded that the aggregate wage and price relations fail to agree with the results presented for the disaggregated two-digit industries. The poor performance of the model in the historical period and the inability of the wage equation to track the wage inflation of the mid-1960s result in an underprediction of wage change. The lower-than-normal wage values then interact in the price equations and result in an underprediction of prices. Thus, the aggregate equations probably yield erroneous estimates of the impact of controls. Second, the apparent contradiction between the industry and aggregate models leaves us somewhat apprehensive about the worth of any macroeconomic relation. The method of data aggregation and poor selection of a model could be causes of some of the disagreement, but a problem of equal importance may be in the inappropriateness of aggregate wage and price equations for the manufacturing sector.[29] This suggests that relationships should not be estimated at such a high level of aggregation.

VII. SUMMARY AND CONCLUSIONS

Our tentative conclusion is that the industry equations are more meaningful than the aggregate ones. Hence, the Economic Stabilization Program had little impact on the manufacturing sector of the economy. The conclusion is labeled tentative because there are several shortcomings in the analytical system and in the two-digit manufacturing data that underlie the simulation results. The models used are somewhat imprecise and limited by the choice of variables in testing various hypotheses relating to price and wage determinations. Simultaneous models for individual manufacturing industries were not constructed, and consequently the total impact of controls could not be ascertained. An attempt was made to estimate the total impact at the aggregate manufacturing level, but the experiment was less than satisfactory. Finally, like most researchers in the field, we were limited in our ability to measure structural shifts in the economy due to controls because there are many short-comings in the use of dummy variables.

APPENDIX: SOURCES OF DATA

All monthly series were transformed into quarterly ones by averaging their values for the three months of each quarter, except shipments, S_t, for which the sum of the monthly values was used.

In tables 1 through 6, the F suffix on a variable indicates that the figures used for the series are for the change between the current quarter and the same quarter a year ago as a percentage of the current quarter: for any series X, the variable XF_t is equal to $(X_t - X_{t-4})/X_{t-4}$. Unless stated otherwise each data source is industry-specific. The suffix FWA indicates that the variable is defined as a four-quarter weighted average of the F series just described: for any series X, the variable $XFWA_t$ is defined as $0.4\ XF_t + 0.3\ XF_{t-1} + 0.2\ XF_{t-2} + 0.1\ XF_{t-3}$, where XF_t is defined as above.

BLS = U.S. Department of Labor, Bureau of Labor Statistics;

BEA = U.S. Department of Commerce, Bureau of Economic Analysis;

NIPA = national income and product accounts of the United States;

Census = U.S. Department of Commerce, Bureau of the Census;

FRB = Board of Governors of the Federal Reserve System;

SIC = Standard Industrial Classification.

PQ_t = index of nonseasonally adjusted output prices for two-digit SIC. The correspondence between the monthly elements of the BLS nonseasonally adjusted wholesale price index (WPI) and the three- and four-digit SICs was established at the four-digit level. These WPIs were then aggregated to the input-output classifications of the 1958 input-output table published in *Survey of Current Business*, weighting by shipments of the corresponding SIC category in 1958. The quarterly series was constructed as a simple average of the monthly series.

Q_t = FRB quarterly series for industrial production for two-digit SIC.

$DINS_t$ = inventory-to-sales ratio for two-digit SIC. Inventories are the BEA adjusted inventory valuation in billions of current dollars. Sales for two-digit SIC are the BEA seasonally adjusted monthly series on sales in billions of current dollars.

W_t = BLS seasonally adjusted monthly index of average hourly earnings of production workers, adjusted to exclude overtime for two-digit SIC.

PIQ_t = index of nonseasonally adjusted input prices for two-digit SIC. Input prices are constructed from the output price indexes by using input-output coefficients as weights. The input price for an industry is the weighted average of output prices, where the weights are the direct input requirements as given in the 1958 input-output table. Allowances are made for intraindustry purchases of inputs and for the purchase of important materials from outside manufacturing.

BAA_t = Moody's yield on Aaa corporate bonds.

SPD_t = special dummy variable equal to 1.0 in 1970 and 2.0 in 1971, to account for unusual profits in 1970 and 1971.

PR_t = BLS nonseasonally adjusted monthly index of consumer prices for all items, with base of 1.0 in 1967.

EM_t = BLS nonseasonally adjusted employment of production workers for two-digit SIC.

QM_t = BLS seasonally adjusted quarterly index of output per man-hour for two-digit SIC with base of 1.0 in 1967.

u_t = BLS seasonally adjusted unemployment rate for all civilian workers.

L_t = BLS seasonally adjusted layoff rate for all manufacturing, per 100 employees.

GPD_t = mid-1960s wage-price guidepost dummy variable constructed to equal 0.25 in 1962I and 1967II, 0.50 in 1962II and 1967II, 0.75 in 1962III and 1967I, 1.0 from 1962IV through 1966IV, and zero in all other quarters.

$ESP1_t$ = ninety-day wage-price freeze, Phase II, and Phase III dummy variable.

$ESP2_t$ = ninety-day wage-price freeze and Phase II dummy variable.

$ESP3_t$ = Phase III dummy variable.

PM_t = quarterly series on profit margins for two-digit SIC. Ratio of NIPA pretax profits to BEA sales for two-digit SIC.

NOTES

1. Whether a firm is a near-perfect competitor, a monopolistic competitor, an oligopolist, or a pure monopolist, the output-price decisions of the firm depend upon the demand schedule as pictured by the firm after any and all allowances for the actions of others. Thus, we are assuming, for purposes of

determining the effect on the planning function of the firm, that the regulations of the various phases did not affect the demand schedule for the firm.

2. The major exemptions from the freeze were raw, unprocessed products and imports. For further details see *Economic Report of the President* (1972) and Weber (1973).

3. Among the more notable were the ones announced by the major steel firms. Following the signing of a new labor contract effective August 8, 1971, which contained average first-year wage increases of about 15 percent, prices were raised on some product lines and announced for the others. These scheduled price increases averaged 8 percent.

4. Under the term limit pricing (TLP) arrangement enacted by the Price Commission in late 1971, Tier I firms were given the option of applying for a weighted average price increase covering all or most product lines for a period of one year without specific commission approval of changes in individual product prices. The weighted average price increase was initially set at 2 percent, but was reduced to 1.8 percent in the spring of 1972. TLP was designed to give flexibility to the price control program and to relieve the limited staff of the commission from processing and approving thousands of individual price requests by large firms with complex product lines. In order to make certain that firms taking advantage of the TLP arrangement would not commit flagrant violations of the rules, they were required to keep records and file quarterly reports. They were also supposed to establish a monitoring procedure that would assure reasonable compliance with the allowable weighted average price increase.

5. From November 15, 1971, to December 31, 1971, the waiting period was only seventy-two hours. Details are presented in Lanzillotti, Hamilton, and Roberts (1975).

6. "Base *price*" is the price that existed during the freeze. The "base *period*" is the best two out of the last three fiscal years. "Profit margin" is pretax profits, before extraordinary income, as a percent of sales. See *Economic Stabilization* (1972).

7. If prices are allowed to increase by the amount of the increase in unit production costs, then profit margins are identical before and after the price increase. This is only true for a single-product firm.

8. For the profit-maximizing firm, either marginal cost (MC) equals marginal revenue (MR) and the constraint is unbinding, or the profit margin (M) is binding and $MC = MR$. In the following proof, P = price, Y = output, PY = value of output, and $C(Y)$ = costs, where costs are a function of output:

Max: $PY - C(Y)$

subject to $M = \dfrac{PY - C(Y)}{PY} \leqslant$ a constant

implies that for the Lagrangian:

$L = PY - C(Y) + \lambda [MPY - PY + C(Y)]$

$\dfrac{\partial L}{\partial Y} = \dfrac{\partial (PY)}{\partial Y} - \dfrac{\partial C}{\partial Y} + \lambda \left[(M - 1) \dfrac{\partial (PY)}{\partial Y} + \dfrac{\partial C}{\partial Y} \right] \leqslant 0; \ \dfrac{\partial L}{\partial Y} Y = 0$

$\dfrac{\partial L}{\partial \lambda} = (M - 1) PY + C(Y) \geqslant 0; \ \dfrac{\partial L}{\partial \lambda} \lambda = 0$

Thus, if $\lambda > 0$; $[PY - C(Y)]/PY = M$. If $Y > 0$, $\lambda = 0$; then $\partial(PY)/\partial(Y) = \partial C/\partial Y$.

9. To show this, let $C = C(Y, \alpha)$, where $\alpha \geq 0$ and $\partial C/\partial\alpha = 1$. If expenditures are purely wasteful the $\partial(PY)/\partial\alpha = 0$. Thus the Lagrangian is

$$L = PY - C(Y, \alpha) + \lambda[MPY - PY + C(Y, \alpha)]$$

and the first-order conditions are:

$$\frac{\partial L}{\partial Y} = \frac{\partial(PY)}{\partial Y} - \frac{\partial C}{\partial Y} + \lambda\left[(M-1)\frac{\partial(PY)}{\partial Y} + \frac{\partial C}{\partial Y}\right] \leq 0; \frac{\partial L}{\partial Y}Y = 0$$

$$\frac{\partial L}{\partial\alpha} = -\frac{\partial C}{\partial\alpha} + \lambda\frac{\partial C}{\partial\alpha} \leq 0; \frac{\partial L}{\partial\alpha}\alpha = 0$$

$$\frac{\partial L}{\partial\lambda} = (M-1)PY + C(Y, \alpha) \geq 0; \frac{\partial L}{\partial\lambda}\lambda = 0$$

Therefore, if $Y > 0$ and $\lambda = 0$, it must be that $\alpha = 0$ and $\partial(PY)/\partial Y = \partial C/\partial Y$. However, $y > 0$, and $\alpha > 0$; then $\lambda = 1$ or $(PY - C)/PY = M$ and $\partial(PY)/\partial Y = 0$.

10. Formally, add $R(\alpha)$ to the constrained optimization problem in note 9, where $1 > (\partial R/\partial\alpha) > 0$ and $\partial C/\partial\alpha = 1$. The Lagrangian and first-order conditions are:

$$L = PY + R(\alpha) - C(Y, \alpha) + \lambda(MPY - PY + C)$$

(a) $$\frac{\partial L}{\partial Y} = \frac{\partial(PY)}{\partial Y} - \frac{\partial C}{\partial Y} + \lambda(M-1)\frac{\partial(PY)}{\partial Y} + \lambda\frac{\partial C}{\partial Y} \geq 0; \frac{\partial L}{\partial Y}Y = 0$$

(b) $$\frac{\partial L}{\partial\alpha} = \frac{\partial R}{\partial\alpha} - \frac{\partial C}{\partial\alpha} + \lambda\frac{\partial C}{\partial\alpha} \leq 0; \frac{\partial L}{\partial\alpha}\alpha = 0$$

(c) $$\frac{\partial L}{\partial\lambda} = MPY - PY + C \geq 0; \frac{\partial L}{\partial\lambda}\lambda = 0$$

Thus, if $Y > 0$ and $\lambda = 0$, then $\partial(PY)/\partial Y = \partial C/\partial Y$ and $\alpha = 0$, since $\partial R/\partial\alpha < \partial C/\partial\alpha$. If $Y > 0$ and $\alpha > 0$, then from (b), $\lambda > 1 - \partial R/\partial\alpha > 0$. From (a), if $\partial C/\partial Y > \partial(PY)/\partial Y$, then $\lambda > 1$; thus $\partial C/\partial Y > \partial(PY)/\partial Y > 0$ at the optimum.

11. Letting $\hat{P}$ be the desired price for target rate-of-return pricing; P, the allowable price under the regulations; $\hat{\Pi}$, profits at $\hat{P}$; and $\hat{M}$, the profit margin at normal output with price $\hat{P}$; then $dP/P \gtrless d\hat{P}/\hat{P}$ as

$$\Sigma f_i\left(\frac{dv_i}{v_i} + \frac{dv_i}{v_i} - \frac{dY}{Y}\right) \gtrless \frac{f_f}{\hat{M}}\frac{dY}{Y}$$

where v_i is the price of the ith factor of x_i, $f_i = v_ix_i/C$, and $f_f =$ the fraction that fixed costs (K) are to total costs. The proof is as follows: at $\hat{Y}$, $\hat{P}\hat{Y} = \Sigma v_i\hat{x}_i + \hat{\Pi}$, and $\hat{r} = \hat{\Pi}/K$, where $\hat{r}$ is the normal rate of return. Thus $d\hat{r} = 0$ implies $d\hat{\Pi} = 0$

$$\frac{d\hat{P}}{\hat{P}} = \frac{\Sigma f_i\left(\dfrac{dv_i}{v_i} + \dfrac{d\hat{x}_i}{x_i} - \dfrac{dY}{Y}\right)}{\dfrac{\Sigma v_i\hat{x}_i}{\hat{Y}}}$$

The allowable percentage increase in price is

$$\frac{dP}{P} = \Sigma f_i\left(\frac{dv_i}{v_i} + \frac{dx_i}{x_i} - \frac{dY}{Y}\right) - f_f\frac{dY}{Y}$$

Thus, $dP/P \gtrless d\hat{P}/\hat{P}$ implies that

$$\Sigma f_i\left(\frac{dv_i}{v_i} + \frac{dx_i}{x_i} - \frac{dY}{Y}\right) \gtrless \frac{f_f}{M}\frac{dY}{Y}$$

12. The relaxation in the profit margin limitation raised from three to five the number of fiscal years from which firms could select the two years they would consider most advantageous in calculating their profit margin base. Moreover, a firm would no longer be constrained by the profit margin rule if its weighted average price increase was not in excess of 1.5 percent a year.

13. Other alternative proxies for labor market tightness are quit rates, layoff rates, unemployment dispersion, or excess labor reserves.

14. The expectation hypothesis can consist of a distributed lag of past price changes (Turnovsky 1972a), actual expectations price data (Turnovsky 1972b), or a nonlinear inflation severity variable (Eckstein and Brinner 1972).

15. Recent analysis of wage determination stems from the work of A. W. Phillips (1958), who related wage changes to the unemployment rate, a proxy for labor market tightness. Modifications have taken several directions. For example, Eckstein and Wilson (1962), Hammermesh (1972), Ashenfelter, Johnson, and Pencavel (1972), Wachter (1970a, 1974), and Okun (1973) have included effects of unions on the relative wage structure, termed "the spillover thesis" or the "relative wage distortion thesis." Kaldor has long considered profits as a causal variable in wage rate determination, based on his theories of economic growth. Thus, Kaldor (1959) argued that Phillips's results probably arose from a correlation between unemployment rates and profits. Among those who have tested the high profits-wages thesis are Levinson (1960), Bhatia (1962), Eckstein and Wilson (1962), Perry (1966), and Perry et al. (1969). Kuh (1967) argued that profits in econometric wage equations were only a surrogate for a more fundamental determinant of wages: productivity. While this may be true at the aggregate level, it need not be so at the industry level. At the aggregate level, if we divide national income into profits and labor income, then by definition the percent change in wages is equal to the percent change in prices plus the percent change in output per man-hour plus the percent change in the output-capital ratio multiplied by the ratio of profits to labor income. Consequently, if the output-capital ratio is constant or changing at a constant rate, K, then $\%\Delta w = K + \%\Delta p + \%\Delta(Y/L)$, where w = wages, p = prices, and Y/L = output per man-hour.

16. This particular weighting of the lag variables is adopted from Eckstein and Brinner (1972). Also, the imposed weighted lags tend to smooth out impacts which produce a dampening of large fluctuations in predicted wages and prices.

17. We are grateful to David Wyss for providing us with the original work sheets, which were helpful in constructing the output and input series. Because of adjustments these are different from those of Eckstein and Wyss (1972).

18. In previous wage and price studies in which simultaneous-equation techniques were used, it was found that the bias associated with reliance on ordinary least squares is quite small in wage and price equations. See Dicks-Mireaux (1961), Eckstein and Brinner (1972), Goldstein (1972), and Rappoport and Kniesner (1974).

19. However, the Durbin-Watson statistics imply autocorrelation due to the presence of an omitted explanatory variable. For a discussion of this in terms of consistency of the estimated coefficients, see McCallum (1973).

20. For a discussion of the impact of cost-of-living adjustments in the periods prior to and during controls, see Stallard and Solnick (1974).

21. There have been various conceptual objections to using the aggregate unem-

ployment rate as a proxy for labor market tightness. Both Gordon (1971) and Perry (1970) have developed alternative measures of labor market tightness. Both measures were tested in the wage equations, and they performed less well than the aggregate measures. It is doubtful that industry-specific measures would perform any better, except in industries with high unemployment and weak labor unions.

22. This particular weighting of the dummy variable is adopted from Eckstein and Brinner (1972) and reflects the relative strength of the guidepost policies over the period of estimation.

23. For the use of ESP1 to determine the direct impact of controls, see Gordon (1972). Explanations of the wage and price impacts of the freeze and Phase II are discussed in Askin (n.d.), Bosworth (1972), and Poole (1973). For a discussion of the adequacy of guidepost dummies, see Perry (1967) and Perry et al. (1969). For a more general discussion of the dummy variable technique see Askin and Kraft (1973) and Rees (1971).

24. Methods of computing the total impact of wage and price controls are elaborated in Askin and Kraft (1973) and Gordon (1972).

25. The four-quarter percent change in the unemployment rate, the manufacturing layoff rate, and the unemployment rate for manufacturing were also tried separately and in combination, but all were inferior proxies for labor market tightness.

26. We use a second-degree polynomial lag with the coefficient constrained to zero in the last period. The linking equation presents the sum of the lag coefficients on PQF_t, where the t statistic is computed from the standard error of the sum.

27. The model trackings for 1959III–1971II are available on application to the authors.

28. The approximation is crude, since we would be comparing a simulated value with a fixed actual value. Under this comparison, the difference could reflect both controls and any simulated error and thus could be an overstatement, depending on whether the simulations underpredict or overpredict wages and prices.

29. While we presented only one macromodel in the paper, we tested and simulated several others. In all of them there were even greater underpredictions of wage changes.

REFERENCES

Ashenfelter, O. C., G. E. Johnson, and J. H. Pencavel. 1972. "Trade Unions and the Rate of Change of Money Wages in United States Manufacturing Industry." *Review of Economic Studies*, April: 27–54.

Askin, A. B. n.d. "Inflation and Enforcement of Phase IV: Prospects and Proposals." Mimeographed.

Askin, A. B., and J. Kraft. 1973. *Econometric Wage and Price Models*. Lexington, Mass.: Heath and Lexington Books.

Averch, H., and J. L. Johnson. 1962. "Behavior of the Firm Under the Regulatory Constraint." *American Economic Review*, December: 1053–1069.

Baumol, W. J., and A. K. Klevorick. 1970. "Input Choices and Rate of Return Regulation: An Overview of the Discussion." *Bell Journal of Economics and Management Science*, Autumn: 162–190.

Bhatia, V. 1962. "Profits and the Rate of Change in Money Earnings in the U.S., 1935–1959." *Economica*, August: 255–262.

Black, S. W., and H. H. Kelegian. 1972. "The Formulation of the Dependent Variable in the Wage Equation." *Review of Economic Studies*, January: 55–59.

Bosworth, B. 1972. "Phase II: The U.S. Experiment with an Incomes Policy." *Brookings Papers on Economic Activity*, no. 2: 343–383.

de Menil, G. 1969. "Nonlinearity in a Wage Equation for United States Manufacturing." *Review of Economics and Statistics*, May: 202–206.

Dicks-Mireaux, L. A. 1961. "The Interrelationship between Cost and Price Changes, 1946–1959." *Oxford Economic Papers*, New Series, October: 267–292.

Eckstein, O. 1968. "Money Wage Determination Revisited." *Review of Economic Studies*, April: 33–44.

Eckstein, O., and R. Brinner. 1972. *The Inflation Process in the United States*. Study prepared for Joint Economic Committee, 92d Cong., 2d sess.

Eckstein, O., and G. Fromm. 1968. "The Price Equation." *American Economic Review*, December: 1159–1183.

Eckstein, O., and T. A. Wilson. 1962. "The Determination of Money Wages in American Industry." *Quarterly Journal of Economics*, August: 379–414.

Eckstein, O., and D. Wyss. 1972. "Industry Price Equations." In O. Eckstein, ed., *The Econometrics of Price Determination*. Washington, D.C.: Board of Governors of the Federal Reserve System.

Economic Report of the President. 1972. Washington, D.C.: U.S. Government Printing Office.

Economic Stabilization. 1972. Title 6. Code of Federal Regulations. Washington, D.C.: U.S. Government Printing Office.

Goldstein, M. 1972. "The Trade-Off Between Inflation and Unemployment: A Survey of the Econometric Evidence for Selected Countries." *Staff Papers, International Monetary Fund*, November: 647–698.

Gordon, R. J. 1971. "Inflation in Recession and Recovery." *Brookings Papers on Economic Activity*, no. 1: 105–166.

———. 1972. "Wage-Price Controls and the Shifting Phillips Curve." *Brookings Papers on Economic Activity*, no. 2: 385–430.

Hammermesh, D. S. 1972. "Market Power and Wage Inflation." *Southern Economic Journal*, October: 204–212.

Kaldor, N. 1959. "Economic Growth and the Problem of Inflation, Part II." *Economica*, August: 287–298.

Kaplan, A. D. N., J. B. Dirlam, and R. F. Lanzillotti. 1958. *Pricing in Big Business— A Case Approach*. Washington, D.C.: Brookings.

Kuh, E. 1967. "A Productivity Theory of Wage Levels—An Alternative to the Phillips Curve." *Review of Economic Studies*, October: 333–360.

Lanzillotti, R. F. 1958. "Pricing Objectives in Large Companies." *American Economic Review*, December: 921–940.

Lanzillotti, R. F., M. Hamilton, and B. Roberts. 1975. *Phase II in Review: The Price Commission Experience*. Washington, D.C.: Brookings.

Levinson, R. 1960. "Post War Movement of Prices and Wages in Manufacturing Industries." *Study of Employment Growth and Price Levels*. Study Paper no. 21, Joint Economic Committee, 87th Cong., 1st sess., pp. 1–26.

McCallum, B. T. 1973. "On Estimation Assuming Nonexistent Autocorrelation."

Paper presented at meeting of Southern Economic Association. Houston, Texas: November.

Mitchell, D. 1974. "Phase II Wage Controls." *Industrial and Labor Relations Review*, April: 351–375.

Okun, A. 1973. "Upward Mobility in a High Pressure Economy." *Brookings Papers on Economic Activity*, no. 1: 207–252.

Perry, G. L. 1964. "The Determinants of Wage Rate Changes and the Inflation-Unemployment Trade-off for the United States." *Review of Economic Studies*, October: 287–308.

———. 1966. *Unemployment, Money Wage Rates, and Inflation*. Cambridge, Mass.: MIT Press.

———. 1967. "Wages and the Guideposts." *American Economic Review*, September: 897–904.

———. 1970. "Changing Labor Markets and Inflation." *Brookings Papers on Economic Activity*, no. 3: 411–441.

Perry, G. L., P. S. Anderson, M. L. Wachter, and A. W. Throop. 1969. "Wages and the Guideposts: Comments and Reply." *American Economic Review*, June: 351–370.

Phillips, A. W. 1958. "The Relationship between Unemployment and the Rate of Change of Money Wage Rates in the United Kingdom, 1861–1957." *Economica*, New Series, November: 283–299.

Poole, W. 1973. "Wage-Price Controls: Where Do We Go From Here." *Brookings Papers on Economic Activity*, no. 1: 285–302.

Rappoport, P. N., and T. J. Kniesner. 1974. "The Illusion of the Shifting Phillips Curve: A Model with Random Coefficients." Proceedings of the Business and Economic Statistics Section of the American Statistical Association.

Rees, A. 1971. *Wage-Price Policy*. New York: General Learning Corporation.

Rowley, J. C. R., and D. A. Wilton. 1974. "Quarterly Models of Wage Determination: Some New Efficient Estimates." *American Economic Review*, July: 27–32.

Stallard, J., and L. Solnick. 1974. "Effect of Escalators on Wages in Major Contracts Expiring in 1974." *Monthly Labor Review*, July: 27–32.

Stein, J., and G. Borts. 1972. "Behavior of the Firm Under the Regulatory Constraint." *American Economic Review*, December: 964–970.

Truett, D., and B. Roberts. 1973. "Classical Production Functions, Technical Optimality and Scale Adjustments of the Firm." *American Economic Review*, December: 975–982.

Turnovsky, S. J. 1972a. "The Expectations Hypothesis and the Aggregate Wage Equation: Some Empirical Evidence for Canada." *Economica*, New Series, February: 1–17.

———. 1972b. "A Test of the Expectations Hypothesis Using Directly Observed Wage and Price Expectations." *Review of Economics and Statistics*, February: 47–54.

Wachter, M. L. 1970a. "Cyclical Variation in the Interindustry Wage Structure." *American Economic Review*, March: 75–84.

———. 1970b. "Relative Wage Equations for U.S. Manufacturing Industries." *Review of Economics and Statistics*, November: 405–410.

———. 1974. "Phase II, Cost-Push Inflation, and Relative Wages." *American Economic Review*, June.

Weber, A. 1973. *In Pursuit of Price Stability*. Washington, D.C.: Brookings.

COMMENTS

Phillip Cagan
National Bureau of Economic Research
and Columbia University

The general purpose of this study is appealing—to estimate the effects of the price and wage controls from disaggregated industry data. Equations are fitted to the precontrols period and then applied to the controls period to determine their residual effect. We can thus estimate the effect on the rate of change of prices and wages during the controls period and the cumulative effect. The cumulative effect is especially pertinent when controls begin with a freeze, because of postfreeze catching up. It might also be desirable to measure the cumulative effect beginning a little before and ending a little after, to catch precontrol anticipatory increases and postcontrol catching up, though this was not done (since not all the data were yet available for the catch-up period). The total effect is important, since controls are likely to redistribute price increases over time but have little lasting effect on the price level.

The authors take aggregate demand as given, of course, and do not go into the important policy issue of whether the imposition of controls changed policy, perhaps leading policymakers to be overly expansionary, as I think did happen in 1972. The price and wage equations cannot answer that question, and we cannot expect them to. I mention this only to remind us that in discussing the technical problems of these equations, we are not answering all the questions raised by controls.

While we are busily engaged in estimating the effect of controls, I keep wondering what effect we are testing for. For a given set of aggregate demand policies, there is a path of prices and wages which the economy tends to follow. What can controls do? They might suppress increases by holding real wages and profit margins down, in which case there will be large catching-up increases afterward, but no lasting departure from the equilibrium path. Economists understand this, even if no one else does. To be sure, the way in which controls are enforced can affect the degree of suppression, as the authors discuss in the first part of their paper, but such effects are fluctuations around the equilibrium path, not changes in the path itself. The important question is, Can the equilibrium path be changed?

For a given aggregate-demand policy, the answer has to be no, but the hope is that suppression will make the imposition of greater monetary and fiscal restraint easier to bear by allowing higher output and lower prices than would otherwise occur. I see little possibility of achieving this by holding down profit margins through suppression of price increases; the effect on output and employment is likely to be adverse. The argument in the paper that a freeze puts a kink in the demand curve of oligopolies, with the result that changes in marginal cost are *unlikely* to cause a change in output, may be correct for the short run, but it overlooks the effect on incentives to invest in greater capacity, which can create supply limitations later on.

A lasting benefit from controls depends upon a suppression of wage increases by preventing either anticipatory increases to future inflation or a catching up to past inflation. This probably works because labor supply does not appear to be reduced, at least in the short run, by a reduction in real wages that comes about through a failure of money wages to rise as fast as the cost of living; at the same time, on the demand side the reduction in real wages stimulates hiring. The crux of the control program lies in the wage effects; the price controls are a smoke screen. Therefore, I do not understand the authors' concluding remarks, which are addressed to improving the enforcement of *price* controls. They are silent on the benefits to be achieved. I can only surmise that they see controls as preventing cost-push price increases. However, I did not think anyone thought that inflation in recent years was a genuine cost-push. Perhaps I am wrong about prevailing opinion; in any event, it seems to me that the evidence is all against the cost-push interpretation.

The three phases of controls do not appear to have produced any lasting benefit because most of the effect is estimated to have been on prices, with little on wages. That is the indication of casual observation of wages and profit margins and of Gordon's econometric analysis.[1] The results of this study, though mixed, do not contradict that conclusion. These are the same as Nadiri's results presented at this conference for phases I and II, though he inexplicably obtains a strong effect for Phase III, which from all appearances was weak.

Looking more closely at the details of the estimates in the paper, we note that the individual equations of price changes are for seventeen industries. The explanatory variables tested were the change in the indexes for wages and for materials price, the change in deficient demand as measured by an inventory-sales ratio (rather than measuring the change in the ratio, deficient demand should be measured as deviations from a normal or average level, though perhaps the change approximates such deviations), the change in output to catch changes in productivity as firms move along their average cost curve, the change in a rate of return to the firm to catch the effect of target-return pricing, and the change in a bond yield to reflect the cost of capital. Variables were dropped if, before correction for serial correlation, they were statistically insignificant. However, those which became insignificant after correction for serial correlation were retained. In the results, the rate-of-return variable was dropped from all the equations; and the bond rate, from all but one. None of the equations has the same set of variables, though most have wages and input prices, and about half have either the variable for output or for deficient demand or both. Still, deficient demand, which should be important in the more competitive industries (though it is strangely important for certain industries in some studies and not in others), is significant and negative only for the competitive lumber industry and the fairly concentrated nonferrous metals industry. The problem of not having significant demand variables in the equations is brought out by imagining that controls operated perfectly to reduce the rate of change of all prices and wages in the economy. Theoretically, the reduction in price change would be matched in the equations by the reduction in wage and input price changes. Then, without any demand variable, the residuals of the equation would not indicate that controls had any effect!

Most aggregate studies take explicit account of labor productivity by including unit labor cost, not just wages, in the price equation. In this and the Eckstein-Wyss study,[2] productivity is assumed to grow at a constant rate and to be incorporated in the constant term. I am perturbed over this difference between the aggregate and disaggregate studies. I am not sure which is correct. However, it is inadequate to assume that productivity and wage changes are correlated in the short run and that the wage coefficient can represent their combined effect, as the authors seem to imply in their statement at the end of section IV, on wage results, in their effort to make sense of a negative wage coefficient.

Aside from a quarrel here and there over details, I have no objection to the general design of their equations, but I am uneasy with the results here and elsewhere based on time series. My main concern is with the fixed lags implicit in these regression equations. My casual inspection of the time series indicates that lags vary from one episode to the next as well as among industries. I am not sure the short time periods of this study avoid the problem. The use of four-quarter weighted changes in the variables probably does not smooth out very much of the differences in lag times. At the moment, traditional techniques use fixed lags, and I have no alternative to recommend, but they can be a source of major difficulty.

Even aside from lags, the dangers of spurious results are high because of common cyclical movements in these variables. The regressions cover the long upward movement in rates of change over the 1960s and contain four or five explanatory variables; they are ripe for spurious correlation. My uneasiness is heightened by the lack of robustness of the results, which differ greatly between the aggregate and disaggregate studies and between small changes in the period of coverage and in specification. If we compare the same sixteen industries covered in the Eckstein-Wyss study for a slightly earlier period, and look just at the common wage and input price variables, the large differences in significance and magnitude of estimates are alarming. Ignoring the size of the coefficients and looking merely at how many of the coefficients agree only in sign and significance, we find five out of sixteen for wages, though a more favorable twelve out of sixteen for input prices (however, even in the latter case, eleven of the industries do not have a significant coefficient for materials prices). To be sure, other variables included in the equations of these two studies are different, but why should their inclusion make so much difference for basic variables like wages and materials cost? Eckstein and Wyss made much of their equations as showing price behavior consistent with a classification of industries by concentration, based on the coefficients of the utilization and rate-of-return variables. Insofar as the present study offers comparison, I see little agreement in classification.

Let me turn now to Nadiri's results presented at this conference. He regresses the variables in level form, not rate of change, but allows for lagged adjustments and, in principle, estimates some of the same parameters. Here again the differences are major. Nadiri generally obtains more significant results, presumably because the level form of his variables is likely to reflect longer-run total effects than the first-difference form used here. In his price equation Nadiri finds a significant wage variable in eight of his twelve industries, but there is less than 50 percent agreement between his study and this one on significance for the eleven industries covered in common, and the same is true for materials cost. For the wage equations, there is the same problem. By comparison with Nadiri, the significance and sign of unemployment agree in only seven of eleven industries and the significance and sign of lagged prices in six of eleven.

So we are hardly yet in a position to say that we have reached a consensus on the specification and general results of these industry equations. I wish that these studies would duplicate the specifications of previous ones, so that we could distinguish among the differences due to the periods covered, the data used, and the specification, and so narrow down the glaring inconsistencies.

Aside from the lack of robustness, the coefficients often flop around from positive to negative from one industry to another. The authors try to cope with this by arguing that the variables are proxies for different effects, which are relatively strong for some industries and weak for others. For example, changes in output, if positive, indicate changes in capacity utilization and reflect excess demand pressures, but if they are negative, they are a proxy for movements along a falling average cost curve. There may be no simple solution to flip-flopping coefficients, but such multiproxy variables are hardly ideal.

In addition, the size of the coefficients is extremely wide-ranging, much more so than is the theoretical effect of the wage and input price variables, which in percentages should have a long-run effect on prices equal to their respective shares in total costs in each industry. Moreover, those for materials cost are generally too low, suggesting that a good part of the lagged effects is not being caught. Materials costs range from 40 to 70 percent of total costs,[3] but the positive regression coefficients range from 8 to 67 percent. The wage coefficients, on the other hand, tend to be much too high.

For the purpose at hand—estimating the effect of controls—all these deficiencies may not matter too much. The equations, even if misspecified, may be adequate to show the residual effect of controls. The results for the dummy variables inserted in the equations to register the effect of controls indicate that only for tobacco did phases I and II have downward effects on price changes that were statistically significant at the 5 percent level. For Phase III, there is a significant result for apparel only. A few other results were statistically significant at the 10 percent level. In several industries the dummies used had significantly positive effects; however this is explained, it gives no support to the effectiveness of controls. Furthermore, a completely different set of industries showed significant effects of controls on profit margins. If controls suppressed prices, it is hard to see why they would not also reduce profit margins in the *same* industries.

What about wages, which I argued above are the crux of the control program? The wage equations, which do show a significant effect of the mild guideposts in the early 1960s in nine industries, do not show a significantly negative effect during phases I–III in *any* of the seventeen industries, and show significantly *positive* effects in four industries! The aggregate effect, using BLS weights for wholesale prices in December 1972 and excluding instruments (SIC 38), is +0.6 percent. This result is hard to swallow, even for someone unsympathetic to the usefulness of controls like me. I'd bet my hat that the control dummies are reflecting catching-up wage increases here, and the problem lies in the use of concurrent values (or, at most, values lagged one quarter) of the cost of living, which imposes too fast an adjustment on its effect.

Rightly skeptical regarding these results, the authors have presented other tests based on aggregate equations. Theirs are much simpler than Gordon's or Nadiri's, for they use only wages and input prices in the price equation and prices, unemployment, and output per man-hour in the wage equation. The control dummies are generally not significant; the only significant one is for wages in Phase III. The interaction effect of combining the price and wage equations, presented in the final table of the paper, shows a zero overall effect on wages, though a positive effect in phases I and II and a negative one in Phase III. I think the sequence is wrong (Phase II was tougher than III), but the overall zero effect seems to me about right. Nadiri's results for aggregate equations in his Table 9 for total manufacturing are not dissimilar for wages, being generally positive in phases I and II and negative only in III.[4] As I argued before, if the effect of controls was all on prices and not on wages, as suggested by these results, it was not lasting.

Let me end with the obvious point we all know but usually leave unsaid: that the data for two-digit industries are probably not accurate enough to reveal the small effects we are looking for. There is considerable mismatching of prices with other variables at the two-digit level, and we may have to disaggregate further. Certainly no one can say that a reason for not doing so is that the results with more aggregate data have been so satisfactory.

NOTES

1. R. J. Gordon, "Inflation in Recession and Recovery," *Brookings Papers on Economic Activity*, no. 1 (1971):105–166; and "Wage-Price Controls and the Shifting Phillips Curve," *ibid.*, no. 2 (1972):385–430.
2. O. Eckstein and D. Wyss, "Industry Price Equations," in O. Eckstein, ed., *The Econometrics of Price Determination* (Washington, D.C.: Board of Governors of the Federal Reserve System, 1972).

3. *Ibid.*, p. 143.
4. These results suffer also, I believe, from a concurrent price variable. Nadiri has an inexplicable positive effect for manufacturing prices, which turns into the correct negative effect for the equation pertaining to the total economy. But what sectors outside of manufacturing were strongly affected by controls?

7

ALBERT A. HIRSCH
U.S. Department of Commerce

Measurement and Price Effects of Aggregate Supply Constraints

The Keynesian notion of short-run full capacity (Keynes identified it with "full employment"), defined as a level of output beyond which "a further increase in the quantity of effective demand produces no further increase in output and entirely spends itself on an increase in the cost unit" (Keynes 1936, p. 303), remains an empirically underdeveloped aspect of macroeconomics. Aggregative measures of capacity utilization and of potential output do exist, of course. Such measures have been used in econometric price equations as "demand pressure" variables, supplementing cost variables. However, as these measures are derived—by a value-added (or similar) weighting of industry or sector utilization rates—they conceal short-run conditions of effective global full capacity or near

NOTE: The author wishes to thank Irene M. Keyes for computational and clerical assistance in preparing this paper and George L. Perry for providing quarterly interpolations of the McGraw-Hill utilization index. I am also grateful to both George Perry and my colleague Bruce Grimm for useful criticism of the preliminary draft of this paper. The analysis and views expressed are the responsibility of the author and are not necessarily endorsed by the Bureau of Economic Analysis or the Commerce Department.

capacity when, in periods of high demand, there are substantial variations among sectors in the degree of utilization or when there are shortages of materials or of specific kinds of labor (throughout the economy or in specific geographic areas), etc.

It is unlikely that as such bottlenecks first develop, aggregate supply becomes suddenly inelastic, since there is always some potential for substitution (by both producers and consumers) by increasing hours of work, running down inventories, deferring replacement of plant and equipment, and so forth. As bottlenecks become increasingly widespread and more critical, aggregate supply slopes upward more and more sharply and with sufficiently strong increases in demand could become practically vertical. In the short run, this could occur when aggregate utilization indexes register less than 100 percent.

When aggregate supply is perfectly inelastic, measured utilization rates fail to reflect the true state of demand and resulting price pressures (with the trivial exception of the case in which demand equals supply just at the point where supply becomes inelastic), since they are ex post rather than ex ante measures.[1] But even in the situation (more likely to be encountered) of near capacity, true demand pressures on prices are likely to be missed by conventionally measured overall utilization rates—even with strongly nonlinear formulations—unless such measures are biased upward for reasons not associated with bottlenecks.

This paper is focused mainly on the problem of measuring utilization near effective capacity and its implications for predicting price behavior. My primary purpose is to develop an index of capacity utilization that takes into account capital capacity (measured at the Standard Industrial Classification two-digit level), though not availability of labor and raw materials, as a cause of supply bottlenecks. A "bottleneck-weighted" index is then used in price equations in place of the ordinary index to determine whether improved performance results.

In section I, theoretical problems associated with measurement of utilization—in particular, the bottleneck problem—are reviewed. In section II, the construction of a bottleneck-weighted utilization index is described. In section III, the ordinary and bottleneck-weighted utilization rates and, as another alternative, the Federal Reserve Board's newly published major materials index of utilization are compared as explanatory variables in regressions for manufactured goods prices. In section IV, the implications of short-run aggregate inelastic supply in relation to the estimated price equations are briefly described. In order to determine such supply limitations, I apply part of a procedure I had previously developed (Hirsch 1972) for imposing supply constraints in the context of a macroeconometric model. A summary section follows.

I. CAPACITY UTILIZATION AND BOTTLENECKS: THEORETICAL ISSUES AND EMPIRICAL MEASUREMENT

Meaning of Capacity

The problems of defining and measuring capacity at the level of the firm have been much discussed and do not need extensive review here (see, e.g., de Leeuw 1962, Klein 1960, and Phillips 1963). Neo-classical theory implies minimum average cost (MAC) as the criterion for the optimum production level and hence of "capacity." On the theoretical level, there is no ambiguity in this concept for the single-product firm or for the multiproduct firm producing a technologically fixed mix of outputs. Empirically, there is much ambiguity if the production process of the firm is not continuous (i.e., does not take place twenty-four hours a day, seven days a week) or if average costs vary little over a wide range of operating rates. Ambiguity also arises in the case of the multiproduct firm for which a choice of mix is available.

The MAC criterion of capacity would be empirically useful in explaining investment and pricing behavior if MAC output were a threshold point such that output increases have a significantly greater impact on the magnitude of investment or price beyond that point than before. Some questionnaire surveys of operating rates include a question on the "preferred" operating rate in an effort to get a measure based on this concept.[2] It is then desirable for regression purposes that a substantial number of observations of the actual operating rate be above the preferred rate, but this is not the case.

De Leeuw (1962) has suggested as an alternative to MAC the level of production at which short-run marginal cost exceeds minimum short-run average cost by some fixed percentage; rapidly rising marginal costs would ensure that there are appreciable upward pressures on prices as capacity is approached.

The actual operating rates reported in utilization surveys are based on capacity in engineering rather than economic terms. For non-continuous-process industries, this involves the concept of the "normal" workweek, with due allowance for normal breakdowns, maintenance, and vacations. For continuous processes, capacity represents the firm's view of maximum physical production potential. It should also be noted that the firm's fixed real assets, i.e., its plant and equipment, constitute the unambiguous basis of capacity measurement; other resources are thus implicitly assumed to be available to the firm in elastic supply.

Bottlenecks and Aggregate Capacity

A problem of fixed capital bottlenecks, or capacity balance, arises in the measurement of capacity utilization basically because of non-homogeneity of capital goods used in interdependent productive processes. The failure of available indexes of capacity utilization to take into account sectoral bottlenecks has been recognized for some time (see, e.g., Klein 1960; Klein and Summers 1966, pp. 49–50; and Phillips 1963). This issue surfaced again in a recent set of papers presented at the Brookings Panel on Economic Activity.[3]

Although there has been no deliberate effort to incorporate bottlenecks into economy-wide or sector-wide measures of capacity utilization, two attempts—by Malenbaum (1969) and by Griffin (1971)—have been made at the industry level. In each case the "industry" consists of multiproduct firms. Three technological aspects of these multiproduct industries are relevant from the standpoint of aggregate capacity measurement: each firm produces a number of distinct products with the same factor inputs; a number of productive processes, each having its own capacity, is available to the firm (industry); the outputs of the various processes are interdependent. Both studies use a linear programming (LP) approach to capacity measurement.[4]

Can a methodology analogous to that of Malenbaum or Griffin be applied to broader aggregates such as total manufacturing or the total private economy? The LP approach depends on the existence of multiple processes for producing the same set of commodities. However, the Standard Industrial Classification divides industry into mutually exclusive groupings by output categories, resulting in a one-to-one correspondence between processes and products (more precisely, product groups). Consequently, in Malenbaum's framework, determination of capacity under the assumption of a fixed mix would reduce the analysis to the trivial one of identifying the bottleneck industry and, under the assumption of a rigid input-output technology, defining the utilization rate of that industry as the one applicable to the economy (or subsector) as a whole. Thus, realistically, no such analogue exists.

Well before the studies of Malenbaum and Griffin, Klein (1960) proposed (but did not apply) an alternative approach for dealing with the bottleneck problem at the level of the whole economy. Klein's procedure, which involves iterative solutions of an input-output system, depends on arbitrary adjustments to final demand as sector after sector reaches its output capacity and on the assumption—rather unrealistic for periods as short as one quarter—that capacity can be expanded in the bottleneck sectors to supply needed additional output to other sectors. Because of its arbitrary and unrealistic aspects, as well as its being hard to apply, there is little to recommend this approach.

Our problem, then, is to develop a simpler, more pragmatic method of dealing with the bottleneck problem at the level of the economy or a broad sector, such as manufacturing, one that is specifically designed to explain price behavior. The method devised for this study makes use of existing capacity utilization estimates by industry. Its formulation depends on the assumed nature of the relationship between capacity bottlenecks and pricing behavior, to which I now turn.

Capacity Bottlenecks and Pricing Behavior

The precise nature of the relationship between capacity bottlenecks and pricing behavior depends on the impact that such bottlenecks have on aggregate supply. Two kinds of bottleneck situations may be postulated.

The first kind is extreme and has already been alluded to in the previous subsection as being simplistic. Full capacity, in the sense of an absolute (short-run) limit on production, has been reached in (at least) one industry which produces exclusively (or almost so) for intermediate use. Then, under a rigid input-output technology, production is limited everywhere; that is, aggregate supply is perfectly inelastic and prices become demand-determined. The extent of price increase depends on the position of the aggregate demand schedule and on lags in the adjustment of prices to market-clearing levels. The industry's, and therefore the economy's, utilization rate would be 100 percent; and so aggregate output could not be increased further. (In this situation the utilization rate becomes an inadequate indicator of excess demand pressure.)

The other (more likely) situation is one in which aggregate supply is not absolutely restricted. That will be the case either if "full" capacity in the bottleneck industry is not an absolute ceiling, but corresponds to a lower output level, such as MAC or de Leeuw's critical ratio of marginal to average cost, or, if it is at a maximum physical production level, there are substitution possibilities for the users—producers or consumers—of the industry's output. Bottleneck formation is thus viewed as a cumulative process, rather than as an abrupt phenomenon, so far as aggregate price behavior is concerned.[5] Accordingly, a utilization index that incorporates bottlenecks should do so in a gradual way. Nonetheless, rising prices in the bottleneck industries are passed on as cost increases to other industrial and final users.

II. A BOTTLENECK-WEIGHTED INDEX

Which Utilization Index Should Be Modified?

Six aggregate utilization series are available, five directly published and one derivable from a capacity index. These represent a variety of methodologies having varying degrees of coverage.[6] Each one has its own peculiar merits and shortcomings. The article by Perry, referred to previously, provides a careful comparison among four measures of capacity utilization in manufacturing: the McGraw-Hill utilization index, utilization as derived from the McGraw-Hill estimates of capacity, the Federal Reserve Board's (FRB) utilization index for total manufacturing, and the Wharton index. The two others are the series presently published by the Bureau of Economic Analysis (SCB 1974b) and the Federal Reserve Board's special index for major materials (Edmondson 1973).

The McGraw-Hill (1972) utilization index is based on an annual survey of operating rates in large manufacturing firms; thus, quarterly values must be derived by interpolation. A separate question in the survey on available capacity together with industry output data provides an independent basis for evaluating capacity utilization. The FRB's manufacturing index is benchmarked on the McGraw-Hill survey, but is analytically derived in that its movements are based on changes in output (as measured by industrial production) and in capital stock. The latter is a composite measure based on a weighted average of the FRB stock estimate and that implied in the McGraw-Hill capacity series. The Wharton index

(Klein and Summers 1966) is obtained entirely analytically by deriving capacity output by linear interpolation between peak output levels.

The new BEA survey is part of the plant and equipment expenditures survey. It is like the McGraw-Hill survey in that it does not attempt to define "capacity" for the respondent, and responses are obtained on a company basis. It differs from the latter in four ways: (1) Beginning in 1968 it is quarterly rather than annual. (2) The sample is larger and includes small and medium-sized as well as large manufacturing firms. (3) Capacity outputs, rather than current values added, are used as weights. (4) Preferred operating rates are regularly reported.

Finally, the FRB major materials index is compiled as a weighted average from utilization rates for twelve basic primary industries, namely, basic steel, primary aluminum, primary copper, man-made fibers, paper, paperboard, wood pulp, soft plywood, cement, petroleum refining, broad-woven fabrics, and yarn spinning. For each industry, utilization is derived by dividing output by "capacity," the latter obtained in physical units from various governmental and private sources.

For purposes of the present study—since it deals with the problem of capacity balance—it is important that the utilization measure be an explicitly capital-oriented one, i.e., that capacity refer unambiguously to the productive capability of plant and equipment, assuming that other resources are available in adequate supply. This criterion precludes use of the Wharton index because capacity there is obtained by linear interpolation of observed peak levels of output for each two-digit industry. Thus, we do not know whether a particular observed peak indicates that "full" (or optimal) use of capital has been reached in that sector or whether it reflects a peak in demand (the "weak peak" case) or inability to expand output further because of labor or materials shortages. Klein's argument (see note 6) that capital capacity bottlenecks are accounted for is therefore a tenuous one. Nonetheless, this may be so in specific instances, and in that case any further attempt to modify the index for bottlenecks would result in an overcorrection.

Since the FRB major materials index covers only a selected set of industries, it does not serve the primary purpose of this paper, which is to derive a modified utilization measure from a comprehensive set of industry data. Nevertheless, as will be seen in the following section, this index turns out to be useful as an alternative measure and as a benchmark against which to judge the adequacy of the series and procedure that are actually used.

This leaves as candidates for the series for modification the questionnaire surveys and the FRB utilization index. The latter is rejected because of apparent flaws in its methodology which result in the implausibly low utilization figures for recent years.[7]

The McGraw-Hill utilization series was found by Perry to have an apparent cyclical reporting bias, i.e., respondents treat marginal facilities differently at different stages of the cycle, ignoring their existence during slack periods but "discovering" them in peak periods.[8] Despite this shortcoming, the McGraw-Hill index was chosen because it appeared to be superior in other important respects. In particular, it is (at least in principle) free of long-run biases that occur when measures of capacity or capital stock are explicitly required for calculation of utilization rates. Such measures may fail to take adequate account of changes in capital intensity or of the use of capital expenditures for "nonproductive" purposes, such as pollution abatement, which have become prominent in recent years. It also does not suffer from the ambiguities and other shortcomings of the Wharton index. In terms of operating rate levels, as distinct from changes, ". . . the McGraw-Hill utilization survey seems the most believable of the available measures [for total manufacturing]" (Perry 1973, p. 731). Using Perry's methodology for quarterly interpolation and extrapolation, estimates were extended through 1973.[9]

The differences between the BEA and McGraw-Hill surveys also represent advantages of the former over the latter. Unfortunately, for price regressions, the BEA survey provides too few observations, even if quarterly interpolations are made for 1966 and 1967, for which only semiannual estimates are available.[10]

Derivation of Bottleneck-weighted Utilization Index

When utilization rates for the various industry components are all moderate, i.e., are substantially below peak observed levels, there is no bottleneck problem and, therefore, no need to depart from standard weighting methods, such as those based on value added or capacity output. However, when important primary or intermediate processing industries are at or near peak levels, average measures become inadequate indicators of demand-induced price pressures. In that case the utilization rate of the bottleneck industries should dominate the overall index. To achieve this, we derive a weighted combination of the published McGraw-Hill index—the "ordinary" utilization rate—and a bottleneck variant. The weights are made variable, so as to shift between the two measures in accordance with the above criteria and with our discussion in the previous section. This procedure also avoids the simplistic approach of defining the overall rate as the highest sector utilization rate.

The bottleneck rate (U_b) is obtained by weighting each industry's utilization rate by the square of the ratio of the industry's output used as manufacturing input to its gross output, using the 1967 input-output table (SCB 1974a, Table 1, p. 38):[11]

$$U_b = \frac{\sum_{i=1}^{N} r_i^2 U_i}{\sum_{i=1}^{N} r_i^2}$$

where U_i is the ith industry's utilization rate, and r_i is the ith sector's relative input weight. A quadratic rather than a linear formulation is used in order to give greater dominance to utilization rates of industries which are largely suppliers for intermediate use. Note, however, that no single industry establishes the bottleneck rate.

The combined or "bottleneck-weighted" index ($\tilde{U}$) is derived as

$$\tilde{U} = \begin{cases} \alpha U + (1 - \alpha)U_b, & U_b > U \\ U, & U_b \le U \end{cases}$$

where $\alpha = \exp\{-[\beta/(0.95 - U_b)]\}$. As U_b approaches 0.95 (just above the maximum of observed values of U_b), α approaches zero and $\tilde{U}$ approaches U_b. As U_b falls below 0.95, α rises rapidly and U begins to receive substantial weight. It receives full weight when U_b is no greater than U; thus the formulation assures that $\tilde{U}$ is always equal to or greater than U. β is an arbitrary parameter set at 0.04. This gives a plausible nonlinear shape to α (see Figure 1). Experimentation with other values of β of the same order of magnitude revealed that $\tilde{U}$ is fairly robust with respect to this parameter.

Figure 2 shows U and $\tilde{U}$ for 1954IV–1973IV. For most of this time $\tilde{U}$ either equals or is only slightly greater than U. $\tilde{U}$ lies substantially above U for most quarters during 1955–1957, 1964–1966, and in 1973. Only for still more restricted periods is $\tilde{U}$ greater than 0.90. Thus, the number of observations for which a spread between $\tilde{U}$ and U could make a substantial difference is distressingly small. Unfortunately, moreover, industry detail is limited in the McGraw-Hill survey; a finer breakdown would result in high relative input weights for certain industries whose importance is obscured by aggregation. For all of these reasons, regression tests of the useful-

FIGURE 1

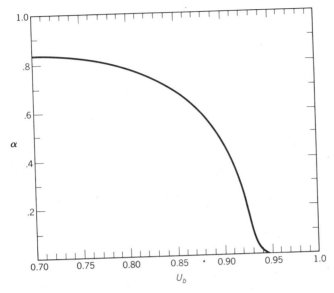

NOTE: U_b = bottleneck rate. For explanation of α, see text.

ness of the bottleneck-weighted index compared to the ordinary index are likely to be sensitive to measurement and specification error; the results reported in the following section should be interpreted in that light.

III. TESTS OF MODIFIED UTILIZATION INDEX IN PRICE EQUATIONS

Role and Form of Capacity Utilization in the Price Equation

Capacity utilization appears in addition to cost variables in various econometric price functions as a "demand pressure" variable. It occurs in various forms, although the connection between its alleged role and the specified form is not always made clear.

There are at least two fairly distinct interpretations of utilization as a price determinant, both related to demand. In the first view, it is a cyclical-state variable representing primarily cyclical variations

FIGURE 2   Utilization Rates: McGraw-Hill and
Bottleneck-weighted, 1954IV–1973IV

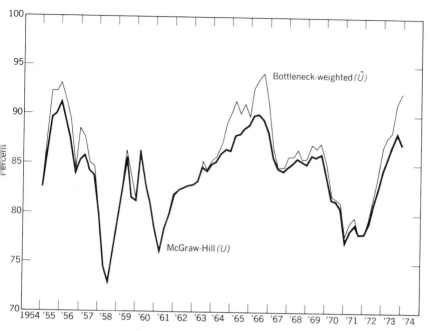

in the degree of effective price competition. As early as 1936,
Harrod pointed out that under monopolistic competition the elasticity of demand for a firm would increase in recession and decline
in prosperity. Moreover, as demand approaches peak levels,
marginal costs may rise sharply.

In the second view, capacity utilization can also represent the
degree of aggregate excess demand. In this role utilization is a disequilibrium variable generating corresponding equilibrating price
adjustments. In discussing the theory underlying their econometric
price equations, Eckstein and Fromm (1968) recognize both roles
of capacity utilization. Alluding (albeit implicitly) to the first role,
they write (p. 1163):[12]

> When the current rate of production is low in relation to the industry's
> capacity, i.e., when the industrial operating rate is low, firms will reduce
> prices as they seek to boost sales and production to permit a better util-
> ization of capacity and thereby to raise profits. Conversely, when pro-
> duction is very high, so that the operating rate of capacity is beyond the
> optimal, signaling the need for additional capacity, firms will increase
> price.

Somewhat further on, with more explicit reference to competitive factors, they note (pp. 1163–1164):

> But some elements of locational or product differentiation attach to the sales of most companies in sufficient degree to create some uncertainty in pricing. When operating rates are high, a firm can feel more confident that an increase in prices will not produce a serious loss in sales. Customers will not be able to establish new supply connections and will therefore be more likely to pay the higher price.

Between these two statements, the excess demand role is recognized (p. 1163):

> When operating rates are high, disequilibrium in product markets will be more frequent and larger. Inevitably, high operating rates are associated with delivery delays, shortages, and changes in the nonprice terms of transactions, such as freight absorption and the provision of "extras." These phenomena, in time, are likely to lead to price change.

In incorporating capacity utilization (the Wharton index is used), however, Eckstein and Fromm make no distinction between these two roles: utilization, in level form, represents both roles in both level and change forms of the price equation. Yet, in principle, at least, the two interpretations call for different forms. The competitive aspect calls for utilization as the argument of a variable markup of price over unit labor cost (or labor and materials costs). That is, the level of utilization occurs in addition to cost variables—either multiplicatively or additively—in an equation explaining the price level. Thus, in a first- or relative-difference form of the price equation, the competitive factor calls for inclusion of the change in utilization rather than the level.[13]

When utilization (U) is an indicator of excess demand, we may specify

$$\frac{\Delta P}{P} = f\left(\frac{q_d - q_s}{q_s}\right) = g(U)$$

where P is price and q_d and q_s are, respectively, quantity demanded and quantity supplied. It is not clear a priori what form $g(U)$ should take. There is little reason to presume the existence of excess demand at low and moderate levels of utilization, while (as noted) at high operating rates disequilibrium in product markets will become more frequent and larger. Thus, a strongly nonlinear form of the level of utilization in an equation explaining the change in price is suggested. Such a form is given by the reciprocal of the complement of utilization, i.e., $1/(1 - U)$, hereafter called the reciprocal complement form.

A problem with this formulation is that if a given level of utilization is sustained indefinitely, excess demand is presumed never to diminish as prices rise in response. Continued price increases imply an ever increasing profit share. For short periods, however, it can be assumed that given the (high) utilization rate, as shortages are eliminated by price increases in some sectors, new shortages can appear in others.

Alternatively, a distributed lag of the change in utilization (or of its reciprocal complement) may be used. In that case, an increase in utilization initially increases the rate of inflation, but gradually the latter returns to its original level. Still another possibility is a variable involving the interaction of the level of capacity utilization (or of its nonlinear transformation) with a more direct demand measure, such as sales or new orders (change form).[14]

Data and Forms of Price Equations Tested

Since the utilization index selected for modification is for manufacturing and the bottleneck-weighted index represents that sector as a whole, it made sense to estimate the price equations for total manufacturing only. The dependent variable is the wholesale price index for manufactured goods.

The basic model, of which the estimated price equations are intended as variants, involves a variable markup over unit labor and materials costs.[15] For an industry one might specify the following level form of the equation:

$$P_i = A(ULC_i + UMC_i)^\alpha [f(U_i)]^\beta (ED_i)^\gamma$$

where ULC_i is unit labor cost, UMC_i is unit cost of materials for the ith industry, $f(U_i)$ is a function of the utilization rate (plausibly the utilization rate itself), representing the cyclically variable competitive effect on the degree of markup over cost, and ED_i is an excess demand variable, which may also contain the utilization rate.

Since the wholesale price index for total manufacturing is an average index for manufacturing industries at all stages of processing, the data could not be aggregated simply by using raw material costs for UMC. At each stage of processing beyond the first, costs of semimanufactures as well as raw materials are reflected in input prices, thus presenting an aggregation problem. Nor does ULC suffice by itself—on grounds that the cost of semimanufactures is absorbed by *ULC* upon aggregation—since *ULC* is obtained from compensation per unit of value-added output. It is, moreover, generally agreed that firms view their labor cost in terms of current wage rates and long-run or "normal" productivity (average output per man-hour). Thus, some specification of normal productivity is required (see, e.g., Schultze and Tryon 1965 and Eckstein and Fromm 1968, pp. 1168–1170).

A relative first-difference formulation can largely avoid these problems of measurement and aggregation, though at the expense of reducing the signal-to-noise ratio. In particular, straight-time average hourly earnings may be used instead of unit labor cost, thus absorbing long-run productivity growth into the constant term and abstracting from cyclical and other short-run variations in the mix of straight-time and overtime hours worked, as well as in productivity. I found, as did Eckstein and Wyss (1972) studying two-digit manufacturing sectors, that straight-time earnings give superior results. In addition, when the wage rate is used in conjunction with the utilization rate, the bias due to correlation between productivity and utilization is avoided.

Two basic kinds of change-form specifications were estimated. In the first, the dependent variable is in relative one-quarter-difference form (i.e., P/P_{-1}) and explanatory variables are given with an imposed lag structure: diminishing weights (0.4, 0.3, 0.2, and 0.1) are applied to values (levels or changes) of all variables from t (current quarter) to $t - 3$. Following Eckstein and Wyss, the alternative specification makes the dependent variable $P/(0.4P_{-1} + 0.3P_{-2} + 0.2P_{-3} + 0.1P_{-4})$. This formulation represents a compromise between a one-quarter change, with its relatively large component of measurement error, and a four-quarter change, which makes no behavioral sense and builds substantial serial correlation into the disturbances. Explanatory variables given in change form are expressed in the same way as the dependent variable; thus, no distributed lag effects are implied. Both types of equations may, of course, involve misspecification of lag structures. However, it was felt that for present purposes, empirical determination of the lag structure would unduly complicate the analysis.

Explanatory variables for the equations whose results are reported below include average straight-time hourly earnings, prices of raw materials used in further processing, various demand variables involving the utilization rate, and—as an alternative to utilization variables—the change in the ratio of unfilled orders to shipments.

The variable used to represent the cyclical state of demand is the change in the utilization rate (ΔU). Alternative transformations of U used to represent excess demand include U, $1/(1 - U)$, and $[1/(1 - U)](NO/NO_{-1})$, where NO is manufacturers' new orders. ΔU must be regarded as possibly representing excess demand instead of (or as well as) the cyclical state of demand in spite of my earlier suggestion that the form of the disequilibrium term should be nonlinear.[16] The statistically "best" formulation, based on the ordinary utilization rate, is then tested with alternative concepts of utilization. (Note, however, that only the excess demand proxy is appropriately thus permuted, since it is not meaningful to incorporate the bottleneck notion into the cyclical state proxy.)

In addition to the ordinary (McGraw-Hill) utilization rate (U) and the bottleneck-weighted rate ($\tilde{U}$), the Federal Reserve Board's major materials index (U_m) was tried as a third alternative. Conceptually, it is more akin to the bottleneck rate (U_b) than to $\tilde{U}$, which represents a compromise between the bottleneck rate and the ordinary rate. However, since it is derived from data sources entirely different from the company surveys that underlie U, it is inappropriate to derive a new bottleneck-weighted rate as a combination of U and U_m, analogous to $\tilde{U}$.

The main reason for including U_m among the tests is that, in contrast to the McGraw-Hill and BEA surveys, the source data are on a product rather than a company basis. Hence, they do not suffer from the distortion that occurs in U_b because of the dispersion of utilization rates for different product lines under the roof of a single company that reports only its average utilization rate. The classification of companies by industry is determined by main activity. If the company mix of products varies over time, U as well as U_b may be distorted.

Empirical Results

Ordinary least squares regressions were run for various specifications of Type I (P/P_{-1}) and Type II (P divided by a weighted moving average of lagged P) forms for 1955IV–1973IV, omitting 1959III, 1959IV, and 1971IV. The first two omissions are to prevent the reduced utilization rates during the 1959 steel strike from distorting the proxy role of that variable. The 1971IV observation is omitted because of the price freeze from mid-August to mid-November (which is essentially reflected in the third-to-fourth quarter change). The subsequent control period is included despite the possible impact of controls on the wage-price relationship because

TABLE 1 Regression Results for Manufactured Goods Prices: Type I

Eq.	Constant	$\frac{AHE}{AHE_{-1}}$	$\frac{PR}{PR_{-1}}$	ΔU	U	$\frac{1}{1-U}$	$\frac{1}{1-U}\frac{NO}{NO_{-1}}$	$\Delta\left(\frac{UO}{S}\right)$	$\bar{R}^2$ [$\bar{S}$] {DW}
1.1	.0769 (0.74)	.7021 (6.34)	.1918 (10.34)	.0280 (0.87)	.0246 (2.38)				0.809 [0.00310] {1.74}
1.2	.0855 (0.83)	.7098 (6.50)	.1969 (10.48)	.0298 (0.95)		.000677 (2.72)			0.813 [0.00306] {1.79}
1.3	.1171 (1.09)	.7209 (6.48)	.1575 (5.75)	−.0273 (0.61)			.0000983 (2.17)		0.806 [0.00312] {1.68}
1.4	.1314 (1.22)	.6471 (5.60)	.2131 (10.72)	.0654 (1.94)				.0102 (2.30)	0.807 [0.00311] {1.74}
1.5	.0741 (0.69)	.7224 (6.32)	.2000 (10.18)	.0391 (1.19)					0.795 [0.00320] {1.61}
1.6	.1125 (1.04)	.6543 (5.67)	.2094 (10.39)		.0223 (2.04)			.0040 (0.90)	0.809 [0.00310] {1.73}
1.7	.1140 (1.07)	.6698 (5.83)	.2074 (10.34)			.000629 (2.30)		.0029 (0.64)	0.812 [0.00307] {1.77}

NOTES TO TABLE 1

The dependent variable is P/P_{-1}, where P = wholesale price index, total manufactures (1967 = 100), and the independent variables are defined as follows:

AHE = average hourly earnings, straight time, for manufacturing production workers;

PR = wholesale price index, crude materials for further processing;

U = capacity utilization for manufacturing (McGraw-Hill);

NO = manufacturers' new orders;

UO = manufacturers' unfilled orders;

S = manufacturers' shipments.

$\bar{R}^2$ = coefficient of multiple determination adjusted for degrees of freedom; $\bar{S}$ = standard error of estimate adjusted for degrees of freedom. DW = Durbin-Watson statistic.

those observations, especially for 1973, involve larger spreads be tween U_b and U than at any other time during the sample period

Table 1 gives regression statistics for various form of Type I equations, using only the ordinary utilization rate.[17] As expected, average earnings and raw materials prices are always highly significant and explain most of the variation in manufactured goods prices. Equations 1.1 through 1.4 each contain the change in utilization together with some excess demand variable. The excess demand variables include the level of utilization, the reciprocal complement multiplied by the relative change in new orders, and the change in the ratio of unfilled orders to shipments. ΔU is clearly not significant in equations 1.1–1.3 and in 1.3 it has the wrong sign. Nor is it significant in equation 1.5, which contains no other excess demand variable, though it is somewhat more potent. In equation 1.4, ΔU occurs together with the change in the ratio of unfilled orders to shipments; there it has borderline significance. Both the ordinary and the nonlinear forms of U are marginally significant at the 5 percent level. Equation 1.2 is slightly superior to 1.1, but is preferred mainly on theoretical grounds (see above). The nonlinear utilization term also does somewhat better than the other two excess demand terms (equations 1.3 and 1.4).

Equations 1.6 and 1.7 are more similar to those tested by Eckstein and Fromm (1968) than are the first five equations. They are less easily justified on the basis of the reasoning presented here, but are included for comparison. The terms involving U do slightly less well in these forms than in equations 1.1 and 1.2, and the orders-shipments term is not significant.

Turning to the Type II equations (shown in Table 2), we find that the ΔU term is not significant and is consistently negative. How-

TABLE 2 Regression Results for Manufactured Goods Prices: Type II

Eq.	Constant	$\dfrac{AHE}{AHE}(L)$	$\dfrac{PR}{PR}(L)$	ΔU	U	$\dfrac{1}{1-U}$	$\dfrac{1}{1-U}\dfrac{NO}{NO_{-1}}$	$\Delta\left(\dfrac{UO}{S}\right)$	$\bar{R}^2$ [S] {DW}
2.1	.1170 (1.71)	.6516 (9.14)	.1790 (15.05)	−.0354 (1.73)	.0555 (4.01)				0.892 [0.00419] {1.44}
2.2	.1471 (2.24)	.6577 (9.62)	.1790 (15.67)	−.0326 (1.71)		.00155 (4.78)			0.900 [0.00403] {1.55}
2.3	.1375 (2.00)	.6798 (9.50)	.1822 (15.25)	−.0288 (1.45)			.00145 (3.88)		0.890 [0.00422] {1.57}
2.4	.1327 (1.84)	.6825 (9.12)	.1784 (14.18)	−.0343 (1.64)				.0234 (2.86)	0.890 [0.00422] {1.57}
2.5	.1366 (1.80)	.6743 (8.56)	.1826 (13.89)	−.0297 (1.35)					0.867 [0.00465] {1.20}
2.6	.1114 (1.62)	.6724 (9.41)	.1719 (14.73)		.0457 (3.57)			.0131 (1.51)	0.891 [0.00421] {1.46}
2.7	.1374 (2.08)	.6752 (9.82)	.1723 (15.32)			.00136 (3.87)		.0110 (1.37)	0.899 [0.00406] {1.55}

NOTE: The dependent variable is in the form $P/P(L)$; for any variable X shown, $X(L) = 0.4X_{-1} + 0.3X_{-2} + 0.2X_{-3} + 0.1X_{-4}$. Terms in U, except ΔU, are in the distributed lag form $0.4U + 0.3U_{-1} + 0.2U_{-2} + 0.1U_{-3}$: ΔU and $\Delta(UO/S)$ are in the form $X - X(L)$.

ever, the other terms improve in significance, while the Durbin-Watson statistics are still acceptable despite the overlapping change form. (The negative coefficients of ΔU suggest that this variable may be capturing short-run productivity effects.) Again, the reciprocal complement form of U does best and has a substantially higher t ratio than in the Type I equations. Hence, a Type II equation form including $1/(1 - U)$ but excluding ΔU was tested as the basis for comparison of different measures of utilization developed in this paper. The reciprocal complement form of U fortunately also allows for maximum differentiation among alternative measures of utilization at periods of peak activity.

The first three lines of Table 3 show regression statistics for price equations with the three utilization variants appearing in the reciprocal complement form and without the nonsignificant ΔU term. The results are disappointing for the bottleneck-weighted index. Equation 3.2, which uses the $\tilde{U}$ variant, yields only negligibly higher values of $\bar{R}^2$ and t ratios for the utilization term than equation 3.1, based on ordinary U. There is also very little difference in the

TABLE 3 Regression Results for Manufactured Goods Prices (Type II) with Alternative Measures of Capacity Utilization, 1955IV–1973IV

Variant of Capacity Utilization	Constant	$\dfrac{AHE}{AHE\ (L)}$	$\dfrac{PR}{PR\ (L)}$	$\dfrac{1}{1-U}$	$\bar{R}^2$ $[\bar{S}]$ $\{DW\}$
U	.1408 (2.11)	.6689 (9.69)	.1742 (15.51)	.00154 (4.66)	0.897 [0.00409] {1.53}
$\tilde{U}$	.1423 (2.16)	.6716 (9.83)	.1732 (15.55)	.00091 (4.85)	0.889 [0.00405] {1.53}
U_m	.3249 (4.66)	.5296 (7.68)	.1323 (10.26)	.00127 (5.99)	0.912 [0.00379] {1.36}
U'	.3050 (4.04)	.5290 (6.97)	.1478 (11.52)	.00224 (4.77)	0.898 [0.00406] {1.22}
$\tilde{U}'$	.3271 (4.70)	.5343 (7.81)	.1237 (9.00)	.00161 (6.05)	0.912 [0.00378] {1.36}

TABLE 4 Regression Results for Manufactured Goods Prices (Type II) with Alternative Measures of Capacity Utilization, 1955IV–1971III

Eq.	Variant of Capacity Utilization	Constant	$\dfrac{AHE}{AHE\,(L)}$	$\dfrac{PR}{PR\,(L)}$	$\dfrac{1}{1-U}$	$\bar{R}^2$ [S] {DW}	RMSE, 1972–1973
4.1	U	.1458 (2.24)	.6917 (10.93)	.1471 (6.44)	.00140 (4.54)	0.792 [0.00362] {1.19}	.0076
4.2	$\tilde{U}$	.1385 (2.16)	.6992 (11.16)	.1497 (6.63)	.00081 (4.68)	0.795 [0.00359] {1.22}	.0073
4.3	U_m	.2934 (4.20)	.5674 (8.80)	.1172 (5.09)	.00113 (5.37)	0.811 [0.00345] {1.08}	.0064
4.4	U'	.2883 (3.85)	.5733 (8.15)	.1212 (5.01)	.00197 (4.57)	0.792 [0.00362] {2.94}	.0077
4.5	$\tilde{U}'$	.2892 (4.13)	.5787 (8.78)	.1173 (5.06)	.00148 (5.26)	0.809 [0.00347] {1.05}	.0057

$RMSE$ = root-mean-square error.

errors of the equation if examination is limited to the periods in which the level of utilization is relatively high and U_b is substantially above U: 1955IV–1957II, 1965I–1966IV, and 1972IV–1973IV.

For each of the equations in Table 3, truncated regressions were also run over the period 1955IV–1971III, thus ending just prior to the period of controls (see Table 4). In addition to the usual statistics, root-mean-square errors $(RMSE)$ of prediction over the period 1972I–1973IV are also shown in the table. These are about the same for equations 4.1 and 4.2 as are the t ratios of the utilization terms.

When the Federal Reserve major materials index is substituted for U and $\tilde{U}$, however (equations 3.3 and 4.3), slightly better fits and substantially higher t ratios for the utilization term are obtained in both the full and truncated regressions. Substitution of U_m also gives a lower $RMSE$ of prediction for the 1972–1973 period.

As noted earlier, U_m is conceptually most comparable to U_b (in contrast to U or $\tilde{U}$). The first two series are plotted in Figure 3. Very similar behavior in both level and movement is observed through 1967III (except during the steel strike of 1959, when U_m dips more

FIGURE 3   Utilization Rates: Bottleneck and Federal Reserve Board Major Materials, 1954IV–1973IV

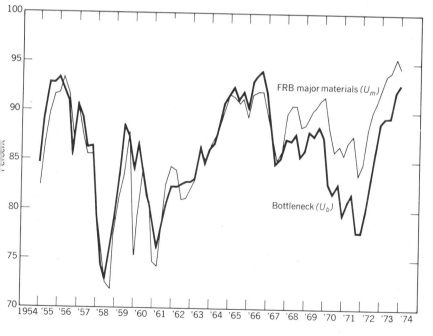

sharply because of the larger weight of steel in the total). In 1967IV, however, U_m takes a large positive jump while U_b increases only moderately. Thereafter, the cyclical movements are roughly parallel, though until 1973 the gap between the two series gradually widens further.

This divergent behavior could be due either to differences in composition and weighting of components of the two series or to basic statistical differences in the component series themselves. The data in Table 5 are intended to shed some light on this question. For each of the U_m components (except steel) and for the most comparable components of the McGraw-Hill series, average utilization rates for the subperiods 1954IV–1967II and 1967IV–1973IV are shown. A consistent pattern of divergence is seen. Whereas most McGraw-Hill average rates either change little or decline somewhat from the first to the second subperiod, those for corresponding major materials components, except primary copper, increase. For petroleum refining, the major materials version shows a much sharper increase. This evidence strongly suggests that the divergence between the McGraw-Hill and major materials indexes after 1967 is statistically grounded.

The cause of the suddenness and persistence of this divergence is hard to pinpoint, particularly since the methods of data collection and construction are fundamentally very different. This behavior does roughly coincide with the onset of rapid growth of antipollution investment expenditures, much of which do not add to productive capacity or which may force early retirement of existing capacity. However, as Perry (1973, p. 721) observes, there is no reason to believe that the McGraw-Hill operating rate survey is biased on either ground "since it represents, ideally at least, a fresh assessment each year of the utilization of available capacity." Indeed, it is the major materials index that uses explicit capacity data from establishment surveys. But capacity is expressed in physical units of output rather than capital. Hence, there should be no bias from misrepresentation of antipollution investment here either.

Another possibility is that there was an increased dispersion of utilization rates among different kinds of output. This would tend to be hidden in the average utilization rates reported by multi-product companies and to bias the bottleneck rate downward. It is hard to believe, however, that this change would have developed so abruptly.

We are thus left uncertain as to which series more accurately portrays the utilization rate of strategic manufacturing industries since the late 1960s. If the McGraw-Hill–based U_b is low for this

TABLE 5 Average Utilization Rate for Selected McGraw-Hill Industries and Corresponding FRB Major Materials Categories, 1954IV–1967III and 1967IV–1973IV (percent)

McGraw-Hill			FRB Major Materials		
Industry	1954IV–1967III	1967IV–1973IV	Industry	1954IV–1967III	1967IV–1973IV
Textiles	90.5	88.0	Broad woven fabric	85.4	87.5
			Yarn spinning	91.7	92.9
Paper and paper products	91.5	91.6	Wood pulp	88.4	92.8
			Paper	92.4	94.6
			Paperboard	87.3	94.4
Chemicals	81.0	80.4	Man-made fibers	81.0	87.4
Petroleum refining	90.3	93.8	Petroleum refining	87.3	94.9
Nonferrous metals	84.5	81.9	Primary copper	73.8	71.1
			Primary aluminum	91.4	94.3
Stone, clay, glass	80.4	79.2	Cement	79.9	82.0

period, there is also a strong presumption that U is low as well, since U_b is generally either above or about the same as U. We have the following (admittedly inconclusive) evidence that U and U_b are biased downward rather than that U_m is biased upward: (1) U_m performed better than U in the price equations. (2) There are anecdotal reports of capacity shortage during 1973, which is not evidenced by the McGraw-Hill series. (3) Still higher levels of utilization appear in the Wharton index for manufacturing as a whole than are shown for major materials.[18]

Proceeding on the *assumption* that U_m is a more accurate measure, we may use it to make a bias correction to U. We next construct a new bottleneck-weighted index ($\tilde{U}'$), using the bias-corrected U series (U') and U_m (in place of U_b). We then test whether $\tilde{U}'$ outperforms U' in the manufacturing price equation (as was expected for $\tilde{U}$ vis-à-vis U). Specifically, it is assumed that the bias correction for overall utilization (U) is the spread between U_m and U_b. Hence, by definition $U' = U + (U_m - U_b)$.

Next, the adjusted bottleneck-weighted index is derived as

$$\tilde{U}' = \begin{cases} \alpha'U' + (1 - \alpha')\,U_m, & U_m > U' \\ U', & U_m \leq U' \end{cases}$$

$$\alpha' = \exp\{-[0.04/(0.96 - U_m)]\}$$

Regressions 3.4 and 3.5 give results using U' and $\tilde{U}'$, respectively, for the whole period; and 4.4 and 4.5, for the truncated one. The adjusted bottleneck-weighted index does give better results than the (adjusted) ordinary index, especially in the longer regression (Table 3), which includes the critical 1973 observations. The *RMSE* of prediction in 1972–1973 (Table 4) is also substantially smaller. Note that the difference $\tilde{U}' - U'$ is virtually the same as the difference $\tilde{U} - U$; but the difference between the reciprocal complements of $\tilde{U}'$ and U' is substantially greater at the higher estimated levels of utilization than for corresponding $\tilde{U}$ and U values. Thus, incorporation of the bottleneck phenomenon, and not simply the higher level of U_m (compared to U and $\tilde{U}$) since 1967, accounts for improved performance.

The difference that incorporation of a bottleneck feature into measurement of capacity utilization makes in explaining inflation during high-capacity periods is indicated in Table 6, which contains results of dynamic predictions of manufactured goods prices made with the parameters of equation 3.5, using alternatively $1/(1 - U')$ and $1/(1 - \tilde{U}')$. Dynamic predictions cover the periods 1955IV–1957II, 1965I–1966IV, and 1972IV–1973IV. The table shows actual percent changes in price levels over each of the

TABLE 6 Actual and Predicted Changes in Manufactured Goods Prices for Selected Periods, Using $\bar{U}'$ and U' of Equation 3.5[a] (percent)

	1955III–1957II	1964IV–1966IV	1972IV–1973IV
1. Actual	6.7	4.7	13.1
2. Predicted ($\bar{U}'$)	5.1	5.4	12.8
3. Error (line 1 minus line 2)	1.6	−0.7	0.3
4. Predicted (U')	4.1	4.1	10.2
5. Error (line 1 minus line 4)	2.6	0.6	2.9
6. Difference (line 2 minus line 4)	1.0	1.3	2.6

[a]Predictions are "dynamic," i.e., predicted rather than actual values of lagged prices are used as they emerge in each period.

periods, predicted changes using each of the two utilization variants, the cumulative errors made in each case, and the difference between the predicted changes. The latter, apart from the overall equation error, indicates the contribution that the bottleneck element makes toward the explanation of inflation, given the estimated equation. In the first and third periods, inclusion of the bottleneck feature substantially reduces the equation error. In the 1972–1973 period, the equation error is small and the difference in predicted changes for the two utilization measures amounts to about one-fifth of the actual price increase.

V. INELASTIC AGGREGATE SUPPLY AND PRICE BEHAVIOR

So far, we have dealt with aggregate capacity measurement in relation to specific bottlenecks. We may think of the specific bottlenecks as constituting near bottlenecks for the economy as a whole: aggregate output is still capable of expanding, though only at higher marginal costs. We shall now briefly consider the case of perfectly inelastic short-run supply, i.e., where bottlenecks are sufficiently widespread to preclude any significant expansion of output whose mix approximates that observed when capacity is reached.

As noted in the introduction, such limits on aggregate output may occur with the measured utilization rate—ordinary or bottleneck-weighted—below 100 percent. This is because labor, delivery, or raw materials bottlenecks can occur as well as those in industrial plant and equipment capacity if growth of demand has been sharp. In this situation, measured capacity utilization—even a bottleneck-weighted variant—does not adequately reflect excess demand pressure.

In an earlier paper (Hirsch 1972) I developed a boundary condition on aggregate output for application to a macroeconometric model. More specifically, this boundary was defined in terms of maximum feasible growth of capacity utilization (as measured by the Wharton index) during any quarter, given the level of utilization during the previous quarter. A function defining the short-run capacity limit was determined on the basis of a scatter diagram, with ΔU plotted against U_{-1}. This boundary condition has the property that the permissible quarterly increase in utilization is less, the higher the level of utilization in the initial quarter. A procedure with a number of arbitrary, built-in rules was devised for adjusting the components of final demand to conform to constrained aggregate output and to raise prices above the levels of the unconstrained solution. Here we derive a similar supply-limit curve, though only for the more limited purpose of determining the possible existence of aggregate supply bottlenecks.[19]

Figure 4 is a scatter diagram of ΔU_m versus U_{m-1} (only positive changes in U_m are plotted). A dashed curve is drawn to fit the outer-most points to suggest an approximate locus of upper limits of increase in utilization. In principle, no points should lie above the curve since, by definition of the limit, no such point is feasible; but by drawing the curve a bit lower, we allow for possible measurement error in the extreme $(U_{m-1}, \Delta U_m)$ pairs, and more points come close to the curve.

This diagram, together with equation 3.5, helps determine whether aggregate supply barriers contributed to inflation under tight capacity conditions. During 1955–1957 $(U_{m-1}, \Delta U_m)$ pairs are near the curve in four quarters: 1955II, 1955III, 1956I, and 1956II. Most of the residuals in equation 3.5 for the high-utilization period 1955IV–1957II are substantially positive, averaging 0.4 percent. During 1965–1966 only one quarter, 1966I, has a point near the curve. Two such quarters, 1973I and 1973III, occur during 1972IV–1973IV. However, the average residuals of 1965I–1966IV and 1972IV–1973IV are not substantially positive: inflation is essentially accounted for by the equation. Much of the 1973 increase is explained by raw materials prices. Thus, I conclude (tentatively) that short-run inelastic supply may well have contributed to inflation during 1955–1957, but not in later periods of high utilization.[20]

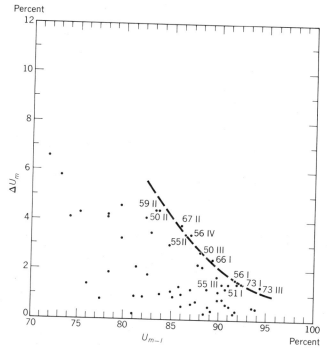

FIGURE 4 Change in Capacity Utilization Rate (ΔU_m) versus Lagged Level (U_{m-1})

SOURCE: Federal Reserve Board major materials index of utilization.

VI. SUMMARY AND CONCLUSIONS

This paper was concerned with one aspect of the more general (and difficult) problem of bringing supply factors within the realm of quantitative macroeconomic analysis. Specifically, balance of capital capacity among manufacturing industries was explicitly taken into account in deriving an aggregate index of capacity utilization. A "bottleneck-weighted" index of utilization was constructed in the belief that it would be more useful as a measure of excess demand than an index aggregated by orthodox weighting methods, especially during the boom phase of a business expansion when demand may well be pressing against capacity.

Initial tests of the modified utilization rate in the context of a price regression equation were disappointing in that they yielded essentially unchanged results compared to the ordinary utilization rate. Only when the two indexes were adjusted for assumed bias, with the Federal Reserve Board's major materials index used as auxiliary information, was there a noticeable improvement in the goodness of fit and statistical significance of the utilization variable. In periods of demand-pull inflation, the bottleneck weighting of the utilization rate (with the bias adjustment) generally reduces the equation error and in 1973 contributes substantially to the amount of total inflation accounted for.

Nonetheless, these findings must be regarded as both tenuous and tentative. First, all capacity utilization data are subject to great uncertainty, and the reciprocal complement form of the utilization variable makes it especially sensitive to errors of measurement. Second, available data on capacity utilization from surveys is broken down into subaggregates that are too broad to identify all important bottlenecks; bottlenecks should also be identified within multiproduct, multiple process industries, as was done by Malenbaum (1969) and Griffin (1971) in measuring capacity for chemicals and petroleum refining, respectively. Third, reporting of operating rates by company rather than by product gives rise to possible bias at the industry level. Fourth, there are relatively few observations for periods of strong demand-pull inflation, when bottlenecks are most likely to occur.

As noted, Perry (1973) has questioned the value of incorporating bottlenecks into an aggregate measure of capacity utilization, pointing out that shortages of labor and raw materials as well as of specific capital may occur and may also affect price behavior. From an aggregative point of view, the degree of capacity balance is clearly an essential consideration in determining available capacity. In this study it has been found (tentatively) that when bottlenecks are built into the utilization index, some improvement in price equations using such an index results. It is, of course, an empirical question— not investigated in this paper—whether a separate bottleneck variable in addition to the ordinary utilization rate would do better.

The problems of specific labor and materials shortages are not readily dealt with. It is not easy, for example, to see how analysis of the impact of the Arab oil embargo could be included as part of a general methodology.[21] This does not, however, vitiate the usefulness of the kind of effort pursued in this paper.

A methodology for defining a limit condition which determines absolute aggregate short-run supply inelasticity was briefly explained and applied to manufacturing capacity. Together with the residuals of the price equation (based on the bottleneck-weighted utilization rate), this provided evidence that aggregate supply limitations in manufacturing accounted for some of the inflation during the period 1955IV–1957II. Again, this conclusion must be regarded as tenuous, depending sensitively on the substantial degree of subjective judgment involved in establishing the limit condition. Here, too, more careful work needs to be done.

NOTES

1. It might be argued that this difficulty is circumvented by using new or unfilled orders, since, unlike output, these are not restricted by physical capacity. However, only a portion of output is produced in response to orders. Moreover, new orders may be delayed or cancelled when existing backlogs are already high.

2. The annual utilization survey conducted by McGraw-Hill (1972) has usually included such a question, and the newer BEA survey (SCB 1974b) regularly obtains such a figure from its respondents.

3. See Klein (1973) and Perry (1973). Klein implies that the Wharton index effectively deals with the problem via its trends-through-peaks approach for measuring capacity "because many or most industries peak approximately together" (p. 744). Perry, however, maintains that bottlenecks should be treated separately from the measurement of capacity utilization. I shall return to this question later.

4. Malenbaum, who studied the bulk organic chemical industry, measures capacity for each process in engineering terms, i.e., as maximum physical capacity. Aggregate capacity for the industry is derived by an LP solution to the problem of maximizing net output along the ray of the observed product mix, subject to input-output requirements, technologically determined joint product proportions, and (fixed) process capacities. Griffin's study (of petroleum refining) also involves process capacity; but aggregate capacity is determined by minimum average cost, which becomes the objective function of the LP model. Griffin analyzes both the fixed and variable mix cases, but the fixed mix used is an analytically derived one for full-employment demand rather than the observed mix.

5. The bottleneck problem in relation to capacity measurement is peculiarly a problem pertaining to price determination. It is not directly relevant, for example, to investment behavior, unless investment is a nonlinear function of the utilization rate. Then the dispersion of utilization rates as well as the aggregate level will matter.

6. The most recently published series is that of the Bureau of Economic Analysis (SCB 1974b); it is accompanied by a convenient synopsis of various measures of manufacturers' capacity utilization.

7. As Perry (1973, pp. 707–708) states: "A serious weakness of the FRB index is that benchmarking to the utilization survey is based on historical statistical relationships that are simple at best and that may change substantially. In particular, estimates for recent years are based on simple time trend estimates of

the drift that are heavily weighted with historical information. The estimates are not currently updated; and even if they were, they would still not adequately reflect any abrupt changes in the relation of investment and capital stock to capacity or in [a] bias in the McGraw-Hill capacity series."

8. This hypothesis is supported by a regression relating (implied) capacity, in log form, to output and capital stock. The null hypothesis of no cyclical reporting bias implies a zero elasticity of measured capacity with respect to output and an (approximately) unitary elasticity with respect to capital stock. Among the four series tested, only the McGraw-Hill utilization-derived capacity measure yielded a significant positive coefficient for output (Perry 1973, pp. 110–111).

9. The methodology for interpolation is as follows: Implicit capacity is measured for each year-end by dividing (industry and total manufacturing) operating rates into the respective component of the Federal Reserve industrial production index (IPI) for December. This is assumed to represent capacity output for the fourth quarter. Capacities for intervening quarters are obtained by interpolation on the assumption of a constant relative growth per quarter. Utilization rates for the first, second, and third quarters are then approximated by dividing, respectively, March, June, and September IPIs by corresponding interpolated capacities.

10. Preliminary regression tests using this series compared with the longer McGraw-Hill series indicated that the BEA sample is inadequate.

11. Input-output sectors were combined to correspond as closely as possible to the McGraw-Hill industrial categories. Separate utilization data for iron and steel ceased to be available after 1961. Therefore, from 1962I on, the basic steel component of the Federal Reserve's major materials index was linked to this series.

12. The discussion is couched, somewhat obscurely, in terms of the influence of the size of the capital stock on price.

13. Evans (1969, pp. 296–297), for example, obtains a variable markup model by assuming a cyclically variable elasticity of demand and profit-maximizing, imperfectly competitive firms. Variable demand elasticity can result from parallel shifting of the demand schedule, with marginal cost not necessarily rising. The form is $P = a_0 + a_1 ULC + a_2 U + a_3 \Theta(U)$, where P = price, ULC = unit labor cost, U = the utilization rate, and $\Theta(U)$ may or may not be linear, depending on the shape of the marginal cost schedule.

14. A variable of this form is used, in a level-form of price equation, in the BEA quarterly model (BEA 1973, sect. IX). The composite variable, along with level of capacity utilization, serves to vary the price markup over unit labor cost.

15. Nordhaus (1972) has criticized econometric price equations for not including capital costs along with labor and materials costs, noting their special relevance for target-return pricing. Only under certain assumptions on underlying production functions and pricing behavior can this omission be fully justified (see, e.g., Evans 1969, pp. 290–292; and Hymans 1972). This sin is perpetuated in the present paper because it was felt that omission of a (complex and hard-to-estimate) cost-of-capital variable does not interfere with the purpose of this section—to make comparisons among alternative concepts of capacity utilization.

16. The form $\Delta[1/(1 - U)]$, which can represent either nonlinearly rising marginal cost near full capacity or excess demand, was also tried, but never found to be significant. It is, of course, highly correlated with ΔU.

17. Similar equations with $\tilde{U}$ and U_m substituted for U in the excess demand terms

were also tried, since comparative results for different specifications might have been different; qualitatively, however, they were not.

18. One may conclude with Perry (1973, p. 731) that the Wharton methodology biases recent levels upward without rejecting the suggestion that perhaps other indexes, including McGraw-Hill's, ought to be higher.

19. U_m rather than U_b is used, since we are tentatively assuming that it more accurately represents a bottleneck utilization rate since 1967. It is also preferred to the bottleneck-weighted index U' because rapid increases in the latter may reflect a shift in weighting from U' toward U_m instead of (or as well as) actual increases in utilization rates.

20. Note the contrast between this accounting for the 1955–1957 inflation and the well-known demand-mix explanation given by Charles Schultze in 1959.

21. In the manufacturing price equations, at least the pass-through of higher oil prices should be captured in the raw materials price variable.

REFERENCES

BEA [Bureau of Economic Analysis, U.S. Department of Commerce]. 1973. A. A. Hirsch, M. Liebenberg, and G. R. Green, "The BEA Quarterly Econometric Model." Bureau of Economic Analysis Staff Paper 22. July.

de Leeuw, F. 1962. "The Concept of Capacity." *Journal of the American Statistical Association,* December: 826–840.

Eckstein, O., ed. 1972. *The Econometrics of Price Determination.* Washington, D.C.: Board of Governors of the Federal Reserve System.

Eckstein, O., and G. Fromm. 1968. "The Price Equation." *American Economic Review,* December: 1159–1183.

Eckstein, O., and D. Wyss. 1972. "Industry Price Equations." In Eckstein, ed. (1972).

Edmondson, N. 1973. "Capacity Utilization in Major Materials Industries." *Federal Reserve Bulletin,* August : 564–566.

Evans, M. K. 1969. *Macroeconomic Activity.* New York: Harper and Row.

Griffin, J. M. 1971. *Capacity Measurement in Petroleum Refining.* Lexington, Mass.: Heath Lexington.

Harrod, R. F. 1936. "Imperfect Competition and the Trade Cycle." *Review of Economic Statistics,* May: 84–88.

Hertzberg, M. P., A. I. Jacobs, and J. E. Trevathan. "The Utilization of Manufacturing Capacity." See SCB (1974b).

Hirsch, A. A. 1972. "Price Simulations with the OBE Econometric Model." In Eckstein, ed. (1972).

Hirsch, A. A., M. Liebenberg, and G. R. Green. "The BEA Quarterly Econometric Model." See BEA (1973).

Hymans, S. H. "Prices and Price Behavior in Three U.S. Econometric Models." In Eckstein, ed. (1972).

Keynes, J. M. 1936. *The General Theory of Employment, Interest, and Money.* New York: Harcourt, Brace.

Klein, L. R. 1960. "Some Theoretical Issues in the Measurement of Capacity." *Econometrica,* April: 272–286.

———. 1973. "Capacity Utilization: Concept, Measurement, and Recent Estimates." *Brookings Papers on Economic Activity,* No. 3: 743–756.

Klein, L. R., and R. Summers. 1966. *The Wharton Index of Capacity Utilization*. Studies in Quantitative Economics, no. 1. Philadelphia: University of Pennsylvania, Economics Research Unit.

McGraw-Hill. 1972. "Business' Plans for New Plants and Equipment, 1972–75." Processed. 25th Annual McGraw-Hill Survey. New York: McGraw-Hill, Economics Department, April 28.

Malenbaum, H. 1969. "Capacity Balance in the Chemical Industry." In L. R. Klein, ed., *Essays in Industrial Econometrics*, vol. 2. Philadelphia: University of Pennsylvania, Economics Research Unit.

Nordhaus, W. D. 1972. "Recent Developments in Price Dynamics." In Eckstein, ed. (1972).

Perry, G. L. 1973. "Capacity in Manufacturing." *Brookings Papers on Economic Activity*, no. 3: 701–742.

Phillips, A. 1963. "An Appraisal of Measures of Industrial Capacity." *American Economic Review, Papers and Proceedings*, May: 275–292.

SCB[*Survey of Current Business*]. 1974a. "The Input-Output Structure of the U.S. Economy." February.

———. 1974b. M. P. Hertzberg, A. I. Jacobs, and J. E. Trevathan. "The Utilization of Manufacturing Capacity." July.

Schultze, C. L. 1959. "Recent Inflation in the United States." In Joint Economic Committee, Study Paper 1, *Study of Employment, Growth and Price Levels*. 86th Cong., 1st sess.

Schultze, C. L., and J. S. Tryon. 1965. "Prices and Wages." In J. S. Duesenberry, G. Fromm, L. R. Klein, and E. Kuh, eds., *The Brookings Quarterly Econometric Model of the United States*. Chicago: Rand McNally.

COMMENTS

George L. Perry
The Brookings Institution

The concepts of industrial capacity and capacity utilization are central to many areas of modern economic analysis. Yet, despite numerous attempts to measure these concepts, involving many different approaches, the measures available to us are far from adequate. As a result, the ingenuity of economists is repeatedly tested when they try to make good use of the information on industrial capacity that is available. Albert Hirsch's paper is the latest example of ingenuity applied to those data.

The two main uses of capacity data by economists are in estimating investment demand and price behavior. Hirsch is concerned with the latter of these. He argues that capacity utilization is likely to be most important for price determination when utilization rates are near effective capacity and supply bottlenecks are likely to appear. Accordingly, he develops a "bottleneck-weighted" index of capacity utilization in manufacturing as a means of capturing the special effects of such supply conditions.

Hirsch rejects as unrealistic the rigid notion of supply bottle-necks implied by an input-output approach. The existence of inventories and of imports and substitution possibilities by both producers and consumers make it unlikely that capacity limits in any one industry can have overriding importance for the pricing of industrial output as a whole. He thus adopts a pragmatic approach to measuring bottleneck effects by forming an index in which utilization rates of all industries enter, but with weights that depend on two characteristics of special importance for price determination. The first is the proportion of an industry's output that is an intermediate product utilized by other industries; the second is a non-linear measure of how near an industry is to its capacity ceiling. Thus, in his measure, an important primary or intermediate processing industry with operating rates at or near peak levels would receive a disproportionately large weight in the measure of aggregate supply conditions. There is no way to test the particular formulation that Hirsch devised, but it looks sensible and captures the effects that he expects should be important.

Over the business cycle, the bottleneck-weighted measure of utilization that Hirsch calculates has the properties one would expect relative to conventional utilization measures. It shows tighter supply conditions than are revealed by conventional measures of utilization in the neighborhood of most business cycle peaks. However, when predictive ability in price equations for manufacturing is compared, there is little to distinguish the bottleneck-weighted index from the conventional utilization measure. He sets out to see what might account for this, and, although his procedure may seem to be excessively ad hoc, I think he is probably on the right track. In the basic utilization series from which he forms his bottleneck index, the degree of utilization in some primary industries was apparently understated in recent years. He cites the new Federal Reserve index of operating rates in major materials industries as some evidence for this and uses the major materials index to adjust both the conventional and the bottleneck-weighted utilization series for bias in recent years. These bias-corrected versions do give a clear verdict in favor of the bottleneck-weighted concept when the corrected series are compared in price equations.

In a later section of his paper, Hirsch specifically looks for speed-limit effects by examining whether price underpredictions are exceptionally large in years when utilization rates are already high and become abruptly higher. He concludes that such effects—which he refers to as short-run inelastic supply situations—were important only in the mid-1950s and not in later inflationary periods. I wish he had pursued this question further. If capacity utilization is already at high levels, it may be difficult to push it still higher, even though demand is growing very rapidly and short-run excess demand problems exist. Hirsch himself had offered this observation earlier in his paper, when he noted that any measure will be an ex post reading of capacity actually utilized.

One wrinkle that Hirsch might have added to his analysis would be a weighting of individual industries that took account of how sensitive their prices were to their own utilization rates. There is some evidence on this sensitivity for industries at different levels of aggregation, and it shows that utilization rates are far more important for pricing in some industries than in others. Indeed, the automobile industry offers an example of pricing behavior that, historically, is inversely related to the degree of capacity utilization. Hirsch's bottleneck concept probably offers a better measure of price pressures than is available from aggregate utilization rates. However, if refined with some allowance for price sensitivity in individual industries, it might be considerably improved.

8

WILLIAM D.
NORDHAUS
Yale University

and

JOHN B.
SHOVEN
Stanford University

A Technique for Analyzing and Decomposing Inflation

I. INTRODUCTION

Although interest in the phenomenon of inflation is both long-standing and widespread, formal analysis has for the most part concentrated on analyzing and projecting broad price level aggregates, such as the wholesale and consumer price indexes and the national output deflators(as an excellent case study, see Eckstein, ed. 1972). Until recently this approach was quite successful, but in the last couple of years most macroeconomic models of price behavior have performed poorly. As is well known, the general inflation of the past two years has been accompanied by significant relative price adjustments and this, in turn, has led to very unusual relationships among the several different price indexes. It is our belief that an examination of the properties and biases of the different price

NOTE: This work was partially supported by the National Science Foundation. We wish to express our thanks to Jeremy I. Bulow, whose long hours of computer programming and other assistance proved invaluable.

indexes, as well as a detailed and disaggregated examination of their components, is necessary for a more complete understanding of the movement of prices over the recent period. In what follows, we will attempt to work out a procedure for this and then outline a preliminary attempt to analyze and decompose the inflation.

The behavior of prices over the past two years has been not only distressing to consumers but equally puzzling to economists and other analysts. The discontinuity in the rate of inflation was the first surprising feature. Over the past two decades, there has never been as rapid an acceleration in price level increases as over the past two years: the consumer price index increased 3.6 percent in 1972, 9.4 percent in 1973, and at an annual rate of 12.7 percent in the first six months of 1974. The last time such a large discontinuity in the rate of inflation occurred was during the Korean War period.

The second extraordinary feature of the recent inflation was that the different price indexes showed widely different rates of inflation. For example, over the entire two-year period July 1972–July 1974, the wholesale price index (WPI) rose 35.1 percent, the consumer price index (CPI) rose 18.2 percent, the seasonally adjusted GNP deflator rose 15.1 percent, and the wage rate of production or nonsupervisory workers likewise rose 15.1 percent. The puzzle is that the historical pattern of the relationships among these series is exactly the opposite, with wages usually rising the most rapidly, followed by the consumer price index and GNP deflator, which, in turn, have risen more than wholesale prices (WPI). What accounts for this inversion in the relationships?

With the WPI rising more than twice as fast as the price of domestic output (represented, say, by the GNP deflator), how is it possible that profits have not been enormously squeezed? This question seems particularly difficult to answer when it is considered that the wholesale sectors as defined by the Bureau of Labor Statistics (BLS) account for approximately one-half of the value added of the economy. As it turns out, much of the puzzle about the relative performance can be explained by the peculiar construction of the wholesale price index. In the next section, we consider the current index, show the bias involved in its construction, and present a preliminary version of an improved index.

A second aspect of this paper, which we deal with in section III, is concerned with accounting for, or decomposing, the inflation experienced in the wholesale sectors, that is, we present a technique for determining how much of the inflation was due to each of a list of exogenous sectors, for example, how much was due to wage rate increases, grain price hikes, or jumps in the price of crude oil? We developed this approach in response to a notion that the recent inflation was somewhat different from previous inflationary episodes. The price increases seemed less strongly fueled by inflationary labor contracts and more concentrated among crude foods and materials. To some extent, all these vague notions are confirmed by the analysis.

II. PROBLEMS OF THE WHOLESALE PRICE INDEX

As stated above, most of the puzzling divergence among the published WPI, the CPI, and the GNP deflator can be explained by the peculiar, and we think faulty, construction of the WPI. The index includes a wide array of goods and services, although exactly which ones are included seems to have been determined in a rather ad hoc manner. These goods and services differ substantially in their stage of manufacture. The index itself is a compilation of a relatively large number of subindexes (or "price-relatives"). It can be represented as

1) $$WPI = \sum_{i=1}^{N} W_i P_i^1 \bigg/ \sum_{i=1}^{N} W_i P_i^0; \quad \sum_{i=1}^{N} W_i = 1.00$$

where W_i is the weight assigned to commodity classification i, P_i^0 is the initial or base-period price for that commodity classification, and P_i^1 is its current price. As the weights are not revised from month to month, but rather are determined by base-period characteristics of the sectors, the WPI is a Laspeyres index and thus generally tends to exaggerate inflation relative to a chain index.

There are, however, much more serious biases constructed into the index. One major flaw of the current WPI is that the weights are proportional to the value of total sales of the various sectors. The problem is that in aggregating the subindexes, price increases experienced by crude products are double and triple counted. For example, when the price of wheat rises, it will influence the WPI as a price increase of wheat, flour, and bread. The more stages of manufacture a crude item goes through, the greater the weight assigned to it. Conversely, the official WPI underweights price movements of items at later stages of manufacture. As long as all prices are changing in a more or less uniform manner, this problem of the WPI weighting system is not apparent. However, if the inflation is particularly acute among crude products and materials, as in the past two years, the index will badly exaggerate the increase in the level of wholesale prices.[1]

It seems to us that the current procedure followed by the BLS is indefensible on economic grounds.[2] It clearly has its roots in historical procedures, for it is only relatively recently that detailed input-output information has been available for construction of a more appropriate index. With the systematic collection of that information, there is no reason not to reconstruct the index in such a way as to avoid the problem of double counting.

In an earlier paper (Nordhaus and Shoven 1974), we presented two alternative indexes for a wholesale price index, one based on value-added weights, the other on net-output weights. The method of construction of value-added weights is self-explanatory. Net-output weights in principle aggregate the entire wholesale sector as if it were a single firm and treat the ratio of the price of that "wholesale firm" to the rest of the economy as the relevant concept. The weights, quite naturally, are proportional to the sales of the "wholesale firm" *to the rest of the economy*; they are "net-output weights" in the sense that they net out sales within the "wholesale firm." The rationale behind this weighting system is that the transaction prices and the circular flow within the "wholesale firm" are irrelevant to nonwholesale buyers; it is only the prices and quantities that exit from the "wholesale firm" that are important.

In this paper, we have presented only the net-output–weighted wholesale price index.[3] The reason for this is that an index with value-added weights may not accurately reflect prices if purchases of the "wholesale firm" from outside itself are significant and move differentially from prices within the wholesale sector. Consider, as an example, a rise in prices due only to an increase in the price of imported petroleum. To take the extreme case, assume that the domestic petroleum industry simply transships petroleum products and, therefore, has no value added. In such a scenario, a net-output price index would reflect the fact that wholesale prices have increased. However, with a value-added index, the petroleum industry would have a zero weight, and therefore the rise in petroleum prices would lead to no (direct) rise in the wholesale price index.[4] It seems to us that the WPI should reflect increases in the prices of "wholesale" goods from whatever source these price increases originate, and for that reason, we prefer a net-output WPI to a value-added index.

In order to compute the net-output weights we used a slightly updated version of the 1967 input-output (I/O) table published by the U.S. Department of Commerce, with the revisions being made in the import coefficients. This table is more recent than the one used in our previous article, and that fact has modified the comparability of the results somewhat. Imports were expanded to five rows and the columns were updated to be consistent with data available for the fourth quarter of 1972.

In the computation of our alternative net-output WPI, the major problem was caused by the lack of correspondence of the input-output sectors of the Department of Commerce with the sectors of the WPI subindexes. In fact, the WPI classification does not match the Standard Industrial Classification (SIC), the Standard Commodity Classification, the United Nations Standard International Trade Classification (SITC), or any other standard classification. This situation necessitated the construction of a concordance between the WPI sectors and the input-output sectors as no monthly price statistics are computed for the latter. This task has been completed, but imperfections in this concordance could introduce some errors into our analysis. The concordance we used is described in detail in Appendix B (on microfiche; see inside back cover).

We computed our net-output WPI for three separate nine-month periods: November 1970–August 1971, the pre-Phase I period; November 1972–August 1973, the same time span two years later, and the period in which grain and agricultural prices rose so substantially; and October 1973–July 1974, the most recent period for which complete data are available. We have also shown the results for the two-year period July 1972–July 1974. The results are given in the following tabulation; the official universe of industries is included:

Time Period	Official WPI (% increase)	Net-Output WPI (% increase)
11/70–8/71	3.61	2.49
11/72–8/73	17.73	12.75
10/73–7/74	16.58	14.30
7/72–7/74	35.09	28.42

In each of the three nine-month periods, the net-output WPI increased less, although the absolute difference is most significant in the November 1972–August 1973 case.

A second problem with the official WPI is that it excludes a very sizable portion of the economy. All services—public and private—are excluded, as are construction, publishing, transportation, communication, much of public utilities, and all of trade. Historically this selection has led to a downward bias, but the opposite was clearly the case in the period November 1972–August 1973. During that period, prices in the excluded sectors went up significantly less than average; for example, in construction and printing and publishing, sectoral prices increased only 5.0 and 7.2 percent, respectively.

There is a real but not terribly profound question involved in the choice of sectors for inclusion in a wholesale price index. Historically, the United States WPI has covered mainly mining, foods, and manufacturing. The omission of services, construction, publishing, transportation, communication, public utilities, and trade was undoubtedly related to the unavailability of price data rather than to any deeply held conviction that these were not "true" wholesale industries. As with the problem of weights, the availability of broader and higher quality data makes the question of the universe of a wholesale price index open for discussion and revision. One possible candidate would be an "industrial" price index that would have the same universe as the widely used industrial production index. We admit that we see little intrinsic merit in a wholesale price index per se; rather the index is of interest insofar as it predicts future trends in the prices of final goods to consumers, firms, or to the economy as a whole.[5]

In attempting to construct a wholesale price index that contains a broader universe of industries, we have included all sectors classified by the Department of Commerce under agriculture, forestry and fisheries, mining, construction, manufacturing, communications, and utilities (these correspond to input-output sectors 1 through 68). We repeat that there is no clear justification for the exact delineation of sectors as regards inclusion or exclusion. Rather, we have tried to construct a broad index of the price level of the business sector of the economy. Using this universe, we calculated the percent change in a net-output–weighted index for the same four periods as above, and the results are displayed in the following tabulation:

| | | Net-Output WPI | |
Time Period	Official WPI (% change)	Official Industries (% change)	I/O Sectors 1–68 (% change)
11/70–8/71	3.61	2.49	3.08
11/72–8/73	17.73	12.75	9.73
10/73–7/74	16.58	14.30	12.94
7/72–7/74	35.09	28.42	24.98

Analyzing the results, one sees that the narrow sectoral span of the official WPI gave a lower estimate of the rate of inflation in the first nine-month period, but resulted in a higher estimate over the other three time intervals. The difference was particularly significant in the November 1972–August 1973 period, as was anticipated above. Comparing the performance of the broadly based net-output WPI with that of the official index, one can draw several conclusions. Most striking perhaps is that the official WPI indicated a rate of inflation 82 percent greater than the broadly defined net-output WPI during November 1972–August 1973. This was, of course, the time span in which grain prices increased so dramatically. A second result, perhaps equally important, is that while the official WPI indicated that the rate of inflation in the wholesale sectors was slightly lower during October 1973–July 1974 than November 1972–August 1973, the net-output WPI indicates the opposite—in fact, indicates the rate to have been some 33 percent greater.

To summarize, it is our opinion that the problems associated with the official wholesale price index should be high on the agenda for official review and revision. There can be differences of opinion as to the proper universe for a wholesale or industrial price index, but the weighting system currently used cannot be defended on economic grounds. In earlier periods, the peculiarities of the official index have not resulted in grossly distorted estimates of the rate of inflation. However, in the last two years, the index has significantly exaggerated price level movements, and consequently, its periodic announcement has probably done the economy a disservice.

II. DECOMPOSING INFLATION

In addition to the perplexing divergence between the WPI and CPI, which we now have gone a long way toward explaining, there still is the question of determining how much of the inflation was due either directly or indirectly to price increases of livestock and agricultural products, how much due to crude oil price increases, and how much was caused by wage rate hikes. In this section, we present a technique for decomposing the inflation, thereby providing some answers to these questions.

In order to accomplish this decomposition of the inflation, we divide the economy into two broad sectors, a "normal-pricing" sector and a "sensitive-pricing" one. We justify this procedure on the ground that firms in much of the economy appear to set prices essentially on the basis of normal, or cyclically adjusted, average costs of production.[6] There appears to be very little price reaction in the normal pricing sector to changes in demand, at least within the range of variation observed over the postwar period. Rather, the response to an increase in demand is an increase in the quantity produced (or in backlogged orders), as well as an increase in the purchases of primary factors, labor, materials, and, eventually, capital. It is only if and when the increased demand for primary factors results in higher input prices that the normal-pricing firms raise their prices.

The second part of the economy is the price-sensitive sector. The prices of these goods are competitively determined. Many of them appear on commodity exchanges and often they are traded on world markets. In these sectors, prices are set by the traditional textbook principles of supply and demand, and these are indeed sensitive, sometimes very sensitive, to the evolution of demand. At present, we do not fully understand why this bifurcation of pricing phenomena occurs, nor is the exact delineation of the two sectors obvious. In what follows, however, we have taken the price-sensitive sector to be relatively small, including mainly crude materials. For the rest of the economy, we assume that the practice is that of normal pricing.

In order to implement our procedure, we have again made use of our slightly updated and revised version of the Department of Commerce's 1967 input-output table. We have assumed that the per-unit-of-output labor coefficients of the various sectors decline through time because of productivity increases. We assumed that the rate of labor productivity growth for each sector was equal to that estimated by Greenberg and Mark (1968) and Egbert (1968) for 1947–1964. All other coefficients are assumed constant over time. Let A be the direct unit input requirement matrix:

$$(2) \qquad A = \begin{bmatrix} A_{11} & \cdots & A_{1n} \\ \cdot & & \cdot \\ \cdot & & \cdot \\ \cdot & & \cdot \\ A_{n1} & \cdots & A_{nn} \end{bmatrix}$$

where A_{ij} is the amount of input i required to produce one unit of output j. Then we know by definition of value added that

$$(3) \qquad \vec{P} \equiv A'\vec{P} + \overrightarrow{VA}$$

where

$$(4) \qquad \overrightarrow{VA} \equiv w\vec{L} + \vec{T} + \vec{\pi}$$

with $\vec{P}$ being the n-dimensional column vector of prices; $\overrightarrow{VA}$, the vector of value added per unit of output; $\vec{L}$, labor requirements per

TABLE 1   Listing of Exogenous Sectors

1. Livestock and livestock products	9. Stone and clay mining and quarrying
2. Other agricultural products	10. Chemical and fertilizer mineral mining
3. Forestry and fishery products	
4. Agricultural, forestry, and fishery services	11. Imported crude foods
	12. Imported manufactured foods
5. Iron and ferroalloy ores mining	13. Imported crude materials
6. Nonferrous metal ores mining	14. Imported semimanufactures
7. Coal mining	15. Imported manufactured goods
8. Crude petroleum and natural gas	

unit of output; w, the wage rate; $\vec{T}$, the vector of indirect business taxes per unit of output; and $\vec{\pi}$, the profit rate, including depreciation, by sector.

The interpretation of equation 3 is that prices equal materials costs plus labor costs, taxes, and profits. Solving that equation for the column vector of prices we obtain the following equation:

(5) $$\vec{P} = [I - A']^{-1}\overline{VA}$$

which gives prices as a function of labor costs, indirect business taxes, and profits (or return to capital).

In contrast to the above procedure, we have split the input-output sectors into two classifications, the exogenous or price-sensitive sectors and the endogenous or normal pricing sectors. An exact list of our fifteen exogenous sectors is contained in Table 1. The cost or price of labor is likewise taken to be exogenous, even though it is clearly not competitively set nor is labor traded on world markets. We have assumed that the other two components of value added— indirect business taxes and profits—are constant per unit of output. Perhaps this is one defect of our procedure, as it would have been more in line with earlier studies to assume that profits are marked up on normal costs.

Consider a rearrangement of the matrix of per unit direct requirements (A) so that the fifteen exogenous sectors are numbered 1 through 15, and the remaining seventy-five, which are considered endogenous, are numbered 16–90. Thus, A is partitioned as follows:

$$A = \begin{bmatrix} A_{11} & \vdots & A_{12} \\ \cdots & \cdots & \cdots \\ A_{21} & \vdots & A_{22} \end{bmatrix}$$

where

A_{11} = 15 × 15 matrix of exogenous inputs into exogenous outputs;
A_{12} = 15 × 75 matrix of exogenous inputs into endogenous outputs;
A_{21} = 75 × 15 matrix of endogenous inputs into exogenous outputs (these coefficients are generally quite small);
A_{22} = 75 × 75 matrix of endogenous inputs into endogenous outputs

Let $\vec{P}_{ex}$ be a 15-dimensional column vector of exogenous prices, and let $\vec{P}_{en}$ be a 75-dimensional column vector of endogenous prices. For a given change in the prices of our fifteen exogenous products, $\Delta \vec{P}_{ex}$, and a change in the price of labor, Δw, equations 3 and 4 imply for the endogenous sectors that

(7) $$\Delta \vec{P}_{en} = A'_{22}\Delta \vec{P}_{en} + A'_{12}\Delta \vec{P}_{ex} + \vec{L}\Delta w + \Delta \vec{T}_{en} + \Delta \vec{\pi}_{en}$$

Again, our hypothesis is that the input-output coefficients are constant except for the assumption made about labor productivity above and that there is no change in per unit taxes or profits, i.e., $\Delta \vec{T}_{en} = \Delta \vec{\pi}_{en} = 0$. We therefore can write our hypothesis in terms of the predicted changes in endogenous prices, $\Delta \vec{P}^*_{en}$, caused by the observed changes in the prices of the exogenous sectors, $\Delta \vec{P}_{ex}$, as follows:

(8) $$\Delta \vec{P}^*_{en} = A'_{22}\Delta \vec{P}^*_{en} + A'_{12}\Delta \vec{P}_{ex} + \vec{L}\Delta w$$

Thus, our theory is that price changes in the endogenous sectors reflect cost changes due to exogenous price movements.[7] Solving equation 8 for $\Delta \vec{P}^*_{en}$, we obtain

(9) $$\Delta \vec{P}^*_{en} = [I - A'_{22}]^{-1}[A'_{12}\Delta \vec{P}_{ex} + \vec{L}\Delta w]$$

Equation 9 gives the 75-dimensional column vector of predicted endogenous price changes, $\Delta \vec{P}^*_{en}$, as a function of the changes in the prices of the exogenous products and labor. The impact of each of the exogenous price changes can be evaluated separately, thus allowing a partial decomposition of inflation in the seventy-five endogenous sectors. Another procedure is to compare $\Delta \vec{P}^*_{en}$ with the observed price changes in these endogenous sectors, perhaps by aggregating both into price indexes.

Our interest, as in the previous section of the paper, is in the sectors that form the official and our revised WPI. Recall that the broadened universe of our WPI included input-output sectors 1–68. The first ten of these are the first ten of our exogenous sectors previously listed in Table 1. The remaining fifty-eight are among the seventy-five endogenous sectors of our model. To give an example of the richness of the technique, a detailed decomposition of the inflation in these fifty-eight sectors is shown in Table 2 for the nine-month period November 1972–August 1973.[8] Clearly our hypothesis is far from perfect, in that the different observed rates of inflation are not perfectly predicted by the direct and indirect cost changes due to price changes in the exogenous sectors. For some sectors the model predicts quite well (note, for example, that, ΔP_{en}^* for item 4, food and kindred products, is 29.93 percent compared to the observed price change of 33.45 percent) while for others, for example, leather products (no. 23), the model does poorly. In order to judge how much of the observed variation in inflation across the fifty-eight endogenous sectors of Table 2 is predicted by our list of fifteen exogenous sectors plus labor, we computed the sample correlation coefficient, i.e.,

$$10) \quad r = \frac{\sum_{i=1}^{58} (\Delta P_{en_i}^* - \overline{\Delta P}_{en}^*)(\Delta P_{en_i} - \overline{\Delta P}_{en})}{\sqrt{\sum_{i=1}^{58} (\Delta P_{en_i}^* - \overline{\Delta P}_{en}^*)^2 \ \sum_{i=1}^{58} (\Delta P_{en_i} - \overline{\Delta P}_{en})^2}}$$

The results for the four periods reported earlier were as follows (r ranges from $+1.0$ to -1.0):

11/70–8/71: +.4351	10/73–7/74: +.5339
11/72–8/73: +.6064	7/72–7/74: +.5952

Perhaps at this point we should emphasize that what our technique offers is an *accounting* for inflation and not an explanation or direct identification of its causes (such as incorrect monetary or fiscal policy). However, the results of the analysis do provide insight into the nature of the price increases (e.g., whether they are largely "labor cost-push," raw materials induced, or "demand-pull") and should be quite useful in suggesting the appropriate anti-inflationary policy instruments.

Returning to Table 2, one encouraging fact we note is that the residuals seem to center around zero, meaning that while the *variation* of price increases across sectors may have been only partially predicted, the *level* of inflation in these fifty-eight sectors has, in fact, been closely predicted. That is, price changes in our relatively short list of exogenous commodities did, on the whole, account for the level of inflation experienced during November 1972–August 1973 in the fifty-eight endogenous sectors that enter our revised WPI.[9] In order to analyze this factor more precisely and to report on the three other periods, we aggregated the data of Table 2 (and the analogous tables for the other time periods) and formed indexes for each of the various columns. In constructing these indexes, we took

TABLE 2 Decomposition of Inflation in Endogenous Sectors 1–58, November 1972 to August 1973

| | Actual % Price Increase (1) | Cost Increase due to[a] | | | | | | Residual Col. 1 less Col. 6 (7) |
		Exog. 1–4 (2)	Exog. 5–10 (3)	Exog. 11–15 (4)	Exog. 16 (5)	Exog. 1–16 (6)	
1. New construction	5.359	0.741	0.330	0.746	1.823	3.639	1.720
2. Maintenance and repair construction	5.359	0.432	0.280	0.483	2.078	3.273	2.086
3. Ordnance and accessories	3.228	0.366	0.235	0.939	1.050	2.589	0.639
4. Food and kindred products	33.453	27.064	0.075	1.673	1.117	29.929	3.524
5. Tobacco manufactures	4.255	15.308	0.030	0.372	0.313	16.023	−11.768
6. Broad and narrow fabrics, yarn and thread mills	16.889	7.697	0.145	2.696	0.667	11.205	5.684
7. Misc. textile goods and floor coverings	3.633	5.123	0.169	2.760	0.671	8.723	−5.090
8. Apparel	2.934	2.590	0.081	3.120	1.516	7.307	−4.373
9. Misc. fabricated textile products	2.839	3.797	0.112	2.275	1.470	7.653	−4.814
10. Lumber and wood products, except containers	19.737	3.894	0.133	1.975	2.046	8.048	11.689
11. Wooden containers	10.270	1.675	0.109	0.924	2.491	5.198	5.072
12. Household furniture	4.657	1.336	0.143	1.228	0.415	3.123	1.534
13. Other furniture and fixtures	7.131	0.691	0.199	0.942	0.430	2.262	4.869
14. Paper and allied products, except containers	7.229	0.985	0.232	1.756	1.416	4.390	2.839
15. Paperboard containers and boxes	7.300	0.387	0.128	5.755	1.109	7.379	−0.079
16. Printing and publishing	2.402	0.562	0.110	0.601	2.469	3.743	−1.340
17. Chemicals and selected chemical products	9.585	0.722	0.845	2.040	−0.153	3.455	6.131
18. Plastics and synthetic materials	4.129	0.734	0.459	1.058	−0.198	2.053	2.077
19. Drugs, cleaning, and toilet preparations	0.676	1.179	0.179	2.053	−0.170	3.241	−2.566

20. Paints and allied products	6.001	2.546	0.400	1.500	-0.190	4.257	1.744
21. Petroleum refining and related industries	16.352	0.180	4.287	1.877	-0.323	6.021	10.332
22. Rubber and misc. plastic products	2.860	0.728	0.186	2.146	1.909	4.969	-2.109
23. Leather tanning and industrial leather products	-5.602	8.491	0.136	2.998	1.651	13.275	-18.878
24. Footwear and other leather products	1.465	2.243	0.090	1.987	2.126	6.445	-4.980
25. Glass and glass products	-1.660	0.311	0.187	1.346	1.323	3.167	-4.827
26. Stone and clay products	3.039	0.331	0.516	1.266	1.207	3.319	-0.280
27. Primary iron and steel manufacturing	3.149	0.206	0.772	2.087	1.513	4.579	-1.430
28. Primary nonferrous metal manufacturing	17.662	0.280	2.557	3.310	1.239	7.385	10.277
29. Metal containers	3.356	0.506	0.450	1.187	1.430	3.572	-0.216
30. Heating, plumbing, and structural metal products	4.435	0.328	0.450	1.642	1.476	3.896	0.539
31. Stampings, screw machine products, and bolts	4.435	0.227	0.390	1.596	1.488	3.702	0.733
32. Other fabricated metal products	3.511	0.280	0.394	2.135	1.347	4.156	-0.645
33. Engines and turbines	2.475	0.258	0.320	3.012	1.253	4.844	-2.369
34. Farm machinery and equipment	2.116	0.268	0.262	2.704	1.278	4.511	-2.396
35. Construction, mining, and oil field machinery	4.038	0.266	0.269	0.940	1.405	2.881	1.157
36. Materials handling machinery and equipment	2.413	0.292	0.301	0.929	1.505	3.026	-0.613
37. Metalworking machinery and equipment	3.710	0.227	0.210	3.319	1.250	5.007	-1.298
38. Special industry machinery and equipment	5.783	0.371	0.255	1.902	1.401	3.928	1.855
39. General industrial machinery and equipment	3.325	0.317	0.306	1.299	1.427	3.349	-0.024
40. Machine shop products	3.325	0.311	0.293	0.686	1.495	2.784	0.541
41. Office, computing, and accounting machines	2.281	0.444	0.133	2.905	1.245	4.726	-2.446
42. Service industry machines	2.281	0.391	0.352	1.071	1.378	3.193	-0.912

TABLE 2 (concluded)

Sector	Actual % Price Increase (1)	Cost Increase due to[a]					Residual Col. 1 less Col. 6 (7)
		Exog. 1–4 (2)	Exog. 5–10 (3)	Exog. 11–15 (4)	Exog. 16 (5)	Exog. 1–16 (6)	
43. Electric industrial equipment and apparatus	1.884	0.372	0.330	0.983	1.157	2.842	−0.958
44. Household appliances	0.926	0.411	0.328	1.114	1.092	2.944	−2.018
45. Electric lighting and wiring equipment	1.859	0.329	0.334	0.906	1.058	2.627	−0.768
46. Radio, television, and communication equipment	−0.541	0.247	0.119	4.403	0.976	5.745	−6.285
47. Electronic components and accessories	1.899	0.322	0.188	3.358	1.074	4.942	−3.043
48. Misc. electrical machinery, equipment, and supplies	1.899	0.297	0.553	1.178	1.131	3.160	−1.261
49. Motor vehicles and equipment	1.709	0.260	0.205	4.598	0.652	5.716	−4.006
50. Aircraft and parts	1.709	0.339	0.231	1.140	1.077	2.787	−1.078
51. Other transportation equipment	3.840	0.391	0.258	3.947	0.797	5.393	−1.552
52. Scientific and controlling instruments	1.402	0.556	0.190	4.168	−0.412	4.502	−3.100
53. Optical, opthalmic, and photographic equipment	1.402	0.214	0.160	4.723	0.317	4.780	−3.378
54. Miscellaneous manufacturing	5.593	0.712	0.224	3.171	0.887	4.994	0.600
55. Transportation and warehousing	2.553	0.394	0.256	0.282	1.729	2.661	−0.108
56. Communications, except radio and TV broadcasting	1.915	0.172	0.045	0.122	−0.063	0.275	1.639
57. Radio and TV broadcasting	4.389	1.290	0.054	0.157	−0.085	1.416	2.973
58. Electric, gas, water, and sanitary services	2.848	0.232	1.112	0.112	−0.039	1.416	1.432

[a] Exogenous sectors 1–4 cover agriculture, livestock, forestry, and fisheries; 5–10, mining and domestic fuels; 11–15, imports; and 16 covers labor.

a set of weights (either the official WPI weights or our net-output weights) and applied them to the vector of observed or calculated price changes. The weights no longer sum to unity, since the fifty-eight sectors of Table 2 account for only 89.9 percent of the official weights and 97.0 percent of the net-output weights. The other weighted commodities are among our list of exogenous goods. The contribution of the endogenous sectors to the change in the WPI is

(11) $$\Delta WPI_{en} = \sum_{i=1}^{58} W_i \Delta P_{en_i}$$

whereas the amount of inflation occurring in the endogenous sectors which is indirectly due to exogenous price changes is

(12) $$\Delta WPI^* = \sum_{i=1}^{58} W_i \Delta P_{en_i}^*$$

This can be written in vector notation as

(13) $$\Delta \overline{WPI}^* = \overline{W}'[I - A'_{22}]^{-1}[A'_{12}\Delta \vec{P}_{ex} + \vec{L}\Delta w]$$

where the weights are zero for components 59 through 75. Equation 11 simply aggregates column 1 of Table 2 into a price index using WPI weights, while equations 12 and 13 do the same thing for column 6. In similar fashion, aggregation can be accomplished for each of the other columns of Table 2.

The results of computing these aggregative indexes are summarized and displayed in percent terms in Table 3. To a large extent, the data in this table answer the questions concerning the composition of inflation. Wide differences are clearly shown. In the earliest period labor was a major contributory factor to inflation, even after we had made corrections for long-run productivity gains. Our list of sixteen exogenous sectors accounts for some 82 to 88 percent of the rather small amount of inflation evident during those nine months, with the residual probably due to the unfortunate construction of profits in our model. In the period two years later (November 1972–August 1973), labor's contribution (exog. 16) is greatly reduced, while agriculture, livestock, forestry, and fisheries (exog. 1–4) account for nearly two-thirds of the inflation. With the net-output weighting system, most of the effects of the price increases show up indirectly (as cost increases in other sectors), whereas with the official weighting system the direct and indirect impacts are comparable. Imports were also a major inflationary factor in this period, accounting for 16 percent of the change in the net-output WPI, largely because of the second and third devaluations of the dollar in early 1973. As we observed casually from Table 2,

TABLE 3 Decomposition of Inflation, Selected Aggregates, Various Periods, 1970–1974

	11/70–8/71		11/72–8/73		10/73–7/74		7/72–7/74	
	Official WPI	Broad Net-Output WPI	Official WPI	Broad Net-Output WPI	Official WPI	Broad Net-Output WPI	Official WPI	Broad Net-Output WPI
Summary Statistics (percent change in WPI)								
Percent change in WPI	3.607	3.078	17.730	9.730	16.582	12.944	35.088	24.979
Amt. due *directly* to exogenous sectors	0.595	0.092	6.089	1.815	0.908	0.246	5.482	1.849
Amt. due to endogenous sectors	3.006	2.986	11.641	7.915	15.674	12.698	29.606	23.130
Amt. due *indirectly* to exogenous sectors	2.539	2.466	9.218	7.545	9.262	7.792	18.969	16.165
Unexplained residual	0.467	0.520	2.423	0.369	6.412	4.906	10.637	6.965

Decomposition of Wholesale Inflation (percent contribution of exogenous sectors)

Agriculture, livestock, forestry, and fisheries (exog. sectors 1–4)								
Direct	14.27	2.67	33.34	18.30	−1.32	0.48	10.84	6.28
Indirect	22.93	19.33	33.07	45.85	−2.73	−2.60	8.75	9.40
Mining and domestic fuels (exog. 5–10)								
Direct	2.40	0.31	1.00	0.36	6.79	1.42	4.80	1.12
Indirect	3.90	4.65	2.68	3.94	13.48	15.03	9.84	11.87
Imports (exog. 11–15)								
Indirect	14.71	15.34	11.01	16.44	37.12	35.61	24.36	24.66
Labor (exog. 16)								
Indirect	29.62	40.81	5.23	11.32	7.98	12.16	11.18	18.67
Total	87.83	83.11	86.33	96.21	61.32	62.10	69.77	72.00
Residual	12.14	16.93	13.67	3.79	38.68	37.90	30.32	28.00
	100.00	100.00	100.00	100.00	100.00	100.00	100.00	100.00

SOURCE: Table 2; see accompanying text.

the list of exogenous sectors accounts for nearly all of the change in the wholesale price level (93 percent), using net-output weights. The technique performs less satisfactorily in analyzing the most recent nine-month period, with the exogenous sectors accounting for only 60 percent of the inflation. The largest inflationary source was imports, accounting for 36 to 37 percent of the total, and this is largely due to the 118 percent rise in the price of imported crude materials. Labor continued to be a relatively minor factor, while agriculture, livestock, forestry, and fisheries actually were deflationary (a fact which the official index exaggerates). The 54 percent price increase in domestic crude oil and natural gas was also a large factor in wholesale inflation.

Clearly, our two-sector, cost-push model of wholesale inflation performed less well in this most recent period. Why? First, the enormous rise in the prices of refined petroleum products was way beyond what could be explained from the rise in crude oil prices according to our price data and input coefficients. While our model shows that the per unit costs of the petroleum industry were up 32.5 percent in those nine months, petroleum prices rose a staggering 77.7 percent, leaving an enormous unexplained residual of 45.2 percent. Part of the explanation may be that, although the price of "old" domestic crude oil was not allowed to rise beyond $5.25 a barrel, product prices rose to the marginal supply price, which in most cases was the import or "new" oil price of approximately $10.50 per barrel. The difference, of course, accounts for the enormous profit increases enjoyed by the oil companies over the past year (1974).

In order to determine the importance of the petroleum price hikes, we did another run of our model in which the price of refined petroleum products was taken as exogenous. Although this procedure is somewhat ad hoc, it can be rationalized as follows: we have taken the price of crude materials as exogenous, but in the case of petroleum the "old" domestic price was frozen. Since product price equalization apparently occurred, the difference between foreign crude prices and the domestic price should be included in the rise of the price of petroleum. Put slightly differently, the frozen price of $5.25 per barrel is a kind of political fiction. Since the oil companies were able to sell the product for a price corresponding to the free market price of about double that, the price freeze had little effect on product prices and merely transferred some of the windfall gains from crude producers to oil refiners. The simplest way to account for this in our analysis is to assume that the model correctly predicts the refined product price and to take the observed refined product price as exogenous.

The effects of this change on the results for October 1973–July 1974 and for July 1972–July 1974 are shown in Table 4. The detailed, disaggregated results for these periods, with the refined petroleum price taken as exogenous, appear as tables A.4 and A.5 in the appendix (on microfiche). Approximately 40 percent of our unexplained residual disappears for the most recent nine-month span, with the new list of seventeen exogenous sectors (those in Table 1 plus labor and refined petroleum products) now accounting for 78 percent of the wholesale inflation. While the percent contribution of "energy resources" to inflation is not explicitly separated out in Table 4, our analysis would indicate that the range of the figure over this time period is from 55 to 60 percent, including both domestic and imported resources. At the same time, the relatively large residual of 22 percent may indicate that some increase in the profit margins of our remaining fifty-seven endogenous sectors was experienced with the final and total elimination of wage and price controls.

The problem of petroleum prices is one reflection of a more serious omission in the technique used here, one that raises several questions for an open economy. The major sectors in which prices are controlled by external forces not taken into account here are those of export- or import-competing goods. Examples would include chemicals and iron and steel. Both of these are highly competitive industries engaged in international trade, and it is clear that, as with raw materials (although in a somewhat attenuated manner), pricing of many of these products is heavily influenced by world markets. It seems likely that movements of foreign prices of such exposed commodities—whether they be competing imports or exports—would lead to similar movements in the domestic prices of these goods (independent of changes in domestic cost factors).

It is likely that this problem with exposed sectors arose in several categories during the October 1973–July 1974 period. If we take as an arbitrary criterion residuals greater than plus or minus 15 percent (from Table A.4), the following eight sectors qualify during this period:

		Residual
18.	Plastics and synthetic materials	+49.819
22.	Leather and leather products	−23.967
9.	Miscellaneous fabricated textile products	−19.294
27.	Primary nonferrous metal manufacturing	+17.293
26.	Primary iron and steel manufacturing	+17.071
28.	Metal containers	+16.984
20.	Paints and allied products	+16.767
17.	Chemicals and selected chemical products	+15.984

Virtually all these industries are "exposed" to the winds of international trade and (except for leather) were in tight demand on world markets. In addition, there was a redirection of demand toward the United States following the 1973 dollar devaluations. So, in summary, it appears to us that the movement in the prices of these eight sectors was accompanied and perhaps heavily influenced by the movement in the world prices of these commodities.

This problem points out one of the chief difficulties in applying our two-sector model for open economies. There is a gray area between the exogenous and endogenous categories—the exposed export- and import-competing sectors—where pass-through pricing breaks down when severe structural shifts occur, such as divergent trends in exchange rate movements, or when relative price adjustments are different in different countries. At present, there does not appear to be any good way to allocate these exposed industries between the exogenous and endogenous categories, and this problem must be listed on the agenda for future work.

There are, of course, other factors that may have contributed to the residual movements in these eight industries. In the first place, the predictions of the model rest on input-output data which are basically seven years old; in addition, the price and input-output data are probably still not matched very well. A second factor was the final lifting of price controls over the past year (1974). We do not have precise information on how important these controls were in the different industries, but the results presented here are consistent with the notion that prices in a few industries were held below their market-determined levels. Finally, we have assumed that there was no movement in markup over cost; however, there may have been some increase in profit margins in those sectors experiencing strong demand. The aggregative data on the gross profits of nonfinancial corporations does indicate an increase in the ratio of before-tax profits to output from 13.8 percent in the third quarter of 1973 to 15.8 percent in the second quarter of 1974. At this stage, it is not possible to sort out how much of this increase was due to the petroleum sector, how much to an increase in inventory profits or underdepreciation due to original-cost basis, and how much to an increase in the markup of the endogenous sectors other than petroleum. Our preliminary view is that the residuals are in part due to increased profit margins (apart from petroleum), but this conjecture must be tested by further analysis.

	7/72–7/74		10/73–7/74	
	Official WPI	Broad Net-Output WPI	Official WPI	Broad Net-Output WPI
Summary Statistics (percent change in WPI)				
Percent change in WPI	35.088	24.979	16.582	12.944
Amount due *directly* to exogenous sectors	9.668	5.551	3.690	2.706
Amount due to endogenous sectors	25.420	19.428	12.892	10.238
Amount due *indirectly* to exogenous sectors	18.033	15.546	8.663	7.418
Unexplained residual	7.387	3.882	4.229	2.820
Decomposition of Wholesale Inflation (percent contribution of exogenous factors)				
Agriculture, livestock, forestry, and fisheries (exog. sectors 1–4)				
Direct	10.83	6.28	−1.32	0.48
Indirect	8.58	9.13	−2.68	−2.53
Mining and domestic fuels (exog. 5–10)				
Direct	4.79	1.12	6.79	1.42
Indirect	4.71	4.95	6.31	6.17
Refined petroleum				
Direct	11.93	14.82	16.77	19.01
Indirect	4.51	7.35	6.34	9.43
Imports				
Indirect	22.63	22.47	34.43	32.29
Labor				
Indirect	10.96	18.34	7.85	11.97
Total	78.94	84.46	74.49	78.24
Residual	21.06	15.54	25.51	21.76
	100.00	100.00	100.00	100.00

SOURCE: See accompanying text.

IV. CONCLUSION

We have presented an analysis of the official wholesale price index, the biases involved in its construction, and a preliminary improved measure of the price level of the wholesale sector. The issues involved here strike us as important, and we conclude that the official WPI has been a very misleading economic indicator during the last two years, as it has estimated the increase in the price level to have been some 40 percent greater than our improved measure indicates (35 percent versus 25 percent).

The second aspect of this paper has involved the development and use of a technique for decomposing the inflation in wholesale sectors into the factors accounting for it. Despite the problems with this approach that we have mentioned, we find the results it provides to be both useful and interesting. The contrasts between the recent and previous periods of inflation have been quantified. Many of the shortcomings of the analysis are not fundamental (for instance, an improved concordance between the price data and input-output sectors can be developed, and more up-to-date input-output tables are possible), and we anticipate making further refinements in the technique. Some extensions and improvements are less easily accomplished (such as accurately determining the appropriate lag structure). Despite this, we anticipate that further refinements will make disaggregated analyses such as this more useful in diagnosing and analyzing the sources and structure of inflation.

NOTES

1. We are by no means the first to point out this particular shortcoming of the WPI (see, for example, Eckstein and Fromm 1959 and Stigler 1961).
2. An index which is even more poorly constructed is the weekly index of crude materials prices, which is simply an unweighted geometric average of spot price relatives.
3. Note that a net-output–weighted price index and a value-added–weighted index would be identical if they covered the entire economy and the economy were closed.
4. Indeed, this is why the GNP deflator, essentially a value-added–weighted price index of domestic output, has been somewhat misleading as an economy-wide price index over the last year or so. It is conceptually quite different from a CPI and should be used accordingly.
5. In another piece of research, John Shoven and David Starrett are attempting to determine the best universe for a WPI and to confirm that an index thus constructed predicts future changes in the CPI better than the official WPI.

6. Evidence for this proposition goes back to Kalecki (1939). Recent confirmations, essentially for manufacturing, have been made by Eckstein and Wyss (1972) for the United States and by Nield (1963) and Godley and Nordhaus (1972) for the United Kingdom.
7. A similar approach to this sort of problem was taken by Eckstein and Fromm (1959) in their study of the direct and indirect impact of steel prices on inflation.
8. The corresponding results for the three periods October 1970–August 1971, October 1973–July 1974, and July 1972–July 1974 are displayed in tables A-1, A-2, and A-3, respectively, in Appendix A (on microfiche).
9. In contrast to a multiple regression procedure, this technique does not guarantee that the mean of the predicted values equals the mean of the observations.

REFERENCES

Ackley, G. 1959. "Administered Prices and Inflationary Process." *American Economic Review, Papers and Proceedings,* May.

Eckstein, O., ed. 1972. *The Econometrics of Price Determination.* Washington, D.C.: Board of Governors of the Federal Reserve System.

Eckstein, O., and G. Fromm. 1959. In Joint Economic Committee. *Steel and Postwar Inflation.* Study Paper no. 2. 86th Cong., 1st sess.

Eckstein, O., and D. Wyss. 1972. "Industry Price Equations." In Eckstein, ed., (1972).

Egbert, A. 1968. "Changing Factor Shares by Industry: Factor Prices and Factor Substitutions." In Kendrick, ed. (1968).

Godley, W., and W. Nordhaus. 1972. "Pricing in the Trade Cycle." *Economic Journal,* September.

Greenberg, L., and J. Mark. 1968. "Sector Changes in Unit Labor Costs." In Kendrick, ed. (1968).

Kalecki, M. 1939. *Essays in the Theory of Economic Fluctuations.* London: Allen and Unwin.

Kendrick, J. W., ed. 1968. *The Industrial Composition of Income and Wealth.* Studies in Income and Wealth 32. New York: National Bureau of Economic Research.

Nield, R. 1963. *Pricing and Employment in the Trade Cycle: A Study of British Manufacturing Industry, 1950–61.* Cambridge, England: Cambridge University Press.

Nordhaus, W., and J. Shoven. 1974. "Inflation 1973: The Year of Infamy." *Challenge,* May/June.

Stigler, G. 1961. In Joint Economic Committee. *Hearings: The Price Statistics of the Federal Government: Review, Appraisal, and Recommendations.* 87th Cong., 1st sess.

NOTE: Appendix A, "Detailed Decomposition of Inflation in Endogenous Sectors," and Appendix B, "The Construction of a Concordance between Available Price Data and Input-Output Sectors," are on microfiche on the inside back cover of the book. Duplicate copies of the fiche can be obtained from Microfiche Systems Corporation, 440 Park Avenue South, New York, N.Y. 10016.

COMMENTS

Clopper Almon
University of Maryland

Nordhaus and Shoven make two distinct points:

The "all commodities" wholesale price index overstates the recent inflation because it double or triple counts the prices of basic commodities.

Eighty to 85 percent of the recent inflation can be explained by the pass-through of hikes in these basic commodity prices and in wages.

Both points are, I think, indisputable, and well and clearly made. Relative to the first, I want to point out only that the Bureau of Labor Statistics agrees with the authors and does, in fact, publish a series with behavior very similar to that of the net-output–weighted index advocated by the authors. Relative to the second point, I shall indicate a few considerations that would further strengthen their argument.

I

The Bureau of Labor Statistics prepares several stage-of-processing price series. The table below shows the growth rates for four of these over the periods selected by Nordhaus and Shoven; it also includes for comparison the growth rates of the "commodities" component of the CPI and the Nordhaus-Shoven net-output indexes:

	Wholesale Price Index						CPI: Com-modities
Period	All Com-modities	Net Output	Finished Goods	Crude Ma-terials	Intermed. Ma-terials	Con-sumer Goods	
11/70–8/71	3.6	2.5	2.3	3.4	4.1	2.1	2.7
11/72–8/73	17.7	12.7	10.8	51.5	10.7	12.9	8.6
10/73–7/74	16.6	14.3	11.7	0.7	23.2	13.4	10.0
7/72–7/74	35.1	28.4	25.7	49.5	40.0	29.4	20.1

Conceptually, the Nordhaus-Shoven index should be close to the finished goods index, and the figures in the table show very similar movements, though the rise in the finished goods index seems to have been slightly slower. The explosion of the crude materials index during the second or "farm" period shows where the source of the inflation in that period lay. Similarly, the hump in the intermediate materials index in the "oil" months showed that the latter inflation had a different cause.

Nordhaus and Shoven also compare the WPI and the CPI. It would be more appropriate to compare the WPI finished consumer goods index with the CPI commodities series. The last two columns of the preceding tabulation show this comparison. One would expect that during the "farm" and "oil" inflations the CPI would rise more slowly than did wholesale prices simply because retailer and wholesaler labor costs were not going up as fast as were farm or oil prices. And, indeed, we find the CPI index rising by only two-thirds of the rise in the corresponding WPI index.

Clearly the BLS offers us some appropriate price indexes. Equally clearly, the press will go on emphasing the all-commodities index, for it is the most nearly all-encompassing. No single stage-of-processing index nor the net-output index will meet the needs of the press, for too many prices are left out. When the price of cotton goes up, *the* wholesale price index should reflect the change even before it shows up in the price of clothes. The original Nordhaus-Shoven use of value-added weights appears to me to come closer to filling the bill than does the net-output index. The trouble with the value-added index, as they point out in the present paper, is that it does not include imports. But why not include imports with "value added" equal to their value? Such an index would measure "prices paid by Americans and their export customers." That seems to be a reasonable concept, attractive to the press and acceptable to the specialist, and clearly better than the hodgepodge which now gets all the attention. Of course, we might need better import price indexes, but we need them anyway.

II

Nordhaus and Shoven have performed a valuable service by showing the great extent to which inflation can be accounted for by pass-through, via input-output relations, of changes in a few commodity prices. I urge the reader to note Tables 3 and 4 carefully and to observe particularly that the residual as a percentage of total price changes is only 3.79 percent for the farm price inflation (Table 3) and only 21.76 percent for the oil inflation (Table 4). My comments will be directed to a few matters which may make these residuals, especially the second, even smaller.

The authors use rates of productivity growth estimated for the period 1947–1964. The rates by input-output industry are all available up through 1972 and show a considerable slowdown after 1964. This overestimate of labor productivity growth helps to explain why all the residuals are positive in tables 3 and 4.

Many of the largest errors in Table 2 and tables A.1–A.5 can be attributed to technical problems. For example:

Table	Sector	Error	Cause
4	5. Tobacco mfg.	−11.7	Tobacco growing has been aggregated with other crops whose prices rose more than its did. Tobacco growing is a separate sector in the 363-order tables of the Bureau of Economic Analysis.
2	6. Fabrics	+5.7	Cotton, which had extra large price increases, was aggregated with other crops. Again, BEA tables provide the separate cotton sector.
2	23. Leather	−18.9	Apparently, the authors used a table that included by-product sales, thereby implicitly assuming that the price of hides moved with the price of meat. It did not.
2	46. Radio and TV equip.	−6.3	Apparently imported radios and TVs have been considered an "input" into domestic radios and TVs, as have imported cars into domestic cars. This treatment would be all right if we were explaining consumer prices, but the WPI includes only the prices of *American-made* radios, TVs, or cars.
2	49. Motor vehicle	−4.0	
2	21. Petro ref.	10.3	If, as appears above, imported crude has been counted as an input into domestic crude and then the crude price taken exogenously as the WPI
A-2	21. Petro ref.	45.2	

Table	Sector	Error	Cause
			for domestic crude, the pass-through process has been strangled. The 8.721 increase due to imports appears to be just the influence of the imported refined products.
A-4	18. Plastics and syn.	49.8	BEA tables treat petrochemical feed stocks produced by petroleum refining as an input into sector 17, chemicals, which then sells them to 18, plastics and synthetics. Consequently, this major cost item to the plastics and synthetics industry was considered to have grown only by the 14.2 percent predicted for sector 17 instead of the 77.7 percent assumed for petroleum refining.

With these corrections, only two errors of more than six points remain in Table 2. The 11.7-point error for 10 (lumber) in the Table 2 results from a special lumber price cycle that has little to do with other prices. By January 1975, however, the lumber and wood products price was down to just 10 percent above the November 1972 level. Clearly, lumber belongs among the price-sensitive sectors, in which "prices are set by the traditional textbook principles of supply and demand" and therefore escape our analysis and must be made exogenous. Finally, there is the 10.3-point error on primary nonferrous metals. Greater detail might make clear what the problem is. Is it the price of gold?

Since Nordhaus and Shoven went to some considerable trouble to make up price indexes for input-output sectors, I gather that it is not as well known as it should be that David Gilmartin of the INFORUM project at the University of Maryland made up such series for a 185-sector table several years ago and that we keep them fairly well up to date. Researchers who need them should get in touch with us. We have used them to estimate distributed lag price equations which are now a part of our INFORUM model. I am, therefore, delighted that this fine paper shows the substantial explanatory power of this approach. What remains to do is to find some explanation for prices in those "traditional textbook" cases.

9

PAUL
WACHTEL

National Bureau of
Economic Research
nd New York University

Survey Measures of Expected Inflation and Their Potential Usefulness

Economists have often treated expectations of price change with benign neglect—acknowledged but largely ignored. However, the inflationary experience of recent years has led to an increased interest in the role of inflationary expectations. It is by now standard procedure to use distributed lag techniques to generate a ready proxy for expectations from past experience. My contention in this paper is that these procedures are often inadequate and that alternatives do exist, namely, the measures of inflationary expectations based on survey data which have begun to attract some research interest in the last few years. This paper is essentially a review of the state of the art of those measures.

The use of past price inflation rates to generate measures of expected rates is both intuitively appealing and easy to implement. Since information about past price change is available at little cost, it is likely to have an important influence on the formation of price expectations. Consequently, adaptive or extrapolative hypotheses

NOTE: The author is grateful to Stanley Liebowitz, Moshe Ben-Horim, and Charles Snow for valuable research assistance and to Rapidata, Inc., for computer time made available to the NBER.

frequently provide adequate proxies for expectations. However, it is erroneous to assume that past price information will always be used in the same fashion or that other information is not used in the formation of expectations.[1] In particular, when the economic situation is changing or unstable, we would expect that additional information would be used in the formation of expectations and that the process by which past history is filtered into an expectation would vary. In either case fixed expectational structures based on past history would be inadequate. However, relevant additional information is available in the price expectations surveys.

In this paper the sources of survey data on price expectations are discussed and the data presented. Then some simple comparisons of the data and their predictive accuracy are presented. The potential usefulness of the data is then demonstrated by showing how price expectations improve upon some standard specifications of price, wage, and interest rate equations and how prices affect consumption behavior. The results do not indicate that expectations series based on survey data can always be substituted for expectations based on simple models of the formation of expectations but they do suggest that the survey data include important additional information. This is particularly true in the period of increasing and variable inflation since 1965.

SOURCES OF SURVEY DATA: LIVINGSTON DATA

The data on inflationary expectations that have attracted considerable attention from researchers are from the survey conducted by Joseph Livingston. Shortly after the Second World War, he began to conduct a semiannual survey of business and academic economists. Their forecasts of economic activity have been published regularly in Livingston's newspaper column, which appears in the Philadelphia *Bulletin*. (However, the data used here were compiled from the actual responses, which were made available by Livingston.) Among other measures of economic conditions, the survey has requested forecasts of the BLS consumer price index (CPI) and wholesale price index (WPI) at six-, twelve-, and sometimes eighteen-month horizons.

The Livingston data have been used in studies of the formation of price expectations (Turnovsky 1970), the effect of price expectations on wages and the Phillips curve (Turnovsky and Wachter 1972), and of Fisher-type interest rate models (Gibson 1972 and

Pyle 1972).[2] In this section, I examine and discuss some of the properties of the data. To keep things manageable, the discussion is restricted to the twelve-month expectations of the CPI. The Livingston survey requests forecasts of the price level and supplies the forecaster with a preliminary figure for two or three months prior to the survey date. As indicated above, Livingston made these figures available to me, as well as the individual responses to the surveys.

Before examining the data a few comments about the survey are in order. First, the number of responses is fairly small and variable. Second, the individuals surveyed have necessarily changed over the twenty-five-year period covered, but a number of economists have been faithful respondents for long periods of time. Third, the individuals chosen are professional economists, often intimately involved in forecasting. They are therefore likely to have more information about prices and should have greater skill in interpreting it than the general public.

Furthermore, it is not a simple matter to calculate the expected rates of inflation from the survey forecasts of the price level. Carlson (1975) has explored this issue, and his observations are worth mentioning. The difficulties can be illustrated by summarizing the survey procedure. For example, in order to prepare a late-December newspaper article Livingston distributes his survey in late November. The questionnaire includes the most recent CPI figures available at that time—originally for September, now for October. It is possible that the respondents have access to a later figure before replying. Livingston tabulates the responses and prepares his article in late December. By that time he is aware of a later CPI figure (now for November), and he often makes an ad hoc correction of the forecasts. The respondents are asked to forecast the level of the CPI for the next December, so responses are really thirteen- or fourteen-month forecasts rather than for one year.

Thus, there are different versions of expected inflation rates as derived from the Livingston survey because of, first, Livingston's adjustments of the data before they are published; and second, the choice of a base figure for calculating the expected rate of inflation. The Livingston-survey expected rates of inflation shown below are based on the following procedures: (a) forecaster responses are used without any corrections; (b) the base figure for calculating the rate of inflation is the figure provided by Livingston on the questionnaire (for a few surveys, Livingston's figure is not available, and the CPI for the month two months prior to the survey is used); (c) it is assumed that the price level forecasts are for a twelve-month horizon. If the forecasts are actually for a fourteen-month period, the rate of inflation is understated by constant proportion (one-sixth).

The one-year expectations of the rate of inflation in the CPI are shown in Table 1. There were 55 semiannual surveys from 1947 through 1973. The mean expected rate of inflation (π^L), the actual inflation rate, and the standard deviation are shown in Figure 1.

FIGURE 1 Livingston Survey: Expectations of One-Year Rate of Inflation in Consumer Price Index, Semiannually, July 1947–December 1973

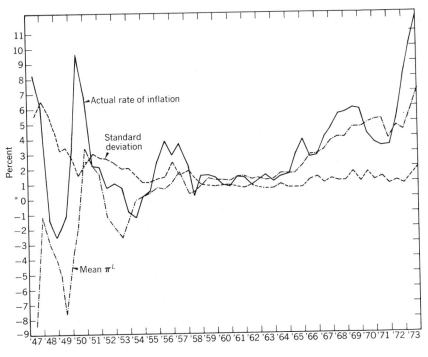

SOURCE: See Table 1.

The first thing to be noticed is the persistence of expectations of price declines from 1947 through June 1954 (except for three surveys taken during the Korean War). The stability of expectations from 1958 to 1965 is also noteworthy. As forecasts of actual inflation the mean expectations do very poorly. Actual inflation exceeds expectations in all but 16 of the 55 surveys (and two of these are due to underpredictions of the effects of the 1971 price freeze). However, it is not at all clear that expectations should, even on average, be unbiased predictors. The expectations held by individuals may well be systematically wrong.

The standard deviation of the distribution can be considered as a proxy for the dispersion of individuals' expectations. It declines throughout the early postwar period, and from 1954–1973 it is under 1.5 percent in all but six surveys. It tends to increase with π^L, but not appreciably. Thus it is not clear from these data that there is a monotonic relationship between the level and dispersion of inflationary expectations. On the other hand, there may be a relationship between the dispersion and the change in expectations. In 1956, 1966, 1967, and 1973 sharp increases in inflationary expectations were followed by a widening dispersion of expectations.

TABLE 1   Livingston Survey: Expectations of One-Year Rate of Inflation in Consumer Price Index, Semiannually, July 1947–December 1973

| Survey Date | π^L | | | | Number of Respondents | Actual Rate of Inflation |
	Mean	Standard Deviation	Skewness	Kurtosis		
7/47	−8.70	5.56	0.97	−0.24	28	8.37
2/47	−1.12	6.57	−0.79	−0.21	32	6.10
7/48	−2.86	5.72	1.34	−0.90	28	−0.42
2/48	−4.05	4.31	−0.46	0.55	32	−2.74
3/49	−5.10	3.24	−0.55	0.31	34	−2.08
7/49	−7.68	3.45	0.04	−0.37	34	−1.12
1/50	−3.99	2.75	−0.42	−0.11	34	3.52
6/50	−1.55	1.60	−0.00	−0.46	43	9.48
2/50	3.45	2.38	−0.88	−0.12	36	6.79
6/51	2.20	3.07	0.39	−0.55	42	2.20
2/51	1.56	2.77	1.80	−0.33	49	1.91
6/52	−1.13	2.72	−0.64	−0.05	44	0.76
2/52	−1.90	2.43	1.28	0.19	53	1.00
6/53	2.52	2.01	2.29	0.18	44	0.75
2/53	−1.26	2.09	0.18	0.24	52	−0.87
6/54	−0.04	1.55	1.49	0.09	48	−0.25
2/54	0.15	1.11	−0.05	−0.30	46	0.37
6/55	0.32	1.03	−0.05	−0.21	48	0.50
2/55	0.72	1.31	7.17	−1.46	51	2.48
3/56	0.67	1.45	4.85	−0.91	45	3.85
2/56	1.01	2.46	7.74	0.99	48	2.91
3/57	1.73	1.53	9.28	−2.13	52	3.59
1/58	0.27	1.80	3.54	−0.75	60	2.12

TABLE 1 (concluded)

Survey Date	π^L				Number of Respondents	Actual Rate of Inflation
	Mean	Standard Deviation	Skewness	Kurtosis		
6/58	0.38	1.30	−0.15	−0.19	58	0.23
12/58	0.93	0.93	0.58	−0.17	60	1.50
6/59	1.33	0.87	0.76	0.81	60	1.50
12/59	1.22	0.76	0.39	0.38	56	1.36
6/60	1.22	0.77	1.28	0.82	52	0.90
12/60	1.14	0.87	1.82	0.38	60	0.78
6/61	1.34	0.75	0.05	0.78	56	1.34
12/61	1.49	0.73	−0.14	0.41	62	1.33
6/62	1.24	0.87	1.39	0.38	57	0.88
12/62	1.34	0.66	2.20	0.94	62	1.21
6/63	1.23	0.57	0.65	0.45	53	1.53
12/63	1.24	0.56	0.32	0.15	58	1.19
6/64	1.54	0.88	3.11	1.33	54	1.40
12/64	1.53	0.61	2.22	0.13	57	1.71
6/65	1.53	0.70	2.37	1.42	52	2.87
12/65	2.14	0.70	0.34	0.57	63	3.79
6/66	2.80	1.15	−0.01	0.73	49	2.48
12/66	2.92	1.33	5.45	−0.91	59	2.54
6/67	3.07	0.99	−0.31	−0.03	49	4.04
12/67	3.75	1.18	3.40	−0.68	56	4.65
6/68	4.00	1.03	1.33	0.73	53	5.43
12/68	4.00	1.01	1.81	−0.04	57	5.58
6/69	4.65	1.64	5.95	1.34	42	5.98
12/69	4.62	1.00	0.04	0.07	49	5.82
6/70	4.89	1.61	−0.24	−0.64	47	4.34
12/70	5.06	1.12	1.15	0.30	49	3.64
6/71	5.12	1.28	1.17	0.80	44	3.41
12/71	3.76	0.79	−0.21	−0.01	57	3.43
6/72	4.70	1.01	0.79	0.76	47	5.15
12/72	4.40	0.78	0.46	0.23	58	7.90
6/73	5.66	1.44	−0.64	3.24	48	10.18
12/73	7.14	1.97	−0.56	1.27	52	12.01

NOTE: Rate of inflation is calculated using the base dates supplied by Livingston when available. Otherwise, the April CPI is used for summer surveys and the October CPI for winter surveys (7/47 to 12/56, 12/59, 12/62 and 12/67). It is assumed to be a twelve-month expectation from this date.

The actual rate of inflation is in each case calculated for the next twelve months from the April prior to summer surveys and the October prior to winter surveys.

The shape of the distribution fluctuates widely. In the early period it tends to be skewed negatively because of the persistence of deflationary expectations. These disappeared by the late 1950s and 1960s, and the distribution becomes peaked, narrowly dispersed, and somewhat skewed to the right. The peakedness remained in most later distributions, although a growing expectation in the late 1960s that the inflation rate would decline led to some negative skewness. The broader dispersion of the distribution in the postwar period, 1947–1950, was accompanied by negative kurtosis (fat tails).

The long-run behavior of the series is suggestive of the way in which forecasters learn from inflation. From 1947 to 1954, expectations were dominated by the lack of any comparable recent experience on which to base them and by fear of the recurrence of deflation. After the 1958 recession, however, expectations adapted rather quickly to the price stability that persisted until 1965. Since 1965, expectations have accelerated with inflation but have not been very accurate forecasts. The mean expectation has been very optimistic in forecasting declines in the inflation rate. There have been large errors in the direction of change in the rate of inflation which has been accompanied by a considerable widening in the dispersion of expectations. From the end of 1968 to the price freeze of 1971 inflationary expectations increased and the dispersion remained narrow, but the forecasted rates never reached the level of actual inflation. All in all, on the basis of this casual examination of the data, I agree substantially with Turnovsky's conclusion that there have been several distinct eras in the postwar history of inflation expectations.

NBER-ASA DATA

Another source of price expectations data, similar to the Livingston series, is the American Statistical Association–NBER survey of forecasters. Forecasts of the implicit GNP price deflator are derived from the real and nominal GNP forecasts. Participants are asked to forecast the current quarter and up to four quarters into the future. A summary of the survey is published by NBER and ASA; the individual survey responses were not readily available.

For comparison with the Livingston series, I present in Table 2 the expected rate of inflation for the next year calculated from the ASA-NBER surveys. However, the data are available for too short a period of time to be used further in this study. The level of the series is often below that of the Livingston series—more than can be accounted for by the difference between the CPI and the im-

TABLE 2   ASA-NBER Survey: Expected Annual Rate of Inflation in GNP Deflator, 1968–1974

Survey Month	Number of Forecasters	Mean	Standard Deviation	Actual Inflation in Next Year
12/68	84	2.99%	0.76%	5.01%
2/69	61	3.08	0.73	5.33
5/69	56	2.96	0.72	5.86
7/69	118	3.33	1.57	5.64
12/69	57	3.88	0.78	5.13
2/70[a]	–	3.98	–	5.35
5/70	48	3.71	2.05	4.94
7/70	53	3.33	0.76	5.00
12/70	121	3.79	1.41	4.61
2/71	53	3.61	0.70	3.50
5/71	56	3.56	0.79	3.69
7/71	74	4.04	1.70 ⎫	2.96
9/71	62	3.09	0.80 ⎭	
12/71	76	3.29	0.91	3.15
2/72	66	3.54	0.73	3.69
5/72	69	3.57	0.94	3.69
8/72	66	3.69	0.84	5.02
12/72	62	3.45	0.78	6.26
2/73	61	3.95	0.99	7.41
5/73	63	4.04	1.09	9.11
8/73	42	4.73	1.30	9.63
12/73[a]	–	5.49	–	10.54
2/74	62	5.79	1.60	11.80
5/74[a]	–	6.18	–	
8/74	53	7.25	1.45	
12/74	52	8.02	1.32	

NOTE: The expected rate of inflation at annual rates for survey quarter t is defined as $80\ (IPD^e_{t+4} - IPD^p_{t-1})/IPD^p_{t-1}$, where IPD^p_{t-1} is the value of the implicit price deflator shown in the issue of the *Survey of Current Business* of the survey month and IPD^e_{t+4} is the expected price level. In 2/69, 5/69, 7/69 and 8/74, IPD^e_{t+3} is the last forecast available.
The actual inflation rate is defined as $100\ (IPD_{t+3} - IPD_{t-1})/IPD_{t-1}$. Revised price data are used.
[a] The individual survey responses were not available, and the rate of inflation was calculated from the median expected price level shown in the ASA-NBER releases.

plicit price deflator (IPD). The series also shows a relatively constant standard deviation.

SURVEY RESEARCH CENTER DATA

A major source of price expectations data that has begun to attract the attention of reseachers in the last two years is the Survey of Consumer Finances (SCF) conducted by the Survey Research Center (SRC). It is fundamentally different from the previously mentioned data in that it is based on a survey of the general public rather than professional forecasters.[3] The SRC has included price expectations questions since the inception of the surveys in 1946.

The SRC surveys were initially annual, but throughout the 1950s at least two or three were held each year, and since the early 1960s they have been held on a quarterly basis. The form of the survey questions has changed somewhat over the years. Furthermore, up to 1966, only directional responses were obtained, but since then point estimates of inflationary expectations have been requested as well. Nevertheless, the SRC data can be used in several ways to construct long time series of inflationary expectations. Series have been analyzed by Juster and Wachtel (1972a, 1972b), Wachtel (1973), Juster (1973), de Menil and Bhalla (1975), and de Menil (1973).

Initially, the SRC survey question was: "What do you think will happen to the prices of the things you buy during the next year [for mid-year surveys: "between now and the end of the year"]—do you think they will go up or down or stay like they are now?" In 1952 the question was changed to "What do you expect prices of household items and clothing will do during the next year or so—stay where they are, go up or go down?" Finally in 1959 the phrasing was changed to: "Now speaking of prices in general, I mean the prices of the things you buy—do you think they will go up in the next year or go down or stay where they are now?" Starting in 1966, respondents expecting price increases were asked, "How large a price increase do you expect? Of course, nobody can know for sure, but would you say that a year from now prices will be about 1 or 2 percent higher or 5 percent or closer to 10 percent than now or what?" These point estimates are not very reliable because respondents tend to agree with one of the suggested answers.

Two basic approaches have been used in the studies noted earlier to construct consistent time series for the expected rate of inflation.

Juster and Wachtel (1972a, 1972b) present a series that is based on the point estimates of the size of expected price increases since 1966. Median values were assigned to each class as presented in the SCF tables. The mean expected increase was used for those who did not know how much of an increase was expected; and zero, for those who expected prices to remain the same or go down, and for don't-know responses. The series was then linked to the pre-1966 data by using the difference between the percentages expecting increases and expecting decreases. Series based on other linking procedures can be found in de Menil and Bhalla and in Juster. The various series differ before 1966 because two basically different types of data are being linked. Therefore, only the post-1966 point estimates are used in this study. The series is shown in Table 3 and is called π^S

TABLE 3 SRC Price Expectations Data, Quarterly, 1946–1967 (percent)

Survey Date	π^S	π^N	σ^N	Actual Inflation in CPI 12 Mos. After Survey Date
1946I		3.83	2.51	
1947I		−2.99	2.81	6.85
1947III		0.23	2.78	9.76
1948I		0.46	3.18	1.71
1948III		2.26	2.64	−2.87
1949I		−4.12	2.61	−1.12
1949III		−2.43	1.75	1.55
1950I		−1.60	2.06	9.49
1951I		5.65	2.28	1.94
1952I		3.03	1.93	1.02
1952IV		−1.16	1.75	0.62
1953I		−0.78	1.77	1.13
1953III		−0.62	1.98	−0.37
1954I		−1.13	1.87	−0.50
1954II		−0.90	1.91	−0.74
1954IV		−1.04	1.99	0.37
1955II		0.43	2.01	1.62
1955IV		1.03	2.09	2.48
1956II		1.63	2.19	3.58
1956IV		2.10	2.02	3.15

TABLE 3 (continued)

Survey Date	π^S	π^N	σ^N	Actual Inflation in CPI in 12 Mos. After Survey Date
1957II		1.53	2.62	2.85
1957IV		1.89	2.83	1.82
1958II		0.53	2.56	0.52
1958IV		1.86	2.33	1.50
1959I		2.15	2.24	1.39
1959II		2.67	2.43	1.72
1959IV		2.99	2.43	1.42
1960I		3.20	2.59	1.54
1960II		2.71	2.60	0.90
1961I		2.29	2.59	0.79
1961II		2.06	2.09	1.29
1961IV		2.07	1.96	1.33
1962I		2.21	2.00	1.27
1962II		2.07	1.96	0.88
1962III		1.79	1.91	1.54
1962IV		2.05	1.95	1.32
1963I		2.74	2.15	1.54
1963II		2.36	1.96	1.53
1963III		2.25	1.89	0.98
1963IV		1.97	1.59	1.30
1964I		2.58	2.08	1.14
1964II		2.32	1.55	1.78
1965I		2.62	1.69	1.92
1965III		2.56	1.66	3.49
1965IV		2.56	1.88	3.58
1966I		4.24	2.37	2.81
1966II	2.74	3.39	2.48	2.69
1966III	3.33	4.91	3.01	2.66
1966IV	a	3.09	2.52	2.84
1967I	2.91	3.75	2.44	3.65
1967II		4.28	2.38	4.02
1967III	3.12	4.00	2.26	4.28
1967IV	3.44	5.02	2.70	4.74
1968II	3.32	4.00	2.26	5.42
1968III	3.47	4.61	2.53	5.63
1968IV	2.99	3.06	2.11	5.93
1969I	3.07	4.03	2.81	6.35
1969II	3.73	5.92	3.50	6.15
1969III	3.74	4.56	2.84	5.63

TABLE 3 (concluded)

Survey Date	π^S	π^N	σ^N	Actual Inflation in CPI in 12 Mos. After Survey Date
1969IV	2.80	3.54	2.94	5.71
1970I	3.53	4.13	2.91	4.83
1970II	3.73	4.65	3.43	4.37
1970III	3.06	3.51	2.94	4.45
1970IV	3.47	4.10	2.90	3.55
1971I	3.50	4.41	3.27	3.69
1971II	3.25	4.09	3.09	3.23
1971III	2.39	1.93	1.99	2.95
1971IV	2.41	2.02	1.92	3.47
1972I	3.04	2.50	1.84	3.88
1972II	2.42	1.90	2.16	5.45
1972III	2.77	2.45	2.13	7.42
1972IV	2.85	2.67	2.10	7.90
1973I	4.19	4.78	3.47	10.03
1973II	3.93	3.02	2.63	10.72
1973III	4.54	3.63	3.53	10.96
1973IV	3.61	2.46	2.69	12.01
1974I	5.44	4.52	2.83	11.10
1974II	4.96	4.29	3.40	9.48
1974III	4.97	3.55	2.57	8.22

NOTE: π^S = Juster-Wachtel series; π^N = SRC data based on normality assumption; σ^N = standard deviation of π^N

[a]Not available; question not asked.

The behavior of π^S from 1966 to 1973 is similar to that of the Livingston series. The forecasts of inflation are consistently too low, and there are several large and erratic declines in π^S without any corresponding decline in the actual rate. In addition, expectations are fairly slow to change. In only 6 of the 34 surveys (1966II–1974III) do expectations increase by 0.5 percent. Examination of the series suggests that expectations can be viewed as extrapolations of a very optimistic perception of current experience. For example, when current economic conditions and policy are perceived to be anti-inflationary, expectations, if not inflation itself, do moderate.

An alternative procedure for constructing a series on inflationary

expectations is to use only the qualitative survey data—the proportion of survey respondents who expect prices to go up, down, or
remain the same. The procedure has been used by Shuford (1970),
by Carlson and Parkin (1975), employing British data from a similar
survey question, and by de Menil (1973). Very briefly, if we assume
that the distribution of expectations among respondents can be described by a two-parameter distribution, the proportions of respondents who assume, respectively, that prices will go up and that
they will go down are sufficient information to identify those
parameters. This is illustrated with a normal distribution in Figure
2. To solve for the mean and standard deviation μ and σ, we need to

FIGURE 2

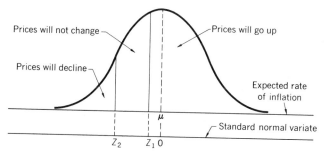

assume the shape of the distribution and the bounds of the
remain-the-same category.[4] Nonresponses can either be ignored or
allocated among the three relevant groups (see Carlson and Parkin
for an elaborate allocation procedure). The bounds of the
nonresponse category can either be chosen arbitrarily or chosen to
scale the resultant expectations series in any way (for example, so
that on average expectations equal actual inflation).

The formal procedure used will be outlined very quickly. Nonresponses were ignored, with the result that the areas in Figure 2
represent proportions of those responding and sum to 100 percent.
Those proportions identify points z_1 and z_2 on the standard normal
variate. Those points are the bounds of the remain-the-same category (unperceived price change) and are assumed to correspond to
± 1.25 percent. The relationship between those points on the standard normal variate and on the expected inflation rate variable is
given by two equations: $z_i = (k_i - \mu)/\sigma$, where $i = 1, 2$ and $k_1 = 1.25$,
$k_2 = -1.25$. They can be easily solved for the mean and standard
deviation of the distribution of expectations:

$$\mu = \frac{1.25(z_2 + z_1)}{z_2 - z_1} \text{ and } \sigma = \frac{2(1.25)}{z_1 - z_2}$$

It is clear from the above that since the bounds of the don't-know category are assumed to be symmetrical, they enter as a scale factor only. The series estimated in this way are shown in Table 3 (π^N and σ^N for the mean and standard deviation, respectively) and plotted in Figure 3. As noted earlier the phrasing of the survey question

FIGURE 3 SRC Price Expectations Data, Quarterly, 1946–1967

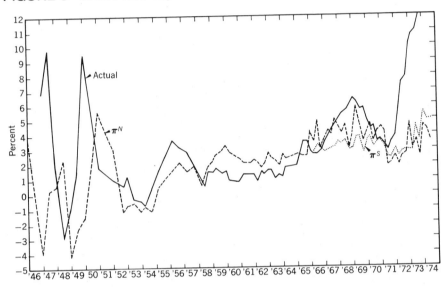

SOURCE: See Table 3.

changed twice. In both cases there are overlaps for which interpolations can be made to obtain two values for a few quarters, and these are used to make a level adjustment.

The normality assumption is useful because it is a two-parameter distribution but it also imposes a rather rigid form on the distribution. My analysis of the actual distribution of responses to the Livingston survey suggests that the distribution is probably not symmetric. The log-normal distribution is therefore used as an alternative.

If x is inflationary expectations in percentages, it is assumed that $(100 + x)$ is log-normal or that $y = \log(100 + x)$ is normally distributed. As before, we can solve for the mean and standard deviation of y. It can be shown (see Naylor et al. 1966) that

$$\mu_x = [\exp(\mu_y + \sigma_y^2)] - 100$$

$$\sigma_x^2 = (\mu_x + 100)^2 [\exp(\sigma_y^2) - 1]$$

Although the series based on the log-normal distribution is very close to the one based on the normality assumption, the former did marginally better in most of the tests run. (The mean of the log-normal series is called π^O and the standard deviation is designated σ^O.)

The expectations data based on the SRC surveys exhibit some characteristics which differ from those of the Livingston series. Expectations of deflation are not as strong in the postwar period, although the expectations series do change erratically. Furthermore, π^N exceeds the actual rate of inflation in the late 1950s.[5] Throughout the 1960s the expected inflation rate based on the normality assumption keeps pace with the actual inflation rate, while π^S lags behind. More recently, both series indicate expectations of more moderate inflation in the recession of 1969. However, these were reversed by the time inflation actually did moderate (prior to the price freeze). The effect of the freeze was overestimated and the current acceleration of inflation completely unpredicted.

FORECAST PERFORMANCE OF EXPECTATIONS

Some simple tests of the predictive accuracy of the various expectations series are shown in Table 4. For these and other tests linear interpolations of the expectations series are used to provide complete series. The forecast test is very simply the regression of the actual inflation rate on the expected rate: $p = \alpha + \beta\pi + u$. Forecasts are unbiased if $\hat{\alpha} = 0$ and $\hat{\beta} = 1$. This is the same as saying that Muth's rational expectations hypothesis holds because rationality is defined by: $p = \pi + \epsilon$.

The equations for π^S show that expectations of inflation derived from the direct responses to the SRC surveys have been a very poor predictor of inflation. However, when the postfreeze period is excluded, the forecasts are not obviously biased, although the relationship disintegrates. The next set of equations tests the forecast reliability of the Livingston series, which is found consistently to underestimate price change. The third set, for π^O, indicates that the behavior of the series is extremely erratic in the various subperiods shown. It is interesting, however, that both the Livingston and SRC data can support the rationality of forecasts hypotheses when the test is restricted to one particular period.[6] It is this particular result that is used by de Menil to argue that expectations are unbiased.

That result is only true of a peculiar time period that spans the relative price stability of the post-Korean War phase and the Vietnam era of price acceleration. The evidence here lends support to the idea that the nature of price expectations changes profoundly from one era to another.

TABLE 4 Forecast Tests of Inflationary Expectations Data (figures in parentheses are standard errors)

	α	β	$\bar{R}^2$	DW	SE
SRC price expectations series (π^S)					
1966II–1973III	−2.96	2.53	.2922	.51	1.91
	(2.31)	(0.70)			
1966II–1971II	1.46	0.92	.0082	.32	1.15
	(2.81)	(0.85)			
Livingston series (π^L)					
1948I–1973IV	2.05	0.57	.2976	.20	2.33
	(0.26)	(0.09)			
1957I–1973IV	−0.16	1.32	.7386	.16	1.34
	(0.30)	(0.10)			
1965I–1973IV	−0.68	1.44	.5089	.14	1.77
	(0.99)	(0.24)			
1957I–1971II	0.46	0.96	.7350	.23	0.86
	(0.21)	(0.08)			
SRC series with log-normal assumption (π^0)					
1948I–1973III	1.47	0.60	.1963	.24	2.36
	(0.34)	(0.12)			
1948I–1955IV	1.46	0.28	.0245	.33	2.85
	(0.51)	(0.21)			
1956I–1973III	0.19	1.06	.2655	.23	2.01
	(0.65)	(0.21)			
1948I–1964IV	1.35	0.21	.0232	.30	2.04
	(0.30)	(0.13)			
1965I–1973III	4.08	0.22	−.0191	.09	2.27
	(1.44)	(0.37)			

NOTE: $\bar{R}^2$ = coefficient of multiple determination adjusted for degrees of freedom; DW = Durbin-Watson statistics; SE = standard error. Actual inflation is defined as $100[CPI(t + 4) - CPI]/CPI$, where CPI is the average value in the quarter. For further explanation, see text.

PRICE EXPECTATIONS AND CONSUMPTION BEHAVIOR[7]

The simplistic view that consumer behavior is neutral with respect to price change has been followed in most econometric studies of consumption. Exceptions include the Branson-Klevorick (BK) study of the money illusion phenomenon and the Juster-Wachtel (1972b) savings rate forecasts. I use the BK framework to analyze the effect of price movements on consumption and to present some evidence based on recent experience. I reached two conclusions: first, in the last eight years, consumers have learned to perceive price changes; and second, consumers react to inflationary expectations by holding back on their expenditures.[8]

There are three ways in which movements in the price level and price expectations can directly effect consumption behavior— money illusion or incorrect price perceptions, intertemporal substitution in consumption patterns, and uncertainty caused by expectations of inflation. Tests for the presence of each of these effects can be specified because the survey data on inflationary expectations are a source of information that is not solely dependent on past prices. For this reason, consumption effects based on price perceptions of past price movements can be distinguished from purely expectational effects. As will be shown, uncertainty resulting from inflationary expectations will cause a permanent decline in consumption; money illusion implies a permanent increase; and intertemporal substitutions imply a temporary increase.

Money illusion in the consumption function arises because the consumer may not perceive, in exactly the same way, changes in real income or wealth stemming from changes in nominal income or emanating from changes in prices. Money illusion can be defined as a tendency to overlook price change. If prices rise and the consumer does not perceive the increase, then he will think that real income is higher than it actually is and consume more than he otherwise would. The implication of this argument is:

$$\frac{d\frac{C}{\rho}}{d\rho}\Bigg|_{\frac{Y}{\rho},\frac{W}{\rho}} > 0$$

where ρ is the price level, and C, Y, and W are respectively nominal consumption, income, and wealth. One point that should be noted is that the money illusion response is not based on price expectations but on perceptions of the existing price level. It requires some consumer ignorance of changes in the price level. We are led to ask, therefore, whether it is reasonable to expect consumers to be ignorant. The answer is affirmative because information about the price level is costly to obtain and difficult to interpret. Information on nominal income and wealth, however, is readily available. It is easy to imagine a situation of moderate price change where the disutility of incorrect price perceptions is relatively small, and it might not pay at all to attempt to gather improved information. However, in time of rapid or large price change the disutility of an incorrectly perceived price level is much larger. In that case, consumers would spend more time and resources in collecting price information. This may or may not enable them to forecast future prices, but it will provide them with better current price information. As a consequence, we would expect less money illusion in inflationary times.

Intertemporal substitution in the pattern of consumption is often suggested as the major consequence of inflation. Simply put, when price increases are expected, purchase plans are advanced. The potential for such intertemporal substitution is limited because for each inflation rate there is an optimal level of inventories of consumption goods. Thus, unless inflation accelerates, consumers will not increase their stocks of goods. There have been very few instances of this type of buying activity in this country.

The third and final possible reaction to price change is the uncertainty effect.[9] We will argue that inflation is a major cause of real-income uncertainty and therefore leads to more saving. Sandmo (1970) demonstrates formally that uncertainty about future income leads to more saving by risk-averse consumers. A higher rate of inflation leads to more real-income uncertainty if the dispersion (variance) of inflationary expectations increases with the rate of inflation. Alternatively, in a society that has difficulty in making adjustments to inflation, an increase in the rate of inflation represents a shift in the state of the world. At a higher rate of inflation there is an overall increase in uncertainty and anxiety. In the face of these attitudes—which should be reflected in an individual's subjective probability distribution of expectations, but not necessarily in the distribution across individuals[10]—the logical response is to build up precautionary balances and to avoid expenditure commitments.

The above hypotheses are tested by estimating the BK version of the life-cycle consumption model with an inflation rate variable:

$$C = \alpha_0 Y^{\beta_1} W^{\beta_2} \rho^{\beta_3} \pi^{\beta_4}$$

Almon lags are used on Y and ρ but not W or π. The price level coefficient can, depending on the shape of the lag distribution, indicate the presence of either money illusion or intertemporal substitutions. π, the expected rate of inflation, which is not found in the BK study, is used to test for the presence of the uncertainty effect; the empirical series used is π^N. The price level (ρ) is the CPI. The real income, wealth, and consumption data are per capita values from the FRB-MIT econometric model data bank.

In Table 5 results are presented for two estimation periods. The Almon lag specifications are the same as those used by BK. The results in the first column correspond rather closely to the preferred BK result. The distributed lag coefficients on the price level are positive (except for a small negative coefficient in the last lag), suggesting a significant degree of money illusion. As the results in the second column indicate, there is little evidence of any uncertainty effect in this period. The coefficient on π^N is negative but not significantly different from zero. These results are not at all surprising. The earlier period was one of unusually stable prices. Consequently, there was little incentive to use resources to obtain price information; in times of stable prices ignorance costs little.

The second set of equations presents the same specification for 1965–1973. The distributed lag on the price level is, in this case,

TABLE 5 Consumption Function Estimates
(figures in parentheses are t statistics)

	1957I–1965IV		1965IV–1973III	
	(1)	(2)	(3)	(4)
Constant	−1.7888	−1.7752	−0.6941	−0.4787
	(9.8)	(9.2)	(4.3)	(2.8)
W	0.1377	0.1477	0.1546	0.1410
	(3.0)	(2.3)	(6.3)	(6.1)
$\Sigma w_i Y_i$	0.5818	0.5756	0.6960	0.7623
	(10.3)	(9.1)	(9.7)	(10.7)
$\Sigma w_i \rho_i$	0.3730	0.3660	0.1020	0.0512
	(6.7)	(5.7)	(2.3)	(1.1)
π^N		−0.0008		−0.0066
		(0.2)		(2.4)
R^2	0.9983	0.9983	0.9987	0.9989
SE	0.00282	0.00287	0.00292	0.00266
DW	2.07	2.05	1.69	1.81

more suggestive of intertemporal substitution than of money illusion. The first three lag coefficients are positive and sum to 0.5009, the succeeding three are negative and sum to -0.6712, and the last is positive. Thus, the initial response to a price increase is a rise in real consumption which is followed by a decline of about the same magnitude later on. The sum of the lag coefficients is positive and more than twice its standard error, suggesting that some money illusion remains after the intertemporal substitutions. However, the amount of money illusion in the later period is only 27 percent of the amount in the earlier one.

When π^N is added to the equation, the sum of the lag coefficients on the price variable is not significantly different from zero. There is no evidence of money illusion, but the lag distribution does suggest that there are intertemporal substitutions. In addition there is strong evidence of an uncertainty effect, that is, consumption declines significantly when the expected rate of inflation increases.

The magnitude of the uncertainty effect is rather small. If the expected rate of inflation increases from 4 to 5 percent (by 25 percent), then real per capita consumption decreases by 0.17 percent. The estimates of money illusion in the early period are, on the other hand, fairly large; a 1 percent price increase leads to an increase of 0.37 percent in consumption.

The combined effect on consumption of money illusion, intertemporal substitution, and uncertainty effects leaves unsettled the question of how prices and price expectations have affected consumption behavior in the past decade. We can examine this question by showing a breakdown of the relative size of the two price effects. We take the log of the BK function above and obtain first differences, with the following result (showing the effects of the variables with distributed lags schematically)

$$\Delta \ln C = \beta_1 \Delta \ln Y + \beta_2 \Delta \ln W + \beta_3 \Delta \ln \rho + \beta_4 \Delta \ln \pi^N$$

The dependent variable is approximately the percent change in predicted real per capita consumption, and the terms on the right-hand side represent the contributions of Y, W, ρ, and π to the prediction. Table 6 shows the percent change in real per capita consumption and the predicted changes due to the effects of price level and inflationary expectations as calculated from the estimates in the last column of Table 5.

The price level effects are positive in most of the quarters since 1966, indicating the presence of some money illusion. As inflation moderates, the lagged negative weights balance out the early positive ones. Large price increases in early 1973, along with those of

1967–1968, led to positive price level effects. When inflation moderated in 1970–1972, the intertemporal substitutions led to negative price level effects.

The expected inflation or uncertainty effects are somewhat erratic because the series itself has many seemingly random

TABLE 6 Contribution of Prices and Inflationary Expectations to Changes in Consumption, Quarterly, 1966–1973 (percent)

	Predicted Change in Real per Capita Consumption	Predicted π Effect	Predicted Price Level Effect
1966II	0.50	−.33	.20
III	0.39	.15	.19
IV	0.47	−.25	.19
1967I	0.75	.31	−.11
II	0.71	−.13	−.23
III	0.73	−.08	.01
IV	0.70	.04	.18
1968I	1.13	−.15	.29
II	1.33	.07	.24
III	0.66	.08	.09
IV	0.61	−.09	.13
1969I	0.71	.27	.13
II	0.47	−.19	.17
III	0.50	−.25	.19
IV	0.40	.17	.16
1970I	0.59	.17	.12
II	0.69	−.10	.07
III	0.71	−.08	−.05
IV	0.48	.19	.05
1971I	0.56	−.10	−.14
II	0.58	−.04	−.13
III	0.22	.05	−.04
IV	0.45	.49	−.04
1972I	1.24	−.03	−.08
II	1.48	−.14	.01
III	0.91	.18	−.01
IV	1.54	−.17	.16
1973I	0.99	−.05	.26
II	0.68	−.39	.43
III	1.01	.31	.59

changes. The effects are negative in only seventeen of thirty quarters because the expected rate of inflation has not increased monotonically. These effects are fairly small—rarely more than 0.2 percent while predicted consumption increases by almost 1 percent per quarter. Finally, it is not uncommon (sixteen out of thirty quarters) for the two price effects to be operating in opposite directions. These results suggest that the relationship between price behavior and consumption is fairly complex and deserving of more study.

EXPECTATIONS AND PRICE CHANGE

Inflationary expectations are likely to affect the actual rate of inflation because they will affect the behavior of price setters throughout the economy. Most prices are less than perfectly and continuously flexible, as they are either set by contract or imply real costs when changes take place (e.g., new catalogues and price labels). Thus, expectations of future inflation will affect current price-setting behavior. The higher the expected rate of inflation, the larger will be the price adjustments made and consequently the higher will be the actual rate of inflation, that is, price changes will reflect anticipated costs and overall expectations of future inflation, as well as current supply and demand conditions. When decision makers throughout the economy expect future inflation, their expectation will be reflected in a higher observed rate of inflation. A similar argument can be made in terms of the variability of the expected rate of inflation. When there is a great deal of uncertainty about future prices, decision makers may move their price increases forward because pricing errors may entail large costs.

Most previous discussions of the effect of inflationary expectations on inflation (e.g., Solow 1969 and Eckstein and Brinner 1972) have been in the overall context of the Phillips-curve trade-off and Friedman's expectations hypothesis. In my discussion here, I have relied implicitly on a similar argument to explain why inflationary expectations will be passed through to the actual rate of inflation. The hypothesis is tested in the context of a price inflation equation that draws upon the current state of the art. The framework is taken, with some modifications, from de Menil (1974), who specifies a single-equation model without any price expectations influence. The above discussion suggests that the inflation rate should, in addition, vary with inflationary expectations. This is the case, as my expectations measures do add to the explanatory power of the model.

The price equation is given by:

$$\Delta \ln P = \alpha_0 + \alpha_1 T + \alpha_2 UC + \alpha_3 \ln Q + \alpha_4 (\ln P_{t-1} - \ln W) + \alpha_5 \pi_{t-1} + u$$

where

P = implicit price deflator for private nonfarm business sector
$\Delta \ln P$ = rate of change in P
T = time trend
UC = trend-adjusted ratio of unfilled orders to capacity (series by Gordon 1971, p. 155; later dates were supplied by Gordon)
Q = output per man-hour for private nonfarm sector
W = compensation per man-hour for private nonfarm sector
π = expected rate of inflation

The expected signs of the coefficients are: $\alpha_1, \alpha_3, \alpha_4 < 0$; $\alpha_2, \alpha_5 > 0$. The rationale for the model will be presented very briefly, as our main interest is in the role of the price expectations variable. The time trend is included to represent the influence of the trend in productivity on price changes. The ratio of unfilled orders to capacity is a short-run demand pressure variable. Current labor productivity enters the de Menil model because it is a determinant of marginal costs in his vintage production model. The major determinant of marginal costs is, of course, the wage rate, which enters with a positive coefficient. To reduce collinearity, the coefficient of W is constrained to be of the same absolute value as that of the lagged price level. The latter is included because lagged adjustments to the optimal price level are expected.

Estimates of the price equation are shown in Table 7. The estimation period, 1955I–1973II, extends four and a half years beyond the estimation period used by de Menil. Nevertheless, the coefficient estimates are remarkably similar to his except for α_3, which is sensitive to the presence of his variable for average age of machinery, which I omit from my specification because data are not available. Thus, equation 1 essentially reproduces the de Menil results. Lagged price expectations are added to the model in equation 2. π^0 is lagged one period to avoid any simultaneity bias. The expectations coefficient is significantly positive, and the other coefficients of the model are essentially unchanged.

In Solow's 1969 lectures at the University of Manchester, he also discusses the effects of price expectations on price change. He uses the familiar adaptive expectations hypothesis to generate price expectations and estimates his price equation for the period 1948–1966. I have not used his specification because the estimates de-

TABLE 7 Price Equations
(figures in parentheses are t statistics)

	1955I–1973II				1955I–1964IV	1965I–1973II
	(1)	(2)	(3)	(4)	(5)	(6)
Constant	.3951	.3656	.3194	.4395	.2348	.8182
	(5.9)	(5.5)	(3.8)	(4.5)	(1.0)	(4.5)
T	-.0004	-.00072	-.00052	-.00066	-.0011	-.0012
	(2.2)	(3.1)	(2.6)	(2.8)	(2.4)	(2.2)
UC	.0176	.0124	.0163	.0152	.0125	.0042
	(6.3)	(3.5)	(5.6)	(3.4)	(2.0)	(0.5)
$\ln Q$	-.0791	-.0682	-.0620	-.0853	-.0348	-.1561
	(5.2)	(4.4)	(3.3)	(3.8)	(0.7)	(4.6)
$\ln P_{t-1} - \ln W$	-.1404	-.1661	-.1349	-.1751	-.1951	-.2912
	(5.5)	(6.1)	(5.3)	(2.3)	(1.9)	(3.5)
π^o_{t-1}		.3302		.3320	.3678	.3421
		(2.3)		(2.3)	(1.0)	(1.8)
$(\bar{\sigma}^o)^2$			.0920			
			(1.5)			
π^X				-.1618		
				(1.0)		
$\bar{R}^2$	0.6924	0.7097	0.6981	0.7101	0.6462	0.6735
SE	0.00222	0.00216	0.00220	0.00216	0.00193	0.00810
DW	2.11	2.19	2.21	2.03	2.33	2.20

Average absolute residuals

1966II–1971II	.00158	.00155
1971III–1973II	.00238	.00203

NOTE: $(\bar{\sigma}^o)^2 = (1/2)[(\sigma^o_{t-1})^2 + (\sigma^o_{t-2})^2]$; $\pi^X = 0.4 \, \Delta \ln P_{t-1} + 0.3 \, \Delta \ln P_{t-2} + 0.2 \Delta \ln P_{t-3} + 0.1 \Delta \ln P_{t-4}$. Other variables are defined in text.

teriorate when the period of fit is extended. However, his preferred equation has a coefficient on the expectations variable of 0.4029, fairly close to my estimate of 0.3302.

The de Menil model[11] is specified as a partial adjustment in $\ln P$: $\ln P = \lambda \ln P^* + (1 - \lambda) \ln P_{t-1}$, where the target price level, P^*, is given by $P^* = e^{\alpha X} P^{e\beta}$, and P^e is the expected price level and X is a vector of the other variables in the model. If P^e is defined as P_{t-1} $(1 + \pi_{t-1})$ and $\ln (1 + \pi) \approx \pi$, the reduced form can be written as the estimated form:

$$\Delta \ln P = \lambda \alpha X + \beta \lambda \pi_{t-1} - \lambda(1 - \beta) \ln P_{t-1}$$

The adjustment coefficient, λ, and the expected price effect, β, can be identified from the estimated equation: $\beta = -\alpha_5/(\alpha_4 - \alpha_5)$, and $\lambda = \alpha_5 - \alpha_4$. Using the estimates in equation 2 of Table 7, the long-run price effect, β, is found to be 0.6653, and the adjustment of prices to the expected level is fairly rapid, although it is incomplete, even in the long run.

A comparison of the survey measure of expected inflation with a more traditional measure based on past inflation is shown in equation 4. An extrapolative measure of inflationary expectations, π^X, is added to the specification. It is defined as a simple weighted average of the actual rate of inflation in the four prior quarters, with linearly declining weights. When both π^0 and π^X are included, the π^X coefficient is negative. Price expectations based on a common extrapolative hypothesis do not add to the explanation of de Menil's thoroughly specified price model. The extrapolative proxy for expectations contains no information about price determination that is not already included in the partial adjustment of prices to their target level. The survey measure of inflationary expectations does, however, add some significant new information to the model. In addition, the π^0 coefficient is remarkably stable when the period of fit is divided into a ten-year span characterized by stable prices and an eight-year inflationary span (equations 5 and 6). Similar results are obtained with the other survey measures derived from the SRC data, but the Livingston series did not enter the price equation significantly, perhaps because every other data point of π^L is an interpolation in the regression estimates.

The effect of the dispersion of expectations on price change is shown in equation 3. The variable $(\bar{\sigma}^0)^2$ is the average of the variances in the expected rate of inflation in periods $t - 1$ and $t - 2$. The coefficient is positive but not quite twice its standard error. π^0 and $(\bar{\sigma}^0)^2$ are collinear and therefore are not both included in the equation. At its peak in 1970IV, $(\bar{\sigma}^0)^2$ is 10.21, some six points higher than the values observed in the early 1960s. Thus, the increase in dispersion accounts for an increase of only 0.55 percent in the rate of inflation.

A final test of the additional information provided by the inflationary expectations variables is shown at the bottom of Table 7. Although the standard error of equation 2, with expected inflation, π^0, included, is only slightly smaller than that of equation 1, without π^0, the residuals are much smaller in the later periods. Particularly in the postfreeze period (1971III–1973II) the average absolute residual is reduced by 17 percent.

WAGE EQUATIONS

The area in which the role of price expectations has received the most attention is the determination of wages. The theoretical controversy—whether the Phillips-curve relationship between labor market conditions and wage changes shifts with price expectations—is by now familiar. It was thrust into prominence by Friedman's presidential speech (1968) and has been the subject of numerous empirical studies as well (see, for example, Perry 1970 and Gordon 1972). Wage determination has also been the testing ground for the Livingston price expectations data (Turnovsky and Wachter 1972) and for the SRC series (de Menil and Bhalla 1975).

The Turnovsky-Wachter article uses the Livingston data on wage and price expectations in several variations of the Phillips relationship augmented by the "expectations hypothesis." Their period of fit is 1949–1969. They find that there is a significant expectations effect on wage inflation and also an error adjustment or catch-up effect. The de Menil paper provides a more rigorous test of the survey data. De Menil takes three wage equations from the literature, each of which has a more elaborate specification than the Phillips curve and a distributed lag specification for the formation of price expectations, and adds the SRC-based survey data as an alternative expectations variable. He finds that the initial specification can be improved upon with the survey data, especially when it is used in the form of a catch-up variable.

In this section similar results are presented with the period of fit extended to include the freeze and postfreeze period through 1973II. It is difficult to determine wage movements over this period and indeed the standard specifications (see Perry 1970 and Gordon

1971) used by de Menil do not hold up. I was unable to find an entirely satisfactory specification based on the standard determinants for wages. Nevertheless, some results using two standard specifications are shown.

First, a standard Phillips-type relationship is shown:

$$\Delta \ln W = \alpha_0 + \alpha_1 U^{-1} + \alpha_2 U_{t-1}^{-1} + \alpha_3 DG + \alpha_4 \Delta \ln SS + \alpha_5 \pi_{t-1} + u$$

where variables not defined in the previous section are

U = standard unemployment rate
DG = dummy variable for the wage-price guideposts: 1962I = 0.25, 1962II = 0.50, 1962III = 0.75; 1962IV–1966IV = 1.0; 1967I = 0.75, 1967II = 0.50, 1967III = 0.25
SS = $1/[1 - 0.5\,(SIN/WY)]$
SIN = contributions for social insurance
WY = wage and salary income

The alternative specification is based primarily on productivity[12] rather than labor market demand (unemployment):

$$\Delta \ln W = \beta_0 + \beta_1 \ln QT + \beta_2 DG + \beta_3 \Delta \ln SS + \beta_4 \pi_{t-1} + u$$

where QT = ratio of output per manhour (Q) to its trend (estimated by $\hat{Q} = 67.15 + 0.5812T$). Both specifications include a dummy variable to reflect the effect of the wage-price guideposts of the Kennedy-Johnson years. Most of the coefficients are significant, indicating that the guideposts reduced wage inflation by perhaps as much as 1.5 percent. Also included is a variable used by Gordon that is designed to reflect the incidence of changes in social security taxes. The coefficients are consistently close to unity, indicating the complete passthrough of payroll taxes to the wage earner.

Estimates of the unemployment rate model are shown in Table 8 and of the productivity model in Table 9. For the whole period of fit both the survey variable (π^o) and the extrapolative formulation (π^x) enter with significant coefficients below 1.0. In the productivity model π^o provides the better fit, and in the unemployment model π^x provides the better fit. However, it is interesting to note that π^o and π^x seem to embody distinctly independent pieces of information, both of which are relevant to wage inflation. This is indicated by the results shown in the third column of each table, which includes both π^o and π^x; both variables enter significantly. In addition, the sum of the two coefficients is very close to 1.0. This suggests that in a long-run static equilibrium situation (where $\pi^o = \pi^x$ because prices have been changing at a constant rate which is perceived) the expectations hypothesis may in fact be justified.

TABLE 8 Wage Equations: Unemployment Rate Model
(figures in parentheses are t statistics)

	1955I–1973II				1955I–1964IV	1965I–1973II
	(1)	(2)	(3)	(4)	(5)	(6)
Constant	0.0042	.0047	0.0047	0.0024	.0069	0.1249
	(1.9)	(2.1)	(2.1)	(0.9)	(1.4)	(3.1)
U^{-1}	0.0920	.1206	0.1183	0.1111	.1010	0.0380
	(2.6)	(3.3)	(3.3)	(2.9)	(2.2)	(0.5)
U_{t-1}^{-1}	−0.0688	−.1067	−0.1090	−0.0861	−.0958	−0.0431
	(1.9)	(2.7)	(2.9)	(2.2)	(1.8)	(0.6)
DG	−0.0031	−.0002	−0.0012	−0.0023	.0013	−0.0054
	(2.8)	(0.2)	(0.9)	(1.8)	(0.8)	(2.8)
$\Delta \ln SS$	1.0586	.9892	1.0297	1.0966	.6134	1.1489
	(3.8)	(3.6)	(2.7)	(4.0)	(1.1)	(4.0)
π_{t-1}^{0}	0.6108		0.3979	0.4413	−.1410	0.7860
	(3.9)		(2.7)	(2.2)	(0.4)	(2.3)
π^{x}		.8191	0.5796		.6820	−0.2700
		(4.2)	(2.7)		(1.7)	(0.7)
$(\bar{\sigma}^{o})^{2}$				0.1648		
				(1.3)		
$\bar{R}^{2}$	0.4141	0.4272	0.4633	0.4207	0.1835	0.4594
SE	0.00390	0.00385	0.00373	0.00387	0.00371	0.00343
DW	1.66	1.88	1.91	1.91	1.91	2.30

Average absolute residuals

1966II–1971III	.00264	.00282	.00253
1971III–1973II	.00330	.00334	.00341

NOTE: Variables are defined in text and in note to Table 7.

TABLE 9 Wage Equations: Productivity Model
(figures in parentheses are t statistics)

| | 1955I–1973II | | | 1955I–1964IV | 1965I–1973II |
	(1)	(2)	(3)	(4)	(5)
Constant	0.0086	.0082	0.0072	.0062	0.0123
	(8.5)	(7.1)	(6.4)	(2.8)	(3.4)
$\ln QT$	0.1073	.0972	0.1043	.1243	0.0662
	(4.5)	(4.0)	(4.6)	(2.2)	(0.1)
DG	-0.0036	-.0007	-0.0021	-.0010	-0.0056
	(3.5)	(0.6)	(4.6)	(0.5)	(2.8)
$\Delta \ln SS$	1.0004	.9751	1.0074	.9266	1.1521
	(3.9)	(3.7)	(1.8)	(0.5)	(2.8)
π_{t-1}^{o}	0.7317		0.5056	.6200	0.7637
	(5.7)		(4.1)	(1.7)	(3.9)
π^{x}		.7635	0.4137	.5136	-0.3649
		(5.1)	(3.2)	(1.1)	(2.5)
			(2.3)	(2.0)	(0.8)
$\bar{R}^2$	.4923	.4588	.5231	.2035	.4693
SE	.00363	.00374	.00351	.00367	.00340
DW	1.80	1.90	1.99	1.81	2.39

Average absolute residuals

	(1)	(2)	(3)		
1966I–1971III	.00270	.00294	.00269		
1971III–1973II	.00250	.00284	.00286		

NOTE: Variables are defined in text and in note to Table 7.

When the period of fit is divided into an early one of fairly stable prices and a later one of inflation, the coefficients of the price expectations variables change. In the early period π^x dominates and in the later one, π^0. The additional information contained in the survey measures of expected inflation is particularly important in the recent past. This can be seen by comparing the average absolute residuals of the different specifications for the Vietnam War and postfreeze periods shown in each table.

The above estimates all utilize π^0. The other survey measures of inflationary expectations series yield similar results. Virtually identical results are obtained with the Livingston series, π^L, in both specifications of the wage equation (π^L did not enter the price equation significantly). The wage equations do not provide a very good explanation of wage behavior in the period for which the SRC data provide direct point estimates. The direct series, π^S, does about as well as π^0 in equations for the post-1966 period and both are clearly preferred to π^x.

Although the models of the wage formation process shown here may not be entirely satisfactory, the results for the inflationary expectations variables are very revealing. In both specifications of the wage equation, the extrapolative measure of expectations and the survey measure appear to provide virtually independent information about price expectations which is relevant to wage behavior. However, in the period of relative price stability, the extrapolative measure is an adequate proxy for actual expectations. In the later period it adds no information not included in the survey measure.

INTEREST RATES

The relationship between price expectations and the interest rate (R) has been widely studied, usually in the context of the Fisher equation: $R = \alpha + \beta \pi$. This approach has been justifiably criticized because no attempt is made to explain changes in the real interest rate due to either structural changes in the economy, which alter the real rate of return, or shifts in the supply and demand of particular financial assets. Nevertheless, I will use the Fisher equation to estimate the effect of expectations on short-term interest rates. Several investigators have extensively explored distributed lag proxies for expectations in the Fisher equation (e.g., Yohe and Karnosky 1969) and the Livingston survey measure of expected inflation (Gibson 1972 and Pyle 1972). Another look at the relationship between price expectations and interest rates is warranted because the possibility that the relationship might be more complex than indicated by the Fisher equation was not explored in the previous studies.

Comparisons of the various survey measures of expected inflation and an extrapolative measure[13] are shown in Table 10. Since financial markets respond quickly to changed conditions, expectations based on the current-quarter survey are used to explain current interest rates. To keep the discussion brief the only interest rate examined here is the commercial paper rate.

For the whole period the survey measure explains more of the variance of interest rates than does the extrapolative forecast.[14] However, it is interesting to note that the standard error (SE) is substantially reduced when both are included. The evidence here strongly suggests that there are two independent types of expectational information, one based on recent experience and one that reflects the forecasts and perceptions of the public. However, the equations that divide the sample period indicate that this is only the case in the post-1965 period. In the earlier period the survey measure dominates π^x completely.

The Livingston series is superior to the SRC series in interest rate determination but inferior in the price and wage equations. This is not surprising, as the expectations of professional forecasts may very well be more important in financial markets, while expectations of the public at large are relevant to overall price and wage determination. The SRC measure based on the respondents' direct estimates is here superior as well, although the difference in the standard errors is not large.

Earlier on in my discussion I suggested that the variance of expectations in survey responses may be a measure of the uncertainty with which expectations are held. This hypothesis is tested in the equation for interest rates, with interest rates taken as reflecting a premium for uncertainty. Another hypothesis is that the effect of inflationary expectations on the interest rate depends on the dispersion of expectations, that is: $\beta = \beta_1 + \beta_2 \bar{\sigma}^2$. Both these hypotheses were tested. For the entire period both can be accepted, although the coefficient on the variance (0.20) is very large. The interaction term suggested by the second hypothesis yields reasonable coefficients, but the effects are difficult to interpret. In the early period, the effect of expectations on interest rates declines with the variance of expectations while in the later period it increases. I will not attempt to justify this difference, but I conclude that the dis-

TABLE 10 Interest Rate Equations
(figures in parentheses are t statistics)

Constant	π^O	π^X	$(\bar{\sigma}^O)^2$	$\pi^O(\bar{\sigma}^O)^2$	$\bar{R}^2$	SE	DW
			1955I–1973II				
1.69	1.02				.6110	1.02	.94
(5.9)	(10.8)						
2.76		0.71			.5275	1.12	.27
(11.9)		(9.1)					
1.56	0.71	0.40			.7228	0.86	.86
(6.4)	(7.2)	(5.5)					
1.15	0.80		0.20		.6601	0.95	.97
(7.3)	(7.3)		(3.4)				
2.12	0.43			0.07	.7031	0.89	.80
(8.0)	(2.9)			(4.8)			
2.46	0.86[a]				.7169	0.87	.40
(13.7)	(13.6)						
			1955I–1964IV				
1.87	0.76				.5602	0.47	.58
(8.5)	(7.1)						
1.86	0.76	0.01			.5484	0.48	.58
(7.9)	(7.0)	(0.1)					
2.01	0.97			−0.06	.5986	0.45	.68
(9.2)	(6.9)			(2.2)			
2.18	1.07[a]				.3423	0.57	.65
(8.2)	(4.6)						
			1965I–1973II				
3.84	0.54				.1596	1.22	.63
(4.9)	(2.7)						
2.60	0.39	0.49			.4213	1.02	.70
(3.6)	(2.3)	(3.9)					
4.41	−0.19			0.08	.4754	0.97	.53
(7.0)	(0.8)			(4.5)			
3.22	0.68[a]				.2967	1.12	.34
(4.5)	(3.9)						
			1966II–1973II				
4.45	0.42				.0849	1.25	.57
(5.0)	(1.9)						
1.97	1.29[b]				.1662	1.19	.69
(1.2)	(2.6)						

NOTE: Variables are defined in text and in note to Table 7.

[a] Variable is π^L.

[b] Variable is π^S.

tribution of expectations does affect interest rates. This relationship clearly merits further study.

CONCLUSION

Several conclusions are suggested by the wide-ranging and somewhat casual examination of survey measures of expected inflation presented here:

1. The recent inflationary experience has clearly established the necessity for better measurement of inflationary expectations. The measures available provide information about expectations that cannot be generated by the expectational hypotheses used in many econometric studies.
2. Survey measures of expectations are not necessarily a substitute for measures based on past experience, but do provide important supplementary information.
3. The dispersion of expectations varies greatly and is probably an important determinant of aggregate behavior.
4. Future work will have to include an examination of the determinants of the apparent variation in adjustments to inflationary experience.

NOTES

1. This has been forcefully stated by Gordon (1972). He points out that after World War II, expectations were based on the previous postwar deflationary experience (1919–1920), rather than the most recent experience.
2. None of the authors presented the data and there are, in fact, alternative versions. A full examination of the data is currently under way by John Carlson of Purdue University, whose comments have helped me avoid some serious errors in this section.
3. The data have been collected from a representative national sample that has included up to 3,500 respondents and has recently included about 1,500.
4. Carlson and Ryder.(1973) are critical of this procedure for two important reasons: (a) sampling variation in the survey responses can have a relatively large effect on the estimated expected rate of inflation and (b) the assumption of constant bounds for the remain-the-same category can lead to some peculiar implications. For example, if more than half the responses are that prices will go up, a shift in responses from remain-the-same to prices-will-go-down will *increase* the mean of the distribution because the variance of the distribution must increase to allow for the smaller percentage in the remain-the-same category, which has fixed boundaries. The increased dispersion shifts the mean *upward in this case.*

5. As noted earlier, the scaling of π^N is determined by the choice of the bounds of the remain-the-same category. The value chosen (1.25) makes the average value of π^N for all the surveys, 1946–1973, somewhat smaller than the average value of actual inflation in Table 3. They would be equal if the bounds were 1.70 (1.50 if the sample ends in 1972).

6. As noted earlier, the scaling of both π^L and π^0 is somewhat arbitrary. The scaling chosen does, of course, determine the size of the slope coefficients and whether the rationality hypothesis is accepted.

7. This section draws heavily on a New York University dissertation in process by Meir Sokoler of the University of Connecticut, who estimated the equations.

8. For a discussion of these issues see Wachtel (1974).

9. Unlike the other two, it is not often discussed in consumer theory although it can easily fit into a theoretical framework. Katona (1960) suggested uncertainty effects based on consumer psychology and Juster and Wachtel offer some crude empirical support. Sandmo (1970) provides a theoretical model of the effect of uncertainty on consumption.

10. The variance of the distribution of expectations across individuals may decrease with the rate of inflation. Individuals will increase their information-gathering activities, and this may mean that they become aware of, and adopt as their own, some consensus forecast.

11. I am grateful to the discussant, George de Menil, for pointing out an error in this discussion as it appeared in the conference paper.

12. In all these single-equation models, the simultaneity inherent in the relationships is overlooked.

13. The extrapolative measure of expectations used in this section is based on the consumer price index (CPI); it is defined as: $\pi^x = 0.4 \ RCPI(t-1) + 0.3 \ RCPI(t-2) + 0.2 \ RCPI(t-3) + 0.1 \ RCPI(t-4)$, where $RCPI = [CPI - CPI(t-4)]/CPI(t-4)$.

14. An Almon lag on the price change can be chosen that will increase R^2. The simple extrapolative forecast is used throughout for simplicity.

REFERENCES

Carlson, John. 1975. "A Study of Price Forecasts." Mimeographed.

Carlson, John A., and Michael Parkin. 1975. "Inflation Expectations." *Economica*, May.

Carlson, John A., and Harl E. Ryder Jr. 1973. "Quantitative Expectations From Quantitative Surveys: A Maximum Likelihood Approach." Paper presented at meeting of the Econometric Society. New York. December.

de Menil, George. 1973. "Rationality in Popular Price Expectations." Mimeographed. Princeton University. August.

———. 1974. "Aggregate Price Dynamics." *Review of Economics and Statistics*, May.

de Menil, George, and Surjit S. Bhalla. 1975. "Direct Measurement of Popular Price Expectations." *American Economic Review*, March.

Eckstein, Otto, and Roger Brinner. 1972. "The Inflation Process in the United States." A Study Prepared for the Use of the Joint Economic Committee, 92 Cong., 2nd sess.

Friedman, Milton. 1968. "The Role of Monetary Policy." *American Economic Review*, March.

Gibson, William E. 1972. "Interest Rates and Inflationary Expectations." *American Economic Review*, December.

Gordon, Robert J. 1971. "Inflation in Recession and Recovery." *Brookings Papers on Economic Activity*, no. 1.

———. 1972. "Wage-Price Controls and the Shifting Phillips Curve." *Brookings Papers on Economic Activity*, no. 2.

———. 1973. "Comment on Interest Rates and Prices in the Long Run." *Journal of Money, Credit, and Banking*, February.

Juster, F. Thomas. 1972–1973. "Savings Behavior, Uncertainty and Price Expectations." In B. Strumpel et al., eds. *Surveys of Consumers*. Ann Arbor: Institute for Social Research, University of Michigan.

Juster, F. Thomas, and Paul Wachtel. 1972a. "Inflation and the Consumer." *Brookings Papers on Economic Activity*, no. 1.

———. 1972b. "A Note on Inflation and the Savings Rate." *Brookings Papers on Economic Activity*, no. 3.

Katona, George. 1960. *The Powerful Consumer: Psychological Studies of the American Economy*. New York: McGraw-Hill.

Klein, Benjamin. 1974. "The Measurement and Social Cost of Inflation: The Recent Inflation and Our New Monetary Standard." Mimeographed. March.

Naylor, Thomas, et al. 1966. *Computer Simulation Techniques*. New York: Wiley.

Perry, George L. 1970. "Changing Labor Markets and Inflation." *Brookings Papers on Economic Activity*, no. 3.

Pyle, David H. 1972. "Observed Price Expectations and Interest Rates." *Review of Economics and Statistics*, August.

Sandmo, A. 1970. "The Effect of Uncertainty on Savings Decisions." *Review of Economic Studies*.

Shuford, Harry L. 1970. "Subjective Variables in Economic Analysis: A Study of Consumers' Expectations." Ph.D. dissertation, Yale University.

Solow, Robert. 1969. *Price Expectations and the Behavior of the Price Level*. England: Manchester University Press.

Turnovsky, Stephen J. 1970. "Empirical Evidence on the Formation of Price Expectations." *Journal of the American Statistical Association*, December.

Turnovsky, Stephen J., and Michael L. Wachter. 1972. "A Test of the 'Expectations Hypothesis' Using Directly Observed Wage and Price Expectations." *Review of Economics and Statistics*, February.

Wachtel, Paul. 1973. "Some Further Evidence on Interest Rates and Price Expectations." Mimeographed. Working Paper. Graduate School of Business Administration, New York University. June.

———. 1974. "Notes on the Psychology of Inflation and Consumer Behavior." Mimeographed. Paper presented to the American Psychological Association. New Orleans, September.

Yohe, William, and D. Karnosky. 1969. "Interest Rates and Price Level Changes, 1952–69." *Federal Reserve Bank of St. Louis Review*. December.

COMMENTS

George de Menil
Princeton University

In this paper, Paul Wachtel presents some evidence regarding the usefulness of survey measures of inflationary expectations. It has long been the accepted view in the economics profession that such measures are largely useless because respondents do not reveal their true attitudes on the questionnaires. This is an empirical question. The validity of any particular measure should be judged on its significance as an explanatory variable in an equation or equations explaining actual behavior. The verdict should *not* be based on anecdotal evidence. Interviewers all have their own stories to tell about the crazy answers people give them, but these are no substitute for good statistical analysis. Wachtel's paper contributes to a small but growing body of evidence suggesting that survey measures of inflationary expectations are a unique and valuable data source.

Wachtel's paper falls into two parts. The first two sections contain a presentation of several existing survey measures of inflationary expectations and a discussion of their characteristics. The remainder of the paper consists of four separate studies of the influence of expectations on consumption, prices, wages, and interest rates.

Two things happen when data is obtained on a variable for which previously there had been no data. First, it is learned that the variable does not behave quite the way it was thought to. Second, the new data open up new directions for research and so make it possible to raise and answer new questions. The four studies in the second part of Wachtel's paper are a good indication of the kind of questions to which survey data on inflationary expectations may provide some answers.

PRESENTATION OF SURVEY MEASURES AND THEIR CHARACTERISTICS

The Data

Wachtel presents five different measures derived from three different data bases. However, he does not do anything with one of the data bases (the ASA-NBER sample of business forecasters) because he judges that it has been available for too short a time period, and therefore I will not talk about it either. This leaves us with the Livingston series and three different series constructed from the Michigan SRC questionnaire. I have nothing to add to his description of the two data sources and will therefore move directly to a discussion of methodological problems associated with their use.

A general caveat is in order for anyone looking at distributions of point-estimate forecasts by individuals. It is that there is a tendency for the responses to cluster around integer values, and this may completely distort the distribution. Wachtel's failure to allow for this phenomenon accounts for the randomness of the skewness and kurtosis measures which he estimates for the Livingston data in Table 1. In a recent paper,[1] John Carlson performs very careful tests of the shape of the distribution of responses to Livingston's questionnaire in which he allows for this tendency to cluster. He finds no evidence of skewness and only mild evidence of kurtosis. He shows that the adjusted distribution fits the normal curve reasonably well, and a t distribution with a small number of degrees of freedom has an even better fit.

The subject of the shape of the distribution of responses brings us to the question of the proper method for interpreting the SRC questionnaire. An economist trying to use the answers to the two SRC questions reported in Wachtel's paper (in the section "Survey Research Center Data") is not automatically provided with a measure of the average expected rate of inflation, or any other moment of the distribution for that matter. He must infer that statistic more or less indirectly from the responses before him. The best way to do that is a matter of some importance. Wachtel, rightly I believe, appears in his paper to look with disfavor upon a procedure which both he and I have at one time used. The rejected method involves assigning values to the interval and end points in the second question asked and computing directly an average for the period from 1966II to the present and then linking that figure in some way to an index of the difference between the percentage of respondents who expect an upturn and the percentage who expect a downturn from the earlier period. There are several good reasons to reject this method. One is that this index does not fully use all the information available for the earlier period. It takes almost no account of variations in the percentage who expect no change. Another reason is the difficulty of appropriately linking two such different series. A third reason to reject the method is that, in my opinion, individuals do not adequately understand the second question. It is a complicated one. There is some evidence of inconsistency in individual answers to this question and two others in the 1970 SRC survey.[2] The general approach, which Wachtel does appear to favor (and I agree with him), is to discard answers from the second question and to infer the mean and variance of the distribution of expected rates of inflation solely from answers to the first question.

The procedure is well explained in the paper in the section on the SRC data. Suffice it to say that an assumption is made about the shape of the underlying distribution and that this assumption makes it possible to infer the desired moments from the responses in percentages.

The choice of the proper assumption regarding the shape of the underlying distribution is an important one, and unfortunately we have little information to guide us in doing so. For lack of anything better, several people who have worked with these data have assumed normality. Carlson, as mentioned above, offers some support for this procedure and raises serious questions about Wachtel's preference for a log-normal distribution with the floor arbitrarily set at -100 percent. One would like to see more evidence to support Wachtel's claim that the two measures are in fact very similar. The results reported in the second part of the paper are based on the log-normal measure.

It is important for users of measures of this kind to be aware of an associated statistical problem, which is present under either the normality or the log-normal assumption. The problem is very thoroughly discussed in an unpublished paper by Carlson and Ryder.[3] The problem is one of measurement error. Briefly, the transformation from percentage responses to the mean of the distribution is nonlinear, and it tends to magnify very significantly the measurement error in the raw percentages whenever, as is often the case in periods of rapid inflation, the sum of the percentage who expect no change and the percentage who expect a downturn falls below roughly 10 percent. The problem is an awkward one because the variance of the resulting measurement error is not constant. A maximum likelihood technique for estimating relations in which a measure such as π^0 or π^N is an explanatory variable has been developed by Yohn.[4] In principle, the equation estimates presented in the second part of Wachtel's paper suffer from neglect of this measurement error problem. In my judgment, however, on the basis of some experimentation by Yohn, this is not likely to change Wachtel's results qualitatively.

Comparison of Different Measures

Wachtel does not provide much systematic comparison of the different series, but the material he presents does throw light on two interesting questions.

The first concerns differences between the Livingston series and the two principal SRC series. (Because Wachtel asserts that the normal and log-normal SRC series do not differ much, I shall not distinguish between them and shall use the term "SRC series" to refer to either one.) It is clear from looking at Wachtel's figures 1 and 3 that the two series are quite different. All kinds of interesting conjectures are suggested by close examination of the two graphs, but Wachtel does not pursue them systematically.

The second question concerns the bias of forecasts or rationality in Muth's sense. This is an important question because of its implications for the Phillips trade-off and because of other implications—as evidenced by a recent spate of theoretical papers on the subject.[5] In Table 4 Wachtel presents results of the Theil test of unbiasness for different series and different time periods. He finds that with the exception of one or two regressions running from the mid-1950s through the early 1970s the series are not rational. However, I feel that his results are marred by a mechanical and unfortunate choice of sample periods. He starts his sample period in several cases in 1948I. For technical reasons which have to do with dramatic changes in the percentage of nonresponses at the end of the Korean War, I have grave misgivings about applying the same construction procedure to the SRC data before and after the Korean War. Moreover, his sample frequently extends through phases I, II, and III. It is true that perfect rationality would in principle include rationality in forecasting the effect of the controls. But I think it is mechanistic and unrealistic to stretch the hypothesis that far, and would have favored stopping the sample period in 1971III. For the period from the end of the Korean War through the Vietnam War, Wachtel does find (as I have also[6]) that the SRC series is very close to unbiased.

INDIVIDUAL STUDIES OF THE EFFECTS OF INFLATIONARY EXPECTATIONS

The more interesting part of Wachtel's paper is the second, which contains the four ministudies of the effect of inflationary expectations on consumption, prices, wages, and interest rates.

Interest Rates

Wachtel extends the results of Gibson and Pyle on the Fisher equation in an original and interesting way, finding among other things that *both* directly measured inflationary expectations *and* a distributed lag of changes in past price together contribute to explaining the commercial paper rate.

Wages

The subject of the effect of inflationary expectations on wage changes has been a controversial one in the Phillips-curve literature ever since Phillips wrote his original paper.

Wachtel constructs two simple but robust wage equations. One is of the Phillips variety; the other he terms a productivity equation. He then examines the effect of inflationary expectations in each one.

He finds again that *both* the SRC series *and* an Almon-type distributed lag contribute significantly to explaining wage changes in both models. When the two measures are introduced together, the sum of their coefficients appears to be insignificantly different from 1.0. Unfortunately, this result is probably sensitive again to what I consider an unfortunate extension of the sample period right through the control period. The very different significance of the distributed lag and the survey measure when the sample is split in 1965I is not adequately explained.

Prices

In an original manner, Wachtel introduces the expected rate of general price change into a markup model of prices given wages. The notion simply is that the target price is a function of unit cost (somehow defined) *and* the expected future general price level. The idea is interesting, and the results are statistically significant, but I find the parameter estimates puzzling. The speed of adjustment doubles, and the estimated trend rate of productivity growth drops from 2.8 percent a year to 0.7 percent. More work on this promising idea is called for.

Consumption

Of the four questions studied by Wachtel, the effect of expected inflation on consumption is the one that has been studied the longest in the literature, and in the light of recent research, I believe it is the most perplexing. Wachtel reports on the work of Meir Sokoler, a thesis student at NYU. Sokoler departs from the earlier work of Juster and Wachtel on the related issue of savings functions and instead takes the Branson and Klevorick money-illusion consumption function as a point of departure. There follows a very convenient and useful separation of the effects of the price level on real consumption into a level or money illusion effect, a substitution effect, and an uncertainty effect—a division long championed by George Katona and his associates.

Where I part company is that π, which in the other studies is used as what it is, a measure of the expected rate of inflation, here is used as a proxy for uncertainty regarding future real income. I think we have to be consistent across equations for the same agents (households in this case). π cannot be a mean forecast in the wage equation and a measure of uncertainty in the consumption function.

CONCLUSION

In summary the four studies support the view that much is to be learned by using direct measures of inflationary expectations—in fact, employing different survey measures for different agents—in explaining actual behavior.

I would like to end with the old story of the drunk and the lamp post. The drunk has been alternately praised and maligned for looking for his lost key solely under the lamp post. I would like to propose another strategy—to turn on more light. And the new source of light I would like to see is additional direct survey measures of economic expectations.

NOTES

1. J. A. Carlson, "Are Price Expectations Normally Distributed?" *Journal of the American Statistical Association,* December 1975.
2. Cf. the appendix of G. de Menil, "The Rationality of Popular Price Expectations," mimeographed (Paris: INSEE, March 1975).
3. J. Carlson and H. Ryder, "Quantitative Expectations from Qualitative Surveys: A Maximum-Likelihood Approach," mimeographed, Purdue University, October 1973.
4. F. Yohn, "A Maximum-Likelihood Technique for Estimation in the Face of

Measurement Error with Nonconstant Variance," mimeographed, Princeton University, May 1975.

5. See the review of this literature in R. J. Shiller, "Rational Expectations and the Dynamic Structure of Macroeconomic Models, A Critical Review" (paper presented to the Conference on the Monetary Mechanism in Open Economics, Helsinki, Finland, August 4–9, 1975).

6. de Menil, "Popular Price Expectations."

10

JACK E. TRIPLETT

U.S. Bureau of
Labor Statistics

The Impact on Econometric Models of the Present Treatment of Smog and Safety Devices in Economic Statistics: A Comment

When theoretical models do not fit the data, the usual procedure is to revamp the theory; but sometimes the problem is less one of the theory not fitting the data, and more nearly one of data that are not appropriate to the theory. Problems that have emerged at several points during this conference lead me to raise the question of whether some of the price and output data being used in econometric models are constructed appropriately for the underlying economic behavior that is being modeled. In particular, builders of econometric models may need to consider carefully present policies concerning the treatment in the statistical series of legally mandated smog devices, safety equipment, and related phenomena. It seems quite possible that the present treatment is appropriate for some uses of the statistics, but not for others. For any econometric model that falls into the latter class, a predictive failure that may appear at first glance to involve a defect in the behavioral or market relationships incorporated into the model may ultimately be traced to a measurement problem either in the data used as inputs or in the data the model is trying to predict.

Although many aspects of the treatment of smog and safety devices in the price indexes and in the national accounts have been carefully considered elsewhere (and need not be reviewed here), implications of their present treatment that are particularly relevant to the subject of this conference seem to have been overlooked in previous debate on the subject. Consider a machinery or vehicles component of the industrial price indexes for which safety or pollution-abatement legislation has required some costly additional equipment that buyers would not have specified had they not been compelled to do so (a long list can be made of such changes in recent years). Under present policy, the BLS treats such legislated changes as a quality improvement, and applies a quality adjustment based on the manufacturing cost of the change (whenever this data can be obtained). Thus, in the industry that experienced the legislated equipment change (call it "Industry A") price statistics will show no increase; and Industry A's output measures—which are usually obtained through deflation of a value aggregate by a price index—will rise by the value of the extra equipment.

At first glance, this seems a consistent treatment: Industry A has, after all, produced something (willingly or not), and used up resources that were required to add the mandatory changes. Treating this resource utilization as a quality change, it has been argued, preserves the measure of Industry A's output, as well as its productivity measures (which are unaffected by the change).

An alternative treatment (which was initially employed by the BLS for 1971 automobile smog-control devices—though later rescinded) is to refuse to allow quality adjustments for such changes, permitting any cost increases associated with the additional equipment to show up as price increases on the product to which they are attached. This treatment implicitly takes the mandatory additional equipment as equivalent to a tax imposed on Industry A's output. Though Industry A used up resources when the mandatory equipment was added to the products it manufactured, under the alternative treatment its output measures would not reflect the additional equipment, and its productivity measures would fall.

The initial debate over the correct treatment of smog-control devices took place mainly within the context of the CPI. Most of the relevant arguments were paraded before an interagency committee which was set up by the Federal Office of Management and Budget to review the matter. The issues are complex—there are prominent economists arrayed on each side—and there is insufficient space to review all the issues here.

Whatever the position of individual committee members on the appropriate treatment within the CPI, there was no debate, so far as I can determine, on the correct treatment of smog-control devices for the analysis of industry price, output, and productivity trends. It was generally agreed that for those purposes, quality adjustment for mandatory equipment was correct. But apparently the debators have overlooked the fact that the decision to handle smog-control devices as quality changes in the price indexes has major implications for the *distribution* of measured output and productivity changes among industries. The decision thus poses major difficulties for the analysis of inflation at the industry level.

To develop this point, consider another industry (call it "B"), which uses the output of Industry A in its own production. We assume that the extra mandatory equipment has no productive value in use in Industry B (or that its value is less than its cost—otherwise, legislation would not have been necessary). What happens to the statistics for Industry B?

Because any extra mandatory equipment added to Industry A's output is currently treated as a quality change (equivalent, in this case, to an output increase) and not as a price change, there will be no recorded rise in Industry B's input prices. The data will in fact show Industry B buying a larger *quantity* of Industry A's output. Thus, using published data, we conclude that Industry B is using more inputs than before to produce the same output, which means that productivity measures for Industry B will decrease. Furthermore, because its costs per unit of output have risen, Industry B's prices will inevitably rise (eventually, if not immediately). But because we have no record, in the input price indexes, of any price increase there, we find that Industry B's prices rose more than the prices of the products it purchases—in other words, more than its measured input costs.

Consider the statistical picture under the alternative. Suppose no quality adjustment for the smog device had been allowed in Industry A. Then we would have observed a decline in measured productivity in Industry A. However, because the smog devices would have raised measures of Industry B's input *prices*, and not the *quantity* of inputs it used up, there would be no impact on Industry B's productivity measures. Moreover, under this alternative (rejected) treatment the data would indicate that any compression on Industry B's profit margins, or increase of its output price, would be associated with increased costs of its inputs, not with (as the present statistics show) increased use of inputs from Industry A per unit of output of B.

Thus, alternative treatments of equipment such as smog-control devices imply two alternative pictures of the distribution of output, price, and productivity changes. The question is: Which alternative scenario gives the most informative picture of economic reality? There is no single answer to such a question, for our definition of "economic reality" will depend on the precise questions being asked of the data. It has been argued, for example, that the present treatment is the appropriate one for the purposes of the national income and product accounts. (Nevertheless, in the unpublished minutes of the deliberations of the interagency committee convened to deal with this question—where national accounts considerations figured prominently—there is no record of consideration given to the question of the *distribution* of productivity and output changes, which is so clearly central to the problem.)

It is clear, however, that the present method of handling pollution-control equipment poses difficult problems for users who wish to employ the data for the analysis of inflation. The present treatment tends to eliminate the effects from the industry in which the change takes place, and distribute them around among the industries that use the equipment. It will be increasingly hard in the future to analyze changes in productivity and prices at the industry level because data on input use and productivity for the *using* industry are made to feel the effects of changes imposed on the supplying industry, whereas data for the supplying industry (where the changes actually occur) are purged of any record of the matter.

There are other analytic objectives for which users must also consider the effect of the smog-control decision on the statistics. For example, price and output measures are important for carrying out studies of consumer demand, of industry demand for inputs, and of substitution among inputs to production. The measures will be inappropriate for such uses if consuming and producing units perceive price and output changes differently from the way they are measured. If consumers, for example, view smog-control devices as an extra cost of acquiring and running an automobile, rather than as an improvement in the quality of cars, then the price indexes as they now exist may not be very relevant in explaining the demand for automobiles. And if business firms take a similar view of those and other mandatory changes on motor vehicles, trucks, and agricultural and industrial machinery, then again, the price indexes as they are now constructed will not adequately explain economic behavior with respect to substitution, demand for inputs, and other production and output decisions. There is as yet little evidence on these matters. Parks,[1] estimating automobile costs for a study of scrapping trends, found large residuals for recent years, which he interprets as evidence that consumers acted as if the cost of automobiles had risen more than the indexes show. This is not conclusive evidence, by any means, but it is consistent with the view that car buyers *act* as if the addition of smog-control and safety devices is a price, not a quality, increase.

Moreover, the performance of price behavior and price prediction models may be additional evidence. If they have performed poorly in recent years, the reason may be that some of the data they are using (and also the series they are trying to predict) have been adjusted for pollution control and safety devices, and the underlying economic behavior that these models are trying to predict may not be consistent with index makers' decisions. On the other hand, product safety and pollution changes have so far probably affected only a small (though growing) proportion of the industrial price indexes, and the problem may not yet be serious enough to throw large-scale econometric models off track. However, those who use industrial price indexes should be aware of this measurement problem and of its possible implications for the appropriateness of the data for their purposes.

NOTE

1. Richard W. Parks, "Determinents of Scrapping Rates for Post War Vintage Automobiles," *Econometrica*, forthcoming.

11

RONALD G. BODKIN
University of Ottawa and Economic Council of Canada

FRANCINE CHABOT-PLANTE
Economic Council of Canada

MUNIR A. SHEIKH
Economic Council of Canada

Canadian Experience with Recent Inflation as Viewed through CANDIDE

In this paper, we employ a large-scale econometric model of the Canadian economy as a tool for studying the generation of inflation during the past fourteen years. Because ours is a medium-term model, we break this total span into three distinct subperiods: 1960–1965, 1965–1970, and 1970–1974. In our analysis we focus on

NOTE: The authors would like to thank their colleagues, Bobbi Cain, Thomas T. Schweitzer, Stephen M. Tanny, and H. E. L. Waslander for numerous comments on this research in the various stages of this paper. Also, the comments of John A. Sawyer and D. J. Daly (the official discussant) on the floor of the conference discussions were both stimulating and useful. Finally, the advice of R. Allen Stewart, head of computer services at the Economic Council of Canada, was very helpful with regard to the numerous computations that this paper entailed. Of course, none of the above is responsible for errors of fact or analysis; that responsibility rests with the authors alone. A version of this paper has already been published in French in *Actualité économique*, autumn 1975, under the title "L'inflation canadienne de la dernière decénnie vue à travers CANDIDE."

the well-known construct of a "trade-off," or Phillips, curve, although our approach to this concept is in the context of our large-scale simultaneous equations model.[1] We shall not defend this construct, which has been the subject of a number of spirited exchanges in the literature in recent years. In any case, our goal in this paper is more modest: the objective is to see whether, and to what extent, the simple concept of a trade-off curve (based, of course, on certain hypotheses to be spelled out later on) remains a valid first approximation, in the context of a large-scale econometric model.[2] Of course, even if it is concluded that the results of an analysis of wage-price-unemployment behavior, in the context of a full model, can really be viewed, at least as a reasonable description, as a trade-off curve, this does not tell us anything directly about the Canadian economy. If the parent model is accepted as a tentatively validated approximation of the Canadian economy, then confidence would be strengthened in the trade-off curves that have been derived from such a model. However, it must be candidly admitted that the existence or nonexistence of such a trade-off curve has been derived from the basic equations of the model, and so this test of the existence of such a curve is really an indirect one. Accordingly, in this paper only an indirect contribution can be made to the debate on this subject.

In the first full section of this paper, we present an extremely brief introduction to CANDIDE Model 1.1. In section II, we analyze the period 1960–1965, utilizing heavily the concept of a trade-off curve as a theoretical simplification and as a basis for the presentation. In section III, we present similar analyses for 1965–1970, when inflationary pressures were much more pronounced in the North American economy. The analysis for 1970–1974 in section IV changes the emphasis of this study to the effects in Canada of price level developments in the United States; it will be recalled that this period includes the New Economic Policy, price controls and decontrols through the various phases of NEP, and worldwide food and oil shortages. In the concluding section, we present both our major conclusions and several caveats, attempting to distill one lesson for policy out of our study.

I. SUMMARY OF CANDIDE MODEL 1.1

CANDIDE Model 1.1 is the second generation of a large-scale model (roughly 2,050 equations for Model 1.1) of a national economy (i.e., a model with no explicit regional detail), fitted to annual data, with a medium-term outlook (for our purposes here, 5–10 years). The acronym represents (in English) *CAN*adian *D*isaggregated *I*nter-*D*epartmental *E*conometric (model or project).[3] In terms of the bare statistics, CANDIDE Model 1.1 has approximately 450 exogenous variables, 616 behavioral equations, 427 input-output identities, and over 1,000 ordinary identities.[4] The technique of parameter estimation was ordinary least squares, with variants such as polynomial (Almon) distributed lags utilized to deal with nondiscrete lag distributions and Hildreth-Lu (autoregressive) transformations employed to handle autocorrelated disturbances, particularly in the context of lagged dependent variables. In general, the sample period for Model 1.1 was 1955–1971, and the behavioral equations have been fitted to national accounts data and concepts that incorporate the 1972 revisions by Statistics Canada, which were important in scope and pronounced in magnitude.

Several striking features of the CANDIDE model may be briefly discussed. First, as the acronym implies, the model is disaggregated in a number of directions, which of course accounts for its large size. Although almost every sector of the model is disaggregated to some extent, the directions in which the disaggregation has been carried furthest include some of the categories of final demand expenditures, output originating (real gross domestic product) by industry, and the price level variables (the implicit deflators associated with the expenditure categories). Secondly, such a large system is obviously computer-oriented. The simultaneous core of CANDIDE Model 1.1 approximates some 1,500 nonlinear equations, and a model of this size would have been quite impossible to handle or even to manage before the age of the high-speed computer.[5]

A third characteristic is that the model is intended, as one might expect from the number of departments and agencies of the Government of Canada that had a hand in its construction,[6] to be a general-purpose one, onto which satellite models can be grafted as a particular need arises. Of course, there are limitations to this principle: the satellite model has to be broadly consistent with the basic model. In other words, CANDIDE is no panacea for all policy problems confronting Canadian government departments, as at times we have had to make quite clear to potential users of the model. In short, a model that is general purpose in nature should not be confused with that nonexistent entity, an all-purpose model.

A fourth striking feature of CANDIDE Model 1.1 is that, like

Model 1.0, it integrates two input-output submodels with conventional econometric modeling. (This has already been indicated in the equation counts above.) An input-output submodel is utilized in each of two places: on the real output side and also on the price side. The price-side I/O submodel will be discussed in the next paragraph. The real-side I/O submodel takes 169 categories of final demand by ultimate use and converts these time series (under the assumption of fixed coefficients) into a time series of final demands for the 105 commodities of the CANDIDE I/O classification. Then a rectangular input-output model is applied, yielding first estimates of gross output and (by another assumption of constant proportions) of value added originating in some sixty-three industries. These first estimates are then subjected to autoregressive correction equations, in order to obviate some of the rigidities entailed in the use of fixed coefficients estimated on the basis of data for a single year, 1961.[7]

Turning to the wage-price sectors of CANDIDE, we note that both wage and price formation (particularly the latter) are heavily cost-oriented. Wage formation takes place in twelve major industries of the Canadian economy. In three of these (manufacturing, construction, and transportation, storage, and communications), the key wage relationship is an industry variant of a wage adjustment function. Thus, a schematic wage adjustment function for these three industries would be:

(1) $\qquad \dot{w}_i = \alpha + \beta(1/U) + \gamma CPI + \delta \dot{w}_{i_{US}} + \epsilon,$

where the Greek letters are parameters, $\dot{w}_i$ is the rate of change of the wage rate in industry i, U is the rate of unemployment (as a proportion of the labor force), $\dot{CPI}$ is the rate of change of the consumer price index, $\dot{w}_{i_{US}}$ is the rate of change of wage rates in a corresponding U.S. industry, and ϵ is a random disturbance. In principle, the total wage bill in these three industries is equal to the product of the wage rate per man-hour multiplied by the total number of man-hours employed in the industry, although in practice inconsistencies in the data bases utilized forced us into ad hoc adjustment relationships. For the remaining nine major industries, the total wage bill (W_i) is explained directly. A typical wage bill function would be the following:

(2) $\qquad \log [W_i/0.5 (CPI + CPI_{-1})] = \alpha' + \beta'X_i + \gamma'E_i + \epsilon',$

where again the Greek letters are parameters, ϵ' is a random disturbance, X_i is the level of real domestic product originating in the ith industry, E_i is the level of industry employment (generally, but not always, in terms of man-hours), and *CPI* is as defined above. Note that the total wage bill has been deflated by the average of the current and the preceding year's consumer price index, on the view that a short lag characterizes this sort of relationship. It might be mentioned that the unemployment rate enters only one of the nine variants of equation 2. Hence it is not quite true to assert that the Phillips curve (relationship between the rate of change of wage rates and the level of the unemployment rate) is built right into all our wage formation equations, as D. J. Daly, our discussant, has asserted. On the other hand, it must be admitted that the model gives the Phillips curve (and the associated trade-off curve) every opportunity to make an appearance.

As noted above, industry price formation is strongly cost-oriented, with the principal explanatory variable being either unit labor costs or unit total costs (which include unit capital costs, or unincorporated business income per unit of real output, or both), depending upon the major industry under consideration. Denote the industry price level (the implicit deflator of real domestic product originating) by P_i, and unit labor costs or unit total costs by UC_i. Then the following is a schematic relationship explaining the determination of the price level of the ith industry's output:

(3) $\qquad P_i = \alpha'' + \beta'' UC_i + \gamma'' Z_i + \epsilon''.$

Again, the Greek letters are parameters, ϵ'' is a stochastic disturbance, Z_i is (depending upon the industry under consideration) either a proxy variable for the direct effects of demand pressures or an indicator of price pressures from the corresponding U.S. industry. (In the case of the price level of mining output, both variants of Z_i appear.) In some major industries, UC_i appears as a distributed lag, rather than simply having a simultaneous influence.

Once the process of domestic industry price formation is complete, we can enter the price-side I/O submodel. (Other relevant independent variables are the prices of competing imports, which are essentially exogenous in CANDIDE Model 1.1, tax and subsidy rates, and several other minor determinants.) The I/O price-side submodel, which is one of pure cost-push, will generate estimates of (most of) the implicit deflators of the domestic final demand categories. Final estimates (in Model 1.1) are then obtained by subjecting these first estimates to an autoregressive correction procedure, analogously to what is done on the side of the estimates of real output by detailed industry emanating from the real-side I/O submodel. At the end of this process, some price-level aggregates are obtained by dividing the relevant current-dollar magnitudes by the appropriate constant-dollar values, which may be interpreted as taking a weighted average (with current weights) of the appropriate component deflators.

Finally, we may note, especially for an American audience, that the model of the U.S. economy that CANDIDE resembles most closely is Ross Preston's Wharton School annual and industry forecasting model.[8] This resemblance is closest with regard to the input-output aspects of the two models, as the CANDIDE treatment has been patterned on that pioneered by Preston. (Indeed, the principal difference between the CANDIDE input-output submodels and the Wharton ones is that a rectangular I/O subsystem is used in the former; and the more usual square system, in the latter.) Of course, there are some differences in the structures of the two models; for example, the links between monetary stocks and final demand functions are much more fully developed in the Wharton model. On the other hand, the foreign trade relationships are much more fully articulated in the CANDIDE models, which is hardly surprising in view of the much more open nature of the Canadian economy. It should be pointed out explicitly that this close resemblance is not accidental; as McCracken acknowledges,[9] the Wharton model was not only an inspiration to the CANDIDE model builders, but Ross Preston and Lawrence R. Klein gave useful counsel during the period of construction of the latter.

II. THE TRADE-OFF DURING 1960–1965

In this section, we take up two important issues:

First, in a directly estimated trade-off relationship, price changes can be derived as a function of the unemployment rate (and possibly some other variables). The unemployment rate is then modified exogenously to find the corresponding price changes, which trace out the trade-off curve. As Kaliski has pointed out,[10] "the several variables included in the wage and price equations can be said, with some exceptions, to be jointly determined in a larger system and thus to occur only in certain specific combinations of values. One cannot, in general, hold some of them constant and vary others." From another point of view, if such a trade-off exists at all, policymakers may want to find out whether or not it is independent of the policy instrument utilized.

The question is then, Can we derive the usual trade-off relationship between changes in prices and the rate of unemployment when we use a jointly determined larger system, such as the CANDIDE model? In a full-scale model we can only make autonomous changes in the exogenous variables or in the constant terms of the behavioral equations. We can then examine the resulting variations in both the unemployment rate and the rate of change of prices and thus derive our trade-off relationship, if it indeed exists.

Second, it is generally agreed that the openness of the Candian economy makes it more susceptible than most countries to foreign economic influences, especially those from the United States. In our trade-off framework, the second question that we want to study is, What happens to our trade-off relationships if we assume that the U.S. economy was experiencing more or less inflation than was actually the case during the sample period 1960–1965?

It is possible to study these issues on a year-to-year basis. Take, for example, some specific year. We have the unemployment rate for that year (*URATE* in the CANDIDE model) and the percent change over the past year in a price level, namely, the implicit deflator of gross national expenditure (*PGNE*), both taken from the *control solution* of the model. This gives us one point for our trade-off curve. Suppose now that we increase government expenditures in that year by a specific amount and obtain another *full-system dynamic solution* of the model. This solution will provide us with new numbers for the rates of inflation and unemployment for that year and hence another point for the supposed trade-off curve. By injecting various amounts of government expenditures into the system, we can generate as many points for our trade-off curve as we wish.

Instead of analyzing results on a year-to-year basis, we preferred to work with five-year averages. We could thus divide our sample period into two five-year subperiods, 1960–1965 and 1965–1970. Furthermore, we felt that five-year averages of the dependent variables that the model generates are more reliable than the simulated values for each year separately, for the simple reason that the impact of the misspecification of any equation (or group of equations) in the model is probably less for a five-year average.

To answer the two questions posed at the beginning of this section, the model was subjected to shocks by changing the following variables in various amounts:[11]

Government current expenditures (*GCURRK* in terms of model
 mnemonics), with a constant supply of high-powered money;
Government expenditure on fixed capital formation (*GFICAK*),
 with a constant supply of high-powered money;

Government transfer payments (*GTR*), with a constant supply of high-powered money;

Government current expenditures (*GCURRK*), with constant interest rates;

High-powered money (*MHPC*).

We were successful in deriving many trade-off curves with the CANDIDE model, consistent with our working hypotheses. It should be mentioned, however, before we present our results, that our model is neo-Keynesian in spirit, and hence it is not surprising that our findings agree broadly with the conclusions implicit in the IS-LM theoretical framework.

The Trade-off with Variations in Government Current Expenditure (with a Constant Supply of High-Powered Money)—GCURRK

To derive our trade-off relationship, we change *GCURRK*[12] by various amounts ranging from +$400 million to −$400 million constant dollars.[13] The results of this experiment are presented in Table 1. Notice that the results clearly indicate that an increase in the unemployment rate is associated with a decrease in the percent increase

TABLE 1   Trade-off under Fiscal Policy (Government Current Expenditure), 1960–1965

Change in *GCURRK* (millions of constant dollars)	*URATE*	Percent Change in *PGNE*
+400[a]	3.25	3.216
+300	3.76	2.877
+200	4.41	2.478
Control solution	5.61	2.002
−200	6.75	1.811
−300	7.31	1.752
−400	7.87	1.702

NOTE: For definition of variables, see text.
[a] We could not keep on injecting $400 million in 1964 and 1965 because the model fails to converge, as *URATE* becomes negative. Therefore, only $300 million are injected in those two years.

in *PGNE;* thus, there *does* exist a trade-off relationship, at least over this particular period.

However, according to the model, a lower *URATE* would not have meant too high a penalty in terms of higher price increases if the government had increased its expenditures on goods and services at that time. Nevertheless, lowering the price pressures, which were a problem only toward the end of that subperiod, would have been an expensive experiment. One can legitimately ask whether these quite optimistic results from the point of view of policymakers would have held, at least to the same degree, if some other fiscal tool had been used.

The Trade-off with Variations in Government Fixed Capital Formation (GFICAK)

According to our experiments, *GCURRK* appears to have been the most effective weapon for fighting unemployment. We have run a number of experiments with government expenditures on fixed capital formation (*GFICAK*) and government transfers (*GTR*). As we had expected, the structure of lags in the model implied by *GFICAK* and its more limited ramifications throughout the economy mean a smaller overall multiplier effect. The experiment with the most stimulation, injection of $400 million, brings mean *URATE* down to 4.33 percent, compared to 3.25 percent with *GCURRK* (Table 2). Again we find the existence of a trade-off rela-

TABLE 2   Trade-off under Fiscal Policy
(Government Fixed Capital
Formation), 1960–1965

Change in *GFICAK* (millions of constant dollars)	*URATE*	Percent Change in *PGNE*
+400	4.33	2.447
+300	4.66	2.309
+200	4.98	2.192
Control solution	5.61	2.002
−200	6.22	1.915
−300	6.53	1.896
−400	6.83	1.881

NOTE: For definition of variables, see text.

tionship. The slope of the trade-off curve that can be derived from this table, based on variations in GFICAK, is slightly flatter than that obtained from Table 1 with GCURRK.

The Trade-off with Variations in Government Transfer Payments (GTR)

Finally, we consider transfer payments from government to persons (GTR). Since GTR is in current dollars, we know that the changes in it are not directly comparable to those discussed above, which are in terms of constant dollars. It is thus not surprising to find a smaller overall effect when using this tool. The results of our various simulations are listed in Table 3. Again, the existence of a trade-off curve is evident, and this curve turns out to be reasonably close to the one derived for GCURRK, above. (Although the figures in Table 3 are closer to those in Table 2, plotting the curves on a graph makes it quite clear that the trade-off curve of this subsection is closer, over the relevant range, to that for GCURRK than for GFICAK.)

TABLE 3 Trade-off under Fiscal Policy (Government Transfer Payments), 1960–1965

Change in GTR (millions of constant dollars)	URATE	Percent Change in PGNE
+400	4.91	2.22
+300	5.09	2.162
+200	5.26	2.106
Control solution	5.61	2.002
−200	5.96	1.933
−300	6.13	1.918
−400	6.30	1.905

NOTE: For definition of variables, see text.

The Trade-off with Variations in Government Current Expenditures (with Constant Interest Rates)

In the previous simulations, we did not obtain the pure fiscal effect, in terms of the IS-LM framework, as the supply of high-powered money remained unchanged and interest rates increased. We now want to keep interest rates unchanged. This is done by making the monetary block exogenous, which means that the observed values of interest rates are used wherever they appear in the rest of the model.[14]

As expected, a comparison of tables 1 and 4 shows that a change of the same magnitude in GCURRK leads to a greater impact on URATE and PGNE if interest rates are kept constant by adjusting the money supply.[15] Any given injection, for example, is more helpful in reducing unemployment, but only at the expense, in the present case, of more inflation. Figure 1 illustrates the effect of keeping interest rates constant in the trade-off between inflation and unemployment. The values of URATE and the percent change in PGNE are almost similar in the two control solutions, one with and the other without an exogenous monetary block. Keeping interest rates constant slightly raises the trade-off relationship for ex-

TABLE 4 Trade-off under Pure Fiscal Policy (Interest Rates Held Constant), 1960–1965

Change in GCURRK (millions of constant dollars)	URATE	Percent Change in PGNE
+300[a]	3.58	3.264
+200	4.23	2.764
Control solution[b]	5.68	2.045
−200	7.01	1.815
−300	7.66	1.737
−400	8.30	1.671

NOTE: For definition of variables, see text.
[a]We could not run a simulation with +400 for the whole subperiod because URATE went below zero in some years and so the model could not converge.
[b]The control solution has slightly different values than in the preceding three tables (and also in Table 5, below), because, with the monetary block exogenous, we have, in effect, a slightly different model.

FIGURE 1   Trade-off under Fiscal Policy (Government Current Expenditure, GCURRK), 1960–1965

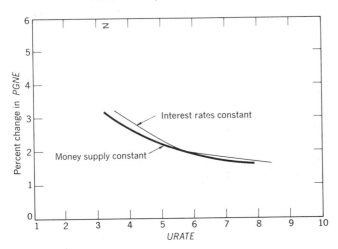

PGNE = GNE (gross national expenditures) deflator.
URATE = unemployment rate.

pansive fiscal policy, but hardly makes any difference for contractionary fiscal policy. This slight change under a stimulative fiscal policy probably occurs because, by holding our interest rates to their observed values and impeding any feedback from the real side of the economy, we may be breaking one of the corrective mechanisms which stabilize the economy under greater demand pressures.

The Trade-off with Variations in High-powered Money (MHPC)

Before launching into the analysis of monetary simulations, we must comment on the linkages between the monetary and real sectors in our model. Following neo-Keynesian tradition, the only such link we have is through interest rates: these are determined in the monetary block, and they enter as explanatory variables in the equations for investment, residential construction, discretionary savings, and some of the consumption categories. Monetary aggregates do not affect anything directly in the model except the complex of interest rates. Thus, given these tenuous links between the monetary and the real sectors and the fact that high-powered money is in current dollars, we generally expect a smaller overall effect for our monetary policy simulation.

A comparison of Table 5 with tables 1, 2 and 4 supports our assertion. However, the changes in *MHPC* have a greater impact than changes in *GTR*, as is obvious from a comparison of tables 3 and 5.[16]

In Figure 2, we compare the trade-off curve derived from Table 5

TABLE 5 Trade-off under Monetary Policy, 1960–1965

Change in *MHPC* (millions of current dollars)	*URATE*	Percent Change in *PGNE*
+500	4.15	2.565
+400	4.47	2.403
+300	4.78	2.275
+200	5.07	2.170
Control solution	5.61	2.002
−200	6.10	1.870
−400	6.55	1.837

NOTE: For definition of variables, see text.

FIGURE 2 Comparison of Trade-offs under Fiscal (GCURRK) and Monetary (MHPC) Policies, 1960–1965

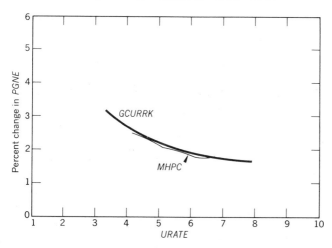

MHPC = high-powered money.

to the one derived by using *GCURRK* in Table 1. Our principal conclusion, at least for this historical period, is that the trade-off curve is relatively independent of the policy—monetary or fiscal—chosen to speed up or slow down the economy.

So far, our model corroborates the conclusions derived from the analysis of neo-Keynesian models, which is not surprising under our assumptions. To fight unemployment, fiscal policy is more effective. But the answer is less clear-cut on price stability. If we wish only to readjust our prices slightly, then monetary policy would do the job. Monetary policy alone will not be successful in achieving a drastic anti-inflationary goal, in the range of variations in the stock of money studied, under the assumptions of our model. We may add, however, that during this particular subperiod, inflation was not an acute problem.

The Trade-off with a Different Price Scenario for the United States, 1960–1965

For an analysis of the impact of U.S. inflation on the Canadian economy, we ask ourselves the following question: What would have happened to the trade-off relationships we derived earlier if the United States had been experiencing inflation at a rate higher than what was actually observed during this period (1960–1965)?

To study this issue, we made exogenous changes in all the prices paid (in U.S. dollars) for goods imported from the United States, which appear as exogenous variables in the model.[17] Assuming that Canada is a small country and hence a price taker in world markets and thus can sell its exports at exogenously determined prices, we change all the prices of goods exported to the United States and the rest of the world (exogenous in our model) by the same margin as the prices of imports from the United States.[18] Specifically, the observed rate of change of all these prices was increased by one percentage point[19] for all years from 1961 to 1965 with 1960 as the base year. A full-system solution of the CANDIDE model incorporating these changes gives us a new control solution and hence new control values of *URATE* and the rate of change of *PGNE* (again working with averages over the five-year subperiod).

Following the same procedure used earlier, we derive a new trade-off curve based on a higher rate of inflation in the United States. The trade-off relationship under this scenario (changes in *GCURRK*) is presented in Table 6. A comparison of this table with Table 1 reveals that a higher U.S. inflation leads to a lower unem-

TABLE 6 Trade-off with Higher U.S. Inflation, Using Fiscal Policy (GCURRK), 1960–1965

Change in GCURRK (millions of constant dollars)	URATE	Percent Change in PGNE
+300	3.41	3.72
+200	4.13	3.09
Control solution	5.37	2.52
−200	6.52	2.16
−300	7.08	2.02
−400	7.64	1.89

NOTE: For definition of variables, see text.

ployment rate in Canada, coupled with more inflation, according to the CANDIDE model. This latter result is consistent with what one would expect, given the extent of the dependence of the Canadian economy on its external environment. A variety of factors may be responsible for lowering the unemployment rate. For example, higher import prices could, among other things, make domestic goods more desirable relative to imported goods. The increase in demand for the former could lead to an increase in their production, consequently generating more employment in these industries.

Figure 3 illustrates much more clearly, however, the effect of additional U.S. inflation on the trade-off curve derived earlier for changes in GCURRK. We observe that higher U.S. inflation at an augmented rate of one percentage point per year shifts the entire trade-off curve upward, so that the annual rate of inflation projected by the model is increased between 0.2 and 0.7 percentage points, depending upon the particular rate of Canadian unemployment under consideration. The new curve is steeper, and so higher amounts of acceleration in the rate of inflation are associated with lower rates of unemployment. Alternatively, if the Canadian government wishes to hold the line at a given rate of increase of the price level, it has to allow for more unemployment at home to cope with the impact of higher U.S. inflation. This may imply roughly a one percentage point increase in the Canadian unemployment rate, as a crude approximation, although this may vary somewhat, depending upon the target rate of inflation selected.

Table 7 can be compared with Table 5 to analyze the impact of a higher rate of U.S. inflation on the trade-off relationship derived by permitting changes in monetary policy. From the table and the corresponding Figure 4, we can derive conclusions similar to those we presented above for *GCURRK*. Because of the differences in the

FIGURE 3 Shift of the Trade-off Curve Resulting from Higher U.S. Inflation under Fiscal Policy (GCURRK), 1960–1965

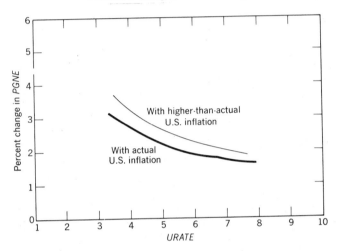

TABLE 7 Trade-off with Higher U.S. Inflation, Using Monetary Policy (MHPC), 1960–1965

Change in *MHPC* (millions of constant dollars)	*URATE*	Percent Change in *PGNE*
+500	3.89	3.18
+400	4.22	2.98
+300	4.53	2.83
+200	4.83	2.71
Control solution	5.36	2.52
−200	5.85	2.38
−400	6.29	2.27

NOTE: For definition of variables, see text.

effectiveness of these policy tools in our model, the magnitudes of the resulting changes are not directly comparable.

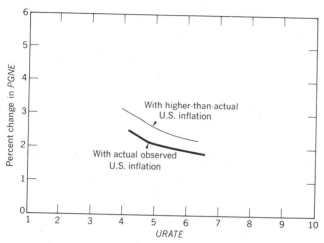

FIGURE 4 Shift of the Trade-off Curve Resulting from Higher U.S. Inflation under Monetary Policy (MHPC), 1960–1965

II. THE TRADE-OFF RELATIONSHIP DURING 1965–1970

Simulations for 1965–1970, when compared to those in the preceding section, permit us to analyze the question of the stability over time of our trade-off curves, following the literature on the Canadian trade-off curve. Working with the full model does not, however, allow us to be as explicit about the factors explaining the shift of the curve as with a small subsystem, even though such an analysis could be important for policy decisions. This is one price that must be paid for a more "realistic" analysis. The second issue considered in this section is the now familiar problem of analyzing the effects of changes in the U.S. environment on the Canadian trade-off curve for 1965–1970. Before proceeding, it is useful to recall that 1966 was a year of full employment for Canada and that inflation was emerging then as a real problem. Even though the rate of unemployment was increasing every year after 1966, inflation did not slow down. Thus, at the end of the 1960s, Canada was facing both a high unemployment rate and considerable inflation. It could thus be anticipated that the trade-off curve would shift up in 1965–1970 compared to 1960–1965.[20]

In Table 8 we list the trade-offs for 1965–1970 derived by utilizing both fiscal and monetary policies for this latter subperiod. A look at figures 5 and 6, which correspond to Table 8, clearly reveals an upward shift of the trade-off curves, whether fiscal or monetary policy is used. Hence a given rate of employment could be achieved only at the cost of higher inflation or, alternatively, a given rate of inflation could only be sustained by generating considerably more unemployment during 1965–1970 than during 1960–1965.

We are now in a position to consider another issue. We may ask about possible differences in cost in terms of additional inflation between the two subperiods, if the objective is to reduce the unemployment rate by a definite amount, e.g., one percentage point.

We turn first to the trade-off relationship derived on the basis of fiscal policy, using Figure 7, which is derived from Figure 5 as follows: In Figure 7, A and B are the respective trade-off curves for 1960–1965 and 1965–1970, and each passes through the origin at

TABLE 8 Trade-offs during 1965–1970

Fiscal Policy (Government Current Expenditures)			Monetary Policy		
Change in GCURRK, with High-Powered Money Held Constant (mill. constant dol.)	URATE	Percent Change in PGNE	Change in MHPC (mill. constant dol.)	URATE	Percent Change in PGNE
			+500	4.02	4.519
+400[a]	2.65	5.402	+400	4.20	4.439
+300	3.08	5.068	+300	4.38	4.370
+200	3.80	4.615	+200	4.55	4.309
Control solution	4.87	4.206		4.87	4.206
−200	5.86	3.923	−200	5.17	4.119
−300	6.34	3.802	−400	5.46	4.044
−400	6.82	3.690	−500	5.60	4.010

NOTE: For definition of variables, see text.
[a] Because 1966 was a full employment year, we could not inject $400 million in the first two years without running into convergence problems. Accordingly, we put in $300 million in 1965 and 1966 and $400 million from 1967 on.

the point of its control solution. The axes of Figure 7 thus represent *variations* in the unemployment rate ($\Delta URATE$) and in the percent rate of increase of prices [$\Delta(\%\Delta PGNE)$].

The relative positions of these two curves can now be used for a

FIGURE 5 Shift of the Trade-off Curve over Time under Fiscal Policy (GCURRK), 1960–1965 and 1965–1970

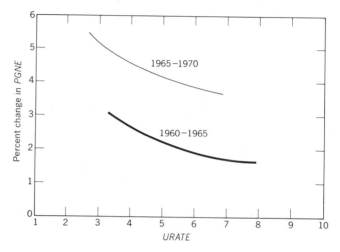

FIGURE 6 Shift of the Trade-off Curve over Time under Monetary Policy (MHPC), 1960–1965 and 1965–1970

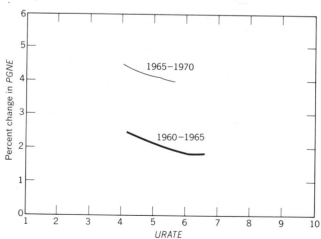

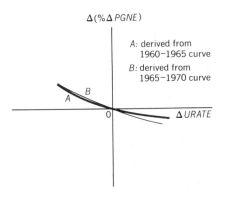

Δ(%Δ PGNE)

A: derived from
1960–1965 curve
B: derived from
1965–1970 curve

Δ URATE

Δ URATE = change over control solution value of URATE.
Δ(%ΔPGNE) = change over control solution value
of percent change in PGNE.

comparative analysis of the opportunity costs for the two sub-periods. We notice that, to the left of the origin, the two curves can hardly be separated. Hence we can draw the conclusion that a given reduction in unemployment in both these subperiods could have been achieved at almost the same cost in terms of inflation. However, to the right of the origin, the slope of curve A is always flatter than that of curve B. This implies that the cost in terms of incremental unemployment of obtaining a reduction in inflation was higher in 1960–1965 than in 1965–1970.

Figure 8 is similarly derived from Figure 6, based on the trade-off curves using monetary policy. Again, curves A and B represent 1960–1965 and 1965–1970, respectively. Here the two curves appear largely to coincide throughout their full range.

To recapitulate, in the two subperiods examined, we found the trade-off curve to be shifting upward over time. An intuitive explanation of this shift is given in footnote 20. We also noticed that such a shift may involve as well a change in the opportunity cost of inflation in terms of unemployment.

Our treatment of the effects of changes in the external economic environment on the Canadian trade-off curves derived for 1965–1970 is similar to what we reported in the previous section for 1960–1965. We again worked with an accelerated rate of increase of U.S. prices equal to one percentage point annually. In Table 9, we

FIGURE 8 Comparison of Relative Costs of
Inflation and Unemployment
under Monetary Policy,
1960–1965 and 1965–1970

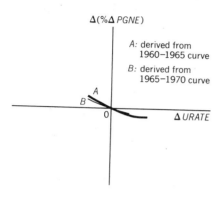

NOTE: Variables are defined in note to Figure 7.

TABLE 9 Trade-off with Assumed Higher U.S. Inflation during
1965–1970

Fiscal Policy			Monetary Policy		
Change in GCURRK (millions of constant dollars)	URATE	Percent Change in PGNE	Change in MHPC (mil. constant dol.)	URATE	Percent Change in PGNE
+300[a]	3.31	5.27	+500	3.84	5.02
+200	3.61	5.13	+400	4.02	4.94
			+300	4.37	4.80
Control solution	4.69	4.69		4.69	4.69
−200	5.69	4.39	−200	4.99	4.59
−300	6.18	4.27	−400	5.28	4.52
−400	6.65	4.15			

NOTE: For definition of variables, see text.
[a] This represents an increase in GCURRK of $300 million in 1965 and 1969, $200 million in 1966–1968, and $400 million in 1970. For explanation, see Table 8, note a.

show the unemployment-inflation trade-offs for Canada for 1965–1970 under these assumptions, for both fiscal and monetary policies. If we compare these results with those of Table 8, we find essentially the same kinds of effects of higher U.S. inflation as were observed for 1960–1965. In particular, the new control solution produces a slightly better performance in terms of unemployment, but coupled with more inflation.

In Figure 9 we compare the trade-off curves based on fiscal

FIGURE 9 Shift of the Trade-off Curve Resulting from Higher U.S. Inflation under Fiscal Policy (GCURRK), 1965–1970

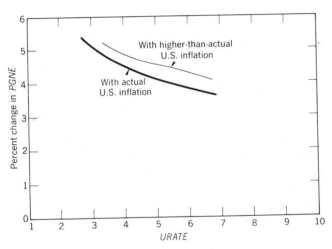

policy with and without increased rates of external inflation in the United States. In mild contrast to the 1960–1965 subperiod, the displacement is a largely parallel one, and an increase in U.S. inflation of one percentage point per year entails an increase in the annual rate of change of Canadian prices equal to four- to five-tenths of a percentage point, largely independent of the rate of unemployment, in the range studied. Similarly, the cost of insulating Canadian prices from additional external inflation is a considerably higher Canadian unemployment rate; due to the curvilinear nature of the trade-off curve, the required increment varies, depending upon the inflation target adopted.

Broadly similar conclusions may be drawn from Figure 10, in which we present the trade-off curves traced out by variations in monetary policy, with and without more rapid U.S. inflation.

FIGURE 10   Shift of the Trade-off Curve
Resulting from Higher U.S. Inflation
under Monetary Policy (MHPC),
1965–1970

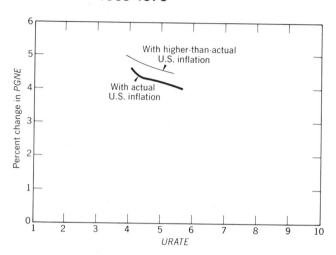

IV. THE PERIOD OF THE NEW ECONOMIC POLICY AND ITS SUCCESSORS, 1970–1974

For 1960–1970, we have been interested in studying the behavior of a trade-off curve given different policy instruments, in testing the stability of the relationship over time, and finally, in raising questions about the impact of the external environment on our tentative conclusions. Since, in the 1970s, inflation has become such an important problem, we decided to devote a section to the effects of the U.S. price picture during 1970–1974 on Canadian economic performance. We not only wanted to know what our own price performance would have been if U.S. prices had increased by one more and one less percentage point than the actual rate, but we suspected that even a constant rate of growth instead of cyclical movements in the rate of price increase in the United States might have caused less harm to Canada.

In order to answer those questions, we first have had to forecast the subperiod 1970–1974 from the model. It is a forecast because the sample period covered by the model ends in 1971. Since data for 1972 were already known, and since we had preliminary figures for 1973 and for the first half of 1974, we decided to use a "tuned forecast"[21] of the period. The values for different variables generated by this forecast are used as a benchmark for the purpose of making comparisons with the results obtained with different scenarios.

To derive these alternative scenarios, we proceed as we did for the sample period, for the increase or reduction in the rate of change of U.S. prices by one percentage point. For the third scenario (the smoothed rate of inflation), the 1970 and 1974 levels of all U.S. prices (and the prices of Canadian exports) remain unchanged, but the price levels for the years in between are generated by applying the geometric average yearly growth rates of those prices during 1970–1974 to base-year (1970) prices. This gives us a group of smoothly increasing price series, in which each percentage yearly increase is constant. There are no longer leads and lags in the peaks of the rate of change of these prices. Of course, this is not to suggest that such a smooth movement of prices would be likely to take place, even in the absence of perverse policies. Nevertheless, such a polar case may be of interest in itself.

Higher Rate of U.S. Inflation

Inflation and Unemployment

Let us have a look first at the results of a higher rate of inflation in the United States. On average over the period, the mean percent change in *PGNE* (6.245) is higher than the control solution (6.057), and there is a decrease in *URATE* from 6.021 percent to 5.845. The bulk of the effect comes in the years 1971 and 1972, after which the economy seems to react very little. We admit that when these prices grow at a rate of 3 or 4 percent (as was the case during 1971 and 1972) the one-percentage-point increase would have more effect than when these prices are already increasing at a rate of 8 percent (as was the case near the end of the period 1970–1974).[22] Comparing the alternative scenario with the control solution, we observe that the mean level of *PGNE* increases by exactly one index point, from 1.479 to 1.489, and not more.

Wages and Industry Prices

Looking at the wage-price subsystem of the model, we find that total-economy wages (per man-hour) change from $4.059 as a subperiod average to $4.094. We expected large effects on Canadian wages and salaries in construction, transportation, and manufacturing industries because the equations for these variables in the model portray a considerable impact of U.S. wages on Canadian wages. On an average over the subperiod, wages per man-hour in construction, transportation, and manufacturing increase more rapidly—by 1.41, 1.74, and 0.14 percentage points,[23] respectively. In other industries, the results seem plausible.[24]

Since our industry prices depend primarily on unit labor costs (according to the model), it is not surprising to find patterns in industry prices analogous to those in industry wages. Thus, the implicit deflators of construction and transportation industries are considerably affected. They show a faster increase—3.06 and 1.98 percentage points, respectively. On the other hand, the deflator for manufacturing industry shows an increase of only 0.32 percentage points.

Foreign Trade

Terms of trade and income are two of the main factors influencing foreign trade. When we made autonomous increases in the prices of goods imported from the United States, we also changed all our export prices (see the discussion in section 2). Thus, there was hardly any change in the terms of trade between the United States and Canada. Furthermore, the U.S. GNP in constant dollars was not changed at all, and the Canadian GNP in constant dollars also is hardly changed in the present simulation. Hence it is not surprising to find that Canadian exports to the United States (in constant dollars) are not much affected on average over the subperiod. The same applies to Canadian imports from the United States.

Canadian exports to and imports from the rest of the world, in constant dollars, also show little change even though, on our assumption, Canadian prices rise relative to the prices of the rest of the world. Such a result can be expected if the goods imported into Canada from the United States and the rest of the world are not good substitutes and if there is little change in Canadian real income. Given virtually no change in these constant-dollar exports and imports, their value in current dollars increases by approximately the same proportion as the autonomous increase we introduced into the prices of goods exported and imported.

Real Growth and Expenditures

As already mentioned, constant-dollar GNP is hardly affected. Thus, the real growth of the economy does not change. Real disposable income, consumer expenditures, investment in machinery and equipment, and investment in nonresidential construction in constant dollars are also not much affected. Investment in residential construction and the number of housing starts fall on average during the four years. We view this result with some apprehension because the housing starts equations have the variable $RTRB3M - RINDB$, which is the difference between the yield on three-month Treasury bills and the long-term industrial bond rate. This variable does not behave properly in the simulations.[25]

Lower Rate of U.S. Inflation

When we reduce U.S. inflation by one percentage point, we succeed in lowering our own average rate of price increases from 6.057 percent to 5.229 percent on the average while at the same time we do not have to pay for it by a higher unemployment rate. We even gain slightly in that respect in that $URATE$ changes from 6.021 percent to 5.909 percent. Once again the average level of $PGNE$ decreases by only slightly more than one index point: 1.464 instead of 1.479. Accordingly, the effect is not evenly spread throughout this particular subperiod. The main components of gross national expenditures[26] in constant dollars hardly change, except for investment in nonresidential construction, which shows an increase of 0.43 percent on average over the subperiod. Real disposable income, also, remains almost completely unchanged. Similarly, Canadian exports and imports in constant dollars do not show any significant changes.

The observations on wages in the case of higher U.S. inflation hold in reverse in the case of lower inflation. This symmetry is consistent with a priori reasoning, but the degree of responsiveness is not at all symmetrical. Industries such as agriculture and manufacturing, which did not show much increase in wages with higher U.S. inflation, now show a less rapid increase of almost two percentage points on average. On the other hand, financial services, public administration, and commercial business wages are less sensitive to an easing of U.S. inflation. For reasons given earlier, this asymmetry in the degree of responsiveness shows up in prices also.

Even Rate of U.S. Inflation

Simulating an even rate of inflation (as defined in the beginning of this section) was probably the most attractive experiment from the

Canadian point of view. It is very difficult to predict intuitively what overall effects an even rate would have for the Canadian economy. As for prices, the observed U.S. GNP deflator increased by 4.718 percent between 1970 and 1971, but then drastic anti-inflationary policies (such as wage and price controls) were successful in lowering it to about 3 percent. Inflation in the United States again increased sharply by the end of the subperiod 1970–1974. Thus, in general, if we transform the U.S. price series (and our export prices as discussed earlier), to incorporate an even rate of inflation, it will lower prices at the beginning of the period, raise them during the middle portion, and leave them nearly unchanged at the end. We expected other prices in the model to be affected similarly in this simulation.[27]

In this trial, we end up with the lowest unemployment rate (among our three simulations) and a lower average rate of price increase than the control solution. For 1970–1974, the unemployment rate decreased from an average of 6.02 percent to an average of 5.74, and the percent increase in the gross national expenditure (GNE) deflator decreased negligibly—from 6.05 percent to 6.02. Thus interestingly enough, simple elimination of the cyclical pattern of U.S. inflation, without even lowering the rate, improves the employment performance of the Canadian economy without any costs in terms of price performance. Indeed, we end up with a slightly lower level of the GNE deflator in 1974 even though, as expected, this level is higher than its level in the control solution for the middle years of the subperiod.

In general, wages per man-hour and industry prices show an increase relative to the control solution. This is not, however, true universally, as manufacturing wages and prices, for example, decline on average relative to control over the subperiod.

Canadian exports to the United States in real terms show an increase relative to control of 0.45 percent on average over the subperiod. This, coupled with the behavior of our transformed prices, increases the nominal value of Canadian exports to the United States during the middle years of the period 1970–1974. Even though exports to the United States, in real terms, show an increase in 1974 compared to the control solution, they show a decline in nominal terms because the decline of export prices relative to control in 1974 is sufficiently large to offset the increase in real terms. Again, in comparison to the control solution, exports to the rest of the world in real terms increase by 0.33 percent and, in nominal terms, exhibit the same behavior as exports to the United States.

On average over the subperiod, imports from the United States in real terms increase by 0.21 percent relative to the control solution. In nominal terms, they show an increase in 1971–1972, and almost no change in 1973–1974. Imports from the rest of the world are not affected much in real terms, but show a small nominal decline during 1972–1974. Consistent with a reduction in unemployment rate, constant-dollar GNP compared to the control solution shows a slight increase —0.25 percent—on average over the subperiod. Real disposable income, consumer expenditures, and investment in machinery and equipment all show slight gains in real terms, but investment in nonresidential construction shows a slight decline. (Again we do not discuss investment in residential construction and housing starts, for reasons already mentioned.) In general, these gains in real terms without much reduction in price increases (and even with some increases in the middle of our subperiod) increase our major nominal aggregates such as disposable income, gross national product, corporate profits, and government revenues.

V. CONCLUDING REMARKS

The principal conclusions of this study may be stated briefly. In a medium-term context within the framework of the CANDIDE model, the trade-off curve does indeed exist: simulations of the model suggest that in a particular historical context with other relevant exogenous variables held constant, demand management policies can generate additional employment only at the expense of an acceleration in the rate of inflation. Alternatively, it can be said that demand contraction would have cut the rate of inflation only at the expense of some increase in the rate of unemployment. Under the regime of a fixed rate of foreign exchange (the only one studied), the trade-off curves derived from the simulations were relatively invariant to the type of demand management instrument (fiscal vis-à-vis monetary policy, or subvariants of fiscal policy) utilized. The curves were sensitive in the expected direction to the assumptions regarding U.S. inflation rates, although in the five-year subperiods analyzed there was far less than a full pass-through of an acceleration of the rate of U.S. inflation. Finally, as has been widely remarked, the trade-off curves derived in this study varied with the historical subperiod studied, and we obtained evidence of the recent upward shift (or shifts) in the Canadian trade-off curve, which has already been widely remarked in a number of discussions.

The caveats and qualifications of this study are less easy to present. A number of shortcuts and simplifying assumptions were utilized in our study, and we attempted to state all of them explicitly in our preceding discussion. Many of those simplifications are debatable ones and, accordingly, could be regarded as shortcomings of this study. Beyond those specific qualifications, we have the general issue of how well the Canadian economy is represented in CANDIDE Model 1.1. This is obviously not a subject that can be treated exhaustively in this discussion. In our forthcoming volume, in which we describe some of the details of CANDIDE Model 1.1, we present a number of points of self-criticism, and other members of the profession will doubtlessly add some other points as well. In our judgment, the CANDIDE model is reasonably well suited for this sort of exercise, even though we must candidly admit that the wage and price sectors are among the weakest portions of the overall model.[28]

Finally, we conclude by attempting to draw one tentative lesson for policy from our study. It will be recalled that a stabilization of the yearly rate of U.S. inflation at the geometric mean rate observed over the subperiod 1970–1974 had favorable effects on the Canadian economy, even though the subperiod mean rate of inflation remained unchanged. We guess that a parallel conclusion would hold for the U.S. economy itself. In other words, we think that the stop-go anti-inflation policy practiced in the United States during those past four years may have been harmful to the North American economies, as contrasted with a more evenhanded policy. (Of course, even for the Canadian economy, the degree of harm has probably been overstated by the polar case we have studied.) It must be admitted that that at the time we wrote our paper, this was little more than a conjecture for the much larger U.S. economy, although we hoped to get some enlightenment on this point at the conference itself.[29] But if this point is correct, it has an obvious and immediate application to demand management and other policies designed to counteract inflation.

NOTES

1. This approach is developed at some length in two of Bodkin's earlier papers: "Wage and Price Formation in Econometric Models," in N. Swan and D. Wilton, eds., *Inflation and the Canadian Experience* (Kingston, Ont.: Industrial Relations Centre of Queen's University, 1971), and "Wage and Price Formation in Selected Canadian Econometric Models," in Otto Eckstein, ed., *The*

Econometrics of Price Determination (Washington, D.C.: Board of Governors of the Federal Reserve System, 1972). As James Tobin indicated in his summary of the Federal Reserve conference (pp. 5–15), the bulk of the papers presented there either focused on or at least touched on the issue of the existence or nonexistence of a long-run trade-off curve in the context of a sophisticated full model of a developed economy.

2. In his comments on Bodkin's "Wage and Price Formation in Econometric Models," John A. Sawyer raised the issue of whether it was legitimate to take the wage and price relationships out of the full model context in which they were embedded (in Swan and Wilton, eds., *Inflation*, pp. 123–126). (He also questioned whether the trade-off relationship, even if it can be shown to exist, is the most useful piece of information that the model builder can give to the policymaker, but that is not our concern here.) In this paper, we have attempted to follow up on Sawyer's first question. In particular, we have tried to do what S. F. Kaliski recommended in a more recent study, although he himself did not carry out the suggested analysis [*The Trade-off between Inflation and Unemployment: Some Explorations of the Recent Evidence for Canada*, Special Study 22 for the Economic Council of Canada (Ottawa: Information Canada, 1972)]. Kaliski asserts: "General considerations suggest that the trade-off or wage-price-unemployment subsector ought to be part of a larger model of the economy" (p. 109). Although the optimum-sized model of the economy for this purpose is still a moot point, there appears to be agreement that it should be larger than the usual two- or three-equation subsystem used to generate the typical trade-off curve, if only because of the important endogeneity of the critical variable, the rate of unemployment.

3. Details of the structure of the model utilized in this study may be found in Ronald G. Bodkin and Stephen M. Tanny, eds., *CANDIDE Model 1.1*, CANDIDE Project Paper 18, Economic Council of Canada for the Interdepartmental Committee (Ottawa: Information Canada, 1975). A statement in some depth of the salient features of the parent CANDIDE Model 1.0 may be found in M. C. McCracken, *An Overview of CANDIDE Model 1.0*, CANDIDE Project Paper 1, published by the Economic Council of Canada for the Interdepartmental Committee (Ottawa: Information Canada, 1973). Further details of Model 1.0 may be found in CANDIDE Project papers 2 through 17, a few of which had not yet been published at the time this paper was written.

4. By comparison, CANDIDE Model 1.0 was somewhat smaller. It had 377 exogenous variables and roughly 1,525 equations, which could be classified into slightly less than 570 behavioral equations, roughly 400 input-output relationships, and roughly 560 ordinary identities.

5. CANDIDE Model 1.1 is block-recursive, with a small number of equations that can be solved prior to the simultaneous core of the model and a small number of equations that can be solved afterward. Within the set of anterior equations, we have a demographic submodel that generates estimates of the Canadian population, households, and major age-sex subgroups from such fundamental determinants as the overall fertility rate, marriage rates, death rates, and net immigration rates. (All these fundamental determinants, except the last, are exogenous in CANDIDE Model 1.1; through the net immigration rates, Canadian population is made responsive to economic conditions, albeit with a lag.) In between the anterior and posterior equations, we have the large simultaneous core, as mentioned in the text.

The software employed to manage the computer files of the model and also to solve the set of nonlinear equations that constitutes the system could be the subject of a full discussion in itself. An introduction to the CANDIDE software may be found in McCracken, *An Overview*, App. A.

6. A brief history of the project may be found in "Foreword to the CANDIDE Model 1.0 Series of Project Papers," which appears in each of the first seventeen CANDIDE Project papers.

7. A summary description of the input-output aspects of CANDIDE Model 1.0 may be found in Ronald G. Bodkin, "The Use of Input-Output Techniques in a Large Scale Econometric Model of the Canadian Economy (CANDIDE)" (paper presented to Sixth International Conference on Input-Output Techniques, Vienna, Austria, April 1974). In turn, this paper was based on CANDIDE Project papers 8 and 12, in which the treatment employed is discussed in some detail. Finally, it must be mentioned that the CANDIDE input-output submodels reflect a heavy input of the labors of the Input-Output Research Division of Statistics Canada. These submodels are essentially a condensation of the large rectangular input-output system described in Statistics Canada (formerly Dominion Bureau of Statistics), *The Input-Output Structure of the Canadian Economy 1961*, Catalogue no. 15-501 Occasional (Ottawa: The Queen's Printer, 1969).

8. Ross S. Preston, *The Wharton Annual and Industry Forecasting Model*, Studies in Quantitative Economics, no. 7 (Philadelphia: University of Pennsylvania, Economics Research Unit, 1972).

9. McCracken, *An Overview*, p. xi.

10. Kaliski, *Trade-off between Inflation and Unemployment*, p. 5.

11. Another important dimension can be added to a study such as ours by also considering whether the exchange-rate regime in operation is fixed or floating. However, we left aside this interesting problem because we feel that the mechanism for determining the exchange rate when the rate floats is too weak in the present CANDIDE model to support such an exercise.

12. In our model, as *GCURRK* is an identity which sums its components, we have to vary all its components according to their relative weights as a mean in the subperiod in order to get an appropriate increase or decrease in *GCURRK*.

13. When we change government expenditures without modifying the supply of high-powered money (as in our first three experiments), we force interest rates to adjust accordingly. The subsequent change in the three-month Treasury bill rate and in all other interest rates linked to this key rate affects investment.

14. Another approach would have been not to hold the monetary block exogenous but to change the supply of high-powered money by a method of trial and error (which in the case of a big model like CANDIDE would be an extremely expensive exercise), until we are successful in keeping the interest rates approximately the same as in the control solution (but never exactly). It can be argued that the observed values of interest rates, which we use in our simulation, still differ from the values of these variables in the previous control solution. These two methods are not perfect substitutes because by keeping the monetary block exogenous we are breaking the normal feedback from the real sector to the monetary sector.

15. Even though we were sometimes successful in our efforts (especially in the case with the monetary block exogenous) to obtain a very low unemployment rate in our simulations, such calculations are, in part, only an academic exercise. We do not believe that Canada would have been successful in keeping its rate of unemployment from diverging from the U.S. rate by more than (say)

1.0 to 1.5 percent, and indeed a larger divergence has never been observed historically.

16. Both *MHPC* and *GTR* are in current dollars. Compared to *MHPC*, changes in *GTR* have relatively little effect in the model because the only channel through which they operate is changes in disposable income, and hence they have only an indirect effect on production.

17. Prices of imports from the United States *in Canadian dollars*, which are endogenous in our model, are simple functions of these exogenous prices and hence are automatically adjusted. Adjusting the exogenous import prices (in U.S. dollars) also changes the prices of competing imported commodities, which are an important determinant of the prices of domestically produced commodities in our price-side input-output submodel.

18. We agree that this is a gross simplification of the interrelationships between U.S. and Canadian prices. In the export of some commodities, such as oil, wheat and some raw materials, Canada probably has some market power in trade. However, in the absence of a known systematic relationship, this is probably the best assumption that can be made. We are thus positing a neutral change in North American markets, in which the prices of U.S. and Canadian exports increase more rapidly by the same number of percentage points on average over the subperiod. This assumption is made essentially for the convenience of the analysis.

19. This increase in price level would thus be cumulative over time. The 1961 increase in price over 1960 would thus be greater by one percentage point compared to historical levels. However, because we increase the 1962 price over the new 1961 price which has already been increased, the new 1962 price will be higher than the 1962 price by more than 1 percent; and indeed, it will be higher by approximately 2 percent. This cumulation of the effects of a higher rate of inflation continues, and has a compound interest effect.

20. In a simultaneous system, each dependent variable depends in general on the totality of the independent variables, and in a dynamic system the independent variables include those that are truly exogenous as well as the lagged values of the endogenous variables that constitute part of the system. Accordingly, at the highest level of generality, it is difficult to pinpoint causal relationships. Nevertheless, after using the model for some time and thus gaining a familiarity with its properties, we can make some more definite statements, provided the reader is willing to accept the results of educated intuition. It would appear that the upward shift of these trade-off curves between the two subperiods would in large part reflect a faster rate of inflation in the United States. (This point is illustrated immediately by a comparison of figures 3 and 4 with 5 and 6.) Secondly, the model has considerable inertia built into it, which reflects presumably similar dynamics in the Canadian economy itself. Once a pronounced movement of wages and prices gets under way, it will tend to perpetuate itself regardless of current economic conditions. This tendency of the model, together with the configuration of a high rate of price change and a low rate of unemployment at the beginning of the period, is a second aspect of a simple explanation of the upward shift in the trade-off curves between the two subperiods. [Footnote added, following critique of D. J. Daly at the conference.]

21. We feel that it is desirable to tune the forecast produced by a model if new information becomes available for some part of the forecast period. The process of tuning the model in the context of our discussion simply means that we do

not always take for granted all the forecasts produced by the model but rather make some adjustments to some of the equations of the model in light of the extra information available, so that the model generates forecasts closer to what is indicated by this new information.

22. A one-percentage-point increase in prices with a 4 percent rate of inflation amounts to a 25 percent increase in the rate of inflation, but compared to an 8 percent rate of inflation, it amounts to an increase of only 12.5 percent.

23. On a year-to-year basis, higher U.S. inflation has an almost negligible impact on wages in the construction industry in 1971 and 1972, but in 1973 and 1974 wages increase more rapidly—by 1.69 and 3.52 percentage points, respectively. This happens mainly because of the lag structure of the U.S. wage rate variable in the equation for construction industry wages. This variable appears to have a coefficient of 1.93 with a one-year lag and 0.68 with a two-year lag.

The percentage-point figures for yearly acceleration in the wage increase in transportation are 1.39, 1.37, 1.88, and 2.27 for 1971–1974, respectively. The sum of the coefficients for the lag structure of the U.S. wage rate variable in this case is 0.643. But the variable that puts such considerable pressure on these wages to rise is the lagged consumer price index, which has a coefficient of 0.917. Such a structure allows us to get more than the one-percentage-point increase as early as the first year, and this effect continues to cumulate over the subsequent years.

In the case of manufacturing, even though the lagged U.S. wage rate appears with a coefficient slightly greater than unity, we do not run into this cumulative process because the lagged dependent variable in this case appears with a negative coefficient (-0.2868) and, in addition, the reciprocal of the unemployment rate as an explanatory variable counteracts some of the pressure from higher U.S. wages.

24. Fishing, however, offers a strange pattern, and this holds for the three simulations and for prices in that industry also. However, this is a relatively small industry, and we need not worry too much about it.

25. Included in the model is a rule that does not allow $RTRB3M$ to diverge too much from a corresponding U.S. interest rate. This condition was introduced as a check for our balance-of-payments constraints. When our rate is above the U.S. rate plus 0.5 percentage points, the former is set equal to this upper limit and when it is less than the U.S. rate, it is reset equal to the U.S. level; in each case, we correct for our supply of high-powered money accordingly. When the system is shocked, $RTRB3M$ diverges widely, after a time, from the U.S. interest rate and hence is kept within the range arbitrarily. In the simulations, the effect showed up in 1973 and after. The same story repeats itself in other scenarios. However, $RINDB$ fluctuates in the simulations, and thus the variable $RTRB3M - RINDB$ creates distortions in the pattern of reactions.

26. Given our experience with the behavior of $RTRB3M - RINDB$, we are not analyzing the effects of this simulation on investment in residential construction and housing (see the preceding footnote).

27. Again, this is not to imply that prices in the United States, particularly prices of U.S. exports, would have behaved in this even fashion in the absence of the alternating patterns of controls and decontrols. (This point has particular force when it is recalled that U.S. export prices were generally not subject to regulation during the period of controls.) However, the examination of a polar case may still be of some interest.

28. As summarized in the two earlier Bodkin papers cited in note 1 above, this relative weakness of the wage-price subsystem is by no means unique to CANDIDE, but appears to characterize the current generation of econometric models almost universally.

29. See, in particular, the comparison papers by Marvin H. Kosters (Chapter 4 in this volume) and by Al-Samarrie, Kraft, and Roberts (Chapter 6). The stimulating Bosworth-Vroman paper (Chapter 3) indicates cogently, in our judgment, the limitations of a strictly empirical analysis of this unique historical experience.

COMMENTS

D. J. Daly
York University

I am glad to see a paper on the topic of recent inflation in Canada for three reasons. First, the subject is of considerable importance to economists, policymakers in government, decision makers in business, and the general public. Second, the paper reflects the use of a large econometric model of final demand, prices, employment, unemployment, and a substantial degree of industrial disaggregation. Finally, the senior author has published widely on applications of econometrics to wage-price and unemployment issues, and has widened his experience by two years in a senior operational role in the Economic Council of Canada.

Let me outline briefly what the authors have done in the paper. This is the first paper on a complete re-estimation of the Canadian CANDIDE model using annual data for 1955–1972. It is a 2,100-equation model with 450 exogenous variables, 625 behavioral equations, more than 400 input-output identities, and over 1,000 ordinary identities. It is thus a large computer-oriented, disaggregated, general-purpose model. It integrates input-output models of relative price determination and employment-output determination by industry. The model is neo-Keynesian and in the tradition of the Brookings and Wharton models for the United States.

In this paper, the authors use the model to simulate a Phillips-type trade-off curve for unemployment and price change. Simulations are made of alternative exogenous patterns on government expenditure change (current, fixed capital formation, and transfer payments) and monetary policy (constant interest rates and variations in high-powered money). The differences in the derived trade-off curves tend to be small, and the curves derived to be only marginally different from those obtained in earlier studies of smaller and simpler models. The authors also did simulations with alternative rates of price change in the United States, with results that indicate that this affected the derived Phillips curves for Canada.

In addition, simulations were made for three different time periods—1960–1965, 1965–1970, and 1970–1974. One important result from the subtime periods was that an outward shift of the Phillips curve was obtained for the 1965–1970 period compared to the previous five years. The authors suggested that the "simple elimination of the cyclical pattern of U.S. inflation, without even lowering the rate, improves the employment performance of the Canadian economy without any costs in terms of price performance."

Since a Phillips-curve relation was used in the specification and estimation of a number of the wage equations at the industry level, it is not surprising that it re-emerges in the aggregative simulations. It is surprising that so much effort went into such a simple point when there are other important topics needing study.

There are five areas that I would like to comment on, some of which relate to this particular Canadian model and the problems of analysis and policy in a small country, and others, to the broader family of models of this kind. A number of the comments raise points of a much broader nature than were covered within this particular conference paper.

My first concern relates to the incomplete documentation in the public domain on the CANDIDE model. The initial results were published two years ago, some of the staff studies related to Model 1.0 are still not published, and we now have the first paper on the next model. With a large, complex model, the sponsoring organization has a responsibility to make the basic information public more quickly than the Economic Council has been doing over the twelve years it has now been in operation. This is the advice I gave consistently when I was inside the organization, and I am now repeating the same advice outside. Ronald Bodkin has some responsibility in this area, and it is to be hoped that the performance on Model 1.1 will be better than it has been on 1.0.

The second question I wanted to raise concerns the stability of the input-output coefficients over time, a question that is relevant to the U.S. models also. Over the years, the assumptions that

Leontieff initially made of stability over time have been softened both in Preston's work for the United States and in the CANDIDE model used here. In the more detailed write-ups on the model (as set out in footnotes 3 and 7 of the paper) it is recognized that the coefficients of the industry technology matrix can change because of technological change, compositional shifts, relative price changes, and possible changes in taste. The procedures used make revisions to take account of changes in the shares of real GDP by industry, but the changes imply a continuation of past observed changes into the future.

What can we say about such procedures to extrapolate changes in the I/O coefficients over a twenty-year period? We do not have a test of this for Canada, but let me draw the attention of the model builders and the audience to a paper by Bea Vaccara and Nancy Simon done at an earlier conference of this body.[1] After standardizing for changes in final expenditures, they found significant changes in I/O coefficients over time, and later work reinforces the earlier results and suggests erratic, rather than systematic, changes in the coefficients. The changes for 1958–1963 are just as large as in their earlier study.

My own view is that the problems will be even *more* acute in Canada than these U.S. data suggest. The Canadian economy is much more open to international trade influences than the U.S. one, and exports and imports are much more important as demand and supply sources for such a small country. Cyclical changes in internationally traded goods are an integral part of the transmission of business cycles. Furthermore, over the period covered by the simulations, new elements have been introduced that were not present over the period used in estimating the model. For example, the Canadian dollar has appreciated about 8 percent since May 1970, and this has significantly affected the profit and price pictures in both export and import-competing industries. Since about 1967, the gap between the two countries in money and real weekly earnings in manufacturing that had persisted since 1900 has almost completely disappeared. This narrowing is partly the result of reductions in tariffs and of the Canada-U.S. trade arrangements. There is no reflection of an allowance for such structural changes in the discussions that I have yet seen on the CANDIDE models.

The third issue I raise concerns estimation procedures and applies to models of this kind, together with a number of the other papers presented at this conference. It relates to the implications of the collective bargaining process for wage settlements and the assumptions made in the basic structural equation estimations. The wage settlement process in unionized industries (covering about 20–25 percent of the Canadian labor force) involves a settlement frequently two or three years ahead, with a larger settlement in the first year. Thus, average hourly and weekly earnings in a particular year (or quarter) reflect developments not only in the current period, but one and two years earlier. The standard practice in estimating is to assume independence in the disturbances in the structural equations, and if estimates are made without allowing for intercorrelation between the independent variables and the residuals, the coefficients and t statistics will be biased. This statistical criticism by Rowley and Wilton of such Phillips-curve estimates made by Perry and Bodkin, Reuber, and others has not been met or mentioned in this paper. It would apply to estimates both of the levels and first differences in wages and to annual as well as quarterly estimates.

Fourth, I wish to point up the shift shown in the Phillips curve between 1960–1965 and 1965–1970. In Bodkin's earlier paper for the Economic Council of Canada, he had argued that the curve was fairly stable and could be used in policy discussions. This paper does not contain a reference to the earlier paper or an explanation of the shift in the second period. At the beginning of section III, it is stated that "working with the full model does not . . . allow us to be . . . explicit about the factors explaining the shift of the curve . . . , even though such an analysis could be important for policy decisions." If those involved in producing the model and the simulations cannot explain and defend the results, the outside professional is bound to be increasingly nervous about projecting the model into a situation of accelerated price developments, no matter what the ultimate or proximate factors in price inflation may be.

Let me just raise one more point. Anderson and Karnosky, in the first paper at this conference, provided a monetary interpretation of inflation. I have read about many past inflationary periods, but I cannot recall any in the industrialized countries which had not been preceded by a period of rapid monetary expansion. It may not be a sufficient interpretation of the last five years, as special circumstances of Vietnam, oil, food prices, and exchange rate changes have clearly been present. Anderson and Karnosky were concerned about a rate of monetary expansion of 6 percent in the United States. For Canada, over the three five-year periods used in the CANDIDE paper, the rates of monetary expansion have been 9.0, 10.25, and 16.4 percent per year compounded (based on an M_2 definition of money supply). These rates are well above the rates of increase in potential output estimated by CANDIDE and earlier methods used by the Economic Council of Canada.

May I suggest that there is a relevant domestic factor in the acceleration in the rate of increase in domestic prices in Canada over the period covered in this paper. More attention to the monetary implications of some of the earlier work by the ECC might have been very useful for government economic policy. The costs of looking at the rates of monetary growth over six- to nine-month periods (by any measure) would have been small, and I think it is undesirable for an agency to put all its eggs in one research basket.

NOTE

1. Bea Vaccara and Nancy Simon, "Factors Affecting the Postwar Industrial Composition of Real Product," in J. W. Kendrick, ed., *The Industrial Composition of Income and Product,* Studies in Income and Wealth 32 (New York: National Bureau of Economic Research, 1968), pp. 19–58.

12

SUNG Y. KWACK
Board of Governors of the
Federal Reserve System

Price Linkage in an Interdependent World Economy: Price Responses to Exchange Rate and Activity Changes

The rate of inflation in major industrial countries has increased steadily from the late 1960s and spread dramatically throughout the world in the last several years. Given the persistence of inflation on a worldwide basis, it is natural to seek for explanations of it from an international point of view. Consequently, the transmission of inflation from one country to another has received increasing attention.[1] In this paper I analyze the behavior of inflation in an individual country in a world of direct price linkages. Such an analysis is useful because it sheds some light on the question of how much the

NOTE: The author is an economist in the Division of International Finance, of the Board of Governors of the Federal Reserve System. The views expressed do not necessarily represent those of the Federal Reserve System. I benefited from the comments of Peter Clark, Dick Berner, John Helliwell, Howard Howe, and Guy Stevens. I am also indebted to the stimulus provided by Gary Fromm, Lawrence Klein, and Thomas Willett, and to Sam Parrillo and Ken Pannell for research assistance.

prices of other countries respond to a change in one country's exchange rate and unemployment rate.

In section I, I specify a model of the direct price linkages in a world economy. The model contains three sectoral equations for individual countries to explain the behavior of domestic prices, import prices, and changes in output levels. In section II, I discuss the estimated equations for twelve industrial countries: Australia, Austria, Belgium, Canada, Finland, Italy, Japan, Netherlands, Sweden, the United Kingdom, the United States, and West Germany. Then the model is tested by examining the results of dynamic simulations within the sample period. Section III contains some estimates of the multipliers on the own- and cross-country inflation rates due to a change in an individual exchange rate and unemployment rate. In addition, the model is used for assessing the contribution of actual changes in the exchange and unemployment rates to the rates of inflation during 1971–1973. The paper is concluded in section IV with a summary of the main results.

I. A MODEL OF INTERNATIONAL PRICE LINKAGES

Price behavior in most industrial countries reflects a variety of factors peculiar to each particular country. None of these countries, however, is isolated completely from the activity of the rest of the world. Thus, it is quite likely that some inflationary pressures originate abroad. In this broad sense, countries can be said to trade not only goods and services with each other but also inflations. Of course, countries differ significantly in their openness, and, thus, the propensity to import or export inflation can be expected to differ markedly among countries.

In seeking explanations for international transmissions of inflation, three types of mechanism can be distinguished: (a) direct, via prices of goods imported and wage rates; (b) indirect, via the changes in the aggregate demand working through the external account; and (c) indirect, via the change in the money supply induced by changes in international reserves. Although the latter two channels are considered to be important, too, I deal with only the first—the direct mechanism of inflation transmission—in this paper.[2]

The model of direct price linkages presented here is basically an extension of the Phillips model of price determination to a world containing many countries trading with each other. It consists of equations determining both domestic and import prices for each country. As shown below, the domestic price of each country is influenced not only by the unemployment rate and output at home, but also by import prices. Import prices of a given country are export prices of other countries to that country, adjusted for the variations in exchange rates. Through this direct relationship, domestic prices in the world are interdependent and therefore determined jointly. Thus, for example, an autonomous increase in the aggregate demand in any one country increases prices in the rest of the world.

In the model estimated below the world consists of n countries. For each country i, the domestic price of consumer goods is denoted by P_i; the wage rate, by W_i; the domestic output level, by Q_i; the import price, by P_i^m; the unemployment rate, by U_i; the exchange rate, defined as the number of U.S. dollars per unit of home currency i, by E_i; and the expected price, by P_i^e. A flex ($\hat{}$) indicates a proportional change in the variable.

Formally, the two structural equations are specified to explain the domestic price and the money wage rate. It is hypothesized that the domestic price is determined by unit labor costs and the import price, and the money wage rate is influenced by the unemployment rate and the expected domestic price.[3] Due to lack of adequate quantitative information, the rate of change in man-hours employed is assumed to be constant. Hence, they are written in a rate-of-change form:

1) $\qquad \hat{P}_i = m_{0i} + m_{1i}\hat{W}_i - m_{2i}\hat{Q}_i + m_{3i}\hat{P}_i^m$

2) $\qquad \hat{W}_i = n_{0i} + n_{1i}U_i^{-1} + n_{2i}\hat{P}_i^e$

To show that the domestic price is determined by the unemployment rate, output, and the import price, after allowing for simultaneous interactions between prices and the wage rate, equations 1 and 2 are solved for $\hat{P}_i$ and $\hat{W}_i$. If the rate of change in actual domestic prices is not equal to the rate of change in expected prices, expected inflation is adjusted for the unanticipated inflation. Such an adjustment continues until actual and expected inflation are equal ($\hat{P}_i = \hat{P}_i^e$). Imposing that equality in the solved reduced-form price equation, we obtain the equation for explaining price behavior in equilibrium, $\hat{P}_i^*$:

3) $\qquad \hat{P}_i^* = k_{0i} + k_{1i}U_i^{-1} - k_{2i}\hat{Q}_i + k_{3i}\hat{P}_i^m$

where $k_{0i} = (m_{0i} - m_{1i}n_{0i})/(1 - m_{1i}n_{2i})$, $k_{1i} = m_{1i}n_{1i}/(1 - m_{1i}n_{2i})$, and $k_{si} = m_{si}/(1 - m_{1i}n_{2i})$ for $s = 2, 3$. It is expected that k_{si} for $s = 1, 2, 3$

are positive, since m_{si} and n_{si} are positive, and $0 < m_{1i}n_{2i} < 1$, based on the available empirical evidence listed in Kwack (1973, p. 5).

The equality of actual and equilibrium prices may not hold at every point in time and adjustment toward such an equality takes some time because there are pecuniary and nonpecuniary adjustment costs associated with institutional rigidities and lack of accurate information. Therefore, it is assumed that the change in actual price is initiated by the changes in equilibrium prices in the current and previous periods. A Koyck-type form is selected as the partial adjustment mechanism, a choice that seems to provide a convenient starting point for empirical implementation. When the partial adadjustment mechanism is incorporated into (3), the following price equation is obtained:[4]

(4) $\qquad \hat{P}_i = \alpha_{0i} + \alpha_{1i}U_i^{-1} - \alpha_{2i}\hat{Q}_i + \alpha_{3i}\hat{P}_i^m + \alpha_{4i}\hat{P}_{i-1}$

where θ_i is the coefficient of adjustment and $\alpha_{1i} = k_{1i}\theta_i > 0$, $\alpha_{2i} = k_{2i}\theta_i > 0$, $\alpha_{3i} = k_{3i}\theta_i > 0$, and $\alpha_{4i} = 1 - \theta_i > 0$.

Generally speaking, the import price of a country is influenced by the demand and supply of the imports. Thus, other things being equal, the domestic prices and levels of activity of both exporting and importing countries determine the import price. However, shifts in the supply schedule caused by changes in output levels may be taken as small, especially in the short run, perhaps because of the limited mobility of productive factors between the traded and nontraded goods sectors. Also, the substitutability in consumption between imports and domestic goods is assumed to be small in the short run. In this case, the import price can be hypothesized as being determined largely by the prices of tradables in exporting countries adjusted for changes in exchange rates and by the income of the importing country.[5] The prices of tradable and nontradable goods are linked within each country through competition in production and consumption. This link ensures that the price of nontradable goods will vary with the price of tradable goods over a longer period of time, and, perhaps, at the same rate of change. On the basis of this relation, the domestic prices of tradables in exporting countries, which are a determinant of the import price, are assumed to be represented by their consumer prices.[6] Hence, we have the following equation for the import price:

(5) $\qquad \hat{P}_i^m = \beta_{0i} + \beta_{1i}\left[\sum_j a_{ij}(\hat{P}_j + \hat{E}_j) - \dfrac{\hat{E}_i}{1 + \hat{E}_i} \right] + \beta_{2i}\hat{Q}_i$

where $a_{ii} = 0$, $1 \geqslant a_{ij} \geqslant 0$ for $i \neq j$ and $\sum_j a_{ij} = 1$.

It is implicit in equation 5 that the aggregate foreign domestic price and the exchange rate are defined as, respectively, averages of the domestic prices and exchange rates of exporting countries, weighted geometrically by their export value shares in the importing country. It will be recalled that the exchange rate of currency j, E_j, is measured by the number of U.S. dollars per unit of currency j. Therefore, the term $\sum_j (a_{ij} - \delta_{ij})\hat{E}_j/(1 + \delta_{ij}\hat{E}_j)$ is a rate of change of the exchange rate of currency i in home currency units, and δ_{ij} is a Kronecker delta having the property $\delta_{ij} = 1$ for $i = j$ and $\delta_{ij} = 0$ for $i \neq j$. Thus, the term serves as a measure of the proportional change in the effective exchange rate. By hypothesis, the signs of both β_{1i} and β_{2i} are positive. The value of β_{1i} is expected to be close to unity if the price elasticity of supply is very large relative to the price elasticity of import demand.[7] Also, the value of β_{2i} is likely to be high when the economic size of the importing country is large, thereby strongly affecting the latter's import price.

Both the unemployment rate and the rate of change in the level of output enter the domestic price equation (equation 4) as exogenous variables. In order to isolate the transmission of inflation due to a change in the activity of a particular country, an equation is introduced in the model for the well-known mapping between unemployment and output, as shown by Okun (1962). Assuming that potential output grows at a constant rate, the specification of Okun's relationship is approximated by:

(6) $\quad \log Q_i = c_{0i}t - c_{1i}(U_i - U_i^{\rho})$

where t is a linear time trend and U_i^{ρ} is the unemployment rate existing at the potential output level. The change in the unemployment rate is derived by differentiating (6) with respect to time:

(7) $\quad \hat{Q}_i = C_{0i} - C_{1i}\Delta U_i$

Equations 4, 5, and 7 are the basis for describing price behavior of an individual country in an interdependent world. Combining the three equations yields:

(8) $\quad \hat{P}_i = \phi_i + \alpha_{1i}U_i^{-1} + \lambda_i \Delta U_i + \sum_j \mu_{ij}\hat{P}_j + \sum_j (\mu_{ij} - \sigma_{ij})\hat{E}_j/(1 + \delta_{ij}\hat{E}_j) + \omega_i P_{i-1}$

where $\phi_i = \alpha_{0i} - \alpha_{2i}c_{0i} + \beta_{0i}\alpha_{3i}$, $\lambda_i = \alpha_{2i}c_{1i}$, $\mu_{ij} = \alpha_{3i}\beta_{1i}a_{ij}$, $\sigma_{ij} = \alpha_{3i}\beta_{1i}\delta_{ij}$, and $\omega_i = \alpha_{4i}$. In equation 8, it can be easily seen that the rate of inflation in country i depends not only on its own unemployment rate and exchange rate but also on the exchange rates and prices of all other countries. To simplify our model for quantitatively analyzing the effect of changes in foreign prices and exchange rates, the constant term (ϕ_i) and ΔU_i are ignored. $\hat{E}_j$ is assumed to be small enough for $1 + \delta_{ij}\hat{E}_j$ to be approximated by 1, and U_i^{-1} is linearized by $1 - U_i$. Thus, equation 8 is simplified to:

(9) $\hat{P}_i = \rho_i U_i + \sum_j \mu_{ij}\hat{P}_j + \sum_j (\mu_{ij} - \sigma_{ij})\hat{E}_j + \omega_i\hat{P}_{i-1}$

where $\pi_i = -(\alpha_{1i} - \lambda_i)$. The signs of the parameters are $\rho_i < 0$, $\mu_{ij} > 0$, $\sigma_{ij} > 0$, and $\omega_i > 0$. The system of equation 8 for n countries can be written as follows:

(10) $\hat{P} = SU + R\hat{P} + [R - T]\hat{E} + L\hat{P}_{-1}$

where $\hat{P}$, U, and $\hat{E}$ are n-dimensional vectors with respective elements $\hat{P}_i$, U_i, and $\hat{E}_i$, for $i = 1,2,\ldots,n$; and S, T, and L are diagonal matrices, with respective elements ρ_i, σ_{ii}, and ω_i. The matrix R has the off-diagonal elements μ_{ij} and diagonal elements 0.

For the countries in the system, the effects on inflation of a change in a predetermined variable can be described by the values of the multipliers implied in (10). Since $[I - R]$ possesses an inverse, the system can be solved for the vector of domestic price inflations, $\hat{P}$:

(11) $\hat{P} = [I - R]^{-1}SU + [I - R]^{-1}[R - T]\hat{E} + [I - R]^{-1}L\hat{P}_{-1}$

where $[I - R]^{-1}S$ and $[I - R]^{-1}[R - T]$ are the impact or short-run multiplier matrices containing the elements of own- and cross-country effects induced by a change in the unemployment rate or exchange rate of a country. Since R is a non-negative matrix, all elements of $[I - R]^{-1}$ are non-negative. Moreover, all elements of $[I - R]^{-1}$ and $[I - R]^{-1}[R - T]$ will not be decreased or will be increased when one element of R increases. This means that the larger the own (diagonal) and cross-country (off-diagonal) effects, the greater is the interdependence of the prices among countries. Also, the own multiplier is generally larger than the cross-multipliers because the μ_{ij} are smaller than unity. So far, the vector of lagged inflation, $\hat{P}_{-1}$, has been treated as exogenous. In the longer run, the $\hat{P}_{-1}$ are considered as endogenous. The system is stable in the long run because each characteristic root of $[I - R]^{-1}L$ is less than 1.0 in absolute value.[8] Thus, the long-run-equilibrium multiplier values of a change in U and $\hat{E}$ are $[I - R - L]^{-1}S$ and $[I - R - L]^{-1}[R - T]$, respectively. L is a diagonal matrix with positive elements, $0 \le \omega_i < 1$. Thus, $[I - R - L]^{-1} \ge [I - R]^{-1}$ because $R + L$ is a non-negative matrix that is greater than R. This proves that the long-run multipliers are not less than the corresponding short-run ones.

It has been shown that a change in the unemployment rate and exchange rate of a given country will result in changes in the inflation rates of all countries. Now consider a special case where the initiating country i is small in the sense $a_{ji} = 0$ for country j. By definition, $a_{ji} = 0$ implies $\mu_{ji} = 0$ for all j, leading to the matrix $R = 0$. Therefore, there are no feedback effects through the induced changes in foreign domestic prices. Consequently, the effect of the initiating country on inflation depends exclusively on the magnitudes of its own parameters, ρ_i, σ_{ii}, and ω_i. Moreover, by introducing the condition $R = 0$ into equation 11, it can be proved that the multiplier values of a change in U_i and $\hat{E}_i$ in this special case are smaller than the values obtained in the case of induced cross-country effects, $R \neq 0$. This is so because $[I - R - L]^{-1} > [I - L]^{-1}$ for the long-run multipliers and $[I - R]^{-1} > I$ for the impact multipliers.

Table 1 is a summary of the direction of the effects of a unit change in the unemployment rate and exchange rate of a particular country. Two points merit special attention. First, a reduction in the unemployment rate of a given country leads to a rise in the rate of inflation of all countries. The resulting increases in the inflation rates become stronger in the presence of cross-country effects ($\mu_{ij} \neq 0$) than the rates expected when the country is small. The reason is that the induced increases in foreign prices result in induced increases in import prices of all countries. Second, an appreciation of a currency against the U.S. dollar lowers that country's domestic price and raises the prices of the other countries, including the United States. However, the reduction in own inflation is smaller when foreign prices also rise, as is the case if $\mu_{ij} \neq 0$, because import prices of the appreciating country then rise.

II. ESTIMATION OF PARAMETERS

Equations 4, 5, and 7 were estimated with annual data for 1957–1973 for each of twelve countries: Australia, Austria, Belgium, Canada, Finland, Italy, Japan, the Netherlands, Sweden, the United Kingdom, the United States, and West Germany. [The data are from *International Financial Statistics* (International Monetary Fund) and the United Nations *Monthly Bulletin of Statistics*.] Except where necessary to obtain reasonable estimates, modifications of the equation specifications were not made. Also, ordinary least squares was employed, ignoring possible simultaneous equation bias. These two simplifications were adopted to avoid a flood of

TABLE 1 Direction of Multipliers

	No Cross-Feedback Effect ($\mu_{ji} = 0$)		Cross-Feedback Effect ($\mu_{ji} \neq 0$)	
	Impact	Long Run	Impact	Long Run
$\dfrac{\partial \hat{P}}{\partial \hat{U}}$	S	$[I - L]^{-1}S = s_i$	$[I - R]^{-1}S = s_i^*$	$[I - R - L]^{-1} = s_i^{**}$
$\dfrac{\partial \hat{P}_i}{\partial \hat{U}_i}$	ρ_i	$s_i > \rho_i(1 + w_i)$	$s_i^* > \rho_i$	$s_i^{**} > s_i^*(1 + w_i)$
$\dfrac{\partial \hat{P}_j}{\partial \hat{U}_i}$	0	0	$s_j^* > \mu_{ji}\rho_i$	$s_j^{**} > s_j^*(1 + w_j)$
$\dfrac{\partial P}{\partial \hat{E}}$	$[R - T]$	$[I - L]^{-1}[R - T] = r_i$	$[I - R]^{-1}[R - T] = r_i^*$	$[I - R - L]^{-1}[R - T] = r_i^{**}$
$\dfrac{\partial \hat{P}_i}{\partial \hat{E}_i}$	$-\sigma_{ii}$	$r_i < -\sigma_{ii}(1 + w_i)$	$r_i^* > -(\sigma_{ii} - \displaystyle\sum_{k \neq 1} \mu_{ik}\mu_{ki})$	$r_i^{**} < r_i^* - w_i\sigma_{ii}$
$\dfrac{\partial \hat{P}_j}{\partial \hat{E}_i}$	0	0	$r_j^* < \mu_{ji}(1 - \sigma_{ii}) + \displaystyle\sum_{k \neq i,j} \mu_{ik}\mu_{ki}$	$r_j^{**} > r_j^* + \mu_{ji}w_j$

NOTE: The information on individual elements, $s_i, r_i, s_i^*, r_i^*, s_i^{**},$ and r_i^{**} is compared with the direction and magnitude obtained by the first-order Taylor approximations, i.e., $[I - L]^{-1}$, $[I - R]^{-1}$, and $[I - R - L]^{-1}$ are compared with the values of $[I + L]$, $[W + R]$, and $[I + R + L]$, respectively.

permutations and alternative specifications. Nevertheless, the estimates presented below are subject to the qualifications that result from the use of ordinary least squares and the existence of some missing variables. In the tables that follow, the numbers in parentheses below the coefficient estimates are t statistics. $\bar{R}^2$ is the coefficient of determination adjusted for degrees of freedom; SEE, the standard error of estimate; and DW, the Durbin-Watson statistic.

Table 2 contains estimates of the price equations for each of the twelve countries. At first glance, most of the estimated equations are reasonable. In particular, both the unemployment rate and import price have significant coefficients with the expected sign in all equations. This seems to confirm that in addition to the unemployment rate, the import price of a country is an important determinant of domestic prices.[9] This finding is consistent with past studies (see Ball and Duffey 1972) in which the import prices are shown to be significant in structural price equations in most industrial countries. The coefficient on the U.S. unemployment rate is larger than that on most of the unemployment rates of other countries. This confirms the finding of previous studies (such as Kwack 1973) that the U.S. trade-off between inflation and unemployment is worse than that abroad. The dummy variables in the equation for the Netherlands and the United Kingdom are designed to capture the income restraint policies, and the dummy variable in the Australia equation is introduced to eliminate the observation for 1973.[10] Note, however, that incomes policies are either perverse, or are introduced in response to strong exogenous price pressures.

When the equation results are closely inspected, however, there are some disturbing elements. The price equation for Canada is not satisfactory, in that the long-run coefficient on the import price, 2.42, is substantially higher than a priori expected maximum value of 1.0 and the estimate of 0.55 in TRACE reported in Bodkin (1972). But, the impact effect, 0.35, is close to TRACE's estimate of 0.45, indicating that the estimated equation can be used for short-term analysis. In addition, the coefficient of the U.K. import price, 0.18, seems to be low. Excluding Canada, the long-run coefficients of import prices range between 0.10 and 0.96. For six of the countries—Australia, Belgium, Canada, Finland, the United States, and West Germany—the coefficients on the one-year lagged price variable are found to be significant. The implied coefficients of adjustment are between 0.15 and 0.65. The estimates seem to be plausible, in view of the existence of institutional rigidities such as escalator clauses and imperfect information.

TABLE 2 Consumer Price Equations,[a] 1957–1973

Country i	α_{0i}	α_{1i}	α_{2i}	α_{3i}	α_{4i}	α_{5i}	$\bar{R}^2$ [SEE] {DW}
Australia[b]	-0.016 (1.89)	0.041 (3.42)		0.409 (3.52)	0.576 (4.07)	0.130 (5.88)	0.877 [0.007] {2.488}
Austria	0.004 (0.32)	0.108 (4.05)	-0.131 (1.25)	0.095 (1.20)			0.611 [0.010] {2.218}
Belgium	-0.010 (1.84)	0.063 (3.38)		0.098 (3.72)	0.754 (6.44)		0.878 [0.005] {2.338}
Canada	-0.021 (2.31)	0.111 (2.53)		0.347 (4.47)	0.857 (5.73)		0.806 [0.007] {1.659}
Finland	-0.014 (0.52)	0.057 (1.58)		0.420 (4.51)	0.342 (1.98)		0.614 [0.019] {1.797}
Italy	-0.004 (0.27)	0.146 (2.40)		0.194 (3.32)			0.592 [0.016] {2.009}

	α_{0i}	α_{1i}	α_{2i}	α_{3i}	α_{4i}	α_{5i}	
Japan	0.050 (3.28)	0.023 (1.57)	−0.169 (3.44)	0.383 (7.60)			0.794 [0.011] {2.196}
Netherlands[c]	0.015 (0.93)	0.025 (1.48)		0.361 (2.54)		0.025 (1.75)	0.462 [0.017] {2.512}
Sweden	0.034 (1.92)	0.038 (1.08)	−0.452 (2.15)	0.389 (3.42)			0.381 [0.016] {2.796}
United Kingdom[d]	0.007 (0.52)	0.062 (2.34)	−0.357 (3.01)	0.174 (3.07)		0.049 (5.04)	0.848 [0.009] {2.136}
United States	−0.014 (2.02)	0.161 (4.92)	−0.125 (3.63)	0.195 (5.91)	0.399 (3.53)		0.898 [0.005] {2.202}
West Germany	0.003 (0.32)	0.008 (1.70)		0.137 (2.75)	0.682 (3.29)		0.696 [0.008] {1.501}

[a]The equation is

$$\log \left[P/P(-1)\right]_i = \alpha_{0i} + \alpha_{1i}(1/U_i) + \alpha_{2i} \log \left[Q/Q(-1)\right]_i + \alpha_{3i} \log \left[P^m/P^m(-1)\right]_i + \alpha_{4i}\{\log \left[P/P(-1)\right]_i\}_{-1} + \alpha_{5i}D_i$$

[b]The sample period is 1959–1973, and $D_i = 0.5$ in 1973.

[c]The unemployment rate enters with a lag of two years, and $D_i = 0.5$ in 1970 and 1971 and 1.0 in 1972 and 1973.

[d]$D_i = 0.5$ in 1969 and 1970, and 1.0 in 1971–1973.

Table 3 contains the equations for explaining import prices as represented by unit value indexes in home-currency units. P_i^r and F_i, are weighted averages of the domestic prices of countries that export to country i and the effective rate for currency i, and are defined in Table 4. The coefficients of the domestic prices abroad adjusted for the exchange rate variations, $P_i^r + F_i$, are between 0.4 and 1.2 for all countries except Austria, Italy, and the Netherlands. The coefficients for these three are close to 1.5, and are not statistically different from 1.0. On the whole, nevertheless, the coefficient estimates seem to overstate the extent to which foreign domestic prices are reflected in import prices. The dummy variable D in the import price equations (except for Austria, Italy, Sweden, and the United States) accounts for the influence of the extraordinary upward surge of raw materials and oil prices that took place in the early 1970s. The output variables are found to be significant or almost so for six countries: Austria, Belgium, Japan, Sweden, the United Kingdom, and West Germany. The results further indicate that import prices are not related to the income of the six remaining countries: Australia, Canada, Finland, Italy, the Netherlands, and the United States. This seems particularly puzzling because the United States, for example, is considered to be a large country, and Sweden, a small one. The results are only tentative because no explicit differentiation is made between tradable and nontradable prices. Nevertheless, the empirical results may very moderately overstate the impact of a change in output levels.

Table 5 presents the results obtained for the unemployment rate equations. First-order Almon-distributed lags on real output are introduced to allow for the possible effects of past changes in real output. The coefficients of current and previous real output levels are negative for all twelve countries, indicating that Okun's relationship holds. The long-run change in the unemployment rate with respect to real output is indicated by the sum of the distributed lag coefficients of current and lagged real output. As expected, the sum of the coefficients varies substantially among countries, ranging from −2.5 for Japan to −47.0 for Canada. However, the estimate for Japan appears to be unrealistic, suggesting that the Okun specification needs to be modified for that country. For the United States, the sum of the coefficients, −31, is in agreement with the estimate of Friedman and Wachter (1974), −29, based on quarterly data for 1954I–1970IV. The constant terms are significant and positive for all countries. Consequently, the explanation of potential output by a time trend is a reasonable first-order approximation.

Even though each individual equation is acceptable, there is no a

TABLE 3 Import Price Equations,[a] 1957–1973

Country i	β_{0i}	β_{1i}	β_{2i}	β_{3i}	$\bar{R}^2$ [SEE] {DW}
Australia	−0.014 (2.74)	0.831 (6.30)		0.012 (1.43)	0.708 [0.012] {2.213}
Austria	−0.071 (3.80)	1.331 (3.46)	0.408 (1.53)		0.504 [0.029] {2.460}
Belgium	−0.071 (2.89)	1.164 (1.83)	0.740 (2.66)	0.071 (2.24)	0.572 [0.040] {1.562}
Canada	−0.006 (0.96)	0.681 (4.44)		0.021 (1.98)	0.670 [0.014] {1.871}
Finland	−0.003 (0.19)	0.465 (3.83)		0.060 (1.86)	0.506 [0.045] {1.945}
Italy	−0.054 (3.61)	1.539 (6.13)			0.696 [0.041] {2.039}
Japan	−0.103 (3.99)	1.129 (2.31)	0.495 (3.02)	0.127 (3.87)	0.558 [0.041] {1.365}
Netherlands	−0.032 (2.75)	1.481 (4.11)			0.498 [0.025] {1.946}
Sweden	−0.033 (2.28)	0.816 (2.51)	0.368 (1.64)	0.034 (1.49)	0.613 [0.024] {2.460}
United Kingdom	−0.048 (4.42)	0.833 (4.86)	0.778 (2.97)	0.057 (2.46)	0.853 [0.027] {2.331}
United States	−0.031 (3.95)	1.231 (8.98)			0.833 [0.020] {2.168}
West Germany[b]	−0.038 (3.15)	0.853 (2.98)	0.219 (1.66)	0.386 (8.62)	0.824 [0.019] {0.941}

[a] The equation is

$$\log [P^m/P^m(-1)]_i = \beta_{0i} + \beta_{1i}\{\log [P^x/P^x(-1) + \log [F/F(-1)]\}_i$$
$$+ \beta_{2i} \log [Q/Q(-1)]_i + \beta_{3i}D_{-2}$$

where D is a dummy variable reflecting structural shifts during 1970–1973, and has 0.5 for 1970 and 1971 and 1.0 for 1972 and 1973.
[b] The dummy variable is 0.5 for 1973 only.

TABLE 4 Foreign Export Prices and Effective Exchange Rates in Each Domestic Currency Unit[a]

Country i	Average Import Value Shares (a_{ij}), 1971											
	AS	AU	BL	CA	FI	IT	JA	NE	SW	UK	US	WG
Australia (AS)	0.0	0.004	0.008	0.053	0.006	0.026	0.222	0.018	0.025	0.261	0.292	0.085
Austria (AU)	0.000	0.0	0.026	0.003	0.008	0.098	0.014	0.043	0.047	0.090	0.034	0.637
Belgium (BL)	0.005	0.005	0.0	0.021	0.005	0.068	0.027	0.234	0.027	0.096	0.123	0.389
Canada (CA)	0.010	0.003	0.005	0.0	0.001	0.013	0.068	0.007	0.009	0.066	0.785	0.033
Finland (FI)	0.004	0.025	0.026	0.007	0.0	0.033	0.030	0.057	0.284	0.211	0.055	0.267
Italy (IT)	0.011	0.039	0.072	0.028	0.007	0.0	0.026	0.098	0.029	0.080	0.174	0.437
Japan (JA)	0.193	0.002	0.010	0.104	0.001	0.016	0.0	0.010	0.010	0.041	0.534	0.070
Netherlands (NE)	0.006	0.008	0.212	0.021	0.009	0.063	0.032	0.0	0.029	0.089	0.158	0.373
Sweden (SW)	0.003	0.030	0.051	0.011	0.091	0.045	0.032	0.073	0.0	0.227	0.114	0.325
United Kingdom (UK)	0.054	0.022	0.045	0.134	0.045	0.059	0.057	0.102	0.100	0.0	0.229	0.156
United States (US)	0.021	0.004	0.028	0.397	0.004	0.049	0.250	0.019	0.016	0.087	0.0	0.124
West Germany (WG)	0.008	0.039	0.170	0.017	0.013	0.189	0.036	0.260	0.045	0.071	0.152	0.0

[a] The estimating equation for foreign export prices (P^x) is

$$\log [P^x/P^x(-1)]_i = \sum\nolimits_j a_{ij} \log [P/P(-1)]_i$$

The estimating equation for effective exchange rates (F_i) is

$$\log [F/F(-1)]_i = \sum\nolimits_j a_{ij} \log [E/E(-1)]_i/\{1 + \log [E/E(-1)]\}_i$$

The diagonal element in the matrix becomes -1.0 when effective exchange rates are calculated.

priori assurance that performance of the system of equations as a whole is satisfactory. If the system does not track price behavior reasonably well, it may not be adequate for policy simulations. A test of this is based on summary statistics derived from the within-sample dynamic simulation for 1957–1973. The mean bias and root-mean-square error for individual equations are given in Table 6. The statistics of mean bias show that the errors generated in the simulation are not severely cumulative and tend to offset each other over time. The values for the root-mean-square error indicate that the import price and output equations for Italy and Japan seem to perform poorly relative to other equations, perhaps because the cyclical behavior of import and consumer prices generated by the low coefficients of real output in the unemployment rate equations differs substantially from the actual movements. Thus, the analysis of the simulation exercises in the following section must be interpreted with caution. Given this caveat, however, the test statistics seem to indicate that the model is able to trace the actual behavior of the rates of change in consumer and import prices and in output.

III. SIMULATION RESULTS: EFFECTS OF EXCHANGE RATE AND UNEMPLOYMENT RATE CHANGES

Different types of dynamic simulation can be carried out to observe the behavior of inflation in all countries in response to a shock to a particular exogenous variable. In each simulation, all other exogenous variables are kept at their actual values. Thus, the differences between the shocked and the control solutions are the estimates of the own- and cross-country multipliers discussed in the previous section. In the following, the model will be simulated over the period 1968–1973 to derive the multipliers of a unit change in the exchange rate and unemployment rate of each country in the system. After these simulations are carried out, two more are performed to ascertain how much of actual inflation rates during 1971–1973 has been associated with actual changes in the exchange and unemployment rates. The model is nonlinear and simultaneous. Consequently, the estimates derived from the simulations depend on initial conditions and the size of shocks.

The model is simulated with a sustained increase of 1 percent in the exchange rate of each country, one country at a time. The multiplier values for domestic and import prices of all countries are

TABLE 5 Unemployment (Okun's Law) Equations,[a] 1957–1973

Country i	γ_{0i}	γ_{1i}	γ_{2i}	γ_{3i}	γ_{4i}	γ_{5i}	$\bar{R}^2$ [SEE] {DW}
Australia[b]	0.496 (3.32)	−10.269 (4.76)					0.607 [0.397] {2.100}
Austria	0.511 (2.01)	−6.288 (2.95)	−4.192 (2.95)	−2.096 (2.95)			0.325 [0.311] {1.084}
Belgium	1.386 (4.66)	−13.96 (5.23)	−10.47 (5.23)	−6.980 (5.23)	−3.490 (5.23)		0.622 [0.487] {0.835}
Canada	2.308 (3.66)	−20.04 (3.60)	−13.36 (3.60)	−6.679 (3.60)			0.428 [0.745] {1.793}
Finland[b]	1.046 (3.81)	−15.09 (4.44)					0.572 [0.457] {2.009}
Italy	0.646 (1.36)	−5.726 (2.21)	−4.295 (2.21)	−2.863 (2.21)	−1.432 (2.21)		0.195 [0.609] {0.683}

	γ_{0i}	γ_{1i}	γ_{2i}	γ_{3i}	γ_{4i}	γ_{5i}	
Japan	0.296	−1.298	−0.865	−0.433			0.194
	(1.97)	(2.20)	(2.20)	(2.20)			[0.163]
							{2.118}
Netherlands	1.120	−7.387	−4.925	−2.462			0.236
	(2.61)	(2.44)	(2.44)	(2.44)			[0.472]
							{1.187}
Sweden	0.550	−10.113					0.672
	(5.32)	(5.81)					[0.191]
							{1.839}
United Kingdom	1.417	−15.31	−12.24	−9.183	−6.122	−3.061	0.484
	(4.11)	(4.00)	(4.00)	(4.00)	(4.00)	(4.00)	[0.383]
							{1.380}
United States	1.311	−12.36	−9.273	−6.182	−3.091		0.496
	(3.68)	(4.09)	(4.09)	(4.09)	(4.09)		[0.712]
							{2.374}
West Germany	0.962	−9.876	−6.584	−3.292			0.545
	(3.57)	(4.49)	(4.49)	(4.49)			[0.403]
							{1.866}

[a] The equation is

$$\Delta U_i = \gamma_{0i} + \sum_{k=0}^{4} \gamma_{1+k,i} \log\left[Q(-k)/Q(-k-1)\right]_i$$

[b] The sample period is 1959–1973.

TABLE 6 Prediction Error Statistics of the Dynamic Simulations, 1957–1973 (fractions)

Country	Mean Bias			Root-Mean-Square Error		
	Consumer Price	Import Price	Output	Consumer Price	Import Price	Output
Australia	.0053	.0007	.0097	.0105	.0093	.0365
Austria	.0002	.0047	.0024	.0110	.0280	.0471
Belgium	.0022	.0028	.0009	.0066	.0400	.0353
Canada	.0012	.0007	.0010	.0101	.0157	.0429
Finland	.0013	.0006	.0115	.0266	.0417	.0383
Italy	−.0004	.0001	.0021	.0144	.0418	.0854
Japan	.0016	.0030	.0027	.0167	.0754	.1600
Netherlands	.0001	.0033	.0021	.0201	.0299	.0581
Sweden	.0006	.0014	.0000	.0130	.0262	.0170
United Kingdom	−.0009	.0046	.0041	.0094	.0303	.0246
United States	.0010	.0019	.0025	.0090	.0214	.0700
West Germany	.0043	.0007	.0007	.0113	.0228	.0504

computed by comparing the solution with the control solution. The own- and cross-country multipliers for domestic prices are summarized in matrix form in Table 7.

Although the table contains a wealth of information, only a few general conclusions can be drawn because of limited space. The reductions in the domestic prices of countries whose currencies appreciate vary from one country to another, as shown by the diagonal elements of the matrix. On the average, a 1 percent appreciation reduces prices by about 0.26 percent in the first year after the policy change and by about 0.36 percent after six years. Thus, the effect on own domestic inflation is substantial. As revealed in the off-diagonal elements, a currency appreciation is accompanied by induced increases in the prices of other countries, although not by an appreciable amount initially. But, the cross-country effects tend to become gradually greater as time passes, because of the lagged adjustments. Since all the cross effects are not found to be zero, the inflationary pressure from a change in currency value can be transmitted abroad.

The sum of the off-diagonal row elements represents the extent to which the prices of receiving countries are influenced. According to the figures shown, changes in the value of the U.S. dollar and West German deutsche mark (DM) are expected to have an appreciable impact on prices in other countries. On the other hand, the sum of the off-diagonal column elements is a measure of the vulnerability of a country's domestic prices to changes in external currency values. Canada, Australia and the Netherlands, for example, are very vulnerable.

As noted earlier, domestic prices are also affected by changes in unemployment rates abroad, not only through inverse changes in unemployment rates but also through changes in the rate of growth of output levels. The multipliers to reveal these influences are also computed by simulations. Table 8 contains the own and cross effects on the domestic prices of all countries of a 1 percent increase in the unemployment rate of each country. As expected, domestic prices in a country tend to fall appreciably in the long run as a result of the simulated increase in its own unemployment rate. As shown by the diagonal elements, in the long run, domestic prices decline by approximately 0.24 percent, on the average. The responses in the first year are mixed, however, depending on whether the positive effect attributable to the induced decrease in the output level (possibly a proxy for lower productivity growth) as described by the Okun equation outweighs the negative effect of the increased unemployment itself.

TABLE 7 Effects of a 1 Percent Appreciation in the Dollar Price of an Initiating Country's Currency on Foreign Consumer Price Inflation[a] (percent)

Initiating Country	Receiving Country												Off-Diagonal Row Sum
	AS	AU	BL	CA	FI	IT	JA	NE	SW	UK	US	WG	
Australia (AS)													
Impact	-0.32	0.0	0.0	0.0	0.0	0.0	0.06	0.0	0.0	0.01	0.01	0.0	0.09
Long run	-0.67	0.0	0.0	0.01	0.0	0.0	0.02	0.0	0.0	0.0	0.01	0.0	0.04
Austria (AU)													
Impact	0.0	-0.12	0.0	0.0	0.01	0.01	0.0	0.01	0.01	0.0	0.0	0.0	0.04
Long run	0.01	-0.10	0.0	0.01	0.01	0.01	0.0	0.01	0.01	0.0	0.0	0.01	0.07
Belgium (BL)													
Impact	0.01	0.01	-0.11	0.0	0.01	0.03	0.01	0.11	0.02	0.01	0.01	0.02	0.24
Long run	0.02	0.01	-0.34	0.02	0.01	0.02	0.01	0.07	0.02	0.01	0.01	0.04	0.24
Canada (CA)													
Impact	0.03	0.0	0.0	-0.21	0.0	0.01	0.06	0.02	0.01	0.02	0.08	0.0	0.23
Long run	0.02	0.0	0.01	-0.92	0.0	0.0	0.01	0.01	0.0	0.0	0.03	0.01	0.09
Finland (FI)													
Impact	0.0	0.0	0.0	0.0	-0.30	0.0	0.0	0.0	0.02	0.01	0.0	0.0	0.03
Long run	0.01	0.0	0.0	0.0	-0.28	0.0	0.0	0.0	0.02	0.01	0.0	0.0	0.04
Italy (IT)													
Impact	0.01	0.01	0.01	0.0	0.01	-0.29	0.01	0.03	0.01	0.01	0.01	0.02	0.13
Long run	0.03	0.01	0.03	0.03	0.01	-0.31	0.01	0.03	0.02	0.01	0.02	0.04	0.24

Japan (JA)													
Impact	0.05	0.0	0.0	0.02	0.01	0.0	−0.40	0.02	0.01	0.01	0.04	0.01	0.16
Long run	0.13	0.0	0.01	0.11	0.01	0.01	−0.33	0.02	0.01	0.01	0.09	0.01	0.41
Netherlands (NE)													
Impact	0.01	0.01	0.01	0.0	0.01	−0.01	0.01	−0.52	0.02	0.01	0.0	0.02	0.09
Long run	0.02	0.01	0.05	0.01	0.01	0.0	0.01	−0.43	0.02	0.01	0.01	0.04	0.19
Sweden (SW)													
Impact	0.01	0.01	0.0	0.0	0.06	0.01	0.01	0.01	−0.29	0.01	0.0	0.0	0.12
Long run	0.02	0.0	0.01	0.01	0.06	0.01	0.01	0.02	−0.28	0.01	0.01	0.01	0.17
United Kingdom (UK)													
Impact	0.08	0.01	0.01	0.02	0.05	0.02	0.03	0.05	0.06	−0.19	0.02	0.01	0.36
Long run	0.18	0.01	0.04	0.09	0.06	0.03	0.05	0.05	0.07	−0.15	0.05	0.03	0.66
United States[b] (US)													
Impact	0.09	0.01	0.01	0.14	0.08	0.08	0.18	0.08	0.02	0.06	−0.21	0.02	0.77
Long run	0.17	0.0	0.05	0.55	0.03	0.12	0.16	0.06	0.04	0.06	−0.29	0.04	1.28
West Germany (WG)													
Impact	0.04	0.08	0.05	0.01	0.07	0.13	0.04	0.19	0.10	0.03	0.03	−0.10	0.77
Long run	0.08	0.05	0.13	0.07	0.07	0.11	0.05	0.15	0.08	0.03	0.06	−0.25	0.88
Off-diagonal column sum													
Impact	0.33	0.14	0.09	0.19	0.31	0.28	0.41	0.52	0.28	0.18	0.20	0.10	
Long run	0.69	0.09	0.33	0.91	0.27	0.31	0.33	0.42	0.29	0.15	0.29	0.23	

[a]The off-diagonal row sum is the effect of the initiating country's rate on foreign consumer prices; the off-diagonal column sum is the effect of foreign countries' rates on the consumer price of the receiving country; the diagonal is the effect of the initiating country's rate on its own consumer price. The impact figure shows the effect of a change in the initiating country's rate on following the change; and the long run, the effect after the sixth year.
[b]In the case of the United States, the dollar is appreciated by 1 percent against the currencies of *all* the other countries.

TABLE 8 Effects of a 1 Percent Increase in the Unemployment Rate of an Initiating Country on Foreign Consumer Price Inflation[a] (percent)

Initiating Country	Receiving Country												Off-Diagonal Row Sum
	AS	AU	BL	CA	FI	IT	JA	NE	SW	UK	US	WG	
Australia (AS)													
Impact	-1.10	0.0	0.0	0.01	0.0	0.01	-0.09	-0.01	0.0	-0.01	-0.01	0.0	-0.14
Long run	-1.85	0.0	-0.01	-0.06	-0.01	-0.01	-0.17	-0.02	-0.01	-0.02	-0.04	-0.01	-0.36
Austria (AU)													
Impact	0.0	0.51	0.0	0.0	0.0	0.01	0.0	0.0	0.01	0.0	0.0	0.0	0.02
Long run	-0.01	-2.54	-0.01	-0.01	-0.02	-0.04	-0.01	-0.02	-0.03	-0.01	-0.01	-0.03	-0.20
Belgium (BL)													
Impact	-0.02	-0.01	-0.78	-0.01	-0.01	-0.03	-0.02	-0.10	-0.03	-0.01	-0.01	-0.02	-0.27
Long run	-0.03	-0.01	-1.44	-0.03	-0.03	-0.05	-0.02	-0.19	-0.04	-0.02	-0.03	-0.09	-0.54
Canada (CA)													
Impact	-0.01	0.0	0.0	-0.41	0.0	-0.01	-0.03	-0.01	0.0	-0.01	-0.04	0.0	-0.11
Long run	-0.12	0.0	-0.02	-1.38	-0.01	-0.03	-0.12	-0.05	-0.02	-0.04	-0.22	-0.02	-0.65
Finland (FI)													
Impact	0.0	0.0	0.0	0.0	-0.29	0.0	0.0	0.0	-0.01	0.0	0.0	0.0	-0.01
Long run	-0.01	0.0	0.0	0.0	-1.12	0.0	0.0	-0.01	-0.03	-0.01	0.0	-0.01	-0.07

Italy (IT)													
Impact	−0.01	−0.01	−0.01	−0.01	−0.01	−0.93	−0.01	−0.04	−0.02	−0.01	−0.01	−0.02	−0.16
Long run	−0.04	−0.02	−0.04	−0.04	−0.02	−0.94	−0.02	−0.05	−0.03	−0.01	−0.03	−0.07	−0.37
Japan (JA)													
Impact	−0.22	−0.01	−0.02	−0.08	−0.02	−0.04	−2.52	−0.07	−0.04	−0.03	−0.17	−0.02	−0.72
Long run	−0.18	0.0	−0.02	−0.16	−0.01	−0.02	−0.88	−0.03	−0.02	−0.02	−0.11	−0.02	−0.59
Netherlands (NE)													
Impact	0.0	0.0	0.0	0.0	0.0	0.0	0.0	0.0	0.0	0.0	0.0	0.0	0.0
Long run	−0.02	−0.01	−0.06	−0.01	−0.02	−0.03	−0.01	−0.62	−0.02	−0.01	−0.01	−0.06	−0.26
Sweden (SW)													
Impact	0.02	0.02	0.01	0.0	0.13	0.02	0.0	0.04	2.43	0.03	0.01	0.01	0.29
Long run	−0.02	−0.01	−0.01	−0.01	−0.06	−0.01	−0.01	−0.02	−0.69	−0.01	−0.01	−0.01	−0.18
United Kingdom (UK)													
Impact	0.06	0.01	0.01	0.01	0.03	0.02	0.01	0.04	0.05	0.74	0.02	0.01	0.27
Long run	−0.11	−0.01	−0.03	−0.06	−0.03	−0.02	−0.03	−0.04	−0.04	−0.49	−0.03	−0.02	−0.42
United States (US)													
Impact	0.0	0.0	0.0	0.01	0.0	0.0	0.01	0.0	0.0	0.0	0.04	0.0	0.02
Long run	−0.32	−0.01	−0.08	−0.80	−0.04	−0.09	−0.32	−0.14	−0.07	−0.06	−1.12	−0.08	−2.01
West Germany (WG)													
Impact	−0.03	−0.05	−0.03	−0.02	−0.04	−0.08	−0.04	−0.12	−0.07	−0.02	−0.03	−0.53	−0.53
Long run	−0.14	−0.11	−0.21	−0.11	−0.13	−0.18	−0.08	−0.29	−0.15	−0.04	−0.10	−1.23	−1.54
Off-diagonal column sum													
Impact	−0.21	−0.05	−0.04	−0.11	0.08	−0.12	−0.17	−0.27	−0.11	−0.06	−0.24	−0.04	
Long run	−1.00	−0.18	−0.49	−1.29	−0.38	−0.48	−0.79	−0.86	−0.46	−0.25	−0.59	−0.42	

[a]See Table 7, note a.

The cross effects, particularly in the long run, appear to be large and negative, as given by the off-diagonal elements. This suggests that the inflationary pressure generated by the increased activity in one country produces inflationary pressures in other countries. While the cross effects of a change in unemployment rates could be exaggerated, as indicated in the previous section, they are definitely sharper and larger than those resulting from currency appreciations. The sums of the off-diagonal row and column elements are also given in Table 8. As expected, the changes in U.S. and German activity strongly affect the inflation in other countries, whereas the inflation in Australia, Canada, Japan and the Netherlands seems to be highly influenced by foreign activity.

One of the interesting conclusions emerging from the discussion on economic policy in an interdependent world is that the achievement of the policy targets of a country is less costly if policy decisions take into account the interactions with other countries.[11] Table 9 contains calculations of the effects of changes in the exchange and unemployment rates of a country upon its own inflation through their impact abroad, in order to see how important the repercussions of interdependence can be. As discussed in the pre-

TABLE 9   Size of Feedback Effects[a] on Domestic Inflation (percent)

	1% Exchange Rate Appreciation		1% Rise in Rate of Unemployment	
	Impact	Long Run	Impact	Long Run
Australia	.01	.0	−.01	−.04
Austria	.0	.0	.0	.0
Belgium	.0	.1	−.01	−.03
Canada	.02	.05	−.01	−.12
Finland	.01	.0	−.01	.0
Italy	.0	.01	.0	−.01
Japan	.02	.03	−.06	−.05
Netherlands	.01	.02	.0	−.02
Sweden	.01	.01	.0	.0
United Kingdom	.0	.01	.0	−.01
United States	.03	.11	.0	−.15
West Germany	.01	.03	−.01	−.05

[a] Feedback effects are defined as the effects estimated with no changes in the consumer price and output rates of all other countries minus the effects with the changes reported in tables 7 and 8. A negative sign indicates addition to the negative effect; a plus sign, offsetting of the negative effect.

vious section, the feedback effect of a currency appreciation tends to offset the initial dampening effect on the inflation of the appreciating country, whereas the feedback effect of a rise in the unemployment rate reinforces the price-dampening effect of the higher unemployment rate in the initiating country. In addition, the estimates reveal that the feedback effect is greater, the larger the country's share in world trade. Although the feedback effects on the whole are smaller than expected, the presence of such repercussion effects suggests that in order to achieve policy targets, it is necessary to take into account the interdependence of countries' rates of inflation.

Finally, simulation experiments are made for 1971–1973 under the assumption that either exchange rates or unemployment rates during the three years are identical to those prevailing in 1970. The results are presented in Table 10.[12] In countries whose currencies have effectively appreciated, domestic prices decreased. For instance, average annual inflation rates in Japan and West Germany were lower by about 2.3 and 0.7 percent than they would have been predicted to be in the absence of currency appreciations. These reductions are substantial; they amount, respectively, to one-third and one-fifth of the predicted inflation rates. Symmetrically, those countries whose currencies have effectively depreciated have experienced increased inflation. For example, the U.S. dollar was effectively depreciated by about 5 percent per year. Accordingly, an annual increase in the U.S. price of about 1.4 percent can be attributed to the devaluation. As shown in the table, the devaluation-induced rise is one-third of the predicted inflation rate, a proportion that is about the same size as that implied in Kwack (1973). On this ground, the U.S. devaluation can be regarded as an important factor in generating inflationary pressure in the U.S. economy.

As shown in the table, annual average unemployment rates in all countries except Austria have increased anywhere from 0.3 to 1.2 percent during the three years. As expected from our finding that a rise in the unemployment rate of a country leads to decreases in the prices of all countries, the increases in unemployment rates would have produced a decline in domestic prices of between about 0.4 and 1.3 percent annually.

Although very informative, my analysis based on the simulations certainly does not deal with all the events that may be regarded as causes of sharply accelerated worldwide inflation during those three years. For example, increases in petroleum and materials prices and upward shifts of natural unemployment rates due to changes in demographic and related factors could have been con-

TABLE 10 Response of Consumer Price Inflation to Changes in the Exchange Rate and Unemployment Rate during 1971–1973 (percent)

Country	Exchange Rate Effect			Unemployment Rate Effect		
	Effective Exchange Rate Change (1)	Consumer Price Change (2)	Relative Magnitude (3)	Unemployment Rate Change (4)	Consumer Price Change (5)	Relative Magnitude (6)
Australia	−3.697	−1.289	0.215	0.533	−1.370	0.233
Austria	−1.293	−0.207	0.038	−0.533	1.037	0.198
Belgium	−1.077	−0.210	0.045	0.467	−0.603	0.133
Canada	−0.047	−0.020	0.005	0.200	−0.397	0.097
Finland	2.753	0.703	0.110	0.433	−0.817	0.129
Italy	3.490	0.973	0.185	0.233	−0.473	0.091
Japan	−5.830	−2.330	0.341	0.100	−0.483	0.071
Netherlands	−1.960	−1.073	0.182	1.267	−0.573	0.098
Sweden	−0.080	−0.027	0.005	0.567	−0.480	0.083
United Kingdom	4.437	0.637	0.078	0.733	−0.933	0.121
United States	5.113	1.363	0.282	0.567	−0.777	0.175
West Germany	−4.670	−0.720	0.173	0.333	−0.623	0.152

NOTE: Column 1—average effective exchange rate change in a country's currency from 1971 through 1973 (negative sign indicates appreciation). The effective appreciation of the U.S. dollar is equivalent to the depreciation of all other currencies.
Columns 2 and 5—average change in consumer price inflation due to the change in the exchange rate (column 2) or unemployment rate (column 5).
Columns 3 and 6—change in consumer price inflation due to the exchange rate (unemployment rate) change as a fraction of the actual inflation.
Column 4—average change in the unemployment rate from 1971 through 1973.

tributing factors.[13] The monetary expansions in the world, either passively or actively, can be said to be associated with the inflation in a sense that persistent inflation over a long period of time is incompatible with the absence of excessive monetary expansions.

IV. CONCLUSIONS

In this paper I attempted to provide a framework for the analysis of price behavior and inflation in an interdependent world. It must be repeated that the model is limited in scope and much remains to be done; sectoral specifications can be improved for individual countries, and real demand and monetary sectors could be incorporated to get more comprehensive conclusions. Nevertheless, the simulation results of the model are useful in increasing our understanding of a phenomenon that has not previously been examined in great detail—the international transmission of inflation.

The major conclusion emerging from this study is that a rise in the exchange rate of a country not only shifts the trade-off relation between inflation and unemployment but also has an inverse effect on such relations in other countries. Consequently, changes in external currency values and activities are transmitted to the rest of the world independent of the effects of changes in aggregate demand and monetary stocks. For a given change in the domestic prices of a country, the more open the initiating country is and the wider its trade relations with other countries, the greater will be the responsiveness of foreign prices. My results seem to suggest that the capability of a country to manage its own inflation may be strengthened if national policymakers take into account the degree of interdependence of prices among countries.

The foregoing results also indicate that a currency depreciation contributes to domestic inflation. That is what is expected when a currency value is depreciated without being accompanied by an appropriate reduction in domestic absorption. If there is worldwide downward rigidity in prices, it seems highly likely that a currency depreciation of an important trading country will give rise to pressures toward a worldwide inflation.

The analysis was carried out in a preliminary way by the use of an aggregative model. Consequently, little attention was paid to differences in rates of inflation between tradable and nontradable goods. A promising avenue for further investigation would be to make an explicit distinction between the two types of goods within a model covering worldwide activity and financial transactions, such as the Project LINK model. For the present, I hope I have shed some light on the interdependence of the economies of industrial nations.

NOTES

1. While a fuller discussion and reconciliation of some works in the area of international transmission of inflation can be found in Sweeney and Willett (1974), an example of the works in this area is found in Haberler (1974). Johnson and Klein (1973, 1974), and Hickman (1974) attempted to examine quantitatively the interdependence of activities among countries in the world, using a LINK model.

2. The transmission channels are spelled out in detail in Sweeney and Willett (1974). Also see Turnovsky and Kaspura (1974) for a thorough discussion on imported inflation in a small country, and Johnson (1973), Laidler (1972), and Parkin (1972) for a monetarist view.

3. These hypotheses are used in some models in the LINK system. No import prices are included in the works of Gordon (1971) and Perry (1970) and the wage-price sectors in most U.S. models in Eckstein, ed. (1972).

4. This specification was applied in Kwack (1974) to explain both U.S. prices and wage rates during 1959I–1972IV. The specification seems to be quite satisfactory, regardless of whether the money stock and government spending are added. Equation 3 was used in Kwack (1973).

5. This is a limiting case of the general specification discussed above that is derived from solving the demand and supply equations, as applied by Amano (1974) to explain export price behavior in industrial countries. While the special form was used here for simplicity, further investigations will be undertaken to examine whether or not the general form reduces specification errors involved in the special form.

6. This assumption is restrictive as discussed by Balassa (1964) because of the difference between the movement of consumer prices (in which prices of non-traded goods are also reflected) and tradable goods prices. However, this assumption simplifies matters a great deal by enabling us to avoid constructing a complicated subsector to show how the two prices are determined.

7. Branson (1972, p. 21) showed that $0 \leq \beta_{1i} = \theta_j/(\theta_j - \epsilon_i) \leq 1$, where ϵ_i = own price elasticity of ith import demand and θ_j = own price elasticity of jth supply.

8. See Goldberger (1964, pp. 373–378) for a mathematical proof of the stability conditions and discussion on multipliers in general.

9. Clark (1974) found the import price to be marginally important in explaining the U.S. GNP deflator, when it was used with the money stock and government expenditures. As noted before, Kwack (1974) found that the coefficients on the import price variable were stable and significant in explaining U.S. deflators for consumption expenditures even in the presence of the money stock. The import prices were important in explaining U.S. and aggregate foreign CPI (consumer price index) behavior, in the study by Kwack (1973).

10. Braun (1974) provided a broad survey of some issues of incomes policy and

discussed actual implementations of incomes policy in industrial countries. One interesting point emerging from her survey is that incomes policies were frequently employed in connection with changes in currency values.

11. See Cooper (1969) for the policy choice of a country in an interdependent world through capital mobility. Duesenberry (1974) pointed out the importance of external factors even in the United States, which external sector was regarded as relatively small.

12. Exchange rates and unemployment rates are treated as exogenously determined, ignoring the activity effect of inflation that is likely to be present in a general equilibrium framework.

13. Nordhaus (1973) investigated how energy requirements will be satisfied and energy prices will affect prices of goods, and Popkin (1974) discussed the impact on the U.S. price level of increasing prices of raw material commodities in the world.

REFERENCES

Amano, Akihiro. 1974. "Export Price Behavior in Selected Industrial Countries." Paper presented at the LINK meeting, Washington, D.C., September.

Ball, R. J., and M. Duffey. 1972. "Price Formation in European Countries." In Eckstein, ed. (1972).

Balassa, Bela. 1964. "The Purchasing Power Parity Doctrine: A Reappraisal." *Journal of Political Economy*, December: 584–596.

Bodkin, Ronald G. 1972. "Wage and Price Formation in Selected Canadian Econometric Models." In Eckstein, ed. (1972).

Branson, William H. 1972. "The Trade Effects of the 1971 Currency Realignments." *Brookings Papers on Economic Activity*, no. 1: 15–58.

Braun, Anne R. 1974. "Three Decades of Incomes Policy: Reflections on the Role of Incomes Policies in Industrial Countries, 1945–74." Manuscript only.

Clark, Peter B. 1974. "An Aggregative Approach to the Domestic Price Effects of Recent U.S. Exchange Rate Changes." August. Manuscript only.

Cooper, Richard N. 1969. "Macroeconomic Policy Adjustment in Interdependent Economies." *Quarterly Journal of Economics*, February: 1–24.

Duesenberry, James S. 1974. "Worldwide Inflation." Paper presented at Conference on the Phenomenon of Worldwide Inflation, American Enterprise Institute of Public Policy Research. Washington, D.C., May 6 and 7.

Eckstein, Otto, ed. 1972. *The Econometrics of Price Determination*. Washington, D.C.: Board of Governors of the Federal Reserve System.

Eckstein, O., and Gary Fromm. 1958. "The Price Equation." *American Economic Review*, December: 1161–1183.

Flanagan, R. J. 1973. "The U.S. Phillips Curve and International Unemployment Rate Differentials." *American Economic Review*, March: 114–131.

Friedman, B. M., and M. L. Wachter. 1974. "Unemployment: Okun's Law, Labor Force, and Productivity." *Review of Economics and Statistics*, May: 167–176.

Goldberger, Arthur S. 1964. *Econometric Theory*. New York: Wiley.

Gordon, R. J. 1971. "Inflation in Recession and Recovery." *Brookings Papers on Economic Activity*, no. 1: 105–108.

Harberger, Arnold C. "Some Notes on Inflation." In Wall (1972).

Haberler, Gottfried. 1974. "Inflation as a Worldwide Phenomenon: An Overview." Paper presented at Conference on the Phenomenon of Worldwide Inflation, American Enterprise Institute for Public Policy Research. Washington, D.C., May 6 and 7.

Hickman, Bert G. 1974. "International Transmission of Economic Fluctuations and Inflation." Paper presented at LINK meeting, in Washington, D.C., September.

International Monetary Fund. International Financial Statistics.

Johnson, H. G. 1973. Further Essays in Monetary Economics. Cambridge: Harvard University Press.

Johnson, K., and Lawrence R. Klein. 1974. "LINK Model Simulations of International Trade: An Evaluation of the Effects of Currency Realignment." Journal of Finance, Papers and Proceedings, May: 617–630.

Kwack, Sung Y. 1973. The Effect of Foreign Inflation on Domestic Prices and Relative Import Prices of Exchange Rate Changes. International Finance Discussion Papers, no. 35. Washington, D.C.: Board of Governors of the Federal Reserve System, November 21.

————. 1974. "U.S. Wage and Price Effects of Import Price Changes." October. Work in progress.

Laffer, A. B. 1974. "The Bitter Fruits of Devaluation." Wall Street Journal, January 10.

Laidler, David E. 1972. "Price and Output Fluctuations in an Open Economy." December. Manuscript only.

Modigliani, F., and E. Tarantelli. 1973. "A Generalization of the Phillips Curve for a Developing Country." Review of Economic Studies, April: 203–223.

Nordhaus, W. D. 1972. "The Worldwide Wage Explosion." Brookings Papers on Economic Activity, no. 2: 431–466.

————. 1973. "The Allocation of Energy Resources." Brookings Papers on Economic Activity, no. 3: 529–571.

Okun, A. M. 1962. "Potential GNP: Its Measurement and Significance." Proceedings of the Business and Economic Statistics Section of the American Statistical Association, pp. 98–104.

Parkin, Michael. 1972. "Inflation, the Balance of Payments, Domestic Credit Expansion and Exchange Rate Adjustment." November. Manuscript only.

Perry, G. 1970. "Changing Labor Markets and Inflation." Brookings Papers on Economic Activity, no. 3: 411–441.

Phelps, E. S. 1968. "Money-Wage Dynamics and Labor-Market Equilibriums." Journal of Political Economy, July/August: 678–711.

Phillips, A. W. 1958. "The Relation Between Unemployment and the Rate of Change of Money Wages in the United Kingdom, 1861–1957." Economica, vol. 25: 238–299.

Popkin, Joel. 1974. "Commodity Prices and the U.S. Price Level." Brookings Papers on Economic Activity, no. 1: 249–259.

Spitäller, Erich. 1971. "Prices and Unemployment in Selected Industrial Countries." International Monetary Fund Staff Papers, November: 538–569.

Sweeney, R. J., and Thomas D. Willett. 1974. "The International Transmission of Inflation: A Survey of Mechanism and Issues." Paper presented at Conference on Bank Credit, Money and Inflation in Open Economies. Leuven, Belgium, September.

Toyoda, Toshihisa. 1972. "Price Expectations and the Short-Run and Long-Run

Phillips Curves in Japan, 1956–1968." *Review of Economics and Statistics*, August: 267–274.

Turnovsky, Stephen J. 1972. "The Expectations Hypothesis and the Aggregate Wage Equation: Some Empirical Evidence for Canada." *Economica*, vol. 38: 1–17.

Turnovsky, S. J., and A. Kaspura. 1974. "An Analysis of Imported Inflation in a Short-Run Macroeconomic Model." *Canadian Journal of Economics*, August: 355–380.

United Nations, *Monthly Bulletin of Statistics*.

Wall, David, ed. 1972. *Chicago Essays in Economic Development*. Chicago: University of Chicago Press.

COMMENTS

John Helliwell
University of British Columbia

INTRODUCTION

The principal objective of Sung Kwack's interesting paper is to specify and estimate a model of the direct transmission of price changes among a group of twelve industrial countries. He wishes to develop the simplest sort of model to explain foreign and domestic changes in prices induced by changes in activity or exchange rates. Monetary influences and changes in trade and capital flows are deliberately left out, while exchange rates come into play only to convert each country's domestic prices into the import prices of its trading partners. In keeping with the spirit of the Kwack paper, I shall share his concentration on the development of models that achieve interdependence while maintaining the simplest feasible structure. I shall proceed in four stages. First, I shall outline the basic structure of the Kwack model, and then describe and interpret his main empirical results. In the third and fourth parts of my presentation I shall first state generally the properties that a model should have if it is to adequately depict the international transmission of inflations, and then suggest some changes to the Kwack model intended to add to its structural aptness without adding unduly to its complexity.

1. BASIC STRUCTURE

For each country, there are three estimated equations; one for the consumer price, one for the price of imports, and one for the unemployment rate. The consumer price equation is intended to represent a price and wage equation pair solved to remove the wage, giving:

(1) $$\dot{P}_i = \alpha_{0i} + \alpha_{1i}(1/U_i) + \alpha_{2i}\dot{Q}_i + \alpha_{3i}\dot{P}_{mi} + \alpha_{4i}\dot{P}_{i,t-1} + \alpha_{5i}D_i$$

where $\dot{P}_i$, $\dot{Q}_i$, and $\dot{P}_{mi}$ are the logarithms of the ratios of country i's consumer price, output in real terms, and import price to their values in the preceding year; U_i is the unemployment rate in country i; and the D_i are dummy variables with values chosen to improve particular equations.

The estimated import price equations are based on weighted averages of the consumer prices in the other eleven countries adjusted for exchange rate changes plus, for some countries, an output influence intended to represent an impact of demand on import prices. The equation is

(2) $$\dot{P}_{mi} = \beta_{0i} + \beta_{1i}\sum_{j=1}^{11} a_{ij}\overline{\dot{P}_j F_j} - \beta_{1i}\dot{F}_j + \beta_{2i}\dot{Q}_j + \beta_{3i}D_j$$

where F_j is (approximately) the number of units of country i's currency required to purchase a unit of country j's currency, and the a_{ij} weights represent the proportion of country i's total 1971 value of imports from the other eleven countries that come from country j. The other variables are as defined for equation 1. This equation merits particular attention because it provides, in conjunction with the import price term in equation 1, the international linkage mechanism of the Kwack model. Note that exchange rate and consumer price changes in country j are assumed to have the same impact on the import prices of country i and that, in general, each country's export prices are assumed to have the same relationship to consumer prices. Note also that the import price being explained is for total imports of country i, while the composite price variable used to explain it comprises domestic prices in only eleven other countries. If prices in the excluded countries are correlated with prices in the included ones, the use of a limited range of country prices as proxies for all others will result in an upward bias of the estimate of the degree of price interdependence among the twelve countries included in the model.

The third equation in the Kwack model provides a tie for each economy between domestic output and the unemployment rate, using the functional form

$$(3) \quad \Delta U_i = \gamma_{0i} + \sum_{K=0}^{i} \gamma_{1+K.i} \dot{Q}_{t-K}$$

For each country, the γ_K weights on Q are forced to decline linearly from the current year to the last year in the lag distribution, but the lag length itself is permitted to vary among countries; ranging from no lag at all for three countries, to two lagged years for five countries, three lagged years for three countries, and four lagged years for the remaining country. The purpose of the unemployment rate equation in the Kwack model is to reduce from three to two the number of exogenous variables for each country, so that it will be possible to simulate the domestic and foreign price consequences of a domestic shock by changing the actual value of a single variable, if the exchange rate is held fixed.

2. SUMMARY OF RESULTS

2.1 Estimated Equations

The single-equation results are shown in Sung Kwack's tables 2, 3, and 5 for the consumer price equations, import price equations, and unemployment rate equations, respectively.

Looking first at the consumer price equations, we note that Kwack's chosen equations contain lags for half of the countries, and that the impact and equilibrium elasticities for import prices are in almost all cases above the import content of consumption expenditure and, in about half the cases, several times the import content. In the light of the difficulties faced by most model builders in obtaining import price coefficients sufficiently high to be plausible, at least with data samples ending by 1970, Kwack's very high estimates are slightly surprising. The suspicion arises that the import prices may be mopping up the residual variance to the extent that import prices are correlated with the excluded variables, such as man-hours employed and capacity utilization, usually found in price equations. Differences in the relative importance of excluded variables are also likely to be part of the explanation for sharply differing coefficients on the lagged dependent variable, ranging from zero in five cases (on what grounds were the lagged dependent variables excluded from these equations?) to 0.75 for Belgium and 0.86 for Canada. These varying lag patterns serve to exaggerate the differences among countries in the role of the import price, giving an equilibrium elasticity of over 2.4 for the effect of import prices on Canadian consumer prices. Kwack points this out as an implausible feature, but uses the equation anyway.

The negative effects of output on consumer prices are also somewhat troubling. Kwack intends output to have a negative sign in the price equation because his theoretical equation contains no capacity utilization term, but has unit labor cost defined with current output in the denominator. For most of the five models in which a negative influence of output enters the price equation, the suspicion arises that an increase in domestic aggregate demand could make prices rise rather than fall.

Turning to the import price equations in Table 3, we find, as one would expect, that foreign prices are the principal determinants. If the aggregate of foreign prices were constructed from just the right components, we would expect import prices to have an elasticity of 1.0 with respect to it. In the estimated equations, the elasticities range from 0.46 to 1.54. These estimates are likely to be subject to biases in opposite directions. On the one hand, export prices in the industrial countries have tended to rise more slowly than consumer prices, and this should produce negative constant terms or coefficients less than 1.0, or both, on the amalgam of foreign consumer prices. All the constant terms are negative, but the average coefficient on the foreign price term is above rather than below 1.0. On the other hand, the exclusion of exports of the nonindustrial world from the mixture of foreign consumer prices results in the omission of most of industrial raw materials, and prices of the latter have more variability than consumer prices.

Finally, in the unemployment, or "Okun's law," equations, there is a disturbing variance among countries in the length of lags and in the elasticities of unemployment with respect to output. In essence, these are employment equations adjusted for activity-induced changes in labor force participation. It would help the reader to assess the equations if these two elements could be separated, so that the comparison between average and marginal employment requirements could be assessed. Furthermore, separate treatment of the labor force would probably help to improve the fit and structural aptness of the equations; it is difficult to tell just what influence the demographic trends and cycles have on the present equations.

2.2 Simulation Results

The simulations reported in tables 6 through 9 are the main substance of the paper, given Kwack's concern with international interdependence rather than the separate structures of national economies.

The first simulation, in Table 6, reports the error characteristics of a control solution for the twelve-country model, using exchange rates, the dummy variables, and national unemployment rates as exogenous variables. The root-mean-square errors range from 0.6 percent to 2.7 percent for consumer prices, from 0.9 percent to 7.5 percent for import prices, and from 1.7 percent to 16.0 percent for output. It would be useful to see which single-equation errors are most responsible for these errors. The initial suspicion must fall on the unemployment equations, which in this model are solved for output changes.

Two types of policy simulation are reported by Kwack. Table 7 contains the results of separate 1 percent appreciations in the value of each country's currency, starting in 1968. In table 8 are found the results of separate simulations of 1 percent increases in national unemployment rates. The sizes of the international feedback effects in the simulations of tables 8 and 9 are shown in Table 9. Finally, Table 10 contains the results of a single simulation from 1971–1973 in which rates of exchange rates and of national unemployment are maintained at their 1970 values.

The appreciation simulations in Table 7 indicate own-country impact effects on consumer prices ranging from −0.1 percent for West Germany to −0.52 percent for the Netherlands. The equilibrium effects range from −0.1 percent for Austria to −0.92 percent for Canada. The differences between impact and equilibrium effects are largely due to cross-country differences in the coefficient of lagged price in the consumer price equation, and not to repercussions from other countries. The figures in Table 9 show that, on average, the own-country long-run price effects would be about 7 percent larger if there were no feedbacks from other countries.

The Table 8 simulations of the domestic and foreign price effects of changes in the unemployment rate show a disturbingly large number (four) of instances where the own-country price effects are initially positive. This result is due to the appearance of output changes with a negative sign in the price equations of the four countries concerned (Austria, Sweden, the United Kingdom, and the United States). In three of the four cases, a 1 percent increase in the unemployment rate causes domestic prices to rise by more than 0.5 percent in the first year, with or without international feedbacks taken into account.

In my view, it would have been more natural to run the activity change simulations by using an output shock, and then tracing the unemployment and price effects of this (perhaps policy-induced) change. This would have given results rather different from those reported by Kwack because the lags in his unemployment-output relation run from output to unemployment rather than in the reverse direction. Using output change as the activity shock would have caused the "perverse" price effects (e.g., rising car prices when demand is falling) to last longer in the four main countries involved. Once the unemployment and output changes have caused changes in domestic prices, they then lead to foreign effects, following the pattern outlined above for Table 8. Since import prices provide the only international linkage in Kwack's system, the results of the activity change provide a poor representation of reality because the most important international effect is (in my view) usually provided by activity-induced trade flows, which in turn act as a means of transmitting inflationary effects abroad. Thus, further analysis of the international price responses of activity changes should await the addition of trade flows to this model, or should be studied within the context of the Project LINK system, in which primary emphasis is placed on activity-induced trade flows as a means of transmitting internationally the employment, output, and price effects of a domestic activity change.

To summarize my analysis of the equations and results of the present version of Sung Kwack's model:

1. The degree of direct price interdependence is probably overstated, for reasons outlined in section 2.1 above. This means that Table 7 probably provides a high estimate of the price effects of exchange rate changes.

2. The international interdependence of activity changes is left out of the model, with the result that the Table 8 results are not a very satisfactory guide to the international price effects of domestic activity changes.

3. Even though the size of the direct international price effects estimated by Kwack is probably overestimated, his calculations of the effects feeding back to the initiating country show them to be too small to substantially alter the domestic effects of the initiating country's policies. A much more important constraint that interdependence places on national policies comes about because of inconsistent policy targets: Country

A initiates a policy that has substantial effects on B, and B responds with a policy that has substantial effects on A. Thus, the main feedback on A arises through Country B's policy responses, which may be much larger (perhaps explosively so) than the reflected effects arising from models, such as Kwack's, that treat policies as exogenous.

3. GENERAL REQUIREMENTS FOR A MODEL OF THE INTERNATIONAL TRANSMISSION OF INFLATIONS

In section 4, I offer a set of specific suggestions for extensions of the Kwack model. The following are what I think to be the general requirements for a fully satisfactory model:

1. Even if the model cannot itself explain the prices of industrial materials from the nonindustrial world, it must allow their impact to be separately accounted for.

2. If the price effects of single or sequential exchange rate changes are to be analyzed effectively, some account must be taken of the effect of monetary policy on domestic price and output levels. Ideally, one would also like to specify the impacts of special drawing rights (SDRs) and other international money on national money supplies and price levels.

3. Minimum international linkage should include trade flows and trade prices, with capital flows left out only because of data limitations and the requirement that the model should be as small as possible.

4. SPECIFIC SUGGESTIONS FOR MODEL CHANGES

I shall start with changes that are either very easy to make or are likely to make a substantial improvement in relation to the effort or equations required.

1. The trade-weighted vector of foreign prices used to explain each country's import prices should use foreign export prices instead of consumer prices and, most important, should specifically include export prices from countries outside the industrial group of twelve, using the appropriate import weights in each case. The estimation of export price equations will facilitate the first step above, and will permit the estimation of feedbacks from exchange rate changes to export prices, or will at least permit the easy application of alternative pass-through assumptions.

2. The present likely overestimation of the effect of import prices in the consumer price equations should be guarded against by explaining the GNP deflator in terms of normal unit labor costs, monetary influences, capacity utilization, and world export prices (to include the possible influence of foreign prices on the domestic value added in tradable goods). The consumer price would then be explained by an appropriately weighted composite of the GNP deflator and the import price.

The following are more extensive revisions, proposed still with an eye to parsimony of structure:

3. Either replace the unemployment rate equations by separate employment and labor force equations, or else redefine the unemployment rate series to remove the variance induced by unusual shifts in the labor force population or in other exogenous factors influencing the measured number of unemployed persons.

4. Add import equations based on output, capacity utilization, and trade prices.

5. If the model is extended further, it would be necessary to develop expenditure equations for the main final demand components, including monetary influences acting directly or through interest rates. If the latter, then a money demand equation is also needed. Exports could be explained as a weighted sum of fractions of other countries' imports, using a trade share matrix based on exogenous or endogenous shares determined by one of the procedures developed in connection with the Project LINK system. If the linkage were further extended to include capital flows, then, but only then, the exchange rates themselves could be made endogenous. At this point, however, the model would begin to resemble an expanded Project LINK system more than a simple structural model of the world economy.

To continue my list any further would impose too much on the principle of model simplicity, overextend an already long commentary, and move too far afield from Kwack's existing model. Perhaps the correct moral to draw is that a structurally accurate model of international inflation must be inherently complex if it is to capture any substantial part of the interplay of raw materials prices and supplies, monetary and exchange market conditions, real supply and demand in national economies, and the roles of trade, capital, and migration movements in the creation and transmission of international inflation.

Index of Authors